1-2-3 2.4: The Complete Reference

1-2-3 2.4: The Complete Reference

Mary Campbell

Osborne **McGraw-Hill**

Berkeley   New York   St. Louis   San Francisco
Auckland   Bogotá   Hamburg   London   Madrid
Mexico City   Milan   Montreal   New Delhi   Panama City
Paris   São Paulo   Singapore   Sydney
Tokyo   Toronto

Osborne **McGraw-Hill**
2600 Tenth Street
Berkeley, California 94710
U.S.A.

For information on software, translations, or book distributors outside of the U.S.A.,
please write to Osborne **McGraw-Hill** at the above address.

1-2-3 2.4: The Complete Reference

1234567890 DOC 9987654321

ISBN 0-07-881853-2

Publisher
Kenna S. Wood

Acquisitions Editor
Elizabeth Fisher

Associate Editor
Scott Rogers

Project Editor
Judy Ziajka

Technical Editor
Chris McClellan

Copy Editors
Vivian Jaquette
Jane Paulsen

Proofreader
Jeff Barash

Word Processing
Valerie Haynes Perry
Lynda Higham

Indexer
Valerie Robbins

Computer Designer
Michelle Salinaro

Illustrators
Susie Kim
Marla Shelasky

Cover Design
Bay Graphics Design, Inc.
Mason Fong

Contents at a Glance

Contents

4

Changing the Appearance of the Worksheet Display 59

5

Basic Worksheet Commands 109

6

Printing with 1-2-3 and Wysiwyg   173

7

1-2-3's Built-In Functions   239

8

Working with Files 339

Part II
1-2-3's Advanced Features

9

Data Management 381

10

Using Data Management Features in the Worksheet Environment 421

11

Working with 1-2-3's Graphics Features 457

**Part III
Enhancing and Expanding 1-2-3**

12
Keyboard Macros 515

13

Command Language Macros 565

14

Using 1-2-3's Built-In Add-Ins 631

Part IV
Appendixes

A

Installing 1-2-3   745

Acknowledgments

I wish to thank the following individuals, without whom this book would not have been possible:

- Elizabeth Reinhardt, for her help with all aspects of the book.

- Margaret Campbell, for creating the screens.

- Liz Fisher, who managed the entire process of making this a book and helped in many ways to produce a quality product.

- Scott Rogers, for all of his help in preparing the chapters for production.

- Chris McClellan, Alene Gansemer, and all the others at Lotus who offered their help in so many ways.

- Judy Ziajka, Vivian Jaquette, Jane Paulsen, and Michelle Salinaro for their help in Editorial and Production.

– Mary Campbell

Introduction

1-2-3 has become an essential tool for many business users. It is hard to conceive of putting together budgets, sales projections, and many other financial projections without the assistance of this package. The wide applicability of this package and its state-of-the-art features have kept it near the top of best-selling software charts since its introduction.

With Release 2.4, you will find that the familiar interface that handles every Release 2.01 command hasn't changed. In addition, you will find many exciting new features that can extend your productivity. This book is designed to steer you in the proper direction so that you look at new options in a logical progression and see how to incorporate these features into your models.

About This Book

1-2-3 Release 2.4: The Complete Reference is designed to serve the needs of both new and experienced 1-2-3 users. Beginning users should start at the beginning of the book and work through the first six chapters. While reading these chapters, you may want to enter some of the examples in your system for practice. These chapters will provide the basic skills for all model building with 1-2-3 and establish a firm foundation from which to explore later topics. Users already familiar with 1-2-3 basics will want to review the table of contents and focus on chapter topics with which they are less familiar, such as data management features, keyboard alternative macros, and command macros.

Experienced 1-2-3 users will also find this volume to be a valuable reference tool, describing all of 1-2-3's many features in detail. You will find discussions of all the

Release 2.01 commands as well as the latest additions for Release 2.4. You can use this book as a source of information about either product if you are using both releases within your organization. Each topic has working examples to go along with the written description. Boxes in the text highlight important summary information, and a thorough index helps you find the precise topics you are looking for.

In addition to its thorough coverage of 1-2-3's features, this book provides information on the Lotus Add-In Manager and the Auditor, Macro Manager, Back-Solver, SmartIcons, Tutorial, and Wysiwyg add-ins.

How This Book Is Organized

This book is divided into four parts. Part One discusses the worksheet and the commands you need to create efficient worksheet models. Part Two focuses on database management and graphics. Part Three looks beyond the basic features to explore macros and the 1-2-3 add-ins that accompany Releases 2.2, 2.3, and 2.4. Part Four consists of four appendixes that offer supplemental information, including installation procedures, a list of LICS codes, and a list of the SmartIcons.

- Chapter 1 provides an overview of Release 2.4's features. If you are already a 1-2-3 user, Chapter 1 will help you focus on the new features that you want to explore first.

- Chapter 2 discusses the Lotus Access System, display, and keyboard. You will learn all about 1-2-3's display in this chapter.

- Chapter 3 has you start entering data in 1-2-3's spreadsheet cells. In this chapter, you will learn about the types of building blocks used in creating a model.

- Chapter 4 introduces you to formatting and the improvements it makes to 1-2-3's spreadsheet. You will learn how to override all the default display characteristics to create the exact display you want. You will use 1-2-3's formats as well as basic Wysiwyg options.

- Chapter 5 describes all of the command options pertaining to the worksheet. You will learn how to determine the status of current settings and how to change options to suit your needs.

- Chapter 6 provides explanations and examples for all of 1-2-3's basic print features as well as for Wysiwyg printing. You will learn how to print formulas, add borders to a printed report, and use background printing to make your work more efficient.

- Chapter 7 describes each of 1-2-3's functions. You can read about just the ones you are interested in or survey all of them to discover new uses for the package.

- Chapter 8 presents everything you need to know about saving and retrieving files. You will learn how to consolidate information in several files and how to save a portion of a worksheet.

- Chapter 9 introduces you to the sort and query features that add data management capabilities to the package. You will learn how to resequence your data and how to extract the data that meets your needs.

- Chapter 10 teaches you how to apply the data management features to the spreadsheet environment. You will learn about automating a "what-if" analysis, generating matrices, and sorting your formulas.

- Chapter 11 teaches you how to display your data graphically in all the new graph formats. You will learn how to use all the graph features, including how to print a graph and how to add a graph to the spreadsheet.

- Chapter 12 introduces keyboard macros and the new Learn feature that records them. Once you learn to save command keystrokes, you can reuse them at will.

- Chapter 13 presents the powerful command language macros that allow you to write programs to automate applications. Each macro command is described and illustrated with an example.

- Chapter 14 describes the Add-In menu and some of the 1-2-3 add-ins that accompany Release 2.4. These add-ins include the Auditor add-in, useful for following the effects of formulas, and the Tutorial add-in, which you can use to help you learn 1-2-3 basics.

- Chapter 15 explains the Wysiwyg add-in. You will learn how to use Wysiwyg spreadsheet publishing features, the Backsolver add-in for working from a result to the value needed to achieve it, and the Icon add-in for customizing pallete 1.

- Appendix A provides installation instructions.

- Appendix B provides a list of the LICS codes.

- Appendix C displays menu trees for 1-2-3 and Wysiwyg commands.

- Appendix D provides a look at the text and graphic versions of Release 2.4's SmartIcons.

Part I

The 1-2-3 Worksheet Reference

Chapter 1

An Introduction to Release 2.4

1-2-3 is one of the most popular packages for microcomputers. Since its introduction, it has set the standard for spreadsheet products on both mainframes and microcomputers. With the introduction of Release 2.4, users have a product that runs on microcomputers as old as the 8088 machines and as new as the machines built with 80486 technology. Lotus added many new features to this release within the confines of DOS and the 8088 machines. Although Release 2.4 does not have all the new features of Release 3, it has many worthwhile additions, including SmartIcons and a spreadsheet publishing Add-In that is preattached to 1-2-3.

Wysiwyg Features

If you have been using 1-2-3 Release 2.3, you might be an avid fan of Wysiwyg's features that offer spreadsheet publishing support. On the other hand, you might not even be aware that Wysiwyg exists. The reason for the different perceptions of Wysiwyg is that it is not part of 1-2-3 itself but an add-in program that can supplement 1-2-3's features. Once attached to 1-2-3, the add-in integration is seamless. With 1-2-3 Release 2.4, the Wysiwyg add-in is automatically attached at startup. This feature gives the screen a more graphical look and also ensures that you can use all the features that your printer supports when laying out your 1-2-3 worksheets.

   If you are already using Wysiwyg, you can skip to the next major section in this chapter and learn about SmartIcons. If Wysiwyg is new to you, review the remaining subsections in this section for an overview of your options.

Formatting Your Worksheet with Wysiwyg

Menu commands allow you to boldface or underline a character, word, or cell entry, whereas 1-2-3 alone does not allow you to change attributes for anything smaller than a row. Just like a professional printer, you can adjust both row height and column width. You can add shading for emphasis to any area of the worksheet. You can outline cells or enclose them in boxes, and you can draw lines anywhere. You can change the color of screen elements such as the background, cell pointer, worksheet frame, or negative values. Also, you can change the display from graphics to text or alter the Zoom factor to display the data as large or small, or you can use a manual sizing factor. Figure 1-1 shows a worksheet in which formatting has been used to change the worksheet's appearance.

Some of these changes to Wysiwyg formats can be made through the SmartIcons, although you must use the Wysiwyg menu to access the full set of features. All of these changes are immediately visible in the worksheet on your screen. Wysiwyg formatting changes will appear in your printout if you use Wysiwyg to print the worksheet.

Special Wysiwyg copy and move commands allow you to reuse formats that have already been assigned to cells. You can also import and export Wysiwyg settings and formats between worksheet files.

Integrating Text and Graphics

Graphs can be included with the printout by adding them to a range on the worksheet before printing. Figure 1-2 shows a worksheet with a graph and text; both text and graphs print on the same sheet. Wysiwyg offers additional features such as the ability

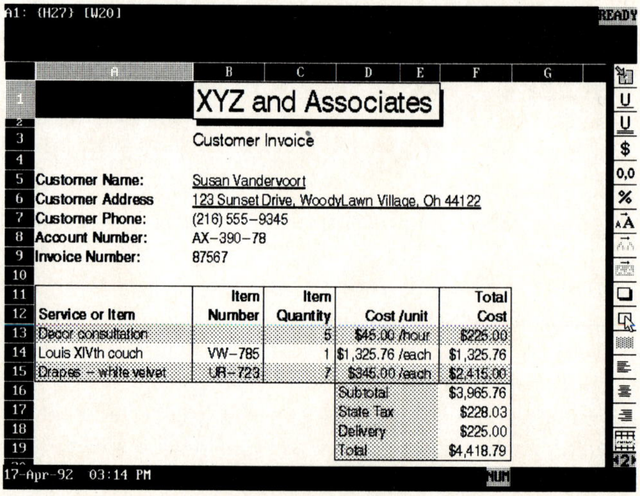

Figure 1-1.   *Formatting changes significantly enhance a worksheet's appearance*

to add graphics to a worksheet from .CGM files, which are discussed later in this chapter.

You can edit any graph to add enhancements and change the appearance. You can change the size of the range where the graph appears, to remove any sizing distortions.

Printing with Wysiwyg

Since Wysiwyg is now automatically attached, the worksheet that you create uses Wysiwyg's default font. Wysiwyg's use of a proportional font lets you fit more text in a cell than you can when you are using 1-2-3 without Wysiwyg. If you detach Wysiwyg, all the text may not fit in the current column width, and you will need to change the width of the column. The same effect occurs when you print the worksheet data with 1-2-3. Although you can see everything on your screen, data may be missing from some columns of your printout since the printout is produced with 1-2-3's font, not Wysiwyg's. You can print from Wysiwyg to get a printout identical to what you see on the Wysiwyg screen, or you can switch to a text display mode to look at the worksheet as it will print in 1-2-3 and then widen the columns.

SmartIcon Palette Offers Efficiency

The SmartIcon palette appears on the right side of your screen in 1-2-3 Release 2.4. It is designed to allow you to perform a task by selecting a picture rather than

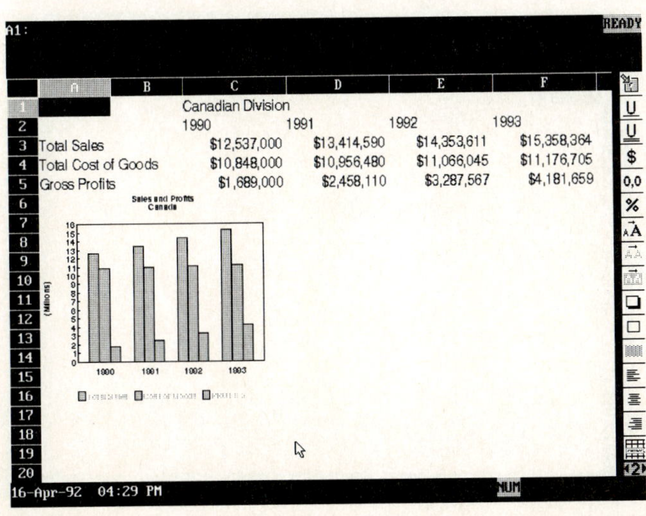

Figure 1-2.   *Worksheet with a graph added*

accessing 1-2-3's menu system. It does not look the same on all systems. If you detach Wysiwyg, your palette will display text, making the icon pictures less detailed in appearance. With Wysiwyg attached, the palette displays graphic images that better represent the task performed when the icon is selected. Also, the number of entries in the palette is affected by whether your monitor supports CGA, EGA, or VGA display modes.

The SmartIcon palette contains icons that correspond to 1-2-3 menu selections. It also contains icons that correspond to Wysiwyg tasks. Most palette selections are designed to operate on a range of cells that you must select prior to selecting the command.

When you first install 1-2-3 on a system with a VGA display, palette 1 will match Figure 1-3. This first palette can be customized. Icons are available that allow you to delete icons and change the order of icons on the custom palette. If you click the right mouse button with an icon highlighted, a brief description of the icon appears at the top of your screen.

You can select an icon with a click of the left mouse button. You can change the active palette by clicking the arrows to the right or left of the palette number at the bottom of the screen. If you want to use the keyboard to select an icon, you must invoke the Icons add-in first. You can then use your Up and Down Arrow keys to highlight different options. You can also use the Left and Right Arrow keys to change the palette that is displayed.

You can attach macro instructions to any of the 12 icons labeled U1 through U12. These are user icons. They can perform any task you can record within the 240-keystroke capacity that can be attached to these icons. The user icons are displayed in

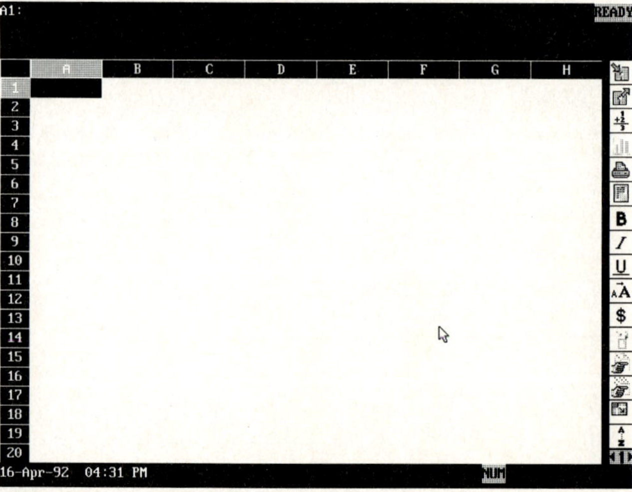

Figure 1-3.   *Default palette 1 visible on a new worksheet*

the last palette and appear as shown in Figure 1-4. You will see these again when macros are discussed later in this chapter.

Expanded Printer Support

1-2-3 Release 2.4 supports printing in landscape mode, where text is printed across the widest part of the page in Wysiwyg. You can think of landscape as turning the page sideways and printing on it in this fashion. Landscape mode is provided for both laser printers and dot matrix printers that support graphic images. This command does not appear in 1-2-3's Print menu; it is located in the Wysiwyg Print Config menu under Orientation.

1-2-3 Release 2.4 also supports printing to an encapsulated PostScript file suitable for incorporation into desktop publishing packages. These files have an .EPS extension and will properly record both text and graphic images.

To create an .EPS file, you must have the PostScript driver installed. You must also select this driver as your printer before selecting Print File from the Wysiwyg menu.

SmartPics to Enhance Worksheet Appearance

SmartPics are .CGM files that contain graphic images. 1-2-3 supplies an assortment of these files that you can incorporate into your worksheets. To be able to access these

Figure 1-4.   User icons displayed in the palette

files, you must transfer Wysiwyg to your hard disk during installation. You may also be able to access some of these files through graphics packages such as Freelance Plus or CorelDraw.

For example, you might want to access an image that you can use for a logo or one that represents comparison data. Figure 1-5 shows a worksheet created with two 1-2-3 graphs and two Metafile images supplied with 1-2-3 Release 2.4. These images

Sales and Profit Report

Canadian Division

	1990	1991	1992	1993
Sales	$12,537,000	$13,414,590	$14,353,611	$15,358,364
Cost of Goods	$10,848,000	$10,956,480	$11,066,045	$11,176,705
Profits	$1,689,000	$2,458,110	$3,287,567	$4,181,659

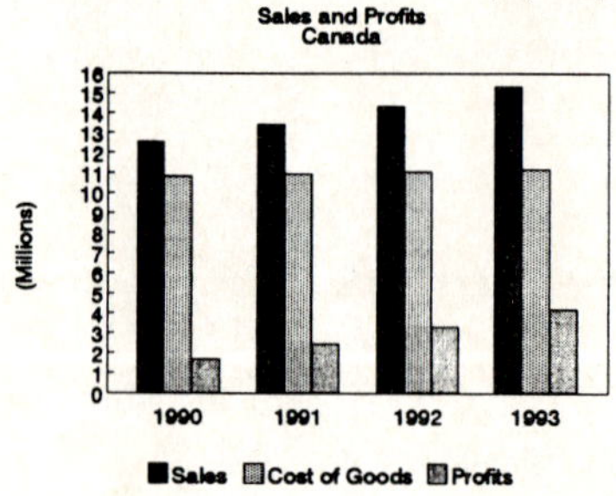

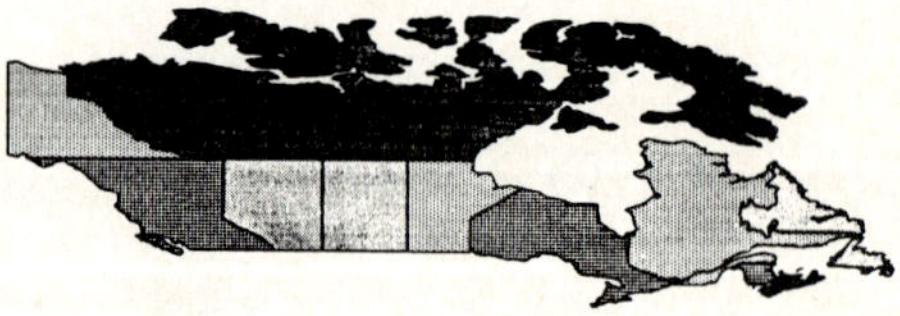

United States Division

	1990	1991	1992	1993
Total Sales	$14,324,000	$15,326,680	$16,399,548	$17,547,516
Total Cost of Goods	$12,978,000	$13,107,780	$13,238,858	$13,371,246
Gross Profits	$1,346,000	$2,218,900	$3,160,690	$4,176,270

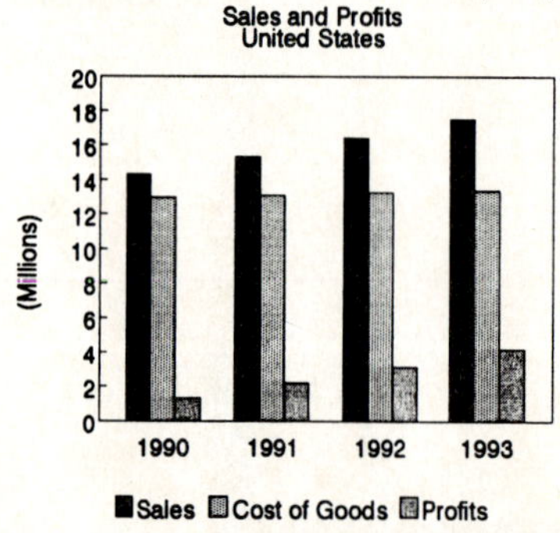

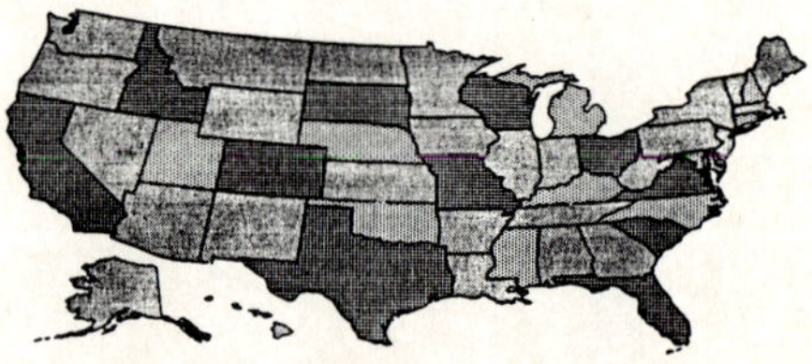

Figure 1-5.   *Worksheet with two graphs and two SmartPics*

were added to the worksheet with the Wysiwyg :Graph Add Metafile command. They can be resized with :Graph Edit if their aspect ratio, or the relationship between length and height, appears distorted.

File Translation Support to Use 1-2-3 Release 2.4 Files in Newly Supported Formats

One strength of Release 2.4 is its ability to read files directly from earlier releases. Releases 2.01, 2.2, and 2.3 use the same .WK1 file format that Release 2.4 uses. If you use your 1-2-3 Release 2.4 data with an earlier release that does not support .FMT files, this data will be ignored. If you use your 1-2-3 Release 2.4 worksheet in Release 2.3 and use Wysiwyg, the .FMT files will be used. Table 1-1 shows all the formats that the Translate Utility now supports.

Backsolver

The Backsolver add-in allows you to look at problems from a different perspective. Rather than providing the assumptions and looking at the result, Backsolver lets you decide what result you want, and then it tells you what value to use for a variable to arrive at the desired result.

Format

1-2-3 Release 1A
1-2-3 Release 2 through 2.4
dBASE II
dBASE III
DIF
Enable 2.0
Multiplan
Supercalc4
Symphony Release 1.0
Symphony Release 1.1 through 2.2
Visicalc

Table 1-1.   Translation Support Available with Release 2.4

Backsolver can tell you whether you can buy a luxury car or a stripped-down basic model based on the payments you can afford. Or, given that you need to make a $10,000 profit, Backsolver can tell you how many units you need to sell to meet your objective.

You enter Backsolver problems the same way as any other 1-2-3 problems. Then you invoke Backsolver and define the various components of the problem. Figure 1-6 shows a Backsolver window where Backsolver is determining how much money you can borrow for a house given a loan term of 30 years, an interest rate of 8 percent, and a monthly payment of $500.

Macros

Macros in 1-2-3 Release 2.4 work the same way they do in earlier releases. The big difference is that now you can create macros and assign them to any of the 12 user icons. This allows you to create 12 of your own SmartIcons to handle tasks such as formatting currency with zero decimal places or formatting a percent with two decimal places. You still have the convenience of the SmartIcon but do not have to accept the predefined options on the icons.

To attach a macro to a user icon you can either enter the keystrokes from the User-Defined Icon dialog box shown in Figure 1-7 or attach a macro that is already

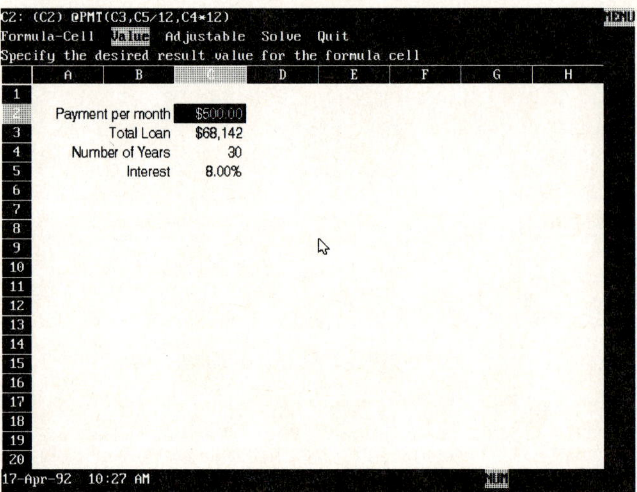

Figure 1-6.   Backsolver window

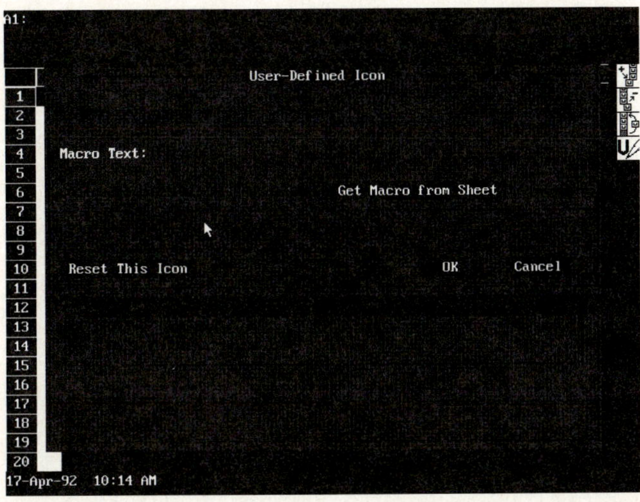

Figure 1-7.   *User-Defined Icon dialog box*

stored on the worksheet. You can use menu commands, keyboards that represent keystrokes, and the advanced macro command {BRANCH}. The total length of the macro cannot exceed 240 characters.

You will want to enter a description as you attach macros to each of the user icons—it is too difficult to remember what each one does if you don't. Then you can read the description for each icon as you point to it.

Chapter **2**

The Access System, Display, and Keyboard

This chapter covers the Lotus Access System—your entry into everything 1-2-3 has to offer. It will also take a detailed look at the screen display and the keyboard. Although this chapter will not require you to type any 1-2-3 commands, you should become comfortable with the keyboard and the information provided by 1-2-3's display as soon as possible; they are designed to assist you in your work with the package.

The Lotus Access System

The Lotus Access System ties together the different programs in the 1-2-3 system. You can use it to enter 1-2-3 and begin working with a worksheet. You can also use the Access System to change your installation selections, print a graph, or translate another data file into a format that is usable in 1-2-3. The main menu for the Access System contains the options 123, PrintGraph, Install, Translate, and Exit. You can choose an option from this menu by typing the first character of the desired selection or by highlighting the desired choice and pressing ENTER.

Highlighting alone does not select a menu option. To avoid a common mistake made by new users, remember to press ENTER *after highlighting your desired selection.*

Just as with any program, you have to load DOS before accessing any 1-2-3 program. If you are using a release prior to 2.4, you may be working with a floppy disk system, which means that you must place a DOS disk in the A drive before turning

13

on your system. This will boot your system, making DOS available in the system memory. When DOS has started you will see the DOS A> prompt on your screen. You then can remove the DOS disk from drive A and insert the 1-2-3 Systems disk. Because Release 2.4 automatically attaches Wysiwyg, a hard disk is required for this release.

If you are working with a hard disk system, you can boot the system by turning it on with the A drive empty. This causes the system to use the operating system information stored on your hard disk. The C> prompt is likely to appear, indicating that the C drive is active. You also want to activate the directory containing the 1-2-3 program files. Thus, if your 1-2-3 files are stored in the directory named 123R24, type **CD\123R24** and press ENTER to make the directory active.

To start the Lotus Access System, you can type **Lotus** and press ENTER. From the Access System you can select the options 1-2-3, PrintGraph, Install, Translate, or Exit.

If you have been given different directions for starting the Lotus Access System by someone at your office, use those special instructions. Differences in the organization structure on your hard disk may necessitate using a different method for starting the program on your machine.

If you want to use a driver configuration file other than 123.SET, you will need to specify the filename. For example, if you want to use a driver configuration file called OFFICE.SET, type **Lotus Office** and then press ENTER.

You can create a number of driver configuration files and use them to establish primary printer or screen displays. Rather than using the menu to change the printer after starting 1-2-3, you can choose the active printer by selecting the .SET file that is appropriate.

Using the Access System makes it easy to transfer from program to program, because you return to the Access System after exiting each program. If you have a hard disk system, you can switch from program to program without having to return to DOS.

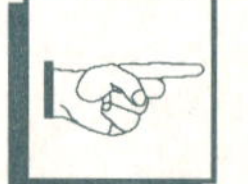

Conserve memory requirements by loading only the program you need rather than using the Access System. To load the 1-2-3 program, type **123** *and press ENTER. To load Translate, type* **trans**; *to load PrintGraph, type* **pgraph**; *to load the Installation program, type* **install**. *If memory is limited, you may need to detach or clear some add-ins from memory with /Add-In Detach or Clear. This is especially true with Release 2.4 because Icons and Wysiwyg are automatically attached.*

Now let's review briefly each of the choices on the Access System menu. This chapter will focus on the 1-2-3 option, since that is the main part of the package. The Translate and PrintGraph options receive additional coverage later in the book. Translate can save valuable time when you want to transfer data between 1-2-3 and another program, and PrintGraph can print a graph that you create with 1-2-3.

1-2-3

1-2-3 is the main option on the Access System menu for all releases. You can select 1-2-3 from the Access System menu or by typing **123** from DOS. This latter approach saves a little memory because the Access System routines do not have to be loaded into memory.

You can use the menu and features of the 1-2-3 program to build spreadsheet models, construct databases, and display graphs on your screen through a series of nested menus. Most of the work you do with the package is done through the 1-2-3 program. The other Access System features are designed to handle more specialized needs, such as translating data and customizing installation settings.

To return to the Access System after working with 1-2-3, simply type /**Q** from 1-2-3's main menu, and then type **Y** to confirm that you wish to exit. With Release 2.2 and above, you have built-in protection against forgetting to save a file. If the current worksheet contains changes that have not been saved, 1-2-3 displays a second prompt before quitting, letting you choose whether or not you wish to save the worksheet. If you initially entered 1-2-3 from the Access System, you return to the Access System menu after quitting 1-2-3. If you entered 1-2-3 directly from DOS, either the A> or C> DOS prompt appears on your screen.

The Wysiwyg and Icons add-ins are automatically attached in Release 2.4. Wysiwyg offers spreadsheet publishing features to create professional-looking spreadsheets, and Icons makes the SmartIcon palette available to perform tasks with a quick mouse selection. These add-ins are very useful, and you will want to keep them attached unless you are creating a large worksheet and are using a machine without expanded memory. You can check the available memory by selecting /Worksheet Status. If only limited memory is available, you will want to save the worksheet with /File Save and then Clear both add-ins from memory with /Add-In Clear. If you want to remove only one add-in, you can use /Add-In Detach and select the add-in that you want to remove. You will free approximately 20K of memory by detaching Icons and 120K by removing Wysiwyg.

PrintGraph

PrintGraph provides a comprehensive range of options for printing or plotting your graphs. Its many menu selections provide options for the final graph printing. With the features of PrintGraph and the Allways or Wysiwyg Add-Ins, you have a full range of options to control graphic output.

You can access PrintGraph from the Access System menu or by typing **pgraph** and pressing ENTER. On a floppy disk system, you must place the PrintGraph disk in the drive.

Like other components of 1-2-3, PrintGraph has a nested menu structure. The menu selections provide the customizing options you can use to print your graph. 1-2-3 can also use the Allways and Wysiwyg Add-Ins. Allways is included in Release 2.2

and Wysiwyg is included in Release 2.3 and 2.4. These Add-Ins let you print a graph as part of a worksheet area.

Translate

Translate permits data interchange between 1-2-3 and other programs by translating files from other programs into a form 1-2-3 can handle, or by translating 1-2-3 files into a variety of other data formats. If you want to access Translate directly, type **trans** and press ENTER.

Once Translate is loaded, a menu appears that allows you to translate from one of the Lotus formats to such formats as DIF (Data Interchange Format), Symphony, or dBASE III, or to translate from one of the other formats to a Lotus 1-2-3 format.

Install

Install is discussed in detail in Appendix A. You can enter the program from the Access System menu or by typing **install** and pressing ENTER. If the Install program is not on a hard disk, insert the Install/Setup disk before attempting to access it.

Exit

When you finish with one of the Access System options, you return to the main Access System menu. To return to DOS, you must use the Exit option.

The Display

1-2-3's screen display is divided into three areas: a control panel at the top of the screen, a worksheet area in the middle, and a status line at the bottom. A *worksheet frame* containing the column names separates the control panel from the worksheet portion of the display. The filename or date display appears at the bottom of the screen below the display of the last row number. Figure 2-1 shows a screen display with all three areas labeled.

If you are using Release 2.3 or 2.4, icons will appear to the right of the worksheet area. They look different depending on whether you are using Wysiwyg mode or text mode. Their appearance will also depend on the resolution of the monitor you are using. These icons are ideally designed for use with a mouse, but in Release 2.4 you can also access them with the keyboard after invoking the Icons add-in.

These icons have limited functionality in Release 2.3 and are designed only to let you move the cell pointer or access help. In Release 2.4 these icons are arranged into SmartIcon palettes. You can choose which palette is in use and even customize the

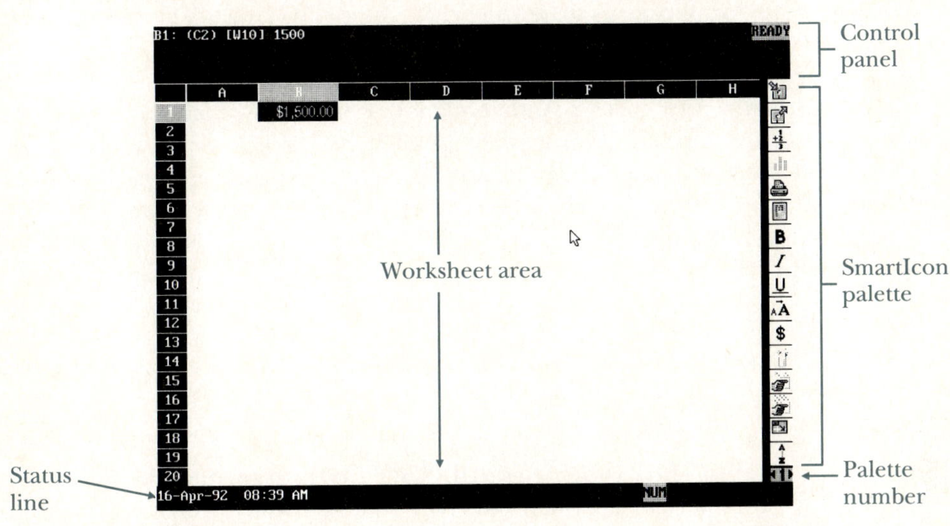

Figure 2-1.   *A screen display*

first palette or attach macros to a user palette. The palette number for the currently selected palette appears at the bottom right corner of your screen. You can click the arrows on either side of this number to increase or decrease the palette number by 1.

The Control Panel

Each of the three lines in the control panel has a specific purpose. The second and third lines are discussed later in this chapter.

The top line provides the greatest number of individual pieces of information. At the far left corner, you'll see the current location of the cell pointer—the highlighted bar visible on the worksheet. 1-2-3 displays the column and row location of the address to give the specific location of the cell pointer in the current worksheet. In Figure 2-1 the cell pointer is in cell B1 (the intersection of column B and row 1), so the top line begins with "B1."

Immediately to the right of the cell pointer location, you can see any special display attributes assigned to the cell. The display attributes 1-2-3 will show include number formatting, cell protection, and column width. If the Wysiwyg Add-In is loaded, abbreviations for Wysiwyg formats will display enclosed in curly braces ({}). After the display attribute information, the content of the cell as it was entered appears. Suppose, for example, that you entered **514.76**. If you decide to display the entry as currency with zero decimal places, you see $515 on the worksheet, but in the control panel you see your original entry.

At the far right corner of the top line, you can see a highlighted area that is the *mode indicator*. This indicator tells you what 1-2-3 is doing and what it expects from you. It can instruct you to wait, correct an error, point to a worksheet location, or tell 1-2-3 what to do next.

Table 2-1 lists the mode indicators and their meanings. Once 1-2-3 is in a certain mode, you must either follow along with its plans or find a way to change the indicator. For example, if the mode indicator reads LABEL, you cannot enter a value entry until you find a way to change the indicator. In some cases this requires eliminating your previous selections and starting over. Many frustrations come from not understanding and watching the mode indicator. In order to maintain a smooth working relationship with 1-2-3, you must stay "in sync" with 1-2-3's mode indicators.

Indicator	Meaning
EDIT	An entry is being edited. EDIT can be generated by 1-2-3 when your entry contains an error and 1-2-3 wants you to edit it. It can also be generated by pressing the F2 (EDIT) key to change a cell entry or by typing an entry in response to a command prompt.
ERROR	1-2-3 has encountered an error. The problem is noted in the middle or lower-left corner of the screen. Press ESC to clear the error message, and then correct the problem specified in the error message.
FILES	1-2-3 wants you to select a filename to proceed.
FIND	The /Data Query Find command is active.
FRMT	The /Data Parse Format-Line is being edited.
HELP	A HELP display is active.
LABEL	1-2-3 has decided that you are making a label entry.
MENU	1-2-3 is waiting for you to make a menu selection.
NAMES	1-2-3 is displaying a list of range or graph names.
POINT	1-2-3 is waiting for you to point to a cell or range.
READY	1-2-3 is waiting for you to make a new request.
SETTINGS	A Release 2.3 or 2.4 dialog box is being edited.
STAT	Worksheet status information is displayed.
VALUE	1-2-3 has decided that you are making a value entry.
WAIT	1-2-3 is processing your last command and cannot begin a new task until the flashing WAIT indicator disappears.

Table 2-1.   Mode Indicators

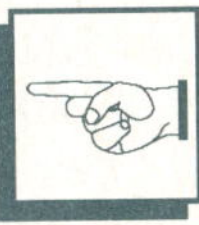

When 1-2-3 does not respond as you expect, check the mode indicator first. If the indicator contains anything other than READY, you cannot start a new request. You might think you are in the middle of making menu selections, but if you check the indicator and see ERROR, you must press ESC to acknowledge the error condition.

Wysiwyg Mode Indicator

If you are using Release 2.4, Wysiwyg is already attached for you. This means that you will be able to type a colon (:) from 1-2-3's Ready mode to display the Wysiwyg menu. Once you begin to use Wysiwyg, the mode indicators in the upper-right corner are Wysiwyg mode indicators. Table 2-2 displays the Wysiwyg mode indicators and what they mean.

The Worksheet

The worksheet occupies most of your display screen. This area serves as a window that allows you to look at the information stored in memory in an orderly format. Although you can always move around on the worksheet to see any row or column, the amount of memory you have on your system limits the number of entries you can make on the worksheet.

Think of the memory in your computer as similar to the workspace on the top of your desk. Just as different-sized desks may hold different numbers of file folders or other information, varied amounts of memory within various computers control the

---

Mode	Meaning
COLOR	You are selecting a color for a graphic that you are editing.
CYCLE	You are cycling through objects on a graph to select one.
DRAG	You are adding a rectangle or ellipse in the graphics editing mode.
PAN	You selected View Pan when editing a graphic.
SELECT	Wysiwyg is waiting for you to select a font, graph, or printer.
SIZE	You selected Transform while editing a graphic.
TEXT	You selected Text Edit.
WYSIWYG	A Wysiwyg menu is active.

Table 2-2.   Wysiwyg Mode Indicators

amount of worksheet data they store. The amount of memory you have in your system dictates whether you have room in memory for one year's budget data or five years' worth. If there is not sufficient room for all your information, you can probably create smaller worksheets with part of the data on each worksheet. You just need to determine a logical way to split the data between worksheet files. Although you can have only one worksheet in memory at a time, you can have as many worksheets as you want on disk. You can also add formulas to link to data in other worksheets.

The worksheet has an orderly arrangement of rows and columns. The row numbers and column letters appear at the top and left side of the worksheet frame in Figure 2-1. Every entry you make on the worksheet is in a specific cell address uniquely identified by the row and column location that make up the actual cell address. Cell entries can be numbers, labels, or formulas. You will learn more about the specific worksheet options in Chapter 3.

The Status Line

The status line, the display area for only date and time in earlier releases of 1-2-3, can now display a filename. The default is to show the date and time, but you may choose Filename from 1-2-3's /Worksheet Global Default Other Clock menu to display the filename. Existing worksheets display the filename as soon as they are retrieved from disk, but new worksheets display the date and time until you have saved them to disk.

Releases before 2.3 and 2.4 will temporarily use the status line to display messages such as "Disk Full" or "Printer Not Ready." In Release 2.3 and above, these error messages appear in a dialog box in the middle of the screen. Proceed by pressing ESC to eliminate the error message and change the ERROR indicator or press F1 for an explanation.

Descriptions also appear in the status line to let you know when certain keys have been pressed or when certain other settings for the package are in use. The seven key indicators and their meanings are as follows:

Indicator	Meaning
CAPS	The CAPS LOCK key was pressed. When the CAPS indicator is on, the alphabetic keys produce capital letters.
END	The END key was pressed and 1-2-3 is waiting for you to press an arrow key.
LEARN	ALT-F5 (LEARN) was pressed, enabling you to save a set of keystrokes. The keys you press will be recorded as a macro on the worksheet.
NUM	The NUM LOCK key was pressed. This key allows you to enter a number from the numeric keypad.
OVR	The INS toggle was pressed, allowing keyboard entries in Overstrike mode rather than Insert mode.

Indicator	Meaning
SCROLL	The SCROLL LOCK key was pressed. This key controls the way information scrolls off your screen. With SCROLL LOCK on, 1-2-3 scrolls the worksheet in the direction indicated. With SCROLL LOCK off, 1-2-3 moves the cell pointer in the direction indicated without scrolling.
STEP	The STEP mode is in effect for macro execution. This mode is activated by pressing ALT-F2. STEP is discussed further in Chapter 12.

Seven additional indicators signal more than just one key press. These indicators and their meanings are as follows:

Indicator	Meaning
CALC	The worksheet needs to be recalculated. Changes have been made to the data that are not yet recalculated in the screen display.
CIRC	The worksheet contains a circular reference, which is a cell that refers back to itself. 1-2-3 provides special help to locate the circular reference with the /Worksheet Status command.
CMD	Appears during the execution of a macro.
MEM	Less than 32K of memory remains.
RO	The status of the current file is Read-Only. This means that you will not be able to save your changes to the same file. To save your changes, you must supply a different filename, path, or both.
SST	This is the macro indicator that appears during single-step execution for a macro. The STEP indicator changes to SST when the macro is pausing for user input. SST is discussed further in Chapter 12.
UNDO	The UNDO feature is enabled, allowing you to press the UNDO (ALT-F4) key to reverse your last action.

Help Features

You can change your screen to an on-line reference source simply by pressing the F1 (HELP) key. 1-2-3 will guess at what your question might be and supply information based on your current task. If you want additional help or help with a different subject, you can use the Help Index or ask for one of the other topics listed at the bottom of the Help screen.

Figure 2-2 lists the help that 1-2-3 provides for entering a value or a formula in a cell. In releases before 2.3, the help screen displays help topics in different colors to

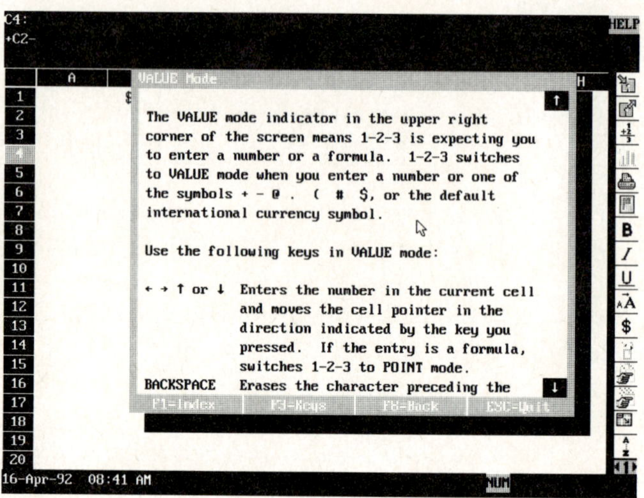

Figure 2-2. *The help screen for entering a value or a formula*

make it easy for you to select additional information. In Release 2.3 and 2.4, additional help topics are in different colors and several function keys are displayed to help you make further selections. You can use F1 to display the Help Index, which in all releases lists the major help topics, F3 to display a list of keys you can use with Help, and F8 to display the help screen you were looking at last.

Since some of the help information is larger than the area 1-2-3 uses to display it, you may need to use the arrow keys and PGDN and PGUP to shift the portion of the help information that appears in the help display. If you are using a mouse, you can click different parts of the screen to select the functions they represent. For example, clicking ESC=Quit on the help screen is the same as pressing ESC.

If Wysiwyg or another Add-In is loaded, pressing F1 displays help information for 1-2-3 unless the Wysiwyg or other Add-In menu is displayed. When an Add-In menu is displayed, pressing F1 displays help information for the Add-In.

The 1-2-3 Menu

Lines 2 and 3 of the control panel can be transformed into a menu of command selections by pressing the slash key (/). You can also activate the menu with the mouse by moving the mouse pointer to the control panel. When the menu is displayed, it initially looks like this:

```
A1:                                                                   MENU
Worksheet  Range  Copy  Move  File  Print  Graph  Data  System  Add-In  Quit
Global  Insert  Delete  Column  Erase  Titles  Window  Status  Page  Learn
```

Menus are the backbone of the 1-2-3 program and are your way of accessing all its features. They are always easily available to you but they will not clutter the screen when you do not need them.

The line beneath the individual menu options displays a description of the current menu selection. You can point to different menu items in line 2. As you move from item to item, the description line (line 3) changes accordingly. For instance, when you point to the Worksheet option in the menu, the second line lists all the specific Worksheet options: Global, Insert, Delete, Column, Erase, Titles, Window, Status, Page, and Learn. These are not completely descriptive of the functions provided, but they do serve as reminders once you learn the commands.

To select a menu item, you can either type a slash followed by the first letter of the menu item (for example, /W for Worksheet) or use the arrow keys to highlight the item, and press ENTER. To select a menu item, point to it and click. When you select a menu item, 1-2-3 invokes the selected command or presents a menu for further selections.

Each subsequent menu level is selected in the same manner as the previous selection, with each level refining your choice further. If you choose a menu item in error, you can back out to the previous level by pressing ESC once. Each time you press ESC, you retreat to the next highest menu level until you are eventually back at READY mode. To back all the way out of the selection with one entry, press the CTRL and BREAK keys simultaneously.

Wysiwyg's Menu

Wysiwyg is an add-in program that supplements 1-2-3 features by adding spreadsheet publishing tasks to what 1-2-3 offers. The letters in Wysiwyg stand for What You See Is What You Get, meaning that what appears on your screen is exactly what will print. When you start 1-2-3 Release 2.4, the Wysiwyg add-in is automatically attached. With earlier releases you must use /Add-In Attach before you can use it. Once Wysiwyg is attached you can type a colon (:) to access its menu, shown here.

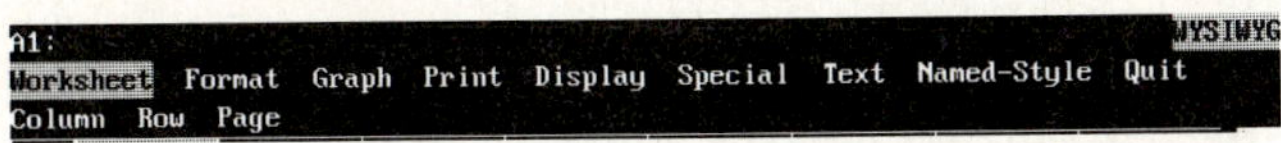

You may be surprised to see that some of the Wysiwyg menu options are represented by the same commands as 1-2-3's menu commands. Different features are offered by the menu, even though at first glance there seems to be duplication. Keep in mind that 1-2-3's purpose is to make 1-2-3 entries and provide basic formatting. Wysiwyg offers significant appearance improvements and lets you integrate text and graphics on one printed page. After activating the Wysiwyg menu, you make selections the same way you make selections from 1-2-3's menu: either by highlighting the desired selection and pressing ENTER or by typing the first letter of the desired selection. Like 1-2-3, Wysiwyg uses a dialog box to allow you to change a series of settings and display the changes on the screen. You will learn more about Wysiwyg in Chapter 15.

Dialog Boxes and Settings Sheets

In Release 2.2, 1-2-3 introduced settings sheets, which appeared for eight groups of commands and displayed the current settings the command options used. In Release 2.3, these settings sheets were expanded and now are entities known as dialog boxes. These dialog boxes are an alternative to using menu commands.

Figure 2-3 shows a dialog box for the /Worksheet Global command. Rather than selecting /Worksheet Global and then selecting other options for it, you can use the dialog box to make all of the worksheet global changes at once. To use a dialog box in Release 2.3 and above, you must select the command that displays it, such as /Worksheet Global, and then either press F2 (EDIT) or point to any part of the dialog box with the mouse and press the left mouse button. You can hide or redisplay a dialog box by pressing F6 (WINDOW). You can still select from the menu at the top of the screen. Selecting from the menu makes the one change and removes the dialog box and menu from the screen.

A dialog box gives you several options. Some options can be used or ignored, such as "Protection on" in Figure 2-3. Options like this one use *check boxes*, which are brackets before the option. If empty, the option is not selected. If filled with an X or

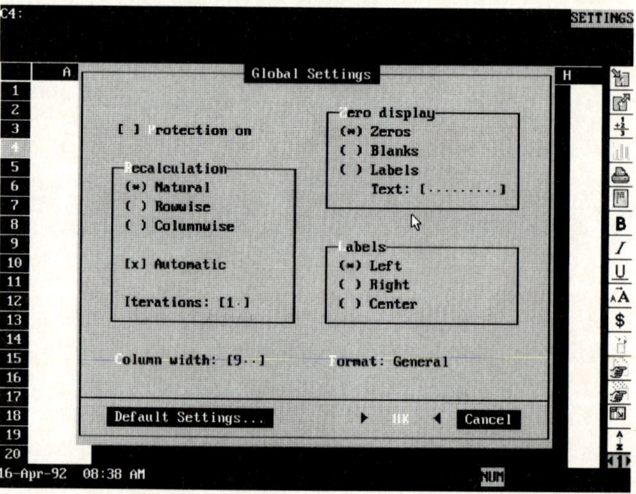

Figure 2-3.   *Dialog box for Global settings*

a period, the option is selected. The selections available with check boxes are not mutually exclusive—more than one can be active at one time.

Options buttons, on the other hand, are mutually exclusive. These shown under the Labels option in Figure 2-3, are indicated with an (*) marking the selected option and empty brackets ( ) marking the ones that are not selected. When you select one from a group you are deselecting the previously selected one.

The third type of selection a dialog box uses is a *text box.* Column width is an example of a text box in Figure 2-3. Text boxes require that you type the entry. You must type an entry that is appropriate for the option that uses the text box. For example, in the Column width text box, you can type any number between 0 and 124.

List boxes provide a list of valid selections. You can move the highlight to the desired selection and press ENTER, or you can click the selection with a mouse.

Pop-up dialog boxes are dialog boxes that offer additional options in response to a selection in the current dialog box.

The last type of option a dialog box uses is a *command button* like the OK and Cancel ones shown in Figure 2-3. Most dialog boxes have OK and Cancel command buttons. OK finalizes the dialog box and Cancel returns all of the selections you have made to their previous settings as if you used ESC. A dialog box may have other command buttons such as the Defaults command button in Figure 2-3, which shows the /Worksheet Global Default dialog box.

You can move between sections of a dialog box using the keyboard or mouse. With a mouse, you only have to point to the option you want to select or deselect and click. With the keyboard, after pressing F2 to edit the settings, you can either use the TAB and arrow keys to move to the option you want, or you can type the letter of the option that is highlighted or is a different color. The dialog box is hierarchical; to select a recalculation option you must select Recalculation before you can select one of the options in the box below it. Also, if you are using the keyboard, you can select or deselect options by highlighting the option and pressing the SPACEBAR. You can toggle the setting to a check box by highlighting it and pressing the SPACEBAR. You can select the OK command button by pressing ENTER again or the Cancel command button by pressing ESC.

When you finish using a dialog box by selecting the OK command button, 1-2-3 returns you to the menu that you invoked to display the dialog box. You can press CRTL-BREAK or ESC several times to return to READY mode without losing your changes.

The Keyboard

You will begin using the keyboard in the next chapter as you make entries in worksheet cells. This section focuses on standard or enhanced keyboards, which are shown in Figures 2-4 and 2-5. There are some differences between these and keyboards of other popular systems. These differences do not require changes in the installation of 1-2-3 or limit your use of the program, but they may affect which keys

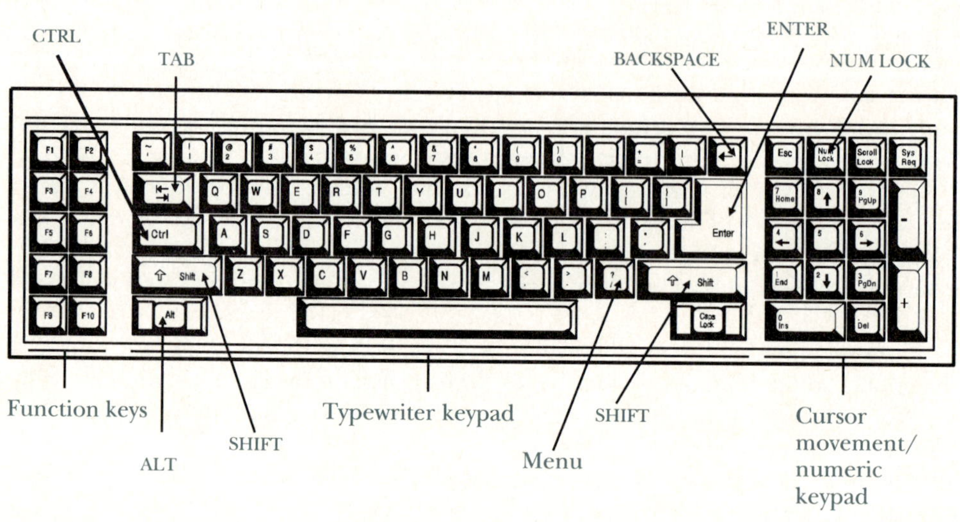

Figure 2-4.   *The IBM standard keyboard*

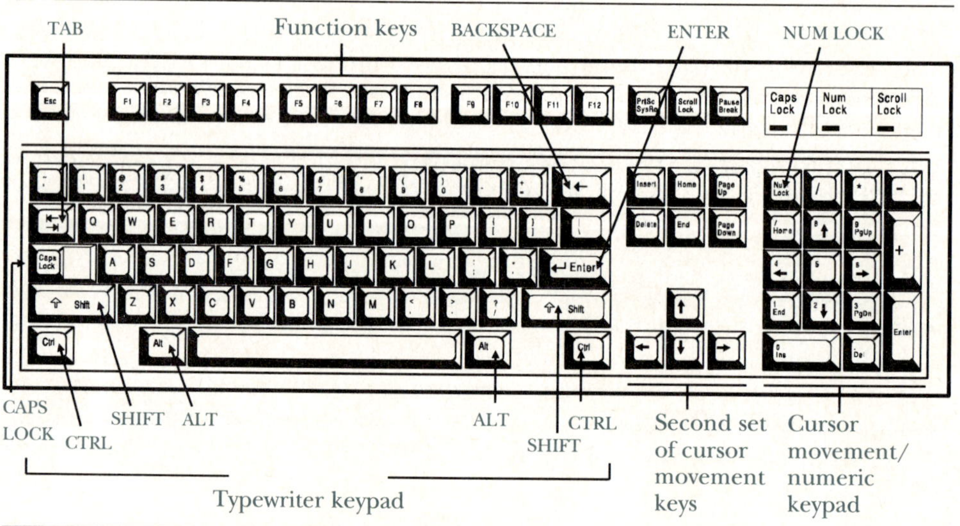

Figure 2-5.   *The IBM enhanced keyboard*

you use to access 1-2-3's features. If you are using a different style of keyboard, you will want to identify where each of the keys mentioned is located on your own keyboard. For example, some keyboards only have a single set of cursor movement keys. On these keyboards, you must press the NUM LOCK key every time you want to switch between using the keys in the keypad for numbers and for cursor movement.

All the keys are discussed in this chapter to provide a single reference source for all keyboard functions. Individual features are pointed out again as needed in later chapters, so you do not have to worry about absorbing all of this information now.

The keyboard has three basic sections. The keys at the far left or along the top of the keyboard are the function keys. These keys are made available to software developers for program-specific use, so there is little consistency among programs in the way function keys are used. Lotus has assigned these keys the special functions shown in Table 2-3. Pressing any of these keys causes 1-2-3 to take the requested

Function Key	Assignment
F1 (HELP)	Provides context-sensitive help.
F2 (EDIT)	Allows you to alter the contents of an entry or activates a dialog box.
F3 (NAME)	Displays a list of your range names or switches between a full or partial screen display of file or range names.
F4 (ABS)	Toggles from a relative address to an absolute or mixed address or enters POINT mode to select a range.
F5 (GOTO)	Moves your cell pointer to the range or cell address you select.
F6 (WINDOW)	Toggles between two windows orhides or displays dialog boxes or settings sheets.
F7 (QUERY)	Repeats the last query operation.
F8 (TABLE)	Repeats the most recent table operation.
F9 (CALC)	Recalculates the entire worksheet.
F10 (GRAPH)	Redraws the most recent graph.
ALT-F1 (COMPOSE)	Creates international characters.
ALT-F2 (STEP)	Executes macros a step at a time.
ALT-F3 (RUN)	Runs selected macro.
ALT-F4 (UNDO)	Undoes the effect of all actions since the last READY indicator if the Undo feature is enabled.
ALT-F5 (LEARN)	Turns Learn on and off.
ALT-F7 (APP1)	Starts an Add-In application.
ALT-F8 (APP2)	Starts an Add-In application.
ALT-F9 (APP3)	Starts an Add-In application.
ALT-F10 (ADDIN) or (APP4)	Displays a menu that allows you to access Add-In applications or starts an add-in application.
CTRL-F1 (Bookmark)	Displays the Help topic you viewed when you last viewed Help.

Table 2-3.   Function Key Assignments with 1-2-3

action. The function keys are used in combination with the ALT key to perform additional tasks.

The keys to the far right serve a dual purpose: They make up the numeric keypad and cursor movement keys. Table 2-4 explains where each of these keys moves the cell pointer. Notice that keys also have direction arrows and other writing on them. This shows their normal function in 1-2-3 when they are used for cell-pointer movement. If you depress the NUM LOCK key, you can also use these keys for numeric entries. Like the CAPS LOCK key, it toggles each time it is pressed. Enhanced keyboards have a second set of cursor movement keys. Depending on the mode indicator, the same key may perform slightly different actions. For example, in READY mode the RIGHT ARROW key moves the cell pointer one cell to the right. In EDIT mode the same key moves the cursor one character to the right, and in MENU mode the next item

Key	Action
HOME	Moves the cell pointer to A1. In EDIT mode, moves to the beginning of the entry.
UP ARROW	Moves the cell pointer up one cell on the worksheet in READY mode. In EDIT mode, finalizes the entry.
DOWN ARROW	Moves the cell pointer down one cell on the worksheet. In EDIT mode, finalizes the entry.
RIGHT ARROW	Moves the cell pointer one cell to the right in READY mode. In EDIT mode, moves the cursor one character to the right.
LEFT ARROW	Moves the cell pointer one cell to the left in READY mode. In EDIT mode, moves the cursor one character to the left.
PGUP	Moves the cell pointer one screen up.
PGDN	Moves the cell pointer one screen down.
END-ARROW key	When the cell pointer is on a cell containing an entry, moves the cell pointer to the end of your entries in the direction indicted by the arrow key. When the cell pointer is on a blank cell, takes the cell pointer in the arrow's direction to the next cell that has an entry. In EDIT mode, moves to the end of the entry.
CTRL-RIGHT or CTRL-LEFT ARROW	Moves your window into the worksheet a full screen to the right or left.
CTRL-HOME	Moves the cell pointer to A1 in the worksheet.
END-HOME	Moves the cell pointer to the last nonblank cell in the worksheet.

Table 2-4.   *Numeric Keypad Functions*

on the menu is highlighted. Although the basic movement is similar in all instances, the effect is not identical.

Let's look at a brief example of the use of these keys. A screen display from 1-2-3 is shown in Figure 2-6. The cell pointer or highlighted area is found in location C3, as shown by the row and column designators at the side and top of the display, and as indicated at the upper-left corner of the control panel. Using the keypad keys moves the cell pointer to new locations. The following table shows the new location of the cell pointer if the listed keys are pressed when the cell pointer is in location C3:

Key Sequence	New Cursor Location
LEFT ARROW	B3
RIGHT ARROW	D3
UP ARROW	C2
DOWN ARROW	C4
END followed by DOWN ARROW	C5
END followed by UP ARROW	C2
END followed by RIGHT ARROW	G3
END followed by LEFT ARROW	B3
PGUP	C1 (Cell pointer cannot move up a screen's worth of rows from its present location)
PGDN	C23
HOME	A1
CTRL-RIGHT ARROW	I3
CTRL-LEFT ARROW	Beeps because it can't scroll screen to the left

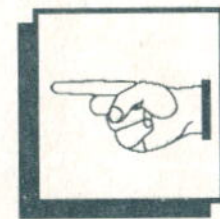

Focus first on the basic keys for cell-pointer movement. There are many keys that allow you to make your way around a worksheet efficiently, but it can be difficult for a novice to remember all the options. Five basic entries are all you need to get started: Press the HOME *key to move to A1, and use the four arrow keys to move in other directions. If you hold down the arrow keys, they repeat and move you around very quickly.*

Although the icon palette in Release 2.4 is designed to provide productivity for mouse users, you can use it with the keyboard as well. You must invoke the Icons add-in by typing **/AI** to select Add-In Invoke, highlighting ICONS, and pressing ENTER. You can use the UP ARROW and DOWN ARROW to highlight any icon in the

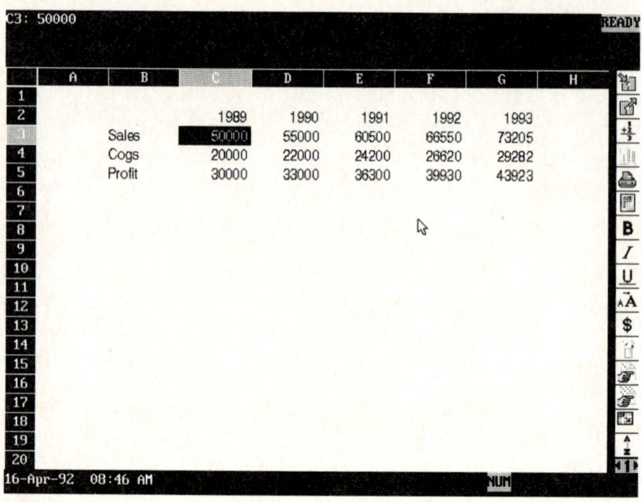

Figure 2-6.   The screen display

current SmartIcon palette and press ENTER to select it. To change the palette number, press the LEFT ARROW or RIGHT ARROW key.

The keys in the center of your keyboard are in most cases identical to the key assignments on a regular typewriter. Table 2-4 lists some of the special keys and additional uses for the regular typewriter keys.

The Mouse

With Release 2.3 and 2.4, you can make selections with a mouse. Assuming the mouse is attached and the software for the mouse is working before you load 1-2-3, the 1-2-3 screen will include a mouse pointer and the SmartIcon panel, which appears on the right edge of the screen. You can change which SmartIcon palette appears by checking the arrows that appear next to the palette number at the lower-right corner of the screen. Later you will learn how to alter options within a palette. In graphic screens such as with the Wysiwyg Add-In, the mouse pointer will look like an arrow. The SmartIcon panel uses solid arrows (◄, ►, ▼, ▲) to represent the arrow keys. If your icon panel displays a question mark, selecting it will give you the same results as pressing F1 (HELP). You can select one of these symbols by pointing to it and clicking the left mouse button. For example, clicking ► is the same as pressing the RIGHT ARROW. If your current palette does not display a question mark or arrows, you can always change the palette.

Include the software that the mouse needs to run in your CONFIG.SYS or AU-TOEXEC.BAT files so it is available every time you load your computer. 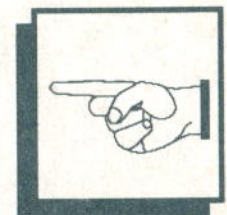

Besides using the icon panel, you can also move to a cell by pointing to it and clicking the cell with the left mouse button. If the cell you want does not appear on the screen and is on the current worksheet, hold down the left mouse button and move the mouse in the direction you want the worksheet window scrolled. This is called *dragging* the mouse. You will also drag a mouse to select groups of cells.

When you use the mouse, the left mouse button represents the ENTER key and the right mouse button represents the ESC key. If your mouse has three buttons, the middle one is generally ignored. If you want, you can switch the buttons with the Install program.

Chapter 3

Entering Data in 1-2-3's Worksheet

Learning how to make entries on 1-2-3's worksheet is one of the most important steps in gaining full use of the package's features. Everything you do with 1-2-3 depends on the entries you make in worksheet cells. These entries are the basis for financial models and projections. They are also the basis for files used in the data management environment because data records are nothing more than a special organization of data entered into worksheet cells. Furthermore, these entries are the basis for graphs because graphs are created by referencing calls in your worksheet.

The Worksheet

In Chapter 2, the discussion of the worksheet display focused on the visible upper-left corner of the worksheet. The 8 columns and 20 rows you saw on the screen are a very small part of the whole worksheet. In its entirety, the Release 2.4 worksheet has 256 columns and 8192 rows. The complete worksheet, though not visible all at once, is organized just like the small section you examined.

Since the worksheet is a replacement for green-bar columnar pads, it may be interesting to make a size comparison. The space for one entry on a green-bar sheet is about 1 1/8 inches by 1/4 inch. If you multiply this area by the number of cells in the 1-2-3 worksheet, you find that the equivalent of your electronic sheet would require a piece of green-bar paper more than 23 feet wide and 170 feet long! The electronic version is certainly more practical in terms of storage space, and it offers the added advantage of automatic recalculation.

1-2-3's worksheet has not always been this large. Release 1A had only 2048 rows. If you are using Release 1A, however, you still have a generous area for performing calculations or storing data.

When you use the Translate utility to convert data between applications, you are limited by the restrictions that apply to the application. For example, if you translate a Release 2.4 worksheet to a release 1A one, the worksheet you will create will only contain the entries stored in A1..IV2048 of the original worksheet (or through row 2048).

Figure 3-1 shows the layout of the electronic worksheet. You can use the screen as a window into any part of a worksheet you want to see. When you move the cell pointer to the extreme edges of the screen and beyond, 1-2-3 scrolls the existing information off the screen to display a new area of the worksheet.

You can make entries in any of the cells on the worksheet, within the memory limitations of your system. Each cell can only contain one entry at a time, however. If you make a second entry in a cell that already contains information, the existing information is replaced by the new information.

Types of Entries

1-2-3 categorizes entries as either label entries or value entries. These two entry types serve as the building blocks for both simple and sophisticated worksheet models. *Label entries* contain at least one text character. Examples include Accounting, Sales, John Smith, 111 Simmons Lane, and 456T78. Even the last example, which is

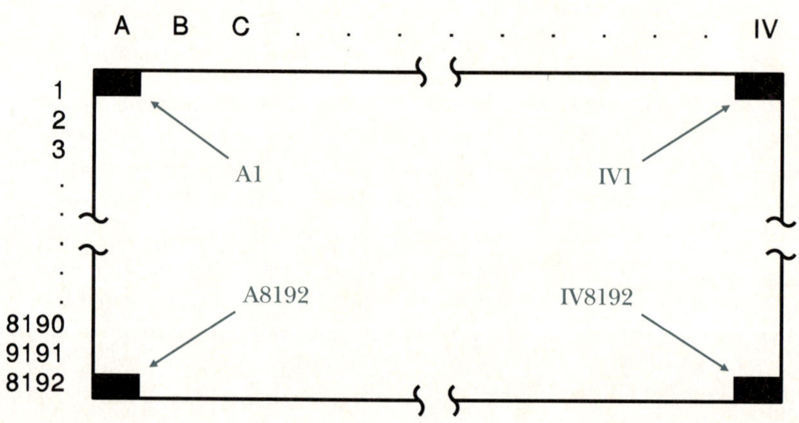

Figure 3-1.   *The worksheet layout*

composed mostly of numbers, has one letter character and therefore is categorized as a label entry. Label entries cannot be used in arithmetic operations. *Value entries, on the other hand, are either numbers or formulas and can be used in arithmetic operations.*

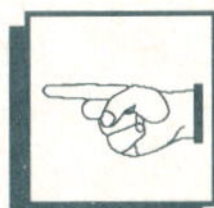

You will learn more about files in Chapter 8, but for now you will want to select /File Save periodically to save the entries that you make on the worksheet. After the first save operation, you will need to confirm that you want to replace the copy on disk with a new copy. The first icon in each SmartIcon palette will request a save operation if you select it. You can access any worksheet file stored on disk with /File Retrieve. This operation will replace the worksheet in memory with the requested file from the disk.

1-2-3 determines the type of entry for a particular cell by reading the first character you type in the cell. Once 1-2-3 determines the entry type, the only way you can change its mind is by either pressing ESC and starting a new entry in the cell or editing the cell to remove or add a label indicator. A *label indicator* is a single character that appears at the front of each label entry and tells 1-2-3 how to display the entry in the cell. You can enter a label indicator or have 1-2-3 generate one for you.

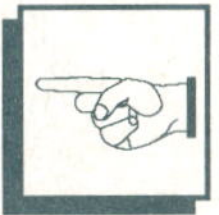

Learn to check the mode indicator as you perform data entry. This can save you considerable time and frustration as you start using 1-2-3. One quick look tells you whether 1-2-3 is treating your entry as a number or a label and allows you to make a quick correction if you need to before completing the entry.

As you make an entry into a cell, 1-2-3 displays the entry on the second line of the control panel at the top of your screen. This line is referred to as the *Edit line.* A sample entry of 17.56 in the Edit line looks like this:

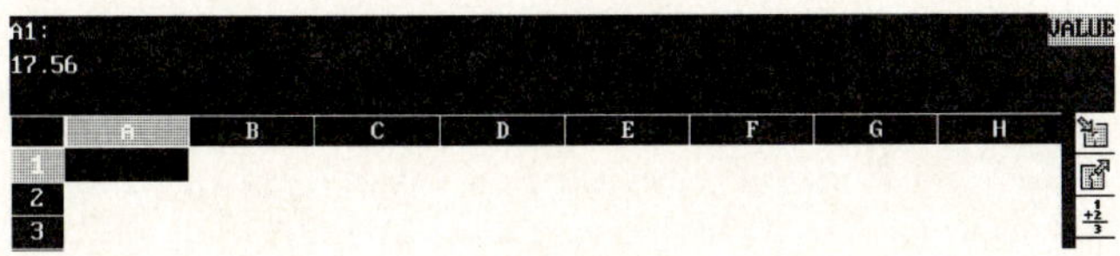

In Release 2.2 and above, as soon as your entry fills the first Edit line, information scrolls off the front of the Edit line to allow you to enter as many as 256 characters. If you want to look at the beginning of a long entry that is not currently visible, press F2 (EDIT) to place yourself in EDIT mode, and then press the HOME key to move to the beginning of the entry.

Once you finish your entry and review its contents in the Edit line, you can finalize it by pressing ENTER or by moving to a new cell. Although the RIGHT and LEFT ARROW keys move within the entry being edited, other keys, such as UP ARROW and PGDN, perform the same functions that they do in READY mode and finalize the edited entry at the same time. Te finalized entry appears in the worksheet cell, as shown here:

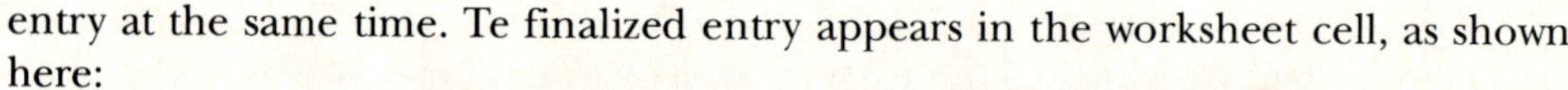
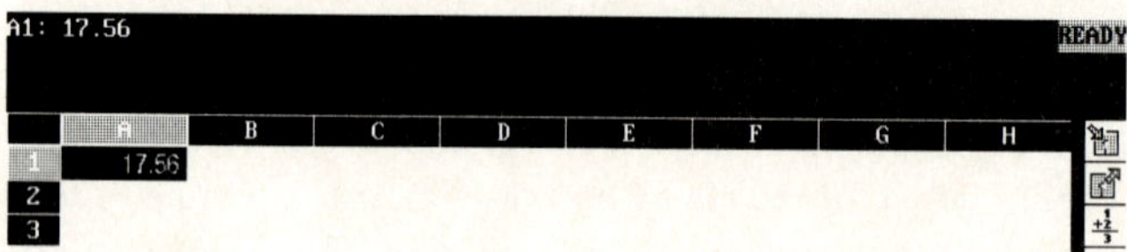

Use the UP *or* DOWN ARROW *key to finalize your entry. You can save a keystroke on most entries if you finalize by moving the cell pointer rather than pressing* ENTER *and then moving to a new cell.*

When the entry is a formula, the result of the formula's calculation appears on the worksheet. For example, if cell A1 contains 10 and A2 contains 5, entering the formula +A1/A2 in cell A3 causes the number 2 to appear in A3 on the worksheet.

Entries other than formulas appear as typed, except that the current format option is applied. For example, if you enter **.4** and the format is Percent, your entry is displayed as 40% in the cell. In the top line of the control panel, however, the entry appears exactly as you typed it.

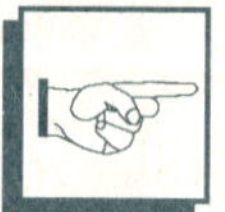
Use the special keys or the mouse introduced in Chapter 2 to position the cell pointer for an entry. Although the arrow keys move you to any location on the worksheet, there are some shortcuts. You can press the F5 *(GOTO) key and then type an address like* **D3** *or* **F2**, *and 1-2-3 immediately positions the cell pointer in the new address. The* END-HOME *key sequence is another useful combination; it takes you to the last entry on the worksheet.*

Label Entries

You use label entries whenever you want to enter text or character data into a worksheet cell. Labels can contain descriptive information as well as character data. As descriptive information, a label might be a report heading containing the company name placed in a cell near the top of the worksheet. Labels can also be column headings indicating the months of the year, row headings indicating account names, or descriptors placed anywhere on the worksheet.

Label entries can also record text data anywhere on the worksheet. Part numbers, employee names, sales territories, and warehouse locations are all examples of data containing text characters. A worksheet to project salaries might contain employee names as label entries. Worksheets that deal with suppliers, inventory items, product sales projections, and client accounts are all likely to have some label entries.

There are no restrictions on the characters you can enter in a label. 1-2-3 supports the full set of characters from the Lotus International Character Set (LICS), including numbers and symbols. LICS codes are the full set of characters that can be represented by Release 2.0 and above; they provide access to international symbols and many special characters not directly accessible from the keyboard. The full set of LICS codes is described in Appendix B.

The character desired can be entered with the @CHAR function described in Chapter 7, or by pressing ALT-F1 (COMPOSE) and then typing the key combination representing the desired character. For example, to generate a cent sign (¢) you can type **@CHAR(162)**, or you can press ALT-F1 and type **c/**. Your display will be the cent sign, not "c/."

The primary rules for label entries are summarized in the box called "Rules for Labels." 1-2-3 displays as much of the label as possible in the cell you use for the entry. If the label is longer than your cell width and the cells to the right are empty, 1-2-3 borrows space from them to permit the complete display of the label. If the adjacent cell is not empty, 1-2-3 truncates the display as soon as it has reached the maximum number of characters that can fit. The extra characters are not lost; they are stored internally and are displayed if the cell is widened or the contents of cells to the right are erased.

When you type a letter as the first entry in a cell, 1-2-3 will add a default label indicator that establishes the entry as a label and controls the display of the entry within the cell when the entry is finalized. The label indicator appears in the top line of the control panel but does not show in the worksheet cell. Only the effects of the indicator appear on the worksheet. If a label begins with a value character, you must enter a label indicator before you type that first character because 1-2-3 determines the entry type by the first character entered in a cell. Value characters are 0 through 9 and . + − $ (@ #.

For example, consider the entries **'134 Tenth Street** and **'213-78-6751**. (The hyphens count as text.) If you do not enter the label indicator, 1-2-3 does not let you

---

Rules for Labels

Labels cannot be longer than 256 characters.

An entry is automatically recognized as a label if the first character is an alphabetic character or any character other than 0 through 9, or any of the following:

. + - $ (@ #

Any entry that contains alphabet letters or editing characters is considered a label, even if it also contains numbers.

When a label begins with a numeric digit or symbol, a label indicator must be typed first.

Labels longer than the cell width borrow display space from the cells to the right if those cells are empty.

finalize the first entry (the address) in a cell. The second entry (the social security number) can be finalized without a label indicator, but it does not appear as a social security number. 1-2-3 interprets the hyphens as minus signs and performs two subtractions, resulting in –6616. You can edit the cell containing this erroneous entry by pressing F2 (EDIT), moving to the front of the entry, and typing a label indicator. This instructs 1-2-3 to treat the minus signs as hyphens (considered text) and display the entry as a social security number.

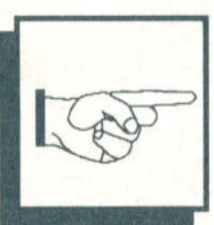

Spaces and special characters (such as £) are treated as labels.

You can use label indicators to control placement of an entry in a cell. 1-2-3 provides five label indicators for this purpose, as the box called "Label Indicators" shows. The apostrophe is the default label indicator—the one 1-2-3 generates for you when you enter character data. It causes an entry to be left-justified within the cell.

The other two label indicators that can be used for entry placement are the double quotation mark (") and the caret (^). The double quotation mark causes label entries to be right-justified, while the caret causes entries to be centered within the cell.

The following steps create entries made using different types of label indicators.

1. The word **Sales** was entered in B1. As soon as the **S** was entered, 1-2-3 changed the READY mode indicator to LABEL. When the entry was completed, the top line of the control panel showed "'Sales" because 1-2-3 added an apostrophe before the word. In the cell the entry was left-justified and appeared without the '.

2. **^Sales** was typed in B2. The caret (^) caused the entry to be centered in the cell.

3. **"Sales** was typed in B3. This caused the entry to be right-justified.

Label Indicators

The label indicator can be changed with a menu command or by typing a different indicator at the beginning of the label entry. The label indicators and their effects are as follows:

'	Left-justified (the default setting)
"	Right-justified
^	Centered
\	Repeat the character that follows until the cell is filled
|	Contains a nonprinting label that is frequently used to send codes to the printer

The resulting entries look like this:

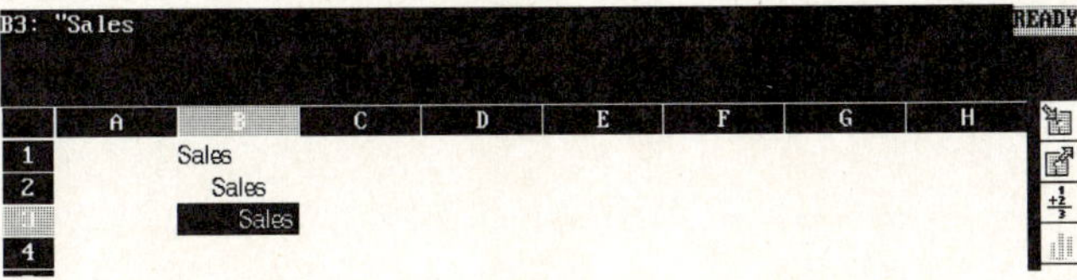

In Chapter 5, you learn how to alter the default label indicator with /Worksheet Global Default Label-Prefix. For now, if you want something other than left-justification, enter the appropriate label indicator before you start typing your entry.

Two additional label indicators perform special functions. The backslash (\) causes the character that follows it to be repeated until the entire width of the cell is filled. For example, entering \– fills the cell with hyphens. Figure 3-2 shows how * was entered to place asterisks in all the cells in one row of a worksheet as a dividing line between the worksheet assumptions and the calculation section.

You can also use the backslash to make multiple characters repeat. Typing \+- results in a pattern of + and – symbols repeated for the width of the cell.

The second special label indicator is the vertical bar (¦), which displays the label on the screen but does not print the entries. This indicator is introduced in Chapter 6 for printing printer control codes in early releases of 1-2-3.

Labels provide readability to a worksheet and allow you to enter text data. Since a worksheet is primarily involved in projections and calculations, however, you clearly also need a way to deal with numeric entries.

Value Entries

Value entries are treated as numeric entries by 1-2-3. They must follow much more rigid rules than label entries. The two basic types of value entries are *numbers* and

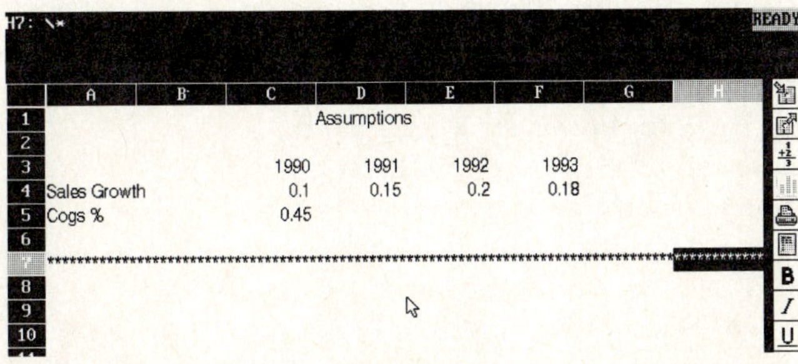

Figure 3-2.   A repeating label entry

formulas. Like labels, numbers are constants; they do not change as the result of arithmetic operations. Formulas are not constants because the results they produce depend on the current values for the variables they reference. The following sections examine each category separately because 1-2-3 handles each differently.

Numbers

The rules for entry of numeric constants are summarized in the box called "Rules for Numbers." Numeric entries do not have a special beginning indicator as labels do, but they can contain only certain characters.

Size   Numbers can be as large as 10^{99} or as small as 10^{-99}. Up to 240 characters can be used to represent the numbers, although you still must adhere to the numeric limits of the package.

You can also use *scientific notation* to enter large numbers. Scientific notation is a method of entering a number along with the power of 10 that it will be multiplied by. In this format, the letter "E" (upper- or lowercase may be used) separates the number from the positive or negative power of 10 that will be used. (Note that the number that follows E must be between −99 and +99.) This kind of notation offers the advantage of representing very large or very small numbers in a minimum of space. Here are some examples of scientific notation:

9.76E+4 = 97,600

6.543e+5 = 654,300

6.71E −02 = .0671

3.86e −5 = .0000386

Rules for Numbers

1 Numbers cannot exceed 256 characters; however, the limitation for decimal accuracy and significant digits is 15.

2 If the first key you press is a number digit or one of the acceptable symbols, + − . ($ @ or #), the entry is treated as a number. Only the following symbols can appear in a number entry: 0 1 2 3 4 5 6 7 8 9 . + − $ @ ( ) E ^ % (the last four of these cannot begin a numeric entry).

3 Only one decimal can be used.

Percentages can either be entered with a decimal as in .15 or with a percent sign as in 15%.

The letter O cannot be substituted for a zero or the letter l for a one. E is the only letter you can use in numbers using scientific notation.

Numbers are always right-aligned.

Entries that you consider numbers may be labels to 1-2-3. It is common to refer to social security numbers, phone numbers, part numbers, and purchase order numbers. Although these entries are called numbers, they may not be number values to 1-2-3 due to the presence of alphabetic characters or special symbols. They must be entered as labels in 1-2-3.

Entry   In one sense, entering numbers is easier than entering labels because you simply type the allowable characters and then press either ENTER or an arrow key. You do not need a special character at the beginning of a numeric entry.

As soon as you type any of the allowable characters, the mode indicator changes from READY to VALUE. Once 1-2-3 has determined that you are entering a value, you must continue entering only allowable characters. If you attempt to finalize an entry containing disallowed characters, 1-2-3 places you in EDIT mode so that you can make necessary corrections. If you realize your error before trying to finalize the original entry, you can use BACKSPACE to remove the incorrect characters or press ESC to eliminate the entire entry. Other time-saving error correction methods are discussed later in this book.

Looking at some numeric entries may clarify the entry process and the way 1-2-3 displays such entries in a cell.

1. With the cell pointer on C1, **.0925** was entered, and the cell pointer was moved to C2 to finalize the entry.

2. **51279** was entered in C2.

3. **4.35E+05** was entered in C3. The entries look like this:

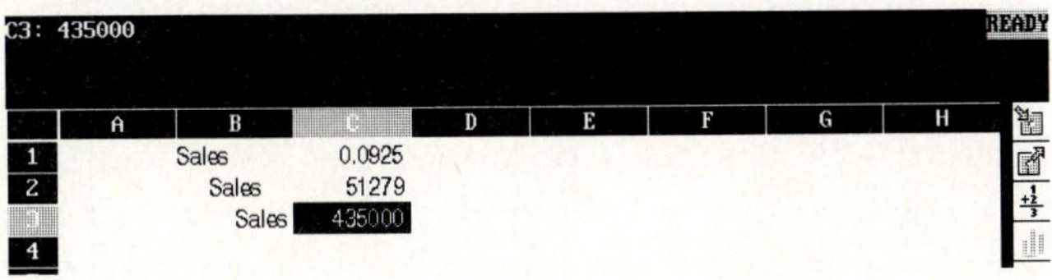

Notice that 1-2-3 converted the third entry to 435000 since the number was not too large for the display area. The first two entries were displayed just as entered, except that a zero was added in front of the decimal in C1.

In these examples the number of decimal places displayed is inconsistent because General format is in effect. General format is the default for all new worksheets. In Chapter 4, you learn how to change the format to display entries as currency, percentages, or with a consistent number of decimal places. In the next section of this chapter you get a closer look at the display with the General format in effect.

Entering Dates and Times   Dates and times are special types of values. Rather than storing dates and times as 12-Jun-92 or 12:57 PM, 1-2-3 stores dates and times as numeric values called *date and time serial numbers*. Dates are recorded as the number of days since December 31, 1899. This means that a date of 12-Jun-92 has a date serial number of 33767 since it is 33767 days away from December 31, 1899. Using date serial numbers allows you to use dates in calculations. For example, by adding 90 to 33767, you can calculate the date serial number of a day 90 days after 12-Jun-92. 1-2-3 can handle dates between January 1, 1900 and December 31, 2099.

1-2-3 records times as the fraction of the day. For example, noon is halfway through the day so it is represented as .5. Using time serial numbers also lets you use time in calculations so you can calculate the difference in times.

To enter dates and times, you will use the date and time functions, covered in Chapter 7. Even though your date and time entries will not initially appear as the dates and times they represent, you can use them in calculations. For example, entering +C4+30 calculates a date that is thirty days after the date stored in C4. To display the date and time serial numbers as the dates and times they represent, you must change the format of the cell containing the date and time serial numbers. Changing the display format is covered in Chapter 4.

Display   The numbers you enter are shown both in the control panel and in the worksheet. They are also stored internally. The form of the numbers may be slightly different in each case. Internally 1-2-3 can store up to 15 significant digits for an entry. If you enter a number with more than 15 significant digits, the displayed number is rounded off to fit within the 15-digit memory limitation. The display on the worksheet depends on the format for the cell and the length of the number in relation to the cell width.

When 1-2-3 displays a number in a cell, it displays all the digits up to one less than the cell width. Numeric entries that are longer than this limit are not handled by borrowing space from cells to the right, as was done with labels. The entries are shown in either scientific notation, rounded form, or as asterisks representing an overflow situation. The cell format and the composition of the number determine the display.

When General format is in effect, 1-2-3 displays the number as entered, if possible. If the integer portion of the number is too large, 1-2-3 converts the display to scientific notation. If the integer portion of the number fits, but some or all of the decimal digits do not, the cell value is rounded to fit within the display. When a column is not wide enough to display the values, they appear as a series of asterisks. The default cell width is nine positions, so you can see that long numbers do not fit unless you expand the width of the column. You will learn how to do that in Chapter 4. To see how 1-2-3 reacts to long numbers, follow these steps:

1. .000000000134 was entered in cell C4. The worksheet display changed this to scientific notation and displayed it as 1.3E–10.

2. 9578000000 was entered in C5. 1-2-3 performed another conversion and shows the entry as 9.6E+09 in the cell. The entry appears in its original form in the control panel.

This illustration shows how 1-2-3 reacted to the long numeric entries:

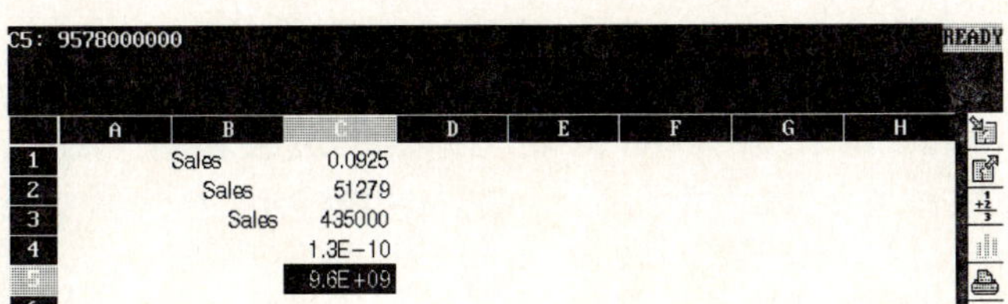

You have no control over either the format in the control panel or the internal storage of a number. In both cases 1-2-3 retains as much accuracy as possible (15 decimal digits is the maximum for the control panel and internal storage).

Formulas

Formulas are the second type of value entry. Unlike number and label entries, their results vary depending on the numbers they reference. Formulas perform calculations to arrive at the proper results. This ability makes formulas the backbone of worksheet features. They allow you to make what-if projections and to look at the impact of changing variable values. To produce an updated result with a formula, you do not need to change the formula. Simply change one of the values the formula references, and the entire formula can be recalculated for you.

Formulas follow the same basic rules as numbers in terms of allowable characters. In addition, formulas also support the use of cell references, range names assigned to a group of cells, and operators that define specific operations to 1-2-3.

1-2-3 has three types of formulas. These formulas are summarized in the box called "Formula Types."

A few rules pertain to all formulas:

- Formulas cannot contain spaces, except for the spaces in range names or string variables.

- The first character of a formula must be one of the following:

  + — (@ # $. 0 1 2 3 4 5 6 7 8 9

- Formulas contain special operators to define the operation you wish performed. Operators are assigned priorities in 1-2-3, as shown in the box called "Operation Priorities."

- Formulas can also contain numeric constants or string constants (such as 77 or "sales total"), cell references (such as F4 or Z3), special built-in functions (such as @MIN), or range names (such as TOTAL).

Arithmetic Formulas

Arithmetic formulas calculate numeric values. These formulas are built with *arithmetic operators* and references to values in other cells. The value references are to the cell address (such as A1 or Z10), a cell in another file on disk, or a name that has been assigned to a cell or cells (such as Cash or Interest). For now, concentrate on references to cells in the current file. Linkages to external files are covered in Chapter 8. You will learn how to assign range names in Chapter 5.

The arithmetic operators used in 1-2-3 are + for addition, – for subtraction, / for division, * for multiplication, and ∧ for exponentiation. An instruction to multiply 3 times 4 would be entered as **3*4**. These operators are listed in the "Operation Priorities" box.

Ignoring 1-2-3's operation priorities causes incorrect formula results. You must use parentheses to group references if you do not want to use the established priorities. A difference in the order of operations can cause a dramatic difference in results.

You should keep some things in mind when entering cell references. In the sample formulas you have seen in this book, you may have noticed a plus sign was placed at the beginning of the formula. To multiply the current contents of C1 by the contents

---

1
2
3

Formula Types

1-2-3 provides three types of formulas for your use: arithmetic, logical, and string.

Arithmetic formulas involve constants, cell references, and the arithmetic operators (+, –, *, /, ∧). Arithmetic formulas calculate the formula entered and return its result. Examples are +A2*A3, or +Sales–Cogs (where Sales and Cogs are names of cells that contain numerical data).

Logical formulas involve cell references, constants, and comparison operators (<, <=, >, >=, =, <>). These formulas evaluate the condition listed to determine whether it is true or false. If the condition is false, the formula returns 0; if true, it returns 1.

String formulas join two or more character strings. To join string variables or constants you can use the concatenation character (&)—for example, +"Sales for the "&"Midwest"&"Region". These formulas can also be constructed with cell references and range names, as long as the cells contain strings.

Functions provide predefined formulas for a variety of calculations, including mathematical formulas, financial calculations, logical evaluations, statistical computations, and string manipulation. Functions begin with an @, and contain a list of specific values for arguments within parentheses.

of C2, you might think that entering **C1∗C2** would work but it will not. The problem here is the initial letter "C." As soon as 1-2-3 realizes **C** has been entered, it flags the cell as a label entry and shows the entry as a label on the worksheet, rather than giving the result of the formula calculation.

You need a formula indicator, and the + is the logical choice because it requires only one additional keystroke and does not alter the formula. (Actually, any numeric character that does not affect the formula result is acceptable.) Therefore, enter + at the front of all formulas that begin with a cell address. The formula just discussed can be entered as **+C1∗C2**.

Blank cells have a zero value. If you reference a blank cell in a formula, the result is the same as referencing a cell that contains a zero. For example, +A1∗A2 equals zero if A1 or A2 contains a zero or if either cell is blank.

Parentheses in arithmetic expressions are the only option for changing the order of operations. For example, in the formula (3+4)∗5, the parentheses take priority. Therefore, 3 is added to 4 first, making the expression 7∗5, or 35.

1-2-3 allows many sets of parentheses in one expression, so you can use them liberally to override the natural priority order. With nested parentheses, the priority

---

Operation Priorities

1-2-3 has a variety of operators for arithmetic, logical, and string formulas. When more than one operator is used in a formula, it is important to know which operation 1-2-3 evaluates first. The following table provides the priority order for each operation within 1-2-3, with the highest number being the highest priority. If several operators in a formula have the same priority, they are evaluated from left to right.

Priority	Operator	Operation Performed
8	(	Parenthesis for grouping
7	^	Exponentiation
6	+, −	Positive and negative indicator
5	/, ∗	Division and multiplication
4	+, −	Addition and subtraction
3	=,< >, <, >, <=, >=	Logical operators
2	#NOT#	Complex not operator
1	#AND#, #OR#, &	Complex and, complex or, and string operator

sequence applies within each set of parentheses. Here is an example of priority order within nested parentheses:

$$4*((1+2)*2)/2+3$$

$$\begin{array}{ccccc} & \uparrow & \uparrow & \uparrow & \uparrow \\ \text{3rd} & & \text{2nd} & & \text{5th} \\ & \text{1st} & & \text{4th} \end{array}$$

You have learned how to build a formula by typing cell addresses and arithmetic operators. This method works well if you are good at remembering the cell addresses you want to use and do not make mistakes in typing. However, a second method of formula construction eliminates both these necessities. This new method lets you point to the cell references you wish to include in the formula and then type only the arithmetic operators. After you type an operator, simply move your cell pointer to the cell whose value you want to include in the formula. Watch the mode indicator change from VALUE to POINT as you move your cell pointer. To finalize the selection of the cell reference, either type the next operator or, if you have reached the end of the formula, press ENTER. If you type another operator, the cell pointer returns to the formula's entry cell, and 1-2-3 then waits for you to move your cell pointer to a new location.

Here is a sample worksheet entry that was developed using the pointing method:

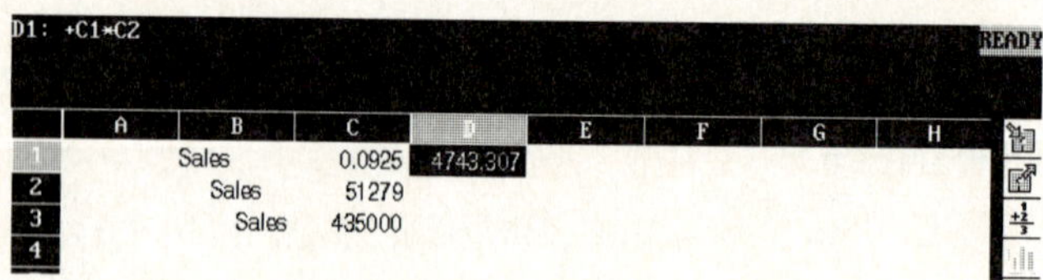

To produce this example the cell pointer was moved to D1, and + was typed. Then the cell pointer was moved to C1, putting 1-2-3 in POINT mode. An asterisk for multiplication was then typed, causing the cell pointer to return to D1. The LEFT ARROW and DOWN ARROW keys were used to move to C2. Finally, pressing ENTER caused the formula to appear in cell D1, as shown in our example.

This may seem like a lot of work compared to typing in cell references. However, once your worksheet becomes large, the pointing method can save considerable time. It speeds up the testing and verification processes for your model because it forces you to visually verify cell references and therefore eliminates many formula errors that could result from incorrect cell references.

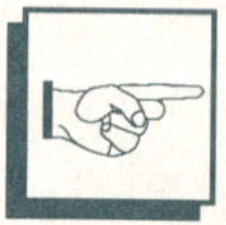

Make the pointing method mandatory for all your formulas on large worksheets. Otherwise you are using mere guesswork. It is too easy to type an incorrect reference. The effects of errors in worksheet entries can be devastating if they are not recognized until after decisions have been made.

Logical Formulas   Logical formulas use *logical operators* to compare two or more values. Such formulas can be used to evaluate a series of complex decisions or to influence results in other areas of the worksheet. As noted in the "Operation Priorities" box, logical operators are = (equal), < > (not equal), < (less than), > (greater than), <= (less than or equal to), and >= (greater than or equal to). The logical operators all have the same priority and are evaluated from left to right in an expression. All the logical operators are lower in priority than the arithmetic operators.

Logical formulas do not calculate numeric results like arithmetic formulas. If the condition that was evaluated is true, 1 is returned; if the condition is false, 0 is returned. For example, if C1 contains .0925, the logical expression +C1>=500 returns 0, since the condition is false.

1-2-3 also has a few *compound operators*. These operators are used either to negate a logical expression or to join two logical expressions. The negation operator #NOT# has priority over the other two compound operators, #AND# and #OR#. These latter operators can join two expressions, as in +C1>=500#AND#C2=50, which returns 1 only if both conditions are true.

The #NOT# operator negates an expression. For instance, the formula #NOT#(A1=2#AND#D2=1) returns 1 for true if the contents of cell A1 are not equal to 2 and/or those of cell D1 are not equal to 1. (If #OR# replaced #AND# in this formula, the formula would be true if both cell A1 were not equal to 2 and cell D2 were not equal to 1.) For practical purposes, you are more likely to use the < > (not equal) logical operator than the more cumbersome #NOT# operator. The formula +A1<>2#AND#D2<>1 is easier to read than the formula #NOT#(A1=2#AND#D2=1), and its meaning is identical.

One application of logical operators in a worksheet is the calculation of a commission bonus. Figure 3-3 shows a calculation on a worksheet to determine the quarterly commission check for salesperson John Smith. The calculation has two components: the regular commission and a bonus for meeting sales quotas.

The regular commission is 10 percent of total sales. The bonus is calculated by product. Each salesperson has a $50,000 quota for each of three products. A bonus of $1000 is given for each product for which the sales quota is met. A salesperson could thus gain $3000 by meeting the quota for all three products.

The following are the steps taken to build the model shown in Figure 3-3:

1. A number of labels were entered in cells B2 and A4 through A8.

2. **John Smith** was entered in C4; and **56000**, **45000**, and **3000** were entered in C5 through C7.

3. The numbers were totaled in C8 by entering the formula **+C5+C6+C7** in that cell.

4. The label **Quotas Met** was entered in E4.

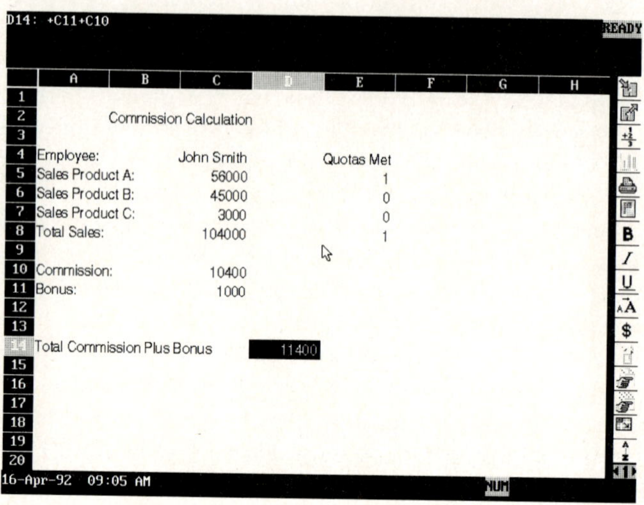

Figure 3-3.   *The formula in D14 shows total compensation*

5. The logical formula **+C5>50000** was entered in E5, so when ENTER is pressed, if sales of product A are greater than 50,000, 1 is returned, but if they are equal to or less than this number, 0 is returned.

6. **+C6>50000** was entered in E6, and **+C7>50000** was entered in E7. Pressing ENTER produces the result of the logical formula in both cases.

7. The total formula, **+E5+E6+E7**, was entered in E8 to determine the number of bonus categories.

8. The labels **Commission:** and **Bonus:** were entered in A10 and A11.

9. **+C8*.1** was entered in C10, and **+E8*1000** was entered in C11.

10. A label for total commission was placed in A14.

11. The final formula was entered in D14 as **+C10+C11**.

String Formulas   With string or text formulas you can join or concatenate two or more groups of characters. This allows you to access and manipulate character data to build headings, correct errors, and convert text formats to a satisfactory format for reporting. There is only one operator for string formulas, the ampersand (&). If you want to join the string "John" with the string "Smith," you could enter the string formula **+"John"&"Smith"** to produce "JohnSmith," or **+"John"&" "&"Smith"** to produce "John Smith." The plus at the beginning indicates the cell contains a formula.

String formulas let you alter data previously entered in a worksheet, so you can use them to correct errors or change formats. For example, if names have been entered in a worksheet with the last name first, and you want to reverse the sequence, you can combine string functions such as @RIGHT, @LEFT, and @MID to produce that result. (String functions are explained in Chapter 7.) String formulas also offer a creative approach to producing new reports by allowing you to join data from two or more locations on your worksheet. For instance, string formulas can be used in combination with cell references to produce more flexible report headings.

Figure 3-4 shows a report heading created by combining string constants and string variables. The formula uses three string constants: "Monthly Statistics for the ", " ", and "Warehouse". These constants are enclosed in quotation marks when entered. The variables are references to cell addresses that contain text data. The two variables here are D5 and D4, which contain Dallas and Timber, respectively.

A string reference to a blank cell (which is equivalent to zero) returns ERR, indicating an error in the formula. You cannot combine numbers and strings in a formula although 1-2-3 has functions that can convert numbers into strings and strings containing digits into numbers.

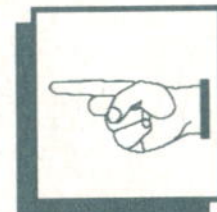

The & operator has the lowest priority of all operators and is in the last priority group with #NOT#, #AND#, and #OR#. This does not diminish the usefulness of these operators; it just means they are the last operators to be evaluated in an expression.

Functions   1-2-3's built-in functions compose a special category of formulas. They can be used alone or as part of a formula you create. The entire algorithm or formula for the calculations represented in a function has been worked out, tested, and incorporated into the package features. 1-2-3 supplies all the operators for a function; all you need to supply are the values that the operators work with. There are functions

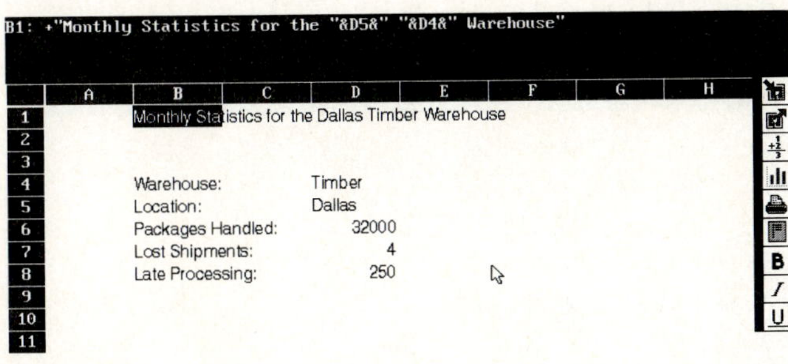

Figure 3-4.   A string formula

to perform arithmetic operations, string manipulation, logical evaluation, statistical calculations, and date and time arithmetic. They all have the same general format and must abide by the same rules. Regardless of the function type, all are regarded as value entries because they are formulas.

All functions start with @. This is followed by a function keyword, which is a character sequence representing the calculation being performed. The keyword is followed by arguments enclosed in parentheses. The arguments define the function's specific use in a given situation. A few of 1-2-3's functions are

@MAX   Calculates the maximum value

@SUM   Calculates a sum or total

@ROUND   Rounds a number to a certain number of decimal places

@NPV   Calculates the net present value

Release 2.4 has more than 90 built-in functions, spanning calculations in financial, mathematical, logical, statistical, string, and other applications. Built-in functions are covered thoroughly in Chapter 7.

Figure 3-5 shows an example of the @SUM function used to produce a total. After entering appropriate numbers and labels, the sum formula was entered in C9 by typing **@SUM(**. The cell pointer was then moved to C6 (the beginning of the range to be summed), and this reference was locked in place as the beginning of the range by typing a period. The cell pointer was next moved to the value in C8. As a last step, the closing parenthesis was typed, and ENTER was pressed to produce the sum. The @SUM function totals all the values between C6 and C8. It is the same as the formula +C6+C7+C8.

If you are using Release 2.4, you can use the SmartSum icon from one of the SmartIcon palettes to sum a preselected range so long as the last cell in the row or column is blank. You can also create a sum without selecting a range by making the current cell the cell where you want the sum. The SmartSum icon is available in the

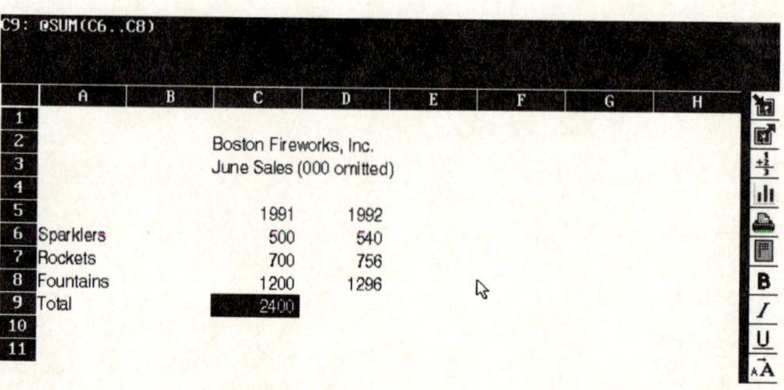

Figure 3-5.   Using @SUM

first palette as well as in other palettes. It is the icon that adds 1 + 2 to total 3 and looks like this:

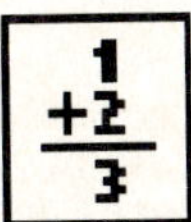

To sum D6 through D8 with this approach, you would move the mouse to D6 and press the left mouse button and drag to D9. Remember: This extra cell is necessary to leave a place for the @SUM entry. Click the SmartSum icon in the SmartIcon palette, and 1-2-3 will place @SUM(D6..D8) in cell D9.

Using the other approach, you could click D9 to make the cell active and then click the SmartSum icon. Unless you need to sum multiple rows or columns, this latter approach is actually the easier. Like the first option, it places the formula @SUM(D6..D8) in cell D9.

How 1-2-3 Treats Formulas

You need to know some facts about formulas beyond the procedure for their entry. 1-2-3 offers a number of recalculation options that affect the timeliness of recalculation and the order of formula evaluation. You are most likely to begin your use of the 1-2-3 package with the default settings, but be aware of alternatives that can enhance your use of the package when you begin to build models with greater sophistication.

With the default settings in Releases 2.3 and 2.4, *minimal recalculation* is used. This gives you a much more efficient method of dealing with recalculation than past releases, which recalculated every formula on the worksheet. This added capability gives 1-2-3 the intelligence to determine which cells require recalculation. Every time you change a variable on a worksheet, only this minimum number of cells is recalculated rather than the entire worksheet. Unless your worksheet is extremely large and has many formulas affected by a change, you hardly notice the amount of time required to perform these calculations. This makes 1-2-3 one of the fastest spreadsheet packages marketed.

Releases 2.2 and above offer further processing efficiency for systems with 8087, 80287, or 80387 math coprocessor chips, because they can automatically recognize and use these chips. The math coprocessor provides noticeable improvements in the speed for worksheets with many calculations and reduces the time involved for recalculation when a worksheet contains numerous trigonometric or mathematical functions.

In addition to fast recalculation, 1-2-3's speed in format changes, cell-pointer movement, window switching, and copying functions sets standards for the other spreadsheet packages. This is not to say that you can never become impatient with the package. If you are like most users, you want no delay at all, but you can take comfort in knowing that 1-2-3 is using the features of your computer to the fullest.

Furthermore, as you will learn in Chapter 5, there is a method to temporarily turn off recalculation when you have data-entry tasks to perform.

Reference Types

The cell address references in 1-2-3's formulas can be relative, absolute, or mixed. These three reference types are covered in detail in Chapter 5 in connection with the /Copy command. They are mentioned here as well, however, because references must be entered in one of the three formats when you type in your original formulas, even though the reference type does not have any effect on the original calculation. The "Reference Types" box provides examples of the three reference type formats.

Notice that the mixed type addresses have several different options, since mixed is a combination of relative and absolute. Only portions of the address are absolute; the other part of the address may vary depending on the location to which it is copied. It is important to know that the way you enter cell references in your original formula can have long-term and widespread consequences if the formula is copied.

Correcting Errors in Entries

1-2-3 offers a variety of error correction techniques, which are summarized in the "Error Correction Methods" box. The method you use mainly depends on whether the entry to be corrected has been finalized (by pressing ENTER or one of the arrow keys).

When an entry is short and has been finalized, retyping is a good correction method. This replaces the incorrect contents of the cell with your new entry. If the Undo feature is active, you can press ALT-F4 (UNDO). This eliminates the effect of your last entry. If Undo is currently disabled, you can enable it after saving the worksheet with /File Save, clearing memory with /Worksheet Erase Yes, and remov-

---

1 2 3

Reference Types

1-2-3 has three different reference types that do not affect the original formula, but do affect the copy operation. You can type the dollar signs where required or add them with the F4 (ABS) key when you are in EDIT, VALUE, or POINT mode. The mixed reference type actually has a number of forms, depending on which parts of the address are held constant and which are allowed to change.

Relative references: A2, B10, Z43

Absolute references: $A$2, $B$10, $Z$43

Mixed references: A$2, $A2

ing any Add-Ins in memory. In Release 2.4 you will need to clear the Wysiwyg and Icons add-ins from memory with /Add-In Clear. If you have a sufficient amount of memory, you do not need to perform these steps before enabling Undo. At this point, use /Worksheet Global Default Other Undo Enable to activate Undo for subsequent use, although it will not help in eliminating the current entry. To make any entry changes, you must retrieve the saved file with /File Retrieve. In Release 2.3 and 2.4 you can press DEL to remove the entry.

One way to quickly fix an unfinalized entry is to press ESC, which makes your entire entry disappear. However, the most common error correction technique for an unfinalized entry is to use the BACKSPACE key. It functions as a destructive backspace, deleting the previous character each time you press it. This approach is ideal when you realize that the last character you typed was incorrect.

Placing yourself in EDIT mode by pressing the F2 (EDIT) key is a good way to correct errors in both finalized and unfinalized entries. It is also useful when the required change is not close to your current position within the entry. When F2 is pressed, the mode indicator in the upper-right corner of the screen changes to EDIT, and a small cursor appears at the end of the entry in the Edit line of the control

---

Error Correction Methods

If data is in the control panel but not yet entered in the cell

- Use ESC to erase the entire entry.

- Use BACKSPACE to delete one character at a time until the erroneous character has been eliminated.

- Press F2 (EDIT), and then use HOME, END, RIGHT ARROW, or LEFT ARROW to move within the entry. Use BACKSPACE to delete the character in front of the cursor and DEL to erase the character above the cursor. INS can be used to toggle between Insert and Overstrike modes.

If data has already been entered in the cell

- Retype the entry; the new entry will replace the old.

- Press F2 (EDIT), and then use HOME, END, RIGHT ARROW, or LEFT ARROW to move within the entry. Use BACKSPACE to delete the character in front of the cursor and DEL to erase the character above the cursor. INS can be used to toggle between Insert and Overstrike modes.

- Press ALT-F4 (UNDO). This will eliminate the entry only if there have been no intervening actions and the Undo feature is enabled.

- In Release 2.3 and 2.4, press DEL.

panel. This small cursor marks your place in the entry as you move within it and make changes. EDIT mode is also a good solution for long, incomplete entries where the error is near the beginning of the entry.

The cell-pointer movement keys take on new functions in EDIT mode, as this table shows:

Key	Effect
HOME	Moves you to the first character in your entry, not to A1 as it does in other modes.
END	Moves you immediately to the last character in your entry. You do not have to press an arrow key to have END take an action, as you do in READY mode.
RIGHT ARROW or LEFT ARROW	Moves you one character at a time in your entry.
BACKSPACE	Still performs its destructive function.
DEL	Also eliminates characters from entries. Rather than deleting the previous character, DEL removes the character above the Edit cursor.

If you have left out a character in an entry, move the cell pointer to the character that follows the desired location, and type the character you wish to add. It is inserted as long as you have not changed the default setting of INSERT mode. (If you want to change this setting so that what you type will overlay an existing character rather than be inserted, press INS. To change the setting back again, just press INS again; this key functions as a toggle switch.)

Let's look at a brief example that uses EDIT mode to make a correction. Suppose that you entered **sales** in B1 and finalized it. To change the first letter of "sales" to a capital, follow these steps:

1. Move the cell pointer back to cell B1.

2. Press F2 (EDIT) to place 1-2-3 in EDIT mode.

3. Press HOME to move to the beginning of the entry and then RIGHT ARROW to move under the "s." (The extra character at the front of the entry is the label indicator.)

4. Press the DEL key to remove the "s" leaving the cell pointer under the "a."

5. Type **S**, and then press ENTER to finalize your corrected entry.

You can also use the error correction techniques to change the justification of a label entry by altering the label indicator that appears at the beginning of the entry. Simply press F2 (EDIT), and then press HOME to move to the front of the entry. Press DEL to remove the label indicator and then type a caret (^). When you press ENTER,

this entry is centered. This same approach works with long label entries and complicated formulas.

Errors can be frustrating, but having several options makes the correction process
as painless as possible.

Ranges

Most of the formulas discussed in this chapter have operated on individual cells. For
example, +C1*C2 multiplies the value in one cell by the value in another cell, and
+C2+F2 adds the values in two cells. The one exception is the use of a range of cells
in the @SUM function example shown in Figure 3-5. When using 1-2-3's built-in
functions and other commands, you often work with more than one cell at a time.
This is not difficult, as long as the range of cells forms a contiguous rectangle. Figure
3-6 presents examples of invalid and valid ranges. The examples on the left are invalid
because the cell groups do not form one contiguous rectangle. Ranges can be large
rectangles of cells, or they can be as small as a single cell.

Specifying a Range

A range specification always includes two cell addresses separated by periods. If you
are typing a range address, you only need to type one period; 1-2-3 supplies the second

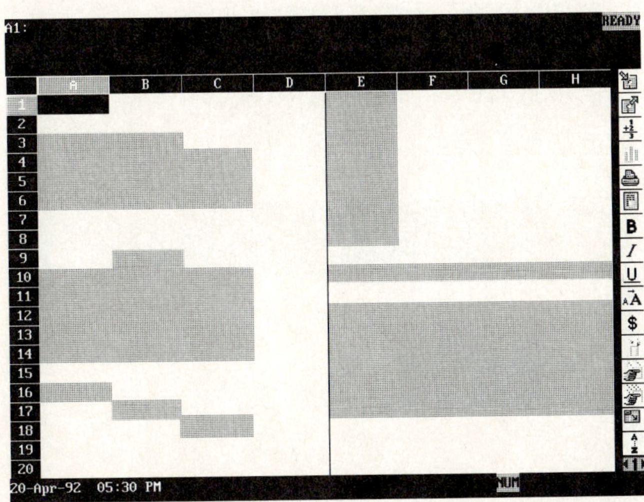

Figure 3-6.   *Invalid and valid ranges*

one. If you are specifying a range address by pointing, and if the address already appears in a range format with two addresses separated by a period, you can use the arrow keys to enlarge or contract a range.

The entries **B1..B10**, **F2..F2**, and **A3..C25** are examples of range specifications. Any single cell address can be changed to a range reference during POINT mode. For example, an entry of **B1** made while 1-2-3 is expecting a range specification appears as B1..B1. With @SUM, type **@SUM(**, point to B1, type a period, and then type). The entry reads @SUM(B1..B1). To expand the range, move the cell pointer down or to the right before typing the closing parenthesis.

To specify the cells of a range, use the cell names of two diagonally opposite corners of the rectangle, separated by one or two periods. For example, the range shown in Figure 3-7 can be entered as **B4.C8**, **B4..C8**, **B8..C4**, **B8.C4**, **C8..B4**, **C8.B4**, **C4..B8**, or **C4.B8**. However, the most common way to represent a range is by specifying the left uppermost cell first and the right lowermost cell last. Also, since 1-2-3 supplies the second period, you might as well save a keystroke and type **B4.C8**.

Cell ranges can be typed just like a single address, highlighted with your cell pointer, or specified with a range name (as explained in Chapter 5).

Preselecting Ranges

With Release 2.3 and 2.4, you can also select cell ranges before you select a command that uses them. To select a range to use from READY mode with the keyboard, move the cell pointer to one corner of the range and press F4 (ABS). This changes 1-2-3 from READY mode to POINT mode. While in POINT mode, press the arrow keys to highlight the range you want, as shown in Figure 3-7. When you have finished highlighting the range, press ENTER. You can also use F4 (ABS) to specify a range when a dialog box is displayed.

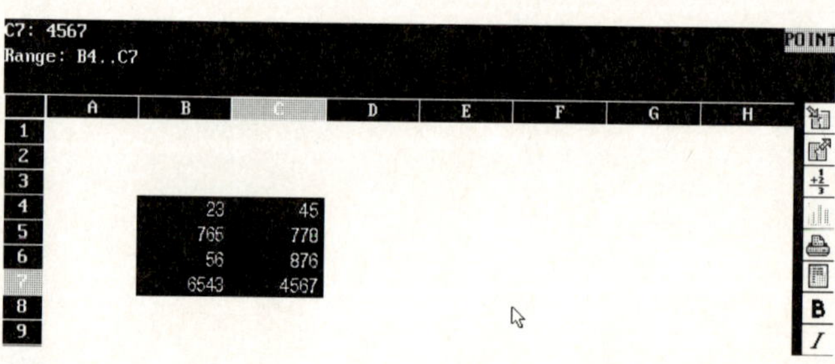

Figure 3-7.   The highlighted range

With a mouse, click one corner of the range and drag the mouse to the opposite corner. With either approach, the range you select will remain selected. When you select a 1-2-3 command that uses a range, 1-2-3 automatically uses the range you have selected. Selecting a range before selecting a command is useful when you want to use the same range for multiple commands—for example, if you want to format and sort the same range, select the range and then perform the two commands. When you select a range before selecting a command that uses a range, you will not see the prompt for the range to use. If a command uses multiple ranges, 1-2-3 uses the preselected range for the first range the command uses.

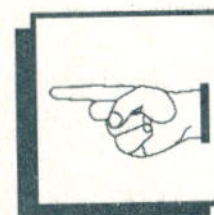

If you have a range highlighted and need to expand or shrink it from the beginning rather than the end, one option is to press ESC and start over. A better approach is to change the range of orientation by typing a period. This makes a different corner of the current range active and allows you to use the arrow keys to push and pull on the range from this corner. For example, the range A1..D10 initially has D10 as the active corner. The first time you press the period, A10 is active, the second time A1, and the third time D1.

Chapter *4*

Changing the Appearance of the Worksheet Display

Using what you have learned up to now, you can make entries on the worksheet that convey useful information. The format of the numeric portion of this information, however, probably is not as attractive as you would like. It has no dollar signs, commas, or aligned decimal points. 1-2-3 can provide these special edit characters for you. The only edit characters you will ever enter are the period (.), used to separate whole numbers from decimal fractions; the percent sign (%), used to represent a percent; and the E or e in scientific notation.

This chapter describes the features 1-2-3 provides for formatting your worksheet and demonstrates global and range formatting options, which give you a choice in the design of all or just a portion of your worksheet. You learn commands to change the width of your worksheet columns when the formats you have chosen require additional display space. You also learn some advanced ways to change 1-2-3's default display options and how to add and delete columns and rows.

Although Chapter 15 presents details of Wysiwyg, you get a glimpse of a few Wysiwyg options here so you can decide whether to skip ahead and make additional format improvements.

Global and Range Changes

1-2-3 has several menu commands and icons for improving the appearance of your worksheet. These commands can work their magic globally, changing the entire

59

worksheet at once, or they can affect only a single range of cells. Global changes like the ones made with the commands available in the /Wordsheet Global menu affect all cells in the worksheet by either altering them or setting the default. For example, the /Worksheet Global Format command changes the appearance of the entire worksheet from the global setting of General to another display format. When you select the new format, 1-2-3 changes every value cell on the worksheet that is not formatted with a range command to the new format. Value entries made on the worksheet after this change also display with the new format.

Range commands, on the other hand, only affect the range of cells you select. For example, the /Range Format command changes the appearance of just the cells within a specified range. A /Range Format option has priority over a /Worksheet Global Format option. This means you can select a /Worksheet Global Format option that matches your needs for most of the worksheet cells and still tailor individual cells to have a different appearance. In Figure 4-1 the /Worksheet Global Format command was used to set the overall format to Currency, and then /Range Format was used to change C3..C5 to Percent format. The years in C7..G7 are entered as centered labels. Changing the global format again would change every numeric worksheet cell except C3..C5. Those cells would not be affected by a worksheet format change because a range format instruction was previously applied to them, and the range format has priority.

In Release 2.4, the SmartIcons let you format a range of cells with either a numeric or Wysiwyg format. You must select the cells to be affected before choosing the icon to change the cell format. Wysiwyg must be attached for you to use the Wysiwyg icon palette options, discussed later in this chapter.

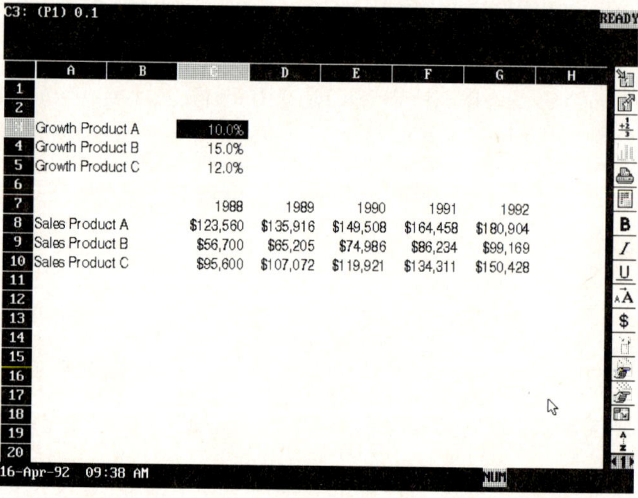

Figure 4-1.   *Combining global and range formats*

Before making a change to your worksheet, you should always determine the extent of the change you want to make. You can then select the command that makes just the amount of change you need. This chapter looks at global changes and range changes separately and takes an in-depth look at each format option that 1-2-3 provides, both for global and range applications.

Worksheet Changes

All /Worksheet commands are accessed through the Worksheet option on the main menu, which looks like this:

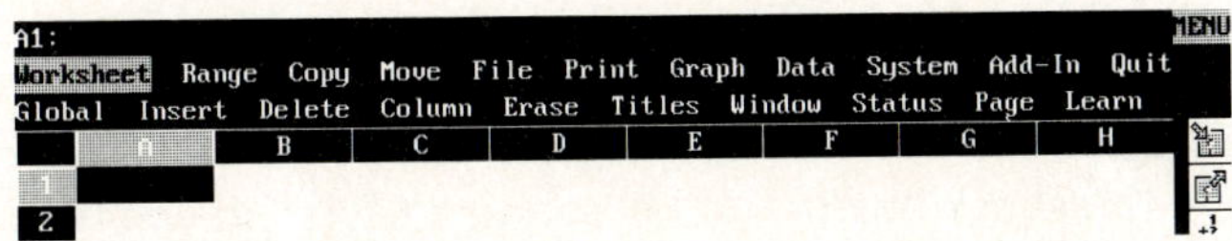

Select Worksheet either by pressing ENTER while the command is highlighted, by clicking Worksheet, or by typing **W**. This chapter discusses the Worksheet menu options that are found under Global, Insert, Delete, and Column.

If you make a series of mistakes and wish to eliminate all entries on your worksheet, you can use /Worksheet Erase Yes. This command makes the ultimate change in worksheet appearance: It clears the screen. Since it also eliminates all the underlying data, affecting more than the display, it is covered in Chapter 5. A similar command, /Range Erase, clears a range in a worksheet; it is also covered in Chapter 5 because it affects the cell entries rather than the display format. You can also use the DEL key or Trash icon to delete the contents of the current cell.

Undoing Worksheet Changes

Release 2.2 and above provide a powerful Undo feature that can return a worksheet to its former status. When Undo is enabled, pressing ALT-F4 (UNDO) reverses all the actions taken since the last time 1-2-3 was in READY mode. Pressing ALT-F4 (UNDO) when Undo is disabled has no effect. The Undo option also has no effect on eliminating a series of actions if another series of actions is executed before you press ALT-F4. In Release 2.4, the fourth icon palette provides an option for undoing the effect of your last actions. This icon looks like this:

Like the ALT+F4 (Undo) option, the effectiveness of this command depends on having Undo enabled.

You can use Undo to eliminate format changes, worksheet insertions and deletions, sorting, the effects of macros, and most other changes that affect the worksheet. Most changes made with Wysiwyg (covered in Chapter 15) can also be undone by pressing F4 (UNDO). External activities like printing or saving a file cannot be undone with Undo within the confines of conventional RAM memory. If you have expanded memory on your machine, 1-2-3 uses it for the Undo buffer needed to maintain the second copy of the worksheet, in case you decide to reverse an action. Most actions can be undone.

To enable Undo, the worksheet must be empty. If you have only conventional memory, no Add-Ins can be attached. In this case, you would detach the add-ins with /Add-In Detach. If you have sufficient expanded memory, you can leave your add-ins attached when enabling Undo. To enable undo, use /Worksheet Global Default Other Undo Enable. To eliminate Undo's actions, use /Worksheet Global Default Other Undo Disable. You can also enable and disable Undo by selecting Undo to mark or unmark the check box in the /Worksheet Global dialog box.

When Undo is enabled, 1-2-3 requires more memory. This means that for some large applications, it is not possible to use Undo. Although most actions can be undone, exceptions are file and print operations, the attachment of Add-Ins, /System, operating system commands, and commands in external programs or Add-Ins. If 1-2-3 does not have sufficient memory to create the copy needed to undo an operation, it displays a prompt and asks you if you still want to proceed.

Insert Commands to Add Rows or Columns

The /Worksheet Insert command adds blank rows or columns to a worksheet. Adding rows and columns is a little like cutting rows and columns from the end of the sheet and pasting them at another location, since the full complement of both rows and columns is in a worksheet from the beginning.

You can use inserted rows and columns to add a heading for a report or to include new or unexpected information. Adding blank rows and columns can also improve your worksheet design by making it more readable. The /Worksheet Insert command is position-dependent, meaning that rows and columns can be added at the cell-pointer location if you position it before entering the command. Position your cell pointer in the column to the right or in the row below where you want to insert. 1-2-3 always inserts columns to the left of the cell pointer and inserts rows above the cell pointer.

After you enter /Worksheet Insert, 1-2-3 asks whether you want to add rows or columns. Make the appropriate selection. 1-2-3 then asks for the range you want to insert, if you have chosen a row or column. You can expand your cell pointer across columns or down rows, covering the number of rows or columns you plan to insert. If you forget to position your cell pointer prior to entering the command, you can always type in the range or use ESC to free the beginning of the range so you can move it. You also have the option of selecting the range before you select /Worksheet Insert and 1-2-3 will add the rows or columns based on the number of rows or columns in the range you select.

In the third icon palette, Release 2.4 provides icons for inserting a row or a column. The icon for inserting rows looks like this:

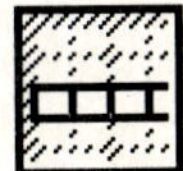

If you select one cell and then click this icon , a blank row is inserted above the selected cell. If you select several cells in the same column and then click this icon, the number of blank rows will be equal to the number of cells selected in one column.

The icon for inserting columns looks like this:

If one cell in one column is selected before clicking the icon, one column is inserted to the left of the selected cell. If multiple cells across a row are selected, the number of columns inserted will be equal to the number of columns in the selected range.

Remember: If you remove Wysiwyg but leave the Icons add-in attached, you can still use the palette, but it will look quite different without the graphics display. 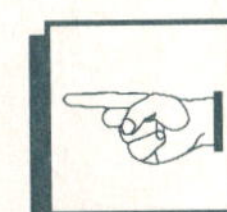

Figure 4-2 shows a worksheet that needs the insertion of additional blank spaces to improve its appearance. To make the insertions, move the cell pointer to A1 to insert blank columns to the left, enter **/Worksheet Insert Column**, and then move the cell pointer to expand the range to B1. When you press ENTER, two new columns are inserted to the left of column A. Next, enter **/Worksheet Insert Row**. Move the cell pointer down to row 3 and press ENTER to add three rows. The final version of the worksheet, after the insertion of both rows and columns, is shown in Figure 4-3.

When columns or rows are inserted in the middle of a range, the range is automatically expanded to allow for the insertions. This applies both to range names

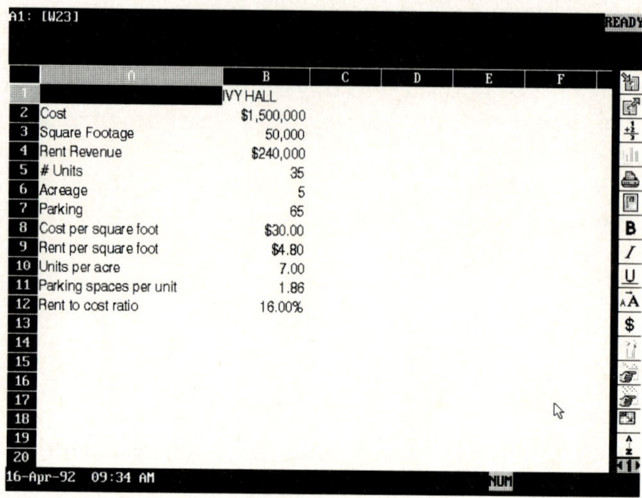

Figure 4-2.   *A sample worksheet needing blank spaces*

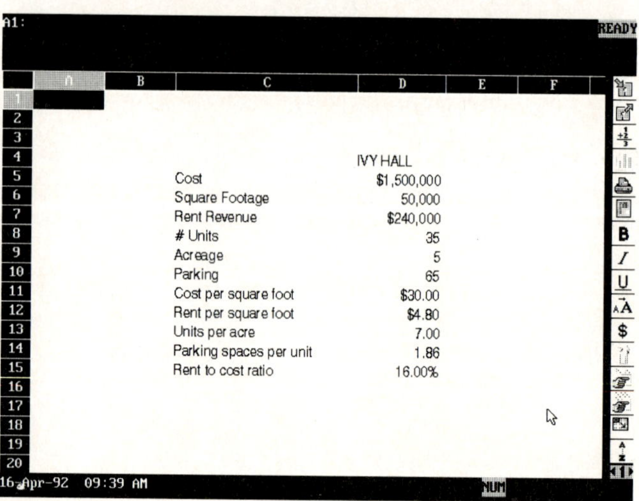

Figure 4-3.   *The worksheet after adding rows and columns*

that have been assigned and to ranges used in formulas. For example, Figure 4-4 shows an @SUM formula for departmental expenses. When two additional rows are inserted in the middle of the range, the formula is automatically adjusted to include two extra cells, as shown in Figure 4-5.

When insertions are made before the first entry or after the last entry, no adjustment is made to the range. Whenever you want to expand a range, therefore,

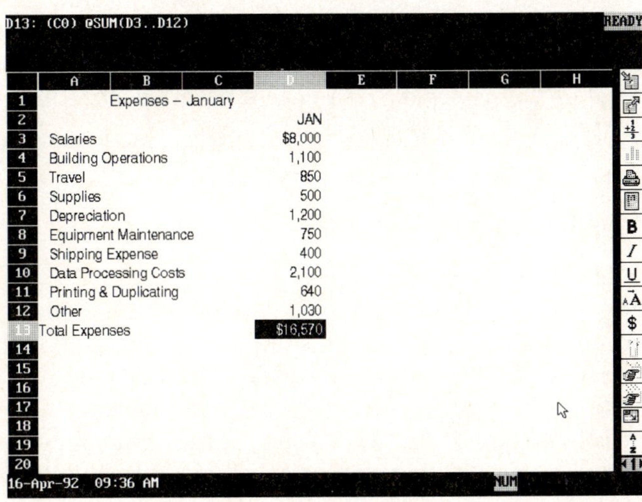

Figure 4-4. *A worksheet computing department expenses*

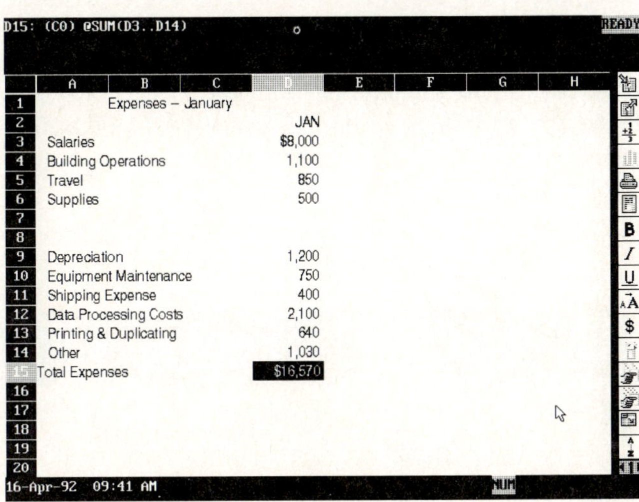

Figure 4-5. *A worksheet after adding two rows*

pick a spot somewhere in the middle of your worksheet. You may even want to design a worksheet with this in mind.

If you plan an application in which you need to total a column of entries, you can add a label at the top and bottom of the entries and include both labels in the total without affecting the result. This approach allows you to use two cells of separating dashes created by entering \- at the top and bottom of the column. Since the range for @SUM extends one cell above and one cell below the actual entries, you can expand the range at the beginning and end of the numeric entries and 1-2-3 will automatically include the rows you insert in the total.

Deleting Rows or Columns

1-2-3 also provides a command that deletes complete rows or columns that are no longer required. As with the Insert command, it is easiest to use the Delete command when you position your cell pointer before selecting the command. If you are deleting rows, place the cell pointer in the uppermost row to be deleted. Note that protected cells cannot be deleted when worksheet protection is enabled.

The rows or columns deleted can be blank, or they can contain worksheet data including formulas. When deleting rows or columns, be sure that the formulas and data in them are not referenced by other worksheet cells. If such references exist, incorrect data may be referenced after the deletion, or an error condition may occur if the new cells are no longer numeric. Figure 4-6 shows the resulting error when a critical column is accidentally deleted.

Before making large-scale deletions, you should save your worksheet to disk or make sure the Undo command is enabled. To enable Undo when it is off, make sure the worksheet is empty. If it is not empty, save the worksheet with /File Save, type the name you want to use for the file, and press ENTER. Next, erase the worksheet with /Worksheet Erase Yes and then enter **/Worksheet Global Default Other Undo Enable**.

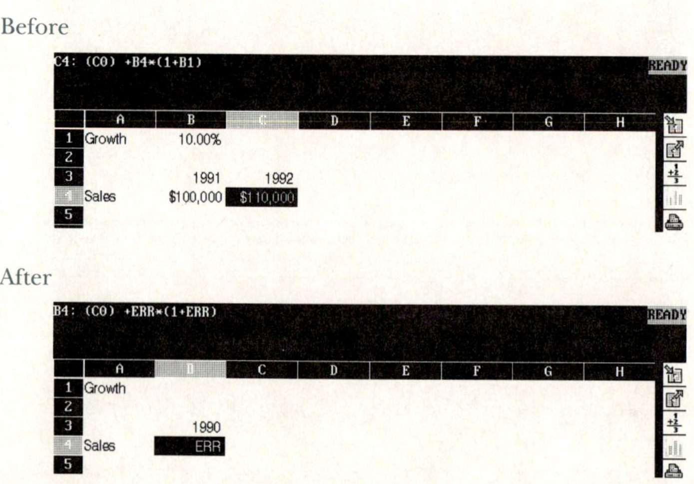

Figure 4-6.   A worksheet before and after deleting critical cells

Figure 4-7 shows a worksheet with extraneous blank columns in locations A through C. To delete these columns, move the cell pointer to A1 and enter /**Work-sheet Delete Column**. To extend the cell pointer to column C, press RIGHT ARROW twice, and then press ENTER. All three columns are deleted with this one command.

Deleting rows is just as easy. For example, you can delete the row containing the building operations expense. Move the cell pointer to that row, enter /**Worksheet Delete Row**, and press ENTER to delete just that one row. The altered worksheet is shown in Figure 4-8. 1-2-3 is able to adjust the @SUM function because the deleted row was taken from the middle of the range.

With Release 2.4 you can delete rows and columns with the SmartIcon palette. You preselect a cell in one or more rows or columns and then select the following icon from palette 3 to delete rows:

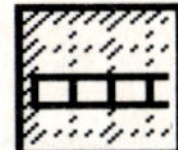

To delete columns, you select this icon:

Column Commands

Every column on a new worksheet is nine positions wide, unless you change the default width. This means that labels with nine characters or numeric entries with

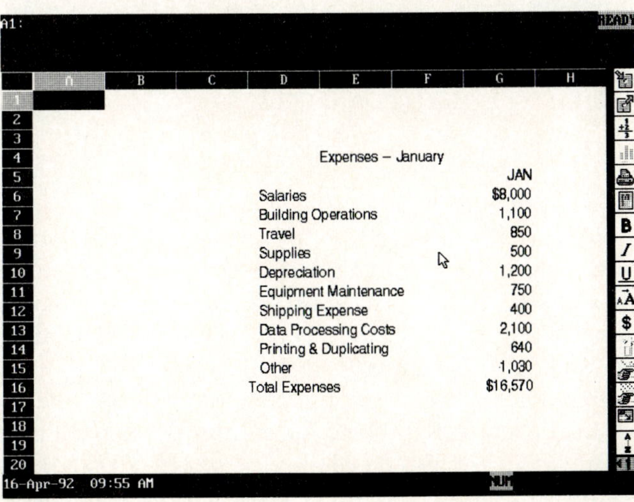

Figure 4-7.   A worksheet with extra columns

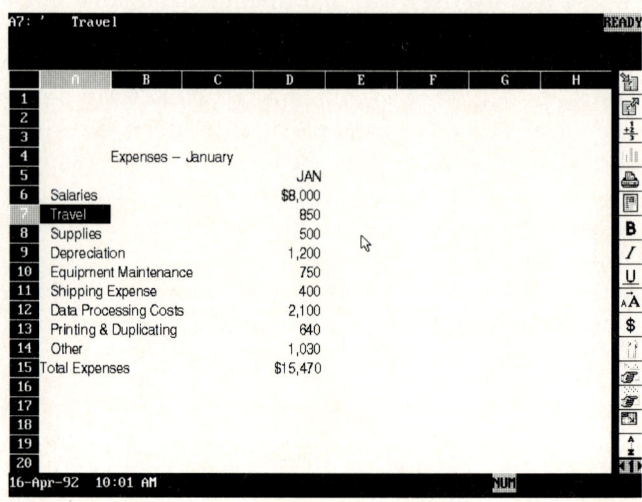

Figure 4-8.   *The worksheet after deleting a row and several columns*

eight digits can be entered in the cell. (Numeric entries are always restricted to one digit less than the cell width.) You can change column widths to widen, narrow, and hide columns using the /Worksheet Column command. The /Worksheet Column menu looks like this:

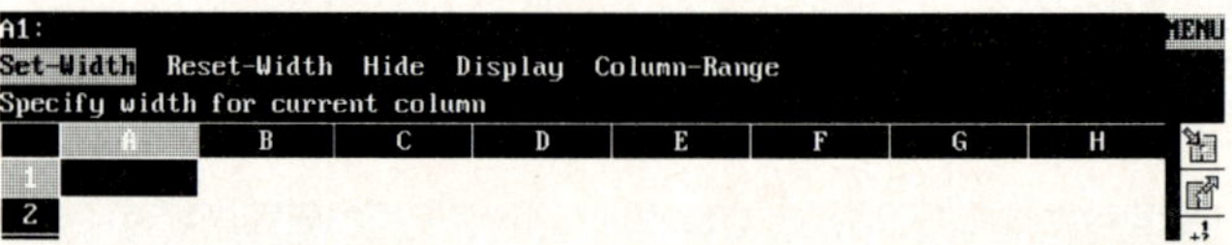

Set-Width

Figure 4-9 shows account names that were entered in column A but are too long to display in that column's default width of 9. As you see in the bottom of the figure, the entries can borrow space from adjacent columns, or column A's width can be changed with Set-Width, so that each entire entry could be shown in that column. This option is especially useful when the label in column A is being truncated because you already have an entry in column B.

First make sure your cell pointer is in column A. Then invoke the command by entering **/Worksheet Column Set-Width**. Next enter the desired number of characters and press ENTER. You can also move with the RIGHT or LEFT ARROW key until the column is the desired width, and press ENTER. With a mouse in Release 2.3, click ◀ and ▶ to change the column width before pressing ENTER. The latter method

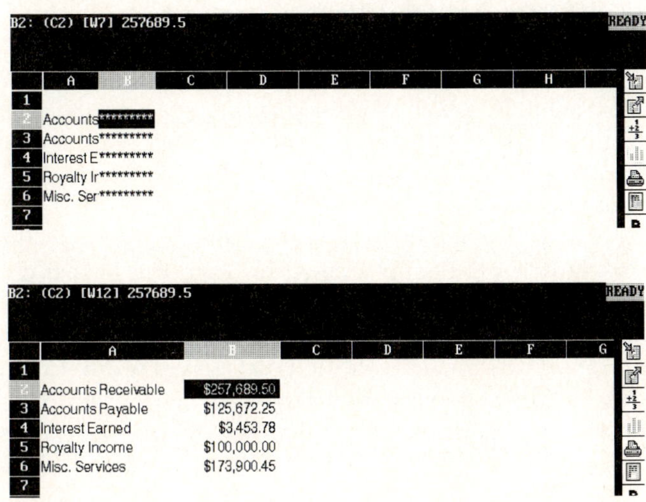

Figure 4-9.   *Currency format with entries that will not fit in cell widened to 12 to show numbers*

is best since a wrong guess about the desired number of characters means you have to start over with /Worksheet Column Set-Width. Figure 4-9 shows column A widened to 21 so the long labels fit within the column width.

If you are using Release 2.3 or 2.4 and have Wysiwyg loaded, you can also change a column's width by dragging the right edge of the column to a new location with the mouse.

The Set-Width option can also be used when numbers are too large to display in the default column width. In the top worksheet in Figure 4-9, numeric entries were made for account balances in column B using the Currency format with two decimal places. 1-2-3 added a dollar sign ($), and a comma after the thousands position. (To produce this format, type **/Range Format Currency**, press ENTER, type **B2..B6**, and press ENTER again.) The asterisks appear in these cells because the values they contain are too wide for the cell width once the dollar sign and comma are added to the existing digits. This column can be widened by typing **/Worksheet Column Set-Width** and pressing RIGHT ARROW three times before pressing ENTER. The bottom worksheet in Figure 4-9 shows the display after the cells were changed to a width of 12.

Reset-Width

Once you have used /Worksheet Column Set-Width to change the width of a column, its width will be different from its neighbors. If that width ceases to be useful, you can return to the global column width with the Reset-Width command. Placing the cell pointer in column C and entering **/Worksheet Column Reset-Width** returns the column to a width of 9, causing the asterisks to reappear.

If you are uncertain about the current global width, you can check it with the dialog box or the /Worksheet Status command. In releases before 2.3, the /Worksheet Status command displays various worksheet settings including the global column width. In Release 2.2 and above, when you select /Worksheet Global, the settings sheet includes the global column width. Chapter 5 provides more information on this dialog box and the /Worksheet Status command.

When the width of a column is changed from the default, the new width is conveniently displayed in the control panel for each cell in that column. In other words, if you place your cell pointer on any cell in a column where a special width has been used, you can see the new width in brackets in the top line of the control panel. For example, [W8] means width 8, [W4] means width 4, and [W25] means width 25. Widths from 1 to 240 can be assigned to any column. The width selected for columns on the screen affects the number of columns that can be viewed on the screen.

Hide and Display

/Worksheet Column Hide allows you to eliminate individual columns from the display. In effect, it cuts a section of the worksheet temporarily. You can use this option to eliminate confidential or proprietary information from the display. Hidden sections can be restored to the display at any time, since the data has not been erased.

Figure 4-10 shows a worksheet before Hide is invoked. To hide columns C and D, place the cell pointer in column C, type **/Worksheet Column Hide** followed by a period, and press RIGHT ARROW and then ENTER. The same worksheet then looks like Figure 4-11. Note that columns C and D have disappeared. The data in the two hidden columns can still be accessed in formulas.

	A	B	C	D	E	F	G	H
1				1991		1992		
2	SS#	Name	Salary	Increase	Salary			
3	213-45-7890	Jones, H	$25,600	7%	$27,392			
4	412-45-8976	Parks, M	$35,750	8%	$38,610			
5	451-90-0224	Boyd, B	$23,400	9%	$25,506			
6	888-88-4567	Able, J	$34,120	10%	$37,532			
7								
8								
9								

Figure 4-10.   *A worksheet before hiding cells*

[worksheet screen image — A1: [W12], READY mode, columns A, B, E, F, G, H, I, J showing:]

	A	B	E	F	G	H	I	J
1			1992					
2	SS#	Name	Salary					
3	213-45-7890	Jones, H	$27,392					
4	412-45-8976	Parks, M	$38,610					
5	451-90-0224	Boyd, B	$25,506					
6	888-88-4567	Able, J	$37,532					
7								

Figure 4-11.   *The worksheet after hiding columns C and D*

While columns are hidden, the only time you will see them is when 1-2-3 is in POINT mode, including when you start POINT mode by pressing F4 or dragging the mouse. When hidden columns temporarily display, asterisks appear next to the column letter as shown in Figure 4-12.

Use /Range Format Hidden to eliminate any range from display and thus display a group of cells as blank. This allows you to hide the information in a row or rectangle on the worksheet.

The /Worksheet Column Display command redisplays hidden columns. After selecting the command, you can select a range containing the columns you want to redisplay and press ENTER.

/Worksheet Column Hide and /Worksheet Delete Column have very different results. When you hide a column it is only eliminated from the display temporarily. When you delete a column, the column and its contents are permanently removed from the worksheet. Other columns are renamed with the letter from the deleted column—but its entries are lost unless you have a retrievable copy of the model on disk or you can undo the column delete.

[worksheet screen image — C1: "1991, Range: C1, POINT mode, columns A, B, C*, D*, E, F, G, H showing:]

	A	B	C*	D*	E	F	G	H
1			1991		1992			
2	SS#	Name	Salary	Increase	Salary			
3	213-45-7890	Jones, H	$25,600	7%	$27,392			
4	412-45-8976	Parks, M	$35,750	8%	$38,610			
5	451-90-0224	Boyd, B	$23,400	9%	$25,506			
6	888-88-4567	Able, J	$34,120	10%	$37,532			
7								
8								
9								

Figure 4-12.   *Selecting columns to redisplay*

Column-Range

To change the width of four or five consecutive columns, you would have to execute Column Set-Width or Reset-Width once for each column that you wish to change. However, Release 2.2 and above offer an additional, far more efficient approach: You can use the /Worksheet Column Column-Range command to change several columns at one time. Figure 4-13 shows a model in which the width of columns D through G was changed to 3. This was accomplished by entering /**Worksheet Column Column-Range Set-Width**, highlighting the columns to change, typing **3**, and pressing ENTER. Using /Worksheet Column Set-Width would have required four separate command entries.

You can use Reset-Width to reset the range of affected columns to the default global column width.

Global Commands

Global commands affect the entire worksheet. Every row, every column, and every cell in each row and column are affected by the changes you make with the /Worksheet Global command options. The options available under the Global menu are shown here:

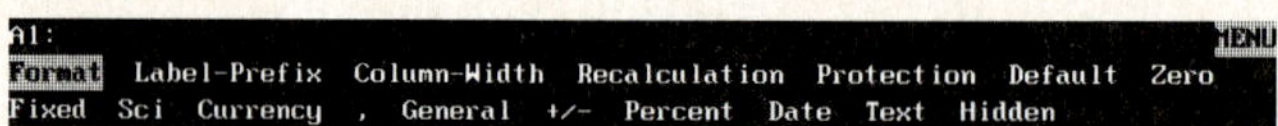

In this chapter you have the opportunity to use Column-Width, Format, Zero, and some of the options under Default. Most of the remaining /Worksheet Global options are covered in the next chapter.

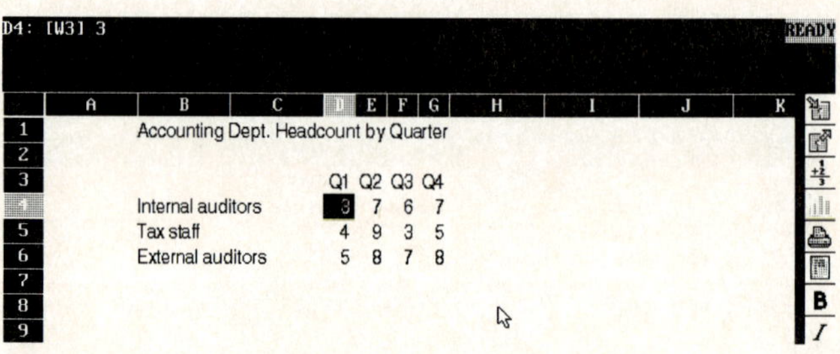

Figure 4-13.   *A worksheet with the width of the columns for D, E, F, and G set at 3*

Column-Width

Changing the column width for the entire worksheet with the /Worksheet Column command is inefficient. 1-2-3 allows you to change the width of every column on the worksheet with one command: /Worksheet Global Column-Width. With this option you can make all the columns on your worksheet any width from 1 to 240, instead of the default setting of 9.

Since this command affects the entire worksheet, there is no need to position your cell pointer before invoking it. The example in Figure 4-14 shows columns of numbers, all of which contain fewer positions than the default setting of 9. Shrinking the size of the columns allows you to display more information on the worksheet. By typing **/Worksheet Global Column-Width 5** and pressing ENTER, you could change the display to match the one shown in Figure 4-15.

Dept	Jan	Feb	Mar	Apr	May	Jun	Jul
100	35	35	34	34	33	33	33
110	15	15	15	15	15	15	15
125	12	12	12	13	13	13	13
135	56	56	55	55	55	54	54
159	65	65	65	65	65	65	63
160	41	39	38	38	38	37	37
175	4	4	4	4	4	4	4

Figure 4-14.   *A worksheet using a default column width of 9*

Dept	Jan	Feb	Mar	Apr	May	Jun	Jul	Aug	Sep	Oct	Nov	Dec
100	35	35	34	34	33	33	33	33	32	32	32	32
110	15	15	15	15	15	15	15	16	16	16	16	16
125	12	12	12	13	13	13	13	13	14	14	14	14
135	56	56	55	55	55	54	54	54	54	54	53	53
159	65	65	65	65	65	65	63	63	63	63	63	63
160	41	39	38	38	38	37	37	37	36	36	35	35
175	4	4	4	4	4	4	4	4	4	4	4	4

Figure 4-15.   *The worksheet using a default column width of 5*

The /Worksheet Column command takes precedence over the /Worksheet Global Column-Width command. You could use both commands if you had a worksheet in which you want all but one column to be narrow. /Worksheet Global Column-Width could set the narrow width for the entire worksheet. You would then move your cell pointer to the column requiring the larger width, type **/Worksheet Column Set-Width**, and specify the width needed for just that column.

Format

Format can also be changed on a global basis. The default setting is General format, but if you want all your entries to be in Currency, Percent, Scientific, or any of the other available formats, every worksheet cell can be reformatted with the /Worksheet Global Format command and the format specification of your choice. Figure 4-16 displays a worksheet created with the General format setting. The appearance of this worksheet can be markedly improved by use of a single command, /Worksheet Global Format Currency. After the initial command sequence, type **0** to indicate zero decimal places and press ENTER. The newly formatted worksheet looks like Figure 4-17.

Any one of the options listed in the "Format Options" box can be used. Some formats require more worksheet space than others, however. If the display turns to asterisks when you change your format, you must widen your columns to accommodate the new format. As previously mentioned, a /Range Format command always takes precedence over a /Worksheet Global Format change.

Zero Display

You can choose how zero values are displayed on the worksheet. In the past, a zero value always resulted in a cell containing a 0. The zero value options in Release 2.2 and above can hide or display zero values or display a label in every zero location on

	A	B	C	D
3		Budget	Actual	Diff.
4	Salaries	120678	125690	−5012
5	Supplies	34578.5	34250	328.5
6	Rent	6789	6955.5	−166.5
7	Postage	325	400.2	−75.2
8	Ins.	1235	1350	−115
9	Legal	4500	5000	−500

Figure 4-16.   *A worksheet using the General format*

	A	B	C	D	E	F	G	H
A1:								READY
1								
2								
3		Budget	Actual	Diff.				
4	Salaries	$120,678	$125,690	($5,012)				
5	Supplies	$34,579	$34,250	$329				
6	Rent	$6,789	$6,956	($167)				
7	Postage	$325	$400	($75)				
8	Ins.	$1,235	$1,350	($115)				
9	Legal	$4,500	$5,000	($500)				
10								

Figure 4-17.　　*The worksheet using the Currency format*

the worksheet. The zero values remain the same so they can be referenced for calculations.

To suppress the display of zeros on the worksheet, use /Worksheet Global Zero Yes. To restore the display, use /Worksheet Global Zero No. To display a label, use /Worksheet Global Zero Label and enter the label. The label you enter can include a label prefix for alignment. In Releases 2.3 and 2.4, you can also use the dialog box to select zero display by selecting one of the option boxes.

Figure 4-18 shows a worksheet with the Zero option set to display "None"; Figure 4-19 shows the same worksheet with Zero suppression set to Yes.

The problem with zero suppression is that 1-2-3 writes over a zero-suppressed cell if you type a new entry there because the cell appears blank. A solution to this problem is discussed in Chapter 5.

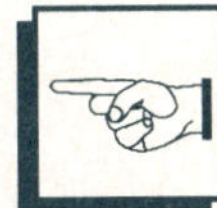

Zeros may still appear in a worksheet, even when Global Zero is suppressing zeros or displaying them as labels. The worksheet displays a zero if it contains a cell that appears as zero due to the cell's format but has a value that is not zero. For example, .1 in a cell formatted as Fixed with 0 decimal places appears as 0. To convert this type of value to actual zeros, use the @ROUND function covered in Chapter 7.

	A	B	C	D	E	F	G	H
B4: 0								READY
1			Absences by Month					
2								
3		Jan	Feb	Mar	Apr	May	June	July
4	Dept 4	None	2	3	2	None	None	1
5	Dept 5	1	1	None	None	None	None	2
6	Dept 7	2	2	2	2	None	None	None
7	Dept 8	None	None	None	None	1	1	None
8	Dept 9	3	3	1	1	None	None	2
9								

Figure 4-18.　　*Displaying zeros as the label None*

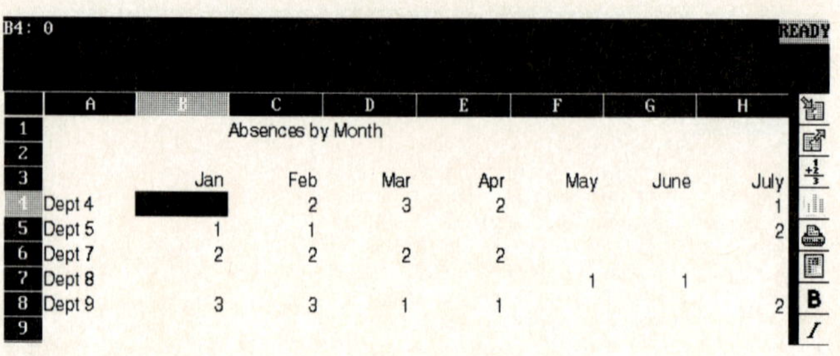

Figure 4-19.   *Hiding zeros*

Format Options

This table provides a quick reference to formatting 1-2-3's features.

Format	Entry	Display
Fixed	5678	5678.00
2 decimal places	−123.45	−123.45
Scientific	5678	5.68E+03
2 decimal places	−123.45	11.23E+02
Currency	5678	$5,678.00
2 decimal places	−123.45	($123.45)
,(Comma)	5678	5,678.00
General	5678	5678
	−123.45	−123.45
+/−	4	+ + + +
	−3	---
	0	.
Percent	5	500%
0 decimal places	.1	10%
Date	31679	24-Sep-91 (D1)
Time	.5	12:00:00 PM (T1)
Text	+A2*A3	+A2*A3

Range Format Commands

Range format commands do just what their name implies: They change the format for a specified range of cells on the worksheet. Any of the valid ranges described in Chapter 3 can be affected. The range can be as small as one cell, or it can be a rectangle of cells.

You can use /Range Format to change the format of any range from the current format setting. You can choose any of the options in the Format Options box.

If you preselect a range, you can use the SmartIcon palettes to apply a few numeric formats to the selected range. Currency, percent, and a thousands separator are available on the predefined palettes. Table 4-1 shows the numeric formats that are selectable from 1-2-3's predefined icon palettes, what they do, and the palette you can use to select them. The palette numbers in the table are the palettes that appear when Wysiwyg is active. Without Wysiwyg, the icons are distributed over eight, rather than six, palettes.

Cells in the current selection that are already formatted in the same format as the icon palette will be reset to the Global format setting. The cells will be reset if the format matches, even if the number of decimal places does not match. For example, if the cells you select are currently formatted as Currency and you choose Percent, they will be formatted as percentages with two decimal places. If the cells are formatted as Percent with one decimal place, they will be reset to the current Global format just as if you had selected /Range Reset for the cells.

Plan your format layout as you plan your worksheet design. You cannot create well-designed models without adequate planning. As you lay out a worksheet design on paper, add color highlighting or some other indication of the formats you want to use. You can make the format changes as a first step in the model creation process.

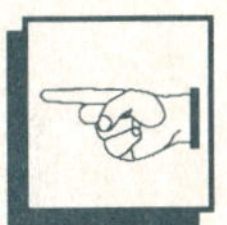

As an example of the /Range Format command in action, consider the worksheet shown in Figure 4-20, which has three different types of entries. Two of these

Icon	Effect	Palette Number
$	Currency with two decimal places	1, 2
0,0	Comma for thousands separator with no decimal places	2
%	Percent with two decimal places	2

Table 4-1.   Numeric Format Palettes

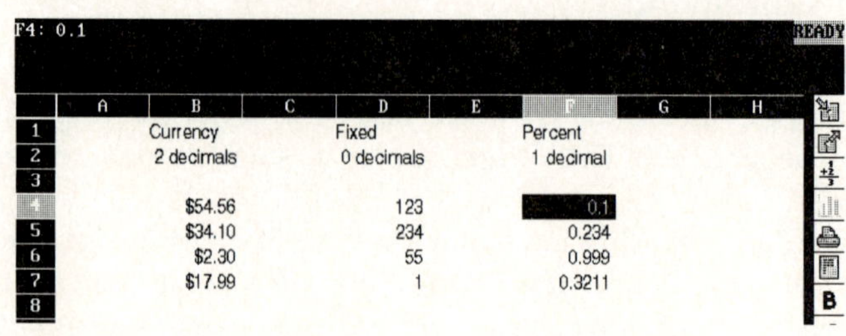

Figure 4-20.   *A worksheet with numbers in different formats*

worksheet entries have already been formatted, and one is in the process of being changed. To change the format of these cells, follow these steps:

1. Move your cell pointer to the upper-leftmost cell in the range you wish to format. Placing the cell pointer in this location allows you to specify the range using only the arrow keys.

2. Type **/Range Format**.

3. Select the Percent format from the menu, either by typing **P** or by pointing and pressing ENTER.

4. If the format requires a certain number of decimal places, either press ENTER to accept the default of two places or enter the desired number of decimal places and then press ENTER. In Figure 4-20, 1 is entered to replace the default.

5. 1-2-3 now requests the range to format. Specify the range by using the RIGHT and DOWN ARROW keys to move to the lower-rightmost cell you wish to format. If you are formatting just one cell, do not move the cell pointer. After all the cells to be formatted are highlighted, press ENTER, and they will be displayed with the new format. The worksheet will then look like Figure 4-21.

Just as with /Worksheet Global Format changes, /Range Format changes do not affect the internal storage accuracy of your numbers and calculated results. Suppose you decide to display an entry with no decimal places, but internally six or more places are stored. When that cell is used in a calculation, the full internal accuracy is applied, because 1-2-3 maintains entries with an accuracy of approximately 15 decimal digits. In Chapter 7, you will learn a way to change the internal accuracy as well with the @ROUND function.

/Range Format commands always take priority over /Worksheet Global Format commands. You can use this fact to your advantage. Before constructing a new worksheet, plan its design. Determine which format you will use more than any other,

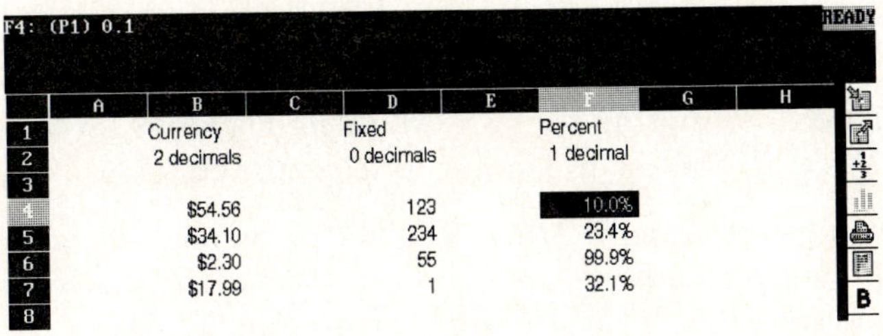

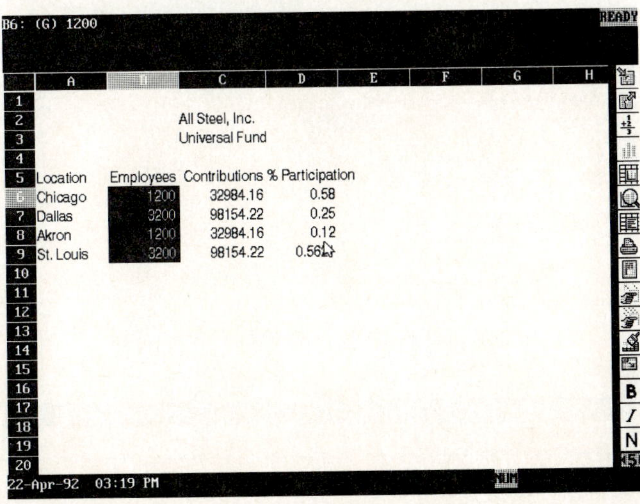

Figure 4-21.   *Formatting percent numbers*

and use /Worksheet Global Format to establish this format. Then, where necessary, use /Range Format commands to alter the format of individual cells or ranges.

The /Range Format commands have a feature not found in /Worksheet Global Format commands. Once a cell has been formatted with a /Range command, the top line in the control panel shows the format for the cell. For example, a display of (F2) means Fixed format with two decimal places, and (C0) indicates Currency format with zero decimal places.

Using SmartIcons to Change the Numeric Format

You can change a worksheet quickly with the icon palettes if they happen to match your needs. If you are working with the worksheet shown in Figure 4-22, you will have

Figure 4-22.   *Worksheet before selecting a SmartIcon*

an opportunity to use the three numeric format icons on the second palette. You can follow these steps to make the changes in Figure 4-22:

1. Move the cell pointer to B6, press F4, select B6..B9 as the range, and press ENTER. (You can also use the mouse to select the cells.)

2. Make icon palette 2 active by clicking the arrows to the right of the palette number. Then select the icon to format with the thousands separator and zero decimal places (this is the icon with a comma and a zero).

3. Select the range C6..C9. Then click the currency icon.

4. Select the range D6..D9. Then select the % icon.

Your model should now match Figure 4-23.

Numeric Format Options

Each of the format options in this section, with the exception of Reset, can be used with either the /Worksheet Global Format or the /Range Format command. Since Reset is used to reverse a /Range Format command by changing the range back to

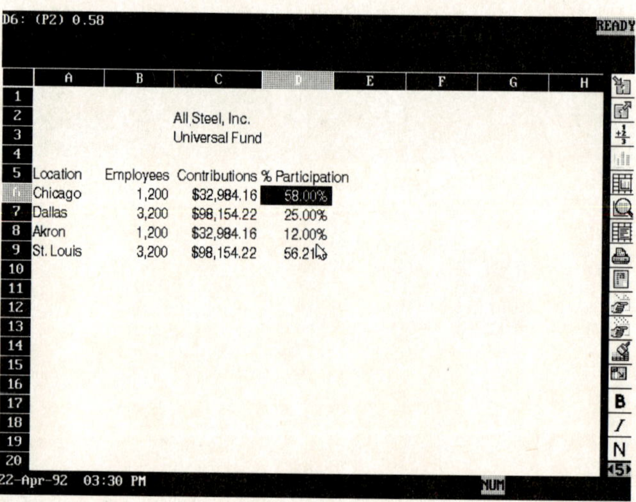

Figure 4-23.   *Worksheet after formatting with SmartIcons*

the global setting, this option is not needed on the /Worksheet Global Format menu. The following format options are summarized for you in the Format Options box. You have already had an opportunity to see how you can apply these options with /Range Format. Three format options are also available in the predefined icon palettes.

Fixed Format

The Fixed format lets you choose the number of places to the right of the decimal point you want to display. Like General format, it does not display dollar signs or commas.

The Fixed format option presents an appealing display when cells have many decimal numbers. This format is particularly useful because it permits numbers to be displayed with the decimals aligned, which General format does not.

If you use the Fixed format option and the numbers you enter or calculate with formulas do not contain a sufficient number of decimal places, zeros are added. Leading zero integers are always added for decimal fraction numbers. If you enter or calculate numbers with more decimal places than have been specified, they are rounded to the appropriate number of decimal places. Any number of 5 or above is rounded upward by 1-2-3.

The following table may help you remember the action 1-2-3 will take in various circumstances.

Entry	Fixed 0	Fixed 2	Fixed 4
7.23	7	7.23	7.2300
8.54	9	8.54	8.5400
3.5674	4	3.57	3.5674
.98	1	0.98	0.9800

After you apply a Fixed format to a range of cells, the control panel displays an indicator, such as (F0), (F2), or (F4). The number following the F (for Fixed) is the number of decimal places that you specified for your display.

Scientific Format

Scientific notation is useful when you need to display very large or very small numbers in a limited cell width. It is used primarily in scientific and engineering applications and would not be acceptable on most business reports. This format displays numbers in exponential notation. You can choose from 0 to 15 decimal places in the first, or multiplier, portion of the expression.

The following table shows entries as they are made in a worksheet cell and the display that results when each three Scientific decimal settings are established for the multiplier:

Entry	Scientific 0	Scientific 2	Scientific 4
100550000	1E+08	1.01E+08	1.0055E+08
7896543	8E+06	7.90E+06	7.8965E+06
.00005678	6E–05	5.68E–05	5.6780E–05

When the /Range Format command is used, the indicator for Scientific is S combined with the number of decimals. It is displayed within parentheses in the same way as the Fixed format indicator; for example, (S0), (S2), and (S4).

Currency Format

The Currency format is used frequently in business reports because they use many dollar figures. This format places a dollar sign ($) in front of each entry. It also adds a comma separator between thousands and hundreds and between millions and thousands. This format shows negative numbers in parentheses.

From 0 to 15 decimal places can be specified for this format, although the most common settings are 0 for whole dollars and 2 to show both dollars and cents. The /Worksheet Global Default Other International command can change the currency symbol, its placement, and the punctuation this format uses.

The following table shows the impact of using different Currency formats on several numeric entries:

Entry	Currency 0	Currency 2	Currency 4
34.78	$35	$34.78	$34.7800
–123	($123)	($123.00)	($123.0000)
1234.56	$1,235	$1,234.56	$1,234.5600

The indicator for the Currency format is C followed by the number of decimal places. Like the other format indicators, this appears in parentheses in front of the cell entry in the control panel.

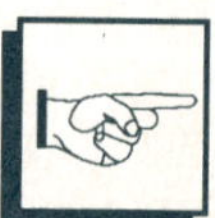

Remember: If you want to use the Currency format with two decimal places, you can use the $ icon in icon palette 2.

Comma Format

The Comma format is just like the Currency format, except it does not use the dollar sign. Just as with the Currency format, negative numbers are shown in parentheses and commas are added as separators. The Comma format is frequently combined with the Currency format for financial statements. As in Figure 4-24, the top and bottom line of a financial statement typically have the dollar sign ($) added, whereas the other numbers are shown in Comma format.

From 0 to 15 decimal places can be shown with this format. Enter the number of decimal places when prompted with the default. If you wish to accept the default (2), just press ENTER.

Here is a sample of the displays created with the Comma format:

Entry	Comma 0	Comma 2	Comma 4
34.78	35	34.78	34.7800
–123	(123)	(123.00)	(123.0000)
1234.56	1,235	1,234.56	1,234.5600

A comma and the number of decimal places are used as the indicator for this format. Thus (,0), (,2), and (,4) represent this format with 0, 2, and 4 decimal places, respectively.

Icon palette 2 contains a 0,0 icon to apply a comma format with zero decimal places to the current selection.

General Format

The General format is the default; it does not provide consistent displays like the other formats. Very large and very small numbers are displayed in scientific format.

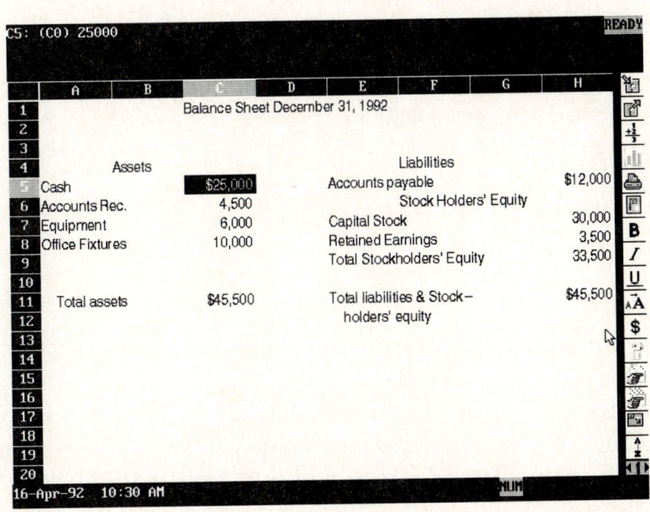

Figure 4-24.   Using the Comma and Currency formats to format numbers

Some numbers appear as they are entered, while others are rounded to a number of decimal digits that fit in the cell width you select. General format display often has varying numbers of decimal places in the entries. There is also no way to establish the number of digits for the multiplier when the Scientific format option is used for very small and very large numbers.

Looking at the way various entries appear in General format can help you decide when it is an appropriate format for your needs:

Entry	General Display
10000000000	1.0E+10
2345678	2345678
234.76895432	234.7689

The indicator for General format is (G). A numeric digit is not present because the format does not use a preset number of digits after the decimal point.

Although it is the default worksheet setting, General format is seldom selected as the display of choice. For most applications you want a more consistent display, even if it does require more room on the worksheet. General format is particularly useful, however, if you are short of space because it automatically converts to scientific notation when the entry becomes too large or too small to fit in the cell width.

+/− Format

The +/− format creates a series of plus (+) or minus (−) signs as a representation of the size of the number in the cell, producing a sort of bar graph. These signs change to asterisks if the size of the bar exceeds the column width. When the value of the cell is zero, a period (.) is displayed on the left side of the cell.

The +/− format creates the following horizontal displays from the entries shown:

Entry	+/−Display
0	.
5	+++++
−4	−−−−
−3.85	−−−

The (+) indicator appears when the cell pointer is on any cell with the +/− format from the /Range Format command.

The +/− format can be used to create a series of small bars to show, for example, growth or decline in sales over a period of time. In this situation you may want to divide the sales figure by 100 or some other appropriate number, so the result can be shown in a reasonable cell width. This approach was used to create the bar graph shown in Figure 4-25.

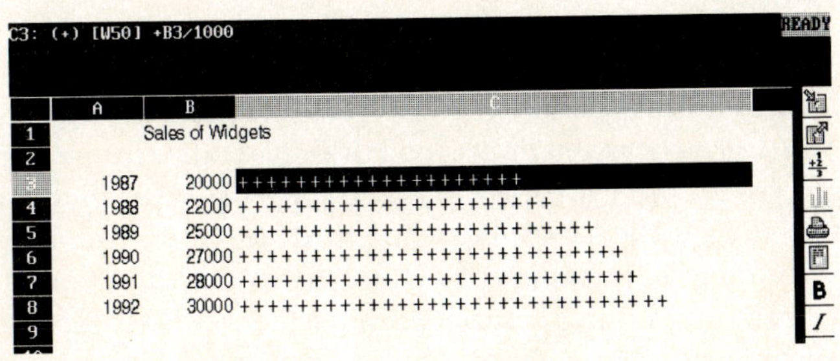

Figure 4-25.   A bar graph created with the +/– format

Percent Format

With the Percent format you can display percentages attractively, with the percent sign (%) added to the end of each cell. The Percent format can be used for applications such as percentage growth rates, interest on loans, and sales increases. You can choose any number of decimal places between 0 and 15. This format uses the indicator P followed by the number of decimal digits.

When the Percent format is applied, the number you have entered is multiplied by 100 before the % symbol is added. Thus, an entry of **.1** becomes 10%, and an entry of **10** becomes 1000%. You can see why it is important to enter the correct decimal fraction for the percent you want.

Avoid the common beginner's mistake of entering percentages incorrectly. Many new users attempt to enter 5% by typing a 5 in a cell and formatting it as a percent. 500% appears since percentages are entered as decimal fractions.

In the Percent format the following entries are displayed as shown, depending on how many decimal places you specify:

Entry	Percent 0	Percent 2	Percent 4
5	500%	500.00%	500.0000%
–.089635	–9%	–8.96%	–8.9635%
.45	45%	45.00%	45.0000%
–1	–100%	–100.00%	–100.0000%
.12	12%	12.00%	–12.0000%

Icon palette 3 has a % icon to format the current selection as percentages with two decimal places.

Date/Time Format

This format displays date and time serial numbers as the dates and times they represent. Dates and times are used in a variety of applications, such as to represent shipment receipts, line processing times, loan due dates, appointment dates, or order dates. Chapter 7 covers the functions that you'll use to enter date and time serial numbers. One of the quickest methods is to enter **@NOW**. You'll get the current date and time assuming the computer has the correct date and time.

1-2-3 allows you to enter a single serial number that represents both the date and the time. The whole number portion of the entry represents the date, and the fractional portion of the entry represents the time.

Assuming that @NOW is entered on June 12, 1992 in each of several cells and generates the serial number 33767, here are the displays you will see with different Date formats:

Format	Indicator	Example
DD-MMM-YY	D1	12-Jun-92
DD-MMM	D2	12-Jun
MMM-YY	D3	Jun-92
MM/DD/YY	D4	06/12/92
MM/DD	D5	06/12

When a cell contains both a date and time serial number (like the @NOW function creates), you must decide whether to apply a Date or Time format, since both formats cannot be applied to the same cell. This means that although you can place both a time and a date in a cell, you can see only one at a time. The one you see depends on the format you choose.

Time formats are accessed through the Date format option by selecting Time. There are four Time formats. Two use the AM and PM designation, and the other two are international formats that use a 24-hour day, as in military time. The indicators for times are D6 through D9, which represent the four time formats.

The effect of format selection on the display of time in worksheet cells can be seen in the following table:

Time Serial Number	HH:MM:SS AM/PM	HH:MM AM/PM	Long Intnl.	Short Intnl.
.25	06:00:00 AM	06:00 AM	06:00:00	06:00
.5	12:00:00 PM	12:00 PM	12:00:00	12:00
.75	06:00:00 PM	06:00 PM	18:00:00	18:00

Text Format

Text format displays actual formulas on the worksheet, rather than displaying the results of formula calculations, as happens with all the other formats. Using Text format causes a cell to display exactly what you enter. If your entry is a formula, 1-2-3 also remembers the result of the formula, and the result can be accessed with a reference to the cell.

When the cell pointer is on a cell formatted as text with a /Range command, the indicator (T) appears in the upper line of the control panel.

The Text format can be used to create a documentation copy of a worksheet, containing the actual formulas used in worksheet calculations. For example, to create a documentation copy of the worksheet shown in Figure 4-26, follow these steps:

1. Use **/Worksheet Global Format Text** to set the global format to Text. This does not completely change the display because some of the entries have been formatted with /Range commands, which always override global settings.

2. Use **/Range Format Reset A1..F16** and press ENTER to reset all the Range formats back to global settings.

3. Move your cell pointer to column D. Use **/Worksheet Column Set-Width**, and press the RIGHT ARROW until column D is 39 characters across. Press ENTER to select 39 as the column width. You now have a copy of the worksheet with all the formulas documented. It should look like Figure 4-27. Notice how the previously formatted numbers appear in the General format.

```
D4:  (C2) [W12] @IF(B4<48000,B4*0.0765,48000*0.0765)                    READY
```

	A	B	C	D	E	F
1						TOTAL
2	Name	Salary	Benefits	FICA	FUTA	SAL EXP
3						
4	Jones, Ray	$26,145.83	$3,660.42	$2,000.16	$420.00	$32,226.40
5	Larkin, Mary	$30,691.66	$4,296.83	$2,347.91	$420.00	$37,756.40
6	Harris, John	$15,437.50	$2,161.25	$1,180.97	$420.00	$19,199.72
7	Parson, Mary	$18,240.00	$2,553.60	$1,395.36	$420.00	$22,608.96
8	Smith, Jim	$24,207.50	$3,389.05	$1,851.87	$420.00	$29,868.42
9	Harker, Pat	$35,350.00	$4,949.00	$2,704.28	$420.00	$43,423.28
10	Jenkins, Paul	$48,712.50	$6,819.75	$3,672.00	$420.00	$59,624.25
11	Jacobs, Norman	$12,480.00	$1,747.20	$954.72	$420.00	$15,601.92
12	Merriman, Angela	$38,837.25	$5,437.22	$2,971.05	$420.00	$47,665.51
13	Campbell, David	$44,000.00	$6,160.00	$3,366.00	$420.00	$53,946.00
14	Campbell,Keith	$34,880.00	$4,883.20	$2,668.32	$420.00	$42,851.52
15	Stevenson, Mary	$19,136.25	$2,679.08	$1,463.92	$420.00	$23,699.25
16						
17						
18						
19						
20						

```
16-Apr-92   10:33 AM                                            NUM
```

Figure 4-26.   *A worksheet displaying results of formulas*

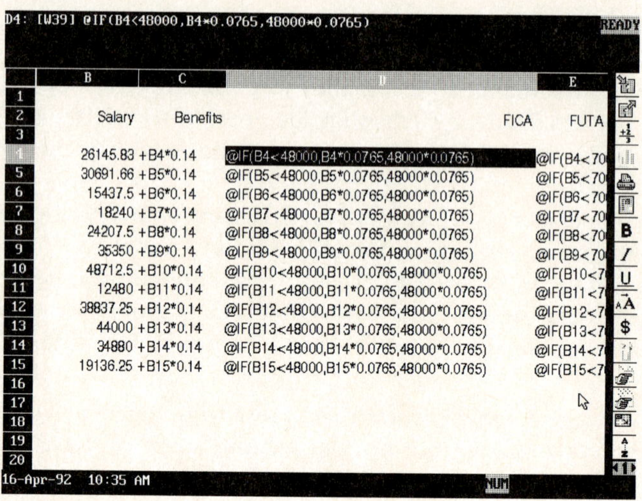

Figure 4-27.   The documentation copy displaying formulas

When you save files, make sure you never save a documentation file under the same filename you used for your original file. If you do, you lose all the formats and column widths that you worked so hard to establish for it. In the next chapter you learn how to print a documentation copy of your worksheet so you have a paper to file away and refer to if your disk copies are ever damaged or destroyed.

Hidden Format

Hidden format causes a cell to display as a blank; that is, 1-2-3 suppresses the display of the cell. The cell's contents have not been lost, even though they do not appear on the worksheet. They are still stored internally and are accessed when you reference the cell in a formula. In fact, the contents of the cell are displayed in the control panel when you move your cell pointer to the cell. You can hide the contents further by enabling worksheet protection as discussed in Chapter 5. When a worksheet is protected and the cell pointer is on a hidden cell, 1-2-3 displays PR in the control panel and does not display the cell entry.

The Hidden format causes all entries regardless of type to appear as blanks. The control panel indicator for a hidden cell, when the format is applied with a /Range command, is (H). In Figure 4-28, you see the cell pointer in a hidden cell and the contents displayed in the control panel.

The main use of hidden cells is in macro applications. If the application is kept completely under macro control, the Hidden format could provide a measure of security. For more about macros, see Chapters 12 and 13.

```
B4: (H) [W13] 26145.83                                    READY

            A          ||        C         D         E         F
  1                                                            TOTAL
  2  Name            Salary   Benefits     FICA      FUTA    SAL EXP
  3
  4  Jones, Ray              [          ] $3,660.42 $2,000.16  $420.00 $32,226.40
  5  Larkin, Mary                         $4,296.83 $2,347.91  $420.00 $37,756.40
  6  Harris, John                         $2,161.25 $1,180.97  $420.00 $19,199.72
  7  Parson, Mary                         $2,553.60 $1,395.36  $420.00 $22,608.96
  8  Smith, Jim                           $3,389.05 $1,851.87  $420.00 $29,868.42
```

Figure 4-28.   Numbers hidden with the Hidden format

Selecting a format option from the icon palette that matches the current format of your selection is equivalent to entering/Range Format Reset to reset the format to the current Global format setting.

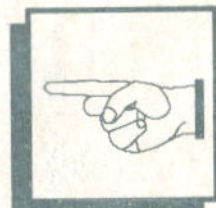

Wysiwyg Format Options Accessible with SmartIcons

In addition to the icons for the numeric formats, the SmartIcons let you access some of Wysiwyg's format options if you have Release 2.4. Although the icons are always present in the palettes, they can be accessed only when Wysiwyg is installed. The formatting changes you make with these icons are visible on the worksheet immediately, but they appear on your printed output only if you use Wysiwyg to print. You can choose options such as boldface, italics, shaded background, underlining with a single or a double line, outlining, and color change. Table 4-2 shows the full set of Wysiwyg options on the palettes.

You will learn all about these formatting features in Chapter 5, but you can use them now to make some quick changes.

All SmartIcon palette options are applied the same way: You select the cells to be affected and then choose the icon option. You can remove any applied Wysiwyg format option from cells by selecting the cells and choosing the icon with an N, for Normal text, without any of the Wysiwyg enhancements. A quick look at a few options shows how these changes can dramatically affect the worksheet shown in Figure 4-29.

Enlarging the Font Size

The *font* is the character style, size, and character set available to you. If you are using the full set of Wysiwyg features discussed in Chapter 15, you can change any of these features by selecting a different font. For now you can use the SmartIcon palette to change the character size to the next largest size. You can choose this option repeatedly to increase the entries in the selected cells by more than one size.

Icon	Effect	Palette Number
B	Displays the selected cell as boldface	1, 5
I	Displays the selected cell as italics	1, 5
N	Removes formatting such as boldface, underlining, and italics	5
U	Underlines entries in the current selection	1, 2
U	Double underlines entries in the current selection	2
(box with drop shadow)	Outlines the current cell or range and adds a drop shadow	2
(box)	Outlines the current cell or range	2
(shaded box)	Adds shading to the current cell or range	2
aA	Displays data in the next font size	1, 2
AA	Displays data in the next color	2
AA	Displays the background in the next color	2

Table 4-2.   Wysiwyg options available on the icon palettes

To enlarge the heading for the worksheet shown in Figure 4-28, select B1..B2 and then click the icon to enlarge the font from palette 1 or 2. In Table 4-2, this icon shows a small A and a large A.

Adding Bold

Adding bold to text makes it stand out from surrounding text. You might want to add bold to the text at the tops of the columns in Figure 4-28 to make it stand out from the column entries. Select cells B4..D4 and then select the icon in palette 1 or 5 that has a large B, for boldface.

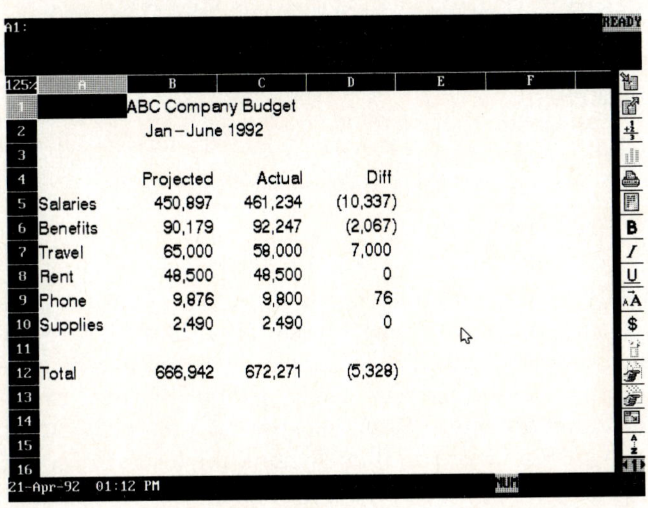

Figure 4-29.   *Worksheet before formatting*

Adding Underlining

When you select either single or double underlining, Wysiwyg underlines only the text within the entries in the selected range. If the cells that were boldfaced in Figure 4-28 are still selected, all you need to do is select the icon with a U and a single underscore in icon palette 1 or 2 to add this option to the cells, too. With Wysiwyg formatting options, you can add as many formatting attributes as you want by continuing to click the icons that represent them. If Undo is enabled, you can always eliminate your last change. Without Undo enabled, you can select the icon representing Normal text (the icon contains an N) to remove all Wysiwyg formatting.

To underline the last detail entry in each column, select B10..D10 and then click the underline icon in palette 1 or 2.

Outlining

When you outline a range, Wysiwyg adds lines around the perimeter of the selected range. In Chapter 15 you will see variations of the outline feature, but the icon palette offers only the full perimeter outline (with or without a drop shadow effect). To add an outline around the Total row, select A12..D12 and then select the outline icon from palette 2. This icon looks like a rectangle.

Shading Cells

Shading adds light gray shading to the selected range. It sets off text from other entries and is often used with the outline feature. To add gray shading to the Total row all you need to do is click the shading icon that follows the outline icon in palette 2.

Figure 4-29 shows the worksheet from Figure 4-28 with all the Wysiwyg changes made from the palettes.

Advanced Features

The options discussed in this section are not features you need to change every day, like the other formatting options, but you may occasionally want to use them. One is the /Worksheet Global Default Other International option, which changes the way 1-2-3 handles punctuation, currency, date and time displays, as well as negative numbers. A related command, /Worksheet Global Other Clock, alters the clock display format on your screen. The third feature, the justification options available under /Range Justify, manipulates a column of text entries in your worksheet. The last option controls whether or not your computer beeps when you make a mistake.

The format changes you make with these options are in effect only for the current session, unless you use the /Worksheet Global Default Update command to make the changes permanent. This command saves your changes in the file 123.CNF, which is used to configure 1-2-3 each time you load it.

The following sections offer a more detailed look at each of these options.

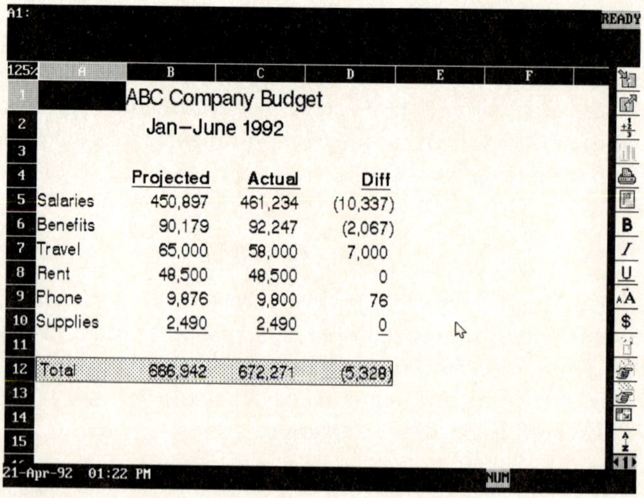

Figure 4-30.   Worksheet after Wysiwyg formatting

International Format Options

The /Worksheet Global Default Other International command customizes the display for numeric punctuation, currency, date, and time.

Punctuation

The numeric punctuation indicators you can control are the decimal point separator, the thousands separator for numbers, and the argument separator in @functions and macro commands. The default point separator is a period (.), but you have the option of changing it to a comma (,). The default thousands separator is a comma and can be changed to a period or a space. The argument separator is initially set as a comma; it can be changed to a period or a semicolon (;).

The Punctuation options are not chosen individually, but rather a combination of three is selected at once as follows:

Option	Point	Argument	Thousands
A (default)	.	,	,
B	,	.	.
C	.	;	,
D	,	;	.
E	.	,	space
F	,	.	space
G	.	;	space
H	,	;	space

The next table shows how each choice affects the display of numbers and the arguments for such @functions as @SUM:

Punctuation Option	Numeric Entry in Currency Format	Function Arguments
A (default)	$1,200.50	@SUM(D2,A8..A10)
B	$1.200,50	@SUM(D2.A8..A10)
C	$1,200.50	@SUM(D2;A8..A10)
D	$1.200,50	@SUM(D2;A8..A10)
E	$1 200.50	@SUM(D2,A8..A10)
F	$1 200,50	@SUM(D2.A8..A10)
G	$1 200.50	@SUM(D2;A8..A10)
H	$1 200,50	@SUM(D2;A8..A10)

International Currency

This option allows you to change the currency symbol from the standard dollar sign ($) to one of the international currency symbols found in the LICS codes. You also may choose to place the symbol at the end of your entry rather than at the beginning, as in the default setting. Examples of currency symbols you may wish to use are those for guilders, pounds, yen, and pesetas. The COMPOSE sequence for these entries is shown in Appendix C.

To change from $ to one of these symbols, invoke /Worksheet Global Default Other International Currency, press ALT-F1 (COMPOSE), enter the appropriate character sequence, and then press ENTER. Once the currency symbol is entered, you can select whether it appears before the number (prefix) or after the number (suffix).

International Date

The international date formats—D4 and D5—can be altered with the /Worksheet Global Default Other International Date command. The initial setting for the international date is MM/DD/YY. This can be changed to three other forms. The choices for this setting and how the settings will affect a sample date are as follows:

Option	Format	D4	D5
A	MM/DD/YY	09/24/92	09/24
B	DD/MM/YY	24/09/92	24/09
C	DD.MM.YY	24.09.92	24.09
D	YY-MM-DD	92-09-24	09-24

International Time

The appearance of the international time formats can be changed with this option. Format D8 shows hours, minutes, and seconds; format D9 shows only hours and minutes. The initial international time setting is HH:MM:SS. Each of the four options is indicated by a letter. The letters, time formats, and examples of the format with the time 12:30:25 PM follow:

Option	Format	D8	D9
A	HH:MM:SS	12:30:25	12:30
B	HH.MM.SS	12.30.25	12.30
C	HH,MM,SS	12,30,25	12,30
D	HHhMMmSSs	12h30m25s	12h30m

Negative

The /Worksheet Global Default International Negative command is a customization feature in 2.2 and above. This option allows you to customize how negative numbers in the Comma or Currency format are displayed. The default setting is to enclose these numbers in parentheses, but once you select this command, you can choose to use a minus sign to affect all the entries in the worksheet.

Update

Any changes made with /Worksheet Global Default Other International commands are in effect only for the current session. The next time you load 1-2-3, the original /Worksheet Global Default settings are in effect. If you wish to make your changes permanent, invoke the /Worksheet Global Default Update command to save your custom settings. This sets your changes to the new global default values, and they are in effect the next time 1-2-3 is loaded into memory.

Deactivating Your Computer's Beep

When you attempt to move the cell pointer beyond the edges of the worksheet or attempt to complete an entry incorrectly, your computer sounds a beep. Other errors also cause your computer to make this same sound, and you can issue the beep tone yourself with a special macro instruction. If you wish to disable the beep sound, you can use the /Worksheet Global Default Other Beep No command to turn it off. Once it is set to No, the beep does not sound regardless of your actions during the current session. You can update this setting with the /Worksheet Global Default Update command.

Clock Display

The clock displays in the bottom line of your screen as long as 1-2-3 does not need this space to display an error message. You also can configure 1-2-3 to display the name of the current file in this area once the file has been saved to disk.

If you would prefer the filename display, you can change the setting for this option with the /Worksheet Global Default Other Clock command. Your choices are Standard, International, None, Clock, or Filename.

Standard displays the date in the long format DD-MMM-YY and the time as HH:MM AM/PM.

Selecting International displays the date in the long international date format and the time in the short international time format. Choosing None eliminates the time display from the screen. The Clock option ensures that the clock display is always on the screen. It uses either Standard or International display, depending on your earlier selection. Choosing Filename displays the filename if the worksheet has one. New files continue to display the clock until they have been saved to disk at least once.

/Range Justify

The /Range Justify command readjusts text in label entries to fit within the width of one or more columns. 1-2-3 moves characters from one label entry to the next with this command.

With this command you can enter one or more long labels in a column and then, after the entry is complete, decide how many columns wide the display of this information should be. The width of the display is determined by selecting a justify range. If that range is two cells wide, for example, the long labels are redistributed so they take up more rows but display only in two columns.

/Range Justify does not provide full word processing support, but it does allow you to write readable documentation on the screen or write a short memo that references worksheet data. It frees you from having to concentrate on the length of your entry as you type. If you want additional word processing support, you can use the Text features of Wysiwyg covered in Chapter 15.

Figure 4-31 contains an example of long labels entered into A1..A6 of the worksheet. Suppose you decide that the display should be confined to columns A through C. (The labels are entered in column A and remain in that location; what you change is the space they borrow for display purposes.) To make the change, take the following steps:

1. Move your cell pointer to the beginning of the range you will use for display— A1 in this example.

2. Type **/Range Justify**.

3. Highlight the cells in the range A1..C1 with the RIGHT ARROW key.

4. Press ENTER. Your justified data should look like Figure 4-32.

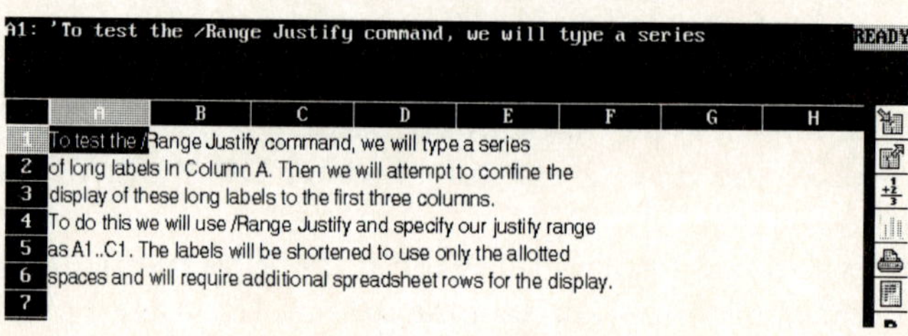

Figure 4-31.   *A worksheet containing long labels*

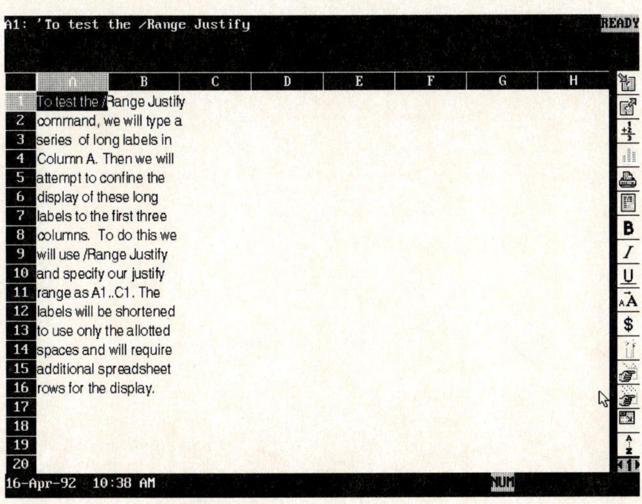

Figure 4-32.   *The worksheet with long labels left justified*

To make the display wider again, move your cell pointer to A1 and start the process over. For example, you might want to specify A1..F1 as the justify range. The first six columns are then used for the display.

Since the label was originally entered in column A, *only* the cell entries in column A are displaced. Even if the justify range includes columns A..C, and there is information in the cells to the right of column A, it is not displaced. For instance, a table in cells B10..C14 would be unaffected by the paragraph rearrangement shown in Figure 4-32. Instead, the label display in column A would be truncated in rows 10 through 14, just as it is when an entry to the right of any long label causes the label display to be truncated.

WORKSHEET DISPLAY

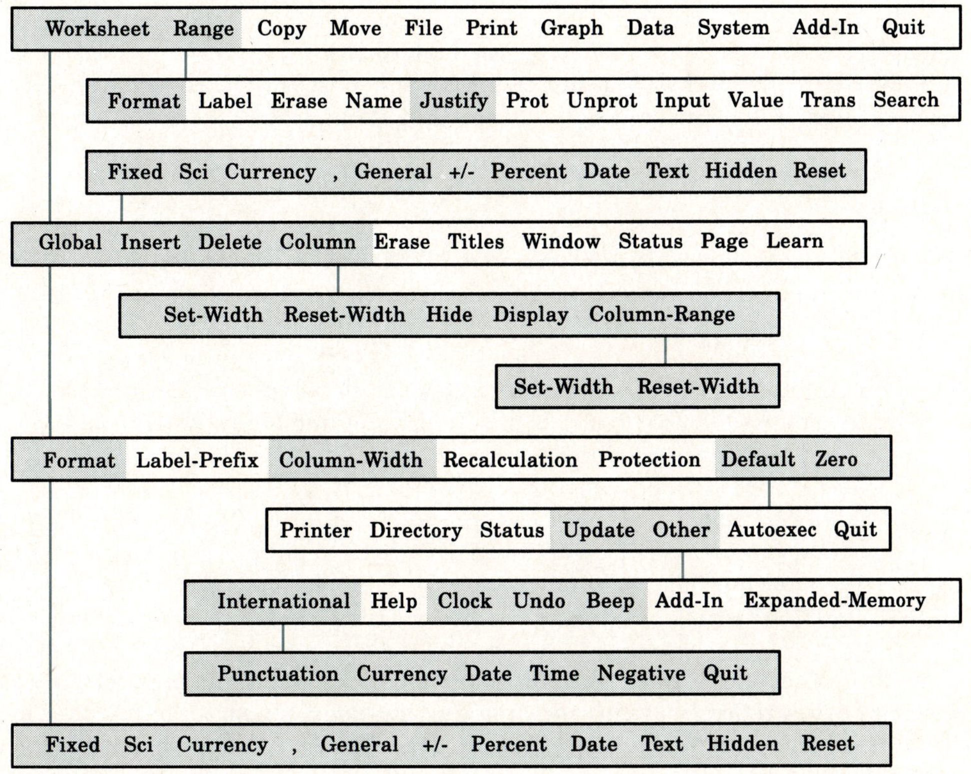

/Range Format

Description

The /Range Format command determines the appearance of numeric entries on your worksheet. With this command you can change the specific display format for one or many cells in a contiguous range on the worksheet. You can choose the number of decimal places displayed (0 to 15) for most formats and determine whether the numeric information is displayed as currency, scientific notation, a date, a time, or one of several other options.

The display format you select does not affect the internal storage of numbers. You can elect to display a number with seven decimal places as a whole number, for example, but all seven places are maintained internally.

Regardless of the format you choose, the column must be wide enough to display your selection. If the column is not wide enough, asterisks (*) appear.

Options

For each format option, you must respond to 1-2-3's prompt concerning the number of decimal places or the Date format you desire. Finally, select the range of cells to format.

Fixed   Fixed format displays all entries with a specific number of decimal places. Two places are the default, but you may select any number between 0 and 15. Examples with three decimal places are .007, 9.000, and 4.156.

Sci   Scientific format displays numbers in exponential form, showing the power of 10 by which the number must be multiplied. From 0 to 15 places can be specified for the number of decimal places. Some examples with two decimal places are 6.78E-20, 4.11E+5, and 0.78E+8.

$ **Currency**   Currency format precedes your entry by a dollar sign ($) and inserts a separator between the thousands and hundreds positions. You may specify from 0 to 15 decimal places for this format; 2 is the default. Negative amounts appear in parentheses. Examples with two decimal places are $3.40, $1,400.98, and ($89.95).

0,0 **, (Comma)**   Comma format is identical to the Currency format, except that Comma lacks the dollar sign. You may specify any number of decimal places between 0 and 15; 2 is the default. Examples with two decimal places are 1,200.00, (5,678.00), and 45.00.

General   General is the default format for 1-2-3. With it the leading zero integer always appears, as in 0.78, but trailing zeros are suppressed. If the number is very large or very small, it appears in scientific notation. Examples of numeric displays with the General format are 15.674, 2.7E+12, and 0.67543.

+/−   +/− format produces a horizontal bar graph showing the relative size of numbers. Each integer is represented by a symbol. For example, −3 is −−−, and 5 is +++++. A period (.) is used to represent 0.

Percent   Percent format displays your entries as percentages. Each entry is multiplied by 100, and a % symbol is added to the end. You may specify from 0 to 15 decimal places; 2 is the default. Examples with two decimal places are 4.00%, 3.15%, and 1200.00%.

Date   The Date option provides a second menu of possibilities, from which you can select the following formats for the date:

D1	(DD-MMM-YY)	08-Sep-91
D2	(DD-MMM)	08-Sep
D3	(MMM-YY)	Sep-91
D4	(MM/DD/YY)	09/08/91
D5	(MM/DD)	09/08

The last two date formats can be changed to several other formats with the /Worksheet Global Default Other International Date command.

Time formats are accessed through the Date format. When you select Time from the Date options, a menu of four Time formats is presented. Two of the formats use the AM and PM designation, and the other two are International formats that use a 24-hour day, as in military time. The formats available for the display of time in your worksheet cells are

(D6) T1	HH:MM:SS AM/PM	06:00:00 AM
(D7) T2	HH:MM	06:00 AM
(D8) T3	Long International	06:00:00
(D9) T4	Short International	06:00

The last two time formats marked can be changed to several other formats with the /Worksheet Global Default Other International Time command.

Text   Text format displays the formulas rather than the result, and formats numbers in a General format.

Hidden   Hidden format causes the selected cells to appear blank on the screen. If you move your cell pointer to a hidden cell, the control panel displays the cell's contents. Cell entries with a hidden format will not appear in the control panel if worksheet protection is enabled.

Reset   This option returns the specified range of cells to the default format setting. Erasing a range on the worksheet with /Range Erase does not affect the format of the cells in the range.

/Range Justify

Description

The /Range Justify command rearranges text in a range. Once a label is entered (for example, a long label entered in cell A1), you can use /Range Justify to redistribute the label so that it is displayed differently. The width of the display is determined by selecting a justify range, which may be one to several cells wide (the maximum is 240 characters) and one to several rows long.

Information in cells to the right of a justify range is not displaced when you use /Range Justify. Instead, the display of a label in the justify range is hidden by the entries—even though the contents of the cells containing the label are not affected.

Options

You have the option of specifying one or more rows for the justify range. If you specify one row, 1-2-3 includes all labels from that row down to either the bottom of the worksheet or the first row that does not contain a label. Cells containing nonlabel entries below the justify range may be shifted up or down, depending on the space requirements for the justified labels.

If you specify more than one row with /Range Justify, you assume the burden of allowing sufficient space for the justification. If there is not enough space in the range you choose, you see the error message "Justify range is full or line too long." With a selection of more than one row for the range, only the labels in the range down to the first nonlabel entry are justified. Also, when you specify more than one row, cells outside the justify range are unaffected.

Note

Do not use this command for cells that have been assigned range names. Although the contents of the cell may be displaced, the range name is still assigned to the same cell.

/Worksheet Column

Description

The /Worksheet Column command allows you to change the characteristics of the worksheet columns. You can use the command to change the column width and to hide and display columns.

Options

Set-Width   After choosing this option, either use the RIGHT and LEFT ARROW keys to change the column width of the current column or type in the exact width desired for that column. Any width between 1 and 240 is acceptable. If you choose a column width narrower than the width of your data, the value data is displayed as asterisks.

Reset-Width   This option returns the width setting for the current column to the default setting; that is, either the initial default of 9 or the setting established with /Worksheet Global Column-Width, if that command has been used.

Hide   This option hides one or many columns, depending on the range you specify for this command. The hidden columns also are not printed, even if the print range spans cells on both sides of them. These hidden columns appear only when 1-2-3 is in the POINT mode; an asterisk appears next to the column letter. Hide does not affect the data in the cells. At any time you can bring the data back into view with the Display option.

Display   This command redisplays one or more hidden columns in the range you select.

Column-Range   This command changes the width in one or more columns on the current worksheet. Column-Range functions the same as the /Worksheet Column Set-Width and Reset-Width commands, except that it allows you to work with more than one column. Any group of adjacent columns on the current worksheet can be changed. The two selections available for this choice are Set-Width and Reset-Width. After selecting either choice, select the range to change and the new width for the range of columns if you select Set-Width.

/Worksheet Delete

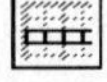

Description

The /Worksheet Delete command allows you to delete unneeded columns and rows.

Options

The /Worksheet Delete command provides two options: Column and Row. You also have the option of deleting one or many columns or rows with one execution of the command. The best approach is to place your cell pointer on the first column or row to be deleted. Enter /**Worksheet Delete Column** or /**Worksheet Delete Row**, and then move your cell pointer to include at least one of the cells in the columns or rows you wish to delete. Deletions from the middle of a range cause 1-2-3 to automatically adjust the range to compensate for the deletions.

Note

A complete column or row must be deleted because 1-2-3 does not provide a feature for deleting part of the selected segment. You may want to make sure that the Undo feature is enabled before deleting, or you can save the file before you begin as a precaution.

/Worksheet Global Column-Width

Description

The /Worksheet Global Column-Width command changes the default column width for the worksheet.

Options

After entering /Worksheet Global Column-Width, either use the RIGHT and LEFT ARROW keys to change the column width or type in the exact width desired. Any width between 1 and 240 is acceptable. You can also set the default column width by entering the global column width in the Column width text box of the /Worksheet Global dialog box.

/Worksheet Global Default Other Beep

Description

This command controls whether 1-2-3 responds to a mistake with a beep sound. When enabled, errors and the macro command {BEEP} cause 1-2-3 to activate your computer's beep sound. When disabled, errors and the macro command {BEEP} have no effect.

Options

The two options for this command are Yes to enable the beep and No to disable it. You can also enable or disable the computer's bell by selecting the Computer bell on check box from the /Worksheet Global Default dialog box.

/Worksheet Global Default Other Clock

Description

This command sets the format for the date and time in the status line.

Options

Standard   This option displays the date as DD-MMM-YY and the time as HH:MM AM/PM.

International   This option displays the date in the current long International format (month, day, and year), and the time in the current short international format (hours and minutes based on a 24-hour clock). The International format options are discussed in more detail under /Worksheet Global Default Other International.

None   This option suppresses the filename or the date and time display in the status line.

Clock   This option causes the clock to display at all times.

Filename   This option displays the filename for saved files or the clock for new worksheets.

/Worksheet Global Default Other International

Description

The /Worksheet Global Default Other International command allows you to customize the display for numeric punctuation, currency, date, and time. You can also select the international settings by selecting from the option boxes for the command options in the /Worksheet Global Default Other International dialog box, described next.

Options

Punctuation   The numeric punctuation indicators you can control are the point separator (the decimal indicator in numbers such as 55.98), the thousands separator for numbers, and the argument separator used in @functions. The default point separator is a period (.), but you have the option of changing it to a comma (,). The initial thousands separator is a comma; it can be changed to a period or a space. The argument separator is initially set as a comma; it can be changed to a period or a semicolon (;). The options are not chosen individually, but rather in a combination of three after you select Punctuation. The options available are shown in the following table:

Option	Point	Argument	Thousands
A	.	,	,
B	,	.	.
C	.	;	,
D	,	;	.
E	.	,	space
F	,	.	space
G	.	;	space
H	,	;	space

Currency   This option selects the currency symbol and placement. Type the currency character you want (the LICS characters are listed in Appendix B, "LICS Codes"). Then select Prefix to display the currency symbol before a number or Suffix to display the currency symbol after a number.

Date   The International Date formats (D4 and D5) can be altered with the Date option under the /Worksheet Global Default Other International Date command. The fourth date format displays month, day, and year and the fifth date format displays the month and day. The initial setting for the International Date (option A) is MM/DD/YY. This can be changed to DD/MM/YY, DD.MM.YY, or YY-MM-DD.

Time   The appearance of the International Time formats can be changed with this option. Format D8 shows hours, minutes, and seconds; format D9 shows only hours and minutes. The initial International Time setting (option A) is HH:MM:SS. The other options to which this setting can be changed are HH.MM.SS; HH,MM,SS; or HHhMMmSSs.

Negative   This option allows you to set 1-2-3 to use either minus signs or parentheses for negative numbers in the Comma and Currency formats.

/Worksheet Global Default Other Undo

Description

This command allows you to enable and disable 1-2-3's Undo feature. When it is enabled, you can reverse (undo) the last command sequence. Before you can enable Undo, you must have all Add-Ins removed and any worksheet erased. Pressing the ALT-F4 (UNDO) key when Undo is disabled has no effect.

Options

The Undo command has two options: Enable and Disable. You can also enable or disable Undo by selecting the Undo on check box from the /Worksheet Global Default dialog box.

/Worksheet Global Default Update

Description

The /Worksheet Global Default Update command allows you to save changes you have made to 1-2-3's default global settings with the /Worksheet Global Default commands. This makes the new settings available the next time you work with 1-2-3. The settings are saved in the 123.CNF file on your 1-2-3 disk. You can also select this command by selecting the Update command button from the /Worksheet Global Default dialog box.

/Worksheet Global Format

Description

The /Worksheet Global Format command allows you to change the default display format for the entire worksheet. All numeric entries on the worksheet use the format chosen with this command, unless they have been formatted with the /Range Format command, which has priority over /Worksheet Global Format.

Options

The options for the /Worksheet Global Format command are the same options as for the /Range Format command (except Reset is not available). You can also select the global format by selecting Format in the /Worksheet Global dialog box and selecting one of the formats in the superimposed box.

/Worksheet Global Zero

Description

This command selects how 1-2-3 displays cells that have a value equal to zero. The options let you display a zero, hide the zero, or display a label such as "Free" in place of a zero.

Options

The /Worksheet Global Zero command presents three options: Yes, No, and Label. The default is No, which displays zero values as 0. Choosing the Yes option hides zero values. The Label option, which is available in Release 2.2 and above, prompts you for a label that 1-2-3 can display for cells that have a zero value. With all these options, the original value (a zero or a formula) still appears in the control panel when the cell is highlighted. You can also select how zero values display by selecting one of the zero display options in the /Worksheet Global dialog box.

/Worksheet Insert

Description

The /Worksheet Insert command can be used to add blank columns and rows to your worksheet. These blank areas can be used to improve readability or to allow for the addition of new information to your worksheet.

Inserts made to the middle of a range of cells automatically expand the reference to a range address or name.

Options

This command provides two options: Column or Row. Columns are always added to the left of the cell pointer location or the range you specify. Rows are always added above the cell pointer or the range you specify. Select a range containing the number of columns or rows you want to add.

Chapter 5

Basic Worksheet Commands

This chapter focuses on menu commands that extend your productivity in using the worksheet. In this chapter you learn additional commands on the Worksheet menus.

You can use /Range commands to name worksheet cells, change the alignment of labels, and erase unneeded entries. Other /Range commands help you find and optionally change entries within formulas or labels. /Range commands let you transpose data from a row layout to a column layout or from a column layout to a row layout. You can also use /Range commands to establish a restricted input area.

The /Copy command and the /Move command improve your skill at developing new worksheets. These commands also require range entries to define your needs to 1-2-3. This chapter introduces you to a variety of new Worksheet options that allow you to use your worksheet data more effectively.

By the time you finish reading this chapter, you will have experience with all Worksheet commands, except those with a very specialized purpose. You will also know which SmartIcons to use to invoke these features if you happen to be working with Release 2.4

Working with Ranges

In Chapter 4, you learned to use some of the /Range commands to change the appearance of your worksheet. In this chapter you expand your range options with commands that allow you to access cells through range names rather than cell addresses. You will also learn /Range commands that can change a worksheet column into a worksheet row. You will find out how to freeze formulas at their existing values for a large or small range of cells. You are introduced to additional commands that alter the worksheet format, either erasing all entries for a range or changing the justification for labels stored in the range. Finally, you learn how to use the new search features that locate matching entries in a formula or label.

Methods of Specifying Cell Ranges

You can tell 1–2–3 in a variety of ways which range you want to work with. With Release 2.3 and 2.4, you have the option of preselecting the range. This is a useful technique when you need to work on the same range of cells with several different commands. You will learn more about methods for preselecting ranges later in the chapter.

To select a range after choosing a command that requires a range, you can press the left mouse button and drag across the cells that you want to include. If you are comfortable using a mouse, this can be the quickest approach to selecting a range. If you prefer to use the keyboard to define your range, the easiest method is using the arrow keys to point to the desired range. Pointing offers the advantage of letting you visually verify the range you have chosen because it highlights the range cells as you expand or contract the range with the arrow keys. Pointing works only when 1-2-3 is in POINT mode after a complete range is suggested. If a command references a single cell, type a period (.) to turn the single cell address into a range, thereby locking the beginning of the range in place at this address. A reference to the cell A1 is A1, whereas a reference to a range consisting of a single cell is A1..A1. You can then expand the range to include additional cells by moving the cell pointer until you reach the end of the range you want.

1-2-3 suggests a range beginning at the location of the cell pointer where you used the /Range Format command in Chapter 4. If your cell pointer is positioned at the beginning of the range, you need only move with the arrow keys to complete the range, as shown here:

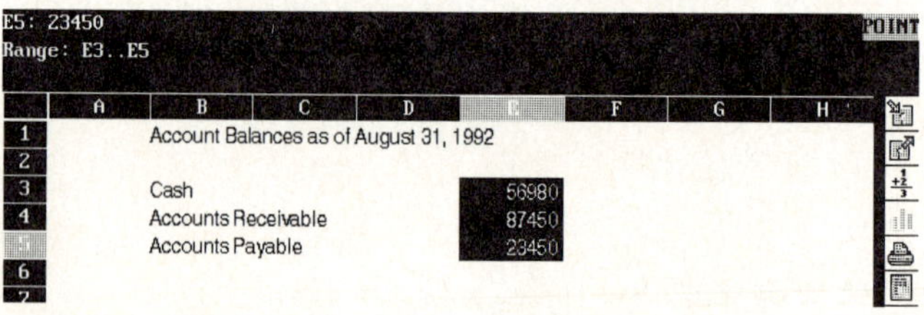

If you forget to position your cell pointer properly before selecting a range, you must unlock the beginning of the range before you can change it. To do this, press ESC and move the cell pointer to the desired location. You must again lock in the beginning of the range by entering a period (.) before you begin to expand the range

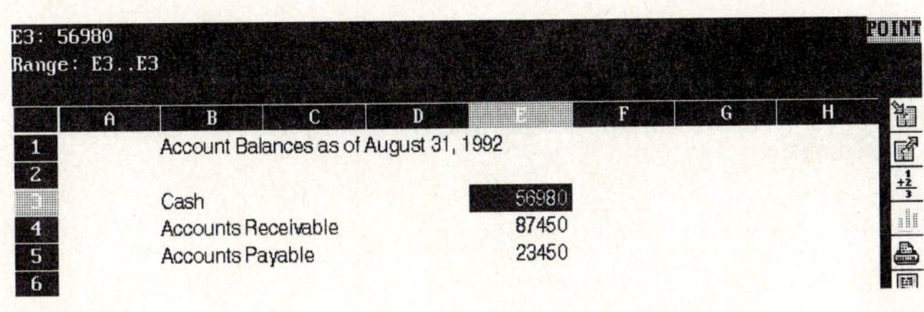

Figure 5-1.   *An example of selecting a range*

with the cell-pointer movement keys. If the beginning of a range is not locked into place, 1-2-3 displays only a cell address as shown here in the To where? entry:

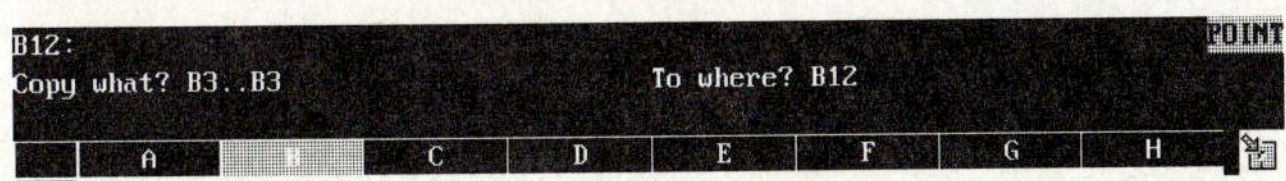

If you then move to the end of the range without locking the beginning in place, only the last cell in the range is highlighted.

You can use other keys in combination with the arrow keys to save time when defining a range. For example, in Figure 5-2 the cell pointer is in A1. If you invoke a command that suggests a range, it displays the range as A1..A1, indicating a single-cell range that begins and ends in cell A1. To select the complete rectangle of cells shown, in response to the prompt for the range, press END followed by RIGHT ARROW. This moves your cell pointer to the last entry on the right. To move to the bottom of the column, press END and DOWN ARROW. This includes all the filled cells in the selected range. You cannot use the SmartIcon palette options to define a range since these options will not work while you are using a menu command.

The END key can be used in other situations with a little planning. Let's say you want to format all the cells in row 3 of Figure 5-3. First move to the beginning of row 3 (cell A3), invoke **/Range Format Fixed**, and press ENTER. The END and RIGHT ARROW keys do not work here because of the breaks in the entries. If you press HOME to move to A1 and then END and RIGHT ARROW, you can then press DOWN ARROW twice for the exact selection you wanted, as you can see in Figure 5-3.

It is preferable to have 1-2-3 generate the cell addresses in a range whenever possible, but you always have the option of typing a cell reference in response to one of the range prompts. With the pointing method or when you type the complete entry, you can type a single period in a reference, and 1-2-3 duplicates it so that two periods display. For example, when you enter **D4.D10** 1-2-3 displays D4..D10.

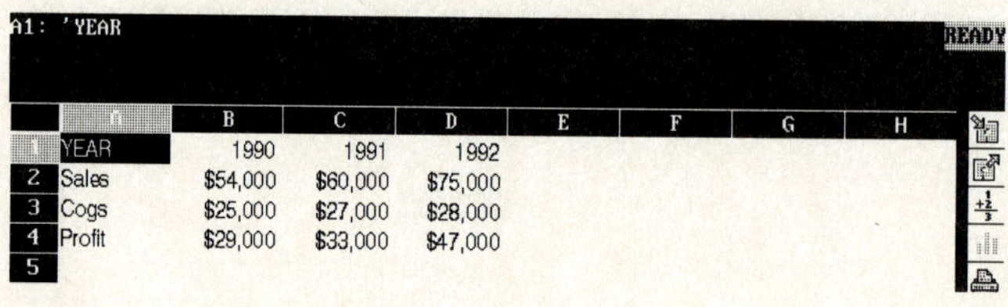

Figure 5-2.   *A worksheet with the cell pointer in A1*

You can enter any two opposite corners of a rectangle of cells to specify a range. Normally, however, the upper-left and the lower-right corners are used for a range (as in A2..F10). Remember, if you type a period after pointing to a range address, 1-2-3 moves the *active corner* (the corner containing the cursor) in the range, allowing you to expand or contract the range from a different side.

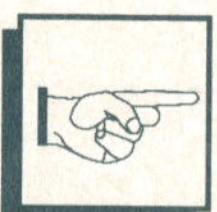

Some commands, such as /Print and /Data Fill (described in Chapters 6 and 8, respectively), remember the last range they used and suggest it for the next use of the command. To change these suggested ranges, you can use ESC to eliminate the range or BACKSPACE to place the cell pointer where it was located before the command was invoked.

Pre-selecting Ranges for Commands

All of the commands that use ranges will give you prompts so that you can select the range you want to use. In Release 2.3 and above, you can select ranges that commands will use before or after you select the command. Preselected ranges can be used for multiple commands without reselecting.

You can select ranges before you select a command by moving to the first cell of the range. With a mouse, drag the mouse from the first cell of the range to the

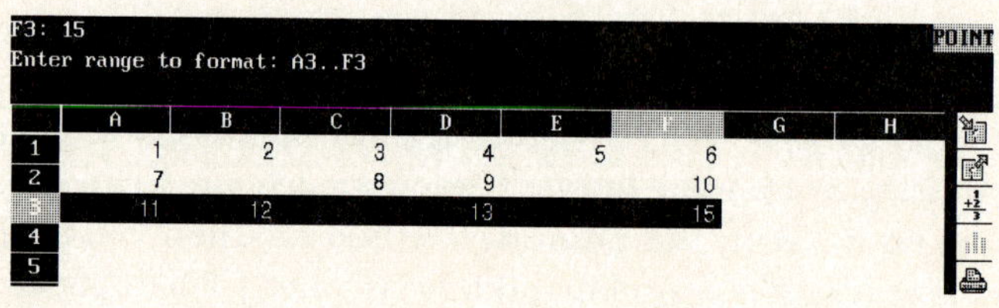

Figure 5-3.   *Using other keys with the END and arrow key combinations*

opposite corner so the cells selected by the range are highlighted. With a keyboard, press F4 (ABS) to switch to the POINT mode. 1-2-3 changes the mode indicator to POINT, and as you press arrow and other cell pointer movement keys the highlighted range expands or contracts. When the range you want to use is selected, press ENTER to return to the READY mode with the range still selected.

After you select a range, the commands that use ranges will not prompt for the range to use but will use the range you have selected. If a command uses more than one range and you select a range before the command, 1-2-3 uses the selected range for the first range of the command and then prompts for subsequent ranges that the command will use.

For example, if you select a range before you select /Copy, 1-2-3 will not prompt for the range that you want to copy but it will prompt for where you want the selected range copied. When you select ranges using F4 or the mouse, the range remains highlighted after you select a command. This lets you apply more than one command to the same group of cells. To unselect the range, press ESC.

Naming Cell Ranges

In some respects, all worksheet cells automatically have names because they have unique cell addresses by which they can be referenced. You are already familiar with column and row addresses such as A2, U7, or AX89. In Release 2.2 and above, you can access a cell in any file on disk if you use a pair of double angle brackets (<< >>) around the filename before the cell address or range name. For example, you could type **+<<BUDGET>>A1** to access A1 in a disk file named BUDGET. A file reference is only required when you are referencing a range in another file.

Although the location of the cell is evident, it is not clear what is contained in a cell named A2, U7, or AX89. Is it the interest rate, the number of employees, or the Los Angeles Dodgers' batting average? It can take time to move the cell pointer every time you need to remember a particular cell's contents.

The /Range Name commands provide a solution to this problem. With these commands you can assign names to ranges of any size, thus providing meaningful information about the contents of the groups of cells they reference. If cell A10 contains sales for 1989, for example, you might assign it the name SALES_89. If cells B3..B25 contain all the expenses for a certain department, you might assign a range name like TOTAL_EXPENSES.

In Release 2.2 and above, file links extend the utility of range names. With links to other files, it is more convenient to access data in other files by using a name like Sales, rather than remembering that you stored it in D13. Also, if you move the contents of the range, using a range name in the file link will ensure the formula always refers to the same data while using a cell address will not.

1-2-3 allows you to assign any name to any range of cells, provided that the name does not exceed 15 characters. Once you assign a range name, you can use it the same way that you would use a cell address. For example, you could create the formula +SALES_89–TOTAL_EXPENSES for a profit calculation using assigned range names. When you include a named range in the formula, 1-2-3 changes the name display to a cell reference when you edit the formula. The box called "A Few Pointers for Creating Range Names" provides some additional tips on range names.

Assigning Range Names

There are two basic methods for assigning range names. Usually you use the /Range Name Create command to enter your range names. When the name you want to use will be assigned to a single cell and already appears in an adjacent cell, you can use the /Range Name Labels command.

Creating New Names

The easiest way to name a range of cells is to move your cell pointer to the upper-left corner of the range. After positioning the cell pointer, enter **/Range Name Create**, type your range name, and press ENTER. If you want to name just the current cell, simply press ENTER again. For a range larger than one cell, move your cell pointer to the lower-right cell in the range and then press ENTER again.

A Few Pointers for Creating Range Names

1-2-3 imposes few restrictions in range naming, but to ensure your names are clear, a few rules are helpful:

- 1-2-3 does not prevent you from using spaces in range names, but you should avoid using them. The name TOTAL SALES could be mistaken for two range names by someone just glancing at a formula, but clearly TOTAL_SALES is one name.

- You are also allowed to use arithmetic operators in range names, but operators also can cause problems. TOTAL*SALES could be confusing as a range name; it might be interpreted as a request for an arithmetic operation that would multiply TOTAL by SALES.

- Another permitted type of name to avoid is a name that could be confused with a cell address, such as CY92 for Current Year 92 data.

- Numbers cannot be used as range names unless they are used in combination with letters. For example, SALES_86 is acceptable, but 56 is not acceptable as a range name.

- Do not name ranges with the same name as @functions, macro commands, or 1-2-3 key names.

Alternatively, you can leave your cell pointer on any worksheet cell, enter **/Range Name Create**, type the range name, and press ENTER. You then type the cell coordinates corresponding to the range or point to the range, and press ENTER again. For example, consider the commands /Range Name Create SALES A1 and /Range Name Create EXPENSES B2..B6. Another possibility for naming B2..B6 is to select the range B2..B6 and then enter **/Range Name Create EXPENSES**.

1-2-3 allows you to assign more than one name to a range. For example, suppose you have data in cells F4..F25 that represent expenses for 1991, and you name this range EXPENSES_91. Now suppose you wish to use these expenses to project the next year's budget. You might want to assign this same range of cells the name PREVIOUS_YR_EXP for use in your budget calculations. 1-2-3 permits you to assign both names.

The worksheet in Figure 5-4 offers several opportunities to use the /Range Name Create command. Suppose you want to name the cells containing the figures for sales and cost of goods sold (Cogs). To do this, place the cell pointer in B3 on the amount for sales and enter **/Range Name Create**. In response to the request for a name, enter **SALES_91** and press ENTER. The next prompt asks for the address of the range you are naming. Since the name is for just this cell, simply press ENTER again. Now move the cell pointer to B4 and repeat the process, using the name COGS_91.

To use these range names move the cell pointer to B5. Type + to start the formula. Press F3 (NAME) to display the range names in the worksheet file like this:

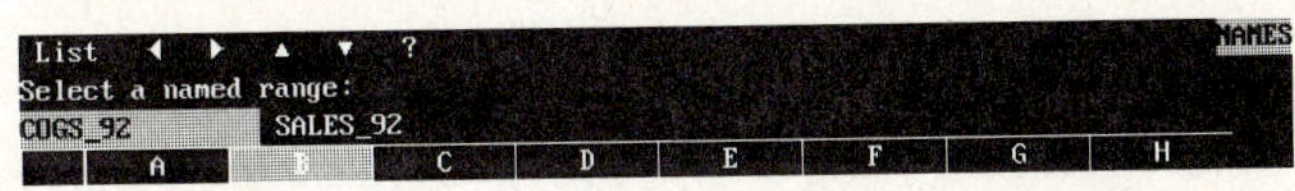

The text in the first line of the control panel displays options you can select. You can select List to use a full screen display, or use the four triangles to move the highlight to the name you want. Do not select since it is not appropriate for this command. Notice the NAMES indicator that 1-2-3 displays when it is listing range names. Highlight SALES_91 and press ENTER. 1-2-3 adds the range name SALES_91 to the formula to represent B3. Type - to continue the formula. Press F3 (NAME), which displays a list of range names. Press ENTER to select COGS_91. Press ENTER again to finalize the formula. Now the worksheet will look like this:

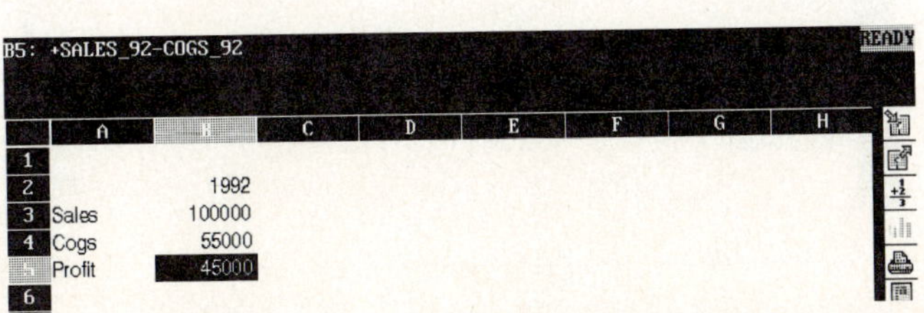

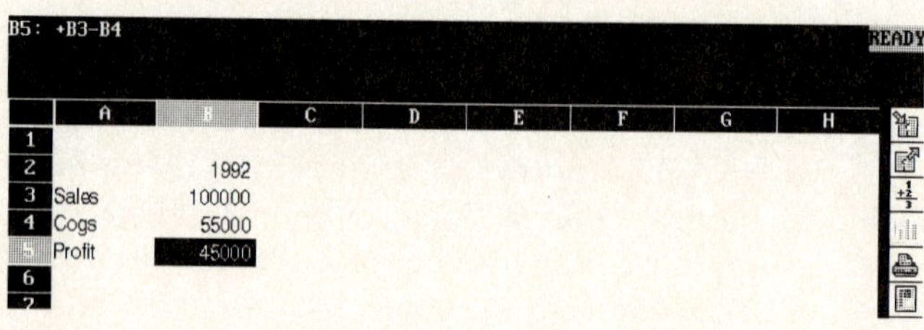

Figure 5-4.   *A worksheet in which range names can be used*

Once a name has been assigned to a cell or a range of cells, you may use this name anywhere you would use a cell or range reference. In addition to formula building, you can use range names when formatting, copying, moving, printing, or graphing data.

Using Existing Worksheet Labels   The /Range Name Labels command can save you data-entry time when you are assigning range names if conditions are right. First, the name you plan to use must already exist on the worksheet as a label entry. It must also be in a cell adjacent to the cell you plan to name. With this command you can assign a range name to only a single cell, so if you are naming more than one cell in a range, you must use the /Range Name Create command. One advantage of /Range Name Labels is that you can use it to assign several range names at once.

The cells in B3..B10 shown in Figure 5-5 can all have range names assigned with one execution of the /Range Name Labels command. To do this, position the cell

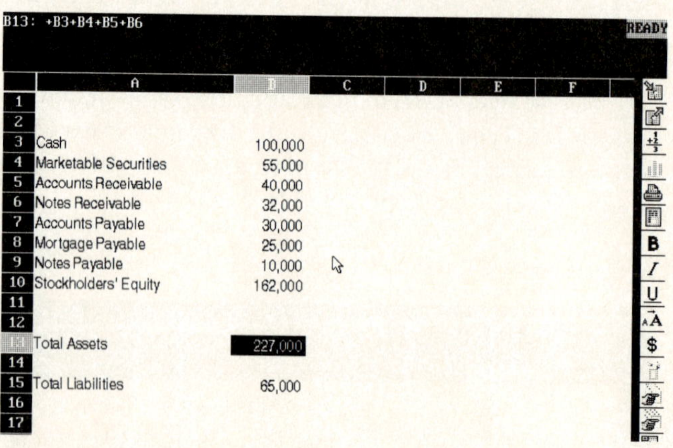

Figure 5-5.   *A range suitable for naming /Range Name Labels*

pointer in A3 and enter /**Range Name Labels**. Since the range of cells you are naming is on the right of the labels, choose Right next. Finally, move the cell pointer to A10 and press ENTER. The range names you will create in this example are CASH, MARKETABLE SECU, ACCOUNTS RECEIV, NOTES RECEIVABL, ACCOUNTS PAYABL, MORTGAGE PAYABL, NOTES PAYABLE, and STOCKHOLDERS' E. These range names are truncated since 1-2-3 has a fifteen-character limit for range names.

Deleting Range Names

Assigned range names use a small amount of 1-2-3's internal memory with 33 bytes required for each range name, regardless of length. If you are not using some of your old range names, consider deleting them to free up the space they use. It is best to delete a range name as soon as you know it is no longer required, because later you may forget whether or not you need it.

To delete a range name, enter /**Range Name Delete**. 1-2-3 then presents a list of all the assigned range names at the top of your screen, just like when you press F3 (NAME). You have the option of typing or highlighting the name you want to delete. In either case, press ENTER after making your selection. This action causes the selected range name to disappear permanently. If any formulas use the range name you deleted, 1-2-3 will automatically replace that range name with the cell or range address the range name represented.

Resetting Range Names

The /Range Name Delete option is ideal when you have only a few names to delete. If you have many names to delete, however, this option is slow. The /Range Name Reset command can speed up the process when you are deleting most or all of your range names. Use /Range Name Reset when you want to start fresh and create all new names. When you have a large number of names and want all but a few deleted, it may be quicker to delete them all and then use /Range Name Create to reenter the names you want to keep, rather than delete the names one by one with /Range Name Delete.

Creating a Table of Range Names

One way to check the range to which a range name is assigned is to list the names on the screen. The /Range Name Table command will build a table of range names and the cell addresses they identify. This table, built in any empty area of the worksheet, can serve as documentation for all the range names used in your worksheet.

Before executing the required command sequence, choose a good table location—one where you cannot overwrite data or important formulas if the table is longer than you expect. When you are ready to create the table, enter /**Range Name**

Table and respond to 1-2-3's prompt by typing in the table location. 1-2-3 permits you to supply just the upper-left corner of the table range and then uses as much space as it needs for the table. Figure 5-6 shows a table created with the /Range Name Table command. Note that the range names are listed in alphabetical order.

Using Filenames with Range Names

Although range names like SALES or B:SALES are the most common form of reference used, you can also use a filename as part of the range name reference when you want to access a range in a file other than the current file. The standard double angle bracket notation (which is << >>) is used around the filename, as in +<<C:\123R23\BUDGET.WK1>>SALES. Unlike the more sophisticated Release 3 linking options that allow you to use a link in a complex formula or function entry, Release 2.2 and above support only cell-to-cell links that place a value from another worksheet into a cell on the current worksheet. You can reference this cell in the current file with other formulas to include the linked value.

Practical Applications for Range Names

Assigning range names may seem like so much extra work that you may wonder why you should bother using them. For very small models they may not be worthwhile, but for larger ones, range names offer a significant payback. They make formulas much more readable. They also help prevent incorrect formula references because you see a descriptive name rather than a cryptic cell address. As data becomes farther removed from the formula location, the payback becomes greater because you cannot see the data and the formula at the same time nor verify the accuracy of the cell addresses used. This is especially true for file links to other worksheets.

	A	B	C	D	E
1				ACCOUNTS PAYABL	B7
2				ACCOUNTS RECEIV	B5
3	Cash	100,000		CASH	B3
4	Marketable Securities	55,000		MARKETABLE SECU	B4
5	Accounts Receivable	40,000		MORTGAGE PAYABL	B8
6	Notes Receivable	32,000		NOTES PAYABLE	B9
7	Accounts Payable	30,000		NOTES RECEIVABL	B6
8	Mortgage Payable	25,000		STOCKHOLDERS' E	B10
9	Notes Payable	10,000			
10	Stockholders' Equity	162,000			
11					
12					
13	Total Assets	227,000			
14					
15	Total Liabilities	65,000			
16					
17					

Figure 5-6.   The output of the /Range Name Table

When range names are used, you can insert columns and rows in the middle of a range, and the range reference is adjusted automatically. The references are also updated if you delete columns or rows from the middle of a range. If you want to see the updated references in a table, however, you must execute /Range Name Table again because this command does not dynamically update the worksheet.

Transposing Data

Sometimes you will want to rearrange a range of entries that you have made in a worksheet. You may change your mind about the best presentation method, or you may want to use an existing worksheet as the basis for a new worksheet, but you must reorganize the presentation to make this possible.

1-2-3 provides the /Range Trans (Transpose) command so you can change data entered horizontally across a row to a vertical column presentation, or vice versa. The command uses a special copy process to automatically transpose column data into a row and row entries into a column. The steps for transposing data are summarized in the box called "Steps for Transposing Data."

Since the /Range Trans command operates on single or multiple rows or columns, it has a wide variety of options. Before using any of these options, you must be sure the formulas in any cells that you are transposing have up-to-date values. If CALC is showing at the bottom of your screen, press F9 (CALC) to recalculate the worksheet before beginning. Also, if the cells that you are transposing contain links to other files, you might want to refresh these links before starting (with /File Admin Link-Refresh). Release 2.2 and above automatically convert formulas to their existing values as they transpose the data. The original cell entries continue to contain formulas, but the transposed entries become values.

To begin the transpose operation, enter **/Range Trans**. Next select a range to transpose—the original location of your data—in response to 1-2-3's prompt, and press ENTER.

Next you are asked to specify where you want the range transposed to. You can enter a range that has the opposite orientation but the same number of entries as the from range. However, the easiest approach is to enter the beginning cell of the to range and let 1-2-3 figure out the size of the range that it needs. 1-2-3 completes the transposition after the entry of the to range. If some of the cells in the to range already contain data, their contents are replaced as a result of the transposition operation.

An example of original worksheet entries for a transposition is shown here:

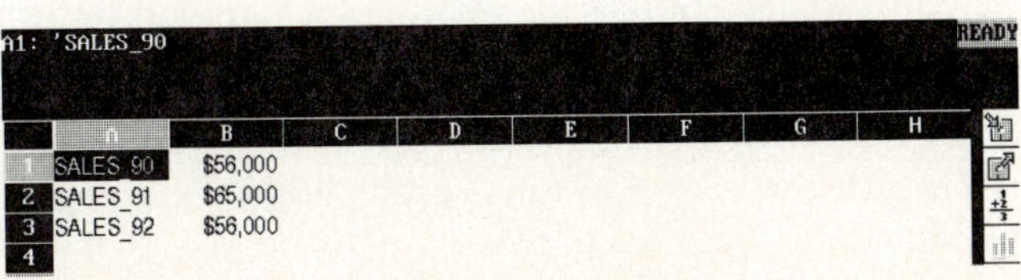

To complete the operation, enter **/Range Trans**, highlight A3..B5, and press ENTER. Highlight D1 as the beginning of the *to* range and press ENTER to complete the transposition. The entries are now displayed horizontally in D1..F2, as shown here:

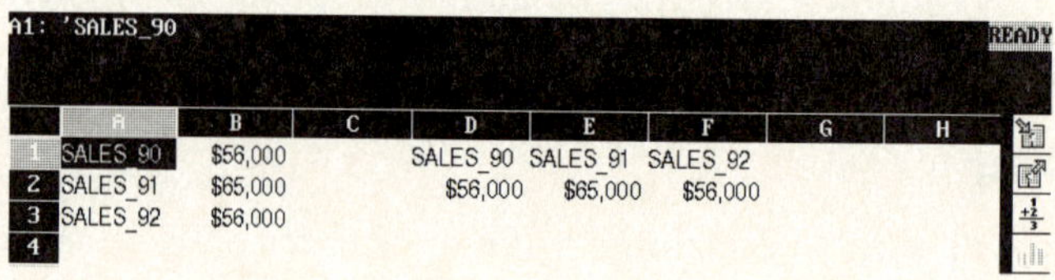

Converting Formulas to Values

At times during the model creation process, you may want to change some of your projections to fixed values, rather than allowing them to be revised each time the worksheet is recalculated. One example is the budgeting process. As you prepare a budget, you want to look at various possibilities. Once the budget is submitted, however, the projections you made are recorded and serve as the target for your operation throughout the budget period. You may want to freeze some of the formulas used to make the budget projection. 1-2-3 provides the perfect way to do this with the /Range Value command.

The /Range Value command copies the values produced by formulas to a new location. It copies only the values displayed in worksheet cells, not the formulas used to produce these values. Thus the original worksheet can still change as new values

---

1
2
3

Steps for Transposing Data

Transposing data in your worksheet allows you to reorganize an entire application without reentering data. Here are the steps you must follow:

1. Use F9 (CALC) and /File Admin Link-Refresh if you need to update calculations or links to external files.

2. Move the cell pointer to the first cell in the range you wish to transpose.

3. Enter **/Range Trans** and use the cursor-movement keys to highlight the entire range containing entries that you want to transpose.

4. Highlight the first cell in the *to* range and press ENTER. The transposition now occurs. 1-2-3 implicitly performs a /Range Value command with the /Range Trans command, since it copies the values instead of the formulas to the *to* range.

are entered for assumptions, but the copy is not affected by changes in the assumptions. To use this command to freeze formula values, use the same range for both prompts for ranges. The original formula values are replaced with fixed values.

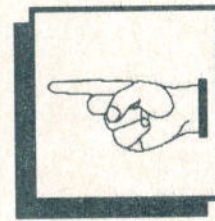

Be sure all your formula values are up-to-date before converting formulas to fixed values. If the CALC indicator appears at the bottom of your screen, press F9 (CALC) to update all formulas before proceeding. If you are referencing linked cells in shareable files, use /File Admin Link-Refresh to ensure the most recent values.

As an example of fixing values, the entry in cell B3 of the following worksheet displays as a number in the worksheet cell but as a formula in the control panel:

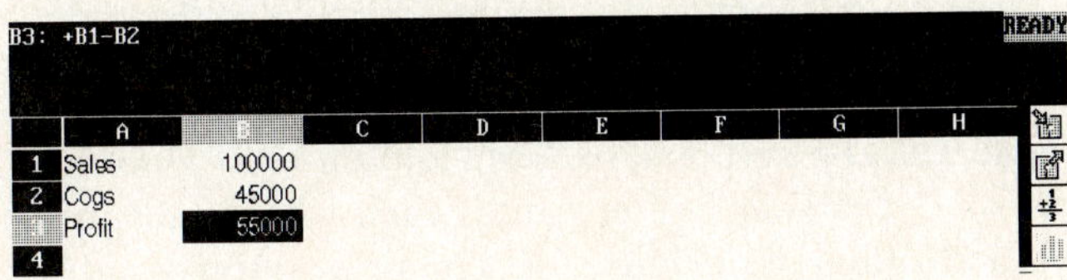

After using /Range Value with B3 as both the from and to ranges, the same cell is now a value:

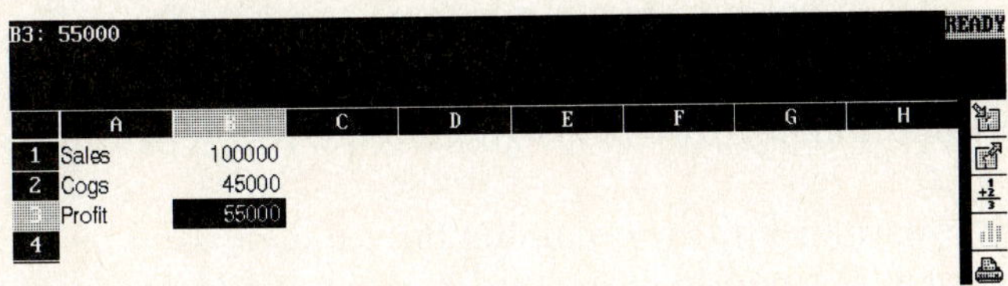

Notice that the worksheet display is the same, but the control panel now shows the cell as containing a value, not a formula.

Changing the Justification of Labels

As a default, 1-2-3 begins labels at the left side of cells. You have already learned that you can change the alignment of an individual label by preceding it with a caret (^) for center justification or a double quotation mark (") for right justification. Using these options can be very time-consuming, however, when you want to change the alignment of a whole range of cells.

The /Range Label command can handle this situation much more efficiently. You simply specify the range in which you want to change the labels and then execute the command. 1-2-3 ensures that existing label entries in the specified cells receive the correct label indicator. Entries made after /Range Label are not entered, and nonlabel entries in the specified cells are not affected. New label entries receive the default label prefix.

Release 2.4 offers SmartIcons on palette 2 that allow you to change the alignment of the selected range. The text in the icon tells you whether right, left, or center alignment will be used. The icons look like this:

With the /Range Label command you can select left, right, or center justification for an existing range of labels. Labels originally entered using the default label prefix of an apostrophe (') are left-justified, as shown in Column A of Figure 5-7. If you enter /**Range Label** and select Right to change the orientation of the labels to the right side of each cell, the results look like Column C of Figure 5-7. Entering the command again and choosing Center causes each label to display in the center of the cell as shown in Column E of Figure 5-7. The Left option could be used to change either of these results back to the original display format.

Erasing Cell Ranges

The /Range Erase command eliminates the entries in a range of cells. It does not matter whether the entries are numbers, labels, or formulas. Using this command does not affect the numeric format assigned to the cell, its width, or its protection status.

Figure 5-8 shows a worksheet containing miscellaneous entries in E1..F5 that are no longer required. To remove these entries, move the cell pointer to E1 and type /**Range Erase**. Then move the cell pointer to F5 to extend the range, and press ENTER

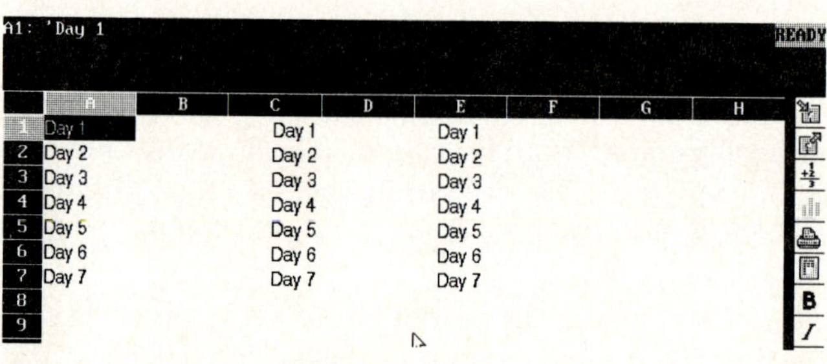

Figure 5-7.   *Labels with different alignments*

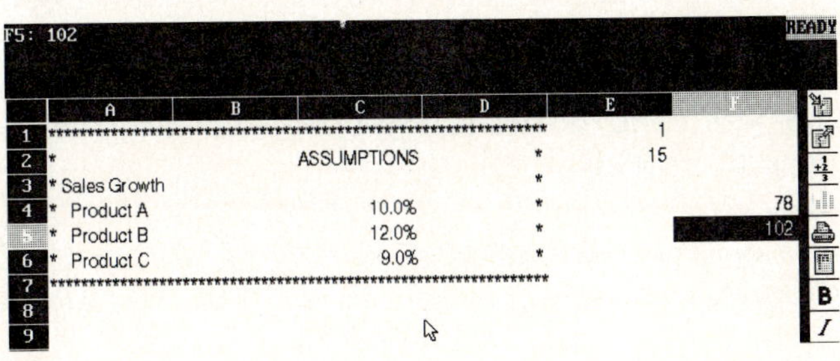

Figure 5-8.   *Extraneous worksheet entries*

to achieve the results shown in Figure 5-9. Note that if worksheet protection has been enabled, the /Range Erase command does not work. If Undo is enabled, you can restore the entries removed with /Range Erase as long as no actions intervene between /Range Erase and the use of ALT-F4 (UNDO). You can also delete the contents of a single cell by pointing to the cell and pressing the DEL key.

Release 2.4 provides a SmartIcon on palette 1 or 4 that looks like a trash can. It provides a function identical to /Range Erase. The contents of the selected cells are erased when this icon is selected.

Protecting Worksheet Cells

A completed worksheet often represents hours or days of work in planning, formula entry, and testing. Once you have created a well-planned and tested worksheet

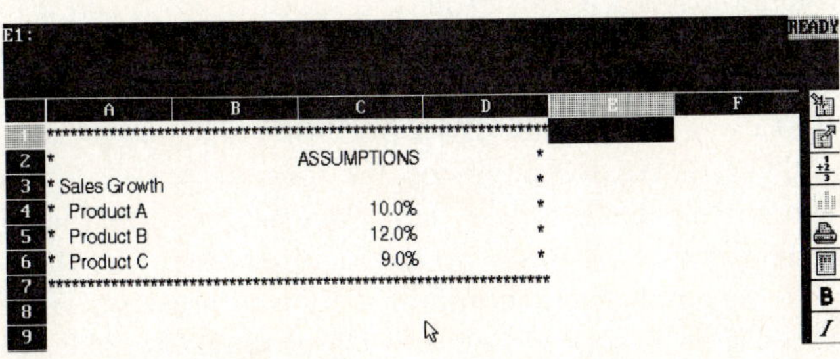

Figure 5-9.   *The results of using /Range Erase*

application, you want to protect it from accidental keystrokes or option selections that could cause you to overwrite formulas or other vital data. 1-2-3 provides features that prevent this damage to important cells. These features can also make other users more comfortable with using models that you create for them, because they know they cannot destroy the models.

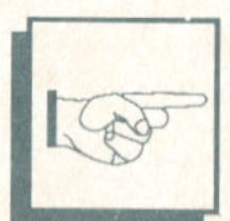

Watch your screen for information about the current Protection status. Look in the control panel for the PR display to identify individual entries with Protected status.

The Protection feature of 1-2-3 lets you determine which cells to protect and which ones can accept entries. There is also an easy way to disable Protection without changing a cell's basic definition as a protected or unprotected cell. Finally, 1-2-3 provides a command that is used in conjunction with Protection to restrict the cell pointer to a single input range on the worksheet.

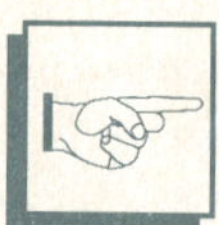

Group input entries in one location where possible. Rather than spread input entries across the worksheet, you should gather them on an input form on one screen when possible. This approach saves operator entry time and makes it easy for you to apply Protection to the cells in all the other locations and eliminate it from the entry cells on the input form.

1-2-3's protection process requires that you first decide which worksheet cells you wish to have protected. All cells are protected as an initial default. If you wish to allow entries in certain cells, you can unprotect them with /Range Unprot. You can then turn on the Protection feature of the package, and these unprotected cells still permit entries.

Deciding What Cells to Protect

1-2-3 establishes a default status of Protected for every worksheet cell. This might sound strange since you can make an entry anywhere on a new worksheet. You can do that because the Protection feature of the package is initially turned off. If you turn on the Protection feature, the Protected status of each cell is energized, and 1-2-3 rejects any additional entries. It is therefore important to decide what cells should accept entries.

You might find it useful to think of 1-2-3's Protection feature as a fence placed around every cell. The fences do not protect the contents of cells in a new worksheet, since none of the fence gates is closed. The /Worksheet Global Protection Enable command closes all the gates, thereby protecting the contents of the cells. Cells that you do not wish to have protected should have their fences torn down with /Range Unprot. Then when the gates are closed with /Worksheet Global Protection Enable, you can still change these cells, because a gate without a fence does not offer effective protection.

The /Range Unprot command strips cell protection from a range of one or many cells. To unprotect a range, enter **/Range Unprot**, and select the range. If you change your mind and decide that a cell should be protected again, enter **/Range Prot** to restore protection for the cell.

Unprotecting a cell highlights it on a monochrome display or changes its color on a color display. Removing protection has no other effect on a cell unless the Global Protection feature (discussed in the next section) is turned on. In addition, a U appears after the cell address in the top line of the control panel when the cell pointer is on an unprotected cell.

Enabling Worksheet Protection

As noted in the analogy established previously, the /Worksheet Global Protection Enable command "closes the gate" on every cell, ensuring that protected cells cannot be altered. It also displays PR in the control panel for every protected cell. In Release 2.2 and above, as soon as you enter **/Worksheet Global**, 1-2-3 displays the worksheet dialog box. The /Worksheet Global screen is more interactive than the /Worksheet Status display because you can make changes through the menu options at the top of it. In Release 2.3 and above, you can use this dialog box to turn on protection by clicking Protection in the dialog box twice—once activates the dialog box and the second time selects Protection. Once protection is enabled, anytime you make an entry in a protected cell, 1-2-3 displays an error message when you try finalizing the entry. You can use the /Range Unprot command even after you enable protection to allow you to make entries into cells.

When you need to turn Protection off after enabling it, enter **/Worksheet Global Protection Disable**. This command allows you to temporarily suspend Protection so you can make a change to a formula, for example.

You can press F2 *in Release 2.3 and above to edit any of the Worksheet Global settings.*

Specifying an Input Range

The /Range Input command is used in conjunction with Protection. The /Range Input command allows you to restrict cell-pointer movement to unprotected cells within the input range. /Range Input is useful for focusing attention on the cells available for entry during data input. The steps for using this command are as follows:

1. Set up the worksheet with all needed labels and formulas. (In other words, design your worksheet before restricting the cell pointer.)

2. Remove Protection from the cells requiring data entry using /Range Unprot.

3. Enter **/Range Input** and select the range of cells in which you want to allow input.

You can edit cells in the specified range or enter new data in them. You can also use ESC, HOME, END, ENTER, F1 (HELP), F2 (EDIT), BACKSPACE, or any of the arrow keys in completing your entries. The cell pointer always remains within the input range, since that is the only area where entries can be made. While /Range Input is in effect, the END and HOME keys move you to the end or the beginning of the input range. Pressing either ESC or ENTER without making an entry ends the /Range Input command. This command is used in the macro environment to assist in automating applications.

Cutting and Pasting

Cutting and pasting can extend your productivity with 1-2-3 by allowing you to move or copy existing entries to new locations. You can thus restructure a worksheet to meet new needs without reentering data. You can also use the /Worksheet Insert and /Worksheet Delete commands, discussed in Chapter 4, to add new columns or rows and to eliminate columns and rows that are no longer required.

Moving Information

Creating a worksheet can be a trial-and-error process during which you attempt to obtain the most effective placement of data. 1-2-3 provides the /Move command that permits you to move a range of cells to another location. The command requires that you specify both a from and a to range. The from range marks the original location of the data to be moved, and the to range is the new location you have selected. 1-2-3 prompts you for these ranges when it is time to enter them. You can use any of the normal methods for specifying a range location, including range names, cell addresses, and pointing.

To specify which range to move for the /Move command, place your cell pointer on the upper-left cell in the range to be moved before invoking the command. This is the easiest method because 1-2-3 assumes that the current cell is the first cell in the range you wish to move. To expand this range, simply move the cell pointer in the direction you want; the beginning cell remains anchored in place. You can also use the mouse or the F4 (ABS) key to select which range to move before you select the /Move command. If you select this option, 1-2-3 uses this as the range to move and prompts for where you want to move it. If you have Release 2.4 and would prefer to use the SmartIcon palette to invoke Move, you can use the icon on palette 1 or 5 that looks like the one shown here.

If you want to change the beginning of the range 1-2-3 suggests, press ESC or BACKSPACE to unlock the beginning of the range. Move your cell pointer to the upper-left cell in the range you wish to move, type a period (.), and move to the end of the range. Alternatively, you can just type a new range when presented with 1-2-3's suggestion. The different releases of 1-2-3 use different prompts for the ranges the command uses but for the /Move command, the first range is always the range to be moved and the second range is where 1-2-3 will move the first range.

Even if you position your cell pointer prior to executing the command, you must move your cell pointer for the to range to move the cell contents, because 1-2-3 suggests the same starting cell that it suggested for from. Since the suggestion is a single cell, you do not need to press ESC to unlock the beginning of the range. Just move to the beginning cell of the range you wish to select or enter the beginning cell from the keyboard. Only the beginning cell needs to be specified, even if many cells are being moved.

The /Move command can be used to move one or many worksheet cells. The example in Figure 5-10 shows a long label that is not in the center of the worksheet. To reenter the label in a more central location would be time-consuming; you can move it more quickly with /Move. Place the cell pointer in A1 and enter /**Move**. Since the first range is the cell-pointer location, press ENTER to accept the current cell address. Then move the cell pointer to C1, and press ENTER to accept C1 as the new range for the data. Figure 5-11 shows the worksheet after the move is complete. Although the label displays in multiple cells, you are able to move it by specifying only one cell each for the two ranges you select with this command.

As another example, suppose that in the worksheet shown in Figure 5-12 you want to move the entries in cells A2..C15 to the right. These cells contain numbers, labels, and formulas. (The formulas are formatted as text so you can see how 1-2-3 adjusts formulas as you move them.) To move all these entries at once, enter /**Move** and the from range **A2..C15**. When the first range is requested, enter **B2**. You only need to use one cell to tell 1-2-3 where to begin the to range; it automatically uses B2..D15 as

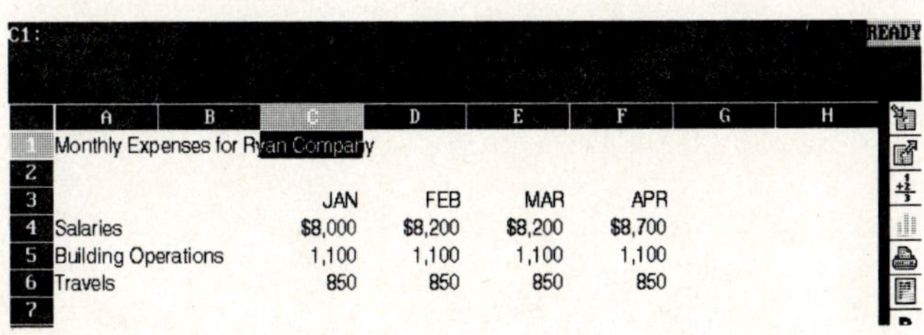

Figure 5-10.   Moving a long label

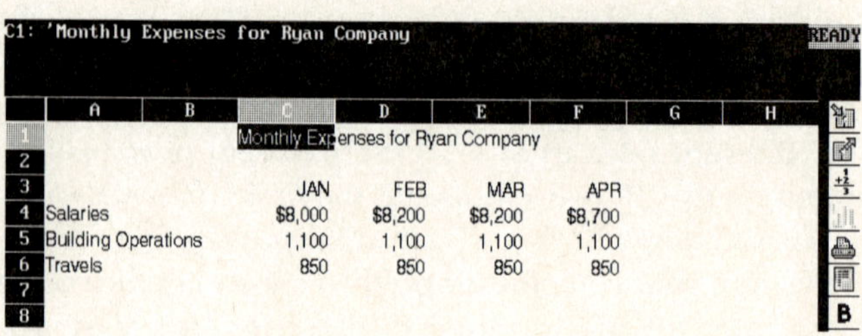

Figure 5-11.   *After moving the label*

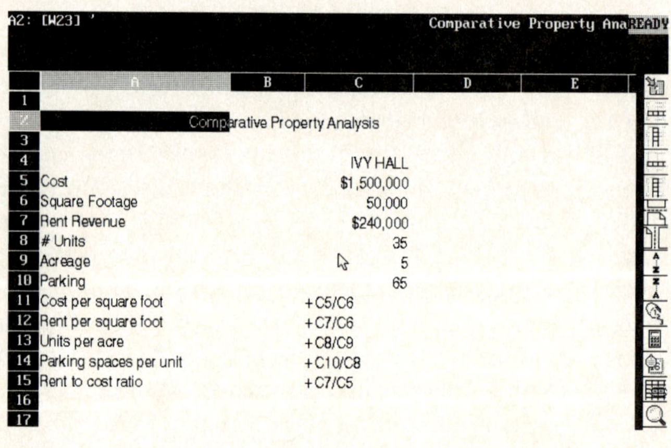

Figure 5-12.   *Entries in A2..C15 to be moved*

the complete to range. Figure 5-13 shows the worksheet after the move, including the way in which the formulas have been adjusted to reflect their new locations. Note also that 1-2-3 is able to handle the overlap between the from and to ranges.

Duplicating Existing Entries

The copying features of 1-2-3 extend your productivity with the package more than any other single feature. /Copy permits you to enter a label, formula, or number in one cell and copy it to many new locations. Icon palette options provide access to

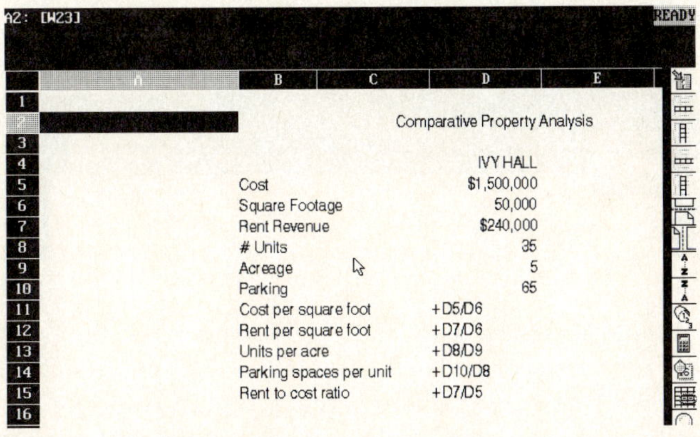

Figure 5-13.   *The result of using /Move*

this type of copy operation as well as to a special copy operation that copies Wysiwyg formatting to other cells. This feature is especially valuable for formulas, since 1-2-3 is able to adjust the formulas to conform to their new locations.

Copy Options

The /Copy command performs its task in a variety of situations. You can copy the contents of one cell to another cell or to a range of many cells. You can speed up the copying process by copying a range of cells to a second range of the same size. This command also can copy a range of cells to a second range whose size is a multiple of the original range. Consider these examples of each of these uses.

Suppose a label entry is placed in cell A1, as in this example:

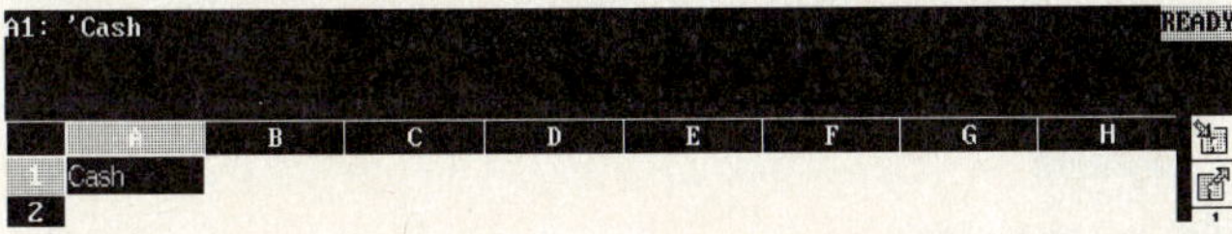

To copy this label to another cell, the easiest approach is to place your cell pointer on A1 before beginning. When you enter /Copy, 1-2-3 asks from what location you want to copy. Since your cell pointer is already positioned on A1, just press ENTER. (If the cell pointer is not where you want it to be, press ESC before moving it to the correct location.) After the location of the cells to copy is specified, 1-2-3's next prompt requests the range where you want the cells to be placed. In the preceding illustration, to copy the label entry to B3, move the cell pointer to B3 in response to this prompt and press ENTER. The completed copy operation generates a second label in B3, as shown here:

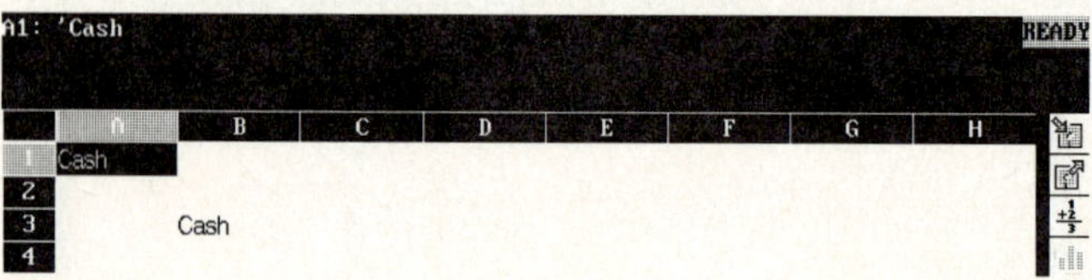

The next example also starts with "Cash" displayed in A1, but this time you want to copy the entry into many cells. The beginning of the operation is the same: Place the cell pointer on A1 and enter /**Copy**. Press ENTER in response to the first range prompt. The entry is to be copied to D1..D5; therefore, when the prompt asking where the range should be copied to appears, move the cell pointer to D1. Type a period (.) to lock the beginning of the range in place. Move the cell pointer down to D5 and press ENTER. The result shown here is the label copied into D1..D5:

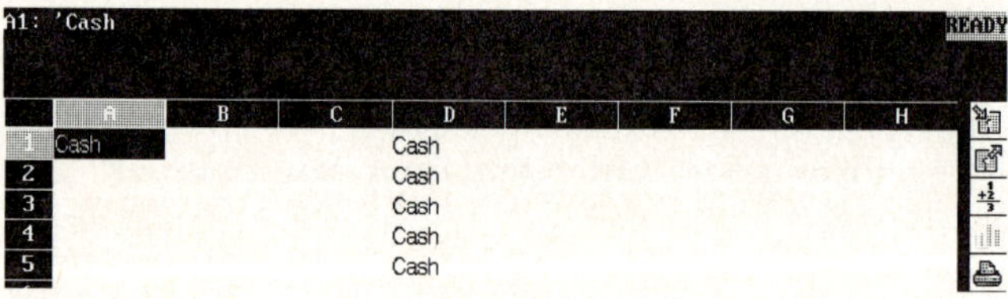

Figure 5-14 shows a worksheet with labels in A1..A13. /Copy can copy these labels to a second range of the same size and shape as the original. The best way to begin is to place the cell pointer in A1, the upper-left cell in the range. Type /**Copy**. Then,

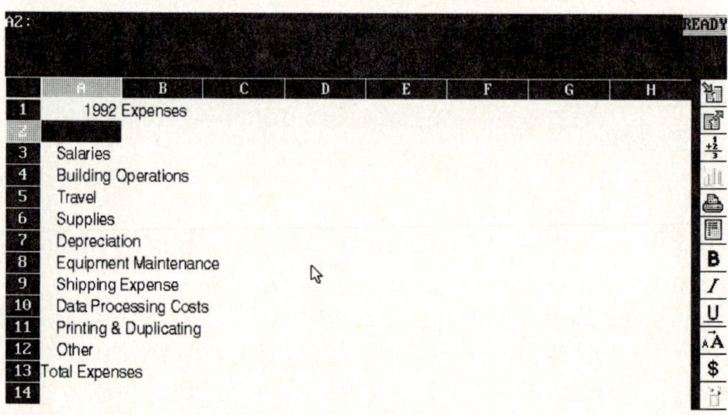

Figure 5-14.   Label entries to be copied

instead of pressing ENTER, move the cell pointer to the bottom of the range to copy. Now press ENTER, and 1-2-3 requests where the range should be copied. At this point, move the cell pointer to E1. Since 1-2-3 knows that the second range must match the first range in size and shape, you need to specify only the upper-left corner of the second range, and then press ENTER. The result is shown in Figure 5-15. With just a few keystrokes, an entire range of label entries has been duplicated much faster than anyone could enter them.

The next use of /Copy is even more powerful, since it copies one row or column of entries to many rows or columns in one operation. To copy the labels found in Figure 5-16, place the cell pointer in A3 and enter /**Copy**. Move the cell pointer to

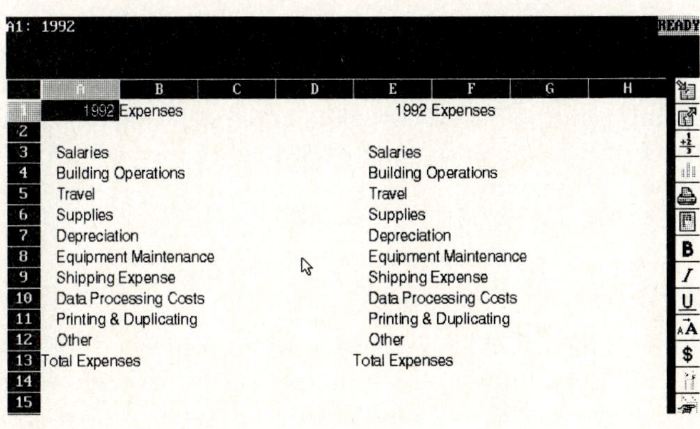

Figure 5-15.   *The result of copying the labels*

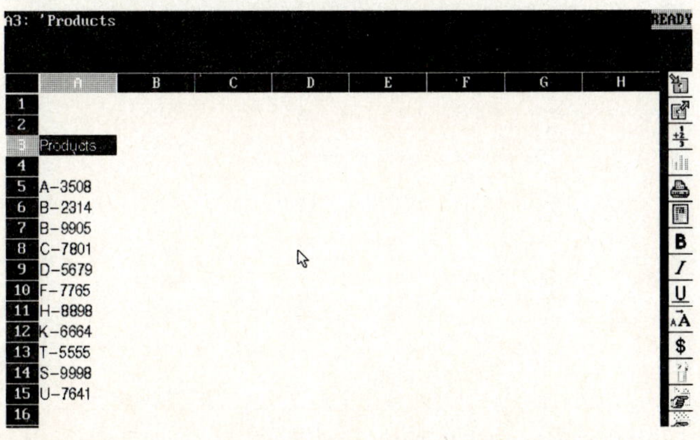

Figure 5-16.   *The column of label entries*

A15 in response to a request for the range to copy, and press ENTER. This time, the labels are to be copied into B3..B15, C3..C15, D3..D15, and E3..E15. When 1-2-3 requests where the cells should be copied, move the cell pointer to the top of the first column where the labels will be copied, B3, and enter a period (.) to lock the beginning of the range in place.

Since 1-2-3 knows it is copying a partial column of labels that extends down to row 15, it needs to be told only how far across the worksheet this partial column should be copied. To do this, move the cell pointer to E1 and press ENTER. The result of this operation is shown in Figure 5-17. While these examples illustrate copying labels, the same steps apply for copying numbers.

Copying Formulas

Copying formulas is another valuable capability. Although the mechanics of copying formulas are the same from your standpoint, it does require adjusting cell references. It is, therefore, important to have a complete understanding of cell addressing. This topic was introduced in Chapter 4, but is expanded in this section to cover the three addressing options completely.

Relative References

Relative references are the addresses generated when you enter regular cell addresses into formulas. A19, D2, and X15 are examples of relative references. This is the normal reference style used with formulas in 1-2-3. When a formula is created with

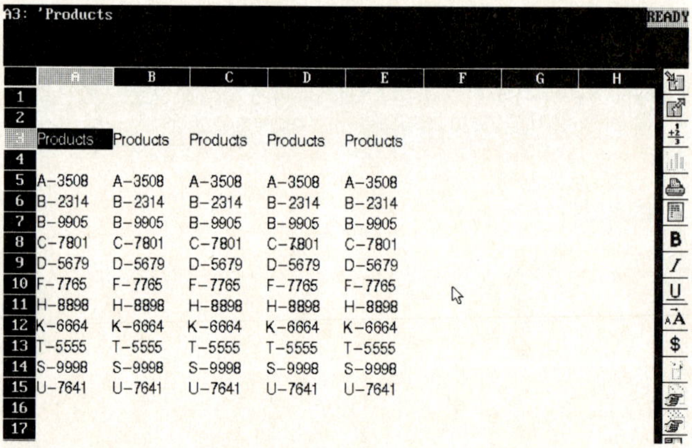

Figure 5-17.   *The result of copying to many locations*

this reference style, 1-2-3 not only records the cell addresses for the formula, but also remembers their relative distance and direction from the cell containing the formula.

For example, when you enter the formula +A1+A2 in A3, 1-2-3 remembers facts that are not shown in the worksheet. Specifically, in the illustration presented here, 1-2-3 remembers the distance and direction that must be traveled to obtain each of the references in the formula:

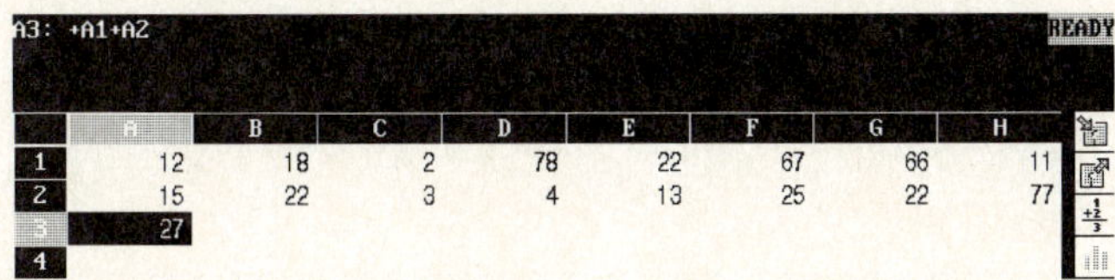

For A1, 1-2-3 knows that this reference is in the same column as the formula result, but is two rows above it. A2 is in the same column, one row above the result. This concept adds great power to the /Copy command. Suppose you want the same type of formula in B3, and you want it to add the values in B1 and B2 together. /Copy can do this because it remembers the directions for the formula's relative references.

To make this transfer, place the cell pointer on A3, enter /**Copy**, and press ENTER. Then move the cell pointer to B3, and press ENTER again. The formula is replicated into B3 and, in addition, adjustments are made that make the formula appropriate for B3, as shown here:

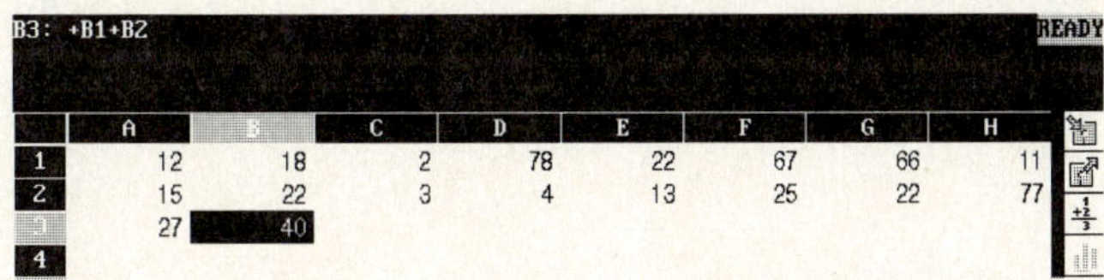

Try this again, but this time copy from B3 across the remainder of the row. Enter /**Copy** with the cell pointer on B3 and press ENTER. Move the cell pointer to C3 as the beginning of the range where the formula will be copied, type a period (.), move the cell pointer to H3, and press ENTER again. Figure 5-18 shows that the appropriate formulas were copied across the row.

Relative references can be used in formulas any time you want the formula adjusted during the copying process. Figure 5-19 shows another worksheet with a column of formulas. To copy the formulas, position the cell pointer on C3 and enter /**Copy**. Then move the cell pointer to C5, which expands the highlighting, and press ENTER. Move the cell pointer to D3, type a period (.), move the cell pointer across to F3, and press ENTER to finalize the to range. Figure 5-20, which contains the result of the copying process, has been changed to a text format so that you can review 1-2-3's work in copying the formulas.

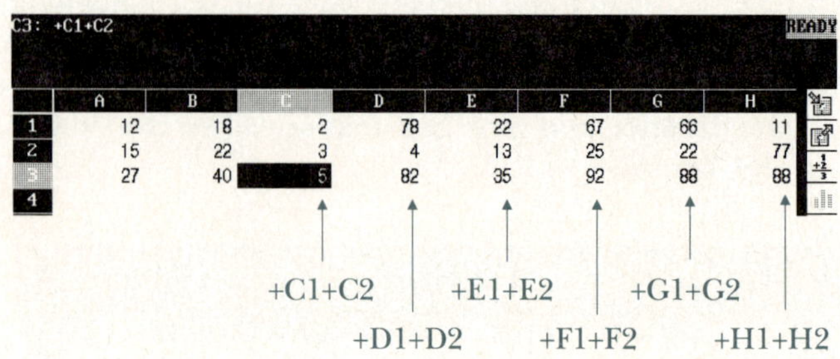

Figure 5-18. *The result of copying formulas across a row*

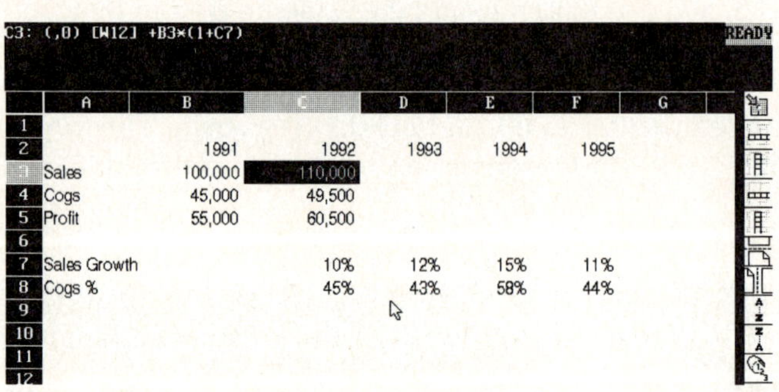

Figure 5-19. *A column of formulas*

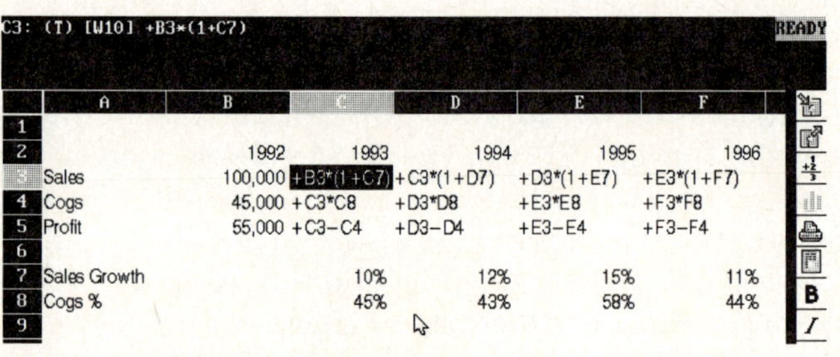

Figure 5-20. *The result of copying formulas, displayed as text*

Absolute References

Absolute references are references that you want held constant. In other words, you do not want these references to be adjusted when they are copied to a different location. This is the kind of reference you want for such entries as a single interest rate, a specific value in an assumption block, or a table that is in a fixed location. Even when you copy this formula to other columns or rows, the absolute address is not updated.

Entering absolute cell references in formulas requires a little more work because absolute references must have a dollar sign ($) in front of both the column and the row portion of the address. $A$4, $F$87, and $X$1 are examples of absolute references. 1-2-3 does not remember the relative direction and distance that must be traveled to obtain these values when they are used in a formula. Instead, it remembers the absolute cell address.

To enter the dollar signs during formula entry, you can type them wherever they are required or you can have 1-2-3 enter them for you. For example, the worksheet in Figure 5-21 requires formulas that use both relative and absolute references, since there are varying sales growth rates but one fixed cost of goods sold (Cogs) percentage that applies to all years. The formulas that were already entered for the 1991 sales used only relative references. The formula for cost of goods sold (row 4) requires both a relative reference to sales for the current year and an absolute reference to the Cogs percentage (cell C8). An absolute reference is required because the same Cogs percentage is used for all years. The formula is +C3*$C$8 for 1991, +D3*$C$8 for 1992, and so forth.

To enter this formula in cell C4 (it will be copied later to other cells in row 4), place the cell pointer in C4 and type +. The first cell reference needed in the formula is the 1991 sales figure in C3, so use UP ARROW to point to C3. Next, since you want to multiply this figure by the Cogs percentage, type *, representing multiplication.

Move the cell pointer to C8 to reference the cost of goods sold percentage. If you needed a relative reference, you would press ENTER now, but since you want an absolute reference to this cell, dollar signs are needed first. 1-2-3 enters them for you from the POINT or EDIT mode if you press F4 (ABS). The first time you press this

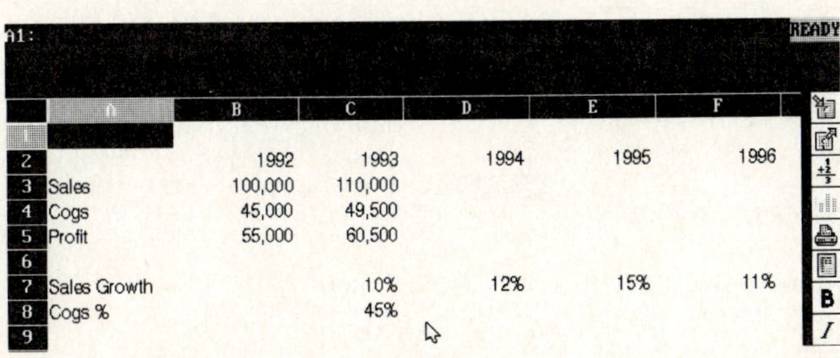

Figure 5-21.   *A model requiring relative and absolute references*

key, the reference becomes $C$8. You can continue to press it to cycle through all the possibilities:

Absolute reference	$C$8	(first time)
Mixed address	C$8	(second time)
Mixed address	$C8	(third time)
Relative reference	C8	(fourth time)

The F4 (ABS) key cycles through the possibilities again if you continue to press it. If the current address you are selecting or editing is a range address, 1-2-3 changes the address of both cell addresses in the range address to absolute, mixed, or relative.

Once the cell reference has the dollar signs added in both positions, press ENTER to accept it. If another arithmetic operation were required in the formula, typing the arithmetic operator would also have accepted the dollar sign placement. (For instance, typing + to continue the formula would accept the $C$8 reference.)

The formula +C3*$C$8 is now entered, containing both an absolute and a relative reference. The result of the calculation is the same as if both relative references had been used. Only when the formula is copied to new locations does the difference become apparent.

Before this is demonstrated, consider one more formula in this example—the one needed to calculate the profit for 1991. This formula is simply +C3-C4, with both references relative. All three years' formulas will be copied at once. To do this, move the cell pointer to the top cell in the range to be copied, C3, and enter /Copy. Move the cell pointer down twice to highlight the entire from range. Next move to D3 as the first location in the to range and type a period (.). Then move across to F3 and press ENTER. Figure 5-22 shows the results of the copying process with the formulas formatted as text so you can see how 1-2-3 has adjusted them as they are copied.

If an absolute reference had not been used for the Cogs percentage, 1-2-3 would attempt to increment the cell reference for each new formula, and blank cells would be referenced for years beyond 1991.

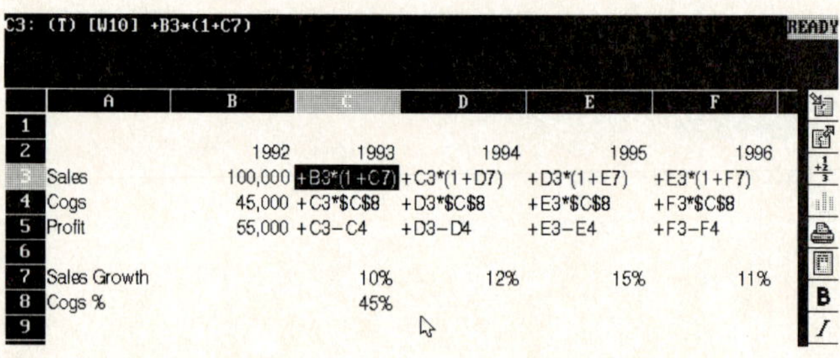

	A	B	C	D	E	F
1						
2		1992	1993	1994	1995	1996
3	Sales	100,000	+B3*(1+C7)	+C3*(1+D7)	+D3*(1+E7)	+E3*(1+F7)
4	Cogs	45,000	+C3*$C$8	+D3*$C$8	+E3*$C$8	+F3*$C$8
5	Profit	55,000	+C3−C4	+D3−D4	+E3−E4	+F3−F4
6						
7	Sales Growth		10%	12%	15%	11%
8	Cogs %		45%			
9						

Figure 5-22. *Formulas from Figure 5-21 displayed*

As you can see from this example, you can combine relative and absolute references to create formulas that meet your exact needs.

Mixed Addresses

1-2-3 has one more reference type that extends the package features still further. This reference type is a *mixed address*, which combines relative and absolute features in one cell reference.

Since a cell address is composed of references to a row and a column, it is possible to make one component absolute while leaving the other relative. This gives you the flexibility, for example, to have the column portion of an address updated when a formula is copied across the page, while keeping the row portion of the same address constant when the formula is copied down the worksheet.

Figure 5-23 shows an application in which the mixed addressing feature is useful. In this worksheet, the 1991 figures are historic numbers, and all projections for subsequent years use these figures as base numbers. Sales projections for each product use the appropriate growth factor from C4..C6. For Product A, for example, the sales figure from 1991 is multiplied by 110%. This formula could be written in cell D11 as +C11*(1+C4). It would work for this one year, but it would cause a problem when copied across to subsequent years, since C4 would be updated to D4, E4, and so on.

Using $C$4 in this formula would present another problem, since the Product A formulas could not be copied down for Product B and Product C. If an absolute reference were used for C4, the copied formulas could not reference C5 and C6. The ideal situation would be to freeze the column portion of the address, but allow the row portion to vary. Mixed addressing provides this capability. When the formula

```
D12:  +C12*(1+$C4)                                                    READY

        A        B        C        D        E        F        G        H
  1  *********************************************************************
  2  *                    ASSUMPTIONS                          *
  3  * Sales Growth                                            *
  4  *   Product A              10.0%                          *
  5  *   Product B              12.0%                          *
  6  *   Product C               9.0%                          *
  7  *********************************************************************
  8  ::
  9
 10                          1992      1993      1994      1995      1996
 11  Sales
 12      Product A         100,000   110,000   121,000   133,100   146,410
 13  Product B              50,000    56,000    62,720    70,246    78,676
 14  Product C              45,000    49,050    53,465    58,276    63,521
 15  Cost of Goods Sold     87,750    96,773   106,733   117,730   129,873
 16  Profit                107,250   118,278   130,451   143,892   158,734
 17
```

Figure 5-23.   An application of mixed addressing

reference is written as $C4, only the column portion of the address is absolute; the row portion can vary during the copy process.

A little thought and planning is required to decide how to construct the address type you need. You might elect to use a different formula for each of the product types. That is all right, but for 25 products the mixed addressing feature saves significant time because it allows you to devise one formula to work for all situations.

The formula devised for D11 is +C11*(1+$C4). Mixed addressing allows this formula to be used for all the sales projections. First copy it down column D to D12 and D13. Then copy the range D11..D13 across column E through column G. The formulas automatically created in E11..G13 are as follows:

    E11: +D11*(1+$C4)
    F11: +E11*(1+$C4)
    G11: +F11*(1+$C4)
    E12: +D12*(1+$C5)
    F12: +E12*(1+$C5)
    G12: +F12*(1+$C5)
    E13: +D13*(1+$C6)
    F13: +E13*(1+$C6)
    G13: +F13*(1+$C6)

Using mixed addressing, you can enter one formula and have 1-2-3 generate the other 11 formulas for you. Although mixed addressing is not useful in all models, its payback under appropriate circumstances is significant enough to make it a desirable part of your model building toolkit.

Using SmartIcon Options for Copying in Release 2.4

Three icons will perform a copy operation for you. Two icons are related to the /Copy command; these copy entries and any related formating. The other Copy icon is designed to work only with the format of the current cell; this icon copies the current cell's format to the other cells in the selected range. You will want to familiarize yourself with these three icons if you are using 1-2-3 Release 2.4.

Specifying the To Location

With a VGA monitor, you can use the seventh icon from the bottom of palette 5 to specify the copy destination for the selected cells. The icon looks like this:

To use this feature, you use the F4 feature or the mouse to select the cells that you wish to copy. Next you select the Copy icon from palette 1 or 5 and specify a To location to end the copy operation.

Copying the Contents of One Cell to Many Locations

Release 2.4 also has an icon palette option for copying the entry in the current cell to many locations within a preselected range. For example, if you have an entry in A2 and want to copy it to all the empty cells within the range A2..D15, one quick click will complete the copy operation if you select the range A2..D15 before clicking the icon. The icon that you use for this task is on icon palette 1 or 5, if you have a VGA monitor, and looks like this:

Copying Cells Formats

The last copy operation does not have an comparable command in 1-2-3's menu since there is no option in the menu for copying only the formats within cells. When you learn all the details of Wysiwyg in Chapter 15, you will find that you can use the Wysiwyg menu to duplicate the same operation. The SmartIcon palette option lets you copy the format of the current cell to all cells in a range. These formats can include numeric format options such as Fixed or Currency as well as Wysiwyg options such as boldface and italics. The cells you are copying the formats to can have entries. These entries will not be affected by the copy operation, except that the cells will take on the format of the current cell immediately.

The icon for copying the format from cells is on palette 5, if you have a VGA monitor, and it looks like this:

To use this icon you must first select a cell that has the format you want to use. In Figure 5-24, January is the only month shown in boldface. You can apply the bold format to the other cells where these format attributes would improve the appearance of the display.

To make the changes, you select B5 and then click the special Copy icon. In response to the prompt, you select C5..G5; all the month names then appear in bold.

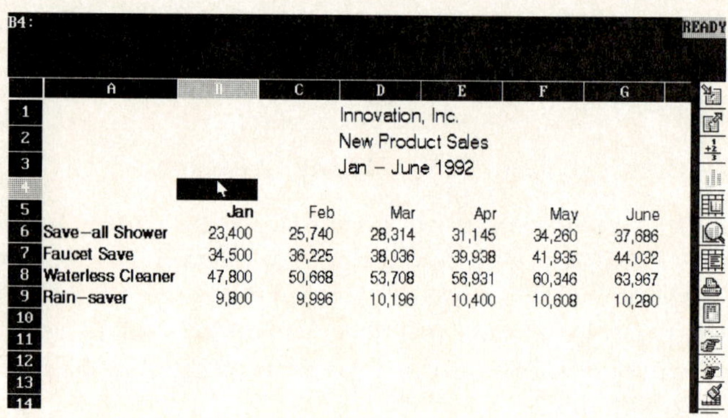

Figure 5-24.   *Only "Jan" appears in boldface*

If cell B5 had other attributes such as underlining or italics, these would have been copied at the same time. Figure 5-25 shows the model after the format is copied.

Using 1-2-3's Search and Replace Features

In Release 2.2 and above, the /Range Search command offers you the ability to search for character strings within formulas and labels. This feature is especially useful in a large worksheet where you need to locate a particular entry but have no knowledge of its cell address. With the Find option you can find the first occurrence of your

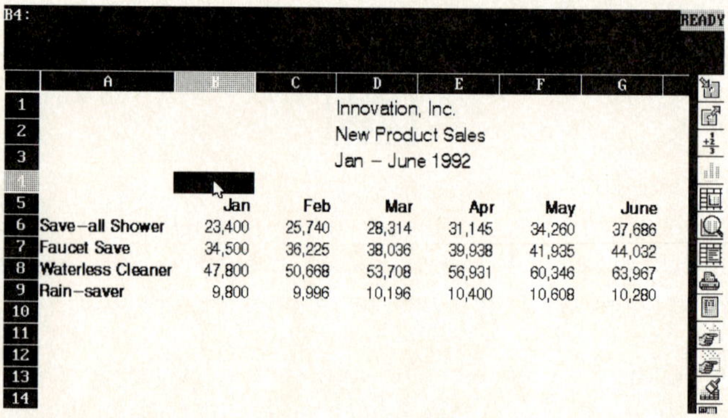

Figure 5-25.   *Worksheet after copying "Jan" formatting*

entry or continue to search through a specified range of the worksheet file. You can use /Range Search to search either formulas, labels, or both.

The /Range Search command offers a Replace option in which you supply a replacement string that 1-2-3 uses as a substitute for the character string you find within matching entries. This feature is useful if you need to replace cell references or range names in a large range of formula entries. You can replace the first occurrence or all occurrences. If you prefer, you can proceed through the selected range, finding one occurrence at a time.

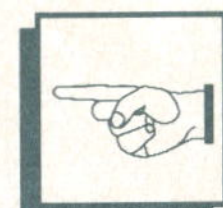

You may want to replace matching entries one at a time until you are certain that the search string you entered is matching correctly. This isn't necessary if you need to change all occurrences of $D$9 to $A$9, because probably you will find only correct matches. But if you choose All and want to change the A in $D$9 to D, searching for A and replacing it with D could be a disaster. Entries like AB10 would be changed to DB10, and all A's in range names would be changed to D's. As a rule, be as specific as possible when doing a replace.

Using Search

The /Range Search command lets you locate a string of characters in a range of formulas or labels. You might want to scan a large range of data for a vendor name or a range name that you are considering deleting. When looking for a range name, use the Formulas option for this command to scan only the cells with formula entries. When looking for text stored in a label cell, you can restrict your search to cells that contain labels.

To find the name Campbell in the data in Figure 5-26, enter **/Range Search** and highlight the cells that contain name entries. This range might be the cells that are visible, or it could include a much longer column or hidden columns. After selecting the appropriate range, press ENTER and type **campbell** (upper- and lowercase are equivalent in a search string, so you do not need to capitalize your entry). Select Labels, and then select Find from the next menu. The first occurrence of the cell containing the first occurrence of the string is highlighted. Select either Next to look for additional occurrences or Quit to end the Find operation.

Using Replace

The Replace option not only locates strings but allows you to replace them with other entries. The data in Figure 5-26 can be used again for this example. To change the second occurrence of the last name Campbell to Camper, you could find the entry, quit, and then change it; or you can use Replace. Begin a replace operation in the same way as a search, by entering **/Range Search**, highlighting the range containing the name entries, and pressing ENTER. Next, type **Campbell** and press ENTER. Select Labels followed by Replace. Type **Camper** and press ENTER. The first occurrence of

```
A1: [W12] 'Last Name                                                    READY
```

	A	B	C	D	E	F	G
1	Last Name	First Name	SS#	Job Code	Salary	Location	
2	Larson	Mary	543–98–9976	23	$12,000	2	
3	Campbell	David	213–76–9874	23	$23,000	10	
4	Campbell	Keith	569–89–7864	12	$32,000	2	
5	Stephens	Tom	219–78–8964	15	$17,800	2	
6	Caldor	Larry	459–34–0921	23	$32,500	4	
7	Lightnor	Peggy	560–55–4311	14	$23,500	10	
8	McCartin	John	817–66–1212	15	$54,600	2	
9	Justof	Jack	431–78–9963	17	$41,200	4	
10	Patterson	Lyle	212–11–9090	12	$21,500	10	
11	Miller	Lisa	214–89–6756	23	$18,700	2	
12	Hawkins	Mark	215–67–8873	21	$19,500	2	
13	Hartwick	Eileen	313–78–9090	15	$31,450	4	
14	Smythe	George	560–90–8695	15	$65,000	4	
15	Wilkes	Caitlin	124–67–7432	17	$15,500	2	
16	Deaver	Ken	198–98–6750	23	$24,600	10	
17	Kaylor	Sally	312–45–9862	12	$32,900	10	
18	Parker	Dee	659–11–3452	14	$19,800	4	
19	Preverson	Gary	670–90–1121	21	$27,600	4	
20	Samuelson	Paul	219–89–7080	23	$28,900	2	

```
22-Apr-92  11:22 AM                                                     NUM
```

Figure 5-26.   *A section of a large worksheet to be searched*

Campbell is not the one you want to replace, so select Next to move to the next occurrence without changing the current entry. The second occurrence highlighted is the one you want, so select Replace to complete the change. Since there are no additional entries, you are finished. You can press ESC to return to READY mode.

Other menu options for Replace are All, which changes all the records at once, and Quit, which returns to READY mode when you do not wish to make further changes.

Use the flashlight icon on palette 4 to invoke the Search and Replace feature.

Making Other Worksheet Changes

Several additional features bring advanced capabilities to worksheet preparation. In this section you look at options that allow you to change label justification for the entire worksheet and to erase the complete worksheet with one command.

Changing Default Label Justification

The default worksheet setting for labels provides left justification for every label entry. This means that an apostrophe (') is generated as the first character of every label entry. As you learned in Chapter 3, you always have the option of centering a label entry by typing the label alignment character, a caret (^). You can also right-justify a single entry by beginning your label entry with a double quotation mark (").

1-2-3 offers further flexibility with the /Range Label command, which lets you change the justification of label entries that are already in cells. But if you want all of your labels to default to a new justification, neither the single entry method nor the Range option is exactly right. For such circumstances, 1-2-3 provides the /Worksheet Global Label-Prefix command to change the default label prefix for every new worksheet entry. To make the change, enter **/Worksheet Global Label-Prefix** and select the left, right, or center justification you want from the menu.

You can also change the default label alignment by selecting the alignment button in the /Worksheet Global dialog box.

With this command, existing entries are unaffected, but new entries have the new label prefix. Just the opposite is true with /Range Label. With both options you should remember that numeric and formula entries are unaffected by changes made to the label prefix.

Erasing the Worksheet

1-2-3 provides a command to erase the entire contents of the worksheet currently in memory. This feature is useful when you have made so many mistakes that you want to wipe the slate clean and start over again, or when you have saved your completed worksheet on disk and want to begin a new application.

Enter **/Worksheet Erase** to request this feature, and 1-2-3 prompts you with a choice of Yes or No. Selecting Yes erases the worksheet; selecting No cancels the command.

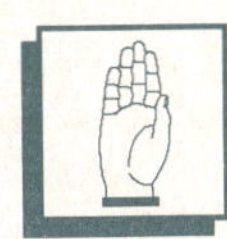

Your only hope for restoring the effect of /Worksheet Erase is by using ALT-F4 *(UNDO), and only then if your Undo feature was enabled at the time of the erase operation and there have been no intervening actions. In other words, once you have erased a worksheet, there is no way to bring the contents of memory back without UNDO, unless you have saved a copy of the worksheet on disk.*

Notice that the cell pointer is initially positioned over the No option on the confirmation screen, so if you accidentally press ENTER without looking, you will not lose your worksheet. To erase the worksheet you will have to take an action—either typing **Y** or pointing to the Yes option before pressing ENTER. Release 2.2 and above will prompt you for a second confirmation if you have made changes since the last /File Save command.

Using Expanded Memory

If you have expanded memory, 1-2-3 can create larger worksheets because it can use part of expanded memory to store some or all of your worksheet. You can select how

1-2-3 uses the expanded memory so if you are creating and using large worksheets 1-2-3 will store more of the information in expanded memory. To set 1-2-3 to store the entire worksheet in expanded memory, select /Worksheet Global Default Other Expanded-Memory Enhanced; with expanded memory this selection lets you create larger worksheets.

If you are not working with worksheets that fully use the enhanced use of expanded memory, select /Worksheet Global Default Other Expanded-Memory Standard; this selection only uses expanded memory for cell contents and stores other types of worksheet information in conventional memory. This use of expanded memory makes 1-2-3 perform faster but the worksheets you create cannot be as large as the ones you can create by storing all of the spreadsheet data in expanded memory (assuming you have enough expanded memory).

Help Access Setting

The first time you press the F1 (HELP) key, the help setting determines how 1-2-3 handles the file 123.HLP. Using the default setting of Removable, 1-2-3 opens the 123.HLP file to display the Help information when you press F1 and closes the file when you press ESC to return to the worksheet. Opening and closing the Help file allows 1-2-3 to run faster. It also allows you to remove the Help disk when you are running 1-2-3 from floppy disks.

With the Instant options, 1-2-3 opens the Help file when you first press F1 (HELP) and closes the file when you quit 1-2-3. This setting provides a quicker response to pressing F1 (HELP) and works better when you are running 1-2-3 from a hard disk. If you are running 1-2-3 from a floppy, you cannot remove the Help disk until you exit 1-2-3. To change to the Instant help access method, enter **/Worksheet Global Default Other Help Instant**. To return to the removable help access method, enter **/Worksheet Global Default Other Help Removable**. These changes do not become permanent until you select Update to save the setting in the 123.CNF file.

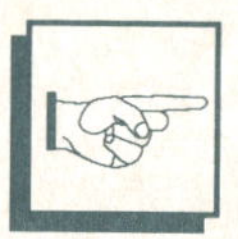

To access Help, you can use the icon that looks like a question mark on palette 2.

Recalculating the Worksheet

1-2-3's recalculation abilities provide the power behind its formula features. A new improved calculation method offers minimal recalculation. The essence of this feature is that 1-2-3 no longer recalculates the entire worksheet every time a new entry is made in a worksheet cell. It only recalculates the formulas affected by the new entry and has the intelligence to determine which cells are affected.

Some tasks—like printing, changing formulas to values with /Range Value, or altering the layout of entries with /Range Trans—should be done only after recalculating the worksheet, if recalculation is set to Manual. 1-2-3 lets you know that the worksheet contains formulas that should be recalculated by displaying the CALC indicator at the bottom of the screen. When you press F9 (CALC), 1-2-3 will do the calculations. All the recalculation options are accessed through the /Worksheet Global Recalculation command or the /Worksheet Global dialog box.

Default Recalculation Settings

1-2-3's recalculation features have three different setting categories, all selected from the following menu:

One group determines whether recalculation is done automatically or only upon request. The second group controls the order in which the worksheet formulas are reevaluated. The last recalculation option specifies how many times each formula is reevaluated during recalculation.

Timing of Recalculation

The default setting for recalculation of a new worksheet is Automatic. This means that any new number, changed number, or new formula causes 1-2-3 to recalculate all worksheet formulas affected by your change. The time needed for this recalculation depends on the number and complexity of the worksheet formulas and the number of formulas affected by your change. You cannot continue with other tasks since your computer's resources are dedicated to the recalculation. If you have a whole series of entries to make and are not concerned with the impact of each individual entry, you can use Manual recalculation, so that 1-2-3 does not do any recalculations until you request them.

To turn off Automatic recalculation, enter **/Worksheet Global Recalculation Manual** or deselect the Automatic checkbox in the /Worksheet Global dialog box. When the Manual option is in force, the worksheet does not recalculate unless you turn Automatic back on or press the F9 (CALC) key. You can also use the calculator icon on palette 3 to recalculate the worksheet. The Manual option can speed up your data entry, since you can enter everything before requesting a recalculation. When you want to return to automatic recalculation, select /Worksheet Global Recalculation Automatic or select the Automatic check box in the /Worksheet Global dialog box.

Order of Recalculation

The default setting for recalculation order is Natural. This means that 1-2-3 examines each worksheet formula for dependencies on other formulas and determines which formulas must be calculated first to provide the results needed by the formulas to be reevaluated next. Natural recalculation order set a new standard for other spreadsheets when it was first introduced. Before that time, the only options were Rowwise or Columnwise recalculation.

Rowwise recalculation evaluates all the formulas in row 1, then all the formulas in row 2, and so on. The problem with this method is that if a formula in row 1 references a value in a row further down the worksheet, the earlier formula references a value from a prior recalculation. The same type of problem occurs with columnwise recalculation when early columns reference values further to the right that have not yet been recalculated. These deficiencies in existing recalculation methods made 1-2-3's Natural recalculation order a welcome addition.

If you want to change the way recalculation is done, enter /Worksheet Global Recalculation, and then either Rowwise, Columnwise, or Natural, or select the Rowwise, Columnwise, or Natural option boxes in the /Worksheet Global dialog box.

You might want to use the other recalculation orders when you import data from another worksheet package. If you bring a model created with another spreadsheet package like VisiCalc into 1-2-3, you might want to retain the recalculation order used with the original model.

Iterations of Recalculation

The default setting for the number of iterations for a recalculation is 1. This means that each formula requiring recalculation is computed once each time the worksheet is recalculated. If you set this number higher than 1, 1-2-3 performs multiple recalculation when the order of calculation is rowwise or columnwise, or if there is a circular reference with Natural recalculation order.

In calculations that involve a circular calculation pattern, one iteration is not sufficient, because each calculation depends on the result of some other calculation, with the final result referring back to one of the earlier calculations. In such situations 1-2-3 is not able to identify a clear recalculation sequence for the formulas. Multiple calculations are required so that each approximates the correct answer a little more closely.

Increasing 1-2-3's iterative count can solve the problem with circular references. This increase means that 1-2-3 recalculates more than once each time the worksheet is automatically calculated or the F9 (CALC) key is pressed.

An example of a circular reference requiring iteration for resolution is shown here:

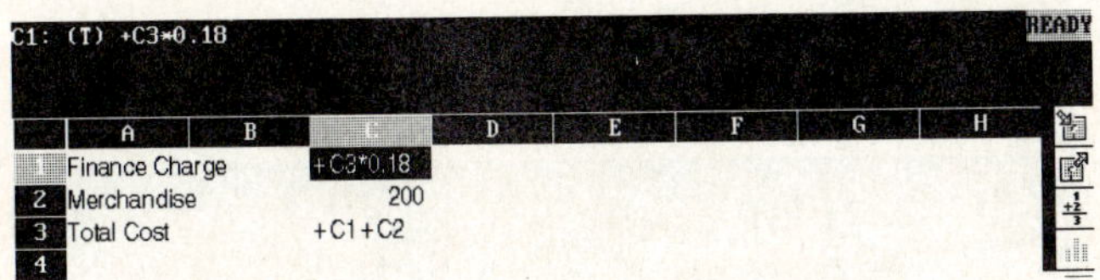

When the formulas are first entered, C3 displays as 0 and C5 displays as 200. Since these two formulas are dependent on each other, each recalculation refines the accuracy of the result. The results after several recalculations with the F9 (CALC) key appear in the worksheet shown here:

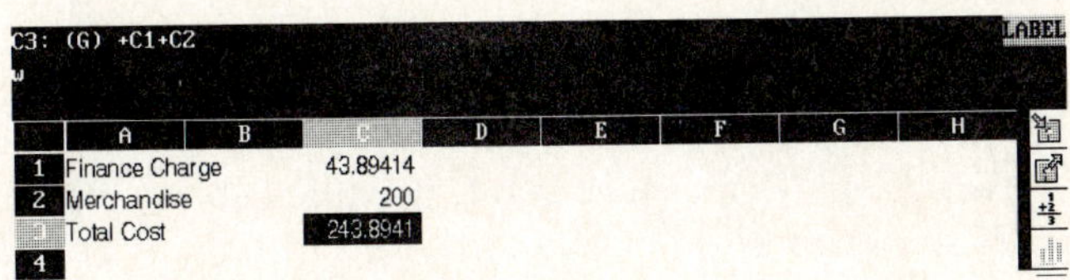

Slight changes continue to occur over the next several recalculations until a final approximation is reached. All these calculations could have been performed the first time the worksheet was calculated if the iteration count had been set higher.

Modifying the Screen Display

1-2-3 has several screen display options that are especially useful for large worksheets. One option allows you to lock the titles or descriptive labels at the side or top of your screen so you can look at data in remote parts of the worksheet and still have these labels in view. Another feature lets you split the screen vertically or horizontally and use each section as a window into a different part of the worksheet.

Freezing Titles

The /Worksheet Titles command presents a menu with the options Both, Horizontal, Vertical, or Clear. With these options you can elect to freeze titles at the top of your screen, the side of your screen, or both. The command is position dependent in that it freezes titles that are above and to the left of the cell-pointer location at the time you invoke the command.

Once titles are frozen on the screen, you cannot use the arrow keys to move into these cells. If you need to make spelling corrections or other changes in these cells,

you can press the F5 (GOTO) key, which temporarily brings two copies of the titles
to the screen, as shown here:

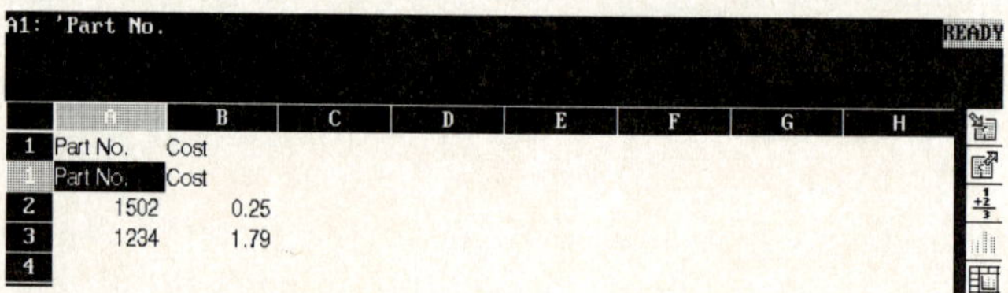

This double title disappears when you scroll away from the title area.

Freezing Horizontal Titles

If you choose /Worksheet Titles Horizontal, the titles above the cell pointer are
frozen. Figure 5-27 shows a section from a worksheet with many entries. If you move
your cell pointer toward the bottom of the entries, the top lines scroll off. The
remaining numbers are difficult to interpret without the column headings in the top
row.

To freeze the labels in row 1, move the cell pointer to A2 on the original screen
and select /Worksheet Titles Horizontal. Now when the cell pointer is moved down
the worksheet, the titles remain visible, as shown in Figure 5-28. Notice that the figure
starts with row 1, which displays the horizontal titles, but the data displayed is from
rows 4 to 22.

Figure 5-27.   *A worksheet with many entries down the worksheet*

```
A22: 1133                                                          READY

         A          B        C        D     E     F     G     H
  1   Part No.     Cost  Warehouse
  4     2134      $1.25      3
  5     5678      $2.35      2
  6     8543      $2.45      1
  7     6752      $5.90      2
  8     3412      $9.99      3
  9     2134      $7.50      3
 10     5432      $6.25      3
 11     8765      $0.59      2
 12     6667      $3.35      4
 13     5567      $2.00      5
 14     5543      $1.00      2
 15     4435      $2.25      2
 16     4432      $3.45      2
 17     7789      $7.80      3
 18     8876      $0.79      1
 19     9931      $2.00      1
 20     4452      $1.50      4
 21     3311      $1.75      5
 22     1133      $1.00      2
16-Apr-92  05:02 PM                                        NUM
```

Figure 5-28.   The titles remain on the screen after freezing

Freezing Vertical Titles

With worksheets that are wider than the screen, you can freeze titles vertically. Doing so allows you to move across the screen into columns far to the right of the normal display and still have identifying labels visible on the left side of the screen. You freeze titles vertically simply by moving your cell pointer to the right of the titles you want frozen and entering /**Worksheet Titles Vertical**.

Freezing Titles in Both Directions

You may want to freeze titles in both directions when the worksheet is both longer and wider than the screen and has descriptive titles at both the top and left sides of the screen. Figure 5-29 shows a portion of a worksheet with many entries. To freeze the titles in both directions, move the cell pointer to cell B3, which is to the right of the side titles and below the top titles, and then enter /**Worksheet Titles Both**. When the cell pointer is moved to J26, causing information to scroll off the top and left of the screen, both sets of titles are still visible, as you can see in Figure 5-30.

Thawing Titles

/**Worksheet Titles Clear** eliminates any titles that you have frozen. This command is not position dependent. It removes the titles regardless of your cell-pointer location. Eliminating titles does not eliminate the data in the cells you were using as titles.

DEPT.	1986	1987	1988	1989	1990	1991	1992
100	51	66	83	82	73	53	43
120	33	93	31	38	29	12	71
130	20	28	95	25	39	78	35
140	88	59	0	33	53	73	56
145	23	31	32	7	22	39	27
150	84	18	72	59	47	76	78
160	64	89	62	55	26	21	54
175	85	22	27	93	46	37	17
180	5	92	17	8	60	73	98
190	21	36	41	76	6	9	57
195	5	65	14	91	83	5	39
200	0	85	41	48	87	13	32
210	62	45	11	60	61	19	52
220	31	23	39	65	31	20	30
225	61	5	38	42	18	74	64
228	50	47	85	1	49	49	57
230	33	96	73	46	9	77	70

Figure 5-29.   *A worksheet with extra width and depth*

DEPT.	1988	1989	1990	1991	1992	1990	1991
160	62	55	26	21	54	42	92
175	27	93	46	37	17	50	45
180	17	8	60	73	98	15	87
190	41	76	6	9	57	94	16
195	14	91	83	5	39	23	87
200	41	48	87	13	32	94	16
210	11	60	61	19	52	23	87
220	39	65	31	20	30	94	44
225	38	42	18	74	64	19	28
228	85	1	49	49	57	100	23
230	73	46	9	77	70	6	9
235	70	73	82	4	2	57	62
240	9	7	88	34	36	18	43
245	5	28	1	9	76	51	28
TOTAL	845	937	910	775	994	820	902

Figure 5-30.   *The titles frozen in both directions*

Adding a Second Window

The /Worksheet Window command allows you to have two windows in your screen display so you can look simultaneously at information in two completely different areas of the current worksheet. You can split the screen into two vertical or horizontal sections and then move your cell pointer within either window to bring whichever cells you choose into view.

If you decide to divide the screen into horizontal or vertical windows, the size of each window depends on the cell pointer location at the time the split is requested. The split is placed to the left of or above the cell-pointer location, based on whether the split is vertical or horizontal.

The /Worksheet Window command produces a menu with the options Horizontal, Vertical, Sync, Unsync, and Clear. Notice there is no option for splitting the screen in both directions at once. This is due to 1-2-3's two-window limitation.

In addition to the Horizontal and Vertical options, the /Worksheet Window options Sync and Unsync decide whether movement in one window causes a corresponding shift of information in the second window.

Splitting the Screen Horizontally

A horizontal screen split is appropriate when you need the entire screen width to show two different sections of a worksheet report. To split the screen horizontally, move the cell pointer to a location within the row immediately below the desired split location. For example, Figure 5-31 shows the cell pointer positioned in Row 12. When you enter /**Worksheet Window Horizontal**, the screen splits into two different windows. The size of the two windows is dictated by the cell-pointer location at the time of the request. Figure 5-32 shows the result of the split. F6 (WINDOW) was pressed to move the cell pointer into the second window.

```
A12: 180                                                              READY
```

	A	B	C	D	E	F	G	H
1		New Employees By Department						
2								
3	DEPT.	1986	1987	1988	1989	1990	1991	1992
4	100	51	66	83	82	73	53	43
5	120	33	93	31	38	29	12	71
6	130	20	28	95	25	39	78	35
7	140	88	59	0	33	53	73	56
8	145	23	31	32	7	22	39	27
9	150	84	18	72	59	47	76	78
10	160	64	89	62	55	26	21	54
11	175	85	22	27	93	46	37	17
12	180	5	92	17	8	60	73	98
13	190	21	36	41	76	6	9	57
14	195	5	65	14	91	83	5	39
15	200	0	85	41	48	87	13	32
16	210	62	45	11	60	61	19	52
17	220	31	23	39	65	31	20	30
18	225	61	5	38	42	18	74	64
19	228	50	47	85	1	49	49	57
20	230	33	96	73	46	9	77	70

```
16-Apr-92  05:08 PM                                                  NUM
```

Figure 5-31.   *The cell pointer positioned for a horizontal window split*

```
A26: 'TOTAL                                                        READY
```

	A	B	C	D	E	F	G	H
1		New Employees By Department						
2								
3	DEPT.	1986	1987	1988	1989	1990	1991	1992
4	100	51	66	83	82	73	53	43
5	120	33	93	31	38	29	12	71
6	130	20	28	95	25	39	78	35
7	140	88	59	0	33	53	73	56
8	145	23	31	32	7	22	39	27
9	150	84	18	72	59	47	76	78
10	160	64	89	62	55	26	21	54
11	175	85	22	27	93	46	37	17

	A	B	C	D	E	F	G	H
19	228	50	47	85	1	49	49	57
20	230	33	96	73	46	9	77	70
21	235	21	99	70	73	82	4	2
22	240	42	66	9	7	88	34	36
23	245	26	55	5	28	1	9	76
24								
25								
26	TOTAL	805	1120	845	937	910	775	994

```
16-Apr-92  05:08 PM                                                  NUM
```

Figure 5-32.   *The horizontally split screen*

Once the screen is split, you can use the arrow keys to move the cell pointer around in either window.

Splitting the Screen Vertically

A vertical screen split is appropriate when you would like the full length of the screen to show sections of the worksheet but do not require the full width. Again, cell pointer position at the time of the request determines the size of the two windows. The split occurs to the left of the column in which the cell pointer is located.

You can split the worksheet shown in Figure 5-33 into two vertical windows at the cell-pointer location. To produce this split, position the cell pointer in column E and enter **/Worksheet Window Vertical**. Press F6 (WINDOW) and move the cell pointer to column I to produce the display shown in Figure 5-33. As it does with the Horizontal option, the cell pointer moves into the second window with F6 (WINDOW). Each time F6 is pressed, the cell pointer moves into the opposite window.

Creating Windows with a Mouse

If you are using a mouse and have loaded the Wysiwyg Add-In as described in Chapter 15, you can use the mouse to create windows. To create horizontal windows with the mouse, point to the upper-left corner of the worksheet frame. Next, hold down the left mouse button and drag the mouse down to where you want the worksheet split into windows. As you drag the mouse, 1-2-3 draws a line to indicate where the

J11: 45   READY

	A	B	C	D		H	I	J	K
1			New Employees By Dep		1				
2					2				
3	DEPT.	1986	1987	1988	3	1992	1993	1994	
4	100	51	66	83	4	43	5	19	
5	120	33	93	31	5	71	12	50	
6	130	20	28	95	6	35	8	26	
7	140	88	59	0	7	56	7	24	
8	145	23	31	32	8	27	59	36	
9	150	84	18	72	9	78	43	80	
10	160	64	89	62	10	54	42	92	
11	175	85	22	27		17	50	45	
12	180	5	92	17	12	98	15	87	
13	190	21	36	41	13	57	94	16	
14	195	5	65	14	14	39	23	87	
15	200	0	85	41	15	32	94	16	
16	210	62	45	11	16	52	23	87	
17	220	31	23	39	17	30	94	44	
18	225	61	5	38	18	64	19	28	
19	228	50	47	85	19	57	100	23	
20	230	33	96	73	20	70	6	9	

16-Apr-92   05:11 PM   NUM

Figure 5-33.   The vertically split screen

worksheet will be split into windows. When you release the left mouse button, 1-2-3 will split the screen into two windows along this line. To create vertical windows, the steps are the same except you drag the mouse to the right instead of down to indicate where you want the worksheet split.

Moving in Both Windows at Once

1-2-3's default setting has its two windows synchronized. This means that if you move in one window, the other window automatically scrolls to match it. With horizontal windows, moving the cell pointer from column A to column Z in one window causes the other window to automatically scroll to column Z. With vertical windows, moving from row 1 to row 120 in one window automatically updates the other window to display row 120.

Moving in One Window at a Time

Sometimes you want information, such as a table, to remain stationary while you move in the other window. You can make this change from either window by entering */Worksheet Window Unsync*. With Unsync, the contents of the two windows are totally independent. If you choose, you can show the same information in both windows. To return to a synchronized mode, invoke */Worksheet Window Sync*. This causes the two windows to move in tandem again.

Clearing the Second Window

When you decide to return to a single window display, enter /Worksheet Window Clear. If the screen was split horizontally, the returning single window obtains its default settings from the top window. If the screen was split vertically, the settings for the left window are used. If you are using Wysiwyg and a mouse, you can also close the windows by dragging the upper-left corner of the worksheet frame so the second window is on top of the worksheet frame for the first window.

Displaying the Current Status of Worksheet Options

When you go back to a worksheet you used earlier, you may not remember all the options you chose for it. Conveniently, 1-2-3 lets you see the settings for all the worksheet options on one screen. You have two commands for looking at the status of these entries. With Release 2.3 and above, you also have dialog boxes.

Enter /Worksheet Status to display the status of the worksheet as shown in Figure 5-34. In releases of 1-2-3 before 2.3, the Worksheet Status screen includes recalculation, cell display and global protection settings that Release 2.3 and above display in the dialog box when you select /Worksheet Global. With this command and dialog

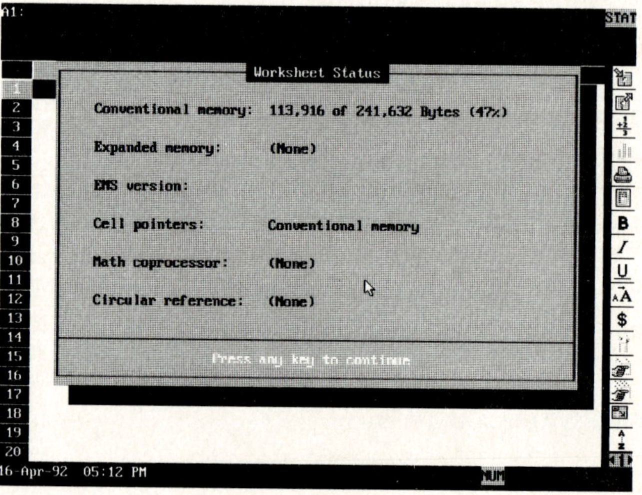

Figure 5-34.   *A Worksheet Status display*

boxes, you can monitor the available memory, the existence of a math coprocessor to speed numeric calculations, the recalculation options, the default options for cell display, the global protection status, and any cell causing a circular reference in the worksheet. The box that is called "A Closer Look at the Status Settings" provides a detailed look at the various status items listed. You cannot change any of the options displayed on the worksheet status screen. In Release 2.3 and above, you can change the settings using the dialog box or with the 1-2-3 commands. The items that can be changed can be altered through /Worksheet Global commands. The other command you can use for displaying 1-2-3 settings is /Worksheet Global Default Status. This command displays the current settings of the commands available by selecting /Worksheet Global Default Status. Figure 5-35 shows the output that this command produces.

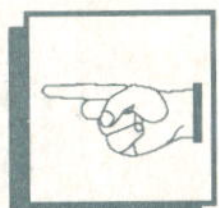

You can use /Worksheet Status, /Worksheet Global Default Status, and dialog boxes to obtain a complete picture of 1-2-3's current settings, including selections, hardware, and system defaults. With Release 2.2 and above, an even better approach is to enter /Worksheet Global for an opportunity to revise any of the modifiable entries on the /Worksheet Status screen through the new dialog box display. A dialog box for the /Worksheet Global Default Status entries is displayed when you enter /Worksheet Global Default. You can change as well as see the status of the entries with this dialog box.

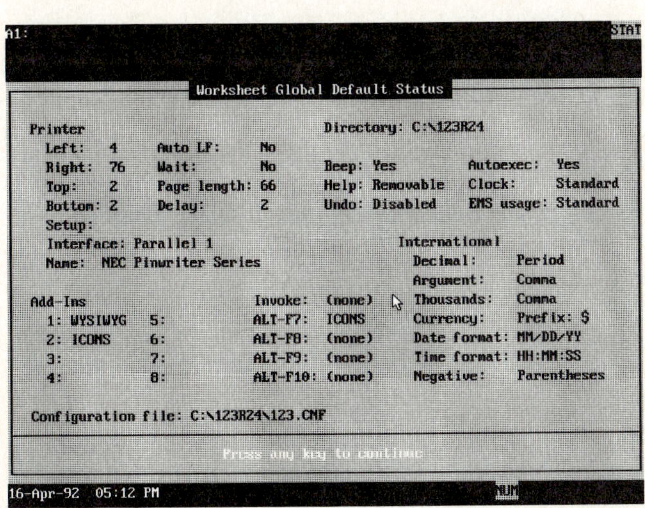

Figure 5-35.   The output from the /Worksheet Global Default Status command

A Closer Look at the Status Settings

The Status screen and /Worksheet Global dialog box monitor a variety of information.

- **Available Memory**: This portion of the display reports the amount of available memory used. 1-2-3 shows conventional and expanded memory separately. This information helps you plan the remainder of your worksheet entries. When memory is almost full, you may have to split your worksheet in two.

- **Math Coprocessor**: Release 2.0 and above support the use of a math coprocessor chip. This section reports whether one of the supported chips is installed on your system.

- **Recalculation**: This section reports on all the recalculation options. You can observe whether recalculation is set at Automatic or Manual. You can also monitor the current recalculation order to see whether it is set at Natural, Rowwise, or Columnwise. The current number of recalculation iterations set to occur is also displayed.

- **Circular Reference**: This section shows you the address of the first cell that is causing the CIRC indicator to appear at the bottom of your screen.

- **Cell Display**: This section provides four different pieces of default information: the global format settings, the current label prefix, the global column width, and whether zero suppression is on or off.

- **Global Protection**: The last area of the Status screen shows whether Global Protection is enabled or disabled.

BASIC WORKSHEET

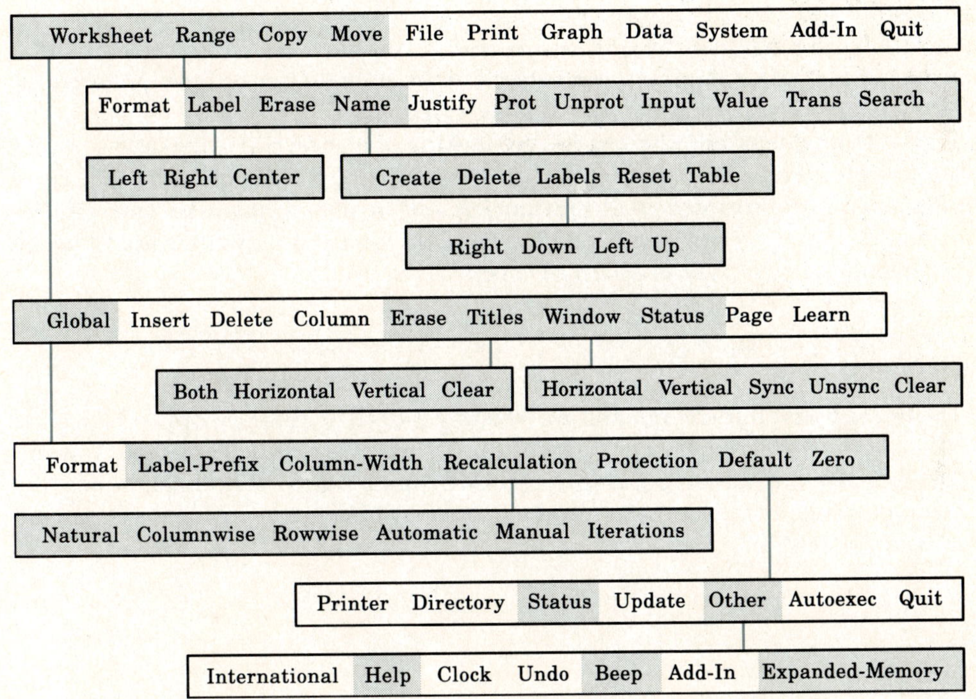

/Copy

Description

The /Copy command is the most powerful command 1-2-3 has to offer. It copies numbers, labels, and formulas to new locations on the worksheet. It can copy one cell or many cells in a range, to either a cell or a range. This command copies the entries and any format assigned to the entries. If Wysiwyg is loaded, any Wysiwyg formats are also copied to the new location. This does not apply to Allways cell formats.

Copying is a simple process that requires telling 1-2-3 only two things: where to copy from and what to copy to.

The from range can be one cell or many. Multiple cells to be copied can be arranged in a row, column, or rectangle. The from range can be typed, referenced with a range name, or highlighted with the cell pointer.

The to range defines whether you are making one or several copies and specifies the exact location where you would like them placed. Each duplication of the from information requires only that the top left cell in the to range be entered. For example, if you were copying A1..A15 to B1..E15, you need only enter **B1..E1** as the to range, since only the top cell in each copy is required.

Options

The two options for this command are selecting the cell or range to copy and selecting where you want one or more copies of the cell or range to be copied to. You can specify ranges by either pressing F3 (NAME), pointing to the range, typing the complete range address, or selecting the range to copy before selecting the command by using F4 (ABS).

/Move

Description

The /Move command moves a range of worksheet entries to any location on the worksheet. This command moves the entries and any format assigned to the entries. If Wysiwyg is loaded, any Wysiwyg formats are also moved to the new location. This does not apply to Allways cell formats. /Move adjusts the formulas to correspond to the new location of the moved cells regardless of the type of cell address so the formulas refer to the same values after moving one or more cells.

Options

This command moves one or many cells to a new location. For example, you can move A2 to B3 by entering /Move A2, pressing ENTER, typing **B3**, and pressing ENTER again. To move a range of cells to a new location, you might enter /Move A2..B6 and press ENTER, and then enter a new destination such as **D2** and press ENTER. You can use any of the options for specifying ranges, such as pressing F3 (NAME), pointing to the range, or typing the complete range address.

/Range Erase

Description

The /Range Erase command eliminates entries you have made in worksheet cells. Protected cells cannot be erased while Worksheet Protection is enabled.

Options

The only option for this command is to specify a single cell or many cells in the range by typing the range reference or highlighting the included cells by pointing.

Note

The /Range Erase command does not affect cell formats. A cell formatted as Currency is still formatted as Currency after /Range Erase is used. (To eliminate a format, use /Range Format Reset to return the range to the default setting.)

/Range Input

Description

This command restricts cell-pointer movement to unprotected cells. To use the command, first construct a worksheet and make sure the desired input cells are unprotected with /Range Unprot. Next, enter /Range Input and select a range of cells for the input area. 1-2-3 will move only to unprotected cells, skipping over the protected ones.

Remember that ranges must be rectangular; this command does not work on input cells scattered across the entire worksheet.

Options

While using the /Range Input command, you can employ many of the cell-pointer movement keys to move among the unprotected cells in the selected area. HOME moves to the first unprotected cell, and END moves to the last unprotected cell. The arrow keys move you within the selected range. ESC cancels an entry, but if you have not made an entry, it ends /Range Input. ENTER finalizes entries, but if no entries have been made, it ends /Range Input. Selections cannot be made from the command menus, although F1 (HELP), F2 (EDIT), and F9 (CALC) are operational.

/Range Label

Description

The /Range Label command changes the justification (placement) of existing worksheet labels. Empty cells in the selected range are not affected by this command. These later entries use the default worksheet setting.

Options

/Range Label has three options: Left, Center, and Right. These selections dictate the label indicator used for existing cell entries. Left changes the label indicator to an apostrophe (') for all entries in the range, and left-justifies them in the cells. Center places a caret (^) at the front of the labels and centers them in the cells. The last option, Right, places double quotation marks (") at the beginning of the labels and right-justifies them in the cells. After selecting one of the options, select the range to apply the new justification unless you already selected a range before entering the command.

/Range Name Create

Description

The /Range Name Create command assigns names to cell ranges. Using names rather than cell addresses makes formulas easier to understand and helps you develop worksheet models that are self-documenting. Range names can be used anywhere cell addresses can be used.

Options

After entering **/Range Name Create**, you have two options: working with an existing range name or entering a new one. If you choose to work with an existing range name, you can select a name from the list of existing range names in the menu and have 1-2-3 highlight the cells that are currently assigned this name. At this point you can use ESC to undo the existing range name assignment and specify a new range name.

To establish a new range name, after entering **/Range Name Create**, type a new range name of up to 15 characters and press ENTER. Next, unless you have selected a range before selecting the command, respond to 1-2-3's prompt for the range by pointing to or entering the range and then pressing ENTER. The range name you choose should be as meaningful as possible.

1-2-3 does not restrict you to a single name for a given range of cells. If a range is used for more than one purpose, you can assign multiple names to it by using /Range Name Create a second time.

/Range Name Delete

Description

The /Range Name Delete command deletes range names that are no longer needed. Each execution of this command removes a single range name. To delete a range name, enter **/Range Name Delete**, point to the appropriate name in the list 1-2-3 provides, and press ENTER. Alternatively, type the name that you wish to delete after entering the command sequence.

/Range Name Labels

Description

The /Range Name Labels command assigns worksheet label entries as range names in certain situations. With this command, each label can be assigned as a name only to a single cell. Furthermore, the label must be in a cell adjacent to the cell you want to assign the name to. If you choose a label that exceeds the 15-character limit for range names, the range name is truncated. The /Range Name Labels command is most useful when you have a column or row of labels and wish to assign each one to its adjacent cell as a range name. One execution of this command can assign all of the range names.

Options

The /Range Name Labels command has four options on a submenu. They let you tell 1-2-3 the direction in which to go for the cell needing assignment of the label. The choices are Right, Down, Up, and Left. After selecting one of the choices, select the range containing the labels to assign to the adjacent cells.

/Range Name Reset

Description

The /Range Name Reset command eliminates all range names in a file at once.

/Range Name Table

Description

The /Range Name Table command lets you access a list of all the range names in a file, and the range to which each name has been assigned.

Options

The only option you have with this command is to specify the upper-left cell of the table. 1-2-3 uses as much space as required, and overwrites worksheet entries if they are present in the cells used for the table.

/Range Prot

Description

The /Range Prot command reprotects cells that you have unprotected with the /Range Unprot command. It allows you to change your mind and reestablish the Protection feature initially provided by 1-2-3 for every worksheet cell. Using the /Range Prot command has no apparent effect on a cell while Protection is turned off. Once Protection is turned on, cells that are protected will not accept entries of any type.

Since /Range Prot must be used in combination with /Worksheet Global Protection, you will also want to read the entry for that command.

Options

The only options for /Range Prot are those for entering the range either before or after you have requested the command. You can type the range address, use POINT mode to expand the cell-pointer to include the entire range, or type the range name that you wish to use.

/Range Search

Description

The /Range Search command performs either a search or replace operation. The command searches for a character string in either formulas or labels, and can optionally be used to replace the string with a new entry.

Options

After specifying the search range and search string, the first set of /Range Search options lets you choose whether to search formulas, labels, or both. Next you tell 1-2-3 to find the string, or find it and replace it with another entry. If you choose Find, 1-2-3 looks for the first occurrence of your entry and highlights it. You can then continue to look for the next occurrence, or quit. If you choose Replace, 1-2-3 asks for the replacement string and highlights the first occurrence of the search string. You are then given the options to confirm this replacement, replace all occurrences of the search string, skip this replacement and move to the next matching string, or quit the /Range Search Replace operation.

This command skips hidden columns but includes cells with a Hidden format.

/Range Trans

Description

The /Range Trans command provides additional flexibility in restructuring a worksheet. It copies data from either a row or column orientation to the opposite orientation; that is, data stored in rows can be copied to columns, and vice versa. Unlike prior releases, Release 2.3 and above copy values in the from range rather than formulas.

Options

The two /Range Trans options control the selection of a range to transpose with either a row or a column orientation. The choice is not made with a menu selection, but rather by specifying a cell range. 1-2-3 interprets this range as having either a row or a column orientation, and produces a to range with the opposite orientation once you select which data you want transposed.

Release 2.2 and above copy the value associated with any cell in the from range, rather than the formula. Earlier releases copied the formula, but would not adjust the formula's references.

/Range Unprot

Description

The /Range Unprot command changes the cell protection characteristics of a range of cells. This command allows entries in the selected cells after Protection is enabled. Unless the /Range Unprot option is used, all worksheet cells have a status of Protected. This means entries cannot be made in the cells once Protection is enabled.

Options

The only option for this command is to select the range to unprotect. You can type the range address, use POINT mode to expand the cell-pointer to include the entire range, or type the range name that you wish to use.

/Range Value

Description

The /Range Value command copies the values of formula cells without copying the formulas. The cells containing the values can be copied to a different range on the worksheet or to the location containing the original formulas. In both cases the cells that receive the data do not contain formulas. They contain only the values resulting from the formulas.

Options

This command provides two options. First, select a range containing the cells with the formulas to be converted. Then select the first cell to which you want to copy the formula's values. Or you can specify the same range for to and from, thus converting the original formulas to their values.

/Worksheet Erase

Description

The /Worksheet Erase command erases the active file from memory. Unless you have Undo enabled or have another copy of the worksheet stored on disk, you will not be able to retrieve the worksheet after using the /Worksheet Erase Yes option.

Options

The command presents a submenu with two options: Yes indicates you want to proceed with the erasure of memory, and No abandons the erase operation. No is the default. In Release 2.2 and above, 1-2-3 presents a second confirmation menu if the worksheet has changed since the Last File Save command.

/Worksheet Global Default Other Expanded-Memory

Description

This command sets how 1-2-3 uses any available expanded memory.

Options

The options for this command allow you to determine how 1-2-3 will handle expanded memory.

Standard   This option sets 1-2-3 to use expanded memory to store only cell contents. This use of expanded memory makes 1-2-3 perform faster than the Enhanced option.

Enhanced   This option sets 1-2-3 to use expanded memory for the entire worksheet. This use of expanded memory allows 1-2-3 to work with larger worksheets than the

Standard option. You can also select this option by selecting the Enhanced expanded memory check box in the /Worksheet Global dialog box (you deselect it to return to Standard, which is the default).

/Worksheet Global Default Other Help

Description

This command sets the Help access method for 1-2-3.

Options

This command has two options, Removable and Instant. Removable, which should be selected if you are using 1-2-3 on a two-disk system, opens the Help file when F1 (HELP) is pressed and closes it when ESC is pressed. Instant opens the Help file the first time F1 (HELP) is pressed and closes it when you exit 1-2-3. You can also select whether the help access method is Instant or Removable by selecting or deselecting the Instant access to help file check box in the /Worksheet Global dialog box.

/Worksheet Global Default Status

Description

The /Worksheet Global Default Status command provides a screen snapshot of the worksheet settings made with /Worksheet Global Default commands. No changes to any of the settings can be made from this screen. Changes can be made to the settings shown in this display through /Worksheet Global Default menu options.

With Release 2.2 and above, the dialog box appears when you enter /Worksheet Global Default.

/Worksheet Global Label-Prefix

Description

The /Worksheet Global Label-Prefix command changes the default label prefix, and therefore changes the default justification (placement in the cell) for all new label entries on the worksheet.

Options

This command has three options: Left, Right, and Center. Left generates a double quotation mark (") as the label prefix; Right generates an apostrophe (') and Center generates a caret (^) at the beginning of each label entry. You can also select the global label prefix by selecting the Left, Right, or Center option box in the /Worksheet Global dialog box.

Note

The /Worksheet Global Label-Prefix command takes a different approach from that of the /Range Label command, which changes the label prefix and justification for existing entries but does not affect new entries into cells within the range. Entries made after the employment of /Range Label use the default label prefix.

/Worksheet Global Protection

Description

The /Worksheet Global Protection command enables Protection for all worksheet cells that have a Protected status or disables Protection for the entire worksheet. The command works with the /Range Prot and /Range Unprot commands to determine which worksheet cells are protected and which are unprotected.

Once Protection has been enabled, you see PR displayed in the control panel when your cell-pointer is in cells that are protected. You cannot make entries in any protected worksheet cells. You cannot make entries in any unprotected worksheet cells. You can continue using 1-2-3 commands that do not affect the entries, such as /Range Format and /Range Unprot.

The color or highlighting created with the /Range Unprot command is maintained. With a color monitor, unprotected cells are highlighted in green, providing a "green light" signaling that you can proceed with entries for that cell. Other cells remain their normal color. With a monochrome display, the unprotected cells are highlighted to indicate that you can make entries in these cells.

Options

This command has two options. The Enable option turns Protection on for the entire worksheet, which allows entries only to those cells that have a status of Unprotected. The second option is Disable, which permits entries to all cells. You can also enable or disable worksheet protection by selecting or deselecting the Protection on check box in the /Worksheet Global dialog box.

/Worksheet Global Recalculation

Description

This command accesses all the recalculation options. With /Worksheet Global Recalculation you can affect the number of recalculations for a worksheet, determine whether recalculation is automatic, and specify the order in which formulas are recalculated.

Options

The options for this command affect three different features of recalculation: Selecting an option box selects the order of recalculation, selecting or deselecting the Automatic check box selects the timing of the recalculation, and typing a number in the text box selects the number of iterations. You can also select recalculation options using the /Worksheet Global dialog box.

Automatic   This option recalculates the worksheet automatically after every worksheet entry. With the more efficient recalculation methods of Release 2.2 and above, only the required recalculations are performed.

Manual   This option turns off the Automatic recalculation feature. When the worksheet uses manual recalculation, the worksheet is only recalculated when you press F9 (CALC) or use the SmartIcon palette option that looks like a calculator.

Natural   This option gives 1-2-3 the responsibility for determining which formula to evaluate first and uses minimal recalculation.

Rowwise   This option disables the Natural recalculation sequence and switches to recalculation by rows.

Columnwise   This option disables the Natural recalculation sequence and switches to recalculation by columns.

Iterations   This option sets the number of times 1-2-3 recalculates circular references formulas. The normal setting for this option is 1.

/Worksheet Status

Description

This command provides a screen snapshot of your current worksheet environment. It allows you to monitor available memory, as well as many of the default worksheet settings. No changes to any of the settings can be made from this screen. Changes to the options that can be altered are made through the /Worksheet Global menu options.

Options

In one sense there are no options for this command because /Worksheet Status has no submenu. A variety of information is presented on the Status screen, however. For releases before 2.3, the status screen tells you the amount of memory, both used and how much is available, the processor, the math coprocessor, recalculation method, recalculation order, number of iterations, the first cell that is part of a circular reference, whether protection is enabled, and the global settings for format, label prefix, column width, and zero display. In Release 2.3 and above, the status screen indicates the conventional and expanded memory used and still available, how 1-2-3 uses expanded memory, the math coprocessor, and the first cell that is part of a circular reference. The other settings are displayed in dialog boxes.

Note

This command is different from the /Worksheet Global Default Status command, which tells you the default settings for each 1-2-3 session.

/Worksheet Titles

Description

The /Worksheet Titles command freezes label information at the top or left side of the screen. This is useful when you have a worksheet that is either wider or longer than the screen. Without the titles frozen on the screen, you would not see any descriptive information as you scroll and move through the worksheet.

The cell-pointer movement keys do not move your cell-pointer to the titles area once it is frozen on the screen. If you want to move there, you must use the F5 (GOTO) key. This displays the title area on the screen twice. When you scroll away from this area, the double view of the titles disappears from the screen.

Options

Both   This option freezes information above and to the left of the cell-pointer on your screen.

Horizontal   This option freezes information above the cell-pointer on your screen.

Vertical   This option freezes information to the left of the cell-pointer on your screen.

Clear   This option frees titles that have been frozen.

/Worksheet Window

Description

The /Worksheet Window command allows you to create two separate windows on your screen. This is an advantage when a worksheet is too large to be viewed on one screen. You can view two different sections of the worksheet through the two windows. The windows' size is controlled by the location of your cell-pointer at the time you request the screen split. When the screen is split vertically, a dividing line replaces one of the worksheet columns; in a horizontal split, the dividing line replaces one of the rows. You can move easily between windows with F6 (WINDOW), which always moves you to the window opposite the one you are in.

Options

Horizontal   This option splits the screen into two horizontal windows. The dividing line is inserted immediately above the cell-pointer.

Vertical   This option splits the screen into two vertical windows. The dividing line is inserted immediately to the left of the cell-pointer.

Sync   This option causes scrolling in the two windows to be synchronized—that is, when you scroll in one window, the other window automatically scrolls along with it. This is the default setting when you create a second window.

Unsync   This option allows you to scroll in one window while the other window remains stationary.

Clear   This option removes the second window from the screen. The window that remains is the top window when the split was horizontal and the left window when the split was vertical.

Note

When Wysiwyg is loaded, you can create windows with the mouse. To create a window, move the mouse pointer to the upper left-corner of the worksheet frame and drag the mouse in the horizontal or vertical direction where you want the window split. As you drag the mouse, 1-2-3 draws a line to display where the window will split. When you release the mouse button, 1-2-3 splits the worksheet into two windows at the selected location. You can change the position of the split by dragging the upper-left corner of the worksheet frame for the second window to a new location. To close a second window, drag the upper-left corner of the worksheet frame so the second window is on top of the first.

Chapter 6

Printing with 1-2-3 and Wysiwyg

Working with your models on the screen is great if you want to make changes and see their immediate impact. But when you have to go to a meeting and reference these same numbers, the screen in your office is no help. Fortunately, 1-2-3 Release 2.4 has extensive print features that allow you to create anything from a quick hard copy of important figures to a professional-looking, multipage report.

If you have an early release of 1-2-3 without Wysiwyg, you will find 1-2-3's print features adequate for your needs; you will not need to print with Wysiwyg's fancy formatting. If you are using Wysiwyg with 1-2-3, you can still use 1-2-3's print features to get a quick draft, but you will want to use Wysiwyg for creating a final printout. To print your worksheet with your Wysiwyg formatting, you must print with Wysiwyg. If you print using 1-2-3, none of the Wysiwyg-controlled formatting features will appear.

Preparation for using the print features of 1-2-3 begins when you install 1-2-3. The installation process creates a driver configuration file that can speak the correct language for your particular printer. You can install up to four printers to use with 1-2-3.

In this chapter, you will work with the 1-2-3 and Wysiwyg commands related to printing. In addition to 1-2-3's Print menu commands, you will learn about other 1-2-3/Worksheet commands that affect printing. By the time you finish this chapter, you should have mastered simple printing tasks, and you should also be familiar with the more advanced print options that Wysiwyg's menu provides.

173

Printing Terminology

Before trying to use print features, you will want to learn the terms that refer to the layout of a page and other print options. Since the same terms are used in both 1-2-3 and Wysiwyg, the printing tasks that you learn in this section can be used regardless of which way you choose to print. Later in this chapter, you will learn to define the settings that affect these print features.

Page Layout Options

Page layout refers to the placement of data and white space on a printed page. Good choices make your material more readable and more effective in conveying your message. In this section, you will learn the correct terminology for defining a page in either Wysiwyg or 1-2-3. You will learn about headers and footers, margins, and other page layout options.

Header and Footer Special Characters

Several characters are essential to creating headers and footers: the vertical bar (|), the at sign (@), the pound sign (#), and the backslash (\). The |, @, and # can be combined with each other and with other text, but not with the \. The cell referenced after the \ can contain the other special characters.

The | character divides the header or footer into three sections. For example, if you enter the header **Accounting Department|Texas Company|Rpt: 8976**, the department name is printed on the left, the company name in the center, and the report identification number on the right.

The @ character represents the current system date.

The # character represents the current page number.

The \ character is followed by a cell address. 1-2-3 then uses the cell's contents for the header and footer. For example, if cell A3 contained

Acme Company—Toy Division|Page #|@

the header entry **\A3** would place "Acme Company—Toy Division" on the left side of the header, the page number in the middle section, and the date at the far right.

Creating Headers and Footers

Headers and footers are lines of text printed at the top and bottom, respectively, of every page of your report. A header or footer may be, for example, a date, company name, report name, department, page number, or a combination of these elements. Except for page numbers, these elements are the same for each page.

Both 1-2-3 and Wysiwyg allow you to use a header and footer of 240 characters each. You can divide both headers and footers into separate segments for the right, left, and center sections of each line. These capabilities allow you to place more than one information element in a header or footer. With 1-2-3 and Wysiwyg, all of the information for a header or footer must fit on one line, so you must consider your line length when planning the contents of a header or footer.

Headers and footers in 1-2-3 are specified through the /Print Printer Options Header and Footer commands or by making entries in the Header or Footer text boxes in the Print Settings dialog box. In Wysiwyg you will use :Print Layout Titles to add or change a header or footer.

Using Special Characters in a Header or Footer

Headers and footers can use four special characters. The special characters you use in headers and footers are summarized in the "Header and Footer Special Characters" box.

To separate the information you are entering into each section of the header or footer, use the vertical bar character (|). Any spaces included between the vertical bars are counted as characters to be included in the heading, and they affect the alignment of the heading sections. For example, to create the heading shown in Figure 6-1, enter

```
Adams & Associates||Rpt. No. 1234
```

```
Adams & Associates                                      Rpt. No. 1234


Description                     Life         Cost Dept
IBM Selectric Typewriter          5          $980 Accounting
Royal Typewriter                  5          $950 Training
Swivel Chair                     10          $345 Check
TI Calculator                     7          $100 Audit
Walnut Desk                      15        $1,200 Cash
Xerox Copier                      3        $2,500 Cash
Xerox Copier                      3        $2,800 Accounting
```

Figure 6-1.   A printout with a header

With Release 2.2 and above and using Wysiwyg, you can retrieve information stored in a worksheet cell for a header or footer. After storing the data in the cell, use the /Print Printer Options Header command and then type a backslash (\) followed by the cell address or range name containing the header characters. For example, if the information you want to use for the header is stored in Z2, you would enter \Z2 in response to the prompt for the header entry. When you use a cell reference for the header or footer, you cannot use the other special header and footer characters. The contents of the cell that you reference, however, can include special header or footer characters; 1-2-3 and Wysiwyg treat the cell's entry just as if you had entered it in the menu prompt for a header or footer.

The pound sign (#) represents the location where you want to add a page number. 1-2-3 page numbering begins with 1 and automatically increments the number for each page. Use the at sign (@) to represent where you would like 1-2-3 to place the current date. 1-2-3 uses the system date, which is stored in your computer's memory. The only way to change this date is to access the DOS DATE command, enter a new date, and then use EXIT to return to 1-2-3. (See Chapter 8 for more information on changing the system date using /System.)

The # and @ characters can be entered in any header or footer segment and can be combined with other text, such as Page No: or Today's Date:. As an example, if you enter the header **Today's Date: @|Page#|Rpt. No. 1234**, the resulting header will look like the top of Figure 6-2.

To automatically date-stamp every page of output you create, use @ to represent the current date in either a header or footer on every worksheet printed.

```
Today's Date: 15-Apr-92          Page 1                    Rpt. No. 1234


Description                 Life          Cost Dept
IBM Selectric Typewriter      5          $980 Accounting
Royal Typewriter              5          $950 Training
Swivel Chair                 10          $345 Check
TI Calculator                 7          $100 Audit
Walnut Desk                  15        $1,200 Cash
Xerox Copier                  3        $2,500 Cash
Xerox Copier                  3        $2,800 Accounting
```

Figure 6-2.   *A printout with a header that includes the date and page number*

Page Size

Neither Wysiwyg nor 1-2-3 can check your printer to determine what size paper is loaded for use. You must determine the size of paper you wish to print on and tell these programs so they can fit the correct amount of information on the page. If you print on a legal-size sheet of paper, with a smaller paper size defined, the full page will not be used. If you try printing on a smaller page with the legal paper size defined, your data will run off the edge of the page.

Wysiwyg specifies page size in inches, just as you probably do. You can choose from one of seven standard paper sizes, or you can specify the measurements of a custom paper size for Wysiwyg, as explained later in this chapter.

1-2-3 defines paper size differently. With 1-2-3, you define how many lines of text will fit on the page, which tells 1-2-3 how long the page is. 1-2-3 can figure this out because normally it uses one default font and a standard setting of six print lines per inch. With 1-2-3, you do not define the width of the page in inches, either. Instead, you specify the margins of the page and 1-2-3 figures out its width, as described in the next section.

Margins

Margins control the amount of white space at the top, bottom, and sides of your printed document. A graphic representation of the page layout, including margins, can be seen in Figure 6-3. To print a narrow range of cells, for example, you can increase the side margin settings to center the output on the paper. To spread a great deal of data across a page, you can use very small side margin settings. You can set the margins separately for the left, right, top, and bottom of pages.

With Wysiwyg you define margins in inches. On standard letter-size paper, 8 1/2 by 11 inches, the usual margins are 1 inch on each side. The worksheet itself only prints in the 6 1/2- by 9-inch area in the middle, evenly surrounded by the margins. The margins, as you can see, measure how far from the edge of the paper the printing can start.

1-2-3 defines top and bottom margins as the number of lines it cannot use on a page. 1-2-3 uses left and right margins to determine the width of the paper in terms of characters. 1-2-3 does not need to know the actual physical width of the paper. It only needs to know where it can print characters. For the left margin, you tell 1-2-3 how many character spaces from the left edge of the paper you want the first character to appear. For example, for a 1-inch left margin, you would set a left margin of 10, since 10 characters of the default font fit in 1 inch. To calculate the right margin, decide how many characters you want to print on a line. Add that number to the left margin count and enter the sum as the right margin. 1-2-3 does not care how many character spaces are left between the last character and the right edge of the paper. It only wants to know where to put the first character in the line, and how many characters it can print for each line.

In Wysiwyg, you set margins with the :Print Layout Margins command. In 1-2-3, margins are set with the /Print Printer Options Margins command.

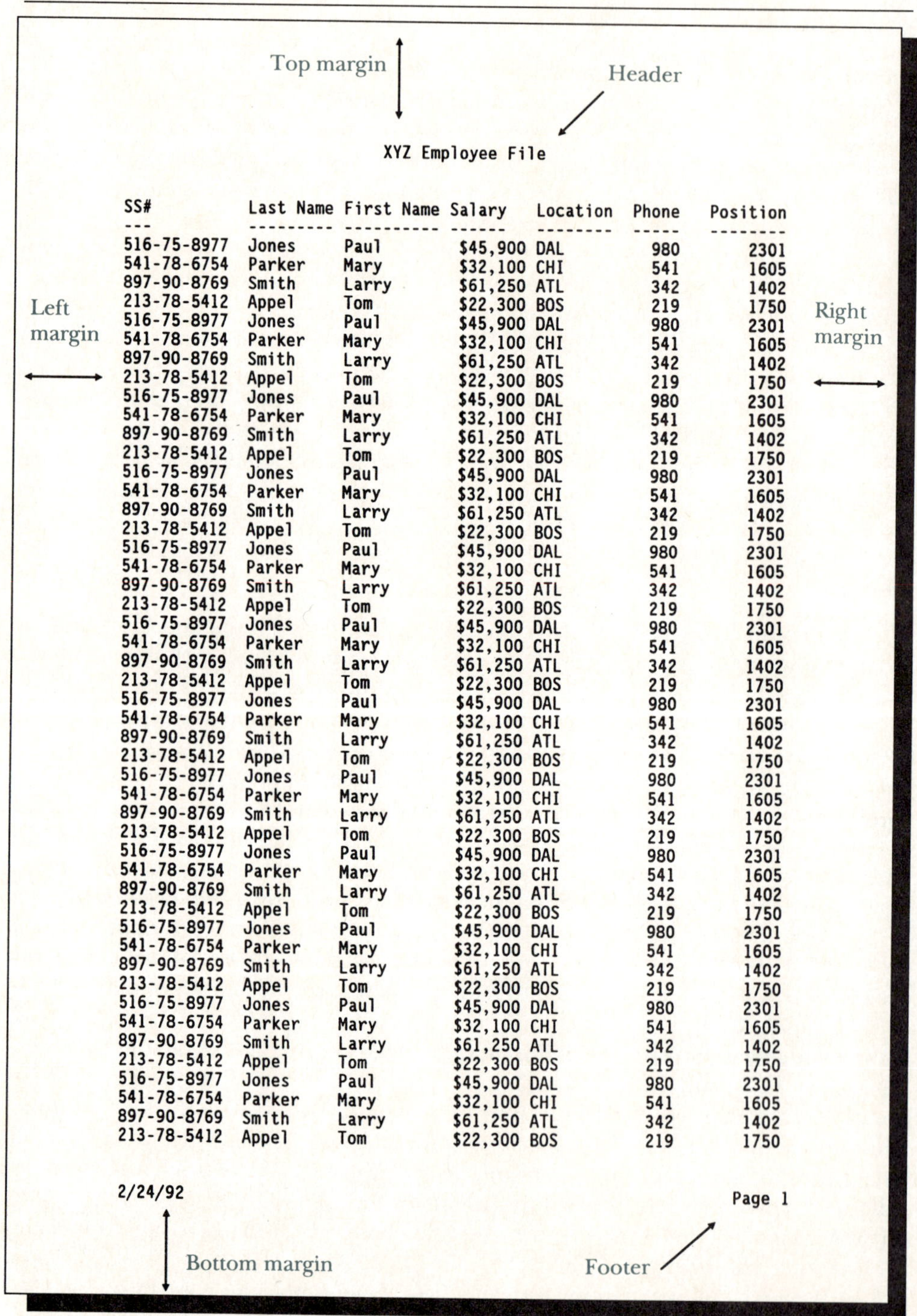

Figure 6-3.   *The page layout*

Borders

You can include the identifying information found at the top of columns and at the left side of rows in your worksheet on every printed page of a report. These cells are called *borders* since they border the data in the worksheet. The information in the borders might be account names or other identifying descriptions. When you print borders, you print descriptive information on each page of a multipage report rather than at the top and sides of only the first page. The descriptive information may be in columns, rows, or both.

This feature is useful if you have used the months of the year as column heads across the worksheet, for example, and have more data than can fit on one printed page. You can print the worksheet with these column heads at the top of each page, if the row containing the months is specified as a border. Similarly, if your report is wider than it is long, you can print the information found at the far left of your worksheet on every page of your report. In Figure 6-4, you can see a report that is three pages wide, listing expenses for the Boston Company for the year. Without the border, the information on the second and third pages would be confusing. When you include the first column as a border on the remaining pages, you make the report much easier to understand.

In Wysiwyg, borders are set with :Print Layout Borders. In 1-2-3, you set borders with /Print Printer Options Borders.

Print Options

You have learned about the settings that control the way your worksheet prints out on a sheet of paper. Next, you need to know about the choices you'll have when printing with both 1-2-3 and Wysiwyg. These choices include your print destination, the range of the worksheet you are printing, and other print options.

Print Destination

You can choose the destination of your printed output. You must decide whether you want the information sent directly to your printer or written to a disk file. With 1-2-3 Releases 2.3 and 2.4, you have four print destination options: the printer, an ASCII file, an encoded file, or an encoded file to print in the background. Earlier releases of 1-2-3 offer only the first two options. With Wysiwyg, you can print to the printer, to an encoded file, or to an encoded file to print in the background.

When you want to save the 1-2-3 output to a file for use by another program, you choose to print to a file. This file is simply the raw data in the ASCII format. No printer codes are included. In Releases 2.3 and above, both Wysiwyg and 1-2-3 let you print to an encoded file, one which includes printer codes for your printer. Printer codes are the codes used to tell the printer when to advance to the next line or where to make the text boldface. With 1-2-3 Release 2.4, you can print to an encapsulated Postscript file (.EPS file) if you have the proper printer driver installed and selected.

```
                                         Boston Company

                              JAN       FEB       MAR       APR
Salaries                    $8,000    $8,200    $8,200    $8,700
Building Operations          1,100     1,100     1,100     1,100
Travel                         850       850       850       850
Supplies                       500       500       500       500
Depreciation                 1,200     1,200     1,200     1,200
Equipment Maintenance          750       750       750       750
Shipping Expense               400       400       400       400
Data Processing Costs        2,100     2,100     2,100     2,100
Printing & Duplicating         640       640       640       640
Other                        1,030     1,030     1,030     1,030
Total Expenses             $16,570   $16,770   $16,770   $17,270
```

```
                              MAY      JUNE      JULY       AUG
Salaries                    $8,700    $7,500    $7,500   $10,000
Building Operations          1,100     1,100     1,100     1,100
Travel                         850       850       850       850
Supplies                       500       500       500       500
Depreciation                 1,200     1,200     1,200     1,200
Equipment Maintenance          750       750       750       750
Shipping Expense               400       400       400       400
Data Processing Costs        2,100     2,100     2,100     2,100
Printing & Duplicating         640       640       640       640
Other                        1,030     1,030     1,030     1,030
Total Expenses             $17,270   $16,070   $16,070   $18,570
```

```
                             SEPT       OCT       NOV       DEC
Salaries                   $10,000   $10,000   $10,000   $10,000
Building Operations          1,300     1,300     1,300     1,300
Travel                         850       850       850       850
Supplies                       500       500       500       500
Depreciation                 1,200     1,200     1,200     1,200
Equipment Maintenance          750       750       750       750
Shipping Expense               400       400       400       400
Data Processing Costs        2,100     2,100     2,100     2,100
Printing & Duplicating         640       640       640       640
Other                        1,030     1,030     1,030     1,030
Total Expenses             $18,770   $18,770   $18,770   $18,770
```

Figure 6-4.   *Three pages of print output using a border at the left edge*

You can also print to the background with 1-2-3 Releases 2.3 and 2.4. When you print to the background, you print your worksheet to an encoded file that prints in the background while you continue to use 1-2-3 or Wysiwyg. The correct information can be read into a file by these programs much faster than your printer can accept the information. Printing in the background reduces the time you spend waiting for a worksheet to print. Now you can get on with your work and take the printout when it is done. If you plan to print in the background with either Wysiwyg or 1-2-3, you need to start the BPrint program before starting 1-2-3. The BPrint program is the program both 1-2-3 and Wysiwyg use for the background printing feature. You cannot load BPrint into memory by selecting the /System command to access the DOS prompt. If you want to print in the background, but do not have BPrint loaded, you may have to exit 1-2-3, load BPrint, and reload 1-2-3. BPrint is the program that actually handles the process of printing while you return to using 1-2-3 and Wysiwyg. If BPrint has not been loaded, you will receive an error message when you attempt to print in the background.

Print Range

Whether you are printing to your printer or to a disk file, you must decide which worksheet cells you want to print. You must specify the range of cells you want to print for 1-2-3 or Wysiwyg. The range of cells you want to print is known as the *print range.* The cells you want to print must be in one contiguous range on the worksheet.

When the print range includes long labels that extend beyond their cells, you must include in the range the cells from which the labels borrow space. This keeps the labels from being truncated in the printout. For example, if G4 contains "Date of Report: March 16, 1990" and the cell width is 9, the label uses G4, H4, and I4 for its display. If all three cells are not included in the print range, 1-2-3 or Wysiwyg prints only the portion of the label that appears in the selected range.

Page Breaks

Both Wysiwyg and 1-2-3 can add page breaks to a worksheet to control the way a large print range is divided into pages. By setting manual page breaks, you can keep information on one page without having to print different sections of the worksheet separately. With Wysiwyg, you can create both horizontal page breaks, which define the bottom of the page, and vertical page breaks, which define the right edge of the page. With 1-2-3, you can create only horizontal page breaks.

Wysiwyg Printing Process (Releases 2.3 and 2.4)

1-2-3 Releases 2.3 and 2.4 come with the Wysiwyg Add-in. Wysiwyg adds professional spreadsheet publishing abilities to 1-2-3. Since 1-2-3 cannot print the formatting added with Wysiwyg, you will want to use Wysiwyg for most of your printing if you are using either Release 2.3 or 2.4. You may use 1-2-3 to print a draft of your worksheet data, since it is quicker, but Wysiwyg is the package that you will use to create professional-looking printouts of your worksheets and graphs.

The basic printing process is quite simple. You need to define the range of cells you want to print and then send them to the printer. Wysiwyg adds all the printer codes that tell the printer to include the different formatting features, such as fonts, shadowing, and colors (if your printer supports colors). Wysiwyg also supports options that let you customize your printing process with much greater sophistication. All Wysiwyg print options are accessed through the :Print menu. Many can also be accessed with the Print Settings dialog box shown in Figure 6-5.

Setting the Print Range

The first step in printing is deciding what you want to print. Once you decide, you must define this range to Wysiwyg as the print range. Wysiwyg prints both text within cells and any graphs or graphic images. You will learn about adding graphs to worksheets for printing with Wysiwyg in Chapter 11, "Working with Graphics Features."

To set the print range, select :Print Range Set. You can either type the range or point to it with the mouse or keyboard. Selecting it before requesting the command is also an option. You can set only one print range at a time. If you set a new range, the old range is automatically cleared.

To see how setting up a print range and printing it works in Wysiwyg, assume that you want to print the first quarter's information from the worksheet shown in Figure

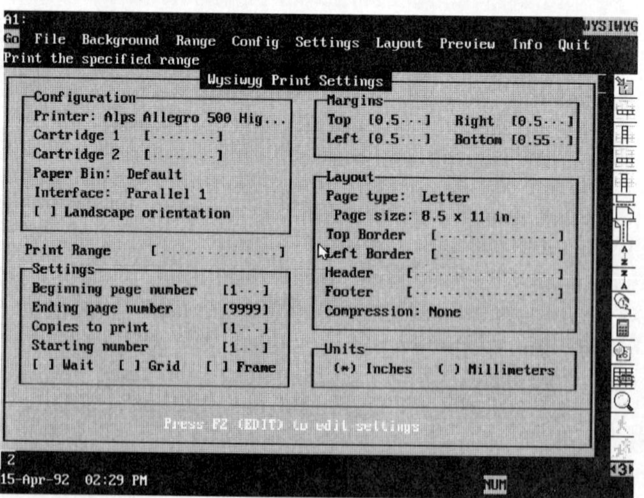

Figure 6-5.   *Wysiwyg's Print Settings dialog box*

6-6. Since you have never printed from this worksheet before, Wysiwyg assumes that the first cell in the print range is the current cell-pointer location. Follow these steps:

1. Position the cell-pointer on cell A6.

2. Type **:PR** to access the Print Range menu.

3. Type **S** to access the Set option.

4. Type a period (**.**) to lock the beginning of the range in place at A6.

5. Move to the end of the information in column A by pressing END followed by the DOWN ARROW twice.

6. Press RIGHT ARROW five times to move to the end of the print range.
    The labels on the left edge of the worksheet and the data for the first three months should be highlighted.

7. Press ENTER to tell Wysiwyg that the range has been selected.

8. Assuming that all of the default settings are acceptable, check to make sure that the printer is turned on and the paper is aligned properly; then select Go from the Print menu.

When you specify a Wysiwyg print range, the range is surrounded by a dotted-line box, as shown in Figure 6-7. If the print range spans multiple pages, an additional dotted line indicates page divisions. Anything that displays within the dotted box will

		JAN	FEB	MAR	APR
					Boston Company
7	Salaries	$8,000	$8,200	$8,200	$8,700
8	Building Operations	1,100	1,100	1,100	1,100
9	Travel	850	850	850	850
10	Supplies	500	500	500	500
11	Depreciation	1,200	1,200	1,200	1,200
12	Equipment Maintenance	750	750	750	750
13	Shipping Expense	400	400	400	400
14	Data Processing Costs	2,100	2,100	2,100	2,100
15	Printing & Duplicating	640	640	640	640
16	Other	1,030	1,030	1,030	1,030
17	Total Expenses	$16,570	$16,770	$16,770	$17,270

20-Apr-92   04:17 PM

Figure 6-6.   Worksheet data for printing

print. Anything outside the box will not appear on the printout. This means that a long label that extends outside the box will not appear in its entirety on the printout.

Printing Your Worksheet

Once you have set the print range, you must simply choose Go to send the range to your printer. Wysiwyg also offers other destinations that you can choose, or you may want to customize the layout with the options described in the next section rather than printing immediately.

Wysiwyg presents three options on the :Print menu that control the print destination. These options are Go, File, and Background. If you select one of these options before specifying a print range, an error message displays indicating that no print range has been selected, which means that Wysiwyg does not know what to print. After you have selected one of these options, the selected print range is printed to the destination you selected.

- Select :Print Go when you want to print to the currently selected printer. If you want to print to another printer, you have to select the printer using the commands discussed in the section "Setting Printer Configurations" later in this chapter.

- Select :Print File when you want to print your print range to an encoded file. An encoded file includes both the raw data and the codes that are sent to the printer indicating how to format that raw data using Wysiwyg's formatting. Every printer uses different codes, so the encoded file can be printed only on

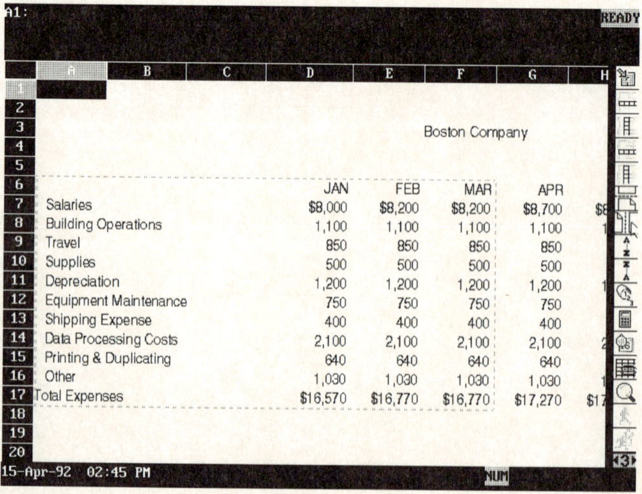

Figure 6-7.   *Wysiwyg marks the print range*

your printer or one just like it. However, you do not need either 1-2-3 or Wysiwyg to print this file. For example, imagine that you do not have a laser printer, but your business associate does; she does not have 1-2-3 or Wysiwyg, however. When you install 1-2-3, you can install the laser printer that your associate uses, even though you do not have one attached to your system. You can print an encoded file with that printer selected, take the encoded file to the other system, and copy the encoded file to the laser printer using the DOS COPY command. This way, you can create a final copy of your document on a laser printer.

Select :Print Background when you want to print your worksheet to an encoded file that prints while you continue working with 1-2-3. By printing in the background, you are increasing your productivity; you can continue working instead of waiting for the file to print. Remember, for background printing, you must load BPrint before starting 1-2-3.

Previewing Your Printed Output

After setting the print range, you can preview how the page will print. You might want to do this to check that you set all the page layout settings correctly. When you choose the command :Print Preview, Wysiwyg displays a graphic representation of the page you have set up. This includes the data that appears in the print range, titles, borders, and other features. When you are finished looking at the preview of the printed page, press ESC.

If you are printing multiple pages, you can view each of the pages by pressing the PGUP and PGDN keys. Pressing the PGUP key displays the previous page, and pressing the PGDN key displays the next page.

Boston Company			
First Quarter Expenses			
	JAN	**FEB**	**MAR**
Salaries	$8,000	$8,200	$8,200
Building Operations	1,100	1,100	1,100
Travel	850	850	850
Supplies	500	500	500
Depreciation	1,200	1,200	1,200
Equipment Maintenance	750	750	750
Shipping Expense	400	400	400
Data Processing Costs	2,100	2,100	2,100
Printing & Duplicating	640	640	640
Other	1,030	1,030	1,030
Total Expenses	$16,570	$16,770	$16,770

Figure 6-8.   *The Print Preview screen*

If you want to look at a page more closely, press F6 {WINDOW} and then press +. The display of the page enlarges. You can see an enlarged print preview display in Figure 6-8. If you want to move to an area of the page that no longer appears on the screen because the page is enlarged, use the arrow keys to move to that area on the page. You can press the + key to continue enlarging the screen up to ten times its original size. When you want to reduce the screen size, press the – key.

Page Layout Options

Before you prepare to print, you may want to lay out the page. When you lay out the pages to print, you can choose a paper size, define the margins, add headers and footers, and specify a border to print on every page, if needed. With Wysiwyg, you can also save a page layout in a file, which you can then recall to use for other worksheets that would use the same page layout. Alternatively, you can revert to the default page layout if you decide that you do not want to use the page layout you have created, or you can create a new default layout. You do not need to use all of these features for a page layout, but they are all available.

The print layout features are accessed by selecting the :Print Layout command. This menu is a sticky menu, which means that you must select Quit to leave it. You can also enter many of the Print Layout options directly into the Print Settings dialog box.

Choosing a Unit of Measurement

You can choose to enter measurements for print settings in Wysiwyg in either inches or millimeters. Specify the unit of measurement you want to use in the Print Settings dialog box. Select either the Inches or the Millimeters option button in the Unit section of the dialog box.

Setting the Paper Size

The :Print Layout Page-Size command specifies the size of paper on which you are printing your worksheet. This command does not actually affect the paper in the printer, but it controls the settings Wysiwyg uses for printing on the paper. After selecting this command, you can choose one of eight options listed. Wysiwyg supports seven standard page sizes and one custom option that lets you define the size of the page. The eight options are summarized in Table 6-1.

Creating a Custom Paper Size   Select the :Print Layout Page-Size Custom command when you are printing on paper that is not one of the standard page-size options. After you select this command, Wysiwyg prompts you for the width of the paper. After you type the width and press ENTER, Wysiwyg prompts for the length. Type the length and press ENTER. Wysiwyg uses the custom paper size you specify for

No.	Name	English	Metric
1	Ltr	8.5" x 11"	216mm x 270mm
2	A4	8.268" x 11.693"	210mm x 297mm
3	80 x 66	8" x 11"	203mm x 270mm
4	132 x 66	13.2" x 11"	335mm x 270mm
5	80 x 72	8" x 12"	203mm x 305mm
6	Legal	8.5" x 14"	216mm x 356mm
7	B5	6.929" x 9.843"	176mm x 250mm
	Custom		

Table 6-1.   Page Size Options in Wysiwyg

printing until you select another page size option. You need to redefine the custom page size each time you select Custom.

You can also set the paper size using the dialog box. When you select Page Type in the dialog box, a pop-up menu box appears, showing the eight page types. Select the appropriate one, and press ENTER. If you select Custom, you are prompted for the width and length of the page in another pop-up dialog box. Respond and press OK twice to return to the Print Settings dialog box.

Specifying Margin Measurements

The :Print Layout Margins command controls the size of the margins. The four Margins options are Left, Right, Top, and Bottom. The Margins menu is a sticky menu, which means that you return to this menu after specifying margin widths. Each margin is set separately, using the currently selected Print Settings measuring system. Select the margin that you wish to define. Then type the margin size you want to use and press ENTER. When you are finished setting all of the margin measurements, select Quit to return to the main :Print Layout menu. You can also set the margins by entering the margin measurements in the Left, Right, Top, and Bottom text boxes under Margins in the Print Settings dialog box.

Adding Titles: Headers and Footers

When you want to create a header or footer or to clear the ones that you previously created, select the :Print Layout Titles command. You can select the options Header, Footer, or Clear from this menu to alter the settings for your header or footer. Select Clear to remove any previously set headers or footers. When you select Header or Footer, you are prompted to enter the text of the title. You can use any of the special features described in the "Header and Footer Special Characters" box earlier in this chapter. These include using a cell address to reference a header or footer stored on the worksheet, using special characters to print in three different sections of the header or footer, and listing a date or page number. The :Print Layout Titles menu is a sticky one, so you need to select Quit to return to the :Print Layout menu.

You can also enter the header and footer by typing them into the Header and Footer text boxes in the Layout section of the Print Settings dialog box. Again, you can use any of the features described previously when entering the header or footer.

Using Borders for Clarity

As you learned earlier in this chapter, borders are rows or columns that are printed on each page to describe the detail entries on the page. You can include borders at the top or the left of the page by selecting the :Print Layout Borders command; choose Left or Top to indicate the border you want to specify. After making the selection, you are prompted to set the range to use as the border. You need to select a range that includes at least one cell from each of the rows or columns that you want to use as part of the border. Figure 6-9 shows a border being set. If you are using only one row, you only need to specify one cell.

You can also enter the range that you want to use for the borders into the Top Border or Left Border text boxes in the Print Settings dialog box. The advantage to using the menu command is that you can see the worksheet and use the pointing method of specifying which columns and rows you want to use for borders, instead of having to remember them.

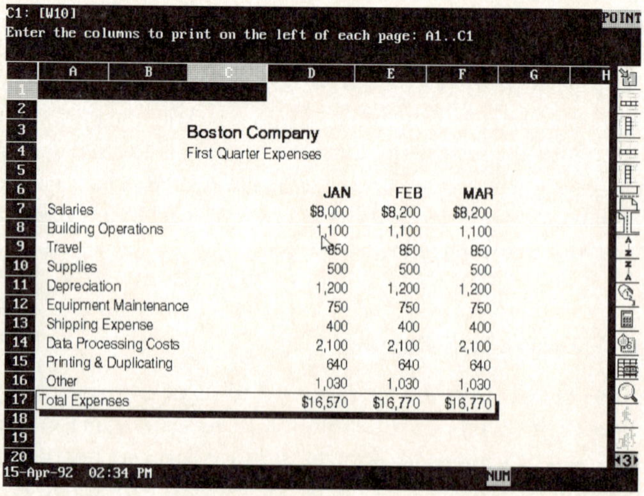

Figure 6-9.   *Entering the columns for the border*

When you want to clear the borders, you can delete the contents of the Top Border or Left Border text boxes in the Print Settings dialog box, or you can select the command :Print Layout Borders Clear. When you select this command, you can choose to clear the contents of the Top, Left, or Both borders. Select the border you wish to clear.

Compressing Your Printout

At times, you may find that you want to change the amount of space that your worksheet and graphics takes on the printed page. You might find that you want to get all of the information used to create a graph on the same page as the graph. To fit all of the information on one page, you can change the font size and other options to control how much room the data takes on the printed page, or you can change the compression with which the print range is printed. By using the :Print Layout Compression command, you can reduce or enlarge the size of the print range not by including or excluding cells, but by shrinking or expanding the characters and charts within the print range. When you alter the compression rate, you define the percentage by which Wysiwyg either reduces or expands your data. You can see in Figure 6-10 how the worksheet shown in Figure 6-4, which required three pages to print, can be compressed to fit on one page.

You can choose either Automatic or Manual compression. When you choose Automatic, Wysiwyg compresses the print range to print on a single page. Wysiwyg can only reduce the print range by a factor of seven. If you want to print a range more than seven times as large as the page, you will need to rearrange the data or use a larger page.

When you select the Manual option, you can set the rate of compression precisely. The degree of compression is expressed in percentages. Therefore, 100 means that the text is not compressed at all. Numbers larger than 100 enlarge the print range so that it uses more room than normal on your page. Numbers smaller than 100 reduce the printed size of the print range. You can specify a compression rate between 15 and 1,000, which equals 15 percent to 1000 percent.

Boston Company

	JAN	FEB	MAR	APR	MAY	JUNE	JULY	AUG	SEPT	OCT	NOV	DEC
Salaries	$8,000	$8,200	$8,200	$8,700	$8,700	$7,500	$7,500	$10,000	$10,000	$10,000	$10,000	$10,000
Building Operations	1,100	1,100	1,100	1,100	1,100	1,100	1,100	1,100	1,300	1,300	1,300	1,300
Travel	850	850	850	850	850	850	850	850	850	850	850	850
Supplies	500	500	500	500	500	500	500	500	500	500	500	500
Depreciation	1,200	1,200	1,200	1,200	1,200	1,200	1,200	1,200	1,200	1,200	1,200	1,200
Equipment Maintenance	750	750	750	750	750	750	750	750	750	750	750	750
Shipping Expense	400	400	400	400	400	400	400	400	400	400	400	400
Data Processing Costs	2,100	2,100	2,100	2,100	2,100	2,100	2,100	2,100	2,100	2,100	2,100	2,100
Printing & Duplicating	640	640	640	640	640	640	640	640	640	640	640	640
Other	1,030	1,030	1,030	1,030	1,030	1,030	1,030	1,030	1,030	1,030	1,030	1,030
Total Expenses	$16,570	$16,770	$16,770	$17,270	$17,270	$16,070	$16,070	$18,570	$18,770	$18,770	$18,770	$18,770

Figure 6-10.   *One page of a printout that uses three pages when uncompressed*

Select the Clear option when you want to remove any compression setting from the print range. You may want to print using compression for a summary report, and then print the full report at the full size for detailed work later. Selecting Clear will quickly return the compression rate to 100, which is full-size.

Restoring the Default

As you customize the page layout settings of a print range, you override the original default settings. The original default settings are designed to be useful for most people most of the time. When you want to return to the default settings, you do not have to reset each of the page layout features individually. Instead, select the :Print Layout Default Restore command. When you select this command, all of the page layout options are reset to the default settings.

If you must frequently customize the page layout in the same fashion, you may prefer to change the default settings to match how you print with 1-2-3 worksheets. When you change the defaults, the new settings you specify appear each time you start 1-2-3, and these are the settings restored when you select the :Print Layout Default Restore command. To change the defaults, first create the set of page layout settings that you would like to use as the default. Then select :Print Layout Default Update. The current settings become the default settings.

Creating a Layout Library File

The :Print Layout Library lets you create, retrieve, or erase a file that contains settings for the layout features. By creating such a layout library file, you can standardize the appearance of your printed worksheets and reports by using the same settings for all of your printed worksheets. When you retrieve a layout library file, all of the print layout settings are set to the settings saved in the file.

To create a layout library file, specify all of the page layout settings. Then select the :Print Layout Library Save command. Enter the name for the layout library file. Do not add a filename extension; Wysiwyg adds an .ALS extension to mark it as a layout library file.

When you want to retrieve a layout library file, select the :Print Layout Library Retrieve command. Highlight the name of the file you want to retrieve and press ENTER. You can delete a layout library file by selecting the :Print Layout Library Erase command and then selecting the name of the file you want to delete.

Adding Manual Page Breaks

One command that can change the appearance of your document is found on the :Worksheet menu rather than on the :Print menu. When you want to insert manual page breaks to tell Wysiwyg where you want to start a new page, you must position the cell pointer at the location where you want the page break and then select the :Worksheet Page command. This command presents you with four options. You can select Row to insert a horizontal page break, Column to insert a vertical page break, or Delete to remove page breaks from your worksheet. Since the :Worksheet Page menu is sticky, the fourth option is Quit, which you can select to return to Ready mode.

The exact position of the page break is determined by the cell pointer location and your selection of Row or Column. When you select Row, a horizontal page break is inserted above the row that your cell pointer is in. This means that the row your cell pointer is positioned in when you select this command is the first row of the new page. When you select Column, the vertical page break appears on the left of the current cell, making the column your cell pointer is in the first column in the new page. In Figure 6-11, you can see Wysiwyg's page break markers, which are dotted lines. The cell pointer has not been moved since the page breaks were inserted, so the current cell will appear in the upper left corner of that page of the printout.

When you want to delete the page breaks inserted with Wysiwyg, you select :Print Page Delete after positioning your cell pointer so that the page break you want to delete is above or to the left of the cell pointer. Any page breaks to the left of or above the cell that the cell pointer is positioned in are deleted.

Setting Printer Configurations

The :Print Config menu commands control the printer to which you are printing the currently selected print range. With these commands, you can specify which type of printer you are using, the port to which the printer is attached to your computer, any font cartridges or cards your printer might have installed, the orientation of the

	F	G	H	I	J	K	L	M
3	Boston Company							
5	MAR	APR	MAY	JUNE	JULY	AUG	SEPT	OCT
6	$8,200	$8,700	$8,700	$7,500	$7,500	$10,000	$10,000	$10,000
7	1,100	1,100	1,100	1,100	1,100	1,100	1,300	1,300
8	850	850	850	850	850	850	850	850
9	500	500	500	500	500	500	500	500
10	1,200	1,200	1,200	1,200	1,200	1,200	1,200	1,200
11	750	750	750	750	750	750	750	750
12	400	400	400	400	400	400	400	400
13	2,100	2,100	2,100	2,100	2,100	2,100	2,100	2,100
14	640	640	640	640	640	640	640	640
15	1,030	1,030	1,030	1,030	1,030	1,030	1,030	1,030
16	$16,770	$17,270	$17,270	$16,070	$16,070	$18,570	$18,770	$18,770

Figure 6-11.   Wysiwyg's page breaks are marked

printing (portrait or landscape), and the bin from which the printer is pulling the paper. By configuring the printer, you make maximum use of the printer features available to you. The :Print Config menu is a sticky menu, so you need to select Quit to return to the :Print menu.

Choosing a Printer

The first step in configuring a printer is to determine which printer you are using. When you select a printer, you are selecting the printer driver file that Wysiwyg uses in printing. The printer driver file includes all of the codes that Wysiwyg uses to tell the computer what to do. If you select the wrong print driver, Wysiwyg and the printer will be speaking different languages to each other, which means that your printout will be garbled, at best.

Use the :Print Config Printer command to select the printer driver you want to use. The printer drivers available are the ones you installed when you installed 1-2-3 and Wysiwyg. If you find that the printer driver for the printer that you are using is not installed, you must exit 1-2-3 and reactivate 1-2-3's install program at the DOS prompt. If you have a hard drive, use the copy of 1-2-3 that is on your hard drive. Select the options that allow you to modify your printer driver set and add the printer drivers for your current printer. If the printer driver that you want to use is already installed, you should highlight it in the Printer List pop-up dialog box that appears when you select the :Print Config Printer command, and then press ENTER. You can also choose the printer driver using the Print Settings dialog box. Select Printer under Configuration, and a Printer List pop-up dialog box appears. Select your printer driver from that dialog box.

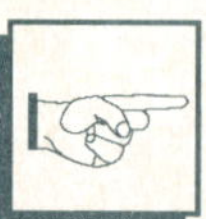

In 1-2-3 Release 2.4, you can create an encapsulated Postscript file (.EPS file) by installing the .EPS driver and then selecting it before printing to a file with Wysiwyg. You can use this .EPS file with any of the desktop publishing programs.

Setting the Printer Interface   After determining what type of printer you are using, you need to tell Wysiwyg where it is. Wysiwyg locates a printer by finding out which port the printer is attached to. When you select the :Print Config Interface command, you are presented with eight selections defining the port or DOS device to which your printer might be attached.

A port is the place where a cable from your printer attaches to your printer. Ports are either parallel or serial, depending on the number of lines in the cable that can carry information to your printer. Usually printers are attached to parallel ports. A DOS device such as LPT1 or COM2 is like a signpost that points the way to the physical port. The advantage to using a DOS device is that by using DOS to change what port the signpost points to, you can change what physical port the DOS device LPT1 is pointing to without having to reattach cables to your machine. This is particularly useful when you are using a network.

For most users, the difference between LPT1 and Parallel 1 is never an issue, and the terms can be used interchangeably. LPT DOS devices point to parallel ports and COM DOS devices to serial ports. Wysiwyg's default setting is that the printer is attached to LPT1. Most systems are assembled this way, and therefore, unless you have multiple printers, you will never need to select a new interface.

You can also select the interface by using the Print Settings dialog box. Select Interface under Configuration, and the Interface pop-up dialog box appears. Select the interface for your printer by selecting the appropriate option button from the pop-up dialog box.

Installing Font Cartridges and Cards   If you want even more fonts to work with, many printers have slots where you can insert a cartridge or card that contains the programming for a font. These cartridges are then used as a font resource for that printer. With Wysiwyg, you can specify which font cartridges your printer has installed, so you can use those fonts in printing your worksheet. If you do not tell Wysiwyg which cartridges are installed, it does not have access to the resources of those cartridges.

Select either the :Print Config 1st-Cart or the :Print Config 2nd-Cart command to select the font cartridges you have installed. After you select either of these commands, you are presented with a series of font cartridge files and must select one. If the cartridge that you have installed in your printer is not on the list of cartridge files, you need to consult the documentation that came with the cartridge to find out how to install it.

When you use the Print Settings dialog box to select the cartridges or cards that your printer has installed, you type the name of the cartridge or card file that is in the font directory into the Cartridge 1 or Cartridge 2 text boxes. You can change which directory is the print font with the :Display Font-Directory command.

Choosing an Orientation   Usually, text is printed across the short width of the paper. This orientation is called *portrait*, because painted portraits are usually taller than they are wide. You may want to print so that the top and bottom edges of the paper are longest. This is called *landscape* orientation, because landscape paintings usually require more width than height. You can see the difference between these orientations in Figure 6-12. Worksheets are often printed with landscape orientation because you are able to print more columns on a single sheet.

The :Print Config Orientation commands control the orientation used when you print. This option is limited by your printer and whether it is capable of printing in landscape mode. To print in landscape mode, your printer needs to be able to rotate fonts to print sideways on paper being fed in normally or to accept paper being fed in sideways while the font prints normally. When you want to change the printing orientation, select the :Print Config Orientation command and choose either Portrait or Landscape. You can also select the Landscape check box under Configuration in the Print Settings dialog box. When this check box is selected, your worksheet prints with the landscape orientation, and when it is not selected, you print with the portrait orientation.

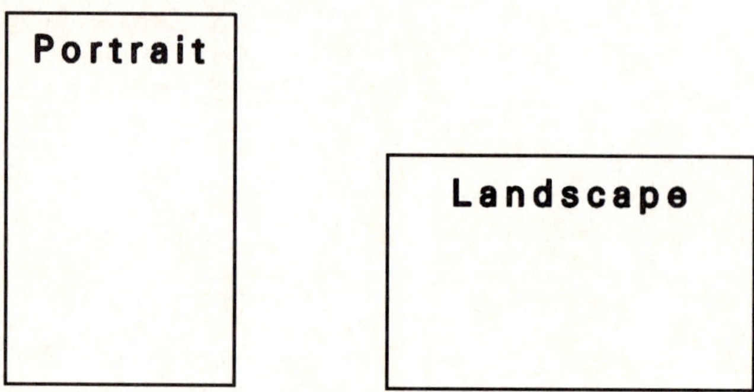

Figure 6-12.   Portrait and landscape orientations

Selecting a Bin   You can set the way a printer with multiple options feeds its paper by selecting :Print Config Bin. You are presented with five options: Reset, Single-Sheet, Manual, Upper-Tray, and Lower-Tray. If your printer only provides one option, there is no need to change this setting.

Select Single-Sheet to use a printer sheet feeder tray. When Wysiwyg uses single-sheet feeding, it places a form feed code at the end of each page. A form feed code advances the printer to the beginning of the next page. If your printer feeds its paper continuously, this will misalign your pages. Select Manual when you need to feed each page separately, using your printer's manual feed options.

If your printer has multiple paper trays, you can specify which tray the paper comes from by selecting either Upper-Tray or Lower-Tray. Wysiwyg instructs the printer to pull paper out of the appropriate bin. Often, each bin is filled with a different type of paper. If your printer does not have multiple trays for paper, selecting one of these options will have no effect. When you select Reset, the bin setting is cleared.

You can also set these features using the Print Settings dialog box. Select Paper Bin under Configuration to open the Paper Bin pop-up dialog box. Select the option button you want to use from this dialog box and select OK to return to the Print Settings dialog box.

Print Settings

In addition to the print layout settings, Wysiwyg offers you several other ways to customize the printing process. You can control the page number of the first page that you are printing or print a specific page from a multipage print range. You can also choose to print multiple copies of the worksheet. You can tell the printer to wait at the end of each page for the next page. You can also include a grid or the frame in the printed copy of your spreadsheet. These features are accessed through the :Print Settings menu.

Controlling Multipage Print Ranges

Sometimes you may not want to redefine your print range, but you do want to print a limited number of pages from a multipage print range. You may find this need while printing off many sections of a large worksheet if each section needs to be printed separately for different reports. It may be easier to control which pages print than to change the print range each time you want to print.

You can select which page number is assigned to the first page in the current print range. For example, if you are printing pages from 1-2-3 to use in a report partially created on a word processor, you may want to control the page number in order to keep it consistent with the page numbers of the word-processed portion of the reports. You may want to do this for reports where you are combining a lot of explanatory material with the worksheets and graphs.

Selecting the First Page   Use the :Print Settings Begin command to select the page in the print range where you want to start printing. When you select this command, you are prompted for the first page to be printed. When the printing begins, this is the first page, but the page numbering stays the same; if the page you have chosen to start with is the fourth page, the page number that appears on the page is still four. Which page you start printing with does not control the page number that appears on the page. To use a different page number, you can select the Beginning Page Number text box under Settings in the Print Settings dialog box and enter the number that you want to appear on the first page that you print.

Selecting the Last Page   Use the :Print Settings End command to select the number of the last page in the print range to be printed. When you select this command, you are prompted to enter the number of the last page that you want printed. Regardless of the size of the print range, when Wysiwyg prints this page, it is the last. You can select the Last Page Number text box under settings in the Print Settings dialog box and enter the number of the last page that you want printed.

Setting the Page Number   Use the :Print Settings Start-Number command to define the page number of the first page of the currently selected print range. When you select this command, you are prompted for a number to apply to the first page of the print range. Remember to count from this number if you choose the first and last page that you want to print from the print range.

Printing Multiple Copies   Usually, you print one copy of a worksheet and then photocopy the rest of the copies that you need. You may find it easier to print multiple copies. If you are printing with a color plotter or a color laser printer, this may be the only way to make color copies, unless you have a color copier as well. Select the :Print Settings Copies command. You are prompted to enter the number of copies you want to print. You can enter a number between 1 and 99 for the number of copies to print at once. You can also enter the appropriate number into the Copies to Print text box under Settings in the Print Settings dialog box.

Print Display Options

The remaining print settings control how the printed copy of your worksheet looks. You can include a *grid*, lines that separate each of the cells. You can also include the *frame*, which labels the rows and columns.

Adding the Grid   When you select the :Print Settings Grid command, the printed copy of your worksheet includes a grid of thin lines marking the boundaries of each of the cells, as shown in Figure 6-13. If one of your cells contains a long label that uses space from other cells, the full label is printed just as it is displayed. The only change is the lines that indicate the edges of the cells. You can see these grid markings when you select the :Print Preview command.

Adding a Frame   The frame is the border along the top and the right side, including the labels for the columns and rows, which you can see in Figure 6-13. The frame does not have grid markings, nor does including the frame in your printout add the grid lines to the document. If you are printing a multipage document, the frame appears on each page.

Resetting Print Settings

When you select the :Print Settings Reset command, all of the settings you specified using commands from the :Print Settings menu are reset to their default settings. This command simply restores all of the default settings for these commands. It does not affect the settings of any other commands.

Displaying the Dialog Box

At times you may want to see the worksheet without the Print Settings dialog box covering it while using the Print commands. To stop displaying the dialog box, select the :Print Info command. To display the dialog box again, reselect this command. The :Print Info command works like a toggle switch, displaying and removing the

	D	E	F	G	H	I	J	K	L	M	N	O
6	$8,000	$8,200	$8,200	$8,700	$8,700	$7,500	$7,500	$10,000	$10,000	$10,000	$10,000	$10,000
7	1,100	1,100	1,100	1,100	1,100	1,100	1,100	1,100	1,300	1,300	1,300	1,300
8	850	850	850	850	850	850	850	850	850	850	850	850
9	500	500	500	500	500	500	500	500	500	500	500	500
10	1,200	1,200	1,200	1,200	1,200	1,200	1,200	1,200	1,200	1,200	1,200	1,200
11	750	750	750	750	750	750	750	750	750	750	750	750
12	400	400	400	400	400	400	400	400	400	400	400	400
13	2,100	2,100	2,100	2,100	2,100	2,100	2,100	2,100	2,100	2,100	2,100	2,100
14	640	640	640	640	640	640	640	640	640	640	640	640
15	1,030	1,030	1,030	1,030	1,030	1,030	1,030	1,030	1,030	1,030	1,030	1,030
16	$16,570	$16,770	$16,770	$17,270	$17,270	$16,070	$16,070	$18,570	$18,770	$18,770	$18,770	$18,770

Figure 6-13.   A Wysiwyg printout using the grid and the frame

dialog box from the screen. When the dialog box is not displayed, you can use the menu commands for specifying settings.

1-2-3's Printing Features

Wysiwyg and 1-2-3 have very similar print features. With the later releases, however, you are going to want to do most of your printing with Wysiwyg because of its advanced spreadsheet publishing abilities. However, even with the later releases, you may find that 1-2-3 is the best choice for drafts or simple reports. The great advantage that 1-2-3 has over Wysiwyg when printing drafts is that 1-2-3 can be printed relatively quickly. Wysiwyg normally takes much longer because of the formatting codes.

This section deals exclusively with 1-2-3's printing commands. You may notice that 1-2-3 does not have the ability to print graphics or graphs. If you want to print graphics or graphs created in 1-2-3 and you do not have Wysiwyg or another Add-In that prints graphs, you need to use the PrintGraph program. For information on using the PrintGraph program to print 1-2-3 graphs, see Chapter 11, "Working with Graphics Features."

Print Destination

The first choice you must make when selecting Print from 1-2-3's main menu is the destination of your printed output. You can choose Printer, which prints to the currently selected printer; File, which prints the print range to an ASCII file; or Encoded, which prints the document to a file, including all the printer codes. Background prints the document to an encoded file and then prints the document afterward, while you continue working with 1-2-3.

When 1-2-3 writes your print file to disk, it assigns the extension .ENC or .PRN to the filename. This distinguishes the print files from the worksheet files on your disk, which have the extension .WK1. If you want to review the contents of your print file, you can use DOS commands such as TYPE to scroll through the output on your screen. You can also use your word processor to view the print file.

You must be sure that the correct printer is selected with the /Worksheet Global Default Printer Name command before you select the Encoded or Background options. This loads the printer driver for 1-2-3. Selecting a printer for Wysiwyg does not select the printer for 1-2-3. Also, to use background printing, you must load the BPrint program into memory, as explained in the Wysiwyg printing section, and run 1-2-3 from a hard disk. Also, the DOS PRINT command must not be loaded into memory. If it is, you must restart your system before you can use background printing in 1-2-3. The BPrint program is run by typing **BPRINT** and pressing ENTER from the DOS command prompt in the 1-2-3 subdirectory. Once you execute this program and it returns a message that BPrint is successfully loaded, you can select Background as a destination for the /Print command.

Once you select a destination, you may select any of the Print options from the Print menu; these options tell 1-2-3 such things as what part of the worksheet you want printed and what left and right margins you want. All of the /Print command options can be used with any destination.

Use 1-2-3 to print when you need a quick printed copy of your worksheet without using Wysiwyg's special formatting.

Print Range

Y̶o̶u̶ specify the cells you want to print through the Range option in the main Print menu shown in Figure 6-14. This figure shows the new Print Settings dialog box that Releases 2.3 and 2.4 use for recording all of your print settings. As you can see from the figure, you can also select the range by making an entry in the Range text box in the dialog box.

To see how this option works, assume you want to print the model shown in Figure 6-15. If you have never printed this worksheet before, 1-2-3 assumes that the starting location for printing is the current cell-pointer location. Therefore, you should position your cell pointer on A1 before typing **/PP** to tell 1-2-3 to print to the printer.

To tell 1-2-3 what range to print, follow these steps:

1. Type **R** to select the Range option.

2. Lock the beginning of the range in place at A1 by typing a period (.).

3. Move to the end of the model by pressing the special key sequence of END followed by HOME. This key sequence moves the cell pointer to the lower-right cell in the range of cells that the worksheet uses.

4. Press ENTER to tell 1-2-3 that the range has been selected.

5. Assuming that all of the default settings are acceptable, check to make sure the printer is turned on and the paper is aligned properly; then select Go from the Print menu.

Your printout should look like the one shown in Figure 6-16. Depending on the printer you are using, your printout may look slightly different.

If you are printing to a file, selecting Go starts the process for writing your information to the disk, but 1-2-3 does not write the final file entries until Quit is selected from the Print menu.

These steps use the default margins and page length. Options to change these and other settings affecting the appearance of your printed output are covered later

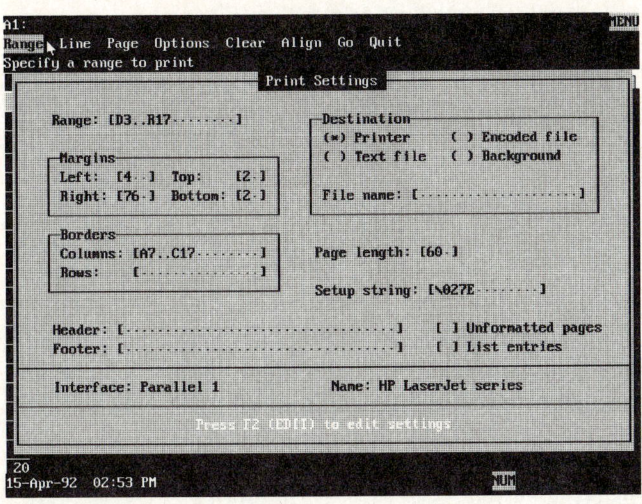

Figure 6-14.   *1-2-3's Print Settings dialog box*

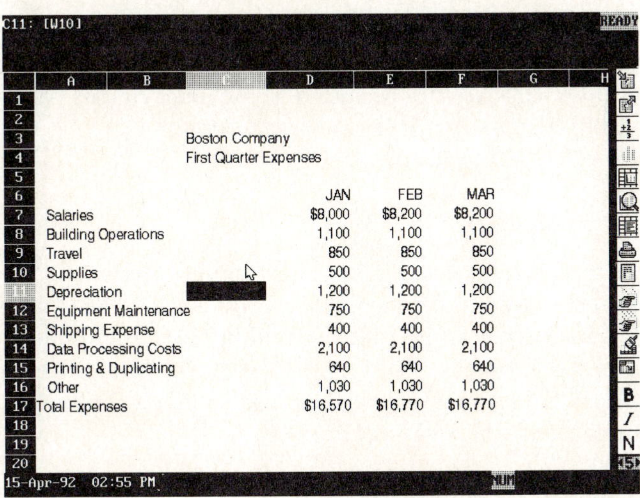

Figure 6-15.   *A worksheet example for specifying print range*

in the chapter. Changes in the default settings would be made between steps 4 and 5 in the print procedure just described.

When the selected range includes long labels that extend beyond their cells, you must include in the range the cells from which the labels borrow space. This keeps

```
                          Boston Company
                     First Quarter Expenses

                                     JAN        FEB        MAR
        Salaries                  $8,000     $8,200     $8,200
        Building Operations        1,100      1,100      1,100
        Travel                       850        850        850
        Supplies                     500        500        500
        Depreciation               1,200      1,200      1,200
        Equipment Maintenance        750        750        750
        Shipping Expense             400        400        400
        Data Processing Costs      2,100      2,100      2,100
        Printing & Duplicating       640        640        640
        Other                      1,030      1,030      1,030
Total Expenses                   $16,570    $16,770    $16,770
```

Figure 6-16.   *The printed output from the worksheet example*

the labels from being truncated in the printout. For example, if G4 contains "Date of Report: March 16, 1990" and the cell width is 9, the label uses G4, H4, and I4 for its display. If all three cells are not included in the print range, 1-2-3 only prints the portion of the label that appears in the selected range.

Changing the Print Range

There may be one additional step in the printing procedure if you have already printed a worksheet before and now want to print a new area from it. This is done by reinvoking /Print Printer Range. 1-2-3 remembers and highlights the last selected range. To select a new range, press ESC or BACKSPACE to change the range address to a single cell address. You can then reposition and anchor again before moving to the opposite corner of the range you want to print.

When the /Print Printer Range command is executed, 1-2-3 remembers and highlights the last range you printed. To expand and contract the print range, move the cell pointer to different corners of the range. To change the corner of the range that is most active, type a period (.); 1-2-3 then moves the active corner in a clockwise direction. (In some cases, the active corner will move in a counterclockwise direction.) The active corner determines the direction in which expansion and contraction of the range occurs. It has a blinking underscore so you can see which corner is affected. The first cell address in the control panel is the anchored corner, and the second address is the corner that you can change.

Controlling the Printer from the Keyboard

1-2-3 provides several methods of controlling the paper in your printer. The three Print menu options involved are Line, Page, and Align. These commands are needed because 1-2-3 does not manage page layouts in the same fashion as Wysiwyg. Wysiwyg thinks of each page as a discrete unit. 1-2-3, since it does not include graphics, font changes, or other advanced formatting features, counts your pages in lines, and prints one line at a time. You have to control what the printer does with the paper, or 1-2-3 might just print all the lines of your worksheet as if they were on a single page.

Advancing Printer Paper a Line at a Time

The /Print Printer Line command moves the paper in the printer up by one line. It acts just as if you used your printer's line feed button, with one important exception. The printer's line feed does not alter the internal line count that 1-2-3 maintains to determine when a new page is needed. The Line command, however, adds 1 to 1-2-3's internal line count, so it will stay in sync with the paper.

1-2-3 assumes that you have positioned your paper at the top of a form before turning your printer on. If you did not, printing starts on the same line on all pages as on your first page, since 1-2-3's line count does not change. The Align command, discussed shortly, can remedy this problem.

Advancing Printer Paper a Page at a Time

The /Print Printer Page command moves the paper in your printer to the top of the next form. When you select this command, 1-2-3 checks its internal line count to determine how many lines must be spaced to complete a full page and reach the top of the next page. The result is similar to pressing form feed with your printer off, except that the Page command prints a footer (if you define one) for the bottom of your page; form feed does not. Like Line, Page assumes that you started printing at the top of a form.

Using Align to Reset the Printer Line Count

The /Print Printer Align command is another page adjustment command. Rather than moving the paper in the printer, it resets the line count to 0 to represent the top of a page, and resets the page number to 1. Every time you position your paper at the top of a new form with /Print Printer Page or the printer control buttons, you should also use Align to tell 1-2-3 to restart the line count for a new page. If you do not remember to use Align, your new page cannot be filled completely, because 1-2-3 continues to use its existing line count even though it does not match the page currently in the printer.

Exiting the Print Menu

Select the /Print Printer Quit command when you finish using the Print menu. All *sticky* menus in 1-2-3—menus that do not automatically disappear when you select a command—provide the Quit option as a means of exiting. Pressing ESC is another way to exit. Leaving the Print menu finishes the print job. If you are printing to a file, it closes the file. If you are printing to a network or to a printer spooler, it directs the network or spooler to begin printing the output.

Printing Options

You have learned about some of the default settings for printing. In this section, you will learn how to tailor printing to the task at hand, making changes that affect only the current session or worksheet. Later, you can reset the default settings according to what you need most of the time and still make temporary changes by using the /Print Printer Options menu.

To temporarily change the appearance of a range before you print it, open a second window with the /Worksheet Window command. Modify the format and column widths in the second window. After printing the range from the second window, close it; 1-2-3 retains the formatting selections from the first window.

Headers and Footers

The /Print Options Header and /Print Options Footer commands in 1-2-3 are used to create Headers and Footers for your 1-2-3 printout. 1-2-3 allows you to use a header or footer with a total width equal to the maximum printed report width of 240 characters. As with Wysiwyg, you can divide both headers and footers into separate segments for the right, left, and center sections of each line as discussed at the beginning of the chapter. 1-2-3 requires that all of the information for a header and footer fit on one line, so you must consider your line length when planning the contents of a header or footer.

Margins

The /Print Printer Options Margins command controls the amount of white space at the top, bottom, and sides of your printed document. Remember that with 1-2-3, margins are measured in terms of lines and characters. The four Margins options are Left, Right, Top, and Bottom. These options get their default values from settings specified with /Worksheet Global Default Printer. A fifth option, None, sets the top, bottom, and left margins to 0, and the right margin to 240. This option is used for printing a worksheet to a file that is later imported into another computer package or for fitting as much as possible on a page.

The default setting for the left margin is 4. The default for the right margin is 76. These numbers indicate the number of characters from the left edge of the paper. You can assign any value to the right and left margin from 0 to 240. The number you use for the right margin must always be larger then the one you use for the left margin; the number indicating the right margin is the number of characters the right margin is from the left edge of the paper. To use values greater than 80, you must use compressed print when the worksheet is printed, a setup string for landscape mode (which prints sideways), or a wide-carriage printer with paper wider than 8½ inches across. The top and bottom margin default is 2 lines, but it can be revised to any number from 0 to 32.

To change any margin setting, simply type the new number after specifying the appropriate Margins option. In Releases 2.3 and 2.4, you can also set the margins by entering the margin in the Left, Right, Top, and Bottom text boxes under Margins in the Print Settings dialog box. The changes you make to the margin settings are saved with the document when you save it to disk after updating the Print options.

Setup String Chart

Setup strings allow you to utilize the full capacity of your printer. You must use a setup string customized for your printer to access the features your printer supports—for instance, to designate a small area of the worksheet or to use a printer feature that 1-2-3's menus do not support.

The following fill-in list serves as a convenient reference for your printer's setup codes once you have looked them up in your printer manual. The section of the printer manual containing the codes is entitled something like "Printer Command Codes." 1-2-3 accepts printer codes using the decimal codes, such as \027\040\115\051\066, or using their equivalent commands, such as \027(s3B. The ESC character must be represented by \027. Add other features to this list as needed so that you have all your codes in one place.

Begin Boldface _____________________

End Boldface _____________________

Begin Emphasized _____________________

End Emphasized _____________________

Begin Italic _____________________

End Italic _____________________

Begin Underline _____________________

End Underline _____________________

Borders

The /Print Printer Options Borders command includes the borders, which are the identifying information found at the top of columns and at the left side of rows in your worksheet, on every printed page of a report. After you select this command, you are given the option of specifying the Top or Left borders. When you select which border you are defining, you are prompted for the range of the border. This range must include one cell from each row or column you want to use as the border.

Using Printer Features

Most printers have a variety of special features that you can access if you "speak the language" of the printer. Wysiwyg may be able to speak the language of the computer directly, but 1-2-3 has the ability to speak the language of most popular printers only if you supply it with the correct entries. Some printers also have features that Wysiwyg cannot access directly.

Using Setup Strings for Printer Features

Unfortunately, not all printer features can be added with the menu commands of either 1-2-3 or Wysiwyg. Each printer has its own language or directions that tell the printer what to do. When you use setup strings, you must look in your printer manual for the language required by that printer model. Look for a set of decimal codes assigned to that printer's features. The "Setup String Chart" box provides a handy form for making a reference list of the printer codes you need. Add your own entries for additional fonts or features and make your own list.

If you want the printer codes to affect all of your output, enter them through the command /Print Printer Options Setup. (If you want to affect the printing of only a small area of the worksheet, you must embed the codes in worksheet cells using a process described later in this section.) To enter the desired printer code or codes as a setup string for the entire print range, enter the command sequence **/Print Printer Options Setup** and press ENTER. If another setup string is already displayed, press ESC before entering a new string. Next, enter the printer code or codes you want, preceding each code with a backslash (\). If your manual only provides a two-digit decimal code, you must precede it with a backslash and a 0.

Printer manuals often provide more than one code to produce the same result. For example, to underline with a Hewlett-Packard LaserJet printer, you can enter the printer control command \027&dD or the decimal code command \027\038\100\068. (Setup strings are very exact, so you must use the same order and case as the printer manual uses.) When the printer manual indicates the ESC key, use \027.

After the complete setup string is entered, press ENTER. Then select Quit from the Options menu and Go from the main Print menu to obtain your printout.

Setup strings can include more than one code. For instance, you may want both underlining and a special font. You may include up to 240 characters in a setup string.

The feature your setup string creates remains in effect, in most cases, until you enter another setup string to turn off or change the feature you selected. For example, the setup string you enter on a Hewlett-Packard LaserJet printer for underlining is \027\038\100\068. The underlining remains in effect until the setup string \027\038\100\064 is entered to turn off the underlining feature or the printer is turned off to erase its memory.

It is also possible to embed setup strings in worksheet cells. The advantage of this approach is that it allows you to change print characteristics more than once while printing a worksheet. Place these entries in blank rows, because the entire row is ignored after the setup string is processed. Setup strings in a worksheet cell must be preceded by two vertical bars (||). For example, to embed \015 in a cell, enter || \015.

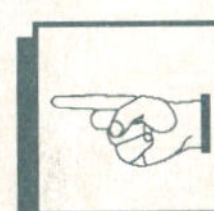

There is an alternative to storing setup strings in worksheet cells to change printer features within a range. Instead, print each area of the worksheet that uses a specific printer feature separately, so you can use the 1-2-3 commands to select printer features. For example, if you want to print the bottom half of the worksheet in compressed pitch, first print the top portion of the worksheet using standard print size. Then, before you print the second half of the worksheet, invoke /Print Printer Options Setup and enter the compressed print string. The rest of the sheet prints in smaller characters.

Page Length

Page length is the number of lines that 1-2-3 can print on a sheet of paper, assuming every line is used. With the default options in effect and 6 lines printed per inch, only 56 lines are printed for a page length of 66. Lines 1, 2, 65, and 66 are reserved for top and bottom margins. Line 3 is left blank for a header, and lines 4 and 5 are blank to make space between header and text. Similarly, line 64 is left blank for a footer and lines 62 and 63 for space. Lines 6 through 61 are used for printing your worksheet data.

You can change the number of lines per page 1-2-3 prints by entering **/Print Printer Options Pg-Length** and then entering the new number of lines 1-2-3 should print on each page. In Releases 2.3 and above, you can also set the page length by entering the number of lines that can fit on the page in the Page Length text box in the Print Settings dialog box. Some printers, such as the Hewlett-Packard LaserJet Series II, can only print 60 lines per page. You will know if you need to change the page length when the page breaks occur at different points on each page.

If you elect to print at 8 lines per inch by using compressed print, you can increase the page length to 88 on an 11-inch sheet of paper. You can reset the default page length with the /Print Printer Options Pg-Length command sequence.

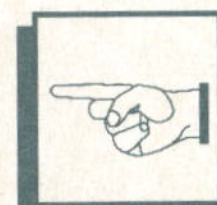

Hewlett-Packard LaserJet printers automatically include a half-inch top and bottom margin. Since this is not included in the page length count, you must change the page length to 60 so your printouts start at the top of every page.

Other Options

The /Print Printer Options Other command allows you to decide whether information will be printed with or without the formatting that has been added to the text. It also allows you to print formulas rather than the information displayed on your screen.

Printing What You See on the Screen

The default setting /Print Printer Options Other As-Displayed causes your printed report to contain the same information you see on the screen if you do not have Wysiwyg attached. This means that the results of formulas are printed just as they are displayed on the screen. The 1-2-3 formats in effect on your screen display are used for the printout, as are the column widths for the currently active window. In short, you have a duplicate of the worksheet portion of the screen display, not including Wysiwyg formatting, except that you are not restricted to screen size for your printout. You are restricted to the limitations of the established page size, however.

Printing Cell Formulas

In Chapter 4, you learned how to display formulas in cells by using the /Range Format Text command. To print a Text format worksheet like the one described in Chapter 4, you could use the As-Displayed option, since the formulas are already displayed. Alternatively, you can use 1-2-3's built-in formula printing option. With this option, you do not have to change the format and width of cells as you did in Chapter 4, because the package does not print the formulas in the shape of the worksheet. Instead, it prints the formulas, one per line, down the page.

If an entire large worksheet is involved, the documentation produced by this approach can be quite a long list. However, this is an excellent way to print the formulas for a smaller range of cells, because it involves so little work on your part. All you have to do is select your print range and then choose Options Other Cell-Formulas. Quitting the Options menu and selecting Go from the Print menu produces a formula listing like the one in Figure 6-17. The formulas print according to the row they are in, in the order A1, B1, C1, A2, B2, C2, and so on.

You can also select the format of the printout by selecting the List entries check box in the Print Settings dialog box instead of selecting Options Other Cell-Formulas from the Print menu. When this check box is not selected, the default Options Other As-Displayed is selected.

Using Format Options for Printing

Like As-Displayed, the Formatted option is another default setting in the Options Other menu. It uses page breaks, headers, footers, and any other 1-2-3 formatting

```
B2:    'Commission Calculation
A4:    'Employee:
C4:    'John Smith
E4:    'Quotas Met
A5:    'Sales Product A:
C5:    56000
E5:    +C5>50000
A6:    'Sales Product B:
C6:    45000
E6:    +C6>50000
A7:    'Sales Product C:
C7:    3000
E7:    +C7>50000
C8:    +C5+C6+C7
E8:    +C8>50000
A10:   'Commission:
C10:   +C8*0.1
A11:   'Bonus:
C11:   1000
A14:   'Total Commission Plus Bonus
D14:   +C10+C11
```

Figure 6-17.   *The cell formulas printout*

you have added to create a professional-looking report. Formatting is used almost every time a report is printed on a printer. Select this option after using the Unformatted option when you want 1-2-3 to return to formatting the output.

Eliminating Formatting from Output

When you write files to disk for use with another program, you often do not want formatting characters added. The other program may not recognize them and may try to process them as data. Choosing the Unformatted option alleviates this problem by causing the files to be written without formatting. This means that 1-2-3 ignores page breaks, headers, footers, and any other formatting you have added to the text.

Usually this option is confined to printing to disk. It might also be used when you print a list that barely runs over to the next page. You might prefer to keep such a list together, even if it prints over the page perforation. You could do this by choosing /Print Printer Options Other Unformatted.

You can also select the Formatted or Unformatted options by selecting or deselecting the Unformatted pages check box in the Print Settings dialog box. When this check box is selected, Unformatted is selected. When this check box is not selected, Formatted is selected.

Saving Print Settings

When a worksheet file is saved, the print settings associated with this file are also saved. Saving a worksheet after setting its margins, setup strings, and other options ensures that you will not have to reenter these settings the next time you use the file.

Clearing Print Settings

The Clear options let you eliminate some or all of the special print settings you have used for a report and return you to the default settings. The four options available on the Clear menu are All, Range, Borders, and Format.

Clearing All Settings

The All option restores the default for all of your print settings, including print range, borders, setup strings, and margins. If you want to be more selective, you can use one of the other three options.

Clearing Range Settings

The Range option eliminates only a range print specification made earlier for the worksheet. Other print options are not affected.

Clearing Border Settings

The Borders option cancels the specification of any rows or columns as borders and removes any frame. Other print options are not affected.

Clearing Format Settings

The Format option returns margins, setup strings, and page length to their default values, but does not affect the range or borders.

Global Printer Defaults

It takes little effort to get a printed copy of your worksheet, because 1-2-3 does much of the preliminary work for you by setting up default values for many of the print options. These default values are available whenever you load 1-2-3. Sometimes, however, you want to change the defaults. You learned in the previous section how to make changes that apply to just one particular worksheet; this section explains how you can make permanent changes to the defaults.

The command you need to change the default values is not found in the Print menu. It is /Worksheet Global Default Printer, which presents the menu shown in Figure 6-18. Besides selecting the different /Worksheet Global Default Printer command options, you can also edit the dialog box and change the entries for the settings you want to change. Changing these options to values that meet your particular daily needs saves time; you don't have to change print options every time you load 1-2-3. Notice the Quit option at the end of this menu, which indicates that this is another menu that remains displayed until you eliminate it with Quit.

Printer Interface

The Default Printer Interface option allows you to specify the default printer interface. The default setting is 1 for a parallel interface; this is the appropriate setting for a parallel printer adapter. Eight other settings are possible. The first three are as follows:

2	Serial 1 for a serial printer with an RS232 interface
3	Parallel 2 for a second parallel printer
4	Serial 2 for a second serial printer

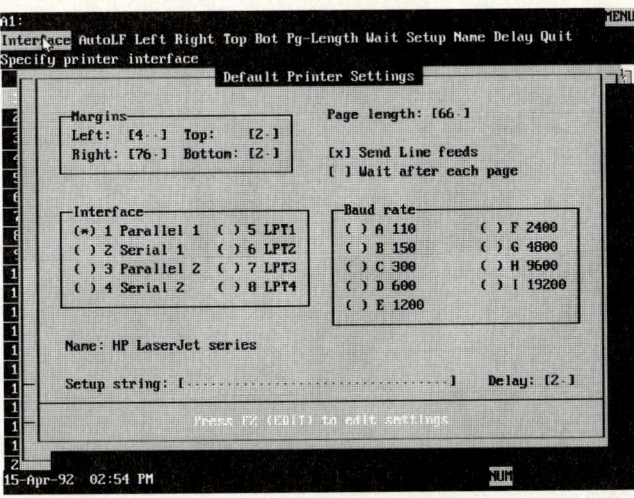

Figure 6-18.   *The /Worksheet Global Default Printer dialog box*

The remaining four options (LPT1 through LPT4) are DOS devices that your system can assign to printers. You must specify additional information concerning your network configuration, such as baud rate, when selecting a serial interface.

Automatic Line Feed

The Default Printer AutoLF option determines whether 1-2-3 needs to generate a line feed after every carriage return. The two options are No, indicating that your printer does not generate line feeds, and Yes, indicating that it does. If your printed output looks the way you want it to, you do not have to worry about this setting. If extra line feeds are being generated, you must set this option to Yes. If line feeds are missing, change it to No.

Left Margin

The Default Printer Left option establishes a default left margin of 4. You can use this option to change the default to any number from 0 to 240.

Right Margin

The Default Printer Right option establishes a default right margin of 76, four spaces in from the right edge of a form that holds 80 characters across. As with the left margin setting, you can use any setting from 1 to 240.

Top Margin

The Default Printer Top option sets the default top margin at 2. You can change this option to allow a default of 0 to 32.

Bottom Margin

The default for the bottom margin is also set at 2. You can change it to any number from 0 to 32, using the Default Printer Bot option.

Page Length

The default setting for Default Printer Pg-Length is 66. This is the correct setting for 8 1/2- by 11-inch paper, assuming printing occurs at 6 lines per inch. You can change the default to any number from 10 to 100.

Paper Feeding

The Default Printer Wait option indicates whether you want to wait for a paper change at the end of each sheet. The default setting is No, which is appropriate for continuous feed paper. Use the Yes setting when you print on single sheets.

Printer Setup

As you saw earlier in this chapter, setup strings are special codes you can transmit to your printer to access its special features. The default setting is no setup string, but if you use certain features regularly, such as the double-strike or compressed print, you can add the appropriate setup string to your printer's default settings. You may also want to use a default setup string to reset the printer so that any changes made to the printer, such as changing the fonts (even when made by other spreadsheet packages), are undone. Use the /Worksheet Global Default Printer Setup command and enter the setup string.

Choosing Your Printer

The Default Printer Name option allows you to specify the name of the printer you want to use if you have more than one. The menu is customized during installation to include the names of your installed printers.

Setting the Printer Error Delay

In Releases 2.3 and 2.4, you can set how soon 1-2-3 alerts you to printer errors when you are printing in the background. Selecting Default Printer Delay and entering a number between 0 and 30 sets the number of minutes 1-2-3 waits until it displays an error message about the printer problem. If you select 0 for the delay, 1-2-3 will wait and not display any printer error messages.

Exiting the Default Printer Menu

The Quit option is the last /Worksheet Global Default Printer menu choice. Aside from repeatedly pressing ESC, Quit is the only way out of the menu.

Saving Global Default Settings

Changing the Default Printer options does not automatically produce a permanent modification. You must first quit the Default Printer menu and choose Update from the prior menu or select the Update command button from the Default Settings dialog box. Update stores the default options in your configuration file, called 123.CNF. This file is on your hard drive. If you have a two-drive system, 1-2-3 writes the updated configuration file on your 1-2-3 disk. Remember to remove the write-protect tab on the backup System disk and place the disk in drive A before selecting Update, so that 1-2-3 can write the configuration file on the disk.

Other Worksheet Commands for Printing

Most of the commands that affect printed output are found under the Print option on the main menu. You have seen that most of the default settings are controlled using the /Worksheet Global Default Printer command. There are two additional commands on the Worksheet menu that affect printing. /Worksheet Column Hide affects the worksheet display and also excludes hidden columns from the printed output. /Worksheet Page inserts a page break anywhere you want in your document.

Using Hidden Columns to Affect Print Range

If you want to omit a column in a range when printing, one method is to split the range into two parts and then print them. The second range prints immediately after the first range. The columns in the second range do not have descriptive information preceding them.

In many instances, it is not possible to fit all of the information in your worksheet across one printed page. You can solve this problem by using the /Worksheet Column Hide feature, discussed in Chapter 4, to choose which columns to print, effectively extending the print features. Figure 6-19 presents part of a worksheet, the result of using /Worksheet Column Hide to eliminate columns D through F. Entering **/Print Printer Range A1..I16** and then selecting Go creates the printed report shown in Figure 6-20.

Using hidden columns is one way to print a second range with descriptive information. It is also useful when some columns contain data that you do not need in your report.

Inserting a Page Break in the Printed Worksheet

In the past, a worksheet with many separate sections could often be a printing nightmare. You had two options: you could sit at the printer and request each section separately, trying to remember to Page and Align during print requests, or you could set up a print macro to do the remembering for you. Neither way was easy.

The /Worksheet Page command makes it possible to split the printing of your reports wherever you want. /Worksheet Page causes 1-2-3 to insert a blank line,

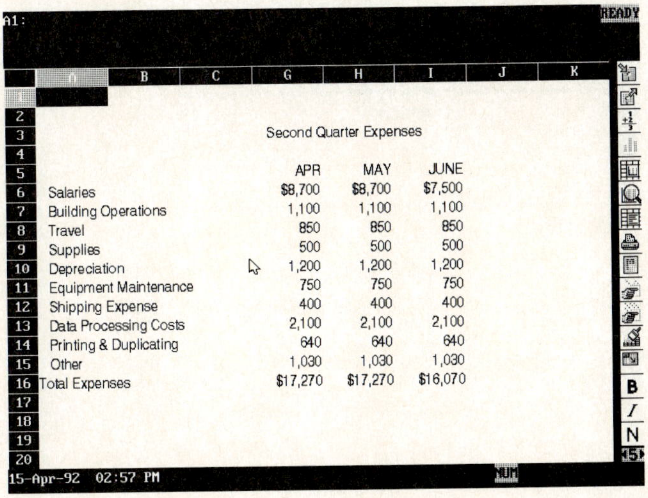

Figure 6-19.   *A worksheet with hidden columns*

	APR	MAY	JUNE
Second Quarter Expenses			
Salaries	$8,700	$8,700	$7,500
Building Operations	1,100	1,100	1,100
Travel	850	850	850
Supplies	500	500	500
Depreciation	1,200	1,200	1,200
Equipment Maintenance	750	750	750
Shipping Expense	400	400	400
Data Processing Costs	2,100	2,100	2,100
Printing & Duplicating	640	640	640
Other	1,030	1,030	1,030
Total Expenses	$17,270	$17,270	$16,070

Figure 6-20.   *The printed output with hidden columns*

adding a page indicator—double colons (::)—at the cell-pointer location. A page break can be manually added by entering |:: on a blank row. (The /Range Erase or

	A	B	C	D	E	F	G	H
1	**							
2	*		ASSUMPTIONS			*		
3	* Sales Growth					*		
4	* Product A		10.0%			*		
5	* Product B		12.0%			*		
6	* Product C		9.0%			*		
7	**							
8	::							
9								
10			1991	1992	1993	1994	1995	
11	Sales							
12	Product A		100,000	110,000	121,000	133,100	146,410	
13	Product B		50,000	56,000	62,720	70,246	78,676	
14	Product C		45,000	49,050	53,465	58,276	63,521	
15	Cost of Goods Sold		87,750	96,773	106,733	117,730	129,873	
16	Profit		107,250	118,278	130,451	143,892	158,734	
17								
18								
19								
20								

Figure 6-21.   *A worksheet showing a page break*

/Worksheet Delete Row commands can be used to erase an unwanted page break.) 1-2-3 ignores anything in the row after the page break.

Figure 6-21 presents a worksheet with a page break inserted. When A1..G16 is selected as the print range, the first seven rows are on the first page and rows 9 through 16 are on the second. The page break indicator causes the page break to occur before the first page is filled.

PRINTING

Worksheet   Range   Copy   Move   File   Print   Graph   Data   System   Add-In   Quit
Printer   File   Encoded   Background
Range   Line   Page   Options   Clear   Aligh   Go   Quit
All   Range   Borders   Format
Header   Footer   Margins   Borders   Setup   Pg-Length   Other   Quit
Left   Right   Top   Bottom   None
As-Displayed   Cell-Formulas   Formatted   Unformatted
Columns   Rows
Global   Insert   Delete   Column   Erase   Titles   Window   Status   Page   Learn
Format   Label-Prefix   Column-Width   Recalculation   Protection   Default   Zero
Printer   Directory   Status   Update   Other   Autoexec   Quit
Interface   AutoLF   Left   Right   Top   Bottom   Pg-Lenth   Wait   Setup   Name   Delay   Quit

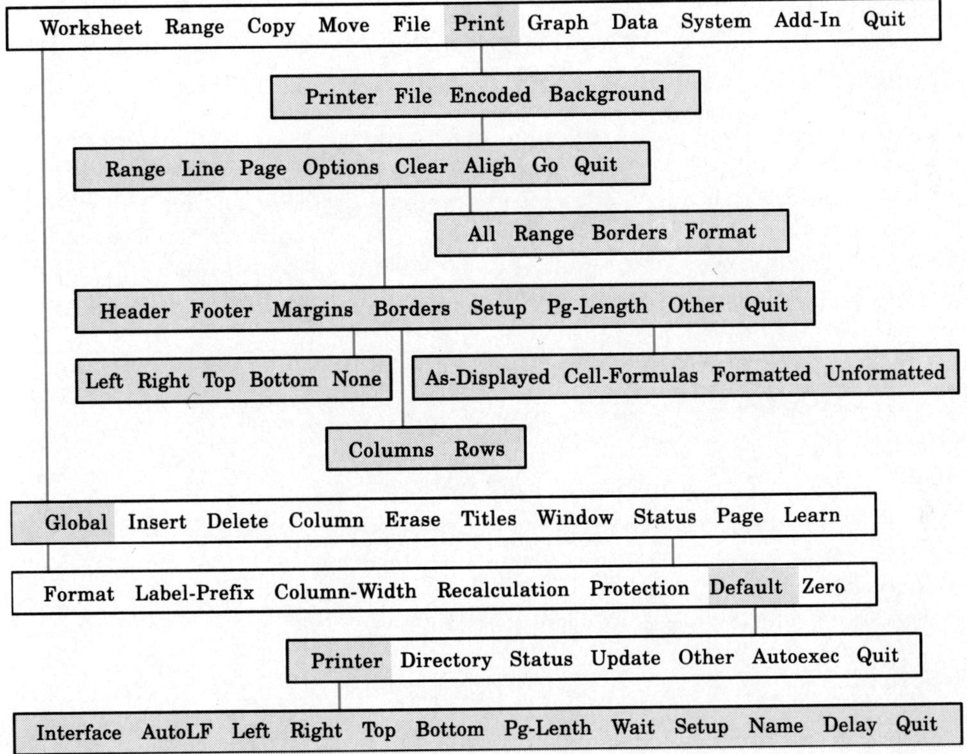

/Print Background

Description

The /Print Background command sends the printed output to an encoded file and then prints it from the background. This command is used so you can print your worksheet and then continue working with 1-2-3 while your printer prints. In Releases 2.3 and above, you can also select this command from the Print Settings dialog box by selecting the Background option button. Before you can use this command, you must load BPrint from the operating system.

Options

Once you select this command, you must enter a filename that 1-2-3 will use to store the printed worksheet. 1-2-3 will add an .ENC extension if you do not provide one. After 1-2-3 finishes printing, 1-2-3 deletes the temporary file. If you select an existing file, you have the Cancel, Replace, and Backup choices that other file commands use. All of the /Print Printer options are also available when you choose /Print Background. This includes the range you print and the other printing options. 1-2-3 does not actually start background printing until you select Go.

/Print Encoded

Description

The /Print Encoded command sends the printed output to an encoded file. This command stores your printed worksheet in a file so you can print it at a later time. In Releases 2.3 and above, you can also select this command from the Print Settings dialog box by selecting the Encoded option button.

Options

Once you select this command, you must enter a filename that 1-2-3 will use to store the printed worksheet. 1-2-3 will add an .ENC extension if you do not provide one. If you select an existing file, you have the Cancel, Replace, and Backup choices that other file commands use. All of the /Print Printer options are also available when you print to an encoded file. This includes the range you print and the other printing options. 1-2-3 does not actually start background printing until you select Go.

/Print File

Description

The /Print File command prints a report to a disk file. In Releases 2.3 and above, you can also select this command from the Print Settings dialog box by selecting the

File option button. This command is useful when your printer is not available. It can prepare data for other programs. You can use the DOS COPY command to print the file.

Options

When you select this command, you must enter a filename to store the data. If you enter an existing file, you must select between the Replace, Backup, and Cancel options. All of the /Print Printer options are also available when you choose /Print File. You can select print ranges and apply any of these other options to them.

/Print Printer

Description

This command prints information from a worksheet file on your printer. In Releases 2.3 and above, you can also select this command from the Print Settings dialog box by selecting the Printer option button. Since 1-2-3 contains default values for most of the Print parameters, printing can be as simple as specifying a print range. When you need greater sophistication or if you would like to tailor a report to your exact needs, you have a variety of options to work with.

Options

The /Print Printer command has the same options as the other /Print [Destination] commands. You can make simple selections such as specifying the range of worksheet cells to print, or you can include more sophisticated information.

/Print Printer Align

Description

This command sets 1-2-3's internal line count to 0. 1-2-3 then assumes that the printer is aligned at the top of the page. Any entries after this point add to the new line count. This command also resets the page number to 1, so a header or footer that prints the page number begins with the correct number. Before you perform this command, you should check that the paper is at the top of the page in the printer.

/Print Printer Clear

Description

This command eliminates special print settings and returns the specified print settings to their defaults. For example, if you have added a setup string, header, footer, and borders to a report and want to print it again without these special features, the Clear option saves you time by eliminating the added settings.

Options

The options for /Print Printer Clear let you decide whether you want to clear all the print settings or just certain ones.

All

This option eliminates all the special entries made through the Print menus. The current print range is canceled. Borders, headers, and footers are all eliminated. Margins, page length, and setup strings are returned to their default settings.

Range

This option cancels only the current print range.

Borders

This option clears both row and column borders.

Format

This option resets the margin, page length, and setup string to the default settings found under /Worksheet Global Default Printer.

/Print Printer Go

Description

This command tells 1-2-3 to begin transmitting the print range to the printer (if Printer was selected) or to a file (if another destination was selected). If you are printing to a file, the file is not fully saved until you select the Quit option or press ESC to return to the READY mode. If you are printing to a printer in a network or to a spooler, the network or spooler does not start printing the print job until you select the Quit option or press ESC to return to the READY mode.

/Print Printer Line

Description

This command generates a line feed. You can print two ranges with only one line between them by entering Line after printing the first range and then selecting the second range and printing it. Line adds 1 to 1-2-3's internal line count.

Note

This command offers an advantage over using the printer's line feed button. Since the Line command increments 1-2-3's internal line count by 1, it keeps the printing of a page in sync with the page's physical length.

/Print Printer Options Borders

Description

The Borders option allows you to print specified rows or columns as borders on every page. When rows and columns are used as a border, you first select either Rows or Columns, and then specify the range of cells you wish to have appear as a border on each page. Be sure not to include the border rows or columns in your print job's print range; otherwise they are printed twice.

Options

Rows

Use this option when you have a report that is too long for one page. Select the rows you want to print as borders on the second and subsequent pages to provide descriptive information on each page. In Releases 2.3 and above, you can also select row borders by entering a cell or range address in the Row text box under Borders in the Print Settings dialog box. Include one cell from each row you want to use.

Columns

Use this option when your report is too wide for one sheet of paper and when the left side of your worksheet contains identifying information that applies to all pages.

You can duplicate the selected column of information at the left side of each page. In Releases 2.3 and above, you can also select column borders by entering a cell or range address in the Column text box under Borders in the Print Settings dialog box. Include one cell from each column you want to use.

Note

If you accidentally select the Borders option, the current row or column becomes a border, depending on whether you choose Rows or Columns. You can easily undo the damage with /Print Printer Clear Borders.

/Print Printer Options Footer

Description

This command adds one line of up to 240 characters at the bottom of each page of a report. The footer text cannot extend for more than one line. Typical footer contents are date, report name or number, company name or department, and page number. In Releases 2.3 and above, you can also enter a footer in the Footer text box in the Print Settings dialog box.

Options

The three options allow an entry to be placed at the left, center, or right section. Entries are separated by the vertical bar character. Use a bar to separate the three sections, even if they are not all used; in other words, a single entry to appear at the right should be preceded by two bars.

You also have the option of using @, \, and #. The # represents the current page number, the \ followed by a cell address represents the contents of the referenced cell, and @ represents the current date.

If you use a \ to reference a cell, you cannot include the other special characters. The cell the footer uses can include the special characters, and the special characters are treated just as if you entered the cell's entry at the menu prompt.

Note

If you include # for the page number, you must use the /Print Printer Align command before printing a second time. Otherwise 1-2-3 starts the second printing of the report with the next page number, rather than beginning again with page 1. Also, to include the footer on the last page, you must use the /Print Printer Page command once 1-2-3 has finished printing the print job.

/Print Printer Options Header

Description

This command allows you to add one line of up to 240 characters at the top of each page of a report. The header text cannot extend for more than one line. Typical header contents are the date, report name or number, company name or department, and page number. In Releases 2.3 and above, you can also enter a header in the Header text box in the Print Settings dialog box.

Options

The options for a header are identical to the options for a footer. See the /Print Printer Options Footer command for a description of the entries you may want to make in a header.

/Print Printer Options Margins

Description

This command controls the amount of blank space at the top, bottom, and sides of a printed page. If you do not make an entry for Margins, the default values are used.

Options

Left

The default setting for the left margin is 4 spaces. You can enter any number from 0 to 240 to establish a new setting. In Releases 2.3 and above, you can also set the left margin by entering the margin in the Left text box under Margins in the Print Settings dialog box. The difference between this number and the right margin sets the number of characters that appear on each line.

Right

The default setting for the right margin is 76. You can enter any number between 1 and 240 to change this margin setting. In Releases 2.3 and above, you can also set the right margin by entering the margin in the Right text box under Margins in the Print Settings dialog box.

Top

The default setting for the top margin is 2. You can change it to any number from 0 to 32. In Releases 2.3 and above, you can also set the top margin by entering the margin in the Top text box under Margins in the Print Settings dialog box. The difference between the top and bottom margins, along with the page length, sets the number of lines 1-2-3 prints on each page.

Bottom

The default setting for the bottom margin is 2. You can change it to any number from 0 to 32. In Releases 2.3 and above, you can also set the bottom margin by entering the margin in the Bottom text box under Margins in the Print Settings dialog box.

None

This option sets the top, bottom, and left margin to 0 and the right margin to 240.

/Print Printer Options Other

Description

This command provides two very different sets of features. First, it lets you decide whether the printed output should be the information as displayed in worksheet cells or the formulas behind the display. Second, this command lets you determine whether print or file output should be formatted or unformatted.

Options

The Options Other command has four options: As-Displayed, Cell-Formulas, Formatted, and Unformatted. The As-Displayed and Cell-Formulas options are opposites, as are Formatted and Unformatted.

As-Displayed

This option prints your worksheet to match the screen display in the active window in terms of cell values, format, and width.

Cell-Formulas

This option causes the cell formulas, rather than their results, to be displayed. The formulas are shown, one per line, down the page. In Releases 2.3 and above, you can also select this option by selecting the List entries check box in the Print Settings dialog box. When this check box is not selected, the As-Displayed option is chosen.

Formatted

This option prints the output with all of your formatting options, such as headers, footers, and page breaks. This is normally the way you want your output to appear when you send it to a printer.

Unformatted

This option strips all the formatting from your data. In other words, information is written to the output device without page breaks, headers, or footers. This option is useful when you are writing the output to a file for use by another program or when you want the printer to ignore page breaks. In Releases 2.3 and above, you can also select this option by selecting the Unformatted pages check box in the Print Settings dialog box. When this check box is not selected, the Formatted option is chosen.

/Print Printer Options Pg-Length

Description

This option determines the number of lines in a page of printed output. The default is 66, but 1-2-3 accepts entries from 10 to 100. (There are not actually 66 lines of printed output on a default page. Remember that top and bottom margins, headers, footers, and the two blank lines below the header and above the footer must be subtracted from the page length to determine the number of printed lines.)

Options

The only option for this command is to enter a page length between 10 and 100. In Releases 2.3 and above, you can also set the page length by typing the number of lines that can fit on the page in the Page length text box in the Print Settings dialog box.

/Print Printer Options Quit

Description

This command exits the Options menu. Since this menu stays displayed for you to make your option selections, you need to select Quit to exit after you have finished.

/Print Printer Options Setup

Description

This command transmits a setup string of control codes to your printer so that you can use the special features the printer offers. These special features may include enlarged, compressed, emphasized, or boldface printing, as well as printing different numbers of lines per inch. The control codes activate printer features that are unavailable from 1-2-3 menus. 1-2-3 does not automatically adjust the other printer settings for changes made with control codes. For example, if the control code setup string activates a different font, 1-2-3 does not adjust the margins to accommodate the different size of the characters. You can also enter a setup string by entering it in the Setup string text box of the Print Settings dialog box.

Options

The printer setup strings you can enter depend upon your printer. A few of the options for a Hewlett-Packard LaserJet printer and its respective setup strings are as follows:

\027(s3B	Start boldface print
\027(s0B	Stop boldface print
\027&dD	Start underline
\027&d@	Stop underline

The decimal codes you need for setup strings can be found in your printer manual. When entering them into 1-2-3, precede each code with a backslash (\) and a 0 if necessary, as in the previous examples.

/Print Printer Page

Description

This command advances the paper to the top of the next form. This keyboard command makes it unnecessary for you to touch the printer, and it prints a footer if one has been specified.

/Print Printer Quit

Description

This command exits the Print menu and places you back in READY mode. Since the Print menu stays displayed while you make selections, you need to select Quit to leave it. Even after printing, you do not return to READY mode until you choose Quit or press the ESC key.

This menu option ends the print job. For network environments and spoolers, it tells the network or the spooler that 1-2-3 is finished sending the print job to the spooler, and that printing can begin. If you are printing to a file, this command closes the file printed.

/Print Printer Range

Description

This command determines how much of the worksheet is printed. Any valid range of cells can be specified, from one cell to the entire worksheet. 1-2-3 decides how much of the range can be placed on one page, based on the margin and page length settings, and carries the remainder of the range over to additional pages.

Options

The only option for this command is to specify a range. The format used for ranges is *cell address..cell address*, where the cell addresses specified are at opposite corners of the range of cells to be printed. For example, if you wanted to print cells A1 through

D10, you could specify the range as A1..D10, D10..A1, D1..A10, or A10..D1. You can select the range by typing the address, using the arrow keys, or using the mouse. If you select a range before using this command, the selected range is automatically used. You can also enter the range by making an entry in the Range text box of the Print Settings dialog box.

/Worksheet Global Default Printer

Description

This command changes the default printer settings. These settings determine the way a document prints if you have not made particular specifications for it through the Print menu. They also determine the default interface between 1-2-3 and your printer. You can make changes to the printer defaults by editing the Default Printer Settings dialog box and making the appropriate entries for the printer settings. Changes made with this command are not permanent unless you save them with /Worksheet Global Default Update.

Options

Interface

This option determines the type of connection between your printer and 1-2-3. There are three basic options with several choices: parallel connection, serial connection, or connection through a local area network. The available options are Parallel 1 (default setting), Serial 1, Parallel 2, Serial 2, LPT1, LPT2, LPT3, and LPT4. If you select one of the serial interface options, 1-2-3 also asks you to specify a *baud rate* (the transmission speed it supports), stop bits, and parity. For 110 baud you must set your printer at 2 stop bits, 8 data bits, and no parity. For speeds other than 110, 1 stop bit is sufficient.

AutoLF

This option specifies whether your printer automatically issues line feeds after carriage returns. Installation sets this to correspond with your printer. If you are getting double-spacing on everything you print, set AutoLF to Yes. If your paper is not advancing as it should, change this setting to No to indicate that the printer does not automatically print line feeds.

Left

This option for the left margin has a default value of 4, but you can change it to any number between 0 and 240.

Right

This option for the right margin has a default value of 76, but you can change it to any number between 0 and 240.

Top

This option for the top margin has a default value of 2 but accepts values between 0 and 32.

Bot

This option for the bottom margin has a default setting of 2 but accepts values between 0 and 32.

Pg-Length

The default page length is 66, but it can be changed to any value between 10 and 100.

Wait

This option sets the default for continuous-feed or single-sheet paper. The initial value is No, indicating continuous-feed paper. If you change it to Yes for single sheets, 1-2-3 waits after each page is printed.

Setup

This option specifies a setup string of control characters to be sent to your printer before every print request. The default is blank, indicating no print control codes. You may supply any valid control codes up to 39 characters in length. The control codes can be obtained from your printer manual. Precede each code with a backslash (\) and also a 0, if necessary, to make a three-digit code.

Name

This option allows you to specify the installed printer to use. The default value is the first printer selected during installation.

Delay

This sets the number of minutes between when 1-2-3 Releases 2.3 and above discover a printer error and when they report it. This is important with background printing. You can enter a number between 1 and 30 for the number of minutes, or you can enter 0 to have 1-2-3 wait indefinitely.

Quit

This option exits the /Worksheet Global Default menu.

/Worksheet Global Default Update

Description

This command saves entries and changes made with the /Worksheet Global Default Printer command to a file called 123.CNF. This file is loaded every time you bring up the 1-2-3 package. You can also select this command by selecting the Update command button in the Default Settings dialog box.

/Worksheet Page

Description

This command inserts an empty row into the current worksheet and puts a page-break symbol (|::) in the current column of the new row. Before you execute this command, position the cell pointer in the first row you want on the new page. This command is equivalent to entering a page-break symbol on an empty row manually. 1-2-3 ignores worksheet contents on the same row with the page-break symbol. To remove the page-break symbol, delete the row, erase the cell, or change the cell's contents.

:Print Background

Description

This command prints your Wysiwyg output in the background so you can continue to work on other tasks. When you print in the background, Wysiwyg stores the printed information temporarily in a file. Before you can use this command, you must execute the BPrint program from DOS.

Option

Your only option for this command is the filename you enter where Wysiwyg temporarily stores the information to be printed. Wysiwyg will add an .ENC extension. If you specify an existing filename, you must select between Cancel and Replace. After you select the name of the file, Wysiwyg will start sending the information to the file. When Wysiwyg has sent all of the information in the file to the printer, Wysiwyg deletes the temporary file.

:Print Config

Description

This command changes print configuration options like font cartridges, printer interface, print bin used, and the print orientation.

Options

Printer

This option selects a printer to use from the list of printers chosen during installation.

Interface

This option selects the connection between the computer and the printer. Select a number between 1 and 9, representing Parallel 1, Serial 1, Parallel 2, Serial 2, LPT1, LPT2, LPT3, COM1, or COM2.

1st-Cart

This option chooses the first font cartridge.

2nd-Cart

This option chooses the second font cartridge.

Orientation

This option selects whether the printer prints in portrait mode, which is standard, or landscape mode, which rotates your print output 90 degrees to print it sideways.

Bin

This option selects the bin from which the printer retrieves the paper for printers with multiple-sheet feed options.

Quit

Returns you to the :Print menu.

:Print File

Description

This command prints your Wysiwyg output to disk rather than to the printer. To print the resulting file, use the DOS COPY command. You do not need 1-2-3 or Wysiwyg to handle printing from disk.

Option

The only option for this command is the filename you enter. Wysiwyg adds .ENC as the file extension. If you specify the name of an existing file, you must select Cancel or Replace. Once you select the name of the file, Wysiwyg starts sending information to the file; you do not need to select Go as you do when printing with 1-2-3.

:Print Go

Description

This command tells Wysiwyg to start printing to the printer.

:Print Info

Description

This command removes or displays the Wysiwyg Print Settings dialog box.

:Print Layout Borders

Description

This command changes the border columns and border rows. These columns and rows will appear on each page printed.

Options

Top

This option chooses border rows for the top of the printed pages. Select a range containing the rows to use.

Left

This option chooses border columns for the left of the printed pages. Select a range containing the columns to use.

Clear

This option removes existing border columns and rows.

Quit

This option returns you to the :Print Layout menu.

:Print Layout Compression

Description

This command sets whether or not printed output will be compressed, and by what percentage.

Options

None

This option prints with no compression.

Manual

This option lets you manually define the extent of expansion or compression. Enter a number less than 100 to compress the output or a number greater than 100 to expand the output.

Automatic

This option compresses the output to fit an entire print range on a page. It uses manual page breaks to determine how much data fits on each page.

:Print Layout Default

Description

This command changes the current page layout or default page layout.

Options

Restore

This option replaces the current settings with the default ones.

Update

This option replaces the default settings with the current ones.

:Print Layout Library

Description

This command maintains a library of page layouts on disk. This allows you to use the same page layout in several worksheets.

Options

Retrieve

This option replaces the current page layout with a layout saved to disk. Select a page layout library.

Save

This option stores the current layout in a file. Enter a name for the page layout library. If the name you specify already exists, you must choose Cancel or Replace to specify whether you want to replace the existing file with the current layout.

Erase

This option permanently removes a layout from the library.

:Print Layout Margins

Description

This command changes any of the margins on the page layout.

Options

You can specify which of the margins you want to change by selecting Left, Right, Top, or Bottom and then entering the distance you want for the margin. You can also choose Quit to return to the Layout menu.

:Print Layout Page-Size

Description

This command specifies the dimensions of the paper you will use for output.

Options

These options select the following predefined page sizes:

1	Letter size (8 1/2 x 11 inches)
2	International A4 size (8 1/4 x 11 11/16 inches)
3	80 column by 66 line listing size (8 x 11 inches)
4	132 column by 66 line listing size (13½ x 11 inches)
5	80 column by 72 line listing size (8 x 12 inches)
6	Legal size (8 1/2 x 14 inches)
7	International B5 size (7 x 9^{13}⁄16 inches)
Custom	This option defines a custom page size. Enter the length and width followed by "in" for inches, "mm" for millimeters, or "cm" for centimeters.

:Print Layout Titles

Description

This command creates or removes a header or footer for every page of output.

Options

Header

This option supplies the header that appears at the top of every page. Enter the header using the same rules as those for headers in 1-2-3.

Footer

This option supplies the footer that appears at the bottom of every page. Enter the footer using the same rules as those for footers in 1-2-3.

Clear

This option removes an existing header or footer, or both.

Quit

This option returns you to the :Print Layout menu.

:Print Preview

Description

This command previews how the print range will appear when printed. After viewing the preview, press any key to display the next page or, on the last page, to return to the :Print menu.

:Print Quit

Description

This command returns you to the READY mode.

:Print Range

Description

This command clears or sets a range for printing.

Options

Set

This option selects the print range. Select any range to print.

Clear

This option eliminates the setting of the print range.

:Print Settings

Description

This command controls how Wysiwyg prints the print range.

Options

Begin

This option specifies the first page to print.

End

This option specifies the last page to print.

Start-Number

This option specifies which page number to use on the first page.

Copies

This option specifies the number of copies to print.

Wait

This option has the printer pause between pages (Yes) or restores continuous printing (No).

Grid

This option chooses whether grid lines that indicate cell boundaries are printed (Yes) or omitted (No).

Frame

This option determines whether the worksheet frame is printed (Yes) or not (No).

Reset

This option restores the default print settings.

Quit

This option returns you to the :Print menu.

:Quit

Description

This command returns you to the READY mode.

Chapter **7**

1-2-3's Built-In
Functions

1-2-3's built-in functions provide ready-made formulas for a wide variety of specialized calculations. They are frequently referred to as @functions because each function must begin with the @ symbol. Since the formulas are already designed and tested, you can have instant reliability when you include them in your models. The built-in functions also allow you to perform calculations like square root and cosine, extending your range of formulas beyond those you can create with the formula operators covered in Chapter 3.

The 93 functions in Release 2.4 are the same functions as those in prior releases with a few exceptions, such as the @ISAAF and @ISAPP functions introduced in Release 2.2. 1-2-3 Release 2.4 introduces a new @ function, @CLEAN, to remove unwanted ASCII characters from 1-2-3 entries. 1-2-3 supports the use of customized functions that are attached through 1-2-3's Add-In manager, which is discussed in Chapter 14.

With Release 2.4, you can enter two @functions with icons on 1-2-3's predefined palettes. If you define macros for entering other @functions, you can use the instructions in Chapter 14 for entering other @functions with user icons.

The functions supplied with 1-2-3 are grouped into eight categories: database, date and time, financial, mathematical, logical, special, statistical, and string. Each of these groups, except the database functions, is covered by category in this chapter. Since the database functions require a knowledge of 1-2-3's data management features, they are covered in Chapter 9. For quick reference, Table 7-1 provides a list of 1-2-3's built-in functions and the category to which each belongs.

Function	Type
@@(*cell*)	Special
@ABS(*number*)	Math
@ACOS(*number*)	Math
@ASIN(*number*)	Math
@ATAN(*number*)	Math
@ATAN2(*x,y*)	Math
@AVG(*list*)	Statistical
@CELL(*attribute string,range*)	Special
@CELLPOINTER(*attribute string*)	Special
@CHAR(*code*)	String
@CHOOSE(*number,list*)	Special
@CLEAN(*string*)	String
@CODE(*string*)	String
@COLS(*range*)	Special
@COS(*number*)	Math
@COUNT(*list*)	Statistical
@CTERM(*interest,future value,present value*)	Financial
@DATE(*year,month,day*)	Date & Time
@DATEVALUE(*date string*)	Date & Time
@DAVG(*input range,offset column,criteria range*)	Database
@DAY(*serial date number*)	Date & Time
@DCOUNT(*input range,offset column,criteria range*)	Database
@DDB(*cost,salvage,value,life,period*)	Financial
@DMAX(*input range,offset column,criteria range*)	Database
@DMIN(*input range,offset column,criteria range*)	Database
@DSTD(*input range,offset column,criteria range*)	Database
@DSUM(*input range,offset column,criteria range*)	Database
@DVAR(*input range,offset column,criteria range*)	Database
@ERR	Special
@EXACT(*string1,string2*)	String
@EXP(*number*)	Math

Table 7-1.   *1-2-3's @ functions*

Function	Type
@FALSE	Logical
@FIND(*search string,entire string,starting location*)	String
@FV(*payment,interest,term*)	Financial
@HLOOKUP(*code to be looked up,table location,offset*)	Special
@HOUR(*serial time number*)	Date & Time
@IF(*condition to be tested,value if true,value if false*)	Logical
@INDEX(*table location,column number,row number*)	Special
@INT(*number*)	Math
@IRR(*guess,range*)	Financial
@ISAAF(*name*)	Logical
@ISAPP(*name*)	Logical
@ISERR(*value*)	Logical
@ISNA(*value*)	Logical
@ISNUMBER(*value*)	Logical
@ISSTRING(*value*)	Logical
@LEFT(*string,number of characters to extract*)	String
@LENGTH(*string*)	String
@LN(*number*)	Math
@LOG(*number*)	Math
@LOWER(*string*)	String
@MAX(*list*)	Statistical
@MID(*string,start number,number of characters*)	String
@MIN(*list*)	Statistical
@MINUTE(*serial time number*)	Date & Time
@MOD(*number,divisor*)	Math
@MONTH(*serial date number*)	Date & Time
@N(*range*)	String
@NA	Special
@NOW	Date & Time
@NPV(*discount rate,range*)	Financial
@PI	Math

Table 7-1.   *1-2-3's @ functions* (continued*)*

Function	Type
@PMT(*principal, interest, term*)	Financial
@PROPER(*string*)	String
@PV(*payment, periodic interest rate, number of periods*)	Financial
@RAND	Math
@RATE(*future value, present value, number of periods*)	Financial
@REPEAT(*string, number of times*)	String
@REPLACE(*original string, start location, # characters, new string*)	String
@RIGHT(*string, number of characters to extract*)	String
@ROUND(*number to be rounded, place of rounding*)	Math
@ROWS(*range*)	Special
@S(*range*)	String
@SECOND(*serial time number*)	Date & Time
@SIN(*number*)	Math
@SLN(*cost, salvage value, life*)	Financial
@SQRT(*number*)	Math
@STD(*list*)	Statistical
@STRING(*number, number of decimal places*)	String
@SUM(*list*)	Statistical
@SYD(*cost, salvage value, life, period*)	Financial
@TAN(*number*)	Math
@TERM(*payment, interest, future value*)	Financial
@TIME(*hour, minute, second*)	Date & Time
@TIMEVALUE(*time string*)	Date & Time
@TODAY	Date & Time
@TRIM(*string*)	String
@TRUE	Logical
@UPPER(*string*)	String
@VALUE(*string*)	String
@VAR(*list*)	Statistical
@VLOOKUP(*code to be looked up, table location, offset*)	Special
@YEAR(*serial date number*)	Date & Time

Table 7-1.   *1-2-3's @ functions* (continued)

All the @functions follow the same basic format. Each has a special keyword or name that tells 1-2-3 which function you want to use. Most also require *arguments* that define your exact requirements for the function in a particular situation. The basic format rules for @ functions are as follows:

- Every function begins with the @ sign.

- The @ sign is followed by a function name or keyword. When entering this name, you must match 1-2-3's spelling exactly. Either upper- or lowercase can be used, although function names are shown in uppercase throughout this chapter.

- You should never use spaces within a function. Always enter **@SUM(A5,A15..A17)**, not @SUM (A5, A15..A17) or @SUM(A5, A15..A17). If you accidentally include a space, 1-2-3 will enter EDIT mode and prompt you to edit the function.

Here are a few general rules that apply to all functions:

- Function arguments must be encased in a set of parentheses.

- Functions that require no arguments do not require parentheses. One example is @RAND, which generates a random number between 0 and 1. The other seven functions that do not require arguments are @PI, @TRUE, @FALSE, @ERR, @NA, @NOW, and @TODAY.

- When a function is used as an argument for another function, you must use a second set of parentheses, because each function must have its arguments enclosed within parentheses. To use the result of @SUM in an @ROUND function, for example, enter the functions like this:

      @ROUND(@SUM(A2..A10),2)

- Functions usually require arguments to be separated by commas. (The separator character can be changed with /Worksheet Global Default International Punctuation, as described in Chapter 4. These arguments can be numeric values, cell addresses, string values, or special codes. The exact requirements for each function are covered in the expanded description of the function later in this chapter.

- Functions are recalculated when they or another cell that affects the function's value is entered or edited. The exceptions to this are the functions @@, @CELL, @CELLPOINTER, @DATEVALUE, @ISAAF, @ISAPP, @NOW, @RAND, @STRING, @TIMEVALUE, and @VALUE. These functions are recalculated every time the worksheet recalculates formulas.

Different functions require different types of arguments and use them in different ways. Here are some of the format rules that pertain to different function types and uses:

- Some functions, such as @SUM, expect a list of arguments that can be entered in any order. @SUM adds together all the entries in its argument list to produce a sum, for example. If you wanted to sum the values in B1..B10, D4, and D7, then you could enter **@SUM(B1..B10,D4,D7)**, **@SUM(D7,B1..B10,D4)**, or any other order of the three entries within the parentheses.

- Arguments that must be provided in a specific order cannot be reordered without causing erroneous results. For example, @ROUND requires two arguments, the number to be rounded and the position. The latter argument tells 1-2-3 how many places from the decimal to round the number. The function must always be written in the form @ROUND(*number,position*), with the numbers or references substituted in the function. If you enter the function in the form @ROUND(*position,number*), an error results.

- Arguments that require a specific argument type cannot have another type substituted without causing an error. For example, the @TRIM function removes leading, trailing, and consecutive spaces from a string and requires a string as an argument. An error results if any argument other than a string is provided.

- For arguments requiring string values, enclose the actual values in double quotation marks, as in **"this is a string"**. For string arguments you can also enter a cell address (C3), a range name (SALES), or a string formula (+B3&"Company Report"). If you need to review string arithmetic, review Chapter 3.

- If a function requires a range as an argument, you can specify the range with a range address (A2..A10), a range name (SALES), or a combination (SALES,A2..A10). If the function expects a range and you enter a single cell reference, 1-2-3 converts the single cell reference to a range address.

- Functions requiring numeric values accept them in many formats. You can use actual values (876.54), cell addresses (A2), range names (INTEREST), formulas (2*A3), functions (@PI), and combinations of the other options (@PI*3+@SUM(D2..D4)+NUMBER).

- 1-2-3 cannot use an external file reference as a function argument. To include values from other files as part of the function in Releases 2.2 and above, you must establish a link to the cell in the other file from within a worksheet. You can then reference the address of this cell as a function argument.

Add-In @functions follow the same basic entry rules as regular @functions, except they must be attached at the beginning of your 1-2-3 session. They cannot be attached once you have worksheet entries. The procedures for working with Add-In @functions are covered in Chapter 14.

You can see how these various kinds of functions and arguments are used as you proceed through the examples in this chapter. You may want to read through the descriptions of all the function groups, or you may prefer to concentrate on particular categories that meet an immediate need. The descriptive paragraphs at the beginning of the section on each function category provide an overview of the types of formulas offered by the functions in the group. The description of each individual function covers its format, its arguments if any, and its use. The functions in each category are covered in alphabetical order.

Date and Time Functions

The date and time functions access, create, and manipulate the serial numbers 1-2-3 uses to represent dates and times. For example, you can use date and time arithmetic in your models to determine elapsed time for a production process, to learn whether a loan is overdue, or to age your accounts receivable.

1-2-3 can handle dates between January 1, 1900, and December 31, 2099. A unique serial number is assigned to each of these days, with the number for January 1, 1900, being 1 and December 31, 2099, being 73050. The serial date number represents the number of days since December 31, 1899. (1-2-3 assigns a serial number to February 29, 1900, even though 1900 was not a leap year.) Although representing every date in terms of its distance from this date in the past may seem a little strange, this is what provides the date arithmetic features of the package. If all dates have the same comparison point, you can subtract one date from another to determine how many days apart they are. This provides an effective method to determine an overdue loan, for example, in that the loan due date can be compared to the current date. If the loan due date is less than the current date, the loan is overdue.

Time of day is represented by fractional serial numbers. Midnight is 0.000, 6:00 AM is .25, noon is .5, 6:00 PM is .75, 11:59:59 PM is .99999, and so on. Serial time numbers can be entered in either decimal (.75) or fraction (3/4) format.

Serial date and time numbers are always used in calculations, but you can use the Format commands to create a more understandable display. Either /Worksheet Global Format or /Range Format can be used to select one of the Date or Time format displays. Since one cell can contain both a whole and a fractional serial number (representing respectively the date and time) but one cell cannot use both a Date format and a Time format, you must decide which you would like displayed.

1-2-3 has five Date format options, two of which offer additional options through the /Worksheet Global Default Other International Date command. There are four Time format options. Two are permanent and two can be altered with the /Worksheet Global Default Other International Time command. For example, the serial number 33507.75 represents 6:00 PM on September 26, 1991. When the cell containing the entry is formatted with Date format 1, it displays as 26-Sep-91. When it is formatted with D6, or Time format 1, it displays as 06:00:00 PM. Review the Date and Time formats in Chapter 4 if you are not familiar with these options.

Some of the date and time functions generate serial numbers (@DATE, @NOW), while others expect them as arguments (@DAY, @YEAR). For those functions that expect serial date numbers as arguments, entering both an integer and fractional serial number causes 1-2-3 to ignore the fractional part of the entry. The integer number portion is ignored if a serial time number is expected. If only the integer portion is entered, the value .0, representing midnight, is used for the time.

For a quick way to enter and format the current date, use the date icon on Wysiwyg palette 3.

@DATE

The @DATE function allows you to create a serial date number when you supply the date components.

Format

@DATE(*year, month, day*)

Arguments

year	A number that is between 0 and 199. 1900 is represented by 0, 1991 by 91, and 2099 by 199.
month	A number from 1 through 12.
day	A number from 1 through 31. The number must be valid for the month chosen. Since month 9 (September) has only 30 days, for example, 31 is an invalid value for the day when 9 is used for the month.

Use

You can use the @DATE function whenever you want to enter a serial date number on a worksheet. Any date used in arithmetic calculations must be in serial form. Figure 7-1 shows an application for the @DATE function. In this example, the charge for each video rental is determined by the number of days a patron has had the video. The date the video is checked out is entered in column C, and the date it is returned is entered in column D. The two serial dates are subtracted, and the result is multiplied by the daily charge of $2.25 to determine the amount the patron should pay. The resulting formula, shown in Figure 7-2, is (+D5–C5)*2.25. The formulas are stored in column E.

```
C5: (D1) [W10] @DATE(92,8,30)                                    READY

          A       B        C          D        E      F      G     H
    1                   Every Rental Videos
    2
    3                        Checked    Checked  Amount
    4   Customer-id   Video    Out        In      Due
    5   21-876         350  30-Aug-92 01-Sep-92  $4.50
    6   23-765         610  30-Aug-92 01-Sep-92  $4.50
    7   34-651         212  01-Sep-92 02-Sep-92  $2.25
    8   11-223         443  01-Sep-92 05-Sep-92  $9.00
    9   56-675         551  02-Sep-92 03-Sep-92  $2.25
   10   77-990         215  03-Sep-92 06-Sep-92  $6.75
   11   11-983         623  04-Sep-92 05-Sep-92  $2.25
   12
```

Figure 7-1.   *A worksheet using @DATE entries*

A Date format is applied to the range of entries in columns C and D, and Currency format is applied to the range of entries in column E. The @DATE function provides a simple method of entering dates without knowing how 1-2-3 records dates. If you want to convert the formula into a value, enter the @DATE function, then press F9 (CALC) to convert the formula to the value it represents.

@DATEVALUE

The @DATEVALUE function returns a serial date number when you supply a date string in one of the five Date formats.

Format

@DATEVALUE(*date string*)

```
E5: (T) [W15] (D5-C5)*2.25                                      READY

          A        B          C              D            E         F
    1                   Every Rental Videos
    2
    3                      Checked        Checked       Amount
    4   Customer-id  Video Out            In            Due
    5   21-876        350 @DATE(92,8,30)  @DATE(92,9,1)  (D5-C5)*2.25
    6   23-765        610 @DATE(92,8,30)  @DATE(92,9,1)  (D6-C6)*2.25
    7   34-651        212 @DATE(92,9,1)   @DATE(92,9,2)  (D7-C7)*2.25
    8   11-223        443 @DATE(92,9,1)   @DATE(92,9,5)  (D8-C8)*2.25
    9   56-675        551 @DATE(92,9,2)   @DATE(92,9,3)  (D9-C9)*2.25
   10   77-990        215 @DATE(92,9,3)   @DATE(92,9,6)  (D10-C10)*2.25
   11   11-983        623 @DATE(92,9,4)   @DATE(92,9,5)  (D11-C11)*2.25
   12
```

Figure 7-2.   *The formulas for @DATE*

Arguments

date string   A string argument in quotes, or a cell reference containing a date in one of the five acceptable Date formats.

Three of the acceptable Date formats are fixed, and two are dependent on the format chosen with /Worksheet Global Default Other International Date. Acceptable date string formats for September 29, 1991, are "29-Sep-91", "29-Sep", "Sep-91", and "29.09.91" if D4 (Date format 4) is set at DD.MM.YY; "9/29/91" if D4 is set at MM/DD/YY; "29/09/91" if D4 is set at DD/MM/YY; and "91-09-29" if D4 is set at YY-MM-DD. Acceptable D5 (Date format 5) options are similar, except only the month and day are shown, as in "09-29".

Use

Use the @DATEVALUE function when you want to perform arithmetic with dates that have been entered in string format. For example, if you enter **@DATEVALUE("23-Oct-91")** in a cell, 33534 is returned. You could then use this value in a formula. Figure 7-3 provides an example of a model using the @DATEVALUE function. It solves the same problem as the model for video charges in Figure 7-1, except that it uses the @DATEVALUE function and string date formats in the function arguments. The formulas to subtract the two dates are located in column E and follow the format of (@DATEVALUE(D5)–@DATEVALUE(C5)) *2.25, as you can see in the control panel of Figure 7-3.

@DAY

The @DAY function extracts the day number from a serial date number.

```
E5: (C2) (@DATEVALUE(D5)-@DATEVALUE(C5))*2.25                        READY

          A          B        C          D          E      F      G      H
    1                        Every Rental Videos
    2
    3                       Checked    Checked      Amount
    4  Customer-id  Video Out   In                  Due
    5  21-876             350 30-Aug-92 01-Sep-92   $4.50
    6  23-765             610 31-Aug-92 01-Sep-92   $2.25
    7  34-651             212 01-Sep-92 02-Sep-92   $2.25
    8  11-223             443 01-Sep-92 05-Sep-92   $9.00
    9  56-675             551 02-Sep-92 03-Sep-92   $2.25
   10  77-990             215 03-Sep-92 06-Sep-92   $6.75
   11  11-983             623 04-Sep-92 05-Sep-92   $2.25
   12
```

Figure 7-3.   *Using @DATEVALUE to work with label (string) dates*

Format

@DAY(serial date number)

Arguments

serial date number   The serial date number of the desired date, which must be between 1 and 73050 to stay within the acceptable range of January 1, 1900, to December 31, 2099.

Use

Use this function whenever you are interested in only the day portion of a date. Used with @DATE, for example, the @DAY function entered as @DAY(@DATE(91,12,14)) returns 14. When @DAY is used with @DATEVALUE, the function that is entered as @DAY(@DATEVALUE("24-Dec-91")) returns a value of 24.

Suppose you want to extract the day from a loan origination date so you can use it to generate payment due dates. @DAY can do this. The dates in Figure 7-4 are generated with @DATE, using a day generated with @DAY. The cell must be formatted with one of the Date formats or the serial date number is displayed. The advantage of this approach is that the same date formulas can be used for all loans, because only the day numbers vary. Naturally you must make some allowance for months with fewer than 31 days. This could be handled with the @IF function, covered later in this chapter.

@HOUR

The @HOUR function extracts the hour from a serial time number, using a military time representation. For example, @HOUR(.75) equals 6:00 PM or 18:00 (on a 24-hour clock).

E3: (D1) [W10] @DATE(92,12,@DAY(C3))   READY

	A	B	C	D	E	F	G
1	Loan		Origination		December Payment		
2	Number	Branch	Date		Date		
3	23419	200	14–Jul–92		14–Dec–92		
4	45617	908	21–Mar–91		21–Dec–92		
5	23145	540	02–Jun–92		02–Dec–92		
6	22231	200	19–Nov–88		19–Dec–92		
7	87654	313	27–Mar–93		27–Dec–92		
8							

Figure 7-4.   Using @DAY

Format

@HOUR(*serial time number*)

Arguments

serial time number	A decimal fraction between 0.000 and 0.9999. You can enter *serial time number* as a fraction or a decimal number. It can be generated by @TIME, @TIMEVALUE, or @NOW.

Use

Use this function whenever you want to work with only the hour portion of a time entry. The function always returns a value between 0 and 23. Used with @TIME, which creates a serial time number when provided with arguments of hour, minute, and second, the function entered as **@HOUR(TIME(10,15,25))** returns 10.

If you want to record the delivery hour for packages received, you might capture the time of receipt and use the @HOUR function to access the specific hour. Figure 7-5 provides an example of using the @HOUR function for this purpose.

@MINUTE

The @MINUTE function extracts the minute from a serial time number.

Format

@MINUTE(*serial time number*)

D3: @HOUR(A3)   READY

	A	B	C	D	E	F	G
1	Time	Package					
2	Received	Number	Recepient	Hour			
3	08:04:06 AM	1761	B. Jones	8			
4	09:11:00 AM	3421	R. Gaff	9			
5	09:30:00 AM	2280	J. Bowyer	9			
6	09:45:00 AM	7891	J. Kiger	9			
7	10:30:00 AM	1975	M. Williams	10			
8	11:05:00 AM	3411	B. Jobes	11			
9	11:15:00 AM	5412	R. Gaff	11			
10	11:55:00 AM	1562	K. Larson	11			
11							

Figure 7-5.   *Using @HOUR*

Arguments

serial time number	A decimal fraction between 0.000 and 0.9999. can enter *serial time number* as a fraction, a decimal number, a cell reference, or a function.

Use

Use this function whenever you want to work with only the minute portion of a time entry. The function always returns a value between 0 and 59. Used with @TIME, which creates a serial time number when provided with arguments of hour, minute, and second, the function entered as **@MINUTE(@TIME(10,15,25))** returns 15.

For example, if you manage a radio station and are interested in recording the exact minutes when you receive calls for hourly radio contests, you could use the @MINUTE function to handle the task. Certain types of contests might generate many calls and immediate winners, whereas other types could be announced throughout the hour before a listener called in with the correct answer. You might want to capture the time of receipt of the winning calls. Figure 7-6 shows the use of the @MINUTE function for this purpose.

@MONTH

The @MONTH function extracts the month number from a serial date number.

Format

@MONTH(*serial date number*)

E3: @MINUTE(C3)   READY

	A	B	C	D	E	F
1	Contest		Time		Minutes	
2	Type	Prize	Of Call	Winner	After Hour	
3	Mystery Guest	$50.00	09:30:00 AM	D. Black	30	
4	Golden Oldies	record	10:05:00 AM	P. Silver	5	
5	Wacky DJ Quiz	$125.00	09:08:00 AM	B. Brown	8	
6	Mystery Guest	$75.00	01:05:00 PM	J. Lyson	5	
7	Unknown Music	dinner	02:13:00 AM	F. Pitts	13	
8	Golden Oldies	record	04:20:00 AM	C. Vernier	20	
9	Wacky DJ Quiz	$150.00	02:18:00 AM	D. Gleason	18	
10	Mystery Guest	$300.00	09:45:00 AM	S. Moore	45	
11	Golden Oldies	record	10:02:00 AM	W. Koone	2	
12	Unknown Music	dinner	12:06:00 PM	R. Stork	6	
13						

Figure 7-6.   Using @MINUTE

Arguments

serial date number The serial date number of the desired date, which must be between 1 and 73050 to stay within the acceptable range of January 1, 1900, and December 31, 2099. The *serial date number* can be generated by another function such as @NOW, @DATEVALUE, or @DATE.

Use

Use this function whenever you are interested in only the month portion of a date. Used with @DATE, the @MONTH function entered as **@MONTH(@DATE (91,12,14))** will return 12. When @MONTH is used with @DATEVALUE, for example, the function entered as **@MONTH (@DATEVALUE("24-Dec-91"))** returns 12.

For example, you could use this function to extract employees' vacation months from historic data, so you could monitor vacation schedules to plan for temporary help. You could use this function to extract the month from the vacation start date. The dates in Column D in Figure 7-7 are used to extract the month number. The advantage of this approach is that the same date formulas can be used for all vacations, as only the month numbers vary.

@NOW

The @NOW function is used to stamp a worksheet cell with the current system date and time. The function does not require any arguments and is simply entered as **@NOW**.

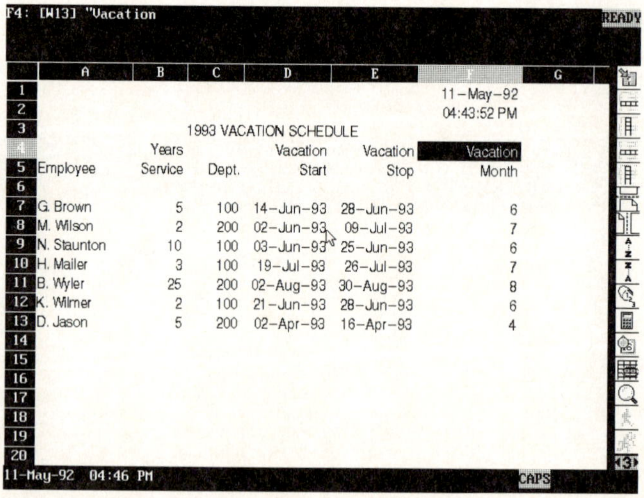

Figure 7-7.   Using @NOW as a date and time stamp

Use

Use the @NOW function whenever you wish to place the current date or time in a worksheet cell. The integer portion of the serial number generated is the current date, and the decimal fraction is the time. @NOW appears as a date if formatted with one of the Date format options, and displays as time if formatted with one of the Time formats.

Figure 7-7 shows a worksheet where two cells, F1 and F2, have @NOW entered in them. One is formatted as a date and the other as a time.

Including these cells in the print range when a report is printed date- and time-stamps the report so you can always identify the most recent copy of the report.

Press F2 (EDIT) followed by F9 (CALC) and then ENTER to freeze the serial date and time number placed in a cell by @NOW and change it to a fixed value.

@SECOND

The @SECOND function extracts the second from a serial time number.

Format

@SECOND (*serial time number*)

Arguments

serial time number   A decimal fraction between 0.000 and .9999. You can enter *serial time number* as a fraction, a decimal number, a cell reference, or a function.

Use

Use this function whenever you want to work with only the seconds portion of a time entry. The function always returns a value between 0 and 59. For example, if cell A3 contains a serial time number representing 11:08:19, @SECOND(A3) equals 19. Used with @TIME, the @SECOND function, entered as @SECOND (@TIME(10,15,25)), returns 25.

@TIME

The @TIME function allows you to create a serial time number when you supply the time components.

Format

@TIME (*hour, minute, second*)

Arguments

hour	A number between 0 and 23. Midnight is represented by 0 and 11:00 PM by the number 23.
minute	A number between 0 and 59.
second	A number between 0 and 59.

Use

Use this function whenever you want to enter time on a worksheet. When you enter time with this function, you can perform arithmetic operations with the time value, since it is stored as a serial time number. If you tried using times stored as labels, you would not get the results you expect since the labels are treated as zeros. You can freeze the serial time number by pressing F9 (CALC) when 1-2-3 is in the EDIT mode.

Figure 7-8 shows a worksheet that uses the @TIME function to record the time vehicles are brought in for repair and the time the work on each is completed. Entering both sets of numbers makes it easy to perform calculations with the time values, and the /Range Format Date Time command allows you to choose a suitable Time display format.

The formulas like +D5-B5 in E5 of Figure 7-8 calculate the difference between the time each car was brought in for repair and the time it was completed. Using the

```
B5: (D7) [W12] @TIME(8,5,0)                                          READY
QUICK CAR REPAIR – Oct. 5, 1992
Job        Time                          Time         Elapsed
Number        In Repair                  Out            Time
1     08:05 AM Tires                  09:17 AM     01:12
2     08:10 AM Brakes                 10:34 AM     02:24
3     08:28 AM Steering               01:18 PM     04:50
4     08:33 AM Lube                   09:44 AM     01:11
5     08:39 AM Transmission           05:21 PM     08:42
6     08:42 AM Brakes                 11:09 AM     02:27
7     08:44 AM Muffler                10:35 AM     01:51
8     08:53 AM Tune–Up                12:35 PM     03:42
9     09:03 AM Brakes                 11:39 AM     02:36
11-May-92   05:02 PM
```

Figure 7-8.   Time arithmetic

Short International format under /Range Format Date Time allows you to show just the hours and minutes (represented by the decimal fraction) for the difference between the two time values.

@TIMEVALUE

The @TIMEVALUE function returns the serial time number, given the string value of the time.

Format

@TIMEVALUE(*time string*)

Arguments

time string   A single string value conforming to one of the acceptable Time formats and enclosed in double quotation marks.

"HH:MM:SS AM/PM" is acceptable because it conforms to D6 (Date format 6), which is the first Time format option. "HH:MM AM/PM" is acceptable because it conforms to the D7 format, which is the second Time format option. Formats D8 and D9 have more than one option and are changeable through the /Worksheet Global Default International Time command. The acceptable formats for D8 and D9 depend on which format is in effect. Chapter 4 provides additional information about Time formats.

Use

Use this function whenever you want to generate a serial time number from a string value. For example, suppose an entry in your worksheet was originally entered as a string, but you decide you want to use it in a calculation of elapsed time. The @TIMEVALUE function makes this possible. It has the same capability to create a serial time number as the @TIME function, but accepts a string for input rather than accepting three separate numeric values for hour, minute, and second. As an example, you might enter **@TIMEVALUE("2:14:14 PM")**, which gives the value 0.5932175926. This value could then be used in a time formula.

Figure 7-9 shows the same worksheet used in Figure 7-8 for the @TIME example, except that all the times are entered as labels. For example, the entry in D5 is '09:17 AM. This means that you must change the formula in column E because you cannot subtract two labels to determine a difference. The formula is changed to use @TIMEVALUE, as shown in cell E5 of Figure 7-9. The entry in this cell is

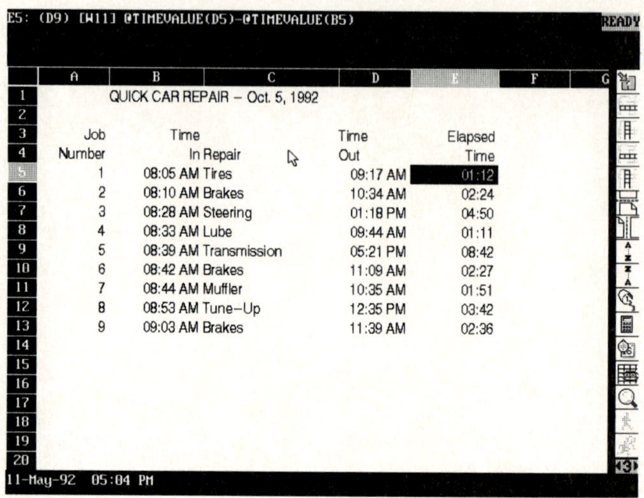

Figure 7-9.   *Working with time labels*

@TIMEVALUE(D5)-@TIMEVALUE(B5), and the cell is formatted in the Short International Time format.

@TODAY

The @TODAY function is used to stamp a worksheet cell with the current system date. The function does not require any arguments and is simply entered as **@TODAY**. It contains the integer portion of the @NOW function. With Releases 2.01 and above, 1-2-3 automatically converts the function to @INT(@NOW).

Use

You can use the @TODAY function whenever you want to place the current date in a worksheet cell. @TODAY creates a date serial number that appears as a date if formatted with one of the Date format options. This feature can prevent the problem of not being able to tell which one of several printed reports is the most current. If the @TODAY function is entered somewhere in every worksheet and included in your print range, you can always identify the most recent copy of a report. As an example, a worksheet can have the following heading:

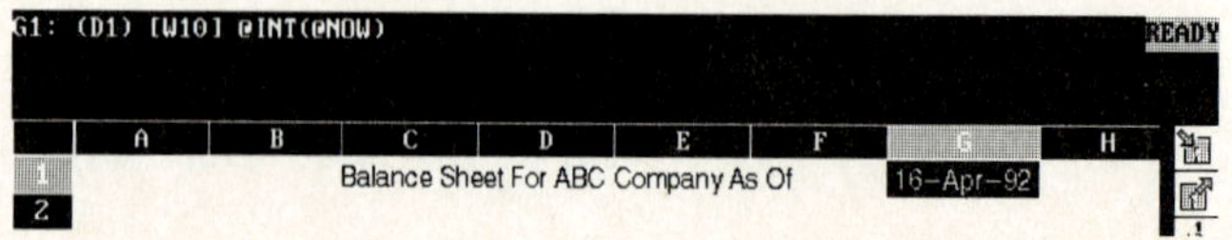

In this worksheet, G1 contains @TODAY, which 1-2-3 displays as @INT(@NOW), and the result is formatted as a date. Including this cell in the print range when a report is printed will date-stamp the report.

Press F2 (EDIT) followed by F9 (CALC) and then ENTER to freeze the serial date number placed in a cell by @TODAY, and change it to a fixed value.

For the same effect as @TODAY with the added bonus of a date format, click the date icon that looks like this: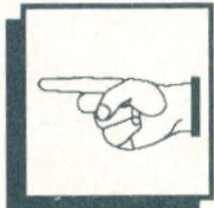

1-2-3 enters a date format in the cell and applies a format of MM/DD/YY unless you set /Worksheet Global Default Other International Date to a different date format.

@YEAR

The @YEAR function extracts the year number from a serial date number.

Format

@YEAR(*serial date number*)

Arguments

serial date number   The serial date number of the desired date, which must be between 1 and 73050 to stay within the acceptable range of January 1, 1900, to December 31, 2099. The *serial date number* can be generated by another function such as @NOW, @DATEVALUE, or @DATE.

Use

Use this function whenever you are interested in only the year portion of a date. Used with @DATE, the @YEAR function can be entered as **@YEAR(@DATE(91,12,14))** to return 91. Used with @DATEVALUE as in **@YEAR(@DATEVALUE("24-Dec-91"))**, the function returns 91.

One sample use for this function is to determine the start year for each of a group of employees. You can reference the date of hire and extract the year number for an easy reference to the anniversary year, as shown in Figure 7-10.

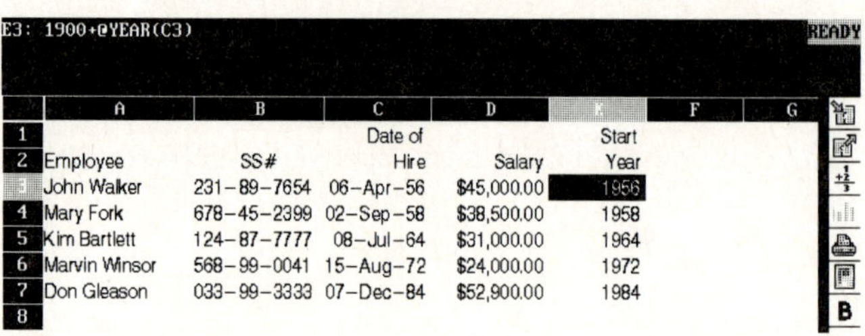

Figure 7-10.   *Using @YEAR*

Financial Functions

The primary use of 1-2-3's financial functions is for investment calculations and other calculations concerned with the time value of money. For example, you can use them to monitor loans, annuities, and cash flows over a period of time. A second group of financial functions calculate depreciation so you can quickly compare the effects of different depreciation methods.

Since many of these functions deal with interest rate calculations, you should be aware of the two acceptable ways of entering interest rates for these calculations. You can always enter a percent as a decimal fraction, for example, .15 for 15%. Your other option is to enter the percent with the percent sign and have 1-2-3 convert your entry to a decimal fraction for internal storage. For example, 15% would be stored as .15.

Many of the financial functions require a term and a rate as arguments. It is important that the same unit of time be used for both arguments. If a term is expressed in years, an annual interest rate should be used. If a term is expressed in months, a monthly interest rate should be used.

@CTERM

Given a present and a future value for an investment, as well as a fixed interest rate, @CTERM computes the number of time periods it takes to reach the future value.

Format

@CTERM(*interest,future value,present value*)

Arguments

interest	The fixed interest rate per compounding period. It can be expressed as a percentage or a decimal fraction within the function, or it can be stored in a cell and referenced with the cell address or a range name. It can also be computed with a formula from within the function.
future value	The value the investment will have at some point in the future. The objective of the @CTERM function is to determine the point at which an investment will reach a specified future value. This argument must be a value or a reference to a cell containing a value.
present value	The current value of the investment. This argument must be a value or a reference to a cell containing a value.

Use

The @CTERM function provides a quick answer when you want to know how long it takes an investment to grow to a certain value. The formula used by the function is as follows:

$$\frac{\text{natural log}\,(\textit{future value/present value})}{\text{natural log}\,(1 + \textit{periodic interest rate})}$$

For example, if you have $5,000 to invest today and feel you can get an 11 percent return on your money, you might want to know how long it would take to triple your investment at that rate. @CTERM (11%/12,15000,5000) provides the answer, assuming the compounding occurs monthly. The result is 120.397 months or 10.03309 years.

@DDB

The @DDB function calculates depreciation expense for a specific period using the double declining balance method.

Format

@DDB(*cost, salvage value, life, period*)

Arguments

cost	The amount you paid for the asset. This argument must be a value or a reference to a cell containing a value.
salvage value	The value of the asset at the end of its useful life. Like *cost,,* this argument must be a value or a reference to a cell containing a value.
life	The expected useful life of the asset; that is, the number of years needed to depreciate the asset from its cost to its salvage value. Normally expressed in years, this argument, too, must be a value or a reference to one.
period	The specific time period for which you are attempting to determine the depreciation expense. Normally the number of the year for which you are calculating depreciation expense, this argument must be a value or a reference to one.

Use

The @DDB function gives you a figure for depreciation expense, using an *accelerated depreciation method* (one that allows you to write off more depreciation expense in the early years of an asset's life). The asset can no longer be depreciated when its *book value* (that is, cost minus total depreciation to date) equals its salvage value.

The formula used in the calculation of double declining balance depreciation is as follows:

$$\frac{\text{book value for the period} * 2}{\text{life of the asset}}$$

1-2-3 makes adjustments in the calculations to ensure that total depreciation is exactly equal to the asset cost minus the salvage value. The @DDB function does not switch to straight-line depreciation when straight-line would be equal or greater.

Figure 7-11 shows the use of this function to determine the proper depreciation expense for each year in an asset's five-year life. The cost of the asset was $11,000, and its salvage value is $1,000.

@FV

The @FV function computes the future value of an investment based on the assumption that equal payments will be generated at a specific rate over a period of time.

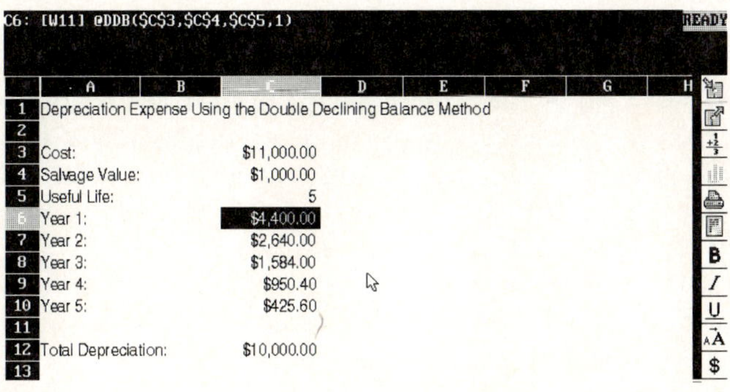

Figure 7-11.   *A double-declining balance depreciation*

Format

@FV(*payment,interest,term*)

Arguments

payment	The amount of the equal payments for the investment. This argument must be a value or a reference to a value.
interest	The periodic interest rate earned by the investment. This argument must be a value or a reference to a value.
term	The number of periods for the investment. This argument must be a value or a reference to a value.

Use

This function is designed to perform calculations for an ordinary annuity. It uses the following formula:

$$\text{payment} * \frac{((1 + \text{periodic interest rate})^{\text{raised to the } n \text{ power}}) - 1}{\text{periodic interest rate}}$$

where *n* is the number of periods.

You can use the @FV function used to calculate the value for an ordinary annuity assuming that you plan to deposit $500 a month for each of the next 36 months and will continue to receive interest on this money at a constant rate of 12 percent compounded monthly. You would enter the formula **@FV(500,1%,36)** to display the result of 21538.43.

This example is based on the premise that interest is paid at the end of the period and that your next contribution is always made on the last day of the period.

The @FV function can be adapted to work with an annuity due (payment is made on the first day of the period), which uses this formula: @FV(payment,interest,term)*(1+interest). Using the same example, your formula is @FV(500,1%,36)*(1+1%). This formula would return 21753.82. This is appropriate when you must make contributions on the first day of the period. Assuming you make annual payments of $5,000 at the beginning of each year and they earn interest at a rate of 10 percent, the value at the end of ten years is represented by the formula @FV(5000,10%,10)*(1+10%), which returns $87,655.83—the value of your annuity after ten years.

@IRR

The @IRR function calculates the internal rate of return on investments.

Format

@IRR(*guess,range*)

Arguments

guess   An estimate of the internal rate of return. Although any number between 0% and 100% will probably work, you encounter situations where the correct internal rate of return cannot be closely approximated. If you think the internal rate of return for an investment is between 15 and 25 percent, 20 percent is a good guess to start with. A series of cash flows that alternate between positive and negative results in more than one internal rate of return. The guess you make affects which of the values is returned. The default for this function is 30 iterations. If 1-2-3 cannot approximate the result within 0.0000001 after 30 attempts, ERR will result.

range   The range of cells containing the cash flows to be analyzed. Negative numbers in this range are considered outflows and positive numbers are inflows. The first number in the range is expected to be negative, since it is the cost of the investment opportunity.

Use

Use the @IRR function whenever you want to find the rate that equates the initial investment with the expected future cash flows generated by the investment. Cash flows must be at equal intervals. If the cash flows are a mixture of positive and negative values, the @IRR function may find multiple internal rates of return. In this case, 1-2-3 returns the internal rate of return closest to the guess.

Figure 7-12 shows the @IRR function used to analyze the stream of projected cash flows shown in A2..A7. As required, the first number in the range is negative, signifying the cost of the investment opportunity. A guess of 12 percent is in D2. The /Range Format Percent command formatted the entries as the percent in D2 and E2. The formula for the internal rate of return is entered in E2 as **@IRR(D2,A2..A7)**. In this example, the function returns 19.58%.

@NPV

The @NPV function computes what you should be willing to pay for a projected stream of cash flows, given your desired rate of return.

Format

@NPV(*discount rate,range*)

Arguments

discount rate	A fixed periodic interest rate used to discount expected cash flows so you can project their worth in today's dollars.
range	The series of cash flows to be discounted. These cash flows do not have to be equal, but they must be evenly spaced over a period of time (monthly, quarterly, and so forth). They are assumed to occur at the end of a period; the first cash flow is received at the end of the first period.

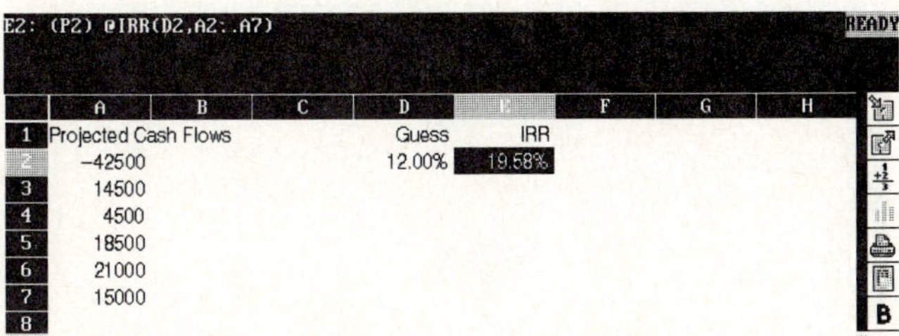

Figure 7-12.   Using @IRR to compute the internal rate of return

Use

This is one of the most frequently used functions in 1-2-3, since it deals with the time value of money.

Figure 7-13 presents a sample use of @NPV. The expected cash flows are shown in B2..G2. Notice from the column headings that these cash flows are received monthly, yet the interest rate in D4 is expressed as an annual rate. Make note of this discrepancy between the time periods of the interest rate and the payments. The difference can be resolved by changing the interest rate to a monthly figure in the function argument. The formula for the calculation is @NPV(D4/12,B2..G2). It produces a result of $57,396.93, indicating that if the discount rate is 15 percent, you should be willing to pay up to $57,396.93 for this investment.

Note

This function is not designed to handle situations where you make an immediate or up-front payment, although you could easily construct a formula to do this. Since the initial payment is already in today's dollars, there is no need to discount it. Your initial outflow can be subtracted from the result of the @NPV function. Using the data shown in Figure 7-13 and assuming the initial cost is $20,000, the formula in D6 is @NPV(D4/12,B2..G2)–20000 and the result is 37396.93.

@PMT

The @PMT function calculates the appropriate payment amount for a loan when given the principal, interest rate, and term.

Format

@PMT(*principal,interest,term*)

```
D6:  (C2) [W11] @NPV(D4/12,B2..G2)                                      READY

        A        B        C        D        E        F        G      H
1                JAN      FEB      MAR      APR      MAY      JUNE
2                5,000    10,000   15,000   10,000   15,000   5,000
3
4  Annual Interest Rate:                    15%
5
6  Net Present Value:               $57,396.93
7
8                                                                       B
```

Figure 7-13.   *The net present value calculations*

Arguments

principal A numeric value representing the amount borrowed. It can be provided as a number or as a cell address, formula, range name, or other function.

interest A numeric value representing the interest rate. It can be provided as a numeric constant in the formula or as a cell reference, formula, or range name.

term The number of payments in the loan term. If monthly payments are made on a loan spanning several years, multiply the years of the term by 12 and use the product for this argument. It can be expressed as a fraction, a formula, a range name, or a cell address.

It is extremely important that the same unit of time be used for both the term and the interest rate. An annual interest rate means a term of a number of years, whereas a monthly interest rate indicates a term consisting of a number of months.

Use

You can use this function whenever you want to calculate the amount of a loan payment. This function makes it easy to calculate your own personal loan tables. Given a specific range of values for the principal and interest rate, you can look at a range of payment amount options and see which are possible given your current monthly income.

Figure 7-14 provides an example of a payment table. Interest rates are entered across row 3. Cells A4..A20 are used for hypothetical principal amounts.

Only one payment formula must be entered; the rest can be copied. **@PMT($A4,B$3/12,240)** is entered in B4. The dollar signs in the arguments are required to keep part of the cell addresses from changing as the formula is copied. $A4 indicates that the column for the reference is absolute, although the row can change. The reverse is true of B$3: the row can change, but the column is constant. B$3 is divided by 12 to convert the annual interest into a monthly interest. The term is 20 years, which equates to 240 monthly periods. The formula can be copied to accommodate the remaining places in the table. You must widen some of the columns in order to fit the currency display in the cells.

Note

Financial institutions calculate payment amounts in a number of ways. The formula used by the @PMT function is as follows:

$$principal * interest / (1 - (1 + interest)^{-n})$$

where n is the number of payments.

```
B4: (C2) [W10] @PMT($A4,B$3/12,240)                                      READY
```

	A	B	C	D	E	F	G
1							
2							
3		9.00%	9.50%	10.00%	10.50%	11.00%	11.50%
4	$100,000	$899.73	$932.13	$965.02	$998.38	$1,032.19	$1,066.43
5	$105,000	$944.71	$978.74	$1,013.27	$1,048.30	$1,083.80	$1,119.75
6	$110,000	$989.70	$1,025.34	$1,061.52	$1,098.22	$1,135.41	$1,173.07
7	$115,000	$1,034.68	$1,071.95	$1,109.77	$1,148.14	$1,187.02	$1,226.39
8	$120,000	$1,079.67	$1,118.56	$1,158.03	$1,198.06	$1,238.63	$1,279.72
9	$125,000	$1,124.66	$1,165.16	$1,206.28	$1,247.97	$1,290.24	$1,333.04
10	$130,000	$1,169.64	$1,211.77	$1,254.53	$1,297.89	$1,341.84	$1,386.36
11	$135,000	$1,214.63	$1,258.38	$1,302.78	$1,347.81	$1,393.45	$1,439.68
12	$140,000	$1,259.62	$1,304.98	$1,351.03	$1,397.73	$1,445.06	$1,493.00
13	$145,000	$1,304.60	$1,351.59	$1,399.28	$1,447.65	$1,496.67	$1,546.32
14	$150,000	$1,349.59	$1,398.20	$1,447.53	$1,497.57	$1,548.28	$1,599.64
15	$155,000	$1,394.58	$1,444.80	$1,495.78	$1,547.49	$1,599.89	$1,652.97
16	$160,000	$1,439.56	$1,491.41	$1,544.03	$1,597.41	$1,651.50	$1,706.29
17	$165,000	$1,484.55	$1,538.02	$1,592.29	$1,647.33	$1,703.11	$1,759.61
18	$170,000	$1,529.53	$1,584.62	$1,640.54	$1,697.25	$1,754.72	$1,812.93
19	$175,000	$1,574.52	$1,631.23	$1,688.79	$1,747.16	$1,806.33	$1,866.25
20	$180,000	$1,619.51	$1,677.84	$1,737.04	$1,797.08	$1,857.94	$1,919.57

```
16-Apr-92   06:47 PM                                                      NUM
```

Figure 7-14.   *Creating a payment table*

@PV

The @PV function determines the present value of an investment, assuming a fixed periodic interest rate and a series of equal payments over a period of time.

Format

@PV (*payment, periodic interest rate, number of periods*)

Arguments

payment	The amount of the equal payments, expressed as a value or a reference to a cell containing a value. Only one value may be referenced because payments are assumed to be equal.
periodic interest rate	The periodic interest rate used to discount the cash flows. This argument must be a value or a reference to a cell containing a value.
number of periods	The term over which the payments will be generated. This argument must be a value or a reference to a cell containing a value.

Use

Use the @PV function whenever you want to determine today's value of money to be received in the future. You can use the function to assess what you should be willing to pay for an investment today, given that it will return a certain amount of money in future periods. You can also use the function to evaluate a lump sum payment as compared to future periodic payments if you have this option on the sale of a property or the receipt of prize money.

For example, assume that you have the option of taking a one-time cash payment of $500,000 versus monthly payments of $5,000 for the next 20 years. To compare the two options you must look at the present value of the future cash flows. This means you must make an assessment of the rate of return you would receive for investing the $5,000 monthly payments. This example assumes that you could get 12 percent compounded monthly. The present value becomes @PV(5000,1%,240). The result indicates that the best decision, without considering the effect of taxes, is to choose the lump sum payment since the present value of the monthly payments is 454097.

@RATE

The @RATE function determines the periodic interest rate that must be earned to increase a specified present value to a future value over a specific term.

Format

@RATE(*future value,present value,number of periods*)

Arguments

future value	The value of the investment at the end of a specified growth period. This argument must be a value or a reference to a value.
present value	The current value of an investment. This argument can contain a numeric value, a formula, or a reference to one of those two options.
number of periods	The compounding periods over which the investment will grow. This reference to argument must be a value or a reference to a value.

Use

The @RATE function is used to determine the periodic interest rate that is required to realize a desired growth rate. If you give the number of periods in months, you get a monthly rate. You can convert this to an annual rate by multiplying by 12.

Suppose you invested $5,000 in a bond maturing in eight years; you could use the @RATE function to calculate the rate of return. This example assumes that the maturity value is $10,000 and that the interest is compounded monthly. The required formula is @RATE(10000,5000,8*12). The rate of return is .72 percent, a monthly rate. To annualize it, multiply by 12 to obtain 8.7 percent.

@SLN

The @SLN function computes the straight-line depreciation for one period in an asset's life. (*Straight-line depreciation* has the same amount of depreciation each year of the asset's life.)

Format

@SLN(*cost,salvage value,life*)

Arguments

cost	The amount paid for the asset. This number can be included in the function or stored in a cell and referenced with an address or range name.
salvage value	The remaining value of the asset at the end of its useful life. This number can be included in the function or stored in a cell and referenced with an address or range name.
life	The number of years of useful life, or the time required to depreciate the asset to its salvage value. This number can be included in the function or stored in a cell and referenced with an address or range name.

Use

You can use the @SLN function whenever you want to depreciate an asset evenly over its useful life, so that the depreciation expense is the same for all years. The formula used by the function is as follows:

$$\frac{cost - salvage\ value}{life}$$

For example, if you purchase a $12,000 machine and estimate its salvage value to be $2,000 at the end of its five-year life, you can use @SLN to calculate its depreciation expense. The formula you would enter is **@SLN(12000,2000,5)**, which returns 2000.

@SYD

The @SYD function computes depreciation expense for an asset using the sum-of-the-years'-digits depreciation method. This is an accelerated depreciation method that depreciates an asset more in the early years of its life.

Format

@SYD(*cost,salvage value,life,period*)

Arguments

cost	The amount paid for the asset. This number can be included in the function or stored in a cell and referenced with an address or range name.
salvage value	The remaining value of the asset at the end of its useful life. This number can be included in the function or stored in a cell and referenced with an address or range name.
life	The number of years of useful life or the time required to depreciate the asset to its *salvage value*. This number can be included in the function or stored in a cell and referenced with an address or range name.
period	Within the useful life of the asset, the year for which you want the depreciation expense calculated. This number can be included in the function or stored in a cell and referenced with an address or range name. It should not be greater than the *life* of the asset.

Use

The @SYD function lets you calculate the sum-of-the-years'-digits depreciation expense for any period in the life of an asset. The formula used by the function is

$$\frac{(cost-salvage)*(life-period \text{ for depreciation expense}+1)}{(life*(life+1)/2)}$$

The worksheet in Figure 7-15 shows the sum-of-the-years'-digits depreciation expense for an asset that was purchased for $12,000 and has a $2,000 salvage value. The cell pointer points to the formula for the depreciation expense in the first year. This calculation uses the formula @SYD($E$3,$E$4,$E$5,1). The worksheet shows

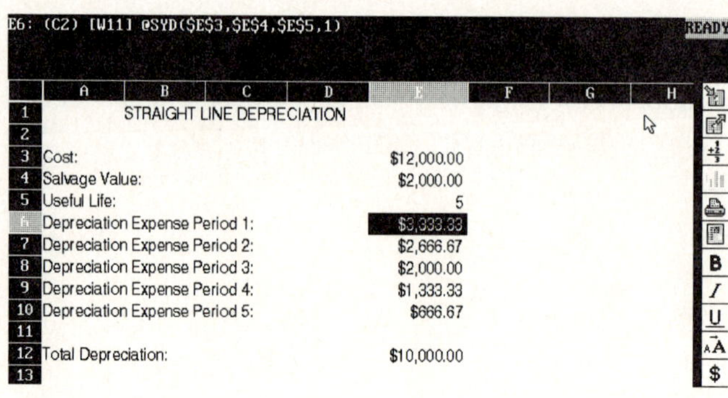

Figure 7-15.   *Computing sum-of-the-years'-digits depreciation with @SYD*

the depreciation expense for the other four years, as well. The only difference in the remaining formulas is in the last argument, which indicates the period for which depreciation expense is being calculated.

@TERM

The @TERM function returns the number of payment periods required to accumulate a given future value if the payment amount and interest rate remain fixed.

Format

@TERM(*payment,interest,future value*)

Arguments

payment	A fixed periodic payment, stored as a number in the function or in a cell that can be referenced by the function.
interest	The fixed interest rate per compounding period. It can be expressed as a percentage or decimal fraction within the function, or stored in a cell and referenced with the cell address or a range name.
future value	The value of the investment at some point in the future. This argument must be a value or a reference to a cell containing a value.

Use

Use the @TERM function to calculate the number of periods required for an ordinary annuity to reach a given value. For example, it permits you to determine how long it will take to save for a dream vacation home or luxury yacht, assuming you set aside a fixed amount at the end of each month.

The formula behind 1-2-3's calculations is

$$\frac{\text{natural log } (1+(\text{future value}*\text{interest}/\text{payment}))}{\text{natural log } (1+\text{interest})}$$

As an example, suppose you set $350 aside at the end of each month for the purpose of accumulating a $25,000 down payment on a vacation home. If the funds are placed in a money market fund paying 10.25 percent annual interest, @TERM will calculate the time required to accumulate the down payment. The formula is @TERM(350,1025/12,25000) and returns 56 months.

Note

This function differs from the @CTERM function in that you must provide the payment amount, not the present value. @CTERM focuses on the number of growth periods required for an investment to reach a specific value, while @TERM is concerned with the number of payment periods for an ordinary annuity. To calculate the term of an annuity due, you must use the formula @TERM(*payment,interest,future value*)/(1+*interest*).

Mathematical Functions

1-2-3's mathematical functions perform trigonometric and other numeric calculations. Their primary use is in engineering, manufacturing, and scientific applications.

The angles the functions work with are all expressed in *radians*, a unit of measure that equates the radius and arc length. If you prefer to work with angles in degrees, multiply radians by 180/@PI to produce the conversion. All angles that you enter for the @SIN, @COS, and @TAN functions should be expressed in radians. If they are in degrees, multiply the degrees by @PI/180 to change them into radians.

@ABS

The @ABS function returns the positive or absolute value of a number.

Format

@ABS(*number*)

Arguments

number   Any value, including references to a cell containing a value. If a string is used for *number,,* an error results.

Use

Use the @ABS function whenever you are interested in the relative size of a number and do not care whether it is positive or negative. A good example might be the need to monitor cash overages and shortages in the registers of a retail establishment. Consistent cash overages and shortages indicate a cash control problem that should be corrected. If you monitored both overages and shortages, adding their + and - signs, they might cancel each other out. Looking at the absolute value of the overages and shortages, however, provides a look at the total amount of the differences.

Figure 7-16 provides a look at a restaurant's cash overages and shortages by adding absolute values. If @ABS had not been used, the positive and negative numbers would have partially canceled each other, making the cash differences seem less of a problem.

@ACOS

The @ACOS function returns the inverse cosine (arccosine) when you provide the cosine of an angle.

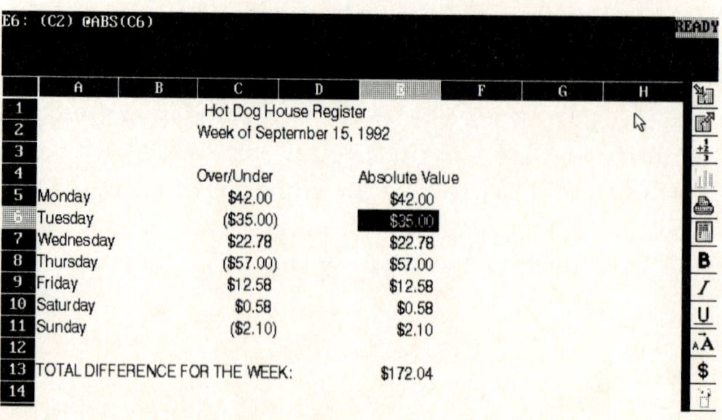

Figure 7-16.   Adding absolute values

Format

@ACOS(*number*)

Arguments

number   The cosine of an angle, which can be in the range of –1 to 1. This numeric value can be provided within the function or through a reference to a cell or range. If you provide a number outside the allowable limits, ERR is returned.

Use

Use the @ACOS function when you know the cosine of an angle but want to know the angle in radians. If you prefer the angle measurement in degrees, you can multiply the result of this function by 180/@PI.

Suppose you were at the top of a cliff in a lighthouse 100 feet above water and wanted to know the angle needed to make a projectile reach a boat approximately 200 feet away (see Figure 7-17). You could find the cosine of the angle by performing the following calculation:

    cos of angle = 100/200
    cos of angle = .5
    @ACOS(.5)*180/@PI = 60 degrees

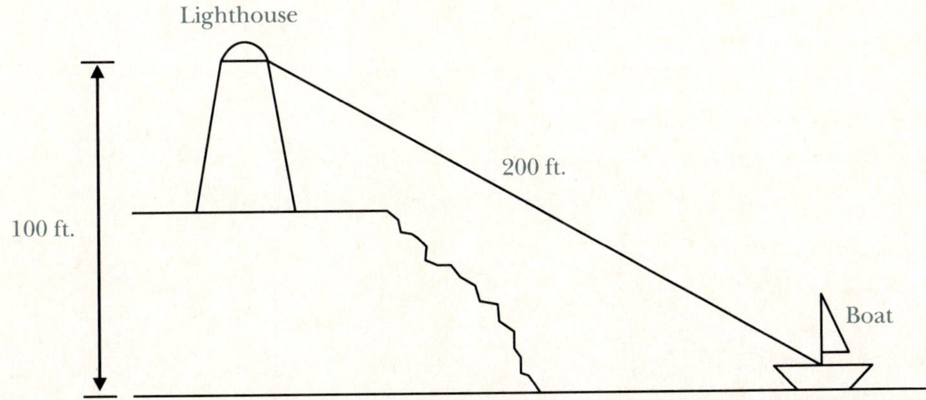

Figure 7-17.   Calculating the angle from the lighthouse to the boat

@ASIN

The @ASIN function is used to determine the arcsine or inverse sine of an angle.

Format

@ASIN (*number*)

Arguments

number   The sine of an angle, which can be in the range of –1 to 1. This numeric value can be provided within the function or through a reference to a cell or range. If you provide a number outside the allowable limits, ERR is returned.

Use

The @ASIN function returns an arcsine between @PI/2 and –@PI/2 and represents an angle in quadrant 1 or 2.

As an example, you can use the @ASIN function to determine the angle of a platform used to roll a barrel into a truck. A diagram of the truck bed and platform is shown in Figure 7-18. The bed of the truck is 3 feet from the ground, and the platform used to roll the barrel is 6 feet long. The sine of the angle between the board and the ground is equal to 3/6, or .5. The equation @ASIN(.5)*180/@PI equals 30 degrees.

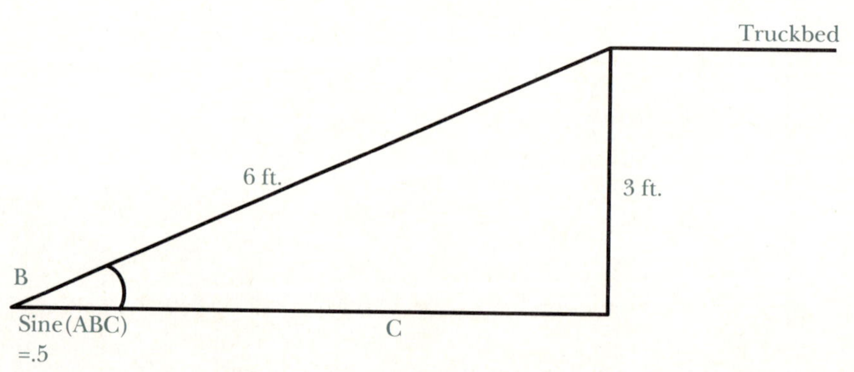

Figure 7-18.   *Using a ramp to get merchandise into a truck*

@ATAN

The @ATAN function calculates the arctangent or inverse tangent of an angle for use in trigonometric problems.

Format

@ATAN(*number*)

Arguments

number   The tangent of an angle, which can be in the range of –1 to 1. This numeric value can be provided within the function or through a reference to a cell or range. If you provide a number outside the allowable limits, ERR is returned.

Use

The @ATAN function returns an arctangent between @PI/2 and –@PI/2 and represents an angle in quadrant 1 or 4.

This function can be used to solve many trigonometric problems. For example, suppose you are playing a championship game of pool and need to pass a ball from point A through point B in the diagram shown in Figure 7-19. The @ATAN function determines the angle at which you should hit the ball.

The location of the ball is 3 inches from the bumper, and the location of the pocket in relationship to the bumper is 4 inches. The tangent between the pocket

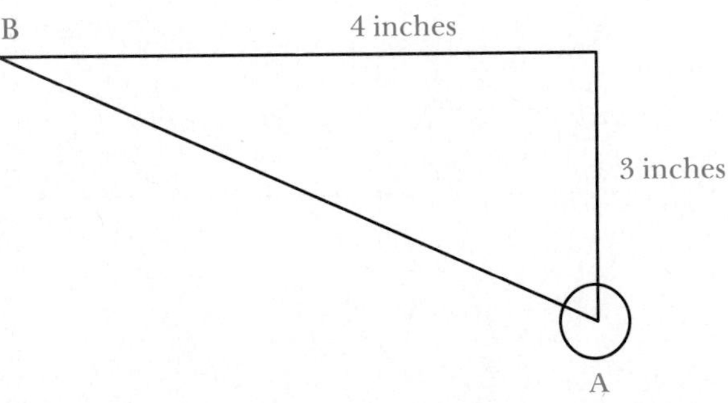

Figure 7-19.   Making the pool shot

and the bumper is equal to 4/3, or 1.333333. @ATAN(1.333333) is .927295 radians. When this is multiplied by 180/@PI, the result is 53.13 degrees.

@ATAN2

The @ATAN2 function returns the 4 quadrant arctangent or the angle in radians whose tangent is y/x.

Format

@ATAN2(x,y)

Arguments

x The x-coordinate of the angle, expressed as a number or a reference to a cell containing a number.

y The y-coordinate of the angle, expressed as a number or a reference to a cell containing a number.

Use

The @ATAN2 function is used to solve trigonometric problems in which you want to differentiate angles found in the first and third quadrants from those found in the second and fourth quadrants. Figure 7-20 shows the values of @ATAN2 for the different quadrants. @ATAN2(1,.5) returns .463647 radians.

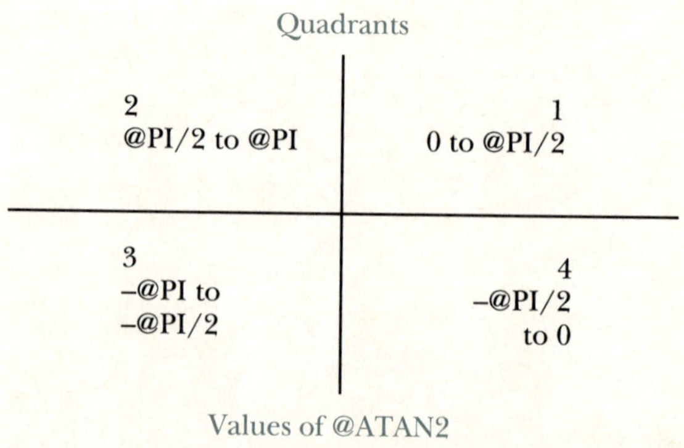

Quadrants

2 @PI/2 to @PI	1 0 to @PI/2
3 –@PI to –@PI/2	4 –@PI/2 to 0

Values of @ATAN2

Figure 7-20.   *Values for @ATAN2 in the different quadrants*

@COS

The @COS function returns the cosine of an angle.

Format

@COS(*number*)

Arguments

number   A number representing the radians in an angle.

Use

Use the @COS function when you have an angle in radians and want to determine the cosine of that angle. This number can assist you in making other determinations, such as distances and other angles. For example, a surveyor can use the @COS function to determine the length of a side of a plot of land in the shape of a right triangle (see Figure 7-21).

The longest side of the plot of land is 50 feet. There is a 60-degree angle at the point of the lot where the surveyor is standing. She would like to know the length of the side on her left (the adjacent side, in mathematics terminology). She constructs the formula COS (60) = x/50. The @COS(60*@PI/180) function returns .5, which can be used to solve for x of 25. @PI/180 was needed because the angle was supplied in degrees.

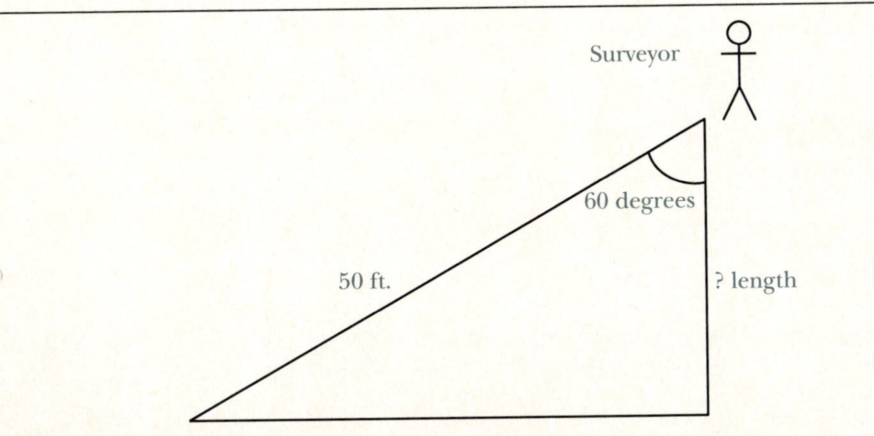

Figure 7-21.   *Determining the length of the side of a plot of land*

@EXP

The @EXP function raises the base *e* (2.718282) to a specific power.

Format

@EXP(*number*)

Arguments

number	The power to which you want to raise *e*. This argument must be a numeric value or a reference to one. *Number* cannot exceed 230 if you wish to display it; it can be as high as 11356 if you just plan to store the number for later calculations.

Use

@EXP is the inverse of @LN and is used whenever you want to raise *e* to a specific power. Here are several examples:

    @EXP(1) equals 2.718282
    @EXP(10) equals 22026.46
    @EXP(@LN(5)) equals 5

@INT

The @INT function allows you to truncate the decimal places in a number to produce a whole number.

Format

@INT(*number*)

Arguments

number	Any value whose integer portion you wish to use. Any digits to the right of the decimal point in *number* are truncated.

Use

Use this function whenever you want to eliminate the decimal portion of a number. It can determine the number of complete batches finished by a production line, for example. In this situation, partial batches may not be of interest, since they would not be ready for shipment. Similarly, if you needed to calculate the number of items that could be produced from a given amount of raw materials, partial items would be of no interest. In both examples, you would not want the number rounded; you would simply want to truncate the decimal portion of the number to look at the number of units. This can be handled with @INT.

The worksheet in Figure 7-22 shows the use of @INT in calculating the number of wallets that can be created from different-sized pieces of cowhide. Partial wallets are not of interest, since one hide cannot necessarily match another.

@LN

The @LN function returns the natural log of a number.

Format

@LN(*number*)

Arguments

number   Any value greater than zero. If *number* is less than zero, ERR is returned.

D4: @INT(A4/$E$1)   READY

	A	B	C	D	E	F	G	H
1	Cowhide needed for 1 wallet –				0.6789 sq. ft.			
2								
3	Available sizes			Wallets Produced				
4		1			1			
5		5			7			
6		10			14			
7		15			22			
8		20			29			
9		25			36			
10								

Figure 7-22.   *Computing the number of finished wallets with @INT*

Use

Natural logarithms are logarithms to the base *e,* where *e* is approximately 2.718282. @LN is the inverse of @EXP, which means that you can incorporate *e* in any calculation with @EXP(1). For example, @LN(@EXP(4)) equals 4, and @EXP(@LN(8)) equals 8. The primary use of logarithms is to make complex calculations less complex. Here are two examples:

    @LN(9) equals 2.197224
    @LN(1.5) equals 0.405465

@LOG

The @LOG function computes the base 10 logarithm of a number.

Format

@LOG(*number*)

Arguments

    number   Any value greater than zero. If *number* is less than zero, ERR is returned.

Use

Like natural logs, base 10 logs are primarily used in scientific or other complex calculations where the rules of logarithms can be used to simplify the math involved. The results returned by 1-2-3 from a few examples of @LOG are as follows:

    @LOG(10) equals 1
    @LOG(100) equals 2
    @LOG(190) equals 2.278753

@MOD

The @MOD function returns the modulus or remainder when a number is divided by another number.

Format

@MOD(*number, divisor*)

Arguments

number	Any positive or negative number or a reference to one.
divisor	Any number other than zero used to divide *number*, as in *number/divisor*.

Use

The @MOD function, which provides the remainder from dividing *number* by *divisor*, is useful in a variety of situations, although creativity is often required to see the applications. For example, this function can be used in conjunction with the date functions covered earlier in the chapter to determine the day of the week. @MOD(@NOW,7) returns a value between 0 and 6, since the @MOD function returns the remainder from a division. If the result is 0, the day is Saturday, and if the result is 6, the day is Friday. Each of the other days is represented by one of the other numbers between 0 and 6.

@PI

The @PI function returns an approximation of the constant π, or 3.14159265. The format of the function is simply @PI, since the function does not require any arguments.

Use

@PI is used frequently in geometric problems involving circumference and area. The circumference of (distance around) a circle is 2*@PI* radius. Given a circle with a radius of 5 inches, you could find the circumference of 31.4 using the formula 2*@PIx5.

@RAND

The @RAND function generates random numbers between 0 and 1. The format of the function is simply @RAND; it has no arguments.

Use

This function is useful for generating test data for simulations. Each time the worksheet is recalculated, the @RAND function takes on a new value. You can create rows and columns of a worksheet with this function to generate data for queuing theory problems or other applications. Each @RAND is a different number, since 1-2-3 uses 15 decimal digits for these numbers.

The worksheet in Figure 7-23 shows numbers generated with the @RAND function. You can control the range of the random number by multiplying the result by a number or adding a number to it. Multiplying @RAND by a factor raises the upper limit to the number you are multiplying by; for example, @RAND*100 provides random numbers between 0 and 100. Adding a fixed number to @RAND raises the lower limit; for example, @RAND*100+50 generates random numbers between 50 and 150.

@ROUND

The @ROUND function is used to round a number in internal storage to a specified number of decimal places.

Format

@ROUND(*number to be rounded, place of rounding*)

```
G3: @RAND*100+50                                                           READY

      A          B         C       D          E       F        G          H
 1   @RAND                             @RAND*100                 @RAND*100+50
 2
 3   0.579094   0.476138            97.37477   87.67271          92.28657   146.0910
 4   0.067969   0.286715            28.01297   95.72851          143.4035   111.2540
 5   0.204075   0.916992            52.79499   12.39471          54.81812   146.1830
 6   0.763783   0.686058            3.650127   30.36549          78.84112   103.3475
 7   0.474741   0.644012            3.003995   97.57856          127.9743   76.88021
 8   0.595361   0.939981            66.22800   75.32957          143.7217   145.9167
 9   0.010055   0.511879            96.46452   46.69364          76.77686   117.6900
10   0.017182   0.506777            36.11253   4.098790          87.53025   71.59018
11   0.461669   0.047225            22.88628   69.28615          63.93095   56.15542
12   0.775428   0.108323            69.94170   41.17698          87.03610   66.83895
13   0.751367   0.927504            90.05336   28.98289          80.54038   146.5553
14   0.803559   0.096597            94.46952   15.49340          90.44011   59.70254
15   0.869464   0.346041            49.12336   65.10377          136.0061   99.82820
16   0.302448   0.586795            45.58583   49.05630          84.66571   57.61228
17   0.896839   0.089000            72.75847   62.80956          112.4757   105.6237
18   0.895714   0.310175            39.07436   63.67290          149.8572   105.6250
19   0.266228   0.902390            25.15109   17.09721          60.40635   119.2963
20   0.000884   0.389751            24.67152   13.54827          90.14776   60.37940
16-Apr-92   06:52 PM                                             NUM
```

Figure 7-23.   Using @RAND

Arguments

number to be rounded

Any value or reference to a value that you want rounded to a specified number of places.

place of rounding

The number of places to the right or left of the decimal point where rounding should occur. The number 5 or higher after the place where 1-2-3 rounds the number causes the number to the left to be increased by one. Using zero for the place of rounding indicates that you want to round to the nearest whole number. Positive numbers indicate rounding to the right of the decimal point, with each higher number moving further to the right. Negative numbers indicate rounding to start at the tens position and move further to the left. For example, Figure 7-24 shows the number 12345.678123 rounded to varying numbers of decimal places in column B, using the formulas in column C.

Use

1-2-3 allows you to display numbers in rounded form if you specify the number of decimal places you wish to see using the Format options (/Worksheet Global Format or /Range Format). However, the full accuracy of the original number, with all its decimal places, is maintained internally. This can cause displayed column totals to seem inaccurate, because the numbers in the column are displayed as rounded while the internal number has greater decimal accuracy. When all this additional decimal accuracy is summed, it can make the total at the bottom of the column disagree with the display of the detail numbers being summed.

The worksheet in Figure 7-25 shows this discrepancy in column E. The figures in column E are a product of column C and column D, but are displayed in Currency format with zero decimal places. The column E figures alone suggest that the total should be $7,041, not the $7,042 shown. The difference of 1 is due to the rounding discrepancy. To solve this problem, more than just a product formula is required. The formula becomes an argument for the @ROUND function, which rounds the product to the nearest whole number (for example, @ROUND (C2*D2,0)). This makes the internal product agree with the display; the sum at the bottom of the column matches the displayed numbers, as you can see in Figure 7-26.

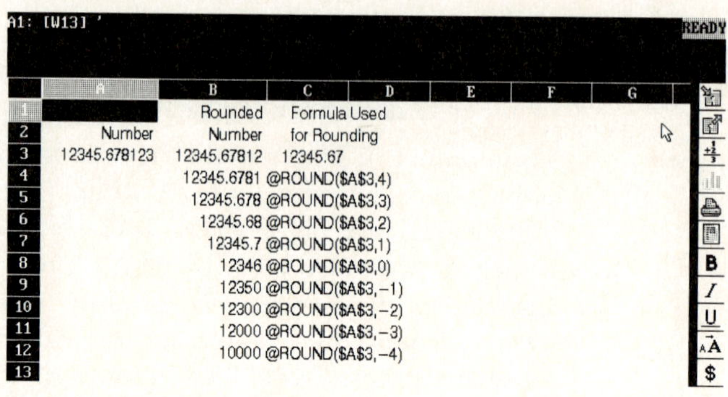

Figure 7-24.   *Using @ROUND*

@SIN

The @SIN function returns the sine of an angle.

Format

@SIN(*number*)

Arguments

number   A number representing the radians in an angle.

Use

Use the @SIN function when you have the measurement of an angle in radians and want to determine the sine of the angle. You can use this information to help make other determinations regarding physical aspects of a problem, such as length or other angles.

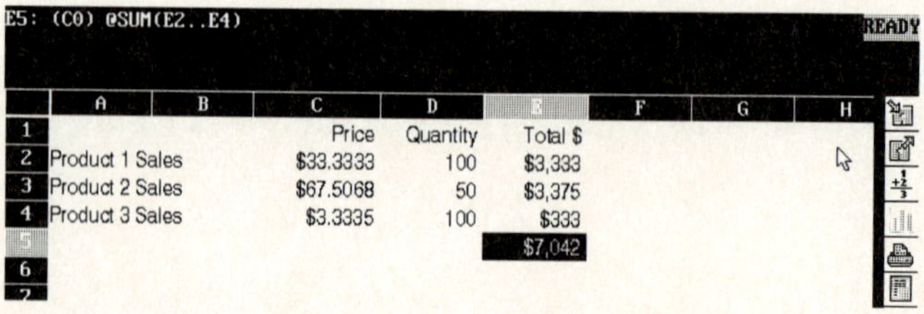

Figure 7-25.   *Discrepancy caused by displaying rounded numbers*

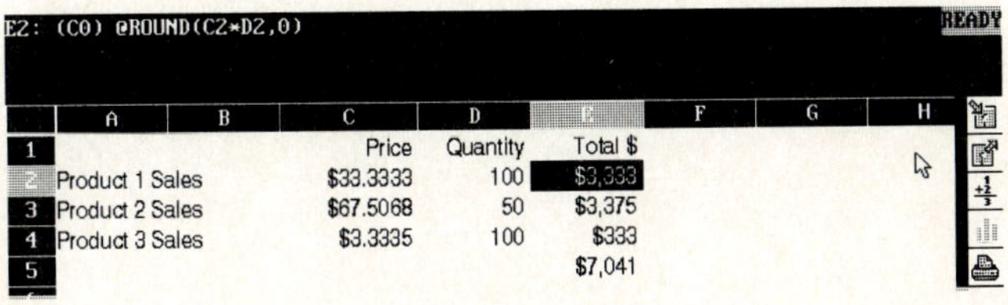

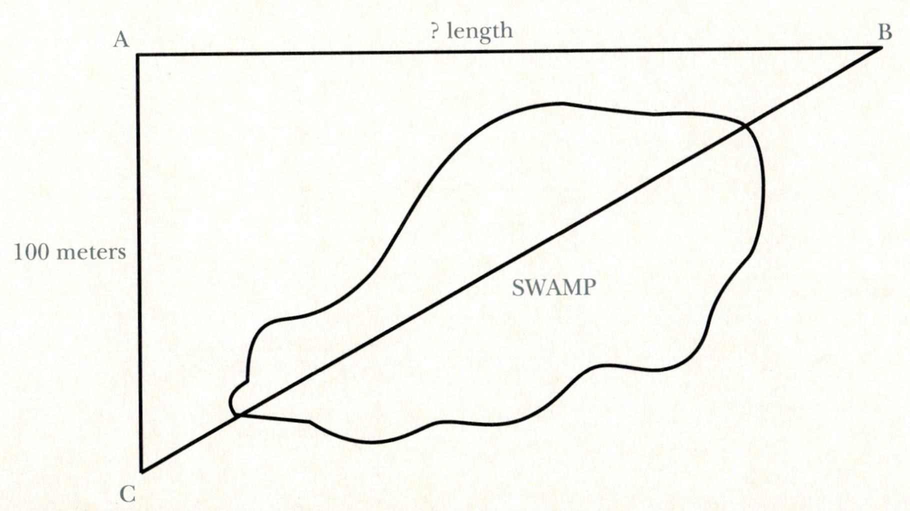

Figure 7-26.   *Rounding numbers to prevent discrepancy*

For example, the diagram in Figure 7-27 shows terrain containing a large swampy area that blocks a road crew from traversing the path from point C to point B. They know that the distance from A to C is 100 meters. If they can determine the distance from B to C, they can use that number in the Pythagorean theorem to determine the distance from A to B. Their entire distance traveled to avoid the swamp would be C to A plus A to B. The angle ABC is 30 degrees.

To calculate the distance from C to B, the crew uses the formula SIN(30)=100/x. Using the @SIN function to determine the sine of 30, @SIN(30*@PI/180) returns .5, and @PI/180 converts 30 degrees to the appropriate number of radians. The distance then is 100/.5, or 200 meters. Using the Pythagorean theorem, $a^2=b^2+c^2$, they get $200^2=100^2+s^2$. This means 40,000 equals 10,000, plus the unknown side squared. The side is thus equal to the square root of 30,000, which they can find with @SQRT(30,000). This function returns 173.2, so the distance from A to B is 173.2 meters.

Figure 7-27.   *Going around the swamp*

@SQRT

The @SQRT function will determine the square root of any positive number.

Format

@SQRT(*number*)

Arguments

number   Any positive integer included in the function or stored in a cell
and referenced with a cell address or range name. If *number* is
negative, ERR is returned.

Use

A number of statistical calculations, the Pythagorean theorem, and economic order
quantity all require square root calculations. Here are a few examples of the way the
square root function operates:

    @SQRT(9) equals 3
    @SQRT(64) equals 8
    @SQRT(100) equals 10

@TAN

The @TAN function returns the tangent of an angle.

Format

@TAN(*number*)

Arguments

number   A number representing the radians in an angle.

Use

The @TAN function returns the tangent, a value useful in solving trigonometric
problems. The diagram in Figure 7-28 requires the @TAN function to determine the

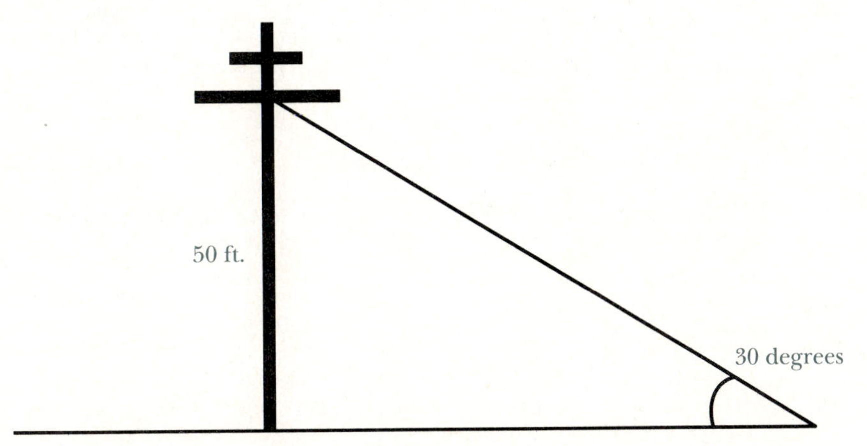

Figure 7-28.   *Guy wires for high-tension power lines*

distance of guy wires for high-tension power lines. The electric company has high-tension wires at the top of a pole 50 feet high and wants to install guy wires from the top of the pole at a 30-degree angle with the ground. The tangent function can be used to determine what distance away from the high-tension wires the guy wires should be attached. The tangent of 30 must be calculated, and, since the angle is measured in degrees, it must also be converted to radians. The formula thus becomes @TAN(30*@PI/180). The height of 50 feet is divided by the result of .5774 to provide a distance of 87 feet.

Logical Functions

1-2-3's logical functions allow you to build conditional features into your models. These functions return logical (true or false) values as the result of condition tests they perform. A value of 0 means false, and a value of 1 means true.

Some of the logical functions are used when ERR (error) and NA (not available) appear as a result of a formula. Both of these values are regarded as numeric and can be tested. This is a particularly important feature because of the ability of NA and ERR to ripple through all the formulas on a worksheet. For example, if NA is used to flag a missing grade for a student, that student's average is shown as NA, and when statistics for all students are combined, the totals also take on the value NA. The functions @ISERR, @ISNA, @ISNUMBER, and @ISSTRING allow you to check for ERR and NA values and stop their effect on the remainder of the worksheet cells by replacing ERR and NA with a value of zero.

The logical functions frequently use logical operators. For example, the expression @IF(A2<>5,3,6) uses a simple operator, and @IF(A1=1#AND#B3=7,5,2) uses a complex operator. These operators are explained in detail in Chapter 3.

@ISAAF

The @ISAAF function checks to see if a particular Add-In @function is attached.

Format

@ISAAF(*name*)

Arguments

name   The name of the Add-In function you want to select. You can enter the argument as a string, a string formula, or as a cell reference as long as the cell contains a label.

Use

The @ISAAF function returns 0 if the function specified as an argument is not defined; 1 is returned if 1-2-3 finds a definition for the @function listed. For example, to check for a function @TAILOR, you would enter **@ISAAF("tailor")**.

@ISAPP

The @ISAPP function checks to see if a particular Add-In is attached.

Format

@ISAPP(*name*)

Arguments

name   The name of the Add-In you want to check. You can enter the argument as a string, a string formula, or as a cell reference as long as the cell contains a label.

Use

The @ISAPP function returns 0 if the Add-In specified as an argument is not attached; 1 is returned if 1-2-3 finds that the specified Add-In is attached. For example, to check for the Allways Add-In, you would enter **@ISAPP("allways")**.

@FALSE

The @FALSE function always returns the logical value 0, permitting you to use it to avoid ambiguity in formulas. @FALSE does not use any arguments.

Use

The @FALSE function is a substitute for zero in formulas. It may seem a lot quicker to type **0** than to type **@FALSE**, but the function is self-documenting and indicates that you want to set up a logical false condition. For example, consider @IF(A3=10,"A3 is equal to 10", @FALSE). If A3 is equal to 10, the string "A3 is equal to 10" is stored in the cell. If A3 is not equal to 10, 0 is stored in the cell.

The worksheet in Figure 7-29 shows @FALSE and its counterpart @TRUE used to determine if the number of items ordered equals the number billed. The formula in D3 checks the numbers ordered and billed for equality and places @TRUE or @FALSE as the value in the cell accordingly. @FALSE displays as 0 and @TRUE as 1. You can then add the 0 and 1 displays to determine how many discrepancies were in the orders. Use the @COUNT function to get an item count for the number of entries in C3..C6, which is 4. This function is placed in C7 as @COUNT(C3..C6). @SUM is then used to total the 0 and 1 displays, returning 3 in D7. Lastly, G9 contains a formula that subtracts D7 from C7 (+C7-D7). The value produced is 1, indicating a discrepancy between number ordered and number billed for one product.

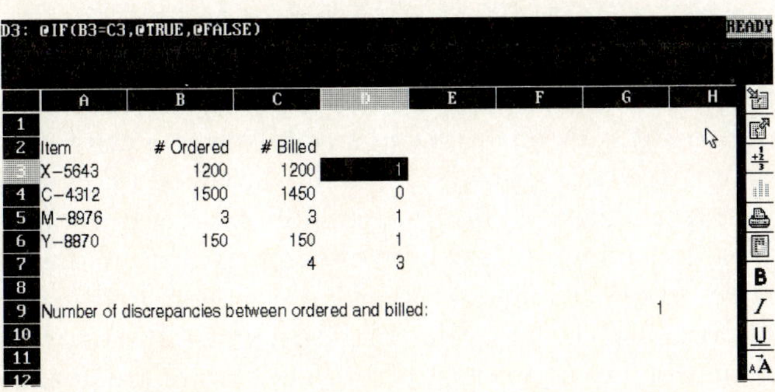

Figure 7-29.   Using @FALSE

@IF

The @IF function permits you to test a logical condition to determine the appropriate value for a cell.

Format

@IF (*condition to be tested, value if true, value if false*)

Arguments

condition to be tested	Any logical expression that can be evaluated as true or false. Examples are A1>=4, D2=H3, and A2+D3<85. The first expression returns a value of true only if A1 contains a value greater than or equal to 4. The logical @IF statement can also work with compound conditions joined by #OR# and #AND#. When this condition is met, the cell containing the @IF takes on the value for true conditions (1); otherwise, it takes on the value for false (0).
value if true	The value the cell containing the @IF statement assumes if the condition is true. This can be either a value or a label. When labels are included in the @IF statement, they must be enclosed in double quotation marks ("). If they are stored in a cell, they can be referenced with a cell address or range name. String formulas are also acceptable as labels. Value entries can be numbers, formulas, or references to cells containing numbers or formulas.
value if false	The value the cell containing the @IF statement assumes if the condition is false. All the conditions listed under *value if true* also apply here.

Use

@IF is one of the most powerful built-in functions because it allows you to get around the limitation of having only one entry in a cell. Now you can set up two different values for a cell and determine which one to use, based on other conditions in your worksheet. You can use this function to establish two discount levels, commission structures, payroll deductions, or anything else requiring more than one alternative.

1-2-3 allows you to nest conditions several levels deep, that is, use a second @IF statement for the true and/or false value in the original @IF. For example, you might want to determine whether a purchase is made by cash or credit and have a code of 1 for cash, assuming that entries without 1 are credit sales. Once the type of sale is determined, you might want to check the amount of the sale to see if it is over the minimum for a discount. The statement might be coded as

```
@IF(TYPE=1,@IF(SALE>1000,.05,.02),@IF(SALE>2500,.04,.01))
```

if TYPE and SALE were named ranges. Regardless of the value for TYPE or SALE, the cell contains a discount amount, but the amount depends on the value of both variables. The following chart shows the appropriate discounts.

Type = 1	Discount
Sale > 1000	.05
Sale < = 1000	.02

Type <> 1	Discount
Sale > 2500	.04
Sale < = 2500	.01

Another example is a calculation of total salary expenses that uses the logical @IF function to calculate FICA and FUTA taxes. The FICA formula in column D of the model shown in Figure 7-30 is the first column that puts the @IF function to work. It has a condition that compares the projected salary to a $48,000 FICA cap (that is, the highest amount of salary on which an employer pays FICA tax). If the projected salary is less than $48,000, FICA tax is calculated as the salary times 7.65 percent. If, however, the salary is equal to or greater than the cap amount, FICA tax is paid on $48,000 at the rate of 7.65 percent.

The FUTA calculation, for unemployment tax, follows a similar pattern. The formula in E4 is as follows:

```
@IF(B4<7000,B4*.06,7000*.06)
```

This states that the FUTA tax is 6 percent of salary if the salary is less than $7,000, but is paid on the cap amount of $7,000 if the salary exceeds that amount.

@ISERR

The @ISERR function checks for a value of ERR in a cell. It returns 1 if the cell contains an error, and 0 if it does not.

Format

@ISERR(*value*)

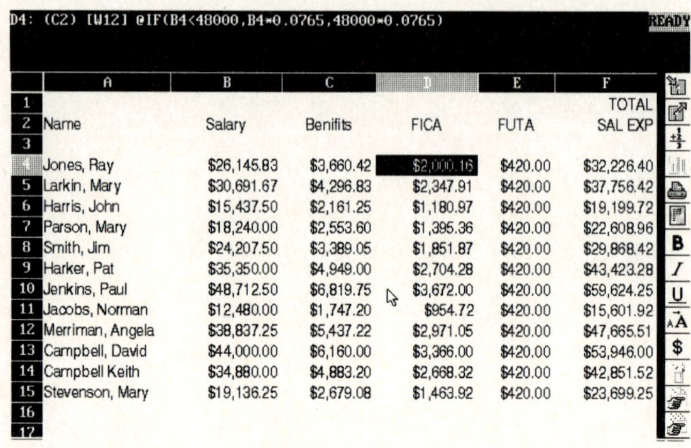

	A	B	C	D	E	F
1						TOTAL
2	Name	Salary	Benifits	FICA	FUTA	SAL EXP
3						
4	Jones, Ray	$26,145.83	$3,660.42	$2,000.16	$420.00	$32,226.40
5	Larkin, Mary	$30,691.67	$4,296.83	$2,347.91	$420.00	$37,756.42
6	Harris, John	$15,437.50	$2,161.25	$1,180.97	$420.00	$19,199.72
7	Parson, Mary	$18,240.00	$2,553.60	$1,395.36	$420.00	$22,608.96
8	Smith, Jim	$24,207.50	$3,389.05	$1,851.87	$420.00	$29,868.42
9	Harker, Pat	$35,350.00	$4,949.00	$2,704.28	$420.00	$43,423.28
10	Jenkins, Paul	$48,712.50	$6,819.75	$3,672.00	$420.00	$59,624.25
11	Jacobs, Norman	$12,480.00	$1,747.20	$954.72	$420.00	$15,601.92
12	Merriman, Angela	$38,837.25	$5,437.22	$2,971.05	$420.00	$47,665.51
13	Campbell, David	$44,000.00	$6,160.00	$3,366.00	$420.00	$53,946.00
14	Campbell Keith	$34,880.00	$4,883.20	$2,668.32	$420.00	$42,851.52
15	Stevenson, Mary	$19,136.25	$2,679.08	$1,463.92	$420.00	$23,699.25
16						
17						

Figure 7-31.   *Calculating FICA with the logical @IF*

Arguments

value   A value, formula, or reference to a cell value.

Use

The @ISERR function is most often used in conjunction with the @IF function, to prevent ERR values from "rippling" through a worksheet. The rippling occurs because any formula that references a cell with ERR will have a result of ERR.

The worksheet in Figure 7-31 shows an ERR for one of the prices in column A. This ERR entry could have been generated by placing @ERR in the cell, or it could be the result of an incorrect formula. When this cell is referenced to supply the unit cost for multiplication, it causes ERR to appear in column C. Again, when the sum is taken in C8, ERR results, since one of the cells in the sum range contains ERR.

To prevent ERR from rippling through the worksheet like this, use the @ISERR function in conjunction with @IF, as shown in column D of Figure 7-31. This allows you to confine ERR to one location.

	A	B	C	D	E	F	G	H
1								
2	Price	Quantity	Total Cost	Total Cost				
3	$3.00	2	$6.00	$6.00				
4	$2.40	4	$9.60	$9.60				
5	ERR	50	ERR	$0.00				
6	$9.25	25	$231.25	$231.25				
7	$10.50	30	$315.00	$315.00				
8			ERR	561.85				
9								

Figure 7-30.   *@IF preventing ERR from rippling through a worksheet*

@ISNA

The @ISNA function allows you to check for a value of NA in a cell. It returns 1 if the cell contains NA, and 0 if it does not.

Format

@ISNA(*value*)

Arguments

value   Normally this is a reference to a cell value, although it may be a formula or a numeric value.

Use

This function is most often used in conjunction with the @IF function to prevent NA values from rippling through all your worksheet formulas.

In some worksheets @NA is used to represent missing data. Any formula that references a cell with a value of NA produces a result of NA. If you would like to prevent the NA value from carrying forward in this way, you can use @ISNA to check for the value NA and substitute a zero or some other value, or you can display an error message to show that the value is missing.

Figure 7-32 shows the @ISNA function used in combination with @IF. The @IF function in E3 checks the condition @ISNA(D3). If D3 is equal to NA, the condition is considered true because @ISNA evaluates as 1. On a true condition, the error message "Missing Unit Price" is displayed. If column D is not equal to NA, column E contains the result of column C times column D.

```
E3: (C2) @IF(@ISNA(D3),"Missing Unit Price",C3*D3)                    READY
```

	A	B	C	D	E	F	G
1							
2	Order Number	Date	Quantity	Price	Total		
3	12760	30–Sep	3	$3.50	$10.50		
4	12781	01–Oct	4	NA	Missing Unit Price		
5	12976	01–Oct	12	$12.20	$146.40		
6	13076	02–Oct	32	$13.75	$440.00		
7	13079	02–Oct	14	$5.25	$73.50		
8	13099	02–Oct	5	$9.84	$49.20		
9	13123	02–Oct	3	NA	Missing Unit Price		

Figure 7-32.   *Checking for missing data*

@ISNUMBER

The @ISNUMBER function allows you to check for a numeric value in a cell. @ISNUMBER returns 1 if the cell contains a number, and 0 if it does not.

Format

@ISNUMBER(*value*)

Arguments

value   Normally this is a reference to a cell value, although it may be a formula or a numeric value.

Use

This function is most often used in conjunction with the @IF function to check whether data entries are of the proper type. For example, an entry of **@ISNUM-BER(56)** in a worksheet cell returns 1, whereas **@ISNUMBER("56")** returns 0. Formulas that return numeric entries will return 1 with this function.

As an example, if you want to check C6 to ensure that a ZIP code was entered as a numeric value, you should use the formula @IF(@ISNUMBER(C6)," ","ERROR -Entry must be numeric"). This formula states that if the entry in C6 is numeric, a blank string will be displayed. If the cell contains a nonnumeric value, an error message appears. This type of error check allows the operator to quickly find errors.

@ISSTRING

The @ISSTRING function allows you to check for a string value in a cell. It returns 1 if the cell contains a string, and 0 if it does not.

Format

@ISSTRING(*value*)

Arguments

value   Normally this is a reference to a cell value, although it may be a formula or a string.

Use

This function is normally used in conjunction with @IF, to test for a string entry during data entry. @ISSTRING("John") returns 1, whereas @ISSTRING(56) returns 0. Since ERR and NA are regarded as numeric values, @ISSTRING(ERR) or @ISSTR-ING(NA) returns 0. You can combine the @IF and @ISSTRING functions as in:

```
@IF(@ISSTRING(C2)," ","Entry is invalid — it is numeric")
```

This formula states that if the entry in C2 is a string, the formula returns a blank label. If the cell contains something other than a string value, an error message appears. With this type of error check you can glance quickly for errors.

@TRUE

The @TRUE function always returns the logical value 1, making this function useful in avoiding ambiguity in formulas. The format of the function is @TRUE; it does not use any arguments.

Use

The @TRUE function is a substitute for the number 1 in formulas. It may seem a lot quicker to type **1** than to type **@TRUE**, but the function is self-documenting and indicates that you want to set up a logical true condition. Here is an example:

```
@IF(A3=10,@TRUE,"A3 is not equal to 10")
```

The worksheet in Figure 7-33 shows @TRUE and its counterpart @FALSE used to determine if the number of items ordered equals the number billed. The formula in D3 checks the numbers ordered and billed for equality and places @TRUE or @FALSE as the value in the cell accordingly. @TRUE displays as 1, @FALSE as 0. You can then add the displays of 0 and 1 to determine how many discrepancies are in the

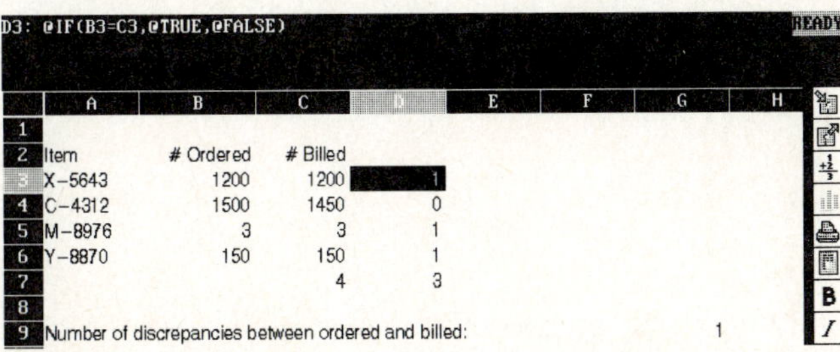

Figure 7-33.   Using @TRUE

orders. Use the @COUNT function to get an item count for the number of entries in C3..C6, which is 4. Then use @SUM to total the 0 and 1 displays, returning 3 in D7. Lastly, G9 contains a formula that subtracts D7 from C7 (+C7-D7). The value produced is 1, indicating a discrepancy in one of the orders.

Special Functions

1-2-3's special functions perform advanced calculations that do not fit neatly into any of the other categories. Some of them extend the capabilities of the logical features by providing a table lookup feature and the ability to choose a value from a list of options. Others can be used to trap errors, create addresses, or determine the number of rows or columns in a range of cells. Still others are able to closely examine the contents of worksheet cells or the current 1-2-3 session, providing information about the cell value or other attributes. The special functions offer a smorgasbord of sophisticated features that can add power to your models. You should examine the functions in this category one by one, gradually adding each of them to your repertoire of 1-2-3 skills.

@@

The @@ function provides an indirect addressing capability that lets you reference the value in a cell pointed to by the cell referenced in the argument of @@.

Format

@@(*cell*)

Arguments

cell   The address of a cell containing a string value that looks like a cell address, such as R10, Z2, or B3; or a range name, such as SALES or PROFIT; or a string formula that creates a string that looks like an address, such as "A"&"A"&"1"&"3", which creates AA13.

Use

The indirect referencing capabilities of the @@ function permit you to set up various values as key variables, and easily change the one you want to use.

The worksheet in Figure 7-34 uses @@ to determine which of the key variable values to use. The model shows the annual sales and commissions for a sales staff. Base commission rate for the company is set at 7 percent, but if it has a profitable year, the company wants the ability to increase the commission percentage. The @@ function provides an easy way to do this. Notice that the formula in C2 is @@($A$10)*B2. A10 in turn contains a reference to one of the commissions in E1..E5. The referenced entry must be a string variable in the form of a cell address. It is currently E4, so the commission is calculated using an 11 percent rate. Changing the commission to another rate merely requires a change to A10.

The worksheet in Figure 7-35 shows that when the entry in A10 is changed to E2, all the commissions are recalculated. Note that a lowercase "e" can be used to reference the cell address.

The @@ function may require F9 (CALC). 1-2-3 returns 0 from @@ if you use the function to refer to a location that contains a formula. Pressing F9 eliminates the problem by forcing 1-2-3 to recalculate the worksheet.

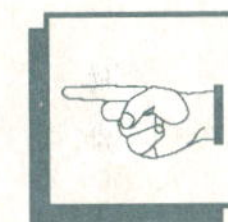

@CELL

The @CELL function allows you to examine characteristics of any worksheet cell, including the format, content, address, and other detail settings.

Format

@CELL(*attribute string,range*)

	A	B	C	D	E	F	G
	Salesman	Total Sales	Commission		7.00%		
2	RKL	$1,500,890.00	$165,097.90		8.50%		
3	HYT	$2,306,789.00	$253,746.79		9.00%		
4	REW	$1,000,950.00	$110,104.50		11.00%		
5	MAC	$957,850.00	$105,363.50		12.00%		
6	DIL	$998,750.00	$109,862.50				
7	SAM	$1,234,750.00	$135,822.50				
8			$879,997.69				
9							
10	e4						
11							
12							

C2: [W12] @@($A$10)*B2   READY

Figure 7-34.   *Using the @@ function to select commission rate*

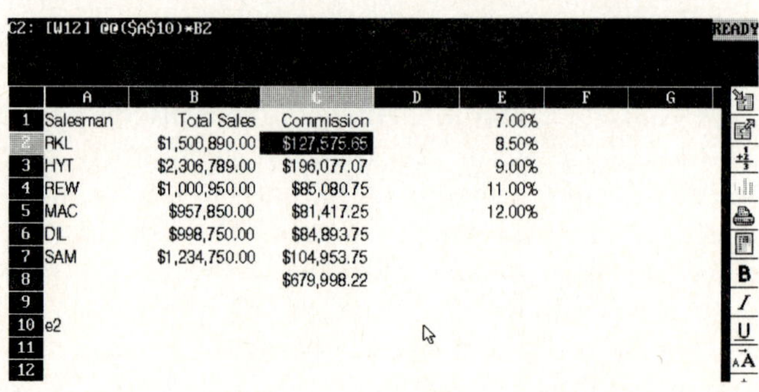

Figure 7-35.   *The worksheet after changing the @@ function argument*

Arguments

attribute string	A character string corresponding to one of the attributes the @CELL function can check, or a reference to a cell containing one. If the characters are included in the function, they must be enclosed in double quotation marks. Acceptable attribute strings and the values they return are listed in the table that follows.
range	A single or multiple cell range, such as A3..A3 or A2..D10. If you enter a single cell address, 1-2-3 converts it to a range address. If the range refers to multiple cells, only the upper-left cell is used.

Attribute String	Results
address	The address of the current cell; for example, $K$3.
col	A number between 1 and 256, representing the column number.
contents	The contents of the cell.
filename	The name of the file in which the cell is located. The complete path is provided.
format	The current format of the cell. Choose from:

C0-C15 for Currency with 0 to 15 decimal places

D1 for DD-MMM-YY

D2 for DD-MMM

D3 for MMM-YY

D4 for MM/DD/YY, DD/MM/YY, DD.MM.YY, or YY-MM-DD

D5 for MM/DD, DD/MM, DD.MM, or MM-DD

Attribute String	Results
	D6 for HH:MM:SS AM/PM
	D7 for HH:MM AM/PM
	D8 for HH:MM:SS, HH.MM.SS, HH,MM,SS, or HHhMMmSSs (all 24-hour)
	D9 for HH:MM, HH.MM, HH,MM or HHhMMm (all 24-hour)
	F0-F15 for Fixed with 0 to 15 decimal places
	G for General
	H for Hidden
	P0-P15 for Percent with 0 to 15 decimal places
	T for Text
	S0-S15 for Scientific with 0 to 15 decimal places
	,0-,15 for Comma with 0 to 15 decimal places
	+ for +/− format
prefix	Label prefix for the cell. The label prefix appears ^ for centered entries, ' for left-justified entries, " for right-justified entries, \ for repeating labels, | for nonprinting labels, and a blank label for an empty or numeric cell.
protect	Protection status of the cell, with 1 representing Protected and 0 representing Unprotected.
row	A number between 1 and 8192 representing the row number.
type	The type of data in the cell. The value types are *b* for blank, *v* for numeric, and *l* for label.
width	A number between 1 and 240 representing the current cell width.

Use

The @CELL function is primarily used in macros, although you may use it any time you wish to examine the contents of a cell closely. It can be combined with the @IF function to test for certain situations and take appropriate actions.

Figure 7-36 provides a look at all the @CELL options. The main entry for examination is in A1. @CELL functions are stored in column C and are shown again in column E as formulas, so you can compare the entry and the result. The formula in C1 reads @CELL ("contents",A1..A1) and returns the contents of 123.45, the exact number entered without the addition of formatting characters. The entry in A11 allows you to check the prefix of a label entry. For example, C11 contains the formula @CELL("prefix",A11..A11) and returns, indicating center justification for the entry.

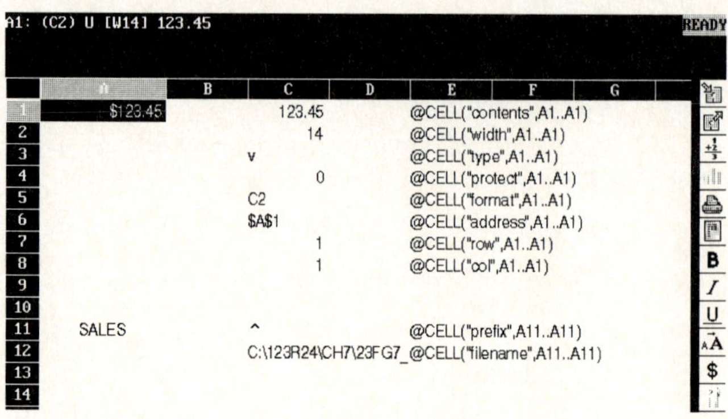

Figure 7-36.   *Using @CELL for a close-up look at a cell*

@CELLPOINTER

The @CELLPOINTER function allows you to examine attributes of the cell where the cell pointer is located. If you move the cell pointer and recalculate, new results are computed.

Format

@CELLPOINTER(*attribute string*)

Arguments

attribute string   A character string corresponding to one of the attributes the @CELLPOINTER can check, or a reference to a cell containing one. If the characters are included in the function, they must be enclosed in double quotation marks. Acceptable attribute strings and the values they return are the same as listed in the table for @CELL.

Use

The @CELLPOINTER function is primarily used in macros, although you may use it any time you wish to examine the contents of a cell closely. It can be combined with the @IF function to test for certain situations and take appropriate actions.

Figure 7-37 provides a look at most of the @CELLPOINTER options. Since the cell pointer is located in A1, the result of @CELLPOINTER provides information about A1. If you were to move the cell pointer to a new location and recalculate the

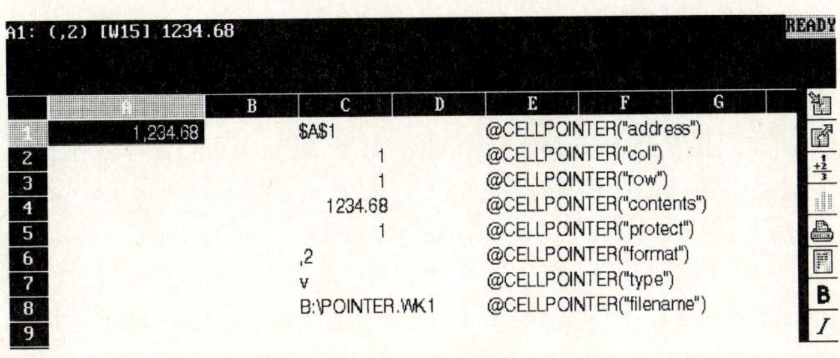

Figure 7-37.   *Examining the current cell with @CELLPOINTER*

worksheet with F9 (CALC) or make another entry, you would get updated results. The @CELLPOINTER functions are stored in column C and are shown again in column E as formulas, so you can compare the entry and the result. For example, the formula in C1 reads @CELLPOINTER("address") and returns $A$1, the address of the current cell.

@CHOOSE

The @CHOOSE function allows you to select a suitable value from a list of values.

Format

@CHOOSE(*number, list*)

Arguments

number   The position number in the list of the value that you wish to use. The first value in the list has a position number of 0. This argument can be a number, formula, or a reference to either. *Number* must be smaller than the number of values in the list. If *number* is not a whole number, 1-2-3 uses only the whole number portion for the argument.

list   A group of numeric or string values that are not limited in number, except that the @CHOOSE function must occupy no more than 240 characters. 1-2-3 lets you mix string and numeric values in one list.

Use

The @CHOOSE function is ideal when you have a set of codes in your data that are consecutive and limited in number. Since every number used to find a number in the list must have a value in the list, the number of values in the list must range from 0 to the largest number used to find a value in the list. For example, if you had codes of 1, 20, 300, and 750, @CHOOSE could not be used; you would have to turn to @VLOOKUP or @HLOOKUP. With consecutive and limited codes, however, @CHOOSE can provide a quick solution for supplying varying values.

Here are a few examples of the @CHOOSE function and the values it returns:

@CHOOSE(0,"Bill","Sally","Tom") equals Bill
@CHOOSE(1,"Bill","Sally","Tom") equals Sally
@CHOOSE(2,B10,A3,C2/4,A3*B4) equals the value C2/4
@CHOOSE(INTEREST,.09,.15,.08,.11) equals .15 when INTEREST equals 1.

The worksheet in Figure 7-38 shows the @CHOOSE function used to determine a shipping cost from a warehouse location. Warehouse 1 adds $5.00 shipping charges, warehouse 2 adds $10.00, warehouse 3 adds $15.00, warehouse 4 adds $3.00, and warehouse 5 adds $20.00.

The warehouse codes are in column A. The item numbers are in column B. The quantity and unit prices are in columns C and D, respectively. The calculation for shipping cost requires the @CHOOSE formula. A dummy value must be used for warehouse 0, since all @CHOOSE lists start with 0. A $0 shipping charge therefore is included in the list. The function is recorded in E2 as @CHOOSE (A2,0,5,10,15,3,20). The cell is formatted as Currency, and the formula is copied down column E. Total cost, shown in Column F, is simply the entry in column C times the entry in column D plus the Shipping cost from column E.

```
E2: (C2) @CHOOSE(A2,0,5,10,15,3,20)                              READY
```

	A	B	C	D	E	F	G
1	Warehouse	Item	Quantity	Unit Price	Shipping	Total Cost	
2	1	2302	3	$50.00	$5.00	$155.00	
3	4	1710	2	$20.00	$3.00	$43.00	
4	5	2350	15	$15.00	$20.00	$245.00	
5	3	3125	13	$3.00	$15.00	$54.00	
6	1	1245	4	$120.00	$5.00	$485.00	
7	4	1111	12	$75.00	$3.00	$903.00	
8	5	2302	4	$50.00	$20.00	$220.00	
9	5	5562	2	$100.00	$20.00	$220.00	
10							

Figure 7-38.   *Choosing the correct value*

@COLS

The @COLS function is used to determine the number of columns within a specified range.

Format

@COLS(*range*)

Arguments

range   A cell range in the format A2..F7 or a range name.

Use

This function is used primarily with range names. For example, you may have a range of cells containing employee information across the columns. By knowing how many columns there are in the range, you can tell how many employees are listed. A few more examples may help you understand this function.

@COLS(A2..H3) equals 8

@COLS(EMPLOYEES) equals 26 when EMPLOYEES refers to the range A3..Z10

@ERR

The @ERR function is used to return the value ERR in a cell and any other cells that reference the cell. The format of the function is @ERR; it has no arguments.

Use

This function is used to flag error conditions. For example, if you combine it with @IF, you can use it to verify that two totals are equal. If the two values are not equal, the cell containing the formula can be flagged with ERR. Such a formula might look like this:

```
@IF(A1=D2,0,@ERR)
```

Another situation where @ERR is useful is in the verification of data input. For example, an appropriate formula here might be @IF(A6<500,0,@ERR). ERR appears if A6 is greater than or equal to 500. Any cells that reference the cell containing @ERR also have a value of ERR.

Note

1-2-3 generates ERR on its own when errors are made in the entry of or in one of the arithmetic operations in a formula. The effect of both ERR conditions is the same, even though they are generated in different ways.

@HLOOKUP

The @HLOOKUP function allows you to search a table for an appropriate value to use in your worksheet. The distinction between this function and the @VLOOKUP function is that @HLOOKUP stores its table across the worksheet in a horizontal orientation, whereas @VLOOKUP uses a vertical orientation for table values.

Format

@HLOOKUP(*code to be looked up,table location,offset*)

Arguments

code to be looked up	The entry in your worksheet that is compared against the table entry. When numeric values are used, 1-2-3 looks for the largest value in the table that is not greater than the code. When string values are used, the search is for an exact match.
table location	A range containing one or more rows on a worksheet. A table is composed of a set of codes and one or more sets of return values in adjacent cells. It can be placed in any area of your worksheet. You want to be sure that it is out of the way of the other data in the spreadsheet. The top row in the range contains the codes, and the subsequent rows contain return values.
offset	A number that determines which row should be consulted for the return value when a matching code is found. The first row beneath the row of codes has an *offset* of 1, the second an *offset* of 2, and so on. Negative offset numbers cause ERR to be returned, as will offset numbers that exceed the range established in the table location. If desired, you may use an *offset* of 0 to return the comparison code.

The process 1-2-3 uses for determining the value to be returned is as follows:

- The specified code is compared against the values in the top row of the table.

- The largest value in the top row of the table that is not greater than the code is considered a match. If the code to be looked up in the table is 3.5, the value adjacent to the 3 is returned.

- The offset is used to determine which value in the column that contains the matching table cell will be returned. If the offset is 0, the matching code value itself is returned. If the offset is 1, the value below the matching value is returned, and so on.

- A code with a value less than the first value in the top row of the table returns ERR.

- A code value greater than the last value in the first row of the table is considered to match the last value.

- If you are using label entries for codes and have label entries in the top row of the table, only exact matches return table values.

Building a table with numeric codes requires that they be in ascending sequence. They are not required to be consecutive numbers, however; nor do the gaps between numbers have to be of a consistent size. With label entries, the codes do not have to be in any special sequence within the table.

Use

Tables are a powerful feature, useful for everything from tax withholding amounts to shipping rates. They are especially valuable because they allow you to look at potential changes in discount or commission structures, with only a few changes to table values and no alterations in your worksheet formulas.

Figure 7-39 shows a table located in cells C2..F7. The following codes return the values shown, assuming the offsets listed are provided:

Code	Offset	Return Value
4.5	1	22
11	2	2
15	3	77
0	1	11
99	1	44
4.5	0	4.5
11	1	22
15	2	3
102	1	44
−1	1	ERR

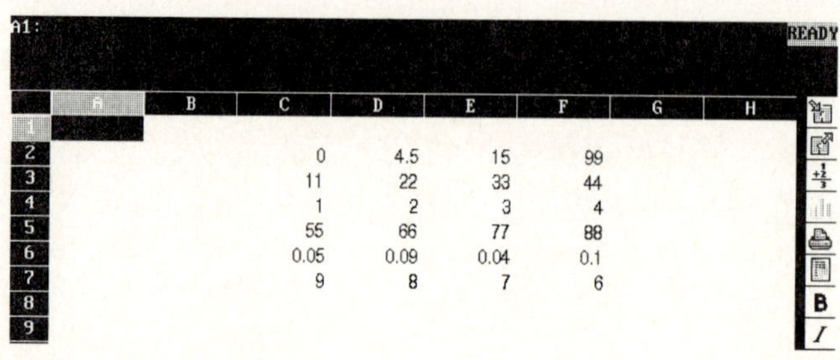

Figure 7-39.   A sample horizontal table

Compare the code against the 0 row of the table when you need an exact match. Remember that 1-2-3 returns a matching value for numeric codes even if there is not an exact match. So, if you only want to use the value returned by @HLOOKUP or @VLOOKUP when the match is exact, compare it against the values with an offset of 0. Your formula might look something like this:

```
@IF(B7=@HLOOKUP(B7,$TABLE,0),@HLOOKUP(B7,$TABLE,1),
"No exact match").
```

@INDEX

The @INDEX function allows you to retrieve a value from a table of codes by specifying the column and row number of the table you want to access.

Format

@INDEX(*table location, column offset, row offset*)

Arguments

table location   The location of the table of codes to be accessed by this function. Unlike the lookup functions, @INDEX does not use a comparison value to access the codes. You must specify a row and column address to obtain the code of your choice.

column offset   The number of the column in the table from which you want to obtain a code. The left-most column in the table range is column 0, with the numbers increasing by 1 for each column to the right that you move. *Column offset* must be within the valid range established for the table. If the number you supply is not a whole number, the decimal portion is truncated.

row offset   The number of the row in the table from which you wish to obtain a code. The upper row in the table is row 0. *Row offset* must be in the relevant range for the table. If it is not a whole number, the decimal portion of the number is truncated.

Use

The @INDEX function can be used whenever your data values are used to access the proper row and column of a table. This type of function works well for quoting insurance rates, shipping charges, and any other calculation in which you can specify the exact code you need from the table.

Figure 7-40 provides an example of a commission application that uses total sales and region values to index the proper commission percentage. The table is located in A1..G3. The row from which the return value is selected is the sales region minus 1, since tables begin with row 0, not row 1. The column from which the return value is selected is calculated as (total sales amount divided by \$10,000) minus 1. The percent obtained from this function is multiplied by the sales figure to determine commissions.

@NA

This function causes NA, meaning "not available," to appear in the cell where this function is entered, as well as in all cells that reference it. The format for the function is @NA; it has no arguments.

Use

The @NA function is used when data is not available for entry in a cell. It serves as a flag for data that must be entered before correct model results can be computed. NA

```
D7: (C2) [W11] @INDEX($A$1..$G$3,(B7/10000)-1,C7-1)*B7          READY
```

	A	B	C	D	E	F	G
1	5.00%	6.00%	7.50%	9.00%	12.00%	15.00%	20.00%
2	6.00%	7.00%	8.00%	9.00%	13.00%	18.00%	25.00%
3	8.00%	9.00%	12.00%	15.00%	18.00%	23.00%	30.00%
4							
5							
6	Salesman	Total Sales	Region	Commission			
7	White	\$50,000.00	2	\$6,500.00			
8	Savage	\$30,500.00	3	\$3,660.00			
9	Greene	\$41,000.00	1	\$3,690.00			
10	Parsel	\$65,000.00	3	\$14,950.00			
11	Murray	\$54,500.00	2	\$7,085.00			
12							
13							

Figure 7-40.   Finding the appropriate value with @INDEX

in one worksheet cell can ripple through a worksheet, since every cell that references a cell containing NA also contains NA.

The @NA function would be useful for an instructor recording student grades. All students who missed an exam would have NA, rather than a score, recorded. Figure 7-41 shows the effect on the grade point average for students with missing grades. At the end of the semester, the instructor can change all grades that are still NA to 0.

Note

The label NA entered in a cell is not equivalent to entering @NA, which produces a numeric rather than a label entry.

@ROWS

The @ROWS function is used to determine the number of rows within a specified range.

Format

@ROWS(*range*)

Arguments

range   A range address or a range name.

```
F4: (F1) @AVG(B4..E4)                                          READY
```

	A	B	C	D	E	F	G
1			Fall Semester — 1991				
2							
3	Student	Exam 1	Exam 2	Exam 3	Final	Average	
4	B. Black	75	NA	82	88	NA	
5	S. Conners	67	78	72	81	74.5	
6	F. Dalton	78	90	89	92	87.3	
7	G. Limmer	88	81	93	87	87.3	
8	S. Melton	67	55	40	60	55.5	
9	P. Stock	67	89	NA	78	NA	
10	J. Zimmer	91	82	75	89	84.3	
11							
12							

Figure 7-41.   *The impact of NA on formulas*

Use

This function is used primarily with range names. For example, you may have a range of cells containing order information with the orders listed down the worksheet. If all the order information were included in one range named ORDERS, you could obtain the number of orders with the function @ROWS(ORDERS). A few other examples may help to show how this function works:

@ROWS(A2..H3) equals 2
@ROWS(EMPLOYEES) equals 8 when EMPLOYEES refers to the range A3..Z10

@VLOOKUP

The @VLOOKUP function allows you to search a table for an appropriate value to use in your worksheet. The distinction between this function and the @HLOOKUP function is that @VLOOKUP stores its table down the worksheet in a vertical orientation, whereas @HLOOKUP uses a horizontal orientation for table values.

Format

@VLOOKUP(*code to be looked up, table location, offset*)

Arguments

code to be looked up — The entry in your worksheet that is compared against the table entry. When numeric values are used, 1-2-3 looks for the largest value in the table that is not greater than the code. When string values are used, the search is for an exact match.

table location — A range containing one or more columns on the worksheet. A table is composed of a set of codes and one or more sets of return values in adjacent cells. It can be placed in any area of your worksheet. You want to be sure that the table location will not interfere with the other data in the spreadsheet. The left column in the range contains the codes, and the subsequent columns contain return values.

offset   A number that determines which column should be used for the return value when a matching code is found. The first column to the left of the column of codes has an *offset* of 1, the second an *offset* of 2, and so on. Negative offset numbers cause ERR to be returned, as will offset numbers that exceed the range established in the table location. If desired, you may use an *offset* of 0 to return the comparison code from the first column of the table.

Figure 7-42 shows a table in A2..D8. The codes are in A2..A8, and the return values are in B2..D8. The process 1-2-3 uses for determining the value to be returned is as follows:

- The specified code is compared against the values in the left column of the table.

- The largest value in the left column of the table that is not greater than the code is considered a match. If the code to be looked up in the table is 3.5, the value adjacent to the 3 is returned.

- The offset is used to determine which value in the column that contains the matching table cell will be returned. If the offset is 0, the matching code value itself is returned. If the offset is 1, the value to the right of the matching value is returned, and so on.

- A code with a value less than the first value in the left column of the table returns ERR.

- A code value greater than the last value in the first column of the table is considered to match the last value.

- If you are using label entries for codes and have label entries in the left column of the table, only exact matches return table values.

	A	B	C	D	E	F	G	H
1								
2	1	5	0.05	12				
3	3	10	0.07	5				
4	5	15	0.09	21				
5	15	20	0.1	14				
6	20	25	0.12	13				
7	35	30	0.13	21				
8	50	35	0.15	17				
9								

Figure 7-42.   *A sample vertical table*

Building a table with numeric codes requires that they be in ascending sequence. They are not required to be consecutive numbers, however; nor do the gaps between numbers have to be of a consistent size. With label entries, the codes do not have to be in any special sequence within the table.

Use

Tables are a powerful feature, useful for everything from tax withholding amounts to shipping rates. They are especially valuable because they allow you to look at potential changes in discount or commission structures, with only a few changes to table values and no alterations in your worksheet formulas.

Figure 7-43 provides a portion of a model to project travel costs. The tables for this model, shown in Figure 7-44, are located in J7..L9 and J12..K15. The first table offers a list of codes that provide an estimate of one night's meal and lodging costs for a travel location on the worksheet, as well as miscellaneous costs such as taxis, phone calls, and so on. The second table lets you assign a second code to a worksheet location, providing an estimate of the airfare costs for reaching that destination. Two tables are needed because the lodging and meal estimates and the travel cost estimates are based on different criteria.

The model in Figure 7-43 contains city names in column A. Column B contains a numeric code for lodging class, which categorizes cities according to their relative costs of living. Column C contains the numeric code for travel cost, assigned on the basis of distance from the origination point. Column D contains the number of trips to the location. This model assumes that all trips are for one night, but you could easily insert another column here to show variable numbers of nights.

LOCATION	LODGING CLASS	TRAVEL COST	# TRIPS	LODGING/ MEALS	AIRFARE	MISC.	TOTAL COST
Dallas	1	2	12	$1,500.00	$3,600.00	$420.00	$5,520.00
Akron	2	2	2	$300.00	$600.00	$90.00	$990.00
Chicago	3	1	3	$525.00	$750.00	$150.00	$1,425.00
Denver	2	2	12	$1,800.00	$3,600.00	$540.00	$5,940.00
Phoenix	2	3	5	$750.00	$1,750.00	$225.00	$2,725.00
Atlanta	2	2	4	$600.00	$1,200.00	$180.00	$1,980.00
New York	3	2	6	$1,050.00	$1,800.00	$300.00	$3,150.00
Portland	2	4	3	$450.00	$1,500.00	$135.00	$2,085.00

Figure 7-43.   An application for a vertical table

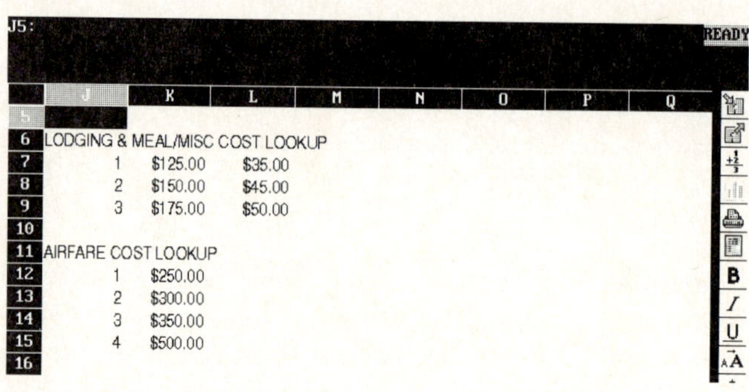

Figure 7-44.   *Vertical tables for the travel cost model*

The next column contains the first lookup formula. From the three arguments in the function, you can see that it looks up B6 in the table with the absolute address of $J$7..$L$9. It uses an offset of 1, referring to the value in the column right next to the code. As a final step, this formula multiplies the returned value by the number of trips, to obtain a total lodging cost for this location.

The next formula, in F6, looks up the travel cost code. This formula is @VLOOKUP(C6,$J$12..$K$15,1). Again the table reference address is absolute, so you can copy the formula down the column for the other cities.

The last lookup formula is in column G. The formulas in this column follow the pattern of the formula in G6, which is @VLOOKUP (C6,$J$7..$L$9,2). The difference between this formula and the first @VLOOKUP formula is that here the offset is 2, indicating that the value two columns away from the code should be returned. Total travel costs for a location are obtained with @SUM(E6..G6).

All the formulas described for this model are valid for the other city entries. They are adjusted automatically if /Copy is used to place them in the other locations.

Statistical Functions

1-2-3's statistical functions perform their magic on lists of values. Frequently these lists are a contiguous range of cells on the worksheet. They can also be a series of individual values or a combination of range and individual values. Blank ranges can be included within the list, but all the values in the blank range count as zeros. When a range has multiple cells, 1-2-3 ignores cells containing blanks. If a single blank cell is used in the list, 1-2-3 assigns a zero to the cell.

The majority of the statistical functions work only with numeric values. @COUNT is the exception, since it counts the number of nonblank cells in a list and also accepts string values.

@AVG

The @AVG function finds the average of a list of values.

Format

@AVG(*list*)

Arguments

list	Any set of numeric values. They can be individual cell references, individual values, or a range of cells. You can also combine the options in one *list*. Examples are @AVG(A2..A9,D4,L2) and @AVG(D4..D15). Note that the components in *list* are separated by commas.

Use

You can use the @AVG function and the worksheet in Figure 7-45 to calculate the average bid amount received from vendors. The vendor bids are shown in B4..B11. If the formula is entered in B13 as @AVG(B4..B11), the result would be $5,837.25.

@COUNT

The @COUNT function determines the number of nonblank entries in a list. A cell that contains a label prefix counts as a nonblank, even though the cell displays as a blank.

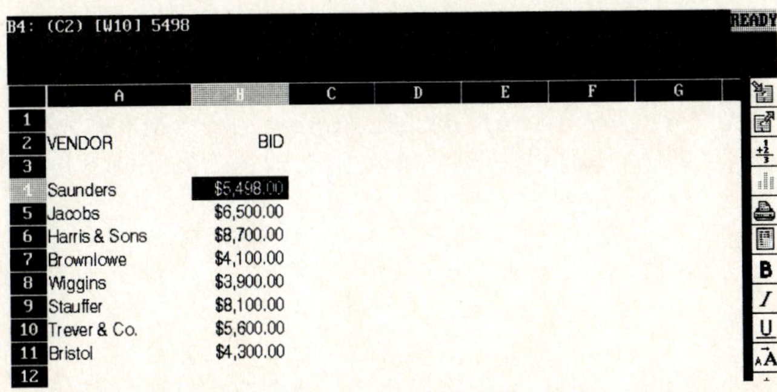

Figure 7-45.   Using @AVG to average vendor bids

Format

@COUNT(*list*)

Arguments

list	Any set of numeric values. They can be individual cell references or a range of cells, although individual cell references may distort your results and should be avoided. A single cell reference increases the count by one, even if the cell is blank. You can also combine the two options in one *list*. Examples are @COUNT (A2..A9,D4,L2) and @COUNT(D4..D15). Note that the components in *list* are separated by commas.

Use

The @COUNT function does not require numeric data. It counts all the nonblank entries in a list, regardless of whether they are values or characters. You can use the worksheet in Figure 7-45 to count the number of bids, using the formula @COUNT(A4..A11), which returns a result of 8.

@MAX

The @MAX function searches a list of values and displays the largest value in the list.

Format

@MAX(*list*)

Arguments

list	Any set of numeric values. They can be individual cell references, individual values, or a range of cells. You can also combine the options in one *list*. Examples are @MAX(A2..A9,D4,L2) and @MAX(D4..D15). Note that the components in *list* are separated by commas.

Use

You can use the @MAX function and the worksheet in Figure 7-45 to obtain the highest bid in a group of vendor bids. Your formula would be @MAX (B4..B11), and returns 8700.

@MIN

The @MIN function searches a list of values and displays the smallest value in the list.

Format

@MIN(*list*)

Arguments

list	Any set of numeric values. They can be individual cell references, individual values, or a range of cells. You can also combine the options in one *list*. Examples are @MIN(A2..A9,D4,L2) and @MIN(D4..D15). Note that the components in *list* are separated by commas.

Use

You can use the @MIN function and the worksheet in Figure 7-45 to find the lowest bid in a group of vendor bids. The bids are located in B4..B11, and you could find the minimum with the function @MIN(B4..B11). The result is $3,900. If you enter additional vendor bids, they are included in the calculation automatically.

@STD

The @STD function is used to determine the population standard deviation of a set of values, or how much variation there is from the average of the values. It is the square root of the variance.

Format

@STD(*list*)

Arguments

list	Any set of numeric values. They can be individual cell references or a range of cells. You can also combine the two in one *list*. Examples are @STD(A2..A9,15,L2) and @STD(D4..D15). Note that the components in *list* are separated by commas. Blank cells within *list* are ignored, but label entries are assigned a value of 0. Including both label entries and single cell references in *list* can cause a problem, because @STD uses a count of the entries as part of its calculation.

Use

The @STD function determines the standard deviation when you have access to the values for the entire population—all the values for the entire group you are studying. If you are measuring the deviation in the weight of packages filled in a plant, for example, population would refer to all packages filled, not just a sample. If you are working with only a sample of the population, use the following formula:

@SQRT(@COUNT(list)/(@COUNT(list)-1))*@STD(list)

The standard deviation calculation determines the amount of variation between individual values and the mean. Suppose, for example, that you determine the average age of your employees to be 40. This could mean that half of your employees are 39 and the other half 41, or it could mean that you have employees whose ages range from 18 to 65. The latter case shows a greater standard deviation because of the greater variance from the mean.

The @STD function uses the following formula:

$$\sqrt{\frac{\sum (x_i - \text{AVG})^2}{n}}$$

where x_i is the ith item in the list and n is the number of items in the list.

As an example, suppose that the Commemorative Bronze Company has made 50 replicas of antique bronze cash registers and wants to determine the standard deviation in the weight of these products. The worksheet in Figure 7-46 shows the list of weights and the formula for the standard deviation.

@SUM

The @SUM function totals a list of numeric values.

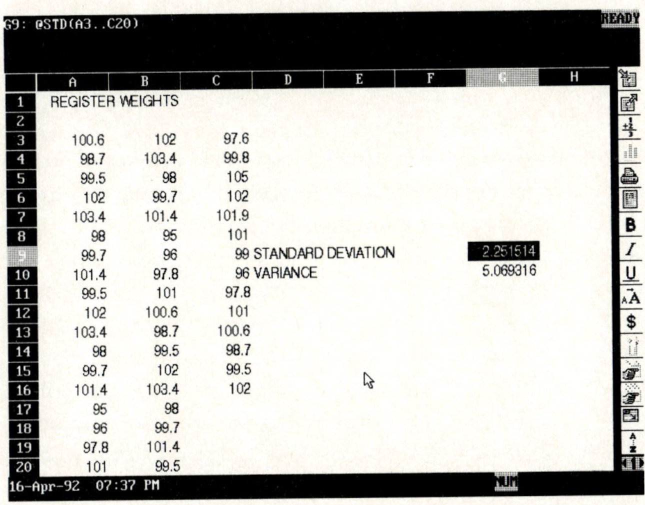

Figure 7-46.   *Using @STD to measure the fluctuations in register weights*

Format

@SUM(*list*)

Arguments

list   Any set of numeric values. They can be individual cell references, individual values, or a range of cells. You can also combine the options in one list. A couple of examples include the lists @SUM(A2..A9,D4,L2) and @SUM(D4..D15). Note that the components in list are separated by commas.

Use

Use the @SUM function to obtain a total of more than two values. It is much more efficient than using addition on each individual component. For example, you can enter @SUM(B4..B11) in place of +B4+B5+B6+B7+B8+B9+B10+B11.

The other advantage offered by @SUM is that when you insert a row or column into the middle of the @SUM range, the range automatically adjusts for the extra entry without changing the formula. For the worksheet in Figure 7-45, you can enter the formula @SUM(B4..B11) to total the bids, which returns the result of 46698.

Release 2.4 provides an icon that can quickly sum both rows and columns. The icon looks like this:

Getting used to the way the SmartSum icon works requires a little practice. Using it seems a bit tricky at first because it is so flexible; it can sum the highlighted cells or the cells *adjacent* to the highlighted cells. As with @SUM, the cells containing the result are not automatically formatted to match the detail entries.

The SmartSum icon can total the adjacent values in a single row or column. To create a total like this, select the cell in which you want the total to appear. It must be in the same row or column as the detail, but you can leave a blank row or column for separation. For example, if you want to total the entries in column C of Figure 7-47, you can select cell C10 or C11, depending on whether you want a blank space between the last detail entry and the total for the column, and then select the SmartSum icon. If you want to total both columns, you can select C10..D10 or C11..D11 to accomplish this in one step.

Computing a row total is just as easy. To total rows, select either E7 or F7 and then select the SmartSum icon. To total all rows at the same time, select either E7..E9 or F7..F9 before selecting the SmartSum icon.

To total both rows and columns in one step, you can select a range including the blank cells where you want the totals stored. You can also include an extra blank row or column to separate the total from the detail with the blank row or column. 1-2-3 always stores the sum in the last column or row of your selection. In the sample model, this would require you to select C7..E10 before selecting the SmartSum icon. All of the totals are added in one easy step to produce the final results, shown in Figure 7-48.

There are several features to be aware of with this palette option. The first is that you can successfully include blank cells in the selected range. 1-2-3 totals the entries in the cells,96

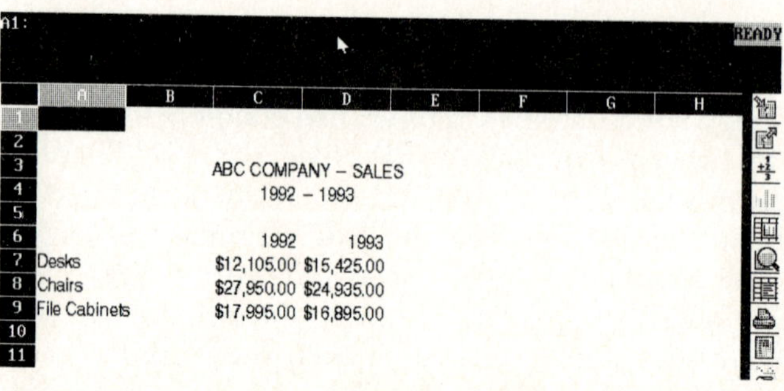

Figure 7-47.   *Worksheet with values to sum*

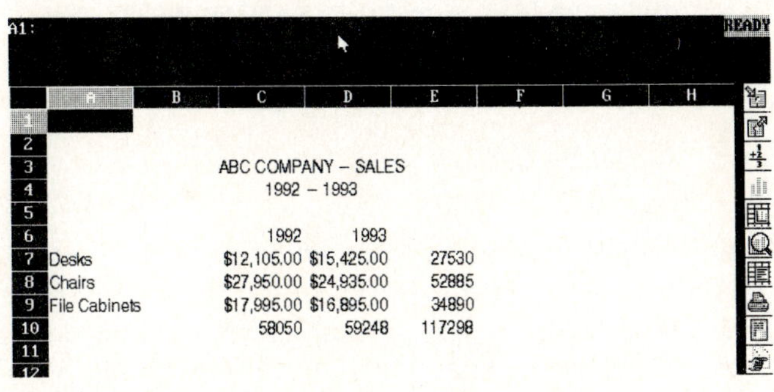

Figure 7-48.   *Summing rows and columns with SmartSum*

including the blank rows or columns. If you were to separate 1992 and 1993 sales figures by a blank column, the sum would still include all the figures.

The other tip is that you can select a row or a column with data and a blank at the end. For instance, if A1 and A2 contain a 7 and A3 is blank and you select A1..A3 and then choose the SmartSum icon, 1-2-3 sums your entries in A1 and A2 and puts the @ SUM function in A3.

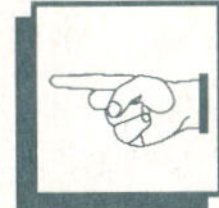

Make it easy to expand your @SUM range reference. Include a cell with a label entry like '---------- at the top and bottom of a column of label entries, and reference these cells as the first and last range entries. This allows you to insert a row at the top or bottom of the range without affecting the accuracy of the computation.

@VAR

The @VAR function computes the population variance of values in a population, or the amount the individual population values vary from the average. The variance is equal to the standard deviation squared.

Format

@VAR(*list*)

Arguments

list	Any set of numeric values. They can be individual cell references or a range of cells. You can also combine the two in one *list*. Examples are @VAR(A2..A9,15,L2) and @VAR(D4..D15). Note that the components in *list* are separated by commas. Blank cells within *list* are ignored, but label entries are assigned a value of 0.

Including both label entries and single cell references in *list* can cause a problem, because @VAR uses a count of the entries as part of its calculation.

Use

The @VAR function determines the variance when you have access to the values for the entire population—the values for the entire group you are studying. If you are measuring the deviation in the weight of packages filled in a plant, for example, population would refer to all packages filled, not just a sample. If you are working with only a sample of the population you must create your own formula, as follows:

@COUNT(list)/(@COUNT(list)-1)*@VAR(list)

The purpose of the variance calculation is to determine the amount of variation between individual values and the mean. Suppose, for example, that you determine the average age of your employees to be 40. This could mean that half of your employees are 39 and the other half 41, or it could mean that the ages range from 18 to 65. The latter case shows a greater variance because of the greater dispersion from the mean.

The @VAR function is biased, since it uses a count as part of its calculation. Specifically, it uses the following formula:

$$\frac{\sum (x_i - AVG)^2}{n}$$

where x_i is the *i*th item in the list and n is the number of items in the list. The number of items is critical in determining if you must modify the formula for a sample of the population. When n is equal to the total population, use @VAR; when n represents a sample of the population, you must use the modified formula.

As an example, suppose that the Commemorative Bronze Company has made 50 replicas of antique bronze cash registers and wants to determine the variance in the weight of these products. The worksheet in Figure 7-46 shows the list of weights. The formula is @VAR(A3..C20), and returns 5.069316.

String Functions

String functions provide a variety of character manipulation formulas that give you flexibility in rearranging text entries. You can work with an entire entry and change its order, or you can use just a piece of a cell entry.

1-2-3's string functions often work with the individual characters in a text string. The numbering system that 1-2-3 uses for the characters in a string may not be what you expect. The character at the far left of a string is regarded as character 0, not character 1. The numbering proceeds with 1, 2, and so on, moving to the right in the character string. Understanding these positions within a string is very important, since you must be sure you are working with the right characters. String position numbers can range from 0 through 239, since a 240-character string is the largest that 1-2-3 can work with.

String position numbers must always be expressed as positive integers. A negative integer causes 1-2-3 to return ERR. Using a number with a decimal causes 1-2-3 to drop the decimal and use only the whole-number portion of the value. No rounding occurs; for example, 1-2-3 truncates a value of 5.6 to 5 when it is used as a position number in a string. The following shows the positions for entries within a label:

```
T h i s    i s    a    s t r i n g
0 1 2 3 4 5 6 7 8 9 | | | | | |
                    0 1 2 3 4 5
```

It is also important to note that the label indicator that begins a string is not assigned a position number. An empty or null string has a length of 0 positions. A cell with a null string contains no entry except a label indicator. It is not the same as a blank cell without a label indicator.

When you use string values as arguments in a string function, you must enclose them in double quotation marks ("). These same entries referenced by a cell address do not require quotation marks, however. For example, if you want to use the character string "This is a string" in the @RIGHT string function to return the last 6 characters on the right, and the entry is stored in D10, you could use @RIGHT(D10,6); but if you put the string itself in the function, it must be written as @RIGHT("This is a string",6).

Some string functions produce numeric results equating to a position in a string, while others produce a string value. You will want to become familiar with the workings of string functions before you indiscriminately combine the results of two string functions. Many of the examples in this section will combine several string functions, however, since this is the way string functions are most commonly used.

@CHAR

The @CHAR function is used to return a character that corresponds to a Lotus International Character Set (LICS).

Format

@CHAR(*code*)

Arguments

code	Any numeric value from 1 to 255. Numbers less than 1 or greater than 255 return ERR.

Use

The @CHAR function converts an LICS code to a displayable and printable character. LICS codes above 127 produce foreign currency symbols, accent marks, and other special characters. If the character represented by the code number you specify cannot be displayed on your monitor, a blank or a character resembling the desired character is substituted.

@CLEAN

The @CLEAN function removes from a string characters that have values of less than 32. These include some special characters that you can import into the worksheet with /File Import.

Format

@CLEAN(*string*)

Arguments

string	A string in quotes, or a cell or range address, or a name that contains a string.

Use

The following example shows the original strings and the strings this function returns:

@CLEAN(" ☺☻ This is ¶|text")

equals

```
This is text.
```

@CODE

The @CODE function returns the Lotus International Character Set (LICS) code number of the first character in the function argument.

Format

@CODE(*string*)

Arguments

string   Any character sequence up to 240 characters. If the characters are included in the function, they must be enclosed in double quotation marks ("). They can also be stored in a cell and referenced with a cell address or range name. Numeric characters can be used as long as they are preceded by a label prefix. This function uses only the first character in the string.

Use

This function finds its primary application in macros working with composed characters. The purpose of the function is to convert characters to their LICS code. Upper- and lowercase characters have different codes. For example, an uppercase A is code 65, but a lowercase a is code 97. Characters using the Wysiwyg font XSymbol will return the LICS code of the character the symbol displays in the other fonts. A few examples of @CODE follow:

    @CODE("$") equals 36

    @CODE("V") equals 86

    @CODE("@") equals 64

@EXACT

The @EXACT function allows you to determine whether two string values are equal.

Format

@EXACT(*string1,string2*)

Arguments

string1	Any character sequence that does not exceed 240 characters. If the string is included in the function, the total length of the formula can exceed 240 characters, so *string1* is restricted to a size that fits within this limitation. If used, the string must also be enclosed in double quotation marks (").
string2	Any character sequence that does not exceed 240 characters. If the string is placed in the function, the total length of the formula cannot exceed 240 characters, so *string2* is restricted to a size that fits within this limitation. If used, the string must also be enclosed in double quotation marks (").

Use

The @EXACT function returns 1 when the two strings match exactly, and 0 when they do not. Everything about the two strings must be the same, including blank spaces and capitalization, or 0 is returned. Although this function can be used by itself, it is normally used with condition tests (that is, with @IF).

Here are some examples of @EXACT:

@EXACT("Mary Brown","MARY BROWN") equals 0
@EXACT("2144","2144") equals 1
@EXACT(2144,"2144") equals ERR, since string1 is a numeric value
@EXACT(A10,"MARY BROWN") equals 1 if A10 contains MARY BROWN

Note

Use @IF and the equal operator (=) if you do not want to have to consider capitalization. As an example, @IF("Tom Jones"="tom jones","True","False") returns True, since the case difference is not considered.

@FIND

The @FIND function permits you to search a character string to find out if a substring (search string) appears within it. If the search string is found, the function returns the starting location of this string.

Format

@FIND(*search string, entire string, starting location*)

Arguments

search string   A character sequence or a reference to a cell containing one. When the characters are included in the function, they must be enclosed in double quotation marks ("). The maximum length of the search string must be less than or equal to the entire string to be searched. Since @FIND is case sensitive, the search string must exactly match a portion of the entire string.

entire string   A character sequence or a reference to a cell containing one. When the characters are included in the function, they must be enclosed in quotation marks ("). The maximum length of this string is 240 characters.

starting location   The position in the entire string where you want to begin your search. Remember that the leftmost character in the string is character 0. The maximum starting location can be one less than the number of characters in the entire string.

Use

Use the @FIND function whenever you want to locate a string within a string. It can be used to identify the location of the blank space between a first and last name, for example. This information, when combined with other string functions, lets you reverse the name entry so that the last name appears first in the cell. ERR is returned when your starting location number is negative or greater than the last position of the entire string, or when the search string is not found.

Here are some examples of @FIND:

@FIND("-","ABF-6785",0) equals 3

@FIND("-","213-46-2389",4) equals 6

@FIND("-","ABF-6785",8) equals ERR

@LEFT

The @LEFT function allows you to extract a specified number of characters from the left side of a string.

Format

@LEFT (*string, number of characters to extract*)

Arguments

string	A sequence of characters included in the function, either by enclosing them in double quotation marks (") or by a reference to a cell address or range name containing the characters.
number of characters to extract	A number representing the characters to be extracted from the string. If you want to extract the first three characters, for example, this number would be 3. ERR results if this number is greater than the number of characters in the string.

Use

The @LEFT function lets you extract one or many characters from a string. It can be used alone or in combination with other string functions. Here are some examples:

```
@LEFT("Lotus 1-2-3",5) equals Lotus
@LEFT("12:30:59",4) equals 12:3
@LEFT("   ABC COMPANY",7) equals ABC preceded by four leading spaces
@LEFT("John Smith",@FIND(" ","John Smith",0)) equals John
```

@LENGTH

The @LENGTH function returns the number of characters in a string.

Format

@LENGTH(*string*)

Arguments

string	A group of characters that can be included in the function (if they are enclosed in double quotation marks) or placed in a cell and referenced. You can also use a string formula as the string. Numeric entries are not allowed and return ERR.

Use

This function can be used to determine the length of an entry you wish to manipulate, to verify input data, or to determine the length of a line. The following examples should clarify the results produced by @LENGTH:

Function	Length
@LENGTH("sales")	5
@LENGTH("profit "&"and loss")	15
@LENGTH(A2) where A2 contains abc	3

@LOWER

The @LOWER function converts strings to lowercase.

Format

@LOWER(*string*)

Arguments

string	A group of characters that can be in upper- or lowercase or mixed upper- and lowercase. The characters can be included in the function if they are enclosed in double quotation marks ("), or they can be placed in a cell and referenced. You can also use a string formula as *string*. Numeric entries are not allowed and return ERR.

Use

This function is valuable when data from several sources must be combined and data entry was not done in a consistent manner. @LOWER is one of the functions that permits you to change the appearance of data without reentering it. You can use it to place all data in lowercase format. Figure 7-49 shows several examples of using the @LOWER function in column C.

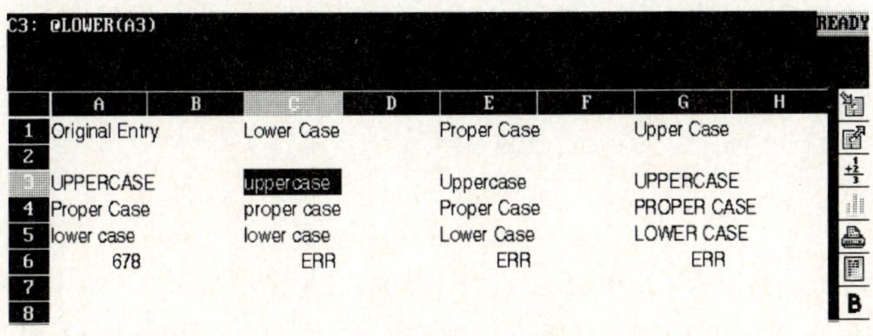

Figure 7-49.   *Converting characters to different cases*

@MID

The @MID function extracts characters from the middle of a string when you specify the number of characters to extract and the starting location.

Format

@MID(*string, start number, number of characters*)

Arguments

string	A group of characters that can be included in the function (if they are enclosed in double quotation marks) or placed in a cell and referenced. You can also use a string formula as *string*. Numeric entries are not allowed and will return ERR.
start number	A number representing the first character position you wish to extract from the string. When you choose this number, remember that the leftmost position in the string is position 0. *Start number* should not be negative. If *start number* is greater than the number of positions in the string, an empty string is returned. @MID("ABC",0,1) returns 1 character from the 0 position in the string: A.
number of characters	A number representing the number of characters you wish to extract from the string. This number can be stored in a cell and referenced by the function through a cell address or range name. When this argument is 0, an empty string is the result. You can set this number at 240 if you do not know how many characters are in the string and you want to extract all of them.

Use

You can use the @MID function whenever you want to extract a portion of a string. The function offers complete flexibility: you can start anywhere in the string and extract as few or as many characters as you wish. Here are two examples:

@MID("abcdefghi",3,3) equals def
@MID("123"&"456",1,240) equals 23456

The worksheet in Figure 7-50 shows @MID used with @LENGTH and @FIND to reverse a name entry. The formula uses the location of the comma plus two characters to identify the beginning of the first name. The number of characters in the first name is the length of the entire entry less the location of the comma. This is

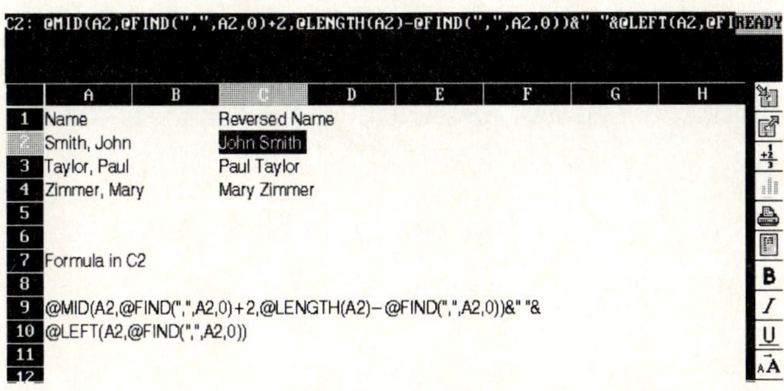

Figure 7-50.   *Reversing name entries with @MID and other string functions*

concatenated with a space and the last name. The last name consists of the characters on the left up to the comma. Creating the correct formula may require a little trial and error if you are not familiar with string functions, but once you have worked it out, you can copy it down the column to reverse all the name entries.

@N

The @N function returns the numeric value of a single cell.

Format

@N(*range*)

Arguments

range   A reference to a range, using either the cell addresses (for example, R2..U20) or a range name. Even though this function uses only the upper-left cell of the range, the argument must be in range format, that is, A2..A2.

Use

The @N function returns the value of the upper-left cell in a range. If the cell contains a label, a 0 is returned. The @N function is useful in macro applications to examine data in a cell. It is also a quick way of excluding label data from your calculations.

The following worksheet shows an example of @N. In this particular example, the range is a single cell.

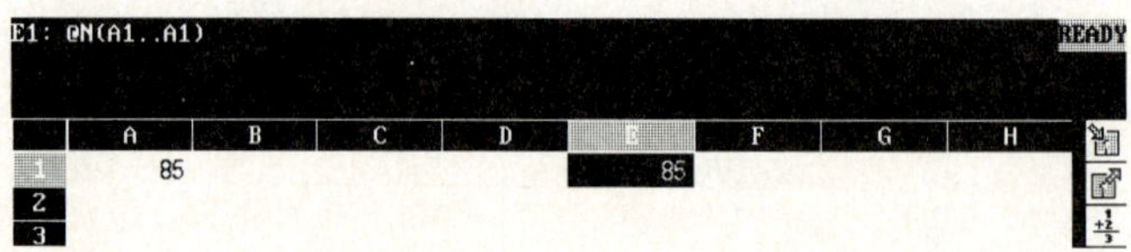

@PROPER

The @PROPER function converts strings to proper case (a format where the first letter of each word is capitalized).

Format

@PROPER(*string*)

Arguments

string	A group of characters that can be in upper- or lowercase, or mixed upper- and lowercase. The characters can be included in the function (if they are enclosed in double quotation marks), or they can be placed in a cell and referenced. You can also use a string formula as string.

Use

This function is valuable when data from several sources must be combined and data entry was not done in a consistent manner. @PROPER is one of the functions that lets you change the appearance of data without retyping it. @PROPER(A2&" "&B3), where A2 contains JOBBARD MILLING COMPANY and B3 contains east dallas division, returns Jobbard Milling Company East Dallas Division. Every word in each string was converted to proper case (lowercase with initial capital). The worksheet in Figure 7-49 shows several additional conversions. Entries are made in column A, and @PROPER formulas are used to obtain the remainder of the display.

@REPEAT

The @REPEAT function is used to duplicate a character string a specified number of times.

Format

@REPEAT (*string, number of times*)

Arguments

string

A series of characters enclosed in double quotation marks (") or a reference to a cell containing a string. *String* can be one character or many.

number of times

A numeric value indicating the number of times to repeat the string

Use

The @REPEAT function can improve the appearance of a worksheet by creating dividing lines between a report's assumptions and the final result. For example, @REPEAT is in one sense similar to the backslash (\) character, since it repeats characters. It differs because the backslash is restricted to filling a single cell, whereas @REPEAT can extend across many worksheet cells. The @REPEAT function can be used in place of the +/− format when you do not want to change the column width. Figure 7-51 shows the REPEAT function used to repeat a character so the resulting string is wider than the column. If you had used a formula like +B3/1000 and the +/− format, you would have had to widen column C so 1-2-3 would not display the column as asterisks.

@REPLACE

The @REPLACE function replaces characters in a string with other characters.

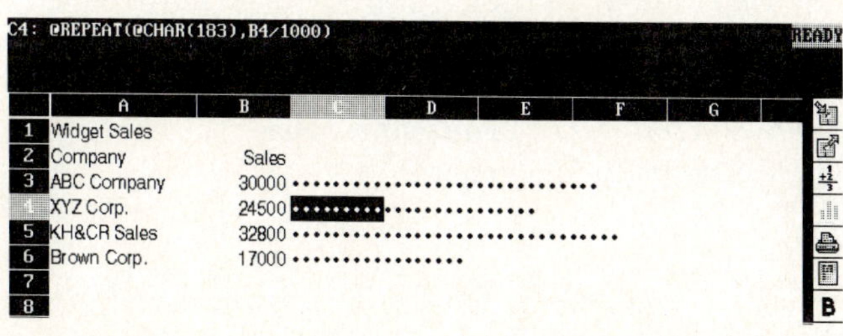

Figure 7-51.   Using @REPEAT

Format

@REPLACE (*original string,start location,# characters,new string*)

Arguments

original string   A series of characters enclosed in double quotation marks (") or a reference to a cell containing a string. The string can be one character or many. It must specify the complete string entry you want to work with.

start location   The position number in the original string where you want the replacement to begin. Remember that the first character in the original string is position 0. If *start location* is greater than the length of *original string,,* the new string is added at the end.

 # characters   The number of characters to remove from the original string. When # *characters* equals 0, *new string* is inserted without removal of any part of original string. When # *characters* is the same as the number of characters in *original string,,* the entire string is replaced.

new string   A series of characters enclosed in double quotation marks (") or a reference to a cell containing a string. The string can be one character or many. When *new string* is an empty string, that is, " ", @REPLACE simply deletes characters from original string.

Use

The @REPLACE function enables you to make changes to a string without retyping the original string. For instance, you can use this function to manipulate a part number into a warehouse location or an account code into a department number. Sample uses might include the following:

@REPLACE("Department 100",11,3,"200") equals Department 200
@REPLACE("Commissions for: ",17,0,"Mary Brown") equals Commissions for: Mary Brown
@REPLACE("AX/1265",2,1,"-") equals AX-1265
@REPLACE("AX/1265",0,7,"-") equals -

Note

To use this function to change text data entered incorrectly, first enter the function in an empty area of the worksheet, referencing the data to be corrected. You must restructure the data in a different location before copying it back, and you want to be sure not to overlay important data in the process of doing so. After the formulas are entered, you can freeze the values in the cells with F2 (EDIT) followed by F9 (CALC). You can then transfer them with /Move. Alternatively, you can use /Range Value to freeze the formulas as values and copy them all in one step. After verifying the accuracy of the data, you can erase the work area that originally contained the formula.

@RIGHT

The @RIGHT function allows you to extract a specified number of characters from the right side of a string.

Format

@RIGHT (*string, number of characters to extract*)

Arguments

string
: A sequence of characters included in the function by enclosing them in double quotation marks (") or by referencing a cell address or range name containing the characters.

number of characters to extract
: A number representing the characters to be extracted from the string. If this number is greater than the number of characters in *string*, the entire string is extracted.

Use

The @RIGHT function lets you extract one or many characters from the right side of a string. It can be used alone or in combination with other string functions. Following are some examples of the function:

    @RIGHT("Lotus 1-2-3",5) equals 1-2-3
    @RIGHT("1:30:59",5) equals 30:59
    @RIGHT("ABC COMPANY   ",8) equals Y with seven trailing spaces

@S

The @S function returns a value as a string.

Format

@S(*range*)

Arguments

range	A reference to a range using either cell addresses (such as R2..U20) or a range name. Even though this function uses only the upper-left cell of the range, the argument still must be in range format (A2..A2).

Use

The @S function is used to return the value of the upper-left cell in a range. If the cell contains a number, a blank cell is returned. This action can prevent the error condition that occurs if strings and numbers are mixed in one formula. If you have any doubt about the contents of a cell you are combining with a string, you can use @S, which will convert the contents of the cell to an empty string entry if it contains a number. For example, using @S in the formula @LEFT(@S(A1)) ensures that the formula will not return ERR even if A1 contains a value.

@STRING

The @STRING function converts numeric values to strings and allows you to specify the number of decimal places to be used for a string.

Format

@STRING(*number,number of decimal places*)

Arguments

number	A numeric value or reference to a numeric value.
number of decimal places	The number of decimal places to be used when the string is created from *number.* If *number* is longer than the specified number of places, rounding occurs. If *number* is shorter, zeros are used for padding.

Use

The primary use of this function is to permit the combination of numeric values with strings in a string formula. If @STRING is not used to convert numbers first, ERR is returned by any such string formula. The @STRING function uses the Fixed format with the number of places you specify to create the resulting string. The @STRING function ignores formatting characters such as commas and dollar signs. Some examples of @STRING are

    @STRING(1.6,0) equals the string 2
    @STRING(12,4) equals the string 12.0000
    @STRING(2.3E+04,2) equals the string 23000.00

If you enter +"The total is "&@STRING(@SUM(B4..B11)) in a cell, the result will be "The total is 46698" assuming the sum of B4..B11 is 46698.

@TRIM

The @TRIM function allows you to strip away extraneous blanks from a string entry.

Format

@TRIM(*string*)

Arguments

string   A sequence of characters included in the function by enclosing them in double quotation marks ("). Or you can reference a cell address or range name that contains the characters.

Use

This function is used to remove trailing, preceding, and multiple internal blanks from a string. It lets you clean up existing entries on a worksheet and establish a consistent format for data storage. @TRIM can be used with string formulas as well as strings. The examples that follow include both types of entries:

    @TRIM("   Sales") equals Sales
    @TRIM(" January "&" Fuel Allowance ") equals January Fuel Allowance.

Notice that @TRIM retains one space between strings separated by an ampersand (&).

@UPPER

The @UPPER function converts lowercase, proper case, and mixed upper- and lowercase character strings to all uppercase.

Format

@UPPER(*string*)

Arguments

string   A group of characters that can be in proper case, lowercase, or mixed upper- and lowercase. The characters can be included in the function (if they are enclosed in double quotation marks) or placed in a cell and referenced. You can also use a string formula as *string*.

Use

This function is valuable when data from several sources must be combined and data entry was not done in a consistent manner. @UPPER is one of the functions that lets you change the appearance of data without retyping it. @UPPER(A2&" "&B3), where A2 contains "Jobbard Milling Company" and B3 contains "east dallas division" returns "JOBBARD MILLING COMPANY EAST DALLAS DIVISION." All of every word in each string is converted to uppercase. Refer back to the worksheet in Figure 7-49 to see several additional conversions. Entries are made in column A, and @UPPER formulas are used to obtain the remainder of the display.

@VALUE

The @VALUE function is designed to convert a string that looks like a number into an actual numeric value.

Format

@VALUE(*string*)

Arguments

string A sequence of characters included in the function by enclosing them in double quotation marks or by referencing a cell address or range name containing the characters. The sequence of characters must look like a number. Acceptable examples are 345.674, 345.1E8, 7, and 7/8 (a fraction). If *string* references an empty cell, 0 is returned.

Use

This function converts strings that look like numbers into actual numeric values so they can be used in calculations. The function removes any leading or trailing blanks from the string. Here are a few examples:

@VALUE("   23.98") returns the number 23.98
@VALUE(Z10) returns 0 if Z10 is blank, and ERR if Z10 contains a label such as abc.

Chapter *8*

Working with Files

The worksheets discussed so far have all been stored in part of your computer's random access memory (RAM). RAM offers the advantage of instant availability for information stored in it. Changes, additions, and deletions to information stored in RAM can be accomplished very quickly. The disadvantage of RAM storage is that it is very volatile. Losing the power to your computer for even a brief instant causes everything stored in RAM to be permanently lost.

A more permanent means of storage is clearly required, and this normally is done with disk files. The 1-2-3 program itself is a file. That is why it is permanently available on your disk. If the program is lost from memory, you can restore it by reloading it from your disk.

This chapter focuses on the data files that contain information on the applications you have created on 1-2-3. You learn how to save, retrieve, and delete files. You also learn to combine files and to perform other file management operations.

Naming and Using Files

1-2-3 uses disk files for the permanent storage of all information. These files can be maintained on either hard or floppy disks. They can be transferred from one disk to another by saving the worksheets to several disks with the /File Save command or by using operating system commands. Because 1-2-3 runs under DOS, the conventions established by DOS for the naming of files must be followed. A comprehensive discussion of rules for filenames and file storage can be found in your DOS manual.

339

Filenames and File Types

The 1-2-3 program creates three types of data files: worksheet files, graph files, and print files. 1-2-3 automatically appends an extension suffix to each filename that allows you to distinguish one file type from another. In addition, 1-2-3 has many files of its own that are part of the program and its various features.

DOS imposes an eight-character limit on filenames, and a three-character limit on filename extensions. A period (.) is used to separate the filename from the extension.

A filename and extension can contain letters, numbers, and many symbols. 1-2-3 automatically changes lowercase characters in your filename entries to uppercase. Symbols are permitted only if the specific release of your operating system allows them. 1-2-3 does not allow spaces in the filename since the operating system does not allow it. An underscore (_) is a better way to separate filenames into words. Examples of valid filenames are SALES, REGION_1, EMPLOYEE, and SALES_85.

If you enter a filename longer than eight characters, 1-2-3 truncates the filename after the eighth character. The filename SALES_REGION_1 thus becomes SALES_RE, which would be identical to truncated versions of SALES_REGION_2, SALES_ REGION_3, and other filenames with the same characters in the first eight positions.

1-2-3 distinguishes file types by the extension added to the file. Each of the 1-2-3 program files and the files you create in 1-2-3 have different extensions to indicate the type of data stored in the file. The three most common types of files and their extensions follow:

File Type	Extension
Worksheet	.WK1 (Releases 2.0 through 2.4)
	.WKS (Release 1A)
Print	.PRN and .ENC
Graph	.PIC

You also have the option of supplying your own extension for any file type. If you supply this extension when you create a file, you must supply it every time you access that file. If you use 1-2-3's default extensions, the package supplies them for you at all times.

Subdirectories

You can create subdirectories for the storage of files. Subdirectories create logical rather than physical divisions for the hard disk and manage the files within a particular directory so it is easy to find related files. The concept of subdirectories is similar to the filing system you may have developed to manage all the memos and other paper information you receive. Just as you cannot throw all this paper in one desk drawer and expect to find something in it with ease, you do not want to randomly place all your files on the hard disk without the organization structure that sub-directories provide.

Using subdirectories lessens the time required for file retrieval because 1-2-3 does not have to search the directory for the entire hard disk to determine the file's location. If you have a hard disk, you are probably already using subdirectories for your other applications.

The first directory on your hard disk is automatic and is called the Root directory. You can store files in the Root directory, or you can create subdirectories immediately beneath it. The latter approach is best because it places all your files within the control of a subdirectory. DOS provides the command MD (or MKDIR) to create new directories at any level within the directory structure.

Within a directory, each filename and extension combination must be unique. You may have two files named BUDGET in a directory, as long as they have different filename extensions. You can use the same filename on a hard disk more than once, as long as the files are in different subdirectories. For example, you can have the filename BUDGET.WK1 in the subdirectory ACCT and the subdirectory FIN. The contents of these files may be the same or different. Even if the files originally contain the same data, they are two separate physical files, and an update to one file does not affect the other.

If you are using subdirectories, 1-2-3 must know the drive and the pathname to find a file. The drive designation is the drive letter followed by a colon (:); for example, A:, B:, or C:. The pathname tells 1-2-3 what directory the file is in. Higher level directories are always listed first. \SALES indicates that the file is in the first-level directory SALES, whereas \SALES\REGION\ONE indicates that the file is several levels down from the top directory in a subdirectory called ONE. If you are not familiar with the ins and outs of subdirectories, review your DOS manual for more detailed information.

The File Menu Options

File is one of the options on 1-2-3's main menu. Most of the commands that manipulate files are options on the File submenu, which is shown in this illustration:

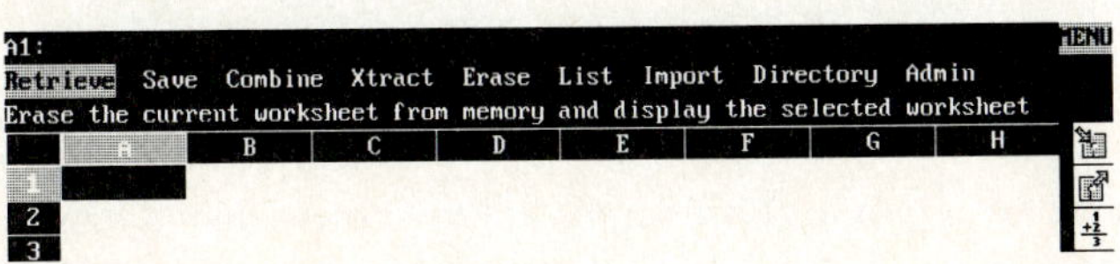

The following sections look at each of these menu options in detail.

Saving a File to Disk

Any worksheet model in RAM must be saved to a disk file if it is to be available in later 1-2-3 sessions. Use the /File Save option to place a copy of the current worksheet on your disk. You use this command to save a new worksheet, as well as an updated, existing worksheet. After entering **/File Save**, type a valid filename at the prompt and press ENTER.

If the current worksheet file has not been saved before, when you invoke **/File Save**, 1-2-3 displays a list of the existing worksheets and prompts for a filename. You can select a filename from the list or enter a new name in response to 1-2-3's prompt, and then press ENTER.

If the file has already been saved in the current session or if it is a file that you retrieved from disk, 1-2-3 suggests that it be saved again under the same name. If you agree, press ENTER. When prompted to confirm this decision, select Replace if you want the current worksheet to replace the existing file. If you want a backup copy of the worksheet, select Backup. The file created has a .BAK extension. If you decide not to save the file, select Cancel to return to READY mode. You can also use the first icon in any of the first five palettes for saving. The icon looks like this:

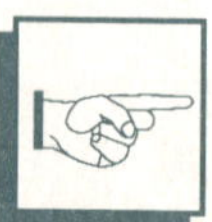

Create a Backup version to retain the original and revised versions of a worksheet. When you use /File Save Backup, 1-2-3 saves the original file with the extension .BAK, and saves the current version with the extension .WK1. This provides access to both versions of the worksheet.

Whether you are saving a new or updated file, you may choose to name it with an existing filename. At the /File Save prompt, you can press ESC. 1-2-3 then provides a file list like the following:

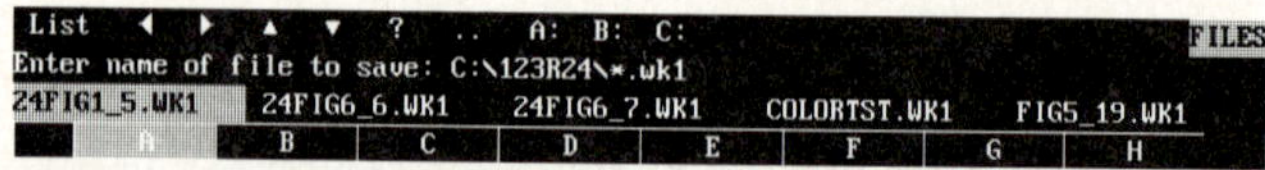

Point to the name you want and press ENTER. Once you select a name, 1-2-3 displays the following prompt:

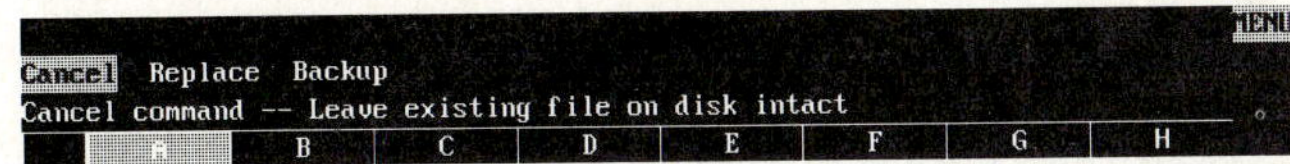

This prompt asks if you wish to cancel the request, replace the file on the disk with the current contents of memory, or back up the original worksheet first before replacing the file on the disk with the current contents of memory. This is the same prompt that appears when you are saving an updated file using the same filename. This prompt is needed because each disk or subdirectory can have only one file with a particular name. When you reuse a name, only the last data you saved remains in the file.

In Releases 2 and above, you can save a file to a different drive or directory by specifying the drive and directory designation along with the filename, as in C:\SALES\REGION\FILE1. If you need to add or delete characters in the current filename and path specification, use the LEFT ARROW and RIGHT ARROW keys to move around.

1-2-3 makes it so easy to save files that you want to save frequently. If your system goes down, you can then retrieve the most recently saved version of the file; it is easier to reconstruct what was lost if it has not been too long since the last save.

Retrieving a File from Disk

The /File Retrieve command retrieves a file from your disk. When 1-2-3 loads a worksheet file into memory, it first erases the worksheet currently in memory. If you have not saved that information on disk, there is no way to bring it back. To retrieve a worksheet, you can use the SmartIcon, shown here:

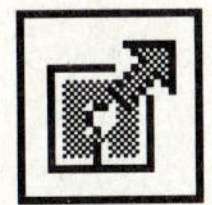

When you enter the /File Retrieve command or click the Smart Icon, 1-2-3 searches the current disk or subdirectory and lists all the files with either a .WK1 (Release 2) or .WKS (Release 1A) extension. As shown here, 1-2-3 displays up to four or five names across the third line of the control panel, depending on the release:

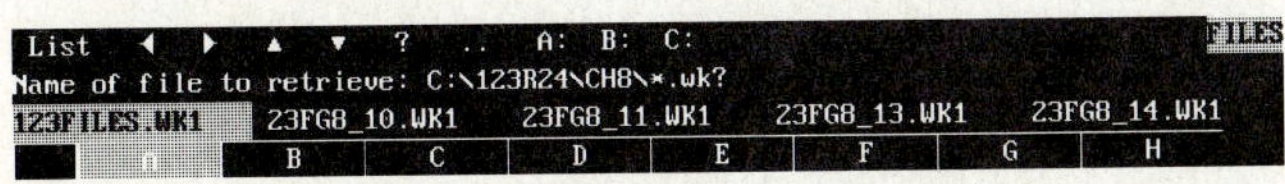

You can use the arrow keys to move across the display, scrolling to additional filenames until you finally cycle through all of them and move back to the beginning of the subdirectory. Pressing the UP ARROW and DOWN ARROW keys moves you a line at a time through the file list. You can press HOME to move to the first file or END to move to the last file in the file list.

If you want to see all the filenames at once, press F3 (NAMES) to see a list like the one in Figure 8-1. Moving to a particular filename displays the date and time that file was saved and its size in the control panel. In Releases 2.3 and 2.4, the top row of the control panel for the /File Retrieve command is to be used with a mouse. List is equivalent to pressing F3 (NAMES) to switch the display of filenames between the control panel and the full screen. You can use the triangles to move to the next filename in the direction of the triangle. The question mark displays help information just as if you had pressed F1. The .. lets you switch to the parent directory. The A: through C: shown in Figure 8-1 let you switch between the available drives with a mouse. To retrieve a listed file, point to the file you want with the mouse and click it, or use the arrow keys and press ENTER.

To retrieve a file in another directory, type the complete pathname for the file. Pressing ESC twice removes the displayed pathname specification. You can also retrieve a worksheet file with an extension other than .WK1 by specifying the extension along with the filename. You can also press BACKSPACE at the /File Save prompt to display the files in the parent directory of the current one. To select a directory in the current one, highlight it in the file list (directory names are at the end) and press ENTER or click it to list the worksheet files in the selected directory.

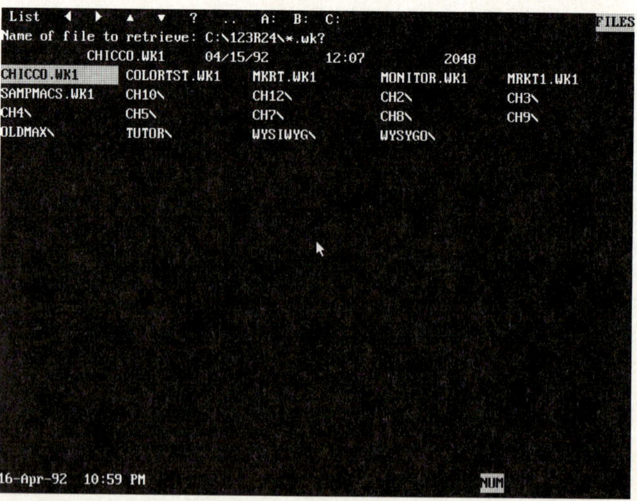

Figure 8-1.   A complete filename display generated with F3 (NAMES)

Using Passwords with Files

Passwords were added in Release 2 to offer a measure of protection for your files. When in effect, a password prevents an operator from retrieving a file without first supplying the correct password.

Passwords are added to a file when it is saved. If you want to specify a password, after entering the filename press the spacebar, type **p**, and then press ENTER, as in SALES P.

1-2-3 then prompts for the password, which can have up to 15 characters. When you type in the password, it is not displayed; your control panel will look like this:

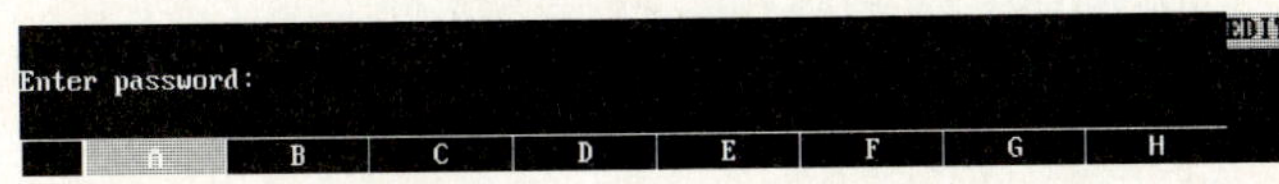

Your use of upper- and lowercase is recorded and must be correctly duplicated when you access the file later. When you press ENTER, you are prompted to enter the password again for verification. If the passwords entered on both occasions are not an exact match, 1-2-3 provides an error message to that effect. The second prompt for the password also offers a way to stop the addition of the password: simply press ESC. Once you have pressed ENTER for the final time, the password is added to the disk, and you must use it whenever you retrieve the file.

To access a file with a password, enter the command you wish to use in working with the file, such as **/File Retrieve**. 1-2-3 then generates a prompt for the password and waits for you to enter it. If you cannot reproduce the password exactly as it was originally entered, including the correct use of upper- and lowercase, 1-2-3 does not retrieve the file and displays an error message.

To change the password of a password-protected file, save the file again. When 1-2-3 displays the filename followed by "[PASSWORD PROTECTED]," press the BACKSPACE key and then the spacebar, and type **p**. 1-2-3 prompts you twice for a new password, just as if you were adding a new password to a new file.

To remove the password of a password-protected file, save the file again. When 1-2-3 displays the filename followed by "[PASSWORD PROTECTED]," press the BACKSPACE key and then ENTER.

Retrieving Files on a Network

When you retrieve a file on a network, you have other considerations; someone else may also be using the file that you want. With worksheet files on a network, only one person is allowed to make changes. Otherwise, the changes made by one person would be undone by another. The privilege to alter a worksheet is called the *reservation.*

1-2-3 is initially set to get the reservation for the file when you retrieve it. If someone else has the reservation, you cannot have it until they relinquish it. When

1-2-3 cannot provide the reservation, it displays an extra prompt asking if you want the file without the reservation. If you select No, the /File Retrieve command is canceled. If you select Yes, 1-2-3 will retrieve the file but you cannot save it using the same filename. 1-2-3 indicates that you cannot save the file with the same name by displaying RO (for read-only) in the status line. You will also see the RO indicator when you release a reservation so someone else can modify the file.

Once you have a reservation, you can release it so someone else can alter the file by selecting /File Admin Reservation Release. Since you will not have the reservation after this command, it is important that you save any changes you want to keep before performing this command. On the other hand, you can try obtaining a reservation when you do not have one by selecting /File Admin Reservation Get. When you perform this command, 1-2-3 attempts to get the reservation. If the reservation is available, the file has not changed since you retrieved it, and you have write access to the file, then the RO indicator disappears. If the reservation is not available, the worksheet stored in the file is different from the one you retrieved, or you do not have write access to the file, then the RO indicator will not disappear. Write access is a privilege granted by the network administrator that allows you to save your changes.

Combining Information from Two Files

The /File Combine options bring information from other worksheet files into your current worksheet. With this capability you can produce budget consolidations, or you can build a new worksheet using components of several existing worksheet files. Unlike /File Retrieve, the Combine options do not erase what is in memory.

The three Combine options are Copy, Add, and Subtract. All three depend on the location of the cell pointer in the current worksheet for the actions they take. The Combine Copy option is essential for transferring data between worksheets. (With Releases 2.2 and above, you can create external links and use the Macro Library Manager discussed in Chapter 12 to transfer data between worksheets.) The /File Combine Add and Subtract options automatically perform arithmetic operations between the contents of the current file and the external file without the need for entering formulas.

Copying Information from a File to a Worksheet

The /File Combine Copy command allows you to replace the contents of current worksheet cells with the contents of cells in a disk file. The replacement begins at the cell-pointer location in the current worksheet, and the extent of the replacement depends on how many cells are being copied from the disk. Values, labels, and formulas can all be copied from the file on disk.

You have two methods for determining the extent of the replacement. You can bring in an entire file, which involves taking each cell in the file that contains a value, label, or formula and replacing an appropriate number of cells in the current worksheet to accommodate the imported data. The location of the cells replaced is determined by the location of the cell pointer at the time of the Combine Copy request and by the contents of the file to be incorporated. Displacement of cells in the current file matches the dimensions of the replacement data, with the base point being the cell-pointer location.

Suppose you have a file named HEADING that is stored on disk and looks like this:

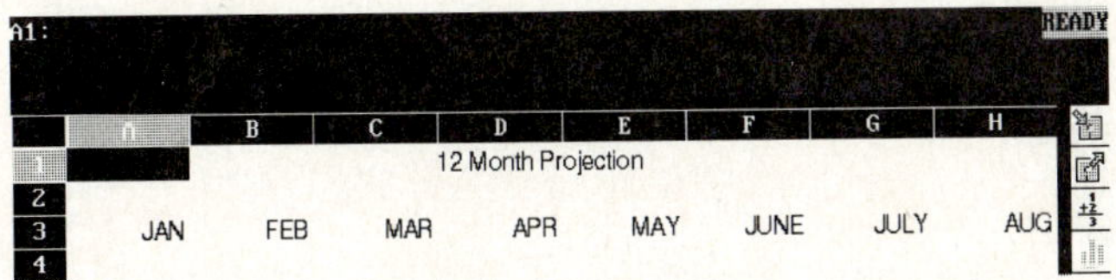

Your current worksheet file looks like Figure 8-2. Move the cell pointer to cell B1 of the worksheet and enter **/File Combine Copy**. Specify the HEADING filename and choose the Entire-File option. The results should look like Figure 8-3. The /File Combine Copy command overwrites the existing contents of cells, starting at B1.

If you only need to copy data once and do not need to update the copy from the external file, use /File Combine Copy. If you want to refresh the copied data, use a formula that contains references to cells that reference external worksheets. You can then update the links at any time with /File Admin Link-Refresh.

If you do not need to copy an entire file, you can use /File Combine Copy's second option, Named/Specified-Range. This option copies only the range of values that you specify. For example, suppose the highlighted range of cells named 91_TOT, shown in Figure 8-4, is saved in a worksheet file called 91_BUD. You want to copy 91_TOT to the column headed 91 Sales on the worksheet shown in Figure 8-5, which already shows 1992 sales and includes formulas to calculate the difference between

Figure 8-2.   *A worksheet without heading entries at the top*

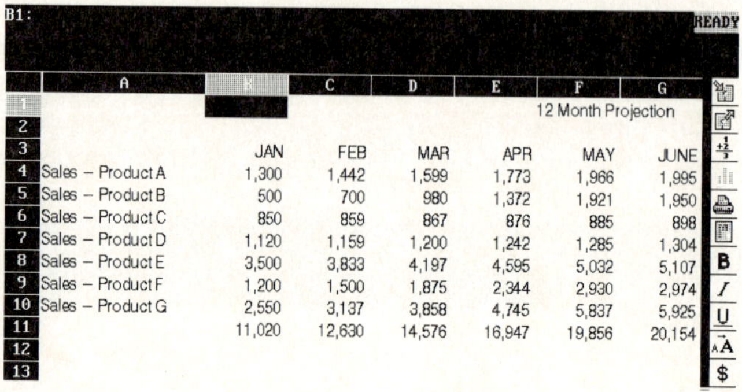

Figure 8-3. *Heading entries added with /File Combine Copy*

91 and 92 sales. Place the cell pointer in B4 of the worksheet in Figure 8-5 and invoke **/File Combine Copy**. Then select Named/Specified-Range and enter **91_TOT** followed by the filename, **91_BUD**. When you're finished, the results should look like Figure 8-6.

Use range names with the /File Combine command, and name the ranges in the file you are combining. Range names are easier to remember. Also, if you give the same name to all the range names that you are combining, it is easier to prevent entering an incorrect range address or range name.

Adding Information from a File to a Worksheet

The /File Combine Add command adds the values of cells in a disk file to corresponding cells in the current worksheet. The addition begins at the cell pointer

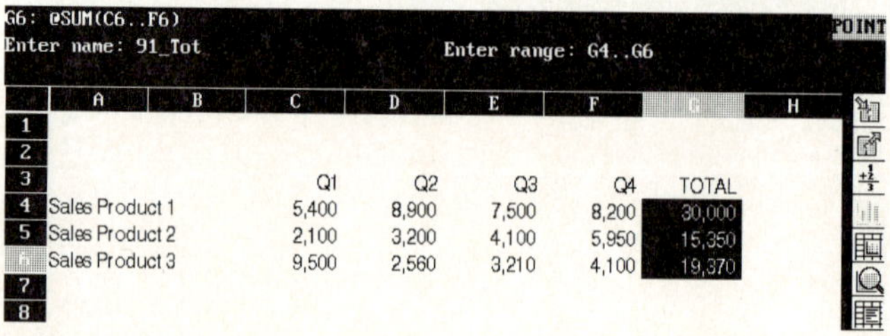

Figure 8-4. *A range named 91_TOT*

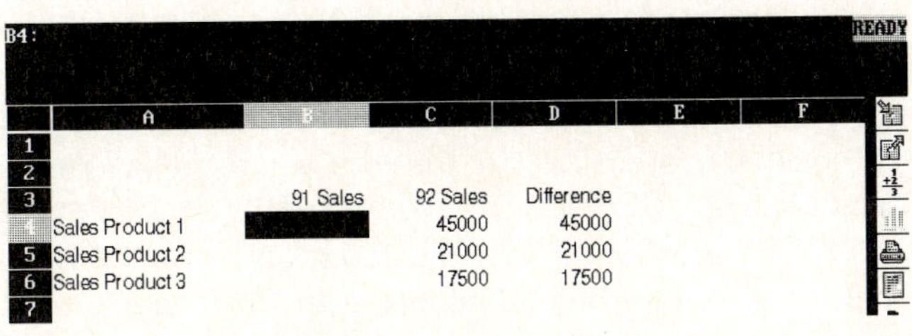

Figure 8-5.   *A worksheet requiring the totals in the named range*

location in the current worksheet, and the extent of the addition depends on the arrangement of cells added from the disk. Only numeric values are involved in the addition process. Labels in the incoming worksheet are ignored, formulas in the incoming worksheet are treated as values, and the label and formula entries in the current worksheet are retained for those cells.

You have two options for determining the extent of the addition. You can choose Entire-File, which adds each cell in the disk file that contains a value to the appropriate cell in the current worksheet. The location of the cells to which the disk file values are added is determined by the location of the cell pointer at the time of the Combine Add request, and by the amount of the displacement (that is, the location of the cell in relation to the beginning of the file) of the particular cell within the file. The same displacement is used to determine the cells that receive the added data, with the base point being the cell pointer location.

The second option is to choose Named/Specified-Range, which adds only the cells in the selected range beginning at the location of the cell pointer in the worksheet.

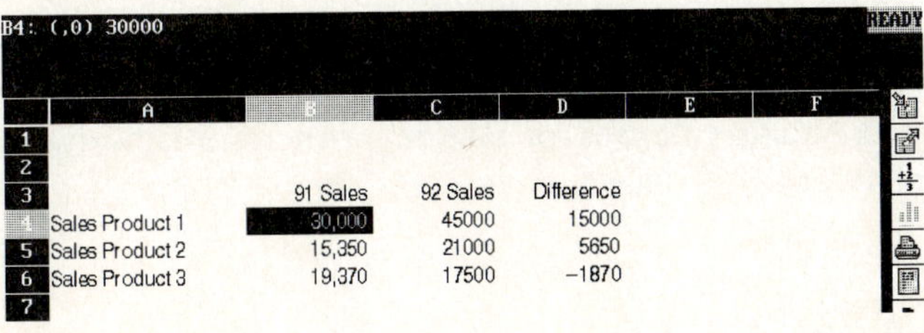

Figure 8-6.   *Adding the named range to the existing worksheet with /File Combine Copy*

/File Combine Add provides one method for budget consolidation. If you have files containing individual department or subsidiary budgets, the /File Combine Add command permits you to put all the figures into one consolidated budget. Figure 8-7 shows portions of the budgets for each department in a company. Notice that the format for all three is identical: this is required if you want to Combine Add entire files. Add the three files one by one to the Total Budget worksheet, shown in Figure 8-8. Because the entire file is being added in each case, you should place your cell pointer in A1 before invoking **/File Combine Add**. The final results are shown in Figure 8-9. The labels and formulas in the total budget worksheet do not change when the other worksheets are added. Any formulas in the worksheets that are added to the current one are converted to their value before being added to the current worksheet.

Subtracting Information in a File from a Worksheet

The /File Combine Subtract command allows you to subtract the values of cells in a disk file from corresponding cells in the current worksheet. The subtraction begins at the cell-pointer location in the current worksheet, and the extent of the subtraction depends on the arrangement of cells from the disk that are being subtracted from the worksheet cells. Only numeric values are involved in the subtraction process. Labels and formulas are ignored, and the label and formula entries in the current worksheet are retained for those cells. /File Combine Subtract does not overlay the contents of existing cells.

You have two options for determining the extent of the subtraction. You can choose Entire-File, which subtracts each cell in the disk file that contains a value from the appropriate cell in the current worksheet. The location of the cells from which the disk file values are subtracted is determined by the location of the cell pointer at the time of the Combine Subtract request, and by the amount of the displacement of the particular cell within the file. The same displacement is used to determine the cells that receive the subtracted data, with the base point being the cell-pointer location. If you choose Named/Specified-Range, only the cells in the selected range are subtracted. This begins at the location of the cell pointer in the worksheet.

The subtraction feature is useful after you have completed file consolidation with the /File Combine Add command. /File Combine Subtract allows you to see the effect of taking the budget figures for one department or subsidiary away from the total, thereby simulating the effect of closing it.

Saving Part of a Worksheet

The /File Xtract command saves part of a worksheet. This command is used to save sections of a worksheet for use in constructing new models or to split a worksheet

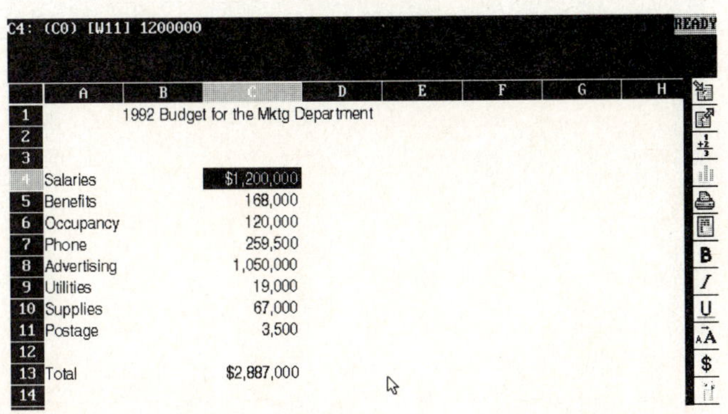

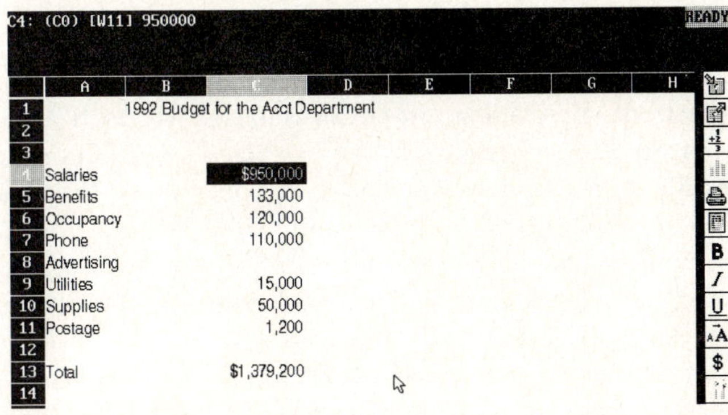

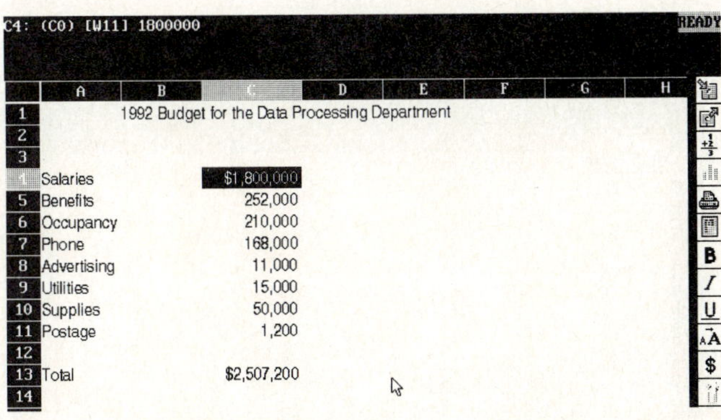

Figure 8-7.   *The department budgets*

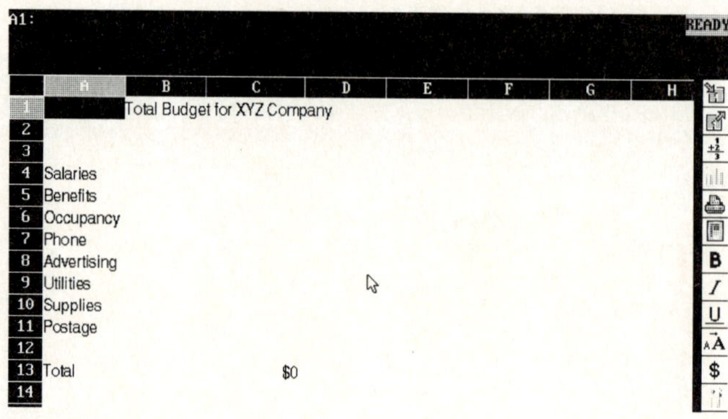

Figure 8-8.   *The total budget worksheet*

into more than one file. Settings established for the current worksheet are saved in the new file.

Worksheet sections are saved as either Formulas or Values. If you choose Values, 1-2-3 saves the values of the formulas in the extracted worksheet rather than maintaining the formulas in the new worksheet. If you choose Formulas, 1-2-3 saves formulas as they are entered, but not the values referenced by the formulas unless they are in the range selected. The formulas in the range you select to extract are adjusted just as if you moved them to the new worksheet. This means that relative, mixed, and absolute addresses are adjusted although they will still be relative, mixed, or absolute addresses in the extracted worksheet. When labels are extracted, the result is the same whether you select Formulas or Values, because labels do not reference other cells.

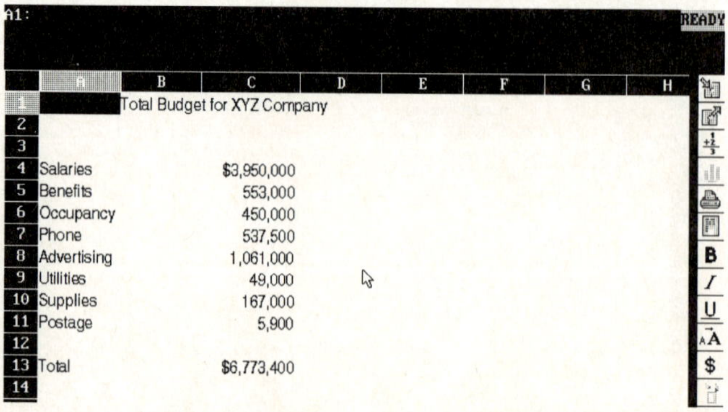

Figure 8-9.   *The result of using /File Combine Add*

Extracting formulas that reference cells outside the extract range offers the biggest potential for error. For instance, you might extract E1..H12, and there might be a formula in E2 that refers to A1. When this reference is adjusted for the new file, it refers to cell IS1 because the reference is computed from A1 of the new worksheet. This cell therefore does not contain what you expected. This is because 1-2-3 adjusts the cell references in formulas as if you were using the /Move command.

The procedure for using either option is to enter **/File Xtract** and choose either Formulas or Values. You are prompted for the filename to use for storage; either type a name or choose one from the list of worksheet files on the disk. You can also make the extracted file password-protected by pressing the spacebar after you name the file and typing **p**. Then you must provide a password, as instructed for password protection with the /File Save command. Next, 1-2-3 prompts you to supply the range of cells to extract by highlighting or typing the address, or supplying a defined range name.

If you choose an existing filename for the extracted file, you must confirm your choice with Cancel, Replace, or Backup. The Replace option erases the original file, and the Backup option renames the original file before storing the extracted data under the specified filename. The other option, Cancel, returns you to READY mode without saving the extract file.

Figure 8-10 shows a worksheet that contains formulas in column E. Suppose you extract the entries in column E and save them as Values. You then place this extract in another worksheet with /File Combine Copy. The result is shown in Figure 8-11, where the formula entries from the previous worksheet appear as calculated values. If you extract the original formulas using the Formulas option, the formulas would become @SUM(IT3..IV3), @SUM(IT4..IV4), and @SUM(IT5..IV5) as they were copied from E3..E5 in the first worksheet to A3..A5 in the extracted worksheet.

Erasing Files from the Disk

From time to time you have files that you no longer require. You can remove them from your disk with the DEL command under DOS, or you can eliminate them from within 1-2-3 with /File Erase. The advantage of /File Erase is that you are still in 1-2-3, so you can retrieve a file and look at it to make sure that you want to delete it.

The /File Erase command requires that you first specify the type of file you want to erase. Choose from Worksheet, Print, Graph, or Other, and 1-2-3 then lists all the files of that type on the disk or in the current directory. 1-2-3 also lists the subdirectory names (if any) for the current directory. You can then change directories.

If you choose Worksheet, all .WK1 and .WKS filenames are displayed. Select Print to see all files with a .PRN suffix. Graph displays files with the .PIC extension. Other causes 1-2-3 to display all the filenames on the current disk or in the current directory. With F3 (NAME), you can switch between listing the filenames in a single line or using the whole screen. To change the extension, press F2 (EDIT) and enter the extension of the files you want to see. The /File Erase command offers wildcard features, just

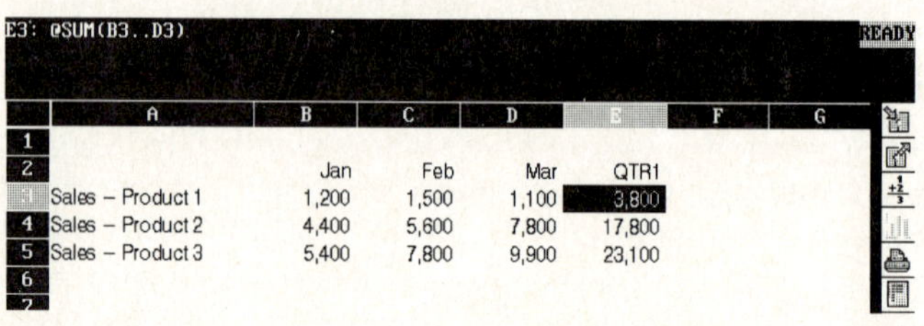

Figure 8-10.   *A worksheet containing formulas*

as DOS does. A question mark (?) can replace any single character in the filename, and an asterisk (*) specifies that any characters are accepted from that point to the end of the filename. For instance, J?N would match JAN, JUN, JON, JEN, and so on. J* would match all of these options, as well as names like JUNE, JANUARY, JOLLY, and JOINT.

After selecting the type of file, pick a filename from the display or enter a name yourself. Once the name is entered, 1-2-3 asks you to confirm your choice by responding with Yes. If you elect not to proceed, select No at the confirmation prompt.

Determining What Files Are on Your Disk

As your list of worksheet models and other 1-2-3 files grows longer, you may have trouble remembering all the files you have on a disk. You can always use the DOS DIR command to see a list of them, but you also have the option of using /File List or /File Admin Table from the 1-2-3 menu.

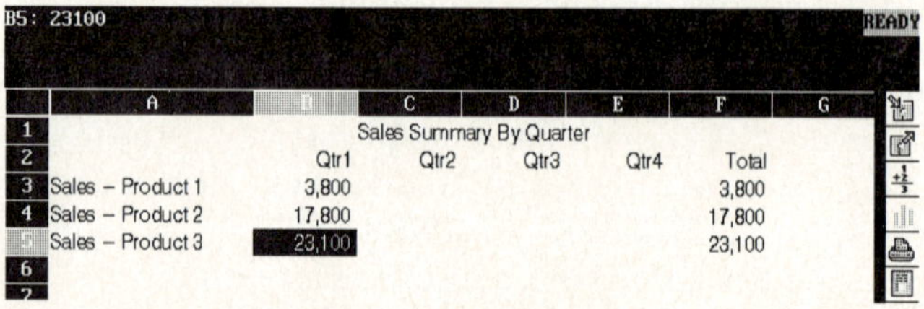

Figure 8-11.   *The result of using /File Combine Copy with values produced by /File Xtract*

Temporarily Listing Files

1-2-3's /File List command lists files on the screen and displays additional information about the highlighted filename. When you enter **/File List**, you are first presented with a menu of file type options. Choose from Worksheet, Print, Graph, Other, or Linked, and 1-2-3 lists all the files of that type on the disk or in the current directory. 1-2-3 also lists the subdirectory names (if any) for the current directory. You can then use the cell pointer to change directories.

If you choose Worksheet, all .WK1 and .WKS filenames are displayed, as shown in Figure 8-12. Select Print for all .PRN files. Graph displays files with the .PIC extension. Choose Other to see all the filenames on the current disk or in the current directory. To change the extension, press F2 (EDIT) and enter the extension of the files you want to see. Releases 2.2 and above provide a new option, Linked, which lists the files for which there are formula references in the current worksheet.

Regardless of the file type selected, pointing to a filename in the list displays the file's size and the date and time it was last saved to disk. The Linked option also includes the pathname of the linked files.

Listing Files on a Worksheet

1-2-3's /File Admin Table command creates a table in the worksheet containing a list of files and related information. The types of files and the information listed for each option matches the /File List command. After selecting the command, choose from Worksheet, Print, Graph, Other, or Linked. If you selected Worksheet, Print, Graph,

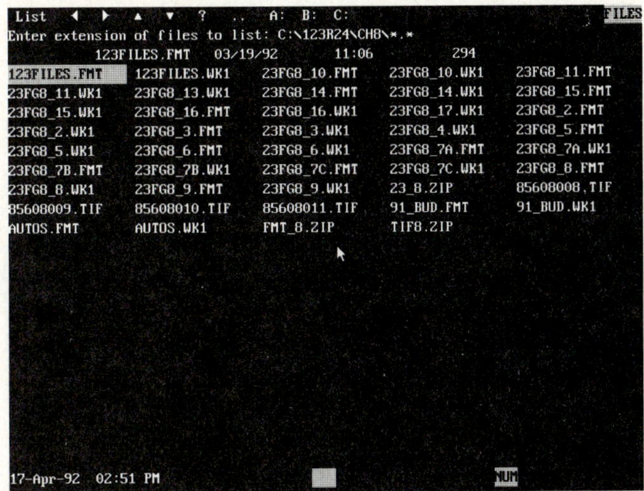

Figure 8-12.   *A list of all the worksheet files on the disk*

or Other, 1-2-3 prompts for the directory of files and will list a prompt such as C:\123R24*.WK?. By editing the pathname, directory, and filename indicator in this prompt, you can determine which files 1-2-3 includes in the table. The selected directory can include the ? and * wildcard characters. For example, if you want all worksheet files that begin with a "P," retype the prompt as **C:\123R24\P*.WK?**.

Once you select the type of files you want to list, 1-2-3 prompts you for the location of the table. Either highlight the cell or type the cell address or range where you want to place the upper-left corner of the table. The table contains as many rows as are needed by the files to be listed, and four columns. The table writes over the worksheet's current contents, so be sure to select an area where the table has plenty of room. Figure 8-13 shows a table created with the /File Admin Table Linked command.

Adding Text Files to the Worksheet

The /File Import command allows you to transfer to your worksheet the data from a word-processing program or other package that generates standard ASCII text input. You must be sure that the word processor does not include special characters in the file. (Most word processors have an option to eliminate special characters from the text file.) A standard ASCII text file is created by 1-2-3 every time you use the /Print File command.

First, move the cell pointer to the first cell where you want the text imported. Then select /File Import Text or /File Import Numbers, and type or highlight the name of the file to import. 1-2-3 looks for filenames that have the extension .PRN. If the file you want to import does not have a .PRN extension, you can rename the file using the DOS RENAME command or enter your own extension at 1-2-3's prompt for the filename.

There are two basic options for importing text data into a 1-2-3 worksheet: Text and Numbers. These options determine how the data is placed in the worksheet.

When you import data as Text, each line of the word-processor document becomes one long, left-justified label. You thus end up with a column of long labels.

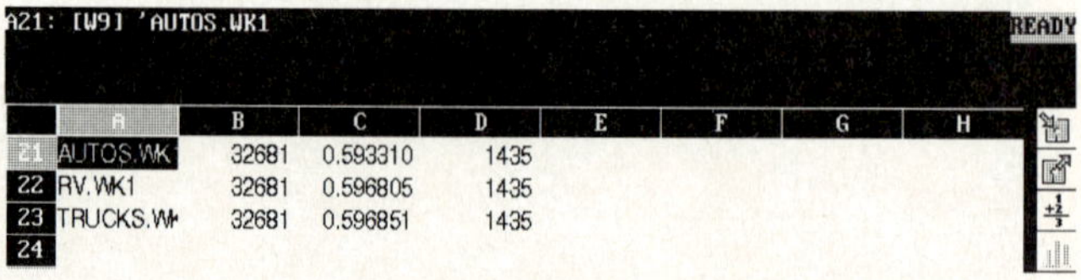

Figure 8-13.   A table created with the /File Admin Table Linked command

Once the data is imported, you can use /Data Parse (covered in Chapter 10) to split the labels into individual pieces.

The Numbers option is for importing delimited data files. If you use the Numbers option, characters enclosed in double quotation marks ("), as well as all numbers, are imported. Blanks and characters not in quotation marks are eliminated in the import process. Each number in a line of the text file generates a numeric cell entry, and each quote-enclosed label creates a left-justified label cell. Entries from the same line of a text file produce entries in the same row of the worksheet, proceeding from left to right of the row with each new entry. Commas separate each piece of data in each line in the imported file.

1-2-3 imposes a size limit on the imported file of 8,192 lines. The maximum number of characters in a cell is 240, so when you use the Text option, each line may contain up to 240 characters; when you use the Numbers option, each entry between commas may contain up to 240 characters.

Figure 8-14 shows text entered into an ASCII file. You have two choices for importing the information into 1-2-3. Place your cell pointer in A1 and use /File Import Text to produce the results shown in Figure 8-15. Notice in the control panel that each of the entries is a long label with the entire line in one label. If you imported the same file using the Numbers option, the resulting worksheet would have 10 in A2, 25 in A3, and 15 in A4. Only the numbers from the Quantity column would be transferred, because the label entries are not enclosed in quotes.

Changing the Current Directory

The /File Directory command changes the disk drive or directory for your current 1-2-3 session. When you enter **/File Directory**, 1-2-3 displays the existing directory. You can press ENTER to accept it, or type a new directory or pathname. If you just want to reach a lower level directory, you can type the new level into the existing directory listing.

```
C:\123R24>type regsales.txt

                    Regional Unit Sales

           Product 1   Product 2   Product 3   Product 4
  Boston       2,565       4,430         130       8,712
  New York     1,890       9,150       8,230       1,100
  Dallas         510       7,842       1,600       9,780
  Chicago      1,009       3,590       2,003       2,135

C:\123R24>
```

Figure 8-14.   *An ASCII file*

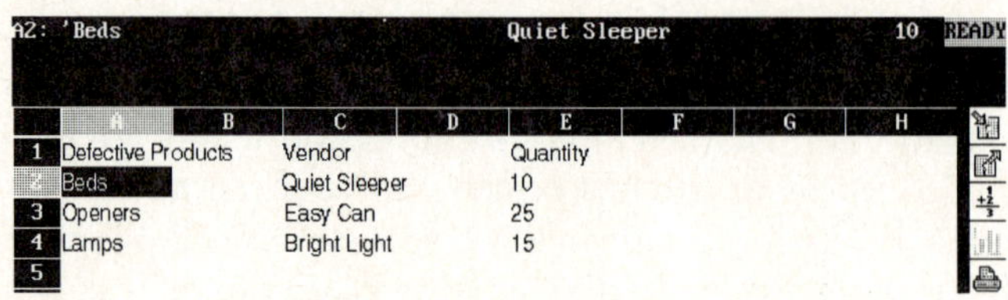

Figure 8-15.   *The results of using /File Import Text*

External File Links

Releases 2.2 and above allow you to establish links between the current worksheet in memory and data stored in cells or ranges on disk. You can use this feature to reference data in another file, and 1-2-3 updates the copy of the data that you reference. In previous releases of 1-2-3, if you wanted to use the data from another worksheet, you could use /File Combine to combine it with the current worksheet. Either way, you needed to continue using /File Combine to refresh the imported data when the data in the other file changed. In Releases 2.2 and above, you can create links to external files, and 1-2-3 updates their values every time you load a file or use the /File Admin Link-Refresh command. If you are using Release 2.3 or 2.4, you will want to look at the Viewer Add-In discussed later in the chapter, which makes creating external file links easier.

To refer to a value in another worksheet file, the cell address or range name is preceded by the filename surrounded by the file delimiter—1-2-3 uses double angle brackets (<<>>). 1-2-3 assumes the file is in the current directory unless a path is provided. If the default filename extension .WK1 is used, there is no need to supply an extension in your link entry. You might enter **+<<SALES>>A1** to link to A1 in the SALES.WK1 worksheet. If you want to establish a link to a worksheet with a .WKS extension, you must specify the extension, as in the entry **+<<SALES.WKS>>A1**.

You can link the current cell in the current worksheet to any other cell in a worksheet on disk. The worksheet can be a 1-2-3 Release 1A, 2.0, 2.01, 2.2, 2.3, or 2.4 worksheet or a Symphony 1.1, 1.2, or 2.0 worksheet. You cannot link to a range of cells. If you specify a range address or a range name referencing multiple cells as the link, 1-2-3 links only to the upper-leftmost cell in the range. To use a linked value in a formula, create an external link formula in one cell and create another formula in another cell that uses the link.

1-2-3 will not let you complete the external file link formula if it finds one of these problems:

- The file or range name in the formula does not exist.

- The file is on a network and is being used by someone else.

- The formula includes other calculations besides the external file links.

- The linked file is password-protected.

- 1-2-3 cannot read the referenced file due to an incorrect file type or other problem.

Figure 8-16 references totals in other worksheets and contains a formula that computes the yearly total for a company with multiple divisions. Each division has its own worksheet file. The upper-left corner of each worksheet contains the summary information for the entire year. The summary worksheet for the entire company adds the different ranges for each of the division's summary worksheets. The summary worksheet uses the most up-to-date values from the supporting worksheets.

When you have links between files, you may want to check occasionally that the numbers are still the most current values. This is a recommended step before you print the worksheet or before you extract values from it to use in another worksheet file, especially if you are using 1-2-3 on a network. To recalculate values from other files, use the /File Admin Link-Refresh command. With this command, 1-2-3 re-checks all formulas in your current worksheet that refer to values in other files. 1-2-3 only checks values from other files when the worksheet containing the formulas is loaded, when the /File Admin Link-Refresh command is performed, or when the cell containing a reference to an external file is edited.

Links to cells that are in turn linked to other cells can cause incorrect results unless the links are updated in the correct order. Links form a hierarchical relationship and must be updated from the bottom up if the file at the bottom is changed. For example, suppose you have files linked as shown in Figure 8-17 and AUTOSLSA has been updated. You must retrieve ALLAUTO to update its link to AUTOSLSA. After saving ALLAUTO, you must retrieve TOTSALES to update its link to ALLAUTO.

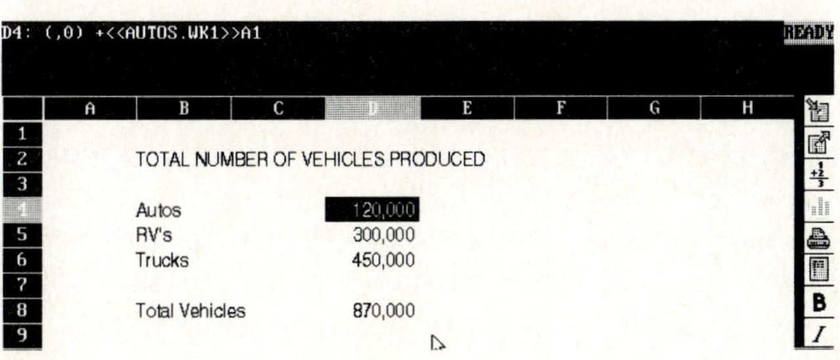

Figure 8-16.   *Referencing other files with external links*

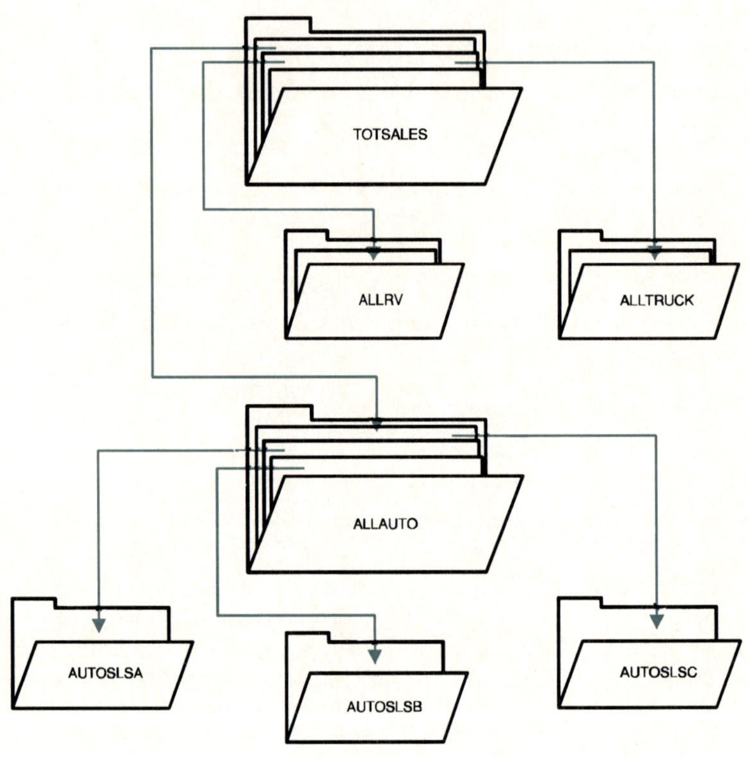

Figure 8-17.   Formula-referencing data from another file

Other Ways to Work with Files

In addition to those on the File menu, 1-2-3 provides several commands and features that are useful in working with files.

Creating a Worksheet File that Loads Automatically

1-2-3 allows you to automatically load a specific worksheet file every time you bring up 1-2-3. The only requirement for creating this special worksheet is that you name it AUTO123 and place it in the default directory.

   With this feature you can create a worksheet that contains help information for your application and documents the names of files to retrieve for different applications, to give one example. Chapters 12 and 13, in discussing macros, give further applications for this feature. It allows you to start an application with no intervention from the operator, which eliminates any possibility of error. As soon as 1-2-3 is brought up, the application is started.

If you want 1-2-3 to load a file as soon as the program is loaded, you can tell 1-2-3 to load a spreadsheet by entering -w and the filename after **123**. For example, if you want 1-2-3 to load the HOUR worksheet file as soon as the program is loaded, type **123 -wHour**. The filename after -w tells 1-2-3 which file to load. You only have to provide an extension for the file if it is not .WK1.

Changing the Default Directory Permanently

The /File Directory command changes the disk drive or directory for the current 1-2-3 session. If you do not change the default directory, it remains specified as the directory in which you installed 1-2-3. To change the default directory, enter **/Worksheet Global Default Directory** and then the directory you want to use. You can also change the directory using a dialog box by selecting /Worksheet Global Default and typing a new entry in the Directory text box. After you press ENTER, this directory is in effect for the remainder of your 1-2-3 session.

To make the change to the default directory permanent, enter **/Worksheet Global Default Update** or select the Update command button in the /Worksheet Global Default dialog box. First, temporarily remove the write-protect tabs from your system disk if you are using 1-2-3 on floppy disks. This saves any worksheet default changes and ensures they will be available for your next 1-2-3 session. The changes are saved in 1-2-3's configuration file, called 123.CNF.

Using Operating System Commands

The /System Command on Releases 2.2 and above accesses DOS commands from within 1-2-3. It allows you to use DOS commands while still retaining your worksheet in memory. The only requirement for using /System is that COMMAND.COM be in the 1-2-3 drive or directory, or in a directory 1-2-3 can access through DOS's PATH command. To access DOS commands, enter **/System**. At the DOS prompt, enter the DOS command of your choice.

For example, suppose you plan to import a file to the worksheet and want to assign it a suffix of .PRN. You can use /System to leave 1-2-3 temporarily and use the DOS RENAME command. Likewise, if you attempt to save a file and the disk is full, you can use /System to access DOS and format a floppy disk, while keeping your current worksheet in memory.

Keep in mind that commands like PRINT, which cause DOS to overlay memory, may erase your worksheet data. Any memory-resident DOS command, such as DIR or COPY, can be used with no problem. However, DOS commands such as GRAPHICS and MODE that require a program to be permanently loaded in memory can cause problems. FORMAT is an externally stored program, but it does not remain permanently resident and thus can be used without problems.

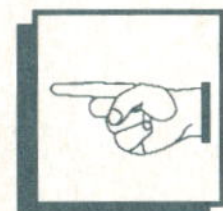

The /System command displays the DOS header shown in Figure 8-18. You can enter your DOS commands as usual. When you are finished with DOS, enter **EXIT** to return to your 1-2-3 worksheet where you left off.

Do not attempt to reenter 1-2-3 by typing 123 at the DOS prompt because 1-2-3 will attempt to load another copy of the worksheet into memory and may not find sufficient memory.

Translating Files from Other Programs

1-2-3 has several options for translating data from one format to another. 1-2-3 includes a separate program, called Translate, to translate file formats that 1-2-3 commands cannot handle. 1-2-3 also has individual translation programs that you can use instead of the menu-driven Translate program. Some of the 1-2-3 commands can also translate data.

1-2-3's Translate Program

The 1-2-3 Translate program provides the ability to translate 1-2-3 files to other file formats, and files from other programs to the 1-2-3 format. Translate can be accessed directly from DOS or through the Lotus Access System.

Select Translate from the Lotus Access System or type **trans** at the DOS prompt. First, you must select the format to translate from. These formats include 1-2-3 Releases up to 2.4, dBASE releases, DIF, Enable, Multiplan, SuperCalc4, Symphony releases, and VisiCalc. After making this selection, you are prompted to choose from the list of to formats, which includes 1-2-3 releases, dBASE releases, DIF and VisiCalc, Enable, Multiplan, SuperCalc4, and Symphony releases. Translate displays a message if the formats you choose do not need translation. You do not need to translate Release 1A files in order to use them with Releases 2.0 and above. Nor do you need to translate Symphony files for use with 1-2-3 Releases 2.01 and above, or files from Releases 2.01 and above for use with Release 3. However, converting to an earlier version of 1-2-3 eliminates new features from the files translated for earlier releases.

Once you select the To and From data formats, 1-2-3 prompts for the filename in the current directory that you want to translate. You can enter the filename directly

```
(Type EXIT and press ENTER to return to 1-2-3)

Microsoft(R) MS-DOS(R) Version 5.00
            (C)Copyright Microsoft Corp 1981-1991.

C:\123R24>
```

Figure 8-18.   A range named 91_TOT

or select it from the list provided. Translate assumes that the translated file (the to file) has the same filename with an appropriate extension for the new data format. You can use asterisks and question marks to translate multiple files, such as BUDGET*.WK1 or *.DBF. When you translate multiple files, Translate uses some settings, such as orientation (DIF format), for all of the files. If the file already exists, Translate asks you if you want to write over the existing file. Select Yes to write over the file or No to abort the translation and return to the file selection list.

If you are translating to DIF format, Translate prompts for a row or column orientation. If you are translating to a dBASE II, dBASE III, or dBASE III+ format, Translate asks if you want to translate a named range or the entire file. If you want a named range, you must enter a range name when Translate prompts for one.

Finally, Translate prompts if you want to continue. Select Yes to translate the file or No to return to the initial Translate menu. Once you instruct Translate to continue, Translate converts the file and returns a message telling you that it did or did not successfully translate the file. To exit the Translate Program, press ESC until Translate asks if you want to leave, and then select Yes.

When Translate translates a file, it only converts the features that are common to both data format types. For example, when Release 2.2 or above converts to Release 1A, it does not convert string functions because they are not part of Release 1A.

Translating with 1-2-3 Commands

Some data formats do not need to be translated with the Translate program because 1-2-3 can translate the data with the /File commands. The /File Retrieve command can retrieve 1-2-3 Release 1A, 2, 2.01, and 2.2 files, as well as Symphony Releases 1.1, 1.2, and 2.0. When Release 2.2 retrieves a Release 1A or Symphony file, it loads the data into memory and creates a file with the same name and a .WK1 file extension. Since this .WK1 file is empty, 1-2-3 deletes it if you do not save the file. The /File Save command can save files in a Release 2.0, 2.01, or 2.2 format because all three programs support a .WK1 extension.

By supplying a .WKS extension with the filename, you can save worksheets in a Release 1A format.

The Viewer Add-In

Releases 2.3 and 2.4 include a Viewer Add-In that makes viewing files, retrieving files, and creating external file links easier. The Viewer Add-In is a scaled-down version of Lotus Magellan, which lets you view files of different formats. You may want to review the Add-In menu described in Chapter 14 before using the Viewer Add-In. Here's a quick description. You can use the Viewer Add-In by selecting /Add-In Attach and then selecting VIEWER.ADN, a key such as 8 for ALT-F8, and Quit to return to READY mode. When you want to use this Add-In, you can press the key combination you selected (ALT-F8 in this example) or select /Add-In Invoke VIEWER.

The Viewer menu has three options: Retrieve, Link, and Browse. Selecting Retrieve will retrieve a worksheet file you select to become the current worksheet. Selecting Link will create an external link formula for you based on the worksheet and cell you select. Browse allows you to look at different files and return to 1-2-3 where you left off when you are finished.

When you select Retrieve and the current worksheet has unsaved changes, 1-2-3 will prompt you if you want to retrieve the file and replace the current worksheet. When you select Link and the current cell has an entry, 1-2-3 will prompt you if you want to replace the entry in the current cell with the external link formula. You can select Yes to continue or No to return to READY mode.

Once you select Retrieve, Link, or Browse, Viewer displays the files of the current directory, as shown in Figure 8-19. You can move between the files on the left side of the screen; the highlighted file's contents will appear on the right side. If you selected Retrieve or Link, only worksheet files are listed, but if you selected Browse, all files are listed.

You can press the RIGHT ARROW key to move from the file list into the worksheet. When you are in the worksheet, you can use all of the keys you would use in 1-2-3 to move to different cells. The control panel displays the cell's contents and formatting information. Cells containing formulas display (formula) and the formula results. You cannot change a worksheet in the Viewer. If a file is password-protected, you cannot see its contents. To return to the file list, press HOME and LEFT ARROW.

```
Lotus Magellan Viewer      Specify file to retrieve and press ENTER      LIST
 ◄ ►  Directory: C:\123R24\*.W??
   <ART>            ▲A1: [W15]                                          READY
   <BUDGET>
   <CH1>                   A          B          C         D         E     ◄
   <WYSIWYG>      1                                     Innovation, Inc.    ►
   1ST_QTR.WK1    2                                     New Product Sales   ▲
   2411_6.WK1     3                                     Jan - June 1992     ▼
   2ND_QTR.WK1    4                                                         ?
   ACCOUNTS.WK1   5                      Jan       Feb       Mar       Apr
   COLORS2.WK1    6   Sav-all Shower   23,400    25,740    28,314    31,145
   COLORTST.WK1   7   Faucet Save      34,500    36,225    38,036    39,938
   DAVID.WK1      8   Waterless Clean  47,800    50,668    53,708    56,931
   DBIV_BAN.WK1   9   Rain-saver        9,800     9,996    10,196    10,400
   FINISH.WK1    10
   FORMAT.WK1    11
   ME12_I5.WK1   12
   NUMBERS.WK1   13
   QTRIVALU.WK1  14
   QTRTOTAL.WK1  15
   SAMPMACS.WK1  16
   START.WK1
  File 9 of 16       FINISH.WK1        3-27-92  10:27a         2,493 Bytes
   F1     F2    F3    F4      F5        [F6]     F7    F8    F9    F10
  Help  Reset            Date Sort  Name Sort
```

Figure 8-19.   *Viewer Add-In showing worksheets*

In the file list, pressing UP ARROW, DOWN ARROW, PGUP, or PGDN changes the file that is selected on the left side. You can also press HOME or END to move to the first or last file in the list. If you want to change the drive or directory of files that 1-2-3 displays, press LEFT ARROW or RIGHT ARROW. Pressing LEFT ARROW changes the directory of files displayed to the parent directory of the current one. Pressing RIGHT ARROW changes the directory of files displayed to the directory the highlight is on. You can only press RIGHT ARROW to change the directory when the highlight is on a directory name, such as <BUDGET> in Figure 8-19. You can also click the arrows and the Enter icon shown in a different color with the mouse instead of pressing the keys. You can press F2 to return to the default directory 1-2-3 uses. You can also use the F5 and F6 function keys to change the order in which the files are listed. Pressing F6 displays files in alphabetical order which is the default. Pressing F5 displays files according to the date and time they were created.

If you are retrieving a file with Viewer, press ENTER when the highlight is on the file you want to retrieve. This is identical to the /File Retrieve command except you can visually check that it is the file you want. If you are creating a link with the Viewer, press ENTER when the highlight is on the file you want to use on the left side and the cell pointer is on the cell you want on the right side. The Viewer Add-In will create the external link formula for you using the selected worksheet and cell. If you are browsing through files, press ENTER when you want to return to READY mode.

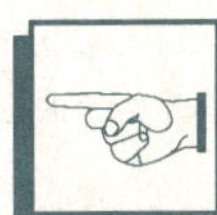

If you want to create a range of link formulas with the Viewer, move the cell pointer to the first cell where you want the link formulas, activate the Viewer Add-In, and select Link. Select the worksheet containing the range of cells that you want to link, and move to the first cell of the range. Select the range by typing a period and pressing the arrow keys or dragging the mouse to cover the cells you want to link, and then press ENTER. For example, if you select the range B10..B13 in the Viewer Add-In, the current cell in the current worksheet and the three cells below it will contain formulas that each link with B10, B11, B12, and B13 in the selected worksheet.

FILES

Worksheet   Range   Copy   Move   File   Print   Graph   Data   System   Add-In   Quit
Retrieve   Save   Combine   Xtract   Erase   List   Import   Directory   Admin
Cancel   Replace   Backup
Text   Numbers
Copy   Add   Subtract
Reservation   Table   Link-Refresh
Formulas   Values
Worksheet   Print   Graph   Other   Linked
Worksheet   Print   Graph   Other
Worksheet   Print   Graph   Other   Linked
Global   Insert   Delete   Column   Erase   Titles   Window   Status   Page   Learn
Format   Label-Prefix   Column-Width   Recalculation   Protection   Default   Zero
Printer   Directory   Status   Update   Other   Autoexec   Quit

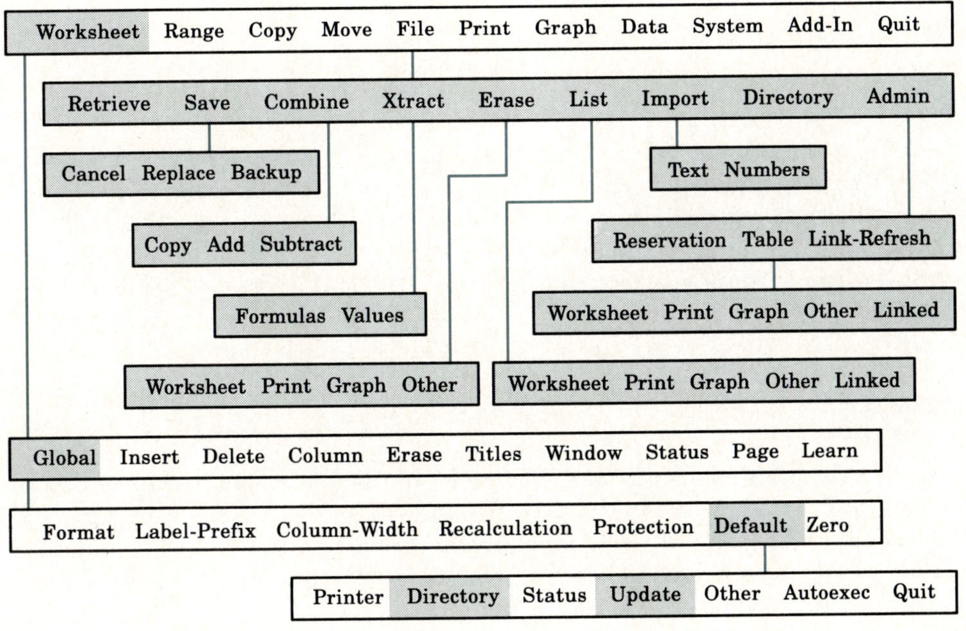

/File Admin Link-Refresh

Description

This command recalculates external file links in the current worksheet that have active links to other files.

/File Admin Reservation

Description

This command gets or releases the file reservation. As discussed earlier, a file reservation is permission from the operating system to save the modified file over the original. File reservations are important in networks since more than one user may want the file. Only one person may have the file reservation at one time. You can tell if you have the file reservation because RO (for read-only) appears in the status line when you do not have it.

Options

Get   The Get option attempts to obtain the file reservation for you if you do not already have it. If 1-2-3 obtains the file reservation for the current worksheet file, the RO indicator disappears. If 1-2-3 cannot obtain the file reservation, the RO indicator stays. Possible reasons for not obtaining the file reservation include someone else using the file, a file change since you last retrieved that file, or your lacking write access to the file.

Release   This option releases the file reservation so someone else can get it. Since you cannot save the file without a reservation, make sure to save the worksheet before selecting this option.

/File Admin Table

Description

This command creates a table that lists all the files of the specified type in the current directory. The table is four columns wide and as many rows long as the directory has file entries. This command can select which files it lists.

Options

This command has five options to select the type of files in the table. The table includes the filenames and extensions, the date serial number when the file was saved last, the time serial number when the file was saved last, and the size. The Worksheet, Print, Graph, Other, and Linked options can further limit which files 1-2-3 lists by modifying the filename skeleton. Once you select the type of files 1-2-3 lists in the table, you must specify where you want 1-2-3 to put the information. This area must be unprotected and blank so that the table does not overwrite worksheet information.

/File Combine Add

Description

The /File Combine Add command adds some or all of the values from a worksheet file to current worksheet values. The addition process uses the cell-pointer location as the upper-leftmost cell to be combined with the first cell in the worksheet or range you are adding. Only cells that are blank or contain values are affected by this process. Cells that contain formulas or labels are unaffected.

The Add option is useful when you are performing a budget consolidation. You can begin with a total budget worksheet that contains nothing more than labels and a few total formulas. As long as all departmental budgets are in exactly the same format as the total worksheet, you can use /File Combine Add once for each worksheet file to produce a budget consolidation. This command can incorporate data from files in Releases 1A through 2.4.

Options

Like the other /File Combine options, Add permits you to combine an entire file or a range. In either case, it begins the combination at the cell-pointer location. The cells in the combined range will have the format of the incoming data.

Entire-File   With this option, every value cell in the worksheet file is added to a cell in the current worksheet. Cell A1 in the file is added to the cell where the cell pointer rests in the current worksheet. Remaining values are added to the cell with the proper displacement from the current cell-pointer location.

When you select Entire-File, the names of the worksheet files on the current directory are displayed. You can either point to one of the filenames or enter another filename you want to use. 1-2-3 assumes that the file has a .WK1 file extension, unless you provide another one or select a filename from the list that has a different extension. Likewise, you can access files on a different drive or in a different directory if you supply the complete pathname.

Named/Specified-Range   With this option, only the cells in the selected range are combined with the cells in the current worksheet starting at the current cell-pointer position. 1-2-3 asks you to specify a range address or range name and then the file that contains this range. The range name you specify must be valid for the filename specified. The rules for entering the filename are the same as for Entire-File.

/File Combine Copy

Description

The /File Combine Copy command replaces some or all values from the current worksheet with values (including formulas and labels) from a worksheet file. The copying process uses the cell-pointer location in the current worksheet as the upper-leftmost cell to be replaced with the first cell in the worksheet or range you are copying. Unlike /File Combine Add, current worksheet cells containing formulas and labels are affected by /File Combine Copy. They are overwritten by the copied information.

The Copy feature is useful when you would like to copy headings and values from an existing worksheet to one you are currently creating. Although formulas can also be copied, you must be sure that the values they require are also copied or an error could result.

Options

Like the other /File Combine options, Copy permits you to combine an entire file or a range. In either case, it begins the replacement at the cell-pointer location. The Entire-File and Named/Specified-Range options were described in the previous section under the /File Combine Add command.

/File Combine Subtract

Description

The /File Combine Subtract command subtracts some or all of the values in a worksheet file from the current worksheet values. The subtraction process uses the cell-pointer location as the upper-leftmost cell to be combined with the first cell in the worksheet or range you are subtracting. Only cells that are blank or contain values are affected by this process. Cells that contain formulas or labels are unaffected.

The Subtract option is useful when you are performing a budget consolidation. You can begin with a total budget worksheet. Then, to see the effect of closing one of a company's departments or subsidiaries, you can subtract the file containing its budget projections from the total. All subsidiary budgets must be in exactly the same format as the total worksheet, however.

Options

Like the other /File Combine options, Subtract permits you to combine an entire file or a named range. The Entire-File and Named/Specified-Range options were described earlier in this chapter under the /File Combine Add command. In either case, it begins the combination at the cell-pointer location. The cells in the combined range will have the format of the incoming data.

/File Directory

Description

The /File Directory command checks or changes the current directory that 1-2-3 is using for file storage and retrieval. With Release 2.4, the current directory is the subdirectory containing the 1-2-3 files, unless another directory has been set as the default. The /File Directory command lets you make a change only for the current session. To change the default directory permanently, use /Worksheet Global Default Directory followed by /Worksheet Global Default Update to save your change.

Options

With this command, you can simply review the current directory setting or change it. To review the setting, simply press ENTER after you have seen the /File Directory display.

To change the directory for the session, first decide if you want to change the complete directory that is designated or to stay in the same directory and just change the subdirectory. You can change the drive, the directory, and the subdirectory with this command. To change the drive, type the drive designator followed by a backslash, for example, **B:** To change the path as well, type the pathname at the same time, for example, **B:\123\SALES**. To change the directory, enter or edit the entry so it contains the new directory information.

/File Erase

Description

The /File Erase command removes one or more files from the disk.

Options

First choose the type of file or files you wish to remove from the disk. These are your options:

Worksheet	Worksheet files with the .WK1 or .WKS filename extension
Print	Print files with the .PRN file extension
Graph	Graph files with a .PIC file extension
Other	Files with any file extension

Once you specify the file type you want to delete, 1-2-3 lists all the files of that type that are on the current drive or directory. You can point to the file you want to delete or type in the filename. If the file you want to delete is on a different drive or in a different directory, change the drive designator and pathname to the path containing the file. After you select the file you want to delete, 1-2-3 prompts for a confirmation. Select Yes to delete the file or No to cancel the command.

/File Import

Description

The /File Import command loads information from an ASCII file into the current worksheet at the cell-pointer location. Standard ASCII files that do not exceed 8,192 rows in length can be imported.

Options

/File Import offers two options: The Text option imports a column of long labels into the worksheet, and the Numbers option can import a combination of numbers and labels. Once you have selected Text or Numbers, 1-2-3 lists the .PRN files in the current directory. To list files with a different extension, type *. followed by the extension you want, and press ENTER. After a filename is selected, 1-2-3 imports the file and places the data starting at the cell-pointer's location.

Text   This option brings each line of the imported text file into the worksheet as a single long label. /Data Parse can then split files imported as text into separate entries, rather than one long label (see Chapter 10 for more information). This option imports up to 240 characters from each line into the worksheet.

Numbers   This option searches the imported file for numbers and for text entries enclosed in quotes. Each number is placed in a worksheet cell as a value, and each text entry in quotes is placed in a cell as a left-justified label. If more than one number or enclosed text entry is found in a line of the text file, more than one column of the worksheet is used. When the next line of the imported file is processed, entries begin again in the same column as the cell pointer on the next row.

Note

Special characters added by some word processors can cause problems. Most word processors have an option that excludes these special characters to produce a standard ASCII file.

/File List

Description

The /File List command lists all the files of the specified type in the current directory. This command creates a temporary listing, rather than the permanent listing the /File Admin Table command creates.

Options

With Releases 2.3 and 2.4, you have five /File List choices:

Worksheet	Worksheet files with the .WK1 or .WKS file extension
Print	Print files with the .PRN file extension
Graph	Graph files with the .PIC file extension
Other	Files with any file extension
Linked	Files to which the current file is linked by formula references

Once you have specified the file type, 1-2-3 displays the filenames of all files of the selected type. For each filename you highlight, 1-2-3 displays the date serial number when the file was last saved, the time serial number when the file was last saved, and the file size at the top of the list. The Linked option includes the pathname of the linked files if the external file link formula includes the pathname.

/File Retrieve

Description

The /File Retrieve command loads a file from disk into the memory of your computer. Any information in memory before the file is retrieved is erased by the loading of the new file.

Options

You can retrieve a file from the current disk or directory, or from a different one if you specify the pathname. You can retrieve password-protected files by supplying the password when 1-2-3 prompts you. 1-2-3 can retrieve files with extensions of .WKS (1-2-3 Release 1A), .WRK (Symphony), .WR1 (Symphony), and .WK1 (1-2-3 Release 2). If the file you need is used in a network environment and 1-2-3 cannot get the file reservation for you, 1-2-3 displays Yes and No selections. Select Yes if you want read-only access to the file or No to cancel the command.

/File Save

Description

The /File Save command allows you to save the current worksheet and any settings you have created for it to a worksheet file.

Options

You can save a worksheet file already on disk to its current path by accepting the default name. To save it to a new name or path, enter another filename or a filename and pathname and press ENTER. To save the worksheet to a new filename, enter the new filename and press ENTER. If you want to use a disk or directory different from the current one, you must specify the complete pathname.

If the file is already saved on the disk, 1-2-3 prompts you with the existing filename. Press ENTER to accept it. The next prompt is a choice between Cancel, Replace, or Backup. Cancel stops the /File Save command and returns you to READY mode. Replace places the current contents of memory on the disk under the existing filename, erasing what was stored in the file previously. Backup copies the previous version of the file to a separate file with the same filename. Then use a .BAK file extension before saving the current version.

This command also allows you to add a password to a file when it is saved. Once a file is saved with a password, you cannot retrieve the file unless you supply the password. After typing the name of the file to be saved, press spacebar and type **p**. 1-2-3 prompts you for a password up to 15 characters long. After you enter it, a prompt will ask you to verify it by entering it again. Passwords are case sensitive, so be sure you enter the password in the upper- or lowercase letters that you want for this password. To abort the password procedure instead of verifying the password, press ESC several times to return to READY mode without saving the file or adding a password.

To change the password, press BACKSPACE to remove "[PASSWORD PRO-TECTED]" when 1-2-3 displays the filename. Then press the spacebar and type **p**. 1-2-3 prompts you for the new password just as if you were adding the password for the first time. To remove password protection from a file, press BACKSPACE to remove "[PASSWORD PROTECTED]" from the display, and then press ENTER.

Note

A file with the name AUTO123 will be retrieved every time you load 1-2-3, as long as it is in the default directory as determined by the /Worksheet Global Default Directory command.

/File Xtract

Description

The /File Xtract command saves a portion of the current worksheet in another worksheet file. Settings established for the current worksheet, such as graph and print settings and range names, are saved in the new file.

Options

The /File Xtract command allows you to save either values or formulas from the range specified.

Formulas   This option saves current worksheet formulas, as well as labels and values, in the worksheet file.

Values   This option saves numbers and labels in the worksheet files. Formulas are evaluated to determine the numbers for saving, but the formulas are not saved. When you copy the values, check to see if the values need to be recalculated or links to external files need to be refreshed.

After choosing Formulas or Values, select the filename from the menu or enter a new name. You can make the extracted file password-protected by adding a space and a **P** and then supplying a password as described earlier under the /File Save command. If you select an existing filename, 1-2-3 asks if you want to cancel the request, back up the existing file, or replace the existing file. The extracted file has a .WK1 extension unless you provide a different one. After you have selected the file to hold the extract, specify the range to be extracted by entering either a range name or range address.

/System

Description

The /System command allows you to use the operating system commands without quitting 1-2-3. This means you can access some of the operating system commands while your 1-2-3 worksheet remains in memory.

Options

Any operating system command that does not overlay memory can be used with /System. Afterward, EXIT returns you to your worksheet.

/Worksheet Global Default Directory

Description

Use this command to specify the directory in which you want 1-2-3 to look automatically for your files. Unless you change it, the default is the directory containing the 1-2-3 files. To make this directory change permanent, use the /Worksheet Global Default Update command.

Options

Normally when you enter /Worksheet Global Default Directory, you specify a new default directory. A second option is to clear the existing entry without entering a new one. In this case, 1-2-3 uses the directory that was current when 1-2-3 was loaded as the default for file storage and retrieval. In Releases 2.3 and above, you can also change the directory by making an entry in the Directory text box in the /Worksheet Global Default dialog box.

/Worksheet Global Default Update

Description

This command saves to the 123.CNF file any changes that you have made to the /Worksheet Global Default settings. If you are using 1-2-3 with floppy disks, the System disk must be in the current drive at the time this command is executed with the write-protect tabs removed. In Releases 2.3 and 2.4, you can also update the worksheet settings by selecting the Update command button in the /Worksheet Global Default dialog box.

Translate Program

Description

The Translate program allows you to exchange data files between 1-2-3 and other popular programs. It is available from the Lotus Access System menu or by entering **trans** from the DOS command prompt.

Options

You have two types of options for the Translate program. You can select from a list of source file formats with the From options and a list of target file formats with the To options.

The From options are as follows:

1-2-3 Release 1A
1-2-3 Releases 2 through 2.4
dBASE II or III
DIF
Enable 2.0
Multiplan
SuperCalc4
Symphony Releases 1.0 through 2.2
VisiCalc

The To options are as follows:

1-2-3 (all releases)
dBASE II or III
DIF (VisiCalc and others)
Enable 2.0
Multiplan
SuperCalc4
Symphony Releases 1.0 through 2.2

Note

You do not need to translate Symphony and Release 1A files for use with 1-2-3 Releases 2 or above because the /File Retrieve command automatically translates these files when it retrieves them.

When you translate one format to another, the Translate program only translates the features common to both the source and target file types. If you are translating a file to a DIF format, you must specify the orientation as row or column. If you are translating a file to a dBASE format, you can select between a named range or the entire file. If you select range, you must provide the range name when Translate prompts for that information.

Part II

1-2-3's Advanced Features

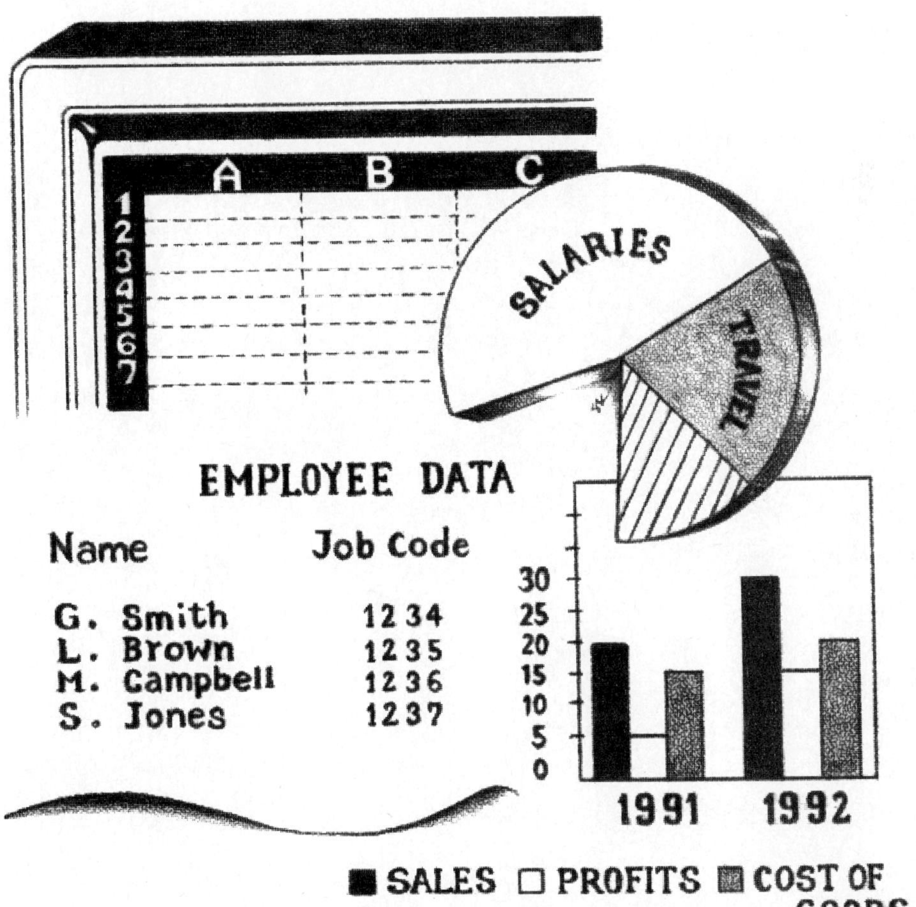

Chapter *9*

Data Management

In one sense, all the work you have done with 1-2-3 up to this point can be considered data management, because it has all involved the management of information recorded on the worksheet. But data management, as defined by 1-2-3, is a special term that refers to the formalized process of design, entry, and retrieval of information from a database.

The world of data management has its own terminology. A *database* is a collection of all the information you have about a set of things—customers, orders, parts in inventory, employees, or anything else. If you create a database of employee information, for example, you want it to contain information about each of your employees. All the information about one employee is one *record* in the database. A record is composed of all the pieces of information you have about one thing in the set, such as one employee. These individual pieces of information in a record are called *fields*. Fields you might want to have in each record in an employee database could include name, address, job classification, date of hire, social security number, department, benefits, and salary. When you design a new database, you need to decide what fields to include in each record.

This chapter describes the /Data commands that permit organization and retrieval of information from 1-2-3's worksheets.

The next chapter examines the /Data commands that add power to the calculations you do on the worksheet. Some of the commands covered in Chapter 10 serve a dual purpose. They work when information management is your only requirement, but they can also lend assistance when your objective is the more traditional use of the worksheet for calculations. In the next chapter you get some hints on using these data management techniques with traditional worksheet applications.

381

The 1-2-3 Database

A 1-2-3 database is a range of cells on a worksheet. It can be in any area of the worksheet, but the field names—that is, the names you use to categorize data—must run across the top row of the range. The records in the database that contain data for each field are placed in the rows immediately following the row of field names. Figure 9-1 is a section of an employee database in A1..F20. The field names are located in A1..F1, and the first database record is located in A2..F2.

As a database manager, 1-2-3 has both strengths and weaknesses compared to other packages. You may find it helpful to look at some ways in which 1-2-3's features differ from those of its competitors.

- All data in your 1-2-3 database is stored in memory while you are working with the database. Unlike other packages that must read data from the disk when you need it, 1-2-3 provides unprecedented quick response to requests for resequencing records and finding those that match specific criteria. This feature does require that you have sufficient memory to hold your entire database at once, however. You need a large memory capacity, a fairly small database, or both.

- 1-2-3's data management commands are similar to its worksheet commands, so they are easy for you to learn. By contrast, other packages may require a significant time investment to master their command structure.

- Most data management packages create formatted screens to enter or review one record at a time. With 1-2-3's macros, you now have the capability to easily design a formatted screen for use with your database.

- Releases 2 and above permit the entry of up to 8,191 records in one database in a worksheet. These limits are sufficient for many applications, but some other database products allow an unlimited number of records within the disk space available.

- 1-2-3 can accommodate up to 256 fields in one database. Some packages allow more and others less.

- 1-2-3 permits each field to have up to 240 characters. Some packages allow more and others less.

Setting Up a Database

The first step in designing a 1-2-3 database is to create a list of fields you want your database to contain. Once you have all the field names recorded, estimate the

```
A1: [W12] 'Last Name                                                    READY
```

	Last Name	First Name	SS#	Job Code	Salary	Location
1	Last Name	First Name	SS#	Job Code	Salary	Location
2	Larson	Mary	543–98–9876	23	$12,000	2
3	Campbell	David	213–76–9874	23	$23,000	10
4	Campbell	Keith	569–89–7654	12	$32,000	2
5	Stephens	Tom	219–78–8954	15	$17,800	2
6	Caldor	Larry	459–34–0921	23	$32,500	4
7	Lightnor	Peggy	560–55–4311	14	$23,500	10
8	McCartin	John	817–66–1212	15	$54,600	2
9	Justof	Jack	431–78–9963	17	$41,200	4
10	Patterson	Lyle	212–11–9090	12	$21,500	10
11	Miller	Lisa	214–89–6756	23	$18,700	2
12	Hawkins	Mark	215–67–8973	21	$19,500	2
13	Hartwick	Eileen	313–78–9090	15	$31,450	4
14	Smythe	George	560–90–8645	15	$65,000	4
15	Wilkes	Caitlin	124–67–7432	17	$15,500	2
16	Deaver	Ken	198–98–6750	23	$24,600	10
17	Kaylor	Sally	312–45–9862	12	$32,900	10
18	Parker	Dee	659–11–3452	14	$19,800	4
19	Preverson	Gary	670–90–1121	21	$27,600	4
20	Samuelson	Paul	219–89–7080	23	$28,900	2

```
23-Apr-92  09:06 AM
```

Figure 9-1.   *A portion of an employee database*

number of characters that each field requires for storage and the number of records in your database. Add the number of characters for each field to get a record total, and then multiply by the number of records. If the potential number of records exceeds 1-2-3's limit, you must find another alternative, such as splitting your database into two separate worksheets. Similarly, if the number of records times the length of one record exceeds the available memory in your system, you cannot proceed with the design process unless you can use multiple files in your application.

Choosing a Location for the Database

The next step is to select an area of the worksheet for storing the database. Here are some considerations to keep in mind as you select a location:

- Allow your database to expand with additional records by choosing an area below calculations and other fixed information in your worksheet.

- Leave plenty of rows below the database blank so it can expand downward.

- If you have sufficient memory and have two databases in one worksheet, start one database in A1 and the other one to the right of and beneath the last record in the first database. This allows you to use the /Worksheet Delete and /Worksheet Insert commands to delete and insert records in either database without affecting the other.

Entering Field Names

Record your selected field names across the top row of the database area. Follow these rules for field names to create a workable database:

- Make sure you record field names in the same order in which they appear in the form you plan to use for data entry. This minimizes the time required for data entry.

- Each field name is placed in one cell and must be unique.

- The names you choose for your fields also are used with some of the other database features; therefore, choose meaningful names. Keep the names short to avoid misspellings when you reenter the field names in other places.

- Do not enter spaces at the end of field names. It is not apparent that you included them, and the names will not match with later entries for other data management features that do not include trailing spaces.

A layout of field names for an employee database might look like this:

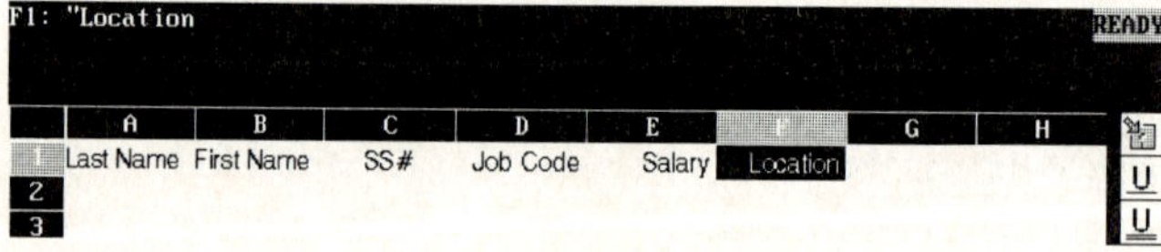

If you are working with Wysiwyg, consider using shading or a different font to highlight field names.

Entering Information

The first database record should begin immediately beneath the row of field names. Do not leave blank lines or use special symbols as divider lines.

All entries in corresponding fields of like records should be of the same type. For example, if a field contains numeric data, the value for that field should be numeric in every like record in the database. Mixing numeric values and labels in a single field causes the two types of data to be separated when records are sorted and when you attempt to select a subset of the records. It is acceptable to leave a field blank within a particular record if you lack data. Figure 9-1 shows an employee database after 20 records have been entered.

As your database grows longer, the field names at the top of your screen will scroll off the screen. You can prevent this by using the /Worksheet Titles Horizontal command to lock the field names in place on your screen. If you have forgotten how this command works, go back to Chapter 5 for a quick review.

If a database becomes too large to fit on a single worksheet, an alternative is to split the records into multiple databases in different worksheets. For example, if a customer database is too large for one worksheet, the customers with last names beginning with A through L may be in the first worksheet's database, and customer names beginning with M through Z may be in the second worksheet's database.

Making Changes

Entries in a database can be changed with any of the techniques you have used on regular worksheets. An entry can be retyped to replace its current value. The F2 (EDIT) key can be used to insert, delete, and replace characters within an entry.

You can use /Worksheet Insert to add a blank row for a new record or add a blank column for another field. The /Worksheet Delete command can be used to remove records or fields. Bear in mind, however, that the entire worksheet is affected by both these commands; it is important to assess potential damage to areas outside the database. One good strategy is to save the file before using insertion or deletion commands. Then, if you have a problem, you can restore the file from disk. Also, the /Copy command can copy field values from other database records.

Sorting Data

1-2-3 provides extremely fast sort features because of the storage of the database in RAM. Any change in sequence can take place at the speed of transfer within RAM, which is considerably faster than sorting records from disk.

All the options you require to specify the records to be sorted, specify the sort sequence, and tell 1-2-3 to begin the sort are located under the /Data Sort command. The menu looks like this:

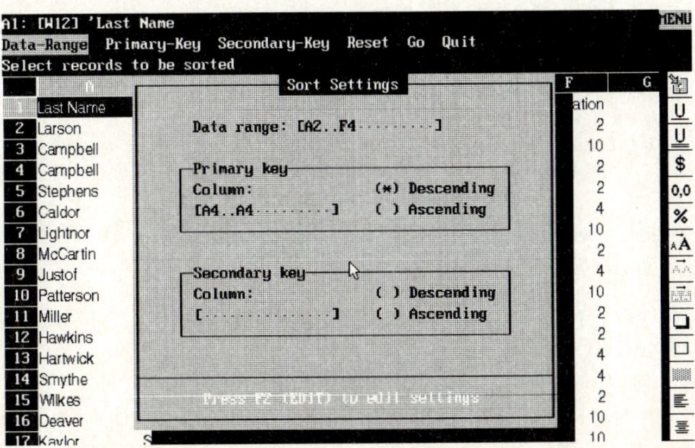

The steps for resequencing your data using the various Sort options are summarized in the box called "Steps for Sorting Your Data." In Releases 2.3 and 2.4, you can use the dialog box to provide the information 1-2-3 needs to sort your data. Remember to press F2 to put 1-2-3 in SETTINGS mode if you want to use the highlighted letters and make the changes from your keyboard.

Determining What Data to Sort

You can sort all the records in your database or just some of them, depending on the range you specify. Always be sure to include all the records' fields in the sort, because excluding some fields causes those fields to remain stationary while the remainder of a record is resequenced. If you ever plan to return your records to their original entry sequence after a sort, you must include a field for the record number. A sequential number can be placed in this field at the time of entry or added later with the /Data Fill command covered later in the chapter.

To set the range for the sort, enter /**Data Sort Data-Range** or select Data range in the /Data Sort dialog box. Then specify the range for the database. Be sure you *do not* include the row of field names. If you do, they will be sorted along with the record values. For the data in Figure 9-1, the data range is A2..F20, which includes all of the records and all of the fields, but omits the field names in the first row.

1
2
3

Steps for Sorting Your Data

Sorting is a quick and easy process, but it requires a sequence of commands from the /Data Sort menu. The steps and commands to use are as follows:

1. Enter /**Data Sort** and choose Data-Range.

2. Highlight (specify) all records and fields to be sorted, but do not include the field names within the range.

3. Select Primary-Key from the Sort menu.

4. Highlight any data value within the column you wish to use to control the sort sequence.

5. If you expect duplicate primary keys within your database, choose Secondary-Key from the Sort menu.

6. Highlight any data value within the column that you wish to use as the tiebreaker if there are duplicate primary keys.

7. Select Go from the Sort menu to have 1-2-3 resequence your data.

Specifying the Sort Sequence

1-2-3 permits you to specify either one or two sort keys. In all cases the *primary key* controls the sequence of the records. The *secondary key* is ignored, even when you specify one, except when duplicate examples of the primary key occur. Then the secondary key is used to break the tie. For both sort keys, you may select whether the values are sorted in ascending or descending order.

Another setting also affects the sort order. This is the collating sequence, which is selected in the Install program. As discussed in Appendix A, there are three options for a collating sequence: Numbers First, Numbers Last, and ASCII. The "Effect of Collating Sequence on Sorting" box describes these options in further detail. To make a change, you must enter the Install program and select a different collating sequence.

Choosing a Primary Sort Key

To specify a primary key, enter **/Data Sort Primary-Key** and type the cell address or point to a cell containing data for a particular field within the database. In Releases 2.3 and 2.4, you can also select the primary key by entering a cell address in the Primary Key Column text box and selecting a Sort order option button. This field (column) becomes your primary sort key. In either case you are prompted to choose the sort order—A for ascending order and D for descending order. When you choose A, the collating sequence you selected with Install is used. When you choose D, the sequence is reversed. The default sort order is Descending or the order you chose for your previous sort. Select the letter for the choice you want and press ENTER.

Setting the sort sequence does not automatically resequence your data. You also must specify the data range and then select Go from the Sort menu.

Choosing a Secondary Sort Key

You can set the secondary key by entering **/Data Sort Secondary-Key** and either pointing to a cell containing a data value for the field you want to sort or by typing the cell address. Then type **A** for ascending or **D** for descending sort order, as you did with the primary key. In Releases 2.3 and 2.4, you can also select the secondary key by entering a cell address in the Secondary Key Column text box and selecting a Sort order option button. The default sort order is Descending or the order you chose for your previous sort.

Starting the Sort

With the data range and at least a primary key selected, you are ready to resequence your data. Now simply select Go from the Data Sort menu, and your data is sorted in

Effect of Collating Sequence on Sorting

The order of your data after a sort is dependent on the collating sequence specified during the Install program. Sort order in the three sequences for ascending order is as follows:

Collating Sequence Option	Sort Order
Numbers last	Blank cells; label entries beginning with letters in alphabetical order; label entries beginning with numbers in numeric sequence; labels beginning with special characters; values.
Numbers first	Blank cells; labels beginning with numbers in numeric sequence; labels beginning with letters in alphabetical order; labels beginning with special characters; values.
ASCII	Blank cells; labels in ASCII order; values. Capitalization will affect the sort order with this choice.

Sorting in descending order reverses the order.

the specified order. 1-2-3 is very quick. With a small database, the sort is complete as soon as you lift your finger after selecting Go.

Figure 9-1 presents part of an employee database with the records in random sequence. Suppose the data range is selected as A2..F20, using /Data Sort Data-Range. Next, the Last Name field (A2) is selected as the primary key, with A for ascending sort order. A secondary key of First Name (B2) is then chosen, with A for ascending sort order. Once Go is selected from the /Data Sort menu, the records are placed in the new sequence shown in Figure 9-2. Notice that the two records with a last name of Campbell are sequenced by first name.

If you decide to leave the Sort menu without completing the sort operation, you must use /Data Sort Quit to get rid of the sticky Sort menu. You do not need this command after a normally completed sort, because /Data Sort Go automatically returns you to READY mode after sorting the data.

Sorting with the SmartIcons

In Release 2.4, you can use 1-2-3's SmartIcons to sort in either ascending or descending order. The icons you can use look like this:

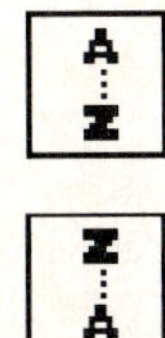

When you choose either of these icons, 1-2-3 looks at the location of the cell pointer to determine the size of the database table that should be sorted. The database table is the contiguous area of cells that includes all database fields and records. 1-2-3 also determines the column to use as a sort key by looking at the column of the selected cell. It will sort in either ascending or descending order, depending on which icon you chose.

Starting Over

Once you have made choices for a sort, 1-2-3 uses these settings as a default. Making a new selection for the data range or either of the sort keys replaces the default. If you want to first eliminate your settings to make sure that you have to reset the data range and primary key before sorting again, you can use /Data Sort Reset. This option eliminates default settings for data range, primary sort key, and secondary sort key.

	Last Name	First Name	SS#	Job Code	Salary	Location
1	Last Name	First Name	SS#	Job Code	Salary	Location
2	Caldor	Larry	459–34–0921	23	$32,500	4
3	Campbell	David	213–76–9874	23	$23,000	10
4	Campbell	Keith	569–89–7654	12	$32,000	2
5	Deaver	Ken	198–98–6750	23	$24,600	10
6	Hartwick	Eileen	313–78–9090	15	$31,450	4
7	Hawkins	Mark	215–67–8973	21	$19,500	2
8	Justof	Jack	431–78–9963	17	$41,200	4
9	Kaylor	Sally	312–45–9862	12	$32,900	10
10	Larson	Mary	543–98–9876	23	$12,000	2
11	Lightnor	Peggy	560–55–4311	14	$23,500	10
12	McCartin	John	817–66–1212	15	$54,600	2
13	Miller	Lisa	214–89–6756	23	$18,700	2
14	Parker	Dee	659–11–3452	14	$19,800	4
15	Patterson	Lyle	212–11–9090	12	$21,500	10
16	Preverson	Gary	670–90–1121	21	$27,600	4
17	Samuelson	Paul	219–89–7080	23	$28,900	2
18	Smythe	George	560–90–8645	15	$65,000	4
19	Stephens	Tom	219–78–8954	15	$17,800	2
20	Wilkes	Caitlin	124–67–7432	17	$15,500	2

Figure 9-2.   The resequenced employee records

Using More Than Two Sort Keys

Although 1-2-3's Sort command supplies only a primary and secondary sort key, you can effectively sort on more than two fields by adding a field to your database. This field contains a string formula that combines two or more of the database fields into one field. Although the usefulness of this approach is dependent on fields having the same number of characters or digits in each entry, it does present a solution to the need for more than two sort keys in some situations.

For example, suppose you need to sort expense data that is coded by expense code, division, region, and branch. The sorted data for this example and the string formula it uses are shown in Figure 9-3. The string formula converts numeric entries to strings with @STRING so they can be combined. The most important field for sorting is listed first in the string formula, continuing across to the least important field in the sort. Once this formula is entered in F2 and copied down the column, you can sort it by selecting a cell from column F for the primary key. After selecting the primary key, you can select Go to sort the records as shown in Figure 9-3.

Generating a Series of Values

The /Data Fill command can save you considerable time when you are preparing a worksheet model. Use it to generate a series of dates, invoice numbers, purchase order numbers, new account numbers, or identification numbers for new employees, for example. You can combine this feature with /Data Sort to create record numbers for a database. Whenever you need to enter a series of data with evenly spaced values in either ascending or descending sequence, /Data Fill can handle the task. The /Data Fill command is often used in conjunction with some of the other Data commands. For example, the next chapter introduces /Data Distribution and /Data

```
F1: [W13] ^Sort-Key                                              READY


         A            B          C         D          E           F          G
   Expense Code    Division    Region    Branch     Amount      Sort-Key
 2 RT-1000             1          1        300      $998.00   11300RT-1000
 3 RF-1265             1          2        200    $6,785.00   12200RF-1265
 4 ST-8978             1          2        200    $1,050.00   12200ST-8978
 5 RX-1254             2          1        110    $1,200.00   21110RX-1254
 6 ST-8978             2          1        110    $2,341.00   21110ST-8978
 7 ST-1100             2          2        500    $7,500.00   22500ST-1100
 8 RX-1254             3          1        100    $1,208.90   31100RX-1254
 9 ST-1100             3          1        110      $560.00   31110ST-1100
10 RF-1265             3          2        610    $2,341.00   32610RF-1265
11
12
```

Figure 9-3.   *The sorted records using four fields with a string formula*

Table, which often use the /Data Fill command to generate a numeric series with regular intervals.

To use /Data Fill, place your cell pointer in the upper-left cell of the row or column in which you want the series generated, and enter /**Data Fill**. Next, enter the range you wish to use for the series. 1-2-3 then prompts you for the first number in the series (the start value) and suggests the default value of 0. You can press ENTER to accept this value, or enter another number.

The prompt for the *increment,* or *step value,* is next. This is the amount to add to each value to generate the next number. To accept the default of 1, press ENTER again; alternatively, enter any positive or negative number for the increment before pressing ENTER.

1-2-3's last prompt is for a stop value. As long as the default stop value of 8,191 is greater than or equal to your planned stop value, you can just press ENTER and allow 1-2-3 to determine a stop value, based on the size of the range and other values you have supplied. If 8,191 is not large enough, enter a new stop value before pressing ENTER.

For example, suppose you need to enter the data for a group of consecutively numbered invoices. Rather than entering the invoice numbers, you can use the /Data Fill command to create them for you. To enter invoice numbers in cells A2..A20 of a worksheet, place your cell pointer in A2 to begin and enter /**Data Fill**. When 1-2-3 prompts for a range, select A2..A20. For the start value, enter **1004**, representing the first invoice number that you want to enter. For the increment, enter **1**.

Remember that there are two situations that stop generation of entries in a fill series. You must ensure that the range is large enough and the stop value is high enough. 1-2-3 stops generating values as soon as either condition is exceeded. Consider what happens if you accept the default stop value of 8,191. This number exceeds the start value, and it also far exceeds the range, so the range is what stops the generation of fill values. The results are shown in Figure 9-4. If you enter **1009** as the stop value, your results are quite different, since the stop value would have been reached before the end of the range. In this case, the /Data Fill command can fill only A2..A7.

You can use the paint can icon on the SmartIcon Palette to fill a selected range with a series of numbers. With a VGA monitor and Wysiwyg, the icon looks like this and is on palette 3:

Selecting this icon fills the selected range with numbers. If you have not defined a Data Fill operation within the current session, 1-2-3 will place 0 in the first cell and increment each succeeding value by 1.

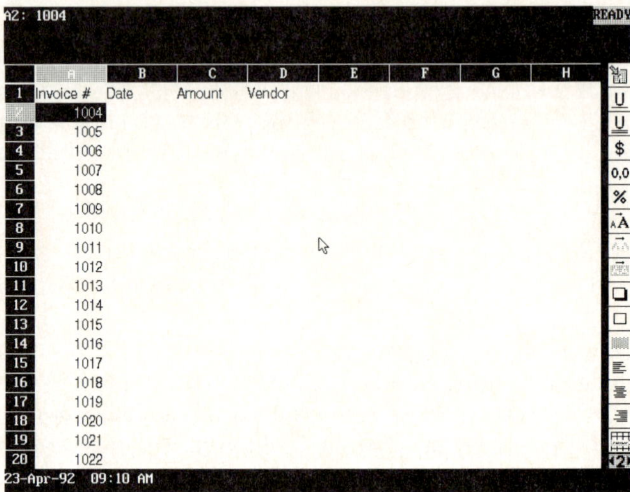

Figure 9-4.   *The result of using /Data Fill for generating invoice numbers*

If you want /Data Fill to fill every cell in the range, make the stop value sufficiently larger than what you expect the last value in the fill range to be.

Adding Record Numbers for Sorting Records

1-2-3 does not have an "unsort" feature. Once you have changed the sequence of your records, there is no command that automatically restores them to their original sequence unless you have Undo enabled. There is a solution to this dilemma, however, if you plan ahead. To each record, you can add a record number field that contains a sequential number based on when the records are added to the database. To return sorted records to their original entry order, you could then simply re-sort based on record number.

You can get 1-2-3 to do the work of sequential record number assignment by using /Data Fill. You have already learned how this command generates any series of numbers that have even increments if you specify the start, stop, and increment values you wish to use.

A look at the command in action with the employee database from previous examples clarifies the steps required for this use. Suppose a blank column has been inserted at the left of the employee database for record sequence numbers, and the field name **Sequence** was entered in A1. Record numbers can keep track of the original entry order for the employee records. To make /Data Fill supply the numbers, follow these steps:

1. Move the cell pointer to A2, the upper-leftmost cell in the range where the numbers will be generated.

2. Enter **/Data Fill** and specify the fill range as **A2..A20** either by pointing or by typing the range reference.

3. At the prompt, enter **1** for the start value.

4. The next prompt is for the step or increment value. Enter another **1** again.

5. The last prompt is for the stop value—the highest number that can be in the series. You could enter **19**, since this is the last value in the range. However, as long as the default stop value is not less than the stop value you want, you can let 1-2-3 generate the exact stop value, based on the range and increment you have supplied. To do this, accept the default of 8,191 by pressing ENTER. You can always use this method when 8,191 is greater than the last value in your series. 1-2-3 will stop when it fills the last cell in the range.

The result of the /Data Fill operation is shown in Figure 9-5.

Using /Data Fill with Dates and Times

You can use the @DATE and @TIME functions to provide a start number for /Data Fill. These commands make the /Data Fill command easier to use with dates and times.

For example, suppose you need to enter a series of dates that are each seven days apart. If the first date you need is January 3, 1991, you can enter **@DATE(91,1,3)** and

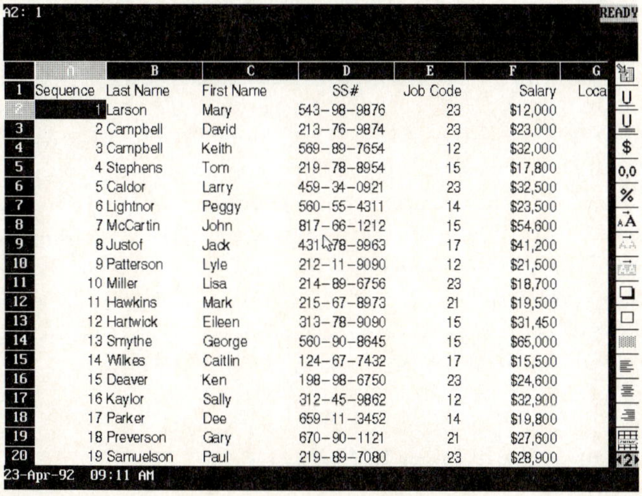

	Sequence	Last Name	First Name	SS#	Job Code	Salary	Loca
1	Sequence	Last Name	First Name	SS#	Job Code	Salary	Loca
2	1	Larson	Mary	543-98-9876	23	$12,000	
3	2	Campbell	David	213-76-9874	23	$23,000	
4	3	Campbell	Keith	569-89-7654	12	$32,000	
5	4	Stephens	Tom	219-78-8954	15	$17,800	
6	5	Caldor	Larry	459-34-0921	23	$32,500	
7	6	Lightnor	Peggy	560-55-4311	14	$23,500	
8	7	McCartin	John	817-66-1212	15	$54,600	
9	8	Justof	Jack	431-78-9963	17	$41,200	
10	9	Patterson	Lyle	212-11-9090	12	$21,500	
11	10	Miller	Lisa	214-89-6756	23	$18,700	
12	11	Hawkins	Mark	215-67-8973	21	$19,500	
13	12	Hartwick	Eileen	313-78-9090	15	$31,450	
14	13	Smythe	George	560-90-8645	15	$65,000	
15	14	Wilkes	Caitlin	124-67-7432	17	$15,500	
16	15	Deaver	Ken	198-98-6750	23	$24,600	
17	16	Kaylor	Sally	312-45-9862	12	$32,900	
18	17	Parker	Dee	659-11-3452	14	$19,800	
19	18	Preverson	Gary	670-90-1121	21	$27,600	
20	19	Samuelson	Paul	219-89-7080	23	$28,900	

Figure 9-5.   The output from using /Data Fill to generate record numbers

get a serial date number of 33241. Assuming you want to enter the dates in cells A2..A20 of the current worksheet, place your cell pointer in A2 to begin, and enter **/Data Fill**. Next, select A2..A20 as the data range to fill. For the start value, enter **@DATE(91   **. Enter **7** for the increment and **45000** for the stop value. Since most dates have serial numbers that are greater than the default stop value of 8,192, you must supply a larger number such as 45,000. The results are shown in Figure 9-6, which has a column width of 10 and is formatted with Date Format 1.

Searching the Database

As your database grows large, it becomes increasingly important to selectively review the information it contains. 1-2-3's /Data Query commands provide the ability to work selectively with information in your database and thus offer an exception-reporting capability; that is, information can be brought to your attention if it is considered to be outside an established norm. You can also use the selective review feature to clean up your database or to create reports.

All the commands required to review information selectively are found in the /Data Query menu shown here:

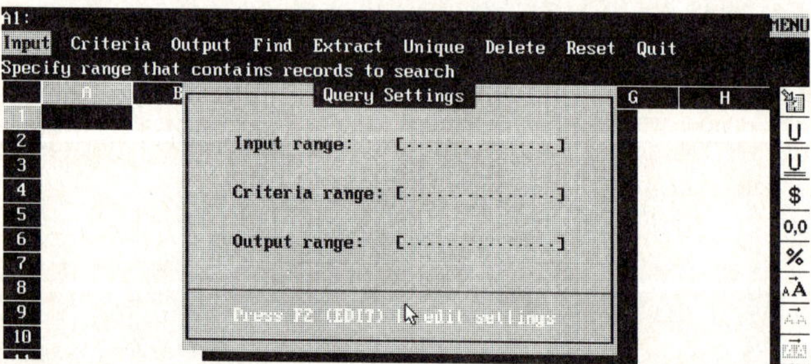

You must use at least three of the /Data Query commands to make a selection. Your database must be specified with /Data Query Input, and your selection criteria identified with /Data Query Criteria before you can select a specific action for the Query command to perform. In addition, database records and selection criteria must be entered on the worksheet before you enter a Query command that uses them. The steps required for using /Data Query commands are summarized in the "Steps for Using /Data Query Commands" box. Each of the Query options is examined in detail in the following sections.

Telling 1-2-3 Where Your Data Is Located

When you use the Query options, 1-2-3 must know where your field names and data records are located. Contrary to the case with /Data Sort, you *must* include the field

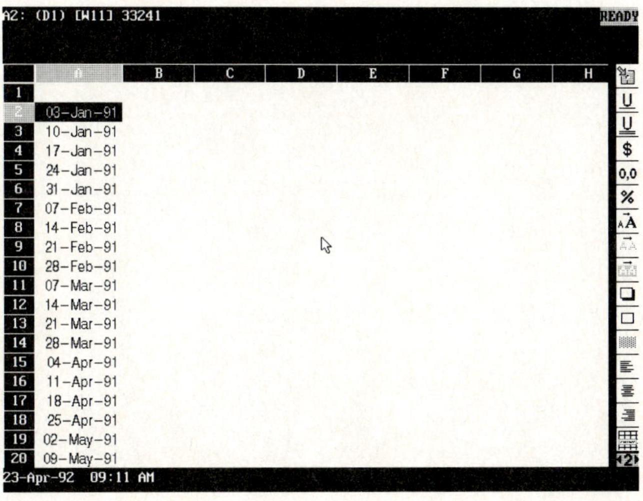

Figure 9-6.   The result of /Data Fill using dates

names when you specify the range. These field names are matched against the field names in the selection criteria area to ensure that selections are correct.

The command you use to specify the location of the database is /Data Query Input. After you enter this command, you can point to your data range or type the required cell references. In both cases, be sure to include the field names, as shown in the selection in Figure 9-7.

Specifying the Desired Records

To determine what records from the database are used to fill your query request, 1-2-3 checks the criteria you specify against each record in the selected database range. Records that do not meet the criteria are not used.

When entering criteria on the worksheet, keep in mind two things. First, criteria must be entered on the worksheet in an out-of-the-way location that does not interfere with the expansion of the database. This action must be taken in READY mode, not from within /Data Query, because once you select /Data Query you cannot make entries on the worksheet. Second, 1-2-3 needs to be told where the criteria are stored by means of the /Data Query Criteria command.

Location of Criteria

When you use one of the /Data Query commands that requires the use of search criteria, you must use the /Data Query Criteria command to tell 1-2-3 the location

```
F20: 2                                                              POINT
Enter input range: A1..F20

        A            B            C          D          E       F      G
 1  Last Name    First Name      SS#       Job Code    Salary   Location
 2  Larson       Mary        543-98-9876      23      $12,000       2
 3  Campbell     David       213-76-9874      23      $23,000      10
 4  Campbell     Keith       569-89-7654      12      $32,000       2
 5  Stephens     Tom         219-78-8954      15      $17,800       2
 6  Caldor       Larry       459-34-0921      23      $32,500       4
 7  Lightnor     Peggy       560-55-4311      14      $23,500      10
 8  McCartin     John        817-66-1212      15      $54,600       2
 9  Justof       Jack        431-78-9963      17      $41,200       4
10  Patterson    Lyle        212-11-9090      12      $21,500      10
11  Miller       Lisa        214-89-6756      23      $18,700       2
12  Hawkins      Mark        215-67-8973      21      $19,500       2
13  Hartwick     Eileen      313-78-9090      15      $31,450       4
14  Smythe       George      560-90-8645      15      $65,000       4
15  Wilkes       Caitlin     124-67-7432      17      $15,500       2
16  Deaver       Ken         198-98-6750      23      $24,600      10
17  Kaylor       Sally       312-45-9862      12      $32,900      10
18  Parker       Dee         659-11-3452      14      $19,800       4
19  Preverson    Gary        670-90-1121      21      $27,600       4
20  Samuelson    Paul        219-89-7080      23      $28,900       2
23-Apr-92  09:13 AM
```

Figure 9-7.   Selecting an input range

of the criteria. (Remember that the criteria themselves must be entered before you select /Data Query.) Leaving blank rows in the criteria range creates a wildcard match with every record in the database. Entering criteria and telling 1-2-3 where they are located with /Data Query Criteria does not show you the matching records, however. A number of other commands can display the matching records, copy them to a new area, or delete them from your database; these commands are explained later in this chapter.

You can choose any location you desire for your search criteria. A popular location is to the right of the database; this allows the criteria area to be expanded to the right and does not interfere with the downward expansion of your database. If your database occupies columns A through M, for example, you may wish to begin your criteria in column R. This allows for the expansion of the database by four new fields before the criteria is moved.

Types of Criteria

You can use a variety of different ways to specify which records in the database you wish to query. You can use values that match your database entries exactly, you can use 1-2-3's wildcard characters to specify only a portion of the entry you are looking for, or you can specify formulas. For matches other than formulas, the name of the field in the database you are searching must appear above the specific entry you are searching for. For formula matches you can use any field name, although for

Steps for Using /Data Query Commands

The /Data Query commands access selected records in your database. Obtaining the results you desire involves some preliminary work, as well as a number of /Data Query options. The required steps are as follows:

1. Enter the Query criteria on your worksheet.

2. If you plan to use the Extract or Unique options, enter the field names you will be copying in the output area of your worksheet.

3. Enter /**Data Query Input** from the Query menu and specify the range for your database, including field names.

4. Select Criteria from the Query menu and specify the location of your criteria.

5. If you plan to use Extract or Unique, select Output and specify the location of your output area.

6. Select the /Data Query option you wish to use: Find, Delete, Extract, or Unique.

7. If you choose Find, press ESC after you have finished browsing in your file, and then Quit to exit the Query menu. If you choose Delete, you must select Yes to confirm the deletions or No to cancel the command.

documentation purposes it is best to use the name of the field referenced in the formula.

For example, if you want to search the last name field in an employee database to find all records with a last name of Smith, your criteria area might look like this:

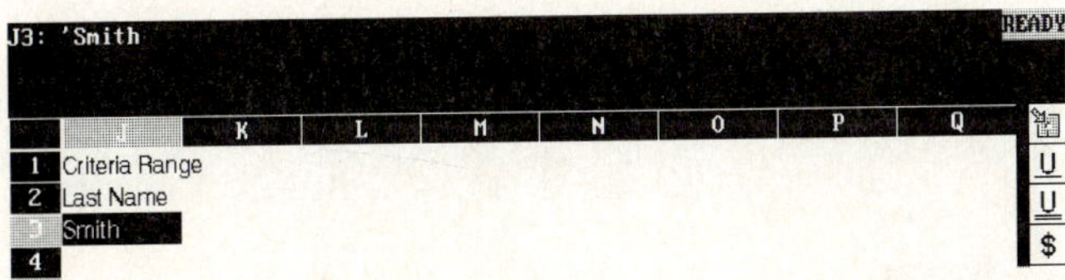

Note that the criteria area is J2..J3. The entry in J1 is documentation. The search value is placed immediately underneath the field name in the criteria area. The field name in the criteria area must be an exact match with the field name in your database. A space at the end of one field name or the other, or a difference in label alignment within the cells, can cause a problem. The safest approach is to copy the field name from its location above the data to the criteria area where you wish to use it.

Note that 1-2-3 is case-sensitive to field names and field entries when the collating sequence used in sorting is set to ASCII.

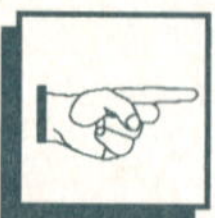

Copy database field names from the database to the criteria range, so the spacing and the upper- and lowercase arrangement of the field names in the criteria match the database.

Values   To search for numeric values in your records, record the desired field name in the criteria area. Underneath this field name enter the value for which you are searching. The criteria value need not have the same format as the values you are looking for. In a search based on the following criteria area, only records for Job Code 23 match as shown here:

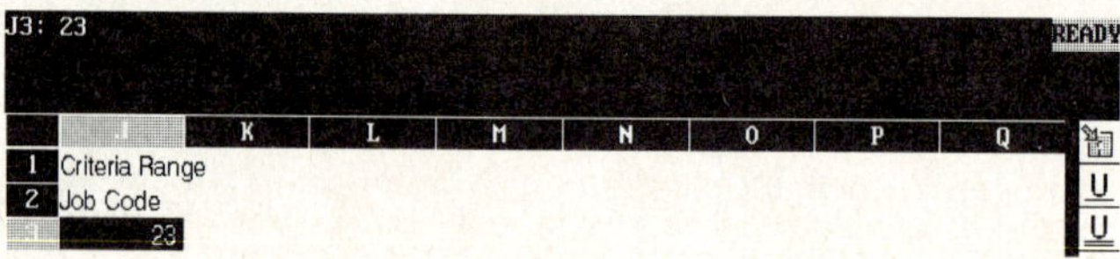

Labels   If you want to match label entries, you can enter them in the criteria exactly as they appear in your database, under the name of the field you wish to search. For example, enter **Last Name** in the criteria area and place **Jones** beneath for 1-2-3 to select records that contain Jones in the Last Name field.

1-2-3 has two special characters that are useful when specifying label criteria. These characters are the asterisk (*) and the question mark (?).

The asterisk (*) at the end of a criteria entry indicates that if the first part of the criteria entry matches a database record, any characters from the location of the * to the end of the database entry can be accepted in the match. For example, the following criteria specify a search of the Last Name field for all records beginning with Sm:

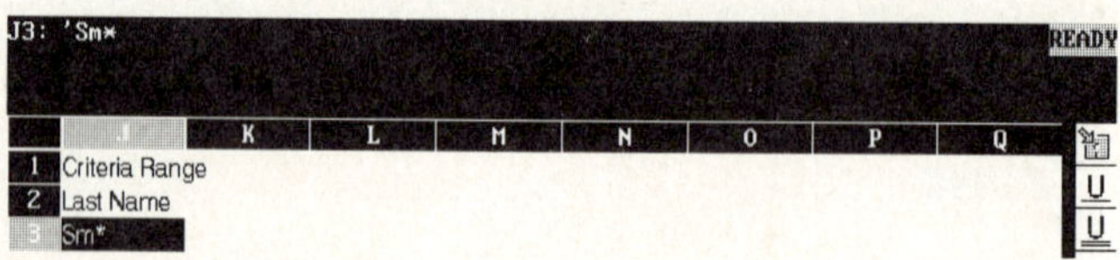

Smith would match, as would Smithfield, Smothers, and Smeltman.

The question mark (?) replaces any one character in an entry. The ? says that you do not care what character comes at that location in the data entry, as long as all the other characters match exactly. For example, the following criteria tell 1-2-3 that you do not care what character is located in the second position of the Last Name field, as long as "B" is the first character, and "tman" the third through the sixth characters of the database entry:

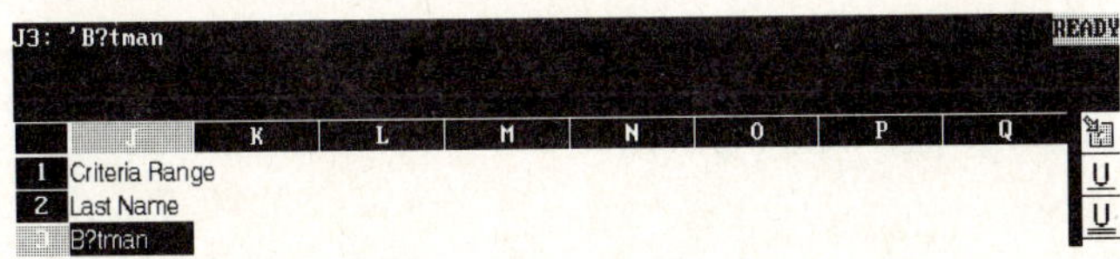

Bitman, Butman, Batman, Botman, and Betman are possible matching entries if records containing these names were in the database. All entries longer than six characters, such as Bitmanson, are rejected.

Formulas   The ability to create formulas to serve as search criteria offers additional query power. Formulas in database queries are logical formulas that 1-2-3 checks against each record in the database to see if the formula is true or false for each. You can use formula comparisons to check for records that contain values with a specific range, and you can even use string formulas in your criteria. When you enter a formula as criteria, the formula is displayed as 0 or 1, depending on whether it evaluates to true or false for the first database record. You may want to format the cell of the criteria area as text, so it is displayed as the formula you entered.

When you create formulas as search criteria, it is not important that the field name above the formula in the criteria area match the field referenced in the formula, although for clarity it is always best to use the proper field name. As you construct your formulas to compare values in the database against a specific value, always reference the first value for the field in the database.

In the example in Figure 9-7, to find all values in the Salary field located in column E that are greater than $25,000, you can use this criteria formula:

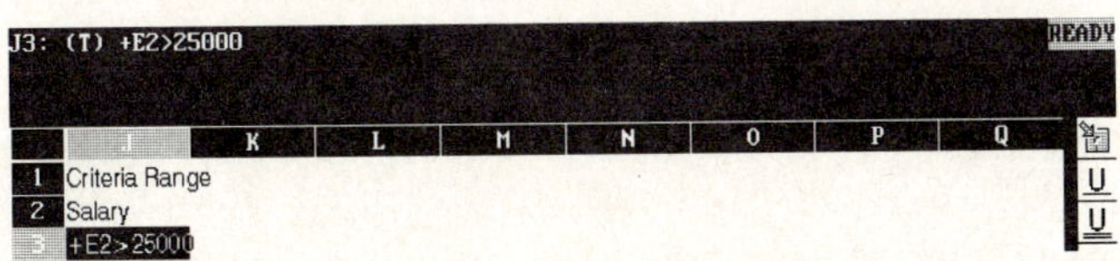

The cell referenced is E2 because it contains the first value in the salary field. Always use a relative reference when referring to database fields. If you use the /Range Name Labels Down command on the field names in the database table, you can also enter the previous formula as **+SALARY>25000** in Releases 2.2 and above, since 1-2-3 substitutes the field values for the field name. Another method of entering this formula is by typing **>25000** in J3 under the Salary field name. When you enter a formula like this, 1-2-3 uses the field name at the top of the criteria. This type of formula is also entered as a label so 1-2-3 will add a label indicator automatically unless you add one.

If you need a criteria formula that compares a database field against a value located elsewhere in the worksheet, use an absolute reference as the reference outside the database. Suppose you want to compare the salaries in Figure 9-7 against the average salary amount stored in M2. This criteria can identify all records in which the salary exceeds the average by $3,000:

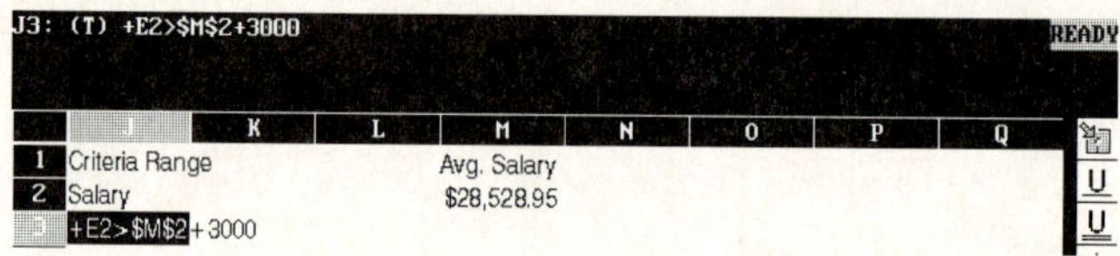

You may need to start a criteria with a less than (<) symbol. Be aware that when you type < in the READY mode, 1-2-3 activates the menus. This feature accommodates foreign-language keyboards, where the slash (/) is in an awkward position. So, to start a formula for a criteria range with a less than symbol, type a label prefix before you type the <.

The complex operators #AND#, #OR#, and #NOT# can also be used in formula criteria. For example, to determine if a salary is less than or equal to $25,000 or greater than or equal to $50,000, use the criteria formula shown here:

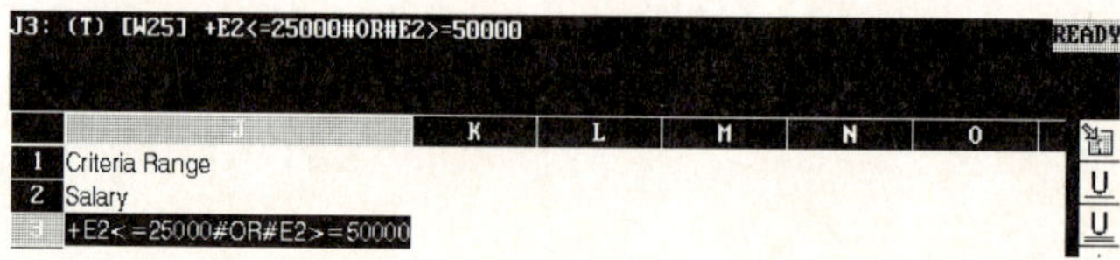

If you use the #AND# operator, the conditions on both sides of the operator must be true for the record to be selected. If you use #OR#, either condition may be true for the record to be selected. #NOT# negates the condition that follows it. When you use a complex operator, you must include the field names or the cell address for the first record. For example, in the previous example, you cannot use the criteria <=25000#OR#>=50000, which will look in the salary column for the string <=25000#OR#>=50000.

Compound Criteria   Whenever you use more than one field in the criteria area, you are using *compound criteria.* 1-2-3 allows up to 32 fields to be used for search criteria at one time. These criteria must be joined by an implied "and" and "or."

If two criteria values are placed on the same row beneath their separate field names, they are joined by an implied "and." The following criteria, for example, select records with the job code equal to 23 and the salary less than $16,000:

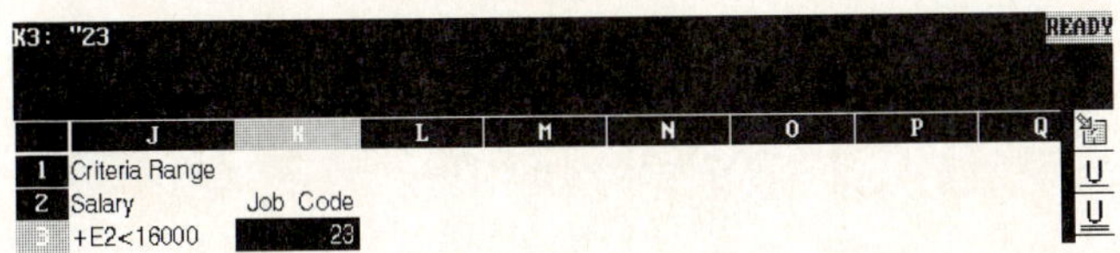

Notice that the field names in the criteria area are placed in adjacent cells. Note also that the criteria types do not have to be the same; one criterion is a formula and the other a value. A database record must meet both criteria to be selected.

If one criteria value is placed one row below the other, the two criteria are joined by an implied "or." Perhaps you want records with a job code of 23 or a salary of less than $16,000. The criteria shown here select records meeting either of these conditions:

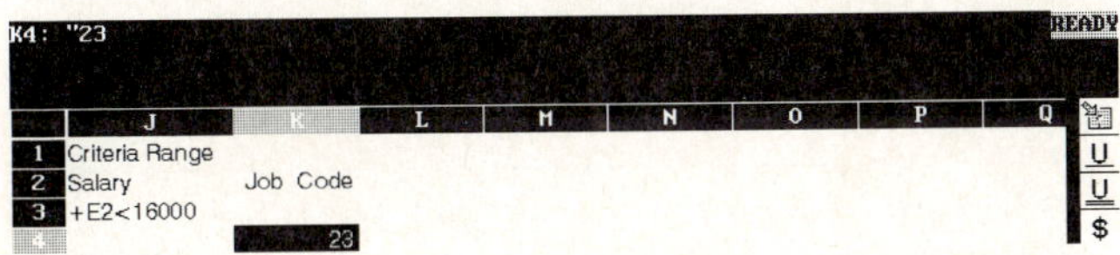

Highlighting Selected Records

Once you have defined your search area and criteria, 1-2-3's /Data Query Find command starts FIND mode, which only lets you move to records that match the criteria. Table 9-1 lists the keys you can use to move through the selected records.

Finding records requires a few preliminary steps. You must define your database, including the field names, with /Data Query Input. You also must enter your search criteria on the worksheet and then define the criteria with /Data Query Criteria. Figure 9-8 shows a database that has been defined with /Data Query Input as A1..E10.

Key	Action
DOWN ARROW	Moves to the next record in the input range that meets the criteria.
UP ARROW	Moves to the previous record in the input range that meets the criteria.
LEFT ARROW	Moves one field to the left in the selected record.
RIGHT ARROW	Moves one field to the right in the selected record.
HOME	Moves to the first record in the input range that meets the criteria.
END	Moves to the last record in the input range that meets the criteria.
ESC	Ends the /Data Query Find operation and returns to the /Data Query menu.
ENTER	Ends the /Data Query Find operation and returns to the /Data Query menu.
F2 (EDIT)	Switches to EDIT mode for the current field in the selected record. Pressing ENTER saves your edits and returns to FIND mode. Pressing ESC cancels the edits and returns to FIND mode.
F7 (QUERY)	Ends FIND mode and returns to the READY mode.

Table 9-1.   *Cell Pointer Movement Keys for Use with /Data Query Find in Database Records*

A1: [W25] 'Description   READY

	A	B	C		D	E	F
1	Description	Life	Cost	Dept	Type	Inv Co	
2	FTY Computer	5	$980	Accounting	Office	5	
3	Dover Typewriter	5	$950	Training	Office	5	
4	Swivel Chair	10	$345	Check	Furniture	5	
5	KL Calculator	7	$100	Audit	Office	5	
6	Walnut Desk	15	$1,200	Cash	Furniture	5	
7	Lanver Copier	3	$2,500	Cash	Processing	5	
8	Lanver Copier	3	$2,800	Accounting	Processing	5	
9	Computer Table	5	$300	Training	Furniture		
10	File Cabinet	10	$450	Audit	Furniture		
11							
12							

Figure 9-8.   *Asset records*

The following criteria are established in A2..A3 to locate records for the Accounting Department:

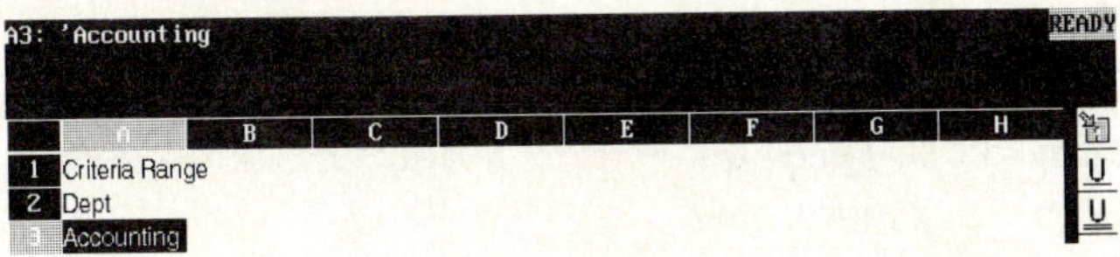

Figure 9-9 shows the first record matching the criteria highlighted on the screen.

The /Data Query Find option is a good one if you need a quick answer to a question concerning data you have stored in your database. The drawback to using it is that all the matching records are not listed at once and cannot be printed out. If you need to do either of these things, use the /Data Query Extract and /Data Query Unique commands.

Writing Selected Records on the Worksheet

1-2-3 provides two commands that make a copy of selected records and fields from your database to another area of the worksheet. You can add headings to these new areas to create an instant report that can be shared with others. Before you can have 1-2-3 copy the database information, however, you must prepare an output location.

Defining an Output Area

First decide on a location and prepare it to receive data. The bottom of the existing database is a commonly selected location. Just make sure you leave some blank rows

Figure 9-9.   Finding records for a specific department

at the bottom of the database to allow for expansion, or you may find yourself moving the output area around to acquire more space. You should also not have any information below the output range since 1-2-3 erases the cells from below the field names in the output range to the bottom of the worksheet before 1-2-3 copies matching records to the output range.

With the location selected, enter the names of the fields you want to copy from matching records. They need not be in the same sequence as the fields in your database, and you do not have to include every field.

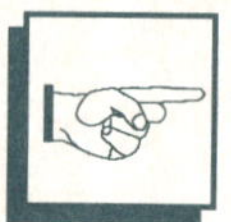

Use the /Copy command to copy field names from the database directly to the output range, so the spacing and letter case of the field names in the criteria match the database exactly. Once you have all the field names, you can delete names of the fields you do not want in the output range.

Once the field names are placed in the output area, you are ready to define its location to 1-2-3. This is done with /Data Query Output. If you define the output area as consisting of only the row containing the field names, 1-2-3 uses the range from the field names to the bottom of the worksheet for writing records that match. It is important that you do not put any worksheet data below the field names.

You can also specify the range for the output area to include a number of blank rows beneath the row of field names. If you use this approach, 1-2-3 stops copying matching database records when the specified output area becomes full. In this case, 1-2-3 only erases the selected range before copying matching records. For example, if you select A100..F110 as the output range, 1-2-3 copies only the first nine records it finds (it uses the first line for the field names). If 1-2-3 cannot fit the selected records into the output range, it displays an error message.

Extracting All Matches

To extract matching records, enter **/Data Query Extract** after you set up the criteria and output areas on your worksheet and define the database, criteria, and output to 1-2-3.

The following preliminary steps are required before using this command. The database in Figure 9-8 is used as an example.

1. Add selection criteria to the worksheet, as shown here:

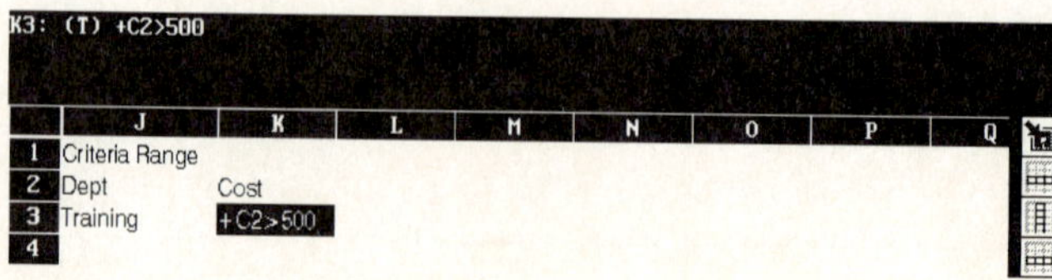

2. Set up the output area on the worksheet to look like this:

3. Enter /**Data Query Input** to define the database as located in A1..E10.

4. Since the Data Query menu remains displayed, all you have to enter is **Criteria** in order to define the criteria location as J2..K3.

5. Define the output area next by entering **Output** and specifying its location of A21..C21 at the prompt.

6. Enter **Extract**, and the following output is produced:

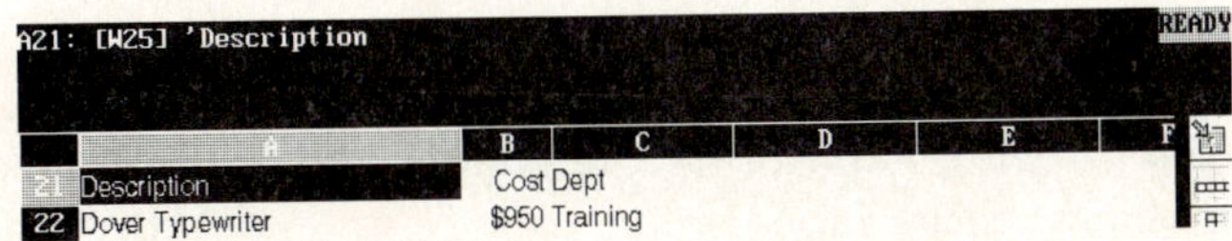

If you want to turn extracted records into a report, you need only add a report title at the top of the extract area and then print the worksheet range containing the report title and the extract.

Writing Only Unique Records

The Unique option is very similar to Extract in that it writes records to the output area. However, it writes only unique records to this area, so if two selected entries are an exact match, only one is written. Uniqueness of records is determined by the fields written to the output area.

Be aware that the number of records written to the output area can be affected by the number of fields you plan to write there. For example, suppose two records are identical in three out of four fields. If the one field that differentiates the two records is included in the output range, the two records are unique and are separately listed in the output range. If the one field that differentiates the two records is not included in the output range, the two records are not unique and are only listed once in the output range.

For instance, consider the following criteria:

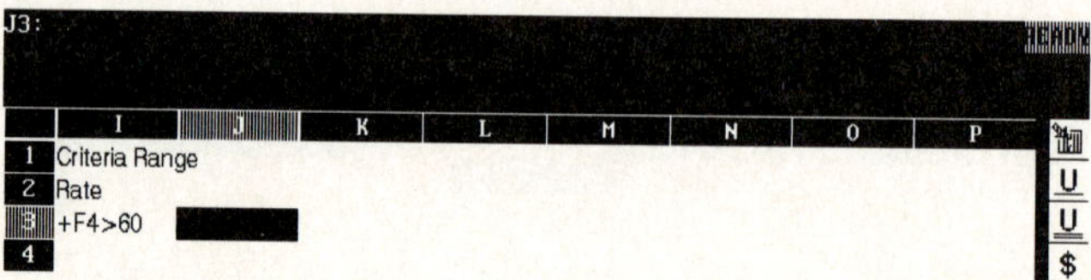

Consider also the database records shown in Figure 9-10. 1-2-3 produced the output shown below when Unique was selected from the /Data Query menu. Note that the Tower College record appears only once, even though several qualifying records for it exist in the database.

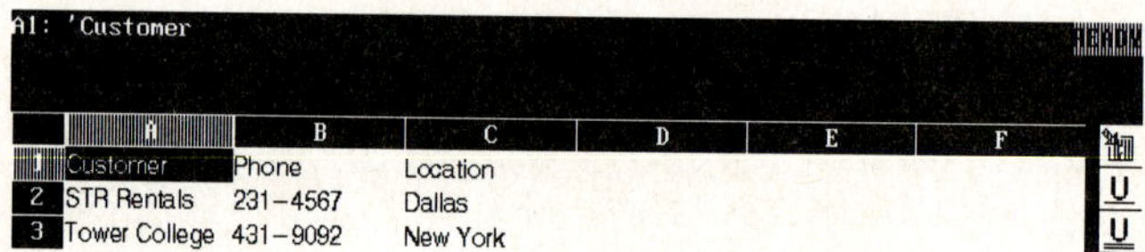

Every time you use the Unique option, the output area is erased so that the newly selected records can be written to it.

Figure 9-10.   *Client billing records*

Deleting Selected Records from the Database

/Data Query Delete is a powerful yet dangerous command. In one easy process it can purge outdated records from your database, but if you make a mistake in entering your search criteria, it can also purge records you still need. You should test your criteria with Find or Extract before selecting the Delete option. In Releases 2.2 and above, you will also need to select Delete to confirm that you want to delete the records or Cancel to cancel the /Data Query Delete command.

If you specify the criteria

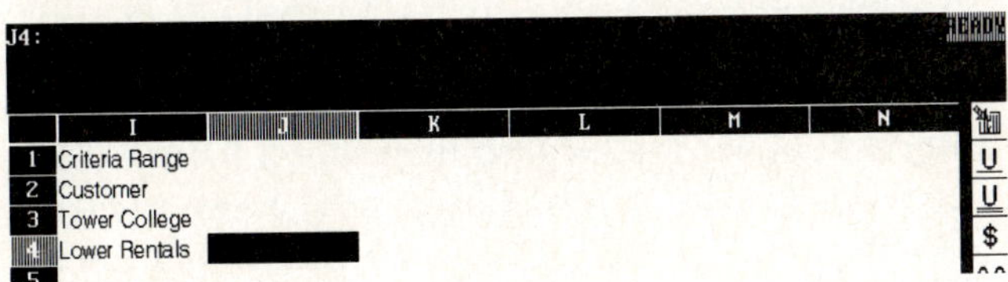

and the database in Figure 9-10, and then choose the Delete option and select Delete for confirmation, only the following records remain in the database:

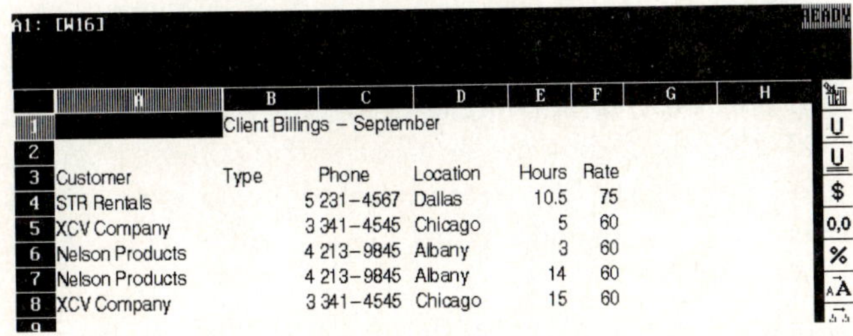

Look at database records before you delete them. Use /Data Query Find or /Data Query Extract to view records the /Data Query Delete command is going to delete. This step prevents you from deleting records that you want to keep.

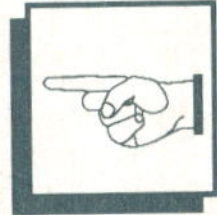

Resetting Selection Options

All the Query specifications can be eliminated with the /Data Query Reset command. This includes the Input range, the Criteria range, and the Output range, if you made one.

Quitting the Query Menu

When you want to leave the /Data Query operation, choose Quit from the Query menu to return to READY mode. This allows you to make new entries for criteria and perform other tasks. To return to /Data Query after making changes, you can reenter through the menu. Alternatively, if you want to use the same choices for Input, Criteria, and Output areas and would like to perform the same query operation as the last one you performed (Find, Unique, Delete, or Extract), simply press F7 (QUERY), and another query is executed.

The Database Statistical Functions

1-2-3's database statistical functions are a special category of functions designed to coordinate with the other data management features. Using criteria you enter on your worksheet, they can perform a statistical analysis on selected records in your database. The criteria used are identical to the criteria for the /Data Query commands, except that you may have many active criteria areas. In fact, it is possible to set up a criteria area for each database statistical function that you use.

Each of the database statistical functions has a letter "D" immediately following the @ in the function name to show that it is a database function. The characters following the "D" indicate the exact task the function performs and also correspond to the name of one of 1-2-3's statistical functions, which are covered in Chapter 7.

All of the database statistical functions have the same format. All of the functions use the format @DFUNCTION (*database range, field offset, criteria range*). The first function argument is the location of the database (including the field names) that is a range name or address. The second is the field used to select which field is used to perform the calculation. This is the number of the column that the function will use. Counting from the left, the first column is 0, the second column is 1, and so on. The third argument is the range address or name containing the criteria.

@DAVG

The @DAVG function averages a selected group of database records.

Use

Use the @DAVG function to average the values in a field in a selected group of records in the database. The database and criteria in Figure 9-11 are used with the @DAVG function in the formula @DAVG(A1..F12,4,A15..A16) to calculate an average salary for employees in job code 23 of $21,550. Note that the database is defined as being located in A1..F12. The field the function uses is the Salary field with an offset of 4, and the criteria used in the selection are located in A15..A16.

@DCOUNT

The @DCOUNT function counts a selected group of database records.

```
A16: [W12] 23                                                          READY

       A              B            C          D          E         F       G
 1  Last Name    First Name      SS#       Job Code    Salary   Location
 2  Larson       Mary        543-98-9876      23      $12,000      2
 3  Campbell     David       213-76-9874      23      $23,000     10
 4  Campbell     Keith       569-89-7654      12      $32,000      2
 5  Stephens     Tom         219-78-8954      15      $17,800      2
 6  Caldor       Larry       459-34-0921      23      $32,500      4
 7  Lightnor     Peggy       560-55-4311      14      $23,500     10
 8  McCartin     John        817-66-1212      15      $54,600      2
 9  Justof       Jack        431-78-9963      17      $41,200      4
10  Patterson    Lyle        212-11-9090      12      $21,500     10
11  Miller       Lisa        214-89-6756      23      $18,700      2
12  Hawkins      Mark        215-67-8973      21      $19,500      2
13
14  Criteria Range
15  Job Code
16                   23
17
```

Figure 9-11.   *Using @DAVG*

Use

Use the @DCOUNT function to count the records in the database that match your selection criteria. The database and criteria shown in Figure 9-11 are used with the @DCOUNT function shown in the formula @DCOUNT(A1..F12,4,A15..A16) to count the last names for records with a job code of 23. Note that the database is defined as being located in A1..F12, the offset to refer to the Salary field is 4, and the criteria used in the selection are located in A15..A16.

Since @DCOUNT counts only records with a nonblank entry in the specified field, choose carefully the field that you count. For example, some records need not have a location assignment, but all records should have a salary.

Another use of @DCOUNT is to determine the size of the output range. For example, assume you want to determine the number of rows you need in an output range for a /Data Query Extract command to extract records with a job code of 23. The @DCOUNT formula in F16 tells you that the output range must include at least five rows—one for the field names and four for the extracted records.

@DMAX

The @DMAX function obtains the maximum value in a field within a selected group of database records.

Use

Use the @DMAX function to obtain the maximum (highest) value in a field for records in the database that match your selection criteria. The database and criteria shown in Figure 9-11 can be used with @DMAX(A1..F12,4,A15..A16) to determine the maximum salary of $32,500 for employees with a job code of 23. Note that the database is defined as being located in A1..F12, the field counted is the Salary field with an offset of 4, and the criteria used in the selection are located in A15..A16.

@DMIN

The @DMIN function obtains the minimum value in a field within a selected group of database records.

Use

Use the @DMIN function to obtain the minimum (lowest) value in a field for records in the database that matches your selection criteria. The database and criteria shown in Figure 9-11 can be used with @DMIN(A1..F12,4,A15..A16) to determine the minimum salary of $12,000 for employees with a job code of 23. Note that the database is defined as being located in A1..F12, the Salary field is used with an offset of 4, and the criteria used in the selection are located in A15..A16.

@DSTD

The @DSTD function determines the standard deviation of a set of values, or how much variation there is from the average of the values. The values used in this calculation are from selected records in the database. Chapter 7 includes more information on standard deviation with the @STD function.

Use

Use the @DSTD function to determine the standard deviation when the selected records comprise the entire population you are measuring.

You can use the database shown in Figure 9-11 and the formula @DSTD(A1..F12,4,A16..A16) to return the result of 7438.581854, which is the standard deviation of salaries for employees in job code 23.

@DSUM

The @DSUM function obtains the total of values in a field within a selected group of database records.

Use

Use the @DSUM function to total up the values in a field for records in the database that match your selection criteria. You can use the database and criteria in Figure 9-11 with the @DSUM(A1..F12,4,A15..A16) function to determine the total of salaries of $86,200 for employees with a job code of 23. Note that the database is defined as being located in A1..F12, the Salary field is selected to total since it has an offset of 4, and the criteria used in the selection are located in A15..A16.

@DVAR

The @DVAR function computes the variance of values in a population, or the amount that the individual population values vary from the average. The records used in the computation are selected from the database with your criteria. Chapter 7 includes more information on variance with the @VAR function.

Use

Use the @DVAR function to determine the variance when the selected records comprise the entire population you are measuring.

You can use the worksheet in Figure 9-11 and the formula @DVAR(A1..F12,4,A15..A16) to get the result of 55332500, which is the variance for salaries of employees with a job code of 23.

DATA MANAGEMENT

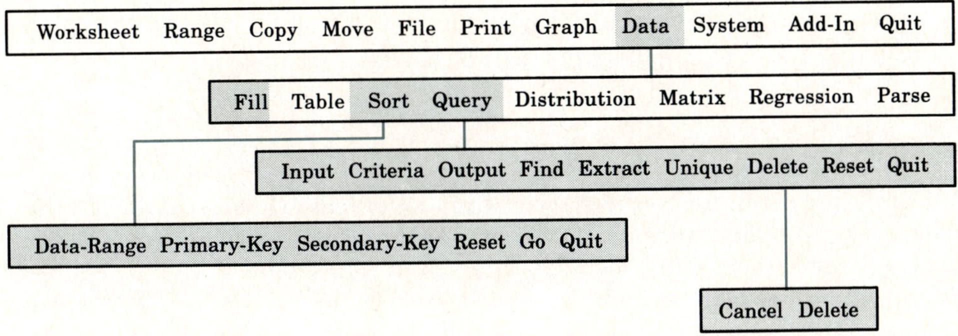

/Data Fill

Description

 The /Data Fill command allows you to produce an ascending or descending list of numbers separated by the same interval. All of the following series can be generated with /Data Fill:

    1 2 3 4 5 6 7 8 9 10 11 12 13 14 15 16
    5001 5006 5011 5016 5021 5026 5031 5036
    90 88 86 84 82 80 78 76 74 72 70 68 66
    03-Jan-92 10-Jan-92 17-Jan-92 24-Jan-92 31-Jan-92

Options

When you use /Data Fill, you must select the range of cells to hold the numeric series. The /Data Fill options include a start value, a stop value, and an increment or step value. The start value is the beginning number in your sequence and has a default of 0 or the value most recently entered. The stop value is the last value in your sequence: its default is 8191 or the last number that fits within the range selected. The increment (step) value is the distance between each pair of numbers in the series; its default is 1 or the value most recently entered. Any of these values can be either positive or negative.

These values can also include functions, @DATE(91,12,13), for example; formulas, such as +@YEAR(@TODAY)+1900; or a cell address, range address, or range name that evaluates to a value, such as A1, which may contain the number 30. If you provide a range name or range address, 1-2-3 uses the cell value in the upper-left corner of the range.

/Data Query Criteria

Description

The /Data Query Criteria command specifies the location of the criteria you have entered on the worksheet for database record selection. You must already have entered criteria on the worksheet when you issue this command.

Options

The only option you have with this command is the method you use to specify the criteria range. Pointing, typing the cell addresses, and using a range name are all acceptable methods of specifying the range.

/Data Query Delete

Description

The /Data Query Delete command searches database records for specified criteria and deletes all the records in the input area that match the criteria. You must first specify the database records with /Data Query Input, and you must already have entered the criteria on the worksheet and specified them with /Data Query Criteria.

Options

The only option for this command is selecting Delete to confirm that you want to delete the matching records or Cancel to cancel this command.

Note

Since the /Data Query Delete deletion process is permanent, be sure to save your file to disk before using the command. This way you can always retrieve the file if you make a mistake in specifying your criteria and delete too many records. Another protective strategy is to use your criteria to extract records (with /Data Query Extract) before using the same criteria for a deletion.

/Data Query Extract

Description

The /Data Query Extract command searches database records for specified criteria and writes all records from the input area that match your criteria to an output area on the worksheet. Preliminary steps that must be completed before using this command are as follows:

- Specify the database records to be searched by using /Data Query Input.

- Enter the criteria for extraction on the worksheet, and specify the criteria with /Data Query Criteria.

- Specify an output area with /Data Query Output.

/Data Query Find

Description

The /Data Query Find command searches database records for specified criteria and highlights one at a time all records from the input area that match those criteria.

Before using this command you must use /Data Query Input to specify the database records to be searched. You must also enter the search criteria on the worksheet and identify them with /Data Query Criteria.

Options

Your options for this command include using the arrow keys to move between matching records and between fields. You can press HOME and END to move to the first and last matching record. To change an entry, move the cell pointer to the entry and make a new entry or press F2 (EDIT) to alter the current one. You can end FIND mode by pressing ENTER or ESC to return to the /Data Query menu or press F7 (QUERY) to return to the READY mode.

/Data Query Input

Description

The /Data Query Input command specifies the location of the database. You should already have entered database records on a worksheet when you issue this command.

Options

The only option you have with this command is the method you use to specify the input range. Pointing, typing the range addresses, and entering a range name are all acceptable methods. The input range should always include the field names at the top of your database.

/Data Query Output

Description

The /Data Query Output command specifies the location of the area you plan to use to store information extracted from a database. You must enter the field names of the fields you want to extract before you issue this command.

Options

You have two options with this command: specifying the entire output area or just the top row. If you specify a one-row output range that includes only the field names,

1-2-3 uses as many rows as it needs for writing data in the columns selected for the output range. Before 1-2-3 copies matching records to the output range, it erases the range from below the output area's field names to the bottom of the worksheet. If you specify a multiple-row output range, 1-2-3 stops extracting records when your output range is full. You can specify the range by pointing, typing the cell addresses, and entering a range name.

/Data Query Quit

Description

This command exits the sticky Data Query menu.

/Data Query Reset

Description

This command clears the range specifications for Input, Criteria, and Output made with the /Data Query command.

/Data Query Unique

Description

The /Data Query Unique command copies records from the input range that match the criteria. Unlike the /Data Query Extract command, this command only includes the first record when several identical records exist. Uniqueness between records is determined solely by the records included in the output range. The output is sorted according to the field values in the output area. Preliminary steps that must be completed before using this command are as follows:

- Specify the database records to be searched by using /Data Query Input.

- Enter the criteria for search on the worksheet, and specify the criteria with /Data Query Criteria.

- Specify an output area with /Data Query Output.

/Data Sort Data-Range

Description

The /Data Sort Data-Range command specifies the location of the records you plan to sort. You should enter database records before you issue this command.

Options

The only option you have with this command is the method you use to specify the input range. Pointing, typing the cell addresses, and entering a range name are all acceptable methods of specifying the range. The sort range should not include the field names at the top of the database. If you accidentally include the field names, they are sorted.

/Data Sort Go

Description

The /Data Sort Go command sorts the records. Before executing this command, you must define the database with the /Data Sort Data-Range command. You must also specify the primary key and any secondary sort keys.

/Data Sort Primary-Key

Description

The /Data Sort Primary-Key command selects the field to use to sort your database records into a new sequence.

Options

Select a cell within the field that you want to use for controlling the sort sequence and specify either ascending or descending sort order.

/Data Sort Quit

Description

This command exits the sticky /Data Sort menu.

/Data Sort Reset

Description

The /Data Sort Reset command cancels the current settings for the primary and secondary sort keys and the data range.

/Data Sort Secondary-Key

Description

The /Data Sort Secondary-Key command selects a field within the database to serve as a tiebreaker whenever there is more than one primary key with the same value. When this situation occurs, the sort operation uses the secondary key to provide a sequence for the records containing the duplicate entries. As an example, you may have an employee file with the last name field selected as the primary key. When you encounter three employees with the last name of Smith and have selected first name as the secondary key, the three Smiths appear in a sequence determined by their first names.

Options

Select a cell within the field that you want to use as the secondary key and specify either ascending or descending sort order.

Chapter **10**

Using Data Management Features in the Worksheet Environment

In Chapter 9 you learned how to use the data management features of 1-2-3 to build your own database of information. In this chapter you'll discover ways that data management commands can assist you with calculations and other worksheet tasks. You'll see some of the same commands used in Chapter 9, such as /Data Sort, but they are presented in a new light. You will also explore more sophisticated features that allow you to handle tasks like regression and sensitivity analysis. These features introduce new commands, such as /Data Table and /Data Regression.

Performing Statistical Analyses with /Data Commands

The statistical options that are part of the /Data commands allow you to perform sophisticated analyses of your data. You can do a sensitivity analysis, a regression analysis, or create a frequency distribution.

421

Sensitivity Analysis

The /Data Table options allow you to quickly substitute a range of values in one or two cells referenced by formulas and to record the results of worksheet calculations at the same time. In other words, /Data Table automates the "what-if" analysis you may have been doing with the package as you plugged in new individual variable values and tried to remember the results from previous iterations. The advantage of this automated approach is that 1-2-3 does all the work, plugs in the values, and remembers the results for you. The results are recorded in a table, as you might guess from the command's name. You can look at these results to see which variables the model is most sensitive to.

The /Data Table command provides three options: a one-way table, a two-way table, and a Reset option that eliminates settings you have made through the other two choices.

One-Way Data Tables

A *one-way data table* allows you to choose a set of values for one variable and record them in a worksheet column. Above and to the right of this column of values you place formulas to be evaluated for each value of the variable. The results are recorded below the formulas to form a complete table.

For example, consider a one-way table you create to use with the worksheet data shown in Figure 10-1. This worksheet computes commissions using the quarterly sales figure for each salesperson times the commission percentage in D1. If you want to change the commission percentage, you probably are interested in what you would have paid out if that commission structure existed in prior periods. You could plug individual values one by one into D1 and monitor the effect on the total commission calculation in C20, but it is faster to have 1-2-3 do the work for you.

You must complete these two preliminary steps before using the /Data Table command. First you must set up the framework for the table. Record the values you want to substitute for D1 in a column. The example in Figure 10-2 uses I4..I19, but you can select any empty location. If you are using values in even increments, you can have /Data Fill generate these values for you. The next step in the setup process is to record the formula or formulas you wish to evaluate, placed one column to the right of the values and one row above them. In this example, to evaluate total commission, a reference to C20 is sufficient. This entry is made in J3. After entering **+C20**, you can format the cell as text to display the formula.

The table at this time looks like the display in Figure 10-2. Enter **/Data Table** and select 1 for a one-way table. Move your cell pointer to I3, the blank cell to the left of the formula and immediately above the values. Select the range I3..J19 for the table location. You can use cell addresses, point with the mouse, or give a range name.

1-2-3's next prompt is for the input cell. This is the cell into which you want to plug the values from the commission percentage column, one by one. For this example, the input cell is D1. When you press ENTER, 1-2-3 takes the first value in the

```
C5: (C0) [W13] +B5*$D$1                                              READY
```

	A	B	C	D	E	F	G
1		Sales Commissions Assuming a 1.50% Commission					
2							
3		Quarterly					
4	Salesperson	Sales	Commission				
5	Rich Roberts	$1,200,987	$18,015				
6	Janet Jolson	$2,134,567	$32,019				
7	Mike Moore	$1,987,600	$29,814				
8	Helen Harn	$3,278,965	$49,184				
9	Tim Torn	$3,451,123	$51,767				
10	Roy Roberts	$2,134,987	$32,025				
11	Kaila Kolson	$1,897,626	$28,464				
12	Herb Horst	$1,750,890	$26,263				
13	Felicia Folly	$2,345,910	$35,189				
14	Ivan Imers	$3,090,152	$46,352				
15	Wilma Walker	$2,186,450	$32,797				
16	Nancy Nait	$2,134,567	$32,019				
17	Edna Edens	$1,678,932	$25,184				
18	Matt McElroy	$890,900	$13,364				
19							
20	TOTAL	$353,054,872	$2,195,457				

```
13-May-92  04:39 PM                              CIRC
```

Figure 10-1.   *A commission schedule*

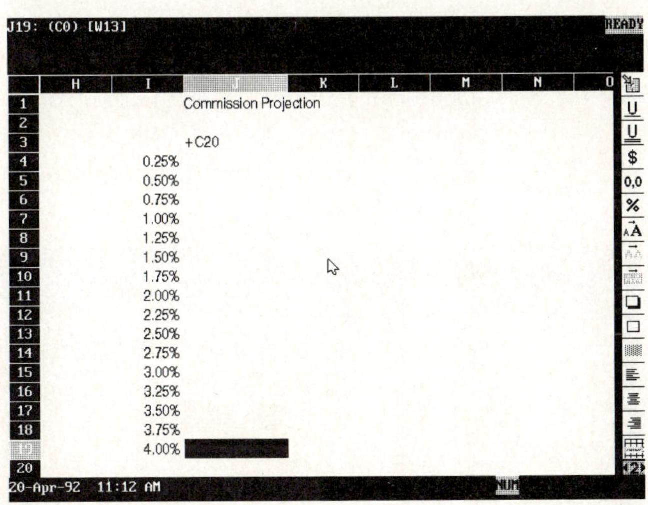

```
J19: (C0) [W13]                                                      READY
```

	H	I	J	K	L	M	N	O
1			Commission Projection					
2								
3			+C20					
4		0.25%						
5		0.50%						
6		0.75%						
7		1.00%						
8		1.25%						
9		1.50%						
10		1.75%						
11		2.00%						
12		2.25%						
13		2.50%						
14		2.75%						
15		3.00%						
16		3.25%						
17		3.50%						
18		3.75%						
19		4.00%						
20								

```
20-Apr-92  11:12 AM                              NUM
```

Figure 10-2.   *An outline of a one-way table*

input column and plugs it into D1 in the model. After the first calculation is completed, 1-2-3 records the result in the table and repeats the process for each of the remaining values. Figure 10-3 shows the level of total commissions at a variety of percentages.

J4: (C0) [W13] 79047							READY

	H	I	J	K	L	M	N	O
1			Commission Projection					
2								
3			+C20					
4		0.25%	$79,047					
5		0.50%	$158,093					
6		0.75%	$237,140					
7		1.00%	$316,187					
8		1.25%	$395,233					
9		1.50%	$474,280					
10		1.75%	$553,326					
11		2.00%	$632,373					
12		2.25%	$711,420					
13		2.50%	$790,466					
14		2.75%	$869,513					
15		3.00%	$948,560					
16		3.25%	$1,027,606					
17		3.50%	$1,106,653					
18		3.75%	$1,185,700					
19		4.00%	$1,264,746					
20								

20-Apr-92   11:12 AM   NUM

Figure 10-3.   *The commission table output*

Be aware that if you change the formulas in your model, the table is not updated to reflect these changes. To update the table values, issue the **/Data Table** command again.

Now consider a second example of a one-way table, this time using more than one formula. Figure 10-4 shows such a model and the completed table. The model

G2: [W10] (F2*(1+$C$7))							READY

	A	B	C	D	E	F	G
1		1991	1992	1993	1994	1995	1996
2	Sales	$23,500	$25,615	$27,920	$30,433	$33,172	$36,158
3	Cogs	$10,575	$11,527	$12,564	$13,695	$14,927	$16,271
4	Profit	$12,925	$14,088	$15,356	$16,738	$18,245	$19,887
5							
6							
7	Sales Growth:		9.00%				
8	Cogs %		45.00%				
9							
10		+G4	+G2	+G3			
11	8.00%	$18,991	$34,529	$15,538			
12	8.25%	$19,212	$34,931	$15,719			
13	8.50%	$19,435	$35,336	$15,901			
14	8.75%	$19,660	$35,745	$16,085			
15	9.00%	$19,887	$36,158	$16,271			
16	9.25%	$20,116	$36,574	$16,458			
17	9.50%	$20,347	$36,995	$16,648			
18	9.75%	$20,580	$37,419	$16,838			
19	10.00%	$20,816	$37,847	$17,031			
20	10.25%	$21,053	$38,279	$17,226			

20-Apr-92   11:14 AM   NUM

Figure 10-4.   *A one-way table with multiple formulas*

projects sales, cost of goods sold, and profit through 1996, using a 9 percent fixed-growth rate for sales and 45 percent as the cost of goods sold percentage.

Suppose you want to look at the impact of variations in the sales growth factor on sales, costs, and profits. Place the variable values in A11..A20. References to the cells containing the formulas you want to evaluate are entered in B10..D10, as +G4, +G2, and +G3. Using Data Table 1, define the table as being in A10..D20 and the input cell as C7. This range must include the formulas in the top row and the input values in the leftmost column. The results are shown in cells B11..D20 of Figure 10-4.

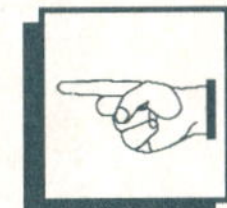

Use F8 *(TABLE) to recalculate tables instead of executing the /Data Table command each time you want to update the values of the formulas. Pressing this key reexecutes the last /Data Table command.*

Two-Way Data Tables

The /Data Table 2 command allows you to build a table in which you supply input values for two variables, instructing 1-2-3 to apply these values when recalculating the worksheet and recording the result of one of the worksheet formulas in the table. This kind of table is referred to as a *two-way data table*. It differs from a one-way table in its use of two sets of variable values and its ability to record the results of only one formula. This command allows you to see which variable the formula being evaluated is most sensitive to.

Like the one-way table, the two-way table requires a significant amount of preliminary work. The example uses a two-way table with the model in Figure 10-5 for payment calculations. The payment calculation is dependent on the amount borrowed, the interest rate, and the term of the loan. The amount borrowed may vary, since it will be equal to the cost of the new home minus the equity from the sale of the existing home. While holding the loan term constant, you can use /Data Table 2 to vary both the equity received from the sale of an existing home and the interest rate.

Figure 10-5.   *The model used in a two-way table*

Values for the first input variable (the interest rate) are stored in one column of the worksheet. If the values are spaced at equal intervals, /Data Fill can be used to generate the column of values. Values for the second input value (equity) are placed one row above the top value for input variable 1 and one cell to the right. The values for input variable 2 are placed across the row. A formula or a reference to one is then placed in the cell at the top of the column used for input variable 1.

In the payment example in Figure 10-6, column H is used for the values for input variable 1. Values are in H2..H17, beginning with 9 percent and, adding increments of .25 percent, ending with 12.75 percent. The equity figures start in I1 with 75,000 and proceed at increments of 2500, ending with 90,000 in O1. Cell H1 contains the formula reference, +D8, representing the payment calculated. If you want this cell to display as a formula, format the cell as text with /Range Format Text.

With these preliminaries accomplished, enter /**Data Table** and choose 2 from the submenu. The first prompt asks for the location of the table, which is H1..O17. The next prompt asks for the cell to use for the first input value, which is D5. Then answer the next prompt with D4, the second input cell. All these locations can be entered as a range, as a range name, or by pointing. After you respond to this last prompt, 1-2-3 provides the results shown in Figure 10-6.

You can use this table of results to determine the monthly payment, as long as the interest rate and the amount of money borrowed are in the ranges established for the table. Locate in column H the interest rate you feel you can obtain for a loan; then use that row to determine your payments at different levels of borrowing. Similarly, you can use the column for any given borrowing level and determine your payments, based on one of the interest rates in column H.

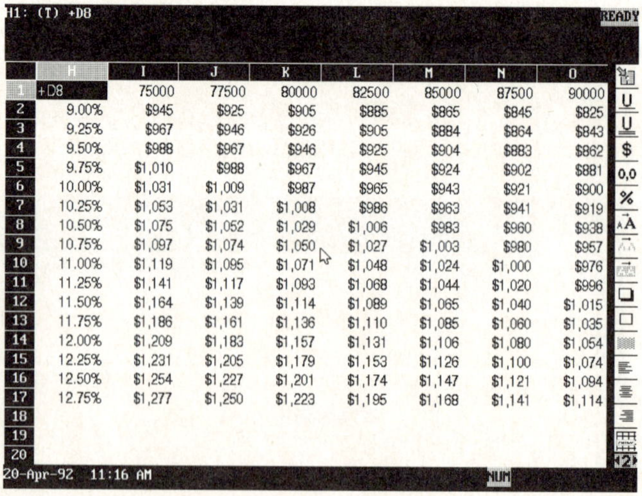

H1: (T) +D8   READY

	H	I	J	K	L	M	N	O
1	+D8	75000	77500	80000	82500	85000	87500	90000
2	9.00%	$945	$925	$905	$885	$865	$845	$825
3	9.25%	$967	$946	$926	$905	$884	$864	$843
4	9.50%	$988	$967	$946	$925	$904	$883	$862
5	9.75%	$1,010	$988	$967	$945	$924	$902	$881
6	10.00%	$1,031	$1,009	$987	$965	$943	$921	$900
7	10.25%	$1,053	$1,031	$1,008	$986	$963	$941	$919
8	10.50%	$1,075	$1,052	$1,029	$1,006	$983	$960	$938
9	10.75%	$1,097	$1,074	$1,050	$1,027	$1,003	$980	$957
10	11.00%	$1,119	$1,095	$1,071	$1,048	$1,024	$1,000	$976
11	11.25%	$1,141	$1,117	$1,093	$1,068	$1,044	$1,020	$996
12	11.50%	$1,164	$1,139	$1,114	$1,089	$1,065	$1,040	$1,015
13	11.75%	$1,186	$1,161	$1,136	$1,110	$1,085	$1,060	$1,035
14	12.00%	$1,209	$1,183	$1,157	$1,131	$1,106	$1,080	$1,054
15	12.25%	$1,231	$1,205	$1,179	$1,153	$1,126	$1,100	$1,074
16	12.50%	$1,254	$1,227	$1,201	$1,174	$1,147	$1,121	$1,094
17	12.75%	$1,277	$1,250	$1,223	$1,195	$1,168	$1,141	$1,114
18								
19								
20								

20-Apr-92 11:16 AM   NUM

Figure 10-6.   *A two-way table for payment calculation*

Using /Data Table with Database Statistical Functions

The /Data Table command can also be used effectively with the database statistical functions covered in Chapter 9. For example, you can use the command's variable values to supply different criteria values to be used with the database functions. These values may be numeric or label entries, depending on the search criteria you are using.

For example, consider the database shown in Figure 10-7. It contains employee records for a variety of locations and job codes. Let's use the /Data Table 2 command to systematically vary the values for these two variables and obtain an employee count for each job code at each location.

The table is created in B22..E28, as shown in Figure 10-8. In B23..B28, job code values 12, 14, 15, 17, 21, and 23 are listed. Locations are displayed in C22..E22 as 2, 4, and 10. The formula used is @DCOUNT(A1..F20,0,J2..K3). The first argument references the database. The second argument references the first column of the database, the Last Name field. That field is a good choice because it is unlikely to be missing from any record. The third argument references a criteria area that you must set up by entering **Job Code** and **Location** in J1 and K1, respectively. Then specify the two cells immediately below these, J2 and K2, as input cells. Initially these input cells will be blank, but as the /Data Table 2 command executes, it supplies values for criteria to compute the selective counts of database records.

With all the preliminary work accomplished, enter **/Data Table 2** and specify the table location as B22..E28, the first input cell as J2, and the second input cell as K2. 1-2-3 then produces the output in Figure 10-9. From this table you can tell how many employees in each job code work at each location.

```
A1: [W12] 'Last Name                                              READY
```

	A	B	C	D	E	F
1	Last Name	First Name	SS#	Job Code	Salary	Location
2	Larson	Mary	543-98-9876	23	$12,000	2
3	Campbell	David	213-76-9874	23	$23,000	10
4	Campbell	Keith	569-89-7654	12	$32,000	2
5	Stephens	Tom	219-78-8954	15	$17,800	2
6	Caldor	Larry	459-34-0921	23	$32,500	4
7	Lightnor	Peggy	560-55-4311	14	$23,500	10
8	McCartin	John	817-66-1212	15	$54,600	2
9	Justof	Jack	431-78-9963	17	$41,200	4
10	Patterson	Lyle	212-11-9090	12	$21,500	10
11	Miller	Lisa	214-89-6756	23	$18,700	2
12	Hawkins	Mark	215-67-8973	21	$19,500	2
13	Hartwick	Eileen	313-78-9090	15	$31,450	4
14	Smythe	George	560-90-8645	15	$65,000	4
15	Wilkes	Caitlin	124-67-7432	17	$15,500	2
16	Deaver	Ken	198-98-6750	23	$24,600	10
17	Kaylor	Sally	312-45-9862	12	$32,900	10
18	Parker	Dee	659-11-3452	14	$19,800	4
19	Preverson	Gary	670-90-1121	21	$27,600	4
20	Samuelson	Paul	219-89-7080	23	$28,900	2

```
20-Apr-92  11:17 AM                                                 NUM
```

Figure 10-7.   An employee database

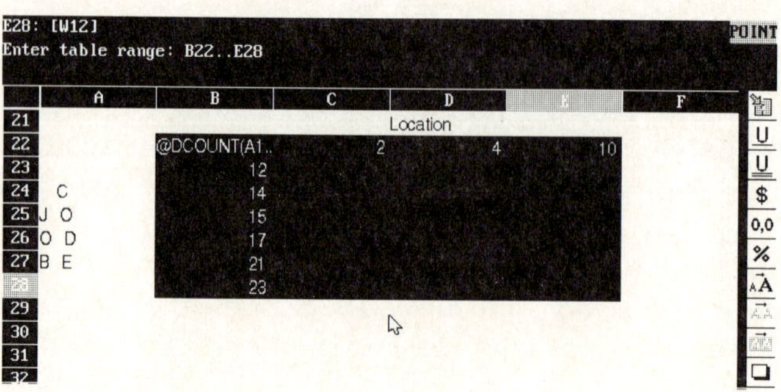

Figure 10-8.   The table range selected

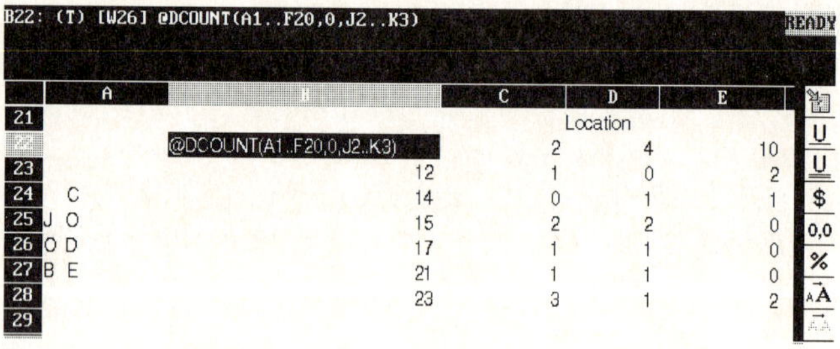

Figure 10-9.   A table created using database tables

Regression Analysis

The /Data Regression command is used to perform a simple regression with one independent variable or a multiple regression with as many as 16 independent variables. You can have up to 8,192 *observations*, or values, for each of your variables. All variables must have the same number of observations, however; you cannot have 8,192 values for one independent variable and 50 values for the dependent variable or another independent variable.

The purpose of this statistical technique is to determine whether changes in the independent variables can be used to predict changes in the dependent variable. This potential interrelationship is described quantitatively with *regression analysis*. Details of the theory behind regression analysis can be found in any business statistics book.

The first step in using regression analysis is recording the values for the dependent and independent variables in columns on your worksheet. Figure 10-10 shows the dependent variable—the sales of Product A—in column A. You can use regression

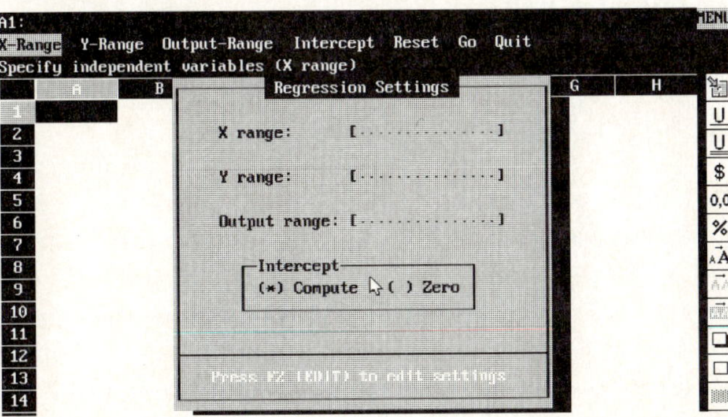

Figure 10-10.   *Regression variables*

analysis to see whether the independent variables for which you have historic data for the same period had an impact on the sales figures for the period. If these variables do seem to have a relationship to the values for sales and you know the values for the other independent variables during the future periods, you may be able to predict sales for future periods.

Suppose the two independent variables selected are disposable income and advertising expense. Column B is Disposable Income, and column C is Advertising Expense.

You are now ready to enter **/Data Regression.** When you do, the following menu and dialog box are displayed.

You must make a number of selections from this menu or dialog box. These are summarized for you in the box called "Creating a Regression Analysis." Your first step is to select the independent variables with the X-Range option. You can specify up to 16 columns of values, with as many as 8,192 total entries in the columns. This example uses B3..C10. You can use a range name, range address, or the pointing method to inform 1-2-3 of your choice.

Creating a Regression Analysis

These steps are required to create a regression analysis:

1. Enter values for the dependent and independent variables in worksheet columns.

2. Enter **/Data Regression**.

3. Choose the X-Range option to select the range containing the independent variables.

4. Choose the Y-Range option to select the column containing the dependent variable.

5. Choose an output range of nine rows and at least four columns. The number of columns should be equal to the number of independent variables plus two.

6. Select the Intercept option and choose Zero for a zero intercept, or select Compute if you want 1-2-3 to compute the intercept. If you have not previously done a regression with a zero intercept during the current session and want the intercept to be computed, you can omit this entry because Compute is the default.

7. Choose Go to create the regression output.

Your next selection is Y-Range. This selection, used to specify the dependent variable, is A3..A10 in this example. This can be specified by entering a range name or cell addresses, or by pointing.

Output-Range is your third selection. You can specify the upper-left cell in the range or the complete range. If you choose to explicitly specify the range, keep in mind that it must be at least nine rows from top to bottom and a minimum of four columns wide—two columns wider than the number of independent variables. If you choose to specify only the left corner, be sure that the space under and to the right of that cell is free, or 1-2-3 overwrites existing data with your regression results. Chose A21 for this example.

The fourth menu choice is Intercept. If you want 1-2-3 to compute the Y-intercept, you can leave this choice blank, since Compute is the default. If you want the intercept set to 0, select Zero.

Once the preliminary setup is finished, enter Go to have 1-2-3 tabulate the regression statistics. The result of the regression for our two variables when 1-2-3 computes the intercept is shown in Figure 10-11. After your analysis is finished, you can use the Reset option to remove previous settings for the command. The Quit option allows you to exit the Data Regression menu.

In general, the higher the R value, the greater the correlation, although you will want to be aware of the number of observations and the degrees of freedom when determining the reliability of your results. All this is explained in more detail in a book on statistics. The results shown in this example include a computed intercept of –60,493.6; a standard error of the estimated Y values; R squared (if you want to know what R is, use @SQRT with R squared as the argument); the number of observations for your variables; the coefficients or slopes for the independent variables; and the standard error for the X coefficients.

You can use the same variable values to do two simple regressions. The variable with the highest R-squared value has the closest relationship to the dependent variable. Figure 10-12 presents two regression output areas. The upper regression output is for disposable income, and the lower regression output is for advertising dollars. The R-squared value for disposable income is higher, which indicates that disposable income is a better predictor of sales than advertising dollars. Since the R-squared value in Figure 10-11 is higher than either output in Figure 10-12, you can assume that both variables together are stronger predictors than either one individually.

You can also use the regression output to help you determine estimated Y values and the best fitting regression line. The formula you would use to estimate the Y values is as follows:

Constant + Coefficient of X1 * X1 + Coefficient of X2 * X2

You can use this formula to project sales values, assuming historical relationships between variables remain the same.

```
A23: [W11] 'Std Err of Y Est                                      READY
```

	A	B	C	D	E	F	G
21		Regression Output:					
22	Constant			−60493.6			
23	Std Err of Y Est			13290.53			
24	R Squared			0.949809			
25	No. of Observations			8			
26	Degrees of Freedom			5			
27							
28	X Coefficient(s)		0.002092	12.75260			
29	Std Err of Coef.		0.000533	5.102853			
30							
31							
32							

Figure 10-11.   *Multiple-regression analysis*

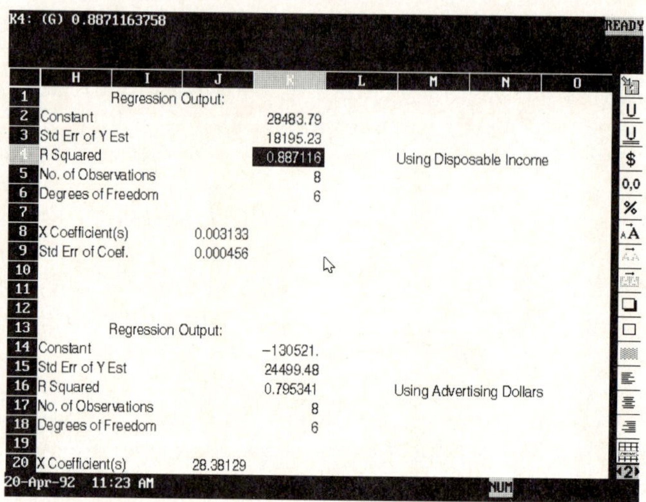

Figure 10-12.   Two simple regression analyses

Frequency Distribution

A *frequency distribution* allows you to count the number of values that fall within specific categories. With the /Data Distribution command features that 1-2-3 provides, you can set up whatever intervals or bins for categorizing your data you want. 1-2-3 will then count the number of entries that fall within each of these intervals.

The frequency distribution table is set up prior to using the command by placing the categories in a location where the column to the right of the categories and the table cells below the last interval are blank. The two cells at the bottom of the table location must be blank to record frequencies greater than the largest specified frequency. All category entries must be numeric and in ascending sequence.

When you enter /**Data Distribution** and tell 1-2-3 the locations of both the data to be categorized and the frequency table, 1-2-3 places each data entry within the range you selected into the smallest category that is equal to or greater than the value in your data. In other words, it adds 1 to the frequency count for that bin. With bin values of 3, 7, and 10, a value of 4 would be counted in bin 7. Each time a value is counted for a category, it increments that category's counter by 1. 1-2-3 ignores labels and cells that are empty. Cells containing @ERR are counted in the last bin, and cells containing @NA are counted in the first bin.

Figure 10-13 is a worksheet that contains commission data in C3..C20. The categories for the frequency count are located in E3..E13. These are arbitrary settings and could have been any set of ascending numbers. The area to the right of these categories is blank, as are cells E14 and F14, which are immediately below the category area. The /Data Distribution command has already been entered, and cells C3..C20 are highlighted in response to 1-2-3's prompt for the range of values

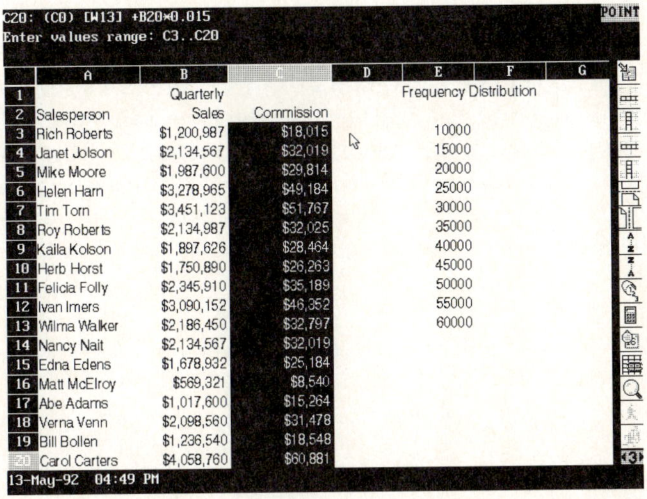

```
C20: (C0) [W13] +B20*0.015                                      POINT
Enter values range: C3..C20
```

	A	B	C	D	E	F	G
1		Quarterly			Frequency Distribution		
2	Salesperson	Sales	Commission				
3	Rich Roberts	$1,200,987	$18,015		10000		
4	Janet Jolson	$2,134,567	$32,019		15000		
5	Mike Moore	$1,987,600	$29,814		20000		
6	Helen Harn	$3,278,965	$49,184		25000		
7	Tim Torn	$3,451,123	$51,767		30000		
8	Roy Roberts	$2,134,987	$32,025		35000		
9	Kaila Kolson	$1,897,626	$28,464		40000		
10	Herb Horst	$1,750,890	$26,263		45000		
11	Felicia Folly	$2,345,910	$35,189		50000		
12	Ivan Imers	$3,090,152	$46,352		55000		
13	Wilma Walker	$2,186,450	$32,797		60000		
14	Nancy Nait	$2,134,567	$32,019				
15	Edna Edens	$1,678,932	$25,184				
16	Matt McElroy	$569,321	$8,540				
17	Abe Adams	$1,017,600	$15,264				
18	Verna Venn	$2,098,560	$31,478				
19	Bill Bollen	$1,236,540	$18,548				
20	Carol Carters	$4,058,760	$60,881				

```
13-May-92  04:49 PM
```

Figure 10-13.   *Commission data*

requiring categorization. When you press ENTER, 1-2-3 prompts you for the location
of the frequency table or bin range. This is E3..F13. You may enter just the column
bin values or the entire table area as your range. Press ENTER, and the completed
table in Figure 10-14 appears. You can interpret the first entry in the table as meaning

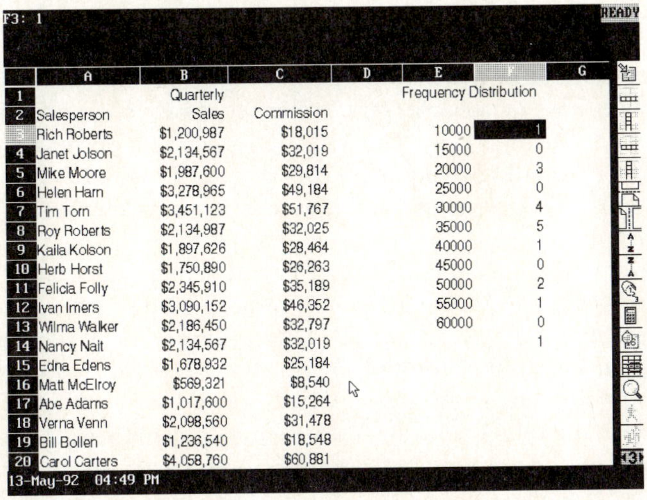

```
F3: 1                                                           READY
```

	A	B	C	D	E	F	G
1		Quarterly			Frequency Distribution		
2	Salesperson	Sales	Commission				
3	Rich Roberts	$1,200,987	$18,015		10000	1	
4	Janet Jolson	$2,134,567	$32,019		15000	0	
5	Mike Moore	$1,987,600	$29,814		20000	3	
6	Helen Harn	$3,278,965	$49,184		25000	0	
7	Tim Torn	$3,451,123	$51,767		30000	4	
8	Roy Roberts	$2,134,987	$32,025		35000	5	
9	Kaila Kolson	$1,897,626	$28,464		40000	1	
10	Herb Horst	$1,750,890	$26,263		45000	0	
11	Felicia Folly	$2,345,910	$35,189		50000	2	
12	Ivan Imers	$3,090,152	$46,352		55000	1	
13	Wilma Walker	$2,186,450	$32,797		60000	0	
14	Nancy Nait	$2,134,567	$32,019			1	
15	Edna Edens	$1,678,932	$25,184				
16	Matt McElroy	$569,321	$8,540				
17	Abe Adams	$1,017,600	$15,264				
18	Verna Venn	$2,098,560	$31,478				
19	Bill Bollen	$1,236,540	$18,548				
20	Carol Carters	$4,058,760	$60,881				

```
13-May-92  04:49 PM
```

Figure 10-14.   *Frequency output*

that there was one entry less than or equal to 10,000. The last 1, in F14, says that there was one entry greater than the largest bin of 60,000.

/Data Distribution provides a quick way to condense data. It is ideal when you want an overall picture of the data within a category. You can also show the result of a frequency distribution in a bar chart or line graph very effectively.

Frequency distribution can be performed for a category of numeric values or on the results of a formula calculation like the one found in this example. The frequency count is not updated as changes occur in the data that was categorized, however. If the data is changed, /Data Distribution must be executed again to update the frequency table.

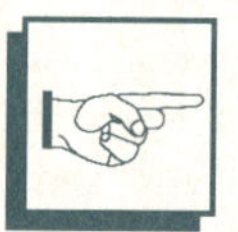

If the bins are the same interval apart, use /Data Fill to quickly create the bins the /Data Distribution command uses.

Matrix Arithmetic

Matrices can be used to solve problems of econometric modeling, market share, and population study. 1-2-3 offers both matrix multiplication and matrix inversion options. The word *matrix* indicates a tabular arrangement of data—something that is quite easy to arrange on a worksheet. Both matrix options allow you to perform sophisticated calculations on the data in these tabular arrangements, without the need for complicated formulas. Although many of the mathematical applications are beyond the scope of this book, two different examples are presented. Thus if matrix algebra is a requirement of your application, you should know how to invoke these capabilities from 1-2-3.

Matrix Multiplication

One of the applications of matrix multiplication is to streamline formulas in which you must multiply a set of variables by another set of variables and add the result of each multiplication together. To illustrate this type of application, consider four different products for which you are trying a number of advertising spots. Each advertising option has a price, and varying numbers of ads are placed for each of the products in various time slots.

Using conventional formulas, determining the total advertising cost for one product would involve multiplying the cost of advertising in time slot 1 times the number of these slots that you purchased. This process must be repeated for each of the advertising slots, each time multiplying the number of slots for the product times the cost of advertising once in that slot. When the cost for each advertising slot has been determined, the values are added together to determine a total advertising cost for the first product. This must be repeated for each of the products. This is a cumbersome process, even when the number of products and potential advertising slots are small.

Matrix multiplication can provide a solution if you can construct your problem according to the rules that matrix operations must follow. After reviewing the rules, you have an opportunity to see them applied to the advertising problem just outlined.

Matrix Multiplication Rules

There are a few rules of matrix multiplication that you must follow. The restrictions are a combination of matrix algebra rules and the limitations of matrix use in 1-2-3.

- Matrix multiplication involves multiplying the values in one matrix by the values in a second matrix. The order in which the multiplication is expressed is critical. Multiplying matrix A by matrix B is not equivalent to multiplying matrix B by matrix A.

- Matrix order is determined by the number of rows and columns in the tabular arrangement of the matrix entries. A matrix with x rows and y columns is an x-by-y matrix. When matrices are multiplied, the number of columns (y) for the first matrix must be equal to the number of rows in the second matrix (x). The easiest way to test this rule is to write the order of the matrices next to each other, as in 5-by-4 and 4-by-6. When the two inner numbers are the same, as in this example, the matrices are compatible and can be multiplied. Rewriting this as 4-by-6 and 5-by-4 produces a set of matrices that are not compatible, which demonstrates that the order in which the two matrices are multiplied is critical.

- The maximum size matrix that 1-2-3 can multiply is 90-by-90.

- Matrices cannot have blank cells and must have a zero inserted in any cell that is blank before you invoke the matrix command.

Entering the Advertising Matrix

In the advertising problem, there are four different products and five different advertising spots. The number of advertising spots for each product is arranged in a 4-by-5 matrix in B11..F14 of the worksheet shown in Figure 10-15. The costs of the spots are arranged in a 5-by-1 matrix in A2..A6. In order for the two matrices to be compatible, the data must be arranged in a 5-by-1 matrix rather than a 1-by-5 matrix. It is expected that results will be stored in B17..B20, and appropriate labels are entered around the worksheet to label all the entries.

The /Data Matrix Multiply command is invoked and the first matrix is highlighted, as shown in Figure 10-15. The next prompt is for the second matrix in A2..A6. Finally, the /Data Matrix Multiply command prompts for the output range. Select B14 and 1-2-3 will use this cell for the first cell of the output range. The results are

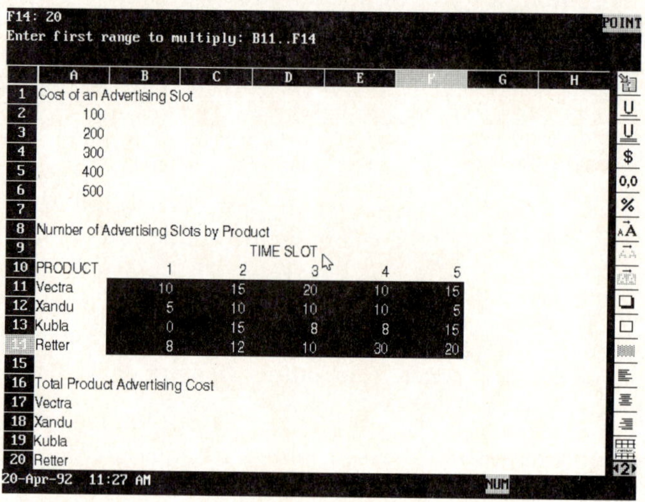

Figure 10-15.   *Highlighting matrix 1*

placed in B17..B20, as shown in Figure 10-16. The figure 21,500 represents the total advertising done for the Vectra product. It is obtained when the matrix operation

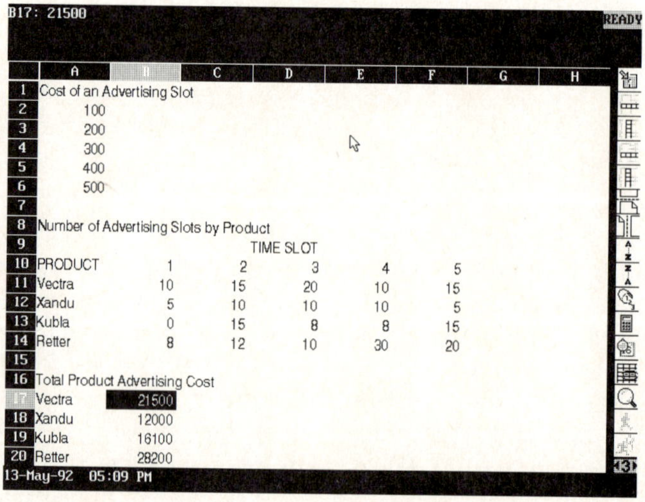

Figure 10-16.   *The result of using /Data Matrix Multiply in B17..B20*

multiplies B11*A2, C11*A3, D11*A4, E11*A5, and F11*A6 and then adds each of these products together. A similar process occurs for Xandu, Kubla, and Retter. All this is accomplished without the need for writing a formula.

Matrix multiplication is quite an operation and can be a real time-saver if it fits your application. One drawback is that the results are not automatically updated when a value in either matrix is changed. To do this updating, you would have to execute /Data Matrix Multiply again. A second potential drawback is that matrices are more difficult to document than formulas and understood less than formulas by most business users. Despite the drawbacks, matrices are a great tool to have for many applications.

Matrix Inversion

Matrix inversion is more difficult, but its potential is even greater. The mathematical concepts behind it are difficult to explain, but in essence they involve the creation of a matrix that is multiplied by your original matrix, resulting in an identity matrix.

In an *identity matrix* all the elements are 0, except one element in each row, which is a 1. The 1 is in a different location in each row. It is easy to remember the location of the 1 for each row, since it is a location identified by the row number. That is, in row 1 the 1 will be in element one, in row 2 the 1 will be in the second element, and so on. You can only invert *square matrices,* which have the same number of columns and rows. 1-2-3 lets you invert matrices up to 90-by-90.

If all this seems confusing, don't worry. You don't really have to understand it all to use the concept. A traditional application for matrix multiplication also uses matrix inversion. It is the same product-mix problem that you solved so often in college algebra. Seeing the solution probably makes you wish you had a copy of 1-2-3 during your college algebra days, when you were trying to solve these with simultaneous equations.

Product-mix problems come in all flavors. Normally there is a limited amount of certain resources, and you have to decide how much of each product to produce. In the sample problem, shown in Figure 10-17, you must determine how much Green Slime and Red Goo to produce. Green Slime requires 2 units of goop and 6 units of gunk. Red Goo takes 8 units of goop and 5 units of gunk. There are 50 units of goop available and 100 units of gunk. The matrix operations allow you to optimize your use of these two raw materials.

First, enter the data of Green Slime and Red Goo in a 2-by-2 matrix. Invert this matrix to create another 2-by-2 matrix to be used in the solution. Store the original matrix in C3..D4, invoke /**Data Matrix Invert**, and highlight this area. Use A7..B8 for the output.

Multiply the resulting 2-by-2 inverted matrix by a 2-by-1 matrix, G3..G4 which contains the available units of each resource. The result is a new matrix, which is stored in A11..A12 and contains the optimal production for each of the products.

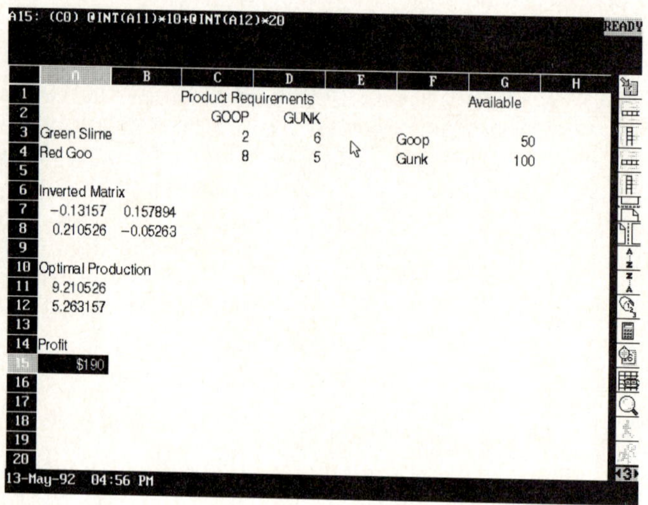

Figure 10-17.   A matrix inversion solving simultaneous equations

Since the profit from Green Slime is $10 a unit and the profit from Red Goo is $20 a unit, multiply the whole units produced for each product by respective unit profit figures. Use the @INT function to access the whole units for the final formula, which is placed in A15. All of the arbitrary locations used in this example are shown in Figure 10-17, which includes the results.

If you are interested in learning more about applications of matrix inversion, look for a reference on linear programming. If you are currently using linear programming, you will be delighted to have these handy techniques incorporated into 1-2-3's features. Even if you currently don't need this type of problem-solving tool, keep it in mind in case such a need arises later.

Splitting Long Labels into Individual Cell Entries

The /File Import command can be used to bring information from an ASCII text file into your 1-2-3 worksheet, as described in Chapter 8. However, it imports this information as a column of long labels, which may not be what you want. Fortunately, the /Data Parse command allows you to split these long labels into various components. These individual pieces can be labels, numbers, or serial time or date numbers.

Using /Data Parse is a multistep process. The steps are summarized for you in the box called "Splitting Text Entries into Cell Values." The options in the /Data Parse submenu and dialog box are as follows:

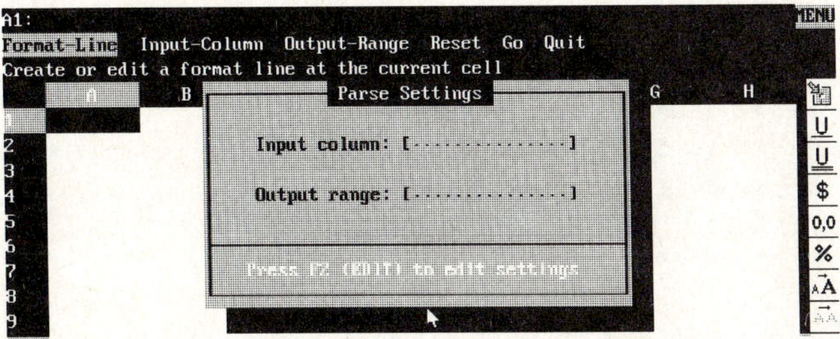

To use /Data Parse, place your cell pointer on the first cell in the column that needs to be parsed and enter /**Data Parse**. Releases 2.2 and above display a dialog box for the entry of information regarding the location of the Input-Column and Output-Range. When the command options are presented, select Format-Line and choose Create from its submenu. 1-2-3 then inserts a blank row above your cell pointer and creates a format line that shows how it splits the label into component pieces.

The characters used in the Format line are as follows:

D   Marks the first character of a date block.

L   Marks the first character of a label block.

S   Marks the first character of a block to be skipped during the parse operation. This character is never generated by 1-2-3, but you can enter it manually through the Edit option.

T   Marks the first character of a time block.

V   Marks the first character of a value block.

>   Indicates that the block started by the letter that precedes this character is continued. The entry that began with the letter continues to be placed in one worksheet cell until a skip or another letter is encountered.

*   Represents a blank space immediately below the character. This position can become part of the block that precedes it.

The pattern established in the Format line is followed in the parsing operation to determine where to split the labels and what type of data is needed for each block. Although you can generate a Format line in multiple locations within your column of labels, you need some consistency in the format of the column for this command to be useful.

If you are not pleased with the Format line generated by 1-2-3, you can edit it with /Data Parse Format-Line Edit. You can add, replace, or delete any part of the Format line after selecting the Edit option. To temporarily remove the dialog box from the screen for a closer look at the top lines of data, use the F6 (WINDOW) key.

Once the format has been established, the remaining steps for using /Data Parse are quite easy. Choose Input-Column, and then either highlight the cells to be parsed

Splitting Text Entries into Cell Values

After importing text into your worksheet, you may need to use /Data Parse to split long labels into individual entries. Follow these steps after using /File Import:

1. Move your cell pointer to the top of the column containing the labels to be parsed, and enter /**Data Parse**.

2. Choose the Format-Line option, and then Create to have 1-2-3 generate a suggested Format line.

3. If the generated Format line requires changes, choose Format-Line Edit and make your changes.

4. Select the Input-Column option and choose the column of labels to be altered; include the Format line in the range.

5. Select the Output-Range option, and choose the top left cell in a blank area large enough to hold the output or else specify a range large enough to hold each of the parsed entries. The width of this area is determined by the number of individual fields in the output. The length is the same as the number of labels being parsed.

6. Select Go.

or type in the address of this column of label entries. Be sure to include the Format line in the range. Then select Output-Range and enter the upper-left cell or the complete range of cells required. If you choose to supply only the upper-left cell, 1-2-3 will determine the space requirements of the output range, overwriting data if necessary. With the first three menu options set, choose Go to have 1-2-3 restructure the long labels into individual cell entries according to the pattern established by the Format line.

The other two options in the Parse menu are Reset and Quit. Reset eliminates any settings you have established for the parsing operation. Quit removes the sticky Parse menu and returns you to READY mode. (Pressing ESC does the same thing.)

A few examples can help clarify the workings of /Data Parse. In this illustration, the entries in A1..A3 are long labels:

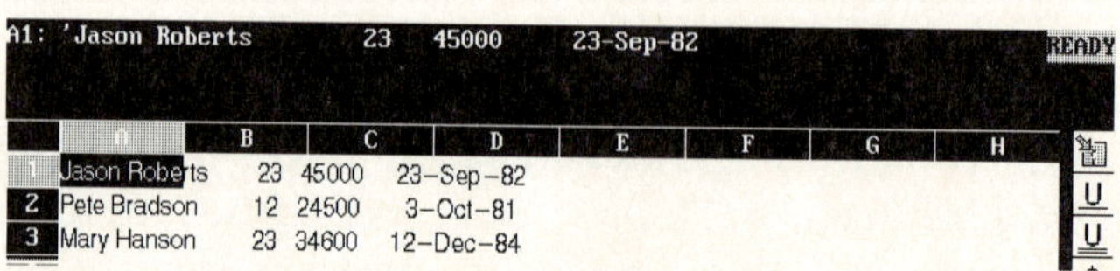

Although at first glance the components of each line appear to be in separate cells, the control panel shows that each line is in fact a single label entry. The steps to parse these labels follow:

1. Move the cell pointer to A1 and enter **/Data Parse Format-Line Create**. 1-2-3 generates a Format line like the one in Figure 10-18. Notice that first names and last names have been treated as separate entries because of the space between them.

2. Choose Input-Column and select A1..A4.

3. To duplicate our example, choose A9 as Output-Range.

4. Select Go, and the output shown in Figure 10-19 is produced.

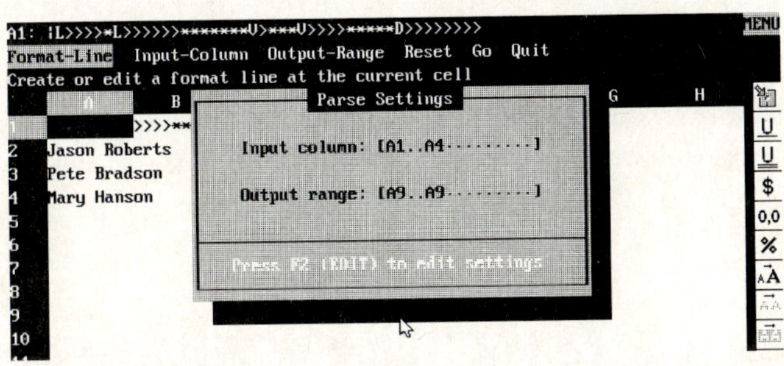

Figure 10-18.   *Caption goes here.*

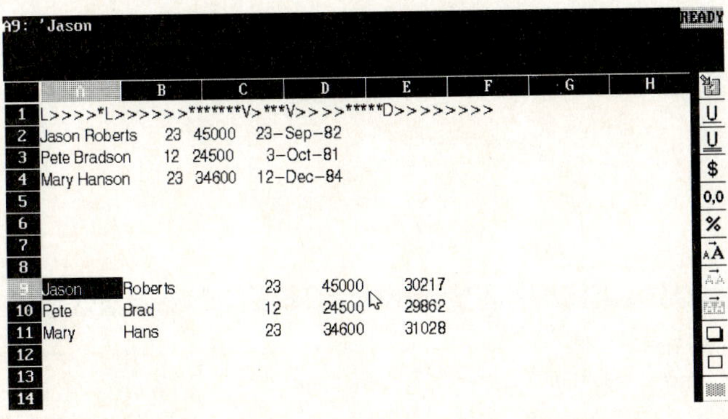

Figure 10-19.   *The output from /Data Parse*

If you do not want the two name components treated as separate entries, choose Format-Line Edit. Then change the Format line to agree with the one in Figure 10-20, and select Go. Notice that the entry "Jason Roberts" is now placed in A9. The display is initially truncated due to the column width, but you can change this easily with /Worksheet Column Set-Width.

Sequencing Worksheet Data

Although the /Data Sort commands were designed primarily for use in the data management environment, they can sometimes be used successfully when your worksheet contains data used solely for calculations. In this section you can look at examples of a successful and an unsuccessful sort for a worksheet application. If you are not familiar with the /Data Sort command, review its features as described in Chapter 9 before trying it with your worksheet data.

Before using /Data Sort, you must assess whether your worksheet is organized so that sorting the data does not cause problems with your formulas. It would be advisable to save your worksheet to disk prior to the sort, just in case you make a mistake and sort formulas that cannot be shuffled without causing an error. Naturally, if you notice the problem right away, ALT-F4 (UNDO) is the easiest solution. If you

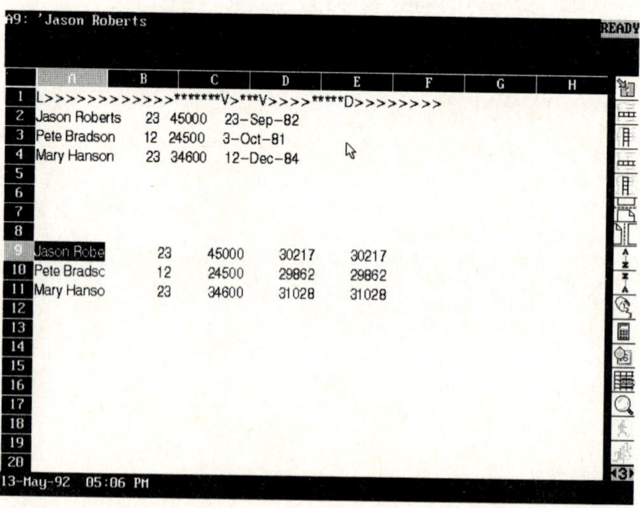

Figure 10-20.   *The output after editing Format line*

enter a command or two before you notice the problem, you will appreciate the backup copy you saved to disk.

As a worksheet is sorted, the rows of your model are placed in a different order. As long as the formulas within each row reference only other variables in that row, the sort does not cause a problem. When formula references point outside the row, however, errors can occur.

Look at the inventory calculations for six months in Figure 10-21; you can see that for each month the new beginning inventory is equal to the inventory at the end of the last period. To obtain the beginning inventory figures, the formula in each month references the appropriate address in the previous month (that is, the prior line of the model). These formulas are shown in Figure 10-22. If you wanted to sequence the data by the sales figure rather than by month, you might decide to try the /Data Sort command. You would use /Data Sort Data-Range and then specify the range as A2..E7. You would select a primary key of D2 (Sales) and then choose Go. The results shown in Figure 10-23 indicate a problem with the references to previous lines. The

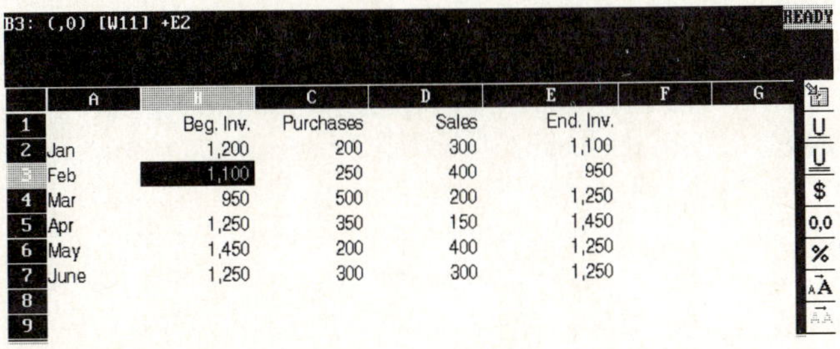

Figure 10-21.   *An inventory database*

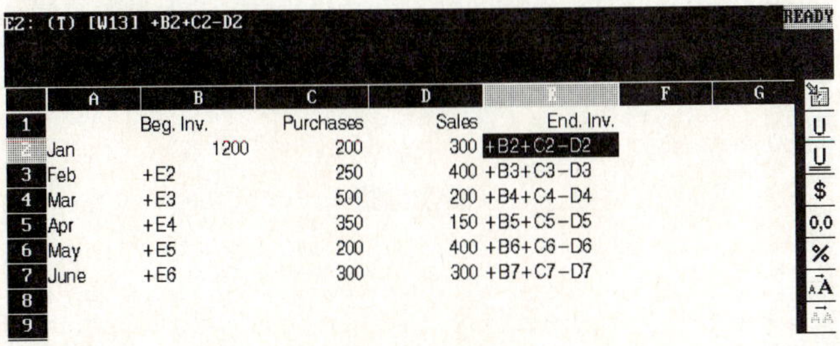

Figure 10-22.   *The text of the inventory database*

```
E2: (,0) [W13] +B2+C2-D2                                    READY
       A          B          C          D          E        F     G
 1              Beg. Inv.  Purchases      Sales   End. Inv.
 2  May       End. Inv.       200          400       (200)
 3  Feb          (200)        250          400       (350)
 4  Jan         1,200         200          300       1,100
 5  June        1,100         300          300       1,100
 6  Mar         1,100         500          200       1,400
 7  Apr         1,400         350          150       1,600
 8
 9
```

Figure 10-23.   *The sorted inventory database*

reason the errors are confined to the top rows is that the original 1200 entry for January is a numeric constant rather than a reference to a previous line.

To avoid this problem, you have two options for sorting the original inventory data. First, you can use /Range Value to freeze the values in column B before sorting. Your other option is to use /File Extract Values to save the portion you want to sort as another file that can be retrieved and sorted separately.

Figure 10-24 shows another worksheet that, at first glance, may appear to have the same kind of problem with the formula in E6. The formula references a table located outside the row of the worksheet. Notice, however, that the formula references the table with absolute addresses. References that are absolute do not change when the sort is performed, so these rows can be sorted without being changed. When /Data Sort is entered and a data range of B6..I13 is specified with a primary key of B6 for location, the results shown in Figure 10-25 are produced.

```
E6: (C2) [W11] @VLOOKUP(B6,$J$7..$L$9,1)*D6                        READY
       A        B        C        D          E          F          G          H
 1
 2
 3            LODGING  TRAVEL       #      LODGING/                          TOTAL
 4  LOCATION  CLASS     COST     TRIPS      MEALS    AIRFARE      MISC.       COST
 5
 6  Dallas       1        2        12    $1,500.00  $3,600.00    $420.00   $5,520.00
 7  Akron        2        2         2      $300.00    $600.00     $90.00     $990.00
 8  Chicago      3        1         3      $525.00    $750.00    $150.00   $1,425.00
 9  Denver       2        2        12    $1,800.00  $3,600.00    $540.00   $5,940.00
10  Phoenix      2        3         5      $750.00  $1,750.00    $225.00   $2,725.00
11  Atlanta      2        2         4      $600.00  $1,200.00    $180.00   $1,980.00
12  New York     3        2         6    $1,050.00  $1,800.00    $300.00   $3,150.00
13  Portland     2        4         3      $450.00  $1,500.00    $135.00   $2,085.00
14
15
```

Figure 10-24.   *A travel worksheet*

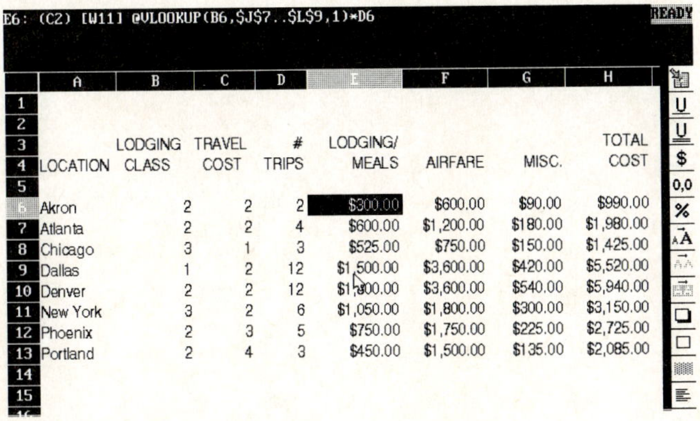

```
E6:  (C2) [W11] @VLOOKUP(B6,$J$7..$L$9,1)*D6                        READY
```

	A	B	C	D	E	F	G	H
1								
2								
3		LODGING	TRAVEL	#	LODGING/			TOTAL
4	LOCATION	CLASS	COST	TRIPS	MEALS	AIRFARE	MISC.	COST
5								
6	Akron	2	2	2	$300.00	$600.00	$90.00	$990.00
7	Atlanta	2	2	4	$600.00	$1,200.00	$180.00	$1,980.00
8	Chicago	3	1	3	$525.00	$750.00	$150.00	$1,425.00
9	Dallas	1	2	12	$1,500.00	$3,600.00	$420.00	$5,520.00
10	Denver	2	2	12	$1,800.00	$3,600.00	$540.00	$5,940.00
11	New York	3	2	6	$1,050.00	$1,800.00	$300.00	$3,150.00
12	Phoenix	2	3	5	$750.00	$1,750.00	$225.00	$2,725.00
13	Portland	2	4	3	$450.00	$1,500.00	$135.00	$2,085.00
14								
15								

Figure 10-25.   *The sorted travel worksheet*

Another situation to watch for is data placed at the side of the data range, like a new field for the database. This data is not moved, since /Data Sort moves only the specified data range.

DATA ANALYSIS

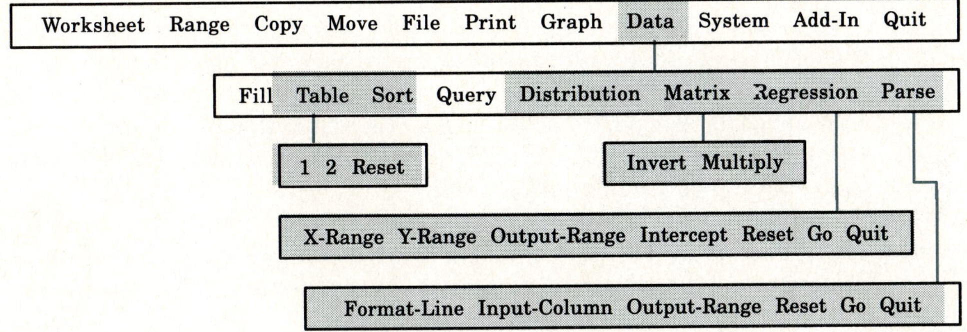

/Data Distribution

Description

The /Data Distribution command permits you to create a frequency distribution table from the values in a range on your worksheet. This table tells you how many values in the range fall within each of the intervals you establish. An area of an active worksheet must be set aside to record the frequency intervals or bins against which your data is analyzed. The frequency for each bin is placed in an adjacent column.

Using the /Data Distribution command requires some preliminary work. First, you must select a location on your worksheet for the bins. 1-2-3 uses the column to the right of the bins for the frequency numbers for each interval, and it uses the row immediately below the last bin for a count of all the values that exceed the last bin value. Second, the values you place in the bins must be in ascending sequence from the top to the bottom of the column you are using.

Here is an example of the way 1-2-3 assigns values to the bins. If you create bin values of 5, 10, and 20, the first bin contains a count of the values in your list that are less than or equal to 5; the second bin contains a count of values greater than 5 and less than or equal to 10; and the third bin holds values greater than 10 and less than or equal to 20. 1-2-3 creates a fourth bin for a count of all values greater than 20. This command ignores blank cells or cells containing the labels. Cells containing @ERR are counted in the last bin, and cells containing @NA are counted in the first bin.

Once /Data Distribution has classified the values in the specified range, a change in one of the values cannot cause a reclassification. To reclassify data after a change, you must enter **/Data Distribution** again. This time you only have to press ENTER in response to 1-2-3's prompts, since 1-2-3 suggests the same ranges you used previously.

Options

The only options you have with this command are the size of the intervals you enter in the bin range and the number of values in the values range.

/Data Matrix

Description

The /Data Matrix command multiplies and inverts matrices. Matrices are tabular arrangements of data with a number in each cell. They are specified by their size. The number of rows is specified before the number of columns. Thus, a matrix with 5 rows and 6 columns is a 5-by-6 matrix. A square matrix has the same number of rows as it has columns.

With 1-2-3's matrix multiplication and inversion options, you can solve problems relating to market share, projecting receivable aging, inventory control, and other modeling problems for the natural and social sciences. The specifics of the theory behind matrix operations are not examined in this book.

Options

The /Data Matrix command provides options for two algebraic matrix operations: multiplication and inversion.

Multiply   This option multiplies the individual components of two matrices according to the rules for matrix arithmetic. It assumes that only two matrices are multiplied and that the number of columns in one matrix is equal to the number of rows in a second matrix. 1-2-3 can multiply matrices up to 90 rows by 90 columns.

When the Multiply option is chosen, 1-2-3 prompts you for the location of the two matrix ranges. You can type the cell addresses, reference the matrices with range names, or use the pointing method for specifying the ranges. When prompted for the output range, you can choose to enter the complete range or a reference to it, or just enter the upper-left cell.

Invert   This option inverts any square matrix according to the rules for matrix algebra. 1-2-3 prompts you for the range of the matrix to invert and the output range. When prompted for the output range, you can enter the complete range or a reference to it, or just the upper-left cell. 1-2-3 can invert matrices up to 90 rows by 90 columns.

/Data Parse

Description

The /Data Parse command creates shorter, individual field values from the long labels stored in worksheet cells. You must use this command after you use /File Import to bring long labels from text files created by your word processor or other program into a column of cells. This column of long labels is limited to descriptive use or a string formula, unless /Data Parse is used to split the long labels into individual fields. Then you can also use the results in numeric formulas and graphs.

Assuming some consistency in the format of the labels, /Data Parse can divide each label into a row of individual values, including label, value, date, and time entries. 1-2-3 makes a suggestion for splitting the label into its individual components, but you have the option of changing this recommendation.

Options

Format-Line   This is the most important option in the /Data Parse command, since it determines how 1-2-3 splits the long labels into individual cell entries. Format-Line has two options you can use to create a new Format line or edit an existing one.

The Create option under Parse Format-Line creates a Format line above the cell-pointer location at the time you make the selection. To ensure that the Format line is positioned correctly, position your cell pointer in the cell for the first long label in your column to be parsed before entering **/Data Parse Format-Line Create.**

1-2-3 places letters and special symbols in the Format line to present its interpretation of the way the long label should be split. The letters and symbols used are as follows:

D	Marks the first character of a date block.
L	Marks the first character of a label block.
S	Marks the first character of a block that is to be skipped during the parse operation. This character is never generated by 1-2-3, but you can enter it manually through the Format-Line Edit option.
T	Marks the first character of a time block.
V	Marks the first character of a value block.
>	Indicates that the block started by the letter that precedes this character is continued. The entry that began with the letter continues to be placed in one worksheet cell until a skip or another letter is encountered.
*	Represents a blank space immediately below the character. This position can become part of the previous block.

After 1-2-3 creates a Format line, you can use the Format-Line Edit option to make changes in it if you wish. 1-2-3 only lets you enter valid Format line characters.

Input-Column   This is the location for the column of long labels imported from an ASCII text file. The range you specify should include the Format line.

Output-Range   This is the location you want to use for the individual entries generated from the long label. You can enter the upper-left cell in an area of the worksheet large enough for the output. 1-2-3 determines how much space is required and writes over cells containing worksheet data if it needs the space.

Reset   This option eliminates the settings for input or output area, so you can start over.

Go   The Go option tells 1-2-3 that you have created and verified the accuracy of the Format line and have defined the location of the input and output areas. It causes the long labels to be parsed according to the specifications given and returns to the READY mode.

Quit   This option tells 1-2-3 that you want to leave the Data Parse menu without parsing the data.

/Data Regression

Description

The /Data Regression command allows you to perform a statistical analysis to see whether two or more variables are interrelated. This command allows you to use from 1 to 16 independent variables for your regression analysis. It estimates the accuracy with which these independent variables can predict the values of a specified dependent variable.

As an example, your dependent variable may be the sales of hot chocolate at a football concession stand. The outdoor temperature and pregame ticket sales are possible predictors of the number of cups of hot chocolate that might be sold at a game. These two factors are your independent variables. By applying regression analysis to historical data for the three variables, you can determine how effective the independent variables are as predictors of the dependent variable. When the regression analysis has been completed, 1-2-3 displays the number of observations, the Y-intercept or constant, the standard error of estimated Y values and X coefficients, R squared, the X coefficients, and the degrees of freedom.

As with many of the other data commands, using /Data Regression involves a few preliminary steps. Your dependent and independent variable values must be placed in columns on the worksheet. Each column must have the same number of entries, and all of them must contain numeric values. You can have a maximum of 8,192 values; this is one value for each row of the worksheet. After these preliminary steps are completed, use the /Data Regression options to complete your analysis.

Options

The Data Regression submenu has the following options.

X-Range   This is the column or columns (16 maximum) that contain the values for your independent variables. Enter cell addresses or a range name, or point with your cell pointer to highlight the selected area.

Y-Range   This is the column containing the values for your dependent variable. Enter a range name or cell addresses, or point to the selected column.

Output-Range   This is the area that contains the results of the analysis. It must be at least nine rows deep and four columns wide, and it must be at least two columns wider than the number of independent variables you are using. You have the option of specifying the entire range or just the upper-left corner. If you use the latter approach, 1-2-3 decides the size of the area to use for the output of the regression analysis. Any existing data in the cells of the output range is overwritten.

Intercept   This is the Y-intercept. You have the option of having 1-2-3 compute this value or setting it to Zero. Compute is the default setting.

Reset   This option eliminates all settings you have established for /Data Regression.

Go   This option completes the regression analysis after you have chosen X-Range, Y-Range, Output-Range, and Intercept.

Quit   This option exits the Data Regression menu and returns you to READY mode.

/Data Sort

Description

This command allows you to sequence information in worksheet cells. The command is covered fully in Chapter 9, because its primary application is for data management. It is mentioned again here because there are selected instances where it can be used in the worksheet environment. These applications are described in this chapter.

Options

The options for /Data Sort are covered in Chapter 9.

/Data Table 1

Description

The /Data Table 1 command allows you to use different values of a variable in formulas. This command provides a structured "what-if" feature that substitutes various values in your formulas and records the result of each value.

The /Data Table 1 command builds what is called a one-way table. This type of table has one set of input values running down its left side. It can evaluate many formulas.

/Data Table 1 requires that you set up a table area in your worksheet. The purpose of the table is to structure the values that you want to plug into an input cell one by one, while recording the impact of these values on the formulas that are also part of the table. To set up the table, place the input values you want to use in a column in a blank area of your worksheet. The row of formulas you want to have evaluated must begin one row above the first input value and one column to the right. You may place new formulas in these cells, or you may reference other cells in the worksheet that contain the desired formulas. For example, to have a formula in A3 evaluated, enter **+A3** in one of the cells in this formula row. You may also want to format the formula cells as text for documentation purposes.

The two sets of entries just discussed create the framework for the table. The column of value cells forms the left edge of the table, with the last entry determining the bottom edge of the table. The row of formulas forms the top of the table, with the last entry in the row marking the right edge.

After the initial setup, you are ready to respond to 1-2-3's prompts to define the location of your table and the cell you want to reference for input.

Options

After your table is defined, tell 1-2-3 the location you have selected for the table. The best way to do this is to position your cell pointer at the upper-left edge of the table before you enter **/Data Table 1**. The table should be a rectangular area that includes all the formulas and all the values you are concerned with. You can use cell addresses, a range name, or the pointing method to communicate the table location.

Next, 1-2-3 asks you what worksheet cell you want to use as an input cell. This is the cell into which 1-2-3 places the input values from the table column, one by one. Using a given value for the input cell, 1-2-3 evaluates each of the table formulas and places the formula result in the column beneath the formula, on the row for the input value being used.

When 1-2-3 has used each of your values, the table is complete with formula results. Depending on the size of your table, this takes up to several minutes. When 1-2-3 has completed the table, the input cell still has its original value; 1-2-3 makes its substitutions behind the scenes without affecting the cell entry. A change to a value in the input table does not cause the table to recalculate. To get recalculation, you must reuse **/Data Table**, or press F8 (TABLE). If you want to reset the table location and input cell before using the command again, use /Data Table Reset to eliminate your previous settings.

/Data Table 2

Description

The /Data Table 2 command allows you to pick any two cells on the worksheet that contain numeric variable values and set up substitution values for these cells, so that the impact of the changes can be measured in the result of a particular worksheet formula. This feature provides a structured approach to "what-if" analysis, in which 1-2-3 does most of the work.

The /Data Table 2 command produces a table that is similar to a one-way table, except that you can substitute values for two variables at once and evaluate only one formula. It allows you to see whether the formula result is more sensitive to changes in variable 1 or variable 2, which provides an easy-to-use sensitivity analysis feature.

/Data Table 2 requires that you set up a table area in your worksheet. The purpose of the table is to structure the values that you want to plug into the two input cells one by one, while recording the impact of these values on the result of a formula that is also part of the table.

To set up the table, place the input values for the first variable in a column in a blank area of your worksheet. The values for the second variable must begin one row above the first input value and one column to the right; place these values across the row. You can use the /Data Fill command to supply them if the increment between values is evenly spaced.

The formula you want to have evaluated for each value of the input variable is placed in the blank cell at the intersection of the row and column of variable values. You may enter either an actual formula or a reference to a worksheet cell containing a formula. For example, to have a formula in A3 evaluated, enter **+A3** in the formula cell. You may also wish to format the formula cell as text for documentation purposes.

The two sets of entries just discussed create the framework for the table. The column of value cells forms the left edge of the table, with the last entry determining the bottom edge of the table. The row of value entries forms the top of the table, with the last entry in the row marking the right edge. To have 1-2-3 complete the table entries for you, enter /**Data Table 2** and respond to 1-2-3's requests for specifications.

Options

After your table is defined, tell 1-2-3 the location you have selected for the table. To facilitate this process, position your cell pointer at the upper-left edge of the table before entering /**Data Table 2**. The table should be a rectangular area that includes the formula and all the values you are concerned with. You can use cell addresses, a range name, or the pointing method to communicate the table location.

Next, 1-2-3 asks you what worksheet cell you want to use as an input cell for the column of values you entered. This is the cell into which 1-2-3 places the input values from the table column, one by one. 1-2-3 then asks what input cell to use for the row of values. 1-2-3 then evaluates the formula shown at the upper-left corner of the table, using each of the possible value combinations for input cell 1 and input cell 2.

When 1-2-3 uses each of your values, the table is complete with formula results. Depending on the size of your table, this takes up to several minutes. When 1-2-3 has completed the table, the input cell still has its original values; 1-2-3 alters the values of the input cell only internally. A change to a value in the input table does not cause the table to recalculate. To get recalculation, you must reuse /Data Table, or press F8 (TABLE). To reset the table location and input cells before using the command again, use /Data Table Reset to eliminate your previous settings.

/Data Table Reset

Description

The /Data Table Reset command eliminates the settings you have established for the table location and input cell. Since 1-2-3 suggests the previous setting the next time you use the command, Reset is convenient when the next table location or input cell setting is far removed from the last use. If you select /Data Table before canceling your previous settings, you must then press ESC and move your cell pointer to the new location to establish new settings. Once Reset is used, your cell pointer remains in its current location.

Chapter 11

Working with 1-2-3's Graphics Features

The graphics features of 1-2-3 allow you to display your worksheet information in a format that is easy to interpret. Rather than presenting all the specific numbers, graphs summarize the essence of your data, so that you can focus on general patterns and trends. When you notice something that warrants further analysis, you can return to the supporting worksheet numbers and look at them more closely.

1-2-3's graphics features are popular because they do not require that data be reentered. Indeed, you can use data already entered for your worksheet, without any changes at all. Nor do you need to transfer data to another program or learn a new system. 1-2-3's graphics menus are just like the other 1-2-3 menus, so you need only learn a few new 1-2-3 commands in order to use the graphics features. They are an integral part of 1-2-3, available from the main menu. After creating your worksheet model, you simply make a few more menu selections to project the data onto a chart.

If you have a color monitor or a graphics card, you can view your graph or chart on the screen. If you have only a monochrome monitor without a graphics card, you cannot view your graph, but you can create graphs and print them.

This chapter explores the various options available through the /Graph command. It also looks at the PrintGraph program and describes the choices you have after your graphic image is saved and ready to print. The Wysiwyg Add-In that accompanies 1-2-3 lets you insert graphs on the worksheet and print them with other worksheet data. Wysiwyg's Graph features are introduced in this chapter and Wysiwyg is covered in its entirety in Chapter 15. These features include adding a graph to a worksheet range and adding other graphic elements to your graphs.

Creating Graphs

Most of the options you need to create, modify, display, and save graphs are located under the /Graph command, available from 1-2-3's main menu. When you select /Graph, you are presented with a menu that looks like Figure 11-1. The dialog box below the menu contains all of the current graph settings. All the changes that you make in the Graph menu are reflected in the dialog box.

The Type option on the Graph menu presents options for selecting the type of graph you want to generate. The specific data to be shown in your graph is accessed through the X, A through F, and Group options. You can use the Options selections to enhance your graph. Various other selections permit you to view, save, and name your graph.

Selecting a Graph Type

To create a graph for the first time, you must make several menu selections. These specify the type of graph you want to see and tell 1-2-3 which data to show in the graph.

When you select Type from the main Graph menu, 1-2-3 offers a choice of seven different types of graphs. You can easily change from one type of presentation to another by returning to the Type menu and choosing another graph type. In Releases 2.3 and above, you can also change the graph type by selecting one of the option buttons under Type in the Graph Settings dialog box. This flexibility allows you to look at your data in a number of presentation formats and select the one that seems

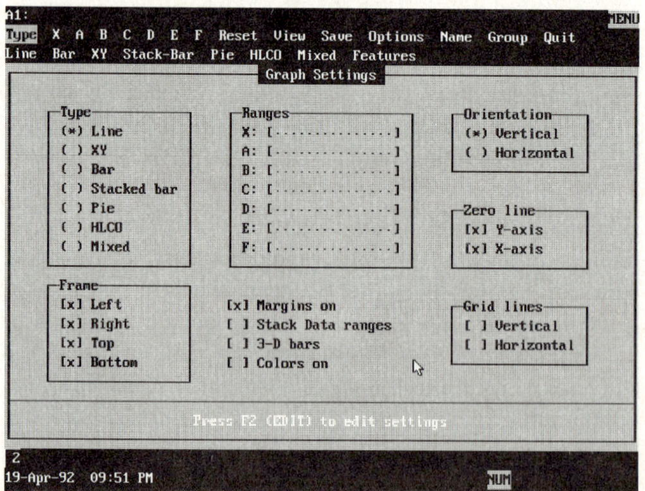

Figure 11-1.   *The Graph menu and dialog box*

to show the data most effectively. If you do not select a graph type, 1-2-3 uses a line graph.

Figures 11-2a through 11-2g present examples of each of the different graph formats. A description of each graph type, along with some suggested uses, is found in the box called "Graph Types for Every Need."

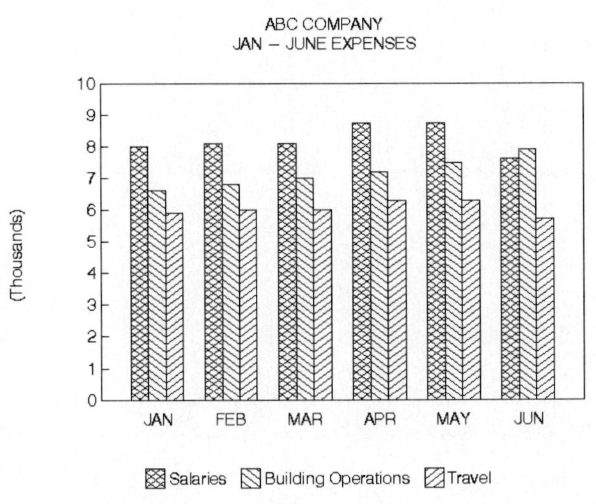

Figure 11-2a.   *A bar graph*

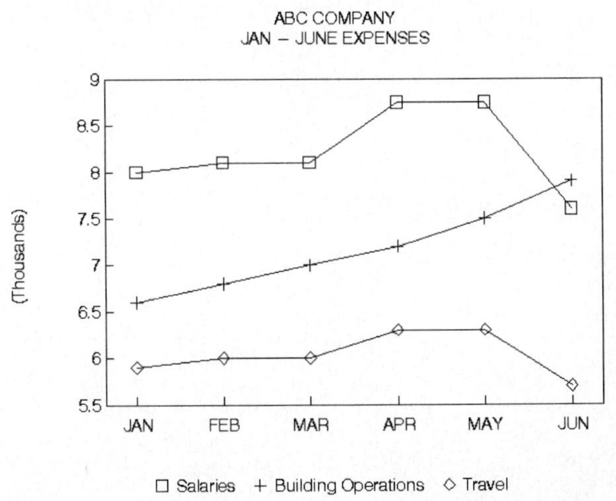

Figure 11-2b.   *A line graph*

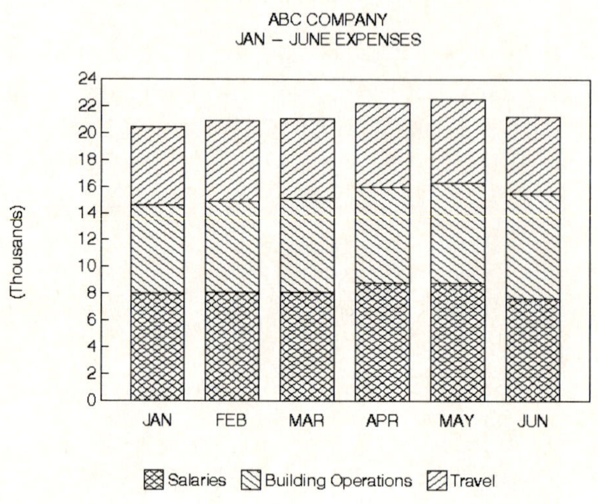

Figure 11-2c.   *A stacked bar graph*

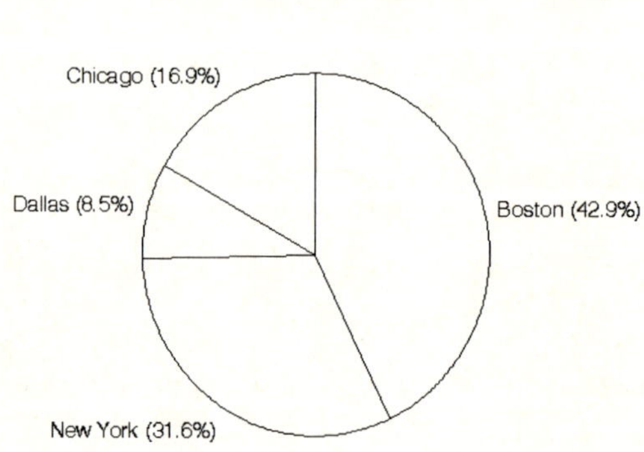

Figure 11-2d.   *A pie chart*

Labeling the X-Axis

After selecting the graph type, you must define the data to be shown on your graph. Use the X option in the main Graph menu to specify a range of cells containing labels

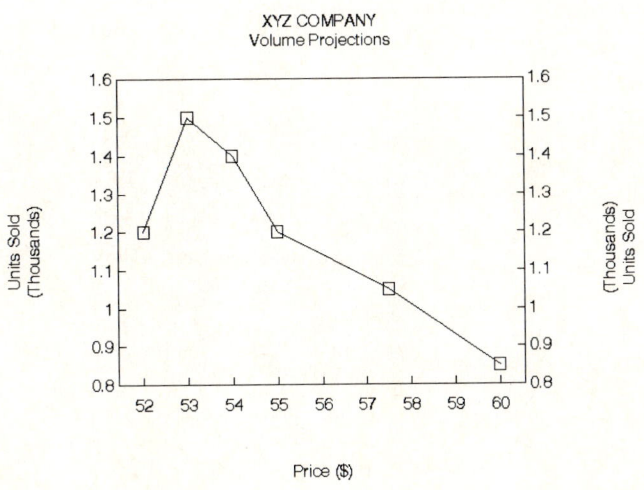

Figure 11-2e. *An XY graph*

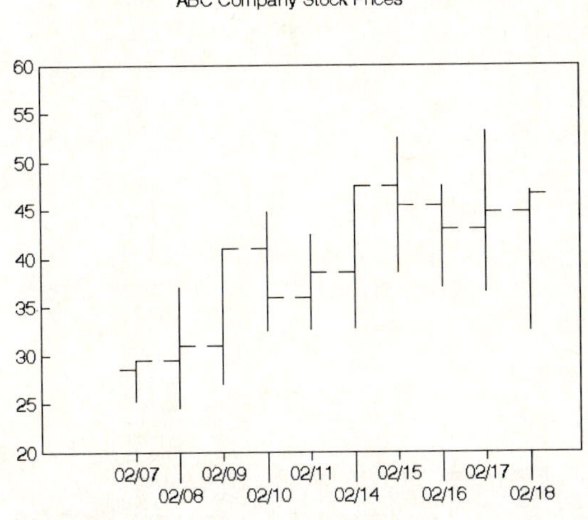

Figure 11-2f. *An HLCO graph*

to be placed along the points on the X-axis or enter a range in the X text box under Ranges in the Graph Settings dialog box. This option works for all graph types except XY and pie charts. The labels may mark the points of the graph for years, months,

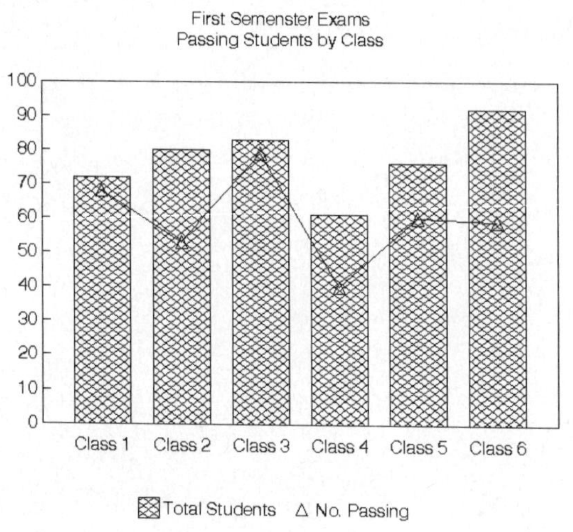

Figure 11-2g.   A mixed graph

or other data values. For example, in Figure 11-3 the cells containing the words "JAN" through "JUNE" were selected as the range after choosing /Graph X. The words in the X range are placed along the X-axis, as shown in Figure 11-4.

For pie charts, the X range labels the sections of the pie. It might list regions, expense categories, or something similar. X range data for a pie chart must be in the same sequence as the data you provide for the A range, which gives the values for the chart.

For XY charts, the X range data is plotted against corresponding Y values provided by the ranges A through F. Again, use /Graph X to specify the range of cells that contains the entries you want to use for the X-axis. For this type of chart, the entries should be values rather than labels.

	JAN	FEB	MAR	APR	MAY	JUNE
Salaries	$8,000	$8,200	$8,200	$8,700	$8,700	$7,500
Building Operations	$6,500	$6,760	$7,030	$7,312	$7,604	$7,908
Travels	$6,000	$6,150	$6,150	$6,525	$6,525	$5,625

Figure 11-3.   ABC Company expenses

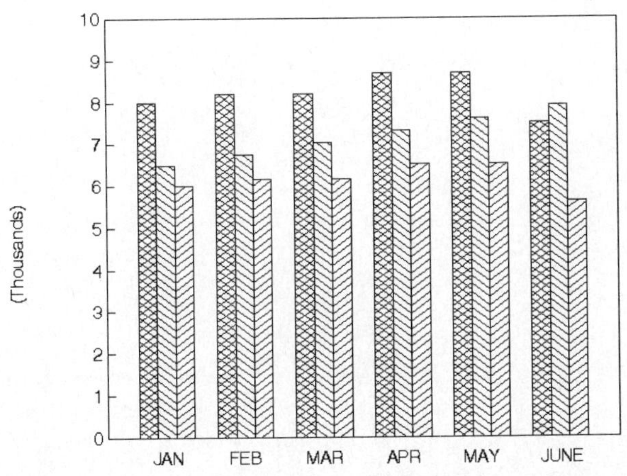

Figure 11-4. *A bar chart showing X range data*

If the range you select for X contains too many characters, 1-2-3 uses two rows, with half of the labels on one row and half on the next row. This creates a display like the one shown here:

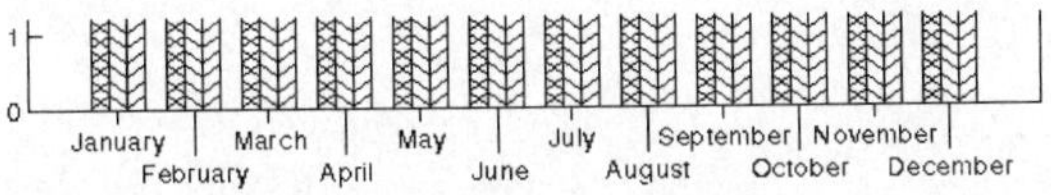

If the X values are too long for two rows, 1-2-3 truncates them if they are labels or displays them as asterisks if they are values. The X-axis can be made easier to read by using fewer or shorter names. You also can use /Graph Options Scale Skip and enter a skip factor that causes 1-2-3 to skip some of the labels in the range. For example, a skip factor of 3 causes every third label in the X range to be used for labeling.

The Y-Axis

In contrast to the X-axis, the Y-axis is labeled automatically once you have selected the data you want to show on your graph. If 1-2-3 needs to represent your data values in thousands or millions to place them on the graph effectively, it makes the conversion and labels the Y-axis appropriately.

Graph Types for Every Need

The variety of graph types provided by 1-2-3 allows you to find a type suitable for presenting almost any kind of data. Here is a description of each type and some suggested uses.

- **Bar**   A bar graph represents the data points in your series with bars of different heights. Although any data can be plotted on a bar graph, it is especially appropriate for comparing the values in several series.

- **Line**   A line graph shows the points of your data range or ranges plotted against the Y-axis. The points may be connected with a line, shown as symbols, or both. The line graph is an excellent choice for plotting trend data over time, such as sales, profit, or expenses.

- **Stacked Bar**   A stacked bar graph places the values in each series on top of each other for any one point on the X-axis. The total height of a bar thus represents the total values in all the series plotted for any given point. A stacked bar graph is an effective presentation vehicle when you wish to see total levels, as well as components levels.

- **Pie**   A pie chart shows one range of values. It represents each value's percentage of the total by the size of the pie wedge assigned to that value. A pie chart effectively shows the relative size of different components. Pie charts are effective for analyzing different kinds of expenses or the contribution to profit from different product lines, for example.

- **XY**   An XY graph plots the values in one series against those in another. An XY graph could be used to plot age against salary, machine repairs by age, or time against temperature, for example.

- **HLCO**   An HLCO chart shows the high, low, close, and open values. For each set of data values for each X-axis value, the HLCO graph has a line from the high to the low value: a projection to the left indicates the open value and one to the right indicates the close value. This graph type is for graphing financial commodities or statistical results.

- **Mixed**   A mixed graph shows up to three data ranges as a bar graph and up to three data ranges as a line graph. Mixed graphs can be used to graph profit from different divisions against sales from different divisions, for example.

Selecting Data for a Graph

1-2-3 permits you to show up to six sets of data values on a graph. A set of data values might represent the sales of a product for a period of months or years, or the number of rejects on a production line for each of the last 16 weeks, to give two examples. Any series of values can be used, as long as they all pertain to the same subject and are organized according to the points labeled on the X-axis. The six different sets of data values are assigned to the A through F series. To expand the two previous examples, the data values might represent sales figures for six different products or production line rejects from six different factories.

To assign a worksheet range to a graph series, select a letter A through F from the Graph menu or select the A through F text box under Ranges in the Graph Settings dialog box. Then type the range address or point to the range (you must press F4 (ABS) in the dialog box to start POINT mode). If you plan to show only one set of data values, choose A and specify the range of cells containing the numeric values you want to have plotted on the graph. If you are creating a mixed graph, the data that you assign to series A through C are graphed as bar graphs and the data you assign to series D through F are graphed as line graphs. To show other sets of data in the graph, select as many of the other range letters as are appropriate, and specify the range of data you want assigned to each. Remember that you do not have to show all your worksheet data on a graph; you can select just those data ranges that are most important. For example, you may have sales, cost of goods sold, and profit data on your worksheet, but you may elect to graph just the profit data.

Figure 11-5 shows the unit sales of four products for the Boston, New York, Dallas, and Chicago regions of a company. To create a graph from this data, enter **/Graph** to invoke the Graph menu, and then select Type. To see the data for Product 1 as a pie chart, choose Pie. Next, select A for the first data range and specify B5..B8 as the range containing the data. Select X next, and specify A5..A8 as the X-axis range.

Pie and HLCO graphs are the only graph types that do not use all six series. Pie charts are special in that they show what percentage each value is of the total. They

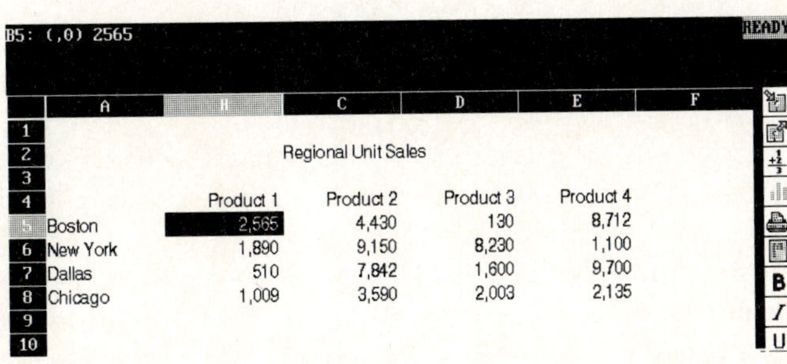

Figure 11-5.   Regional sales data

therefore would not be appropriate for multiple sets of data. A pie chart uses the A range for your data values and the X range to label the sections of the pie. 1-2-3 can use the B range to change the appearance of the pie "slices," as discussed later in the chapter.

HLCO graphs are another type of specialized graph. An HLCO graph only uses the A through D series and each series is graphed differently from the others. An HLCO graph uses the A series as the high values, the B series as the low values, the C series as the close values, and the D series as the opening values. 1-2-3 graphs this type of data by drawing a line from the high to the low value for each value of the X-axis data and draws a perpendicular line to the left to indicate the opening value and a perpendicular line to the right to indicate the closing value, as you can see from the HLCO graph in Figure 11-2f.

Multiple Data Ranges in a Graph

A quicker method of assigning graph ranges is the /Graph Group command, which defines the data groups for several data ranges at once. This reduces the number of steps required to create a graph.

For example, assume that you want to create a line graph using the data in Figure 11-5. Enter **/Graph Group**; 1-2-3 then prompts for the range that you want to divide into data ranges for the graph. You can enter the range by typing a range address, typing a range name, or pointing to the cells. Next 1-2-3 asks if you want to divide the data for the graph according to columns or rows. For the data in Figure 11-5, you can select A5..E8 as the range and divide it by columns. This makes A5..A8 the X range, B5..B8 the A range, C5..C8 the B range, D5..D8 the C range, and E5..E8 the D range. The city names are placed along the X-axis. The sales for each product are thus assigned to different data ranges in the line graph.

An alternative approach is to select B4..E4 as the range and divide it by rows. This makes B4..E4 the X range, B5..E8 the A range, B6..E6 the B range, B7..E7 the C range, and B8..E8 the D range. In this case, the product names are placed along the X-axis, and the sales for each city are plotted as different ranges in the line graph.

Using /Graph View

When you are ready to see the graph you have created, select View from the main Graph menu. This is all that is required to create a basic graph. It is wise to view the graph before proceeding further. This gives you the opportunity to spot problems, such as when the data ranges you have selected are too dispersed to be shown on one graph. An extreme example is a pie chart with one section constituting 99 percent of the total and several others splitting the remaining 1 percent among them. In a bar or line graph showing multiple data sets, you encounter a similar problem if one data set had values in the hundreds and others had values in the millions. You do not want to spend time creating titles, legends, and other enhancements if your basic graph is not usable, so check it with /Graph View first.

Another option is to press F10 (GRAPH) at any point, including while you are using other /Graph commands. Once the graph is displayed, pressing any key returns you to where you were before you viewed the graph. In releases before 2.3, you could only use F10 (GRAPH) to display the current graph from READY mode.

Enhancing the Basic Graph Type

While Release 2.4 has only seven basic graph types, its enhancements to the basic graph types will make 1-2-3 seem like it has more. Some of these graph type enhancements include: rotating the axes, stacking data ranges, changing the graph frame, and adding or removing the zero line. These features are available by selecting /Graph Type Features. The menu this command presents includes Vertical, Horizontal, Stacked, Frame, 3D-Effect, and Quit. This menu does not disappear until you select Quit to return to the main Graph menu.

Setting the Orientation of the Axes

All of the graphs, except pie charts, start with the X-axis on the bottom of the graph and the Y-axis on the left side. You can switch these two axes and make the Y-axis horizontal and the X-axis vertical. To rotate the axes, select Horizontal from the Graph Type Features menu. Figure 11-6 shows the bar graph from Figure 11-2a with its axes rotated. If you decide you want the X-axis on the bottom of the graph again, use the /Graph Type Features Vertical command. The other graph enhancements that affect an axis' display remain with the axis, so when you rotate the axes, the enhancements rotate with the axis (you will learn about these later).

Stacking the Data Ranges

The Stacked bar graph type option creates a graph with the values placed on top of each other, instead of next to each other, or in the same area, like in a line graph. Previous releases of 1-2-3 stacked bar graphs but with Releases 2.3 and above you can also stack the values for other graph types. When you select Stacked, 1-2-3 prompts for a Yes or No selection. If you select Yes, 1-2-3 stacks the data range values for bar, line, mixed, and XY graphs like the graph shown in Figure 11-7. In this graph, the data labels are added, as described later, so you can see how 1-2-3 adds the series to a graph on top of the other series in the graph. To discontinue stacking, enter /Graph Type Features Stacked and select No.

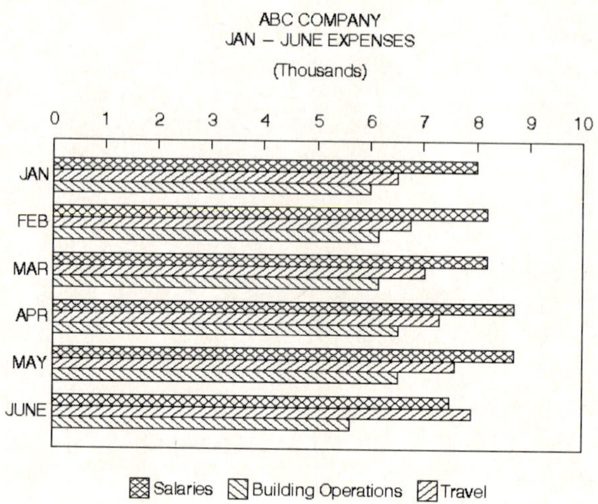

Figure 11-6.   *Bar graph with rotated axes*

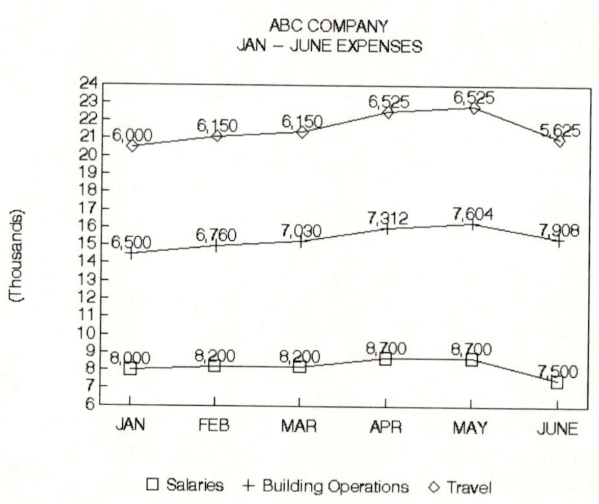

Figure 11-7.   *Stacked line graphs*

Setting the Graph Frame

Release 2.4 has many options for the frame around the graph area. Initially, 1-2-3
draws a frame on all four sides of the area where the data is graphed. 1-2-3 also leaves

a blank area between the left and right edge of the frame and where the graphed data starts to appear. This is called *margins*. A graph also shows where zero is on the graph. You can change these initial settings.

The frame is changed by selecting /Graph Type Features Frame and selecting All, Left, Right, Top, or Bottom to select where you want the graph to have a frame. You can also select None to remove the currently selected graph frame. You can use the dialog box to select the sides of the graph data that have a frame by selecting to mark or unmark the Left, Right, Top, and Bottom check boxes under Frame in the Graph Settings dialog box.

The margin can be removed so the graph data's left and right edges will be the frame. This means that in bar graphs, the first bar will be alongside the Y-axis. In line graphs, the data points for the first X-axis value will be on the Y-axis. To remove the margin, select /Graph Type Features Frame Margins No to mark or unmark the Margins on check box in the Graph Settings dialog box. If you later want to add the margins back to the graph, select /Graph Type Features Frame Margins No or select the Margins on check box in the Graph Settings dialog box.

1-2-3 usually marks where zero belongs on the Y-axis for all graph types except pie graphs and on the X-axis for XY graphs. If you are not concerned about showing the zero level for an axis, you can have 1-2-3 remove it. For example, if you want to show how series fluctuate between 1,000 and 1,100, you do not need to show the zero level on the axis; omitting the zero line in this case also gives the axis more room between 1,000 and 1,100. To remove a zero line from an axis, select /Graph Type Features Frame Zero-Line, X-axis or Y-axis, and No, or select to unmark the X-axis or Y-axis check box below Zero-line in the Graph Settings dialog box. To add the zero line back to an axis, select /Graph Type Features Frame Zero-Line, X-axis or Y-axis, and Yes, or select the X-axis or Y-axis check box below Zero-line in the Graph Settings dialog box.

Adding a Three-Dimensional Effect

The bar, stacked bar, and mixed graphs can be enhanced by giving them a three-dimensional appearance. Figure 11-8 shows a bar graph that has a three-dimensional appearance added to it. You can add a three-dimensional appearance to a graph containing bars by selecting /Graph Type Features 3D-Effect Yes or by selecting the 3-D bars check box in the Graph Settings dialog box. If you want to return to the two-dimensional graph appearance, select /Graph Type Features 3D-Effect No to unmark the 3-D bars check box in the Graph Settings dialog box.

Enhancing the Basic Display

Once you are sure that your data can be shown effectively with the graph type you selected, you will most likely want to make some changes to improve its appearance.

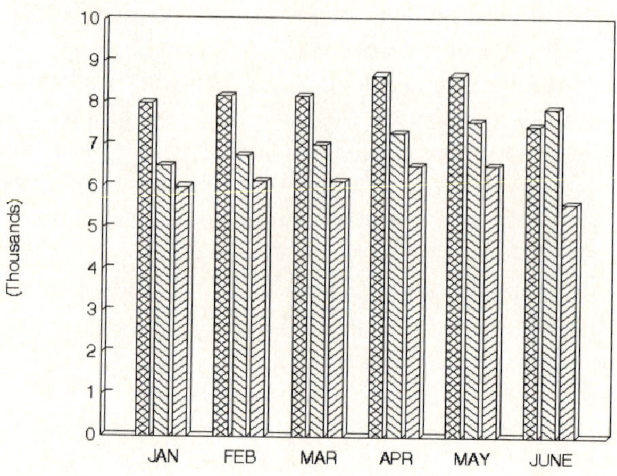

Figure 11-8.   *A bar graph with 3-D effect added*

1-2-3 offers plenty of enhancement options, from colors and hatch patterns to exploding a pie chart or adding titles and legends on any type of graph. Some of the commands needed to produce graph enhancements are options on the main Graph menu, but most are shown on the Graph Options menu shown here:

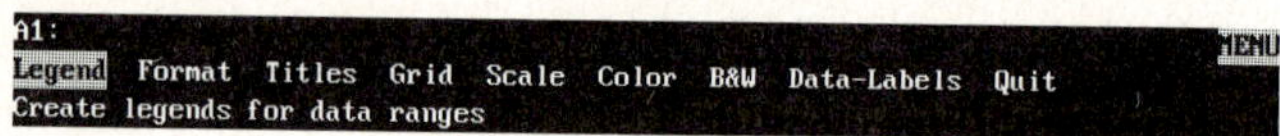

Pie Chart Enhancements

Normally the B graph data range is used to specify a second set of data for your graph. With a pie chart, however, the B range can specify the color or hatch pattern for the individual pieces of the pie. The B range offers code numbers from 1 through 8 representing different colors or hatch patterns. For example, Figure 11-9 shows the hatch patterns 1-2-3 uses for each of the eight hatch pattern values. These hatch patterns are useful for a monochrome display and for printing to a printer that cannot print colors. The same numbers (1 through 8) represent available colors when 1-2-3 displays or prints the graph in color.

In a pie chart, the B data range assumes a special function. In addition to determining color or hatch mark patterns, it can also *explode* a section from the pie. Any pie slice can be exploded by adding 100 to the color or hatch pattern code number for the slice.

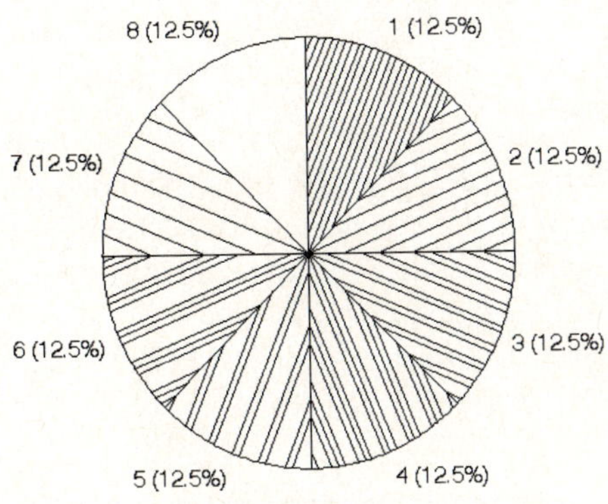

Figure 11-9.   *Hatch mark patterns*

You can add hatch pattern codes to the data shown in Figure 11-5 by adding 1, 2, 103, and 4 to the cells F5..F8. When the B range is selected and F5..F8 is used as the range, the pie chart changes the hatch patterns it uses, as you can see in Figure 11-10.

Figure 11-10 shows the pie chart exactly as it appears in your display after you add these hatch pattern codes. Notice that the section for Dallas is pulled away from the

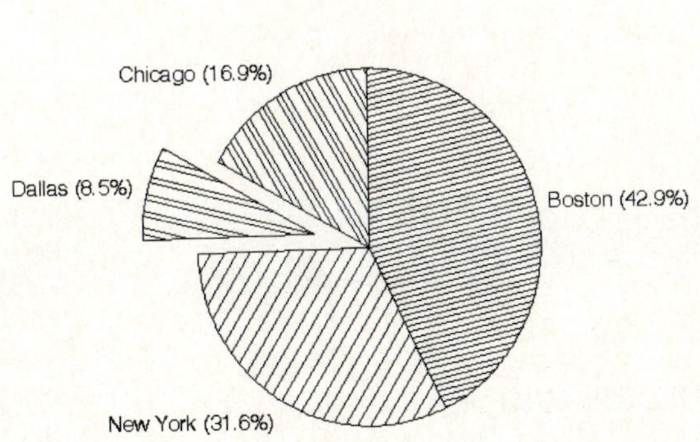

Figure 11-10.   *A shaded pie chart*

center, or exploded. This is accomplished by using 103 for the B range value for this pie slice.

Adding Descriptive Labels

Figure 11-11 shows a bar graph created by selecting Bar from the Graph Type menu. This graph has been enhanced with titles at the top, values along the Y-axis, X-axis data labels, and legends. Adding this type of extra description to a chart makes it convey your message more effectively.

The data used to create this graph is shown in Figure 11-12. The numeric values for January through June are assigned to the A, B, and C data ranges. The months

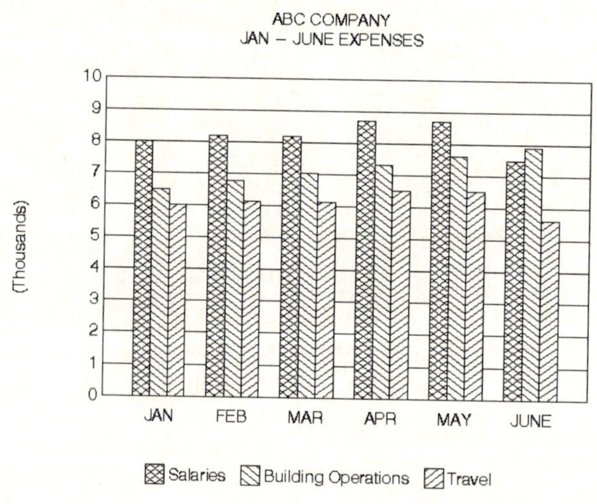

Figure 11-11.   *A bar graph with titles and legends added*

A5: [W23] 'Salaries

	JAN	FEB	MAR	APR	MAY	JUNE
			ABC Company			
Salaries	$8,000	$8,200	$8,200	$8,700	$8,700	$7,500
Building Operations	6,500	6,760	7,030	7,312	7,604	7,908
Travel	6,000	6,150	6,150	6,525	6,525	5,625

Figure 11-12.   *The ABC Company data*

are assigned to the X range. You can select all of the ranges at once by entering the /Graph Group command, selecting B4..G7 as the range, and selecting Rowwise to divide B4..G7 into graph data ranges according to rows.

Adding Legends

A *legend* provides a description for each of the ranges shown on a graph. (You saw an example in Figure 11-11.) If you create a line graph with symbols marking the data points in the range, the legend defines these symbols at the bottom of your chart. If you create a graph with hatch patterns indicating each series, the legend defines each series by placing a small box filled with the hatch pattern at the bottom of the chart and adding a description next to the box.

Legends are added using the /Graph Options Legend command, which lets you select from A through F for the data series or Range to assign legends for multiple series. In Releases 2.3 and above, you can also assign legend text using the text boxes under Legends in the Graph Legends & Titles dialog box, which is available when you select Legends & Titles in the Graph Settings dialog box. Enter the letter corresponding to the data range for which you want to specify a legend. You also can select Range, if the text that you want for all of the legends is predefined in a range in the worksheet.

1-2-3 prompts you for the legend description for that data series. The legends used for Figure 11-11 were Salaries, Building Operations, and Travel for the A, B, and C ranges, respectively. If the legend you want to use appears in a worksheet cell, you have an alternative entry method. Rather than typing the legend at the prompt, you can enter a backslash (\) followed by the cell address or range name of the cell containing the legend data. For example, entering \A5 tells 1-2-3 to use the text in cell A5 as the legend.

1-2-3 has a 19-character limit for the legends that you type directly. While 1-2-3 does not limit the number of characters you can enter for a legend by entering a cell address, the legend text that appears in the graph is limited by the amount of space used for the other legends.

If you select Range, 1-2-3 prompts you for the worksheet range containing the predefined legends. You can enter this range by typing a range address or name, or by pointing to the cells you want to use. For example, for the legends in Figure 11-11, you could have selected Range and entered A5..A7. 1-2-3 assigns the first cell as the A range legend, the second cell as the B range legend, and so on, until it runs out of cells or graph data ranges.

Adding Titles

1-2-3 has four title options, all accessible through the /Graph Options Titles command. Titles appear at the top of the chart or along the X- or Y-axis. Like graph legends, you can either type the title text yourself or type \ and a cell address to use the contents of that cell. You can enter up to 39 characters in the graph titles prompts but you can create longer titles by referencing a cell. In Releases 2.3 and above, besides using the /Graph Options Titles command to add titles to a graph, you can also add graph titles by entering the title text or the \ and cell address in the text boxes under Titles in the Graph Legends & Titles dialog box, which is available when you select Legends & Titles in the Graph Settings dialog box.

The first title appears at the top of the graph. For example, the first line title of the graph in Figure 11-11 was generated by entering /**Graph Options Titles First**, and then **ABC COMPANY**.

A line for a second label is also reserved at the top of the graph. To place an entry in this location, enter /**Graph Options Titles Second**. The entry **JAN - JUNE EXPENSES** was typed at the prompt for the second line title in our example.

Titles can also be given to the X- or Y-axis. These labels normally describe the quantities being measured. The Y-axis title might be Dollars and the X-axis title might be Sales, for example. If you enter a value for the Y-axis title, it is placed vertically on the graph to the left of the Y-axis. (The same character limit applies to this title.) An X-axis title is stored horizontally below the X-axis.

Adding Grid Lines

If you have a number of points on a graph, it may be difficult to identify the exact X and Y values for each point on the line. To make such identification easier, 1-2-3 can add vertical and horizontal lines that originate at the axes and extend upward and to the right. These lines are called *grid lines,* since using them in both directions forms a grid pattern across your graph.

The menu for Grid is obtained by entering /**Graph Options Grid**. The Grid options can be used with all graph types except the pie chart, since grid lines across a pie chart would detract from your ability to interpret the graph. The Grid menu contains four options. Choose Horizontal to add horizontal lines across the graph. This is especially effective for bar graphs, since it enables you to more accurately interpret the tops of the bars. Figure 11-13 presents a bar graph to which horizontal lines were added by entering /**Graph Options Grid Horizontal**. Vertical bars extend upward from the X-axis points. They are more effective on a line or XY graph than on a bar graph. To add them enter /**Graph Options Grid Vertical**. To add grid lines in both directions, enter /**Graph Options Grid Both**. Figure 11-14 shows a line graph with grid lines in both directions. You can remove grid lines without changing the rest of your graph simply by entering the command sequence /**Graph Options Grid Clear**.

In Releases 2.3 and above, you can add grid lines using the Horizontal and Vertical check boxes under Grid lines in the Graph Settings dialog box. Selecting one of the check boxes adds grid lines in the direction you select and unmarking one of the check boxes removes them in that direction.

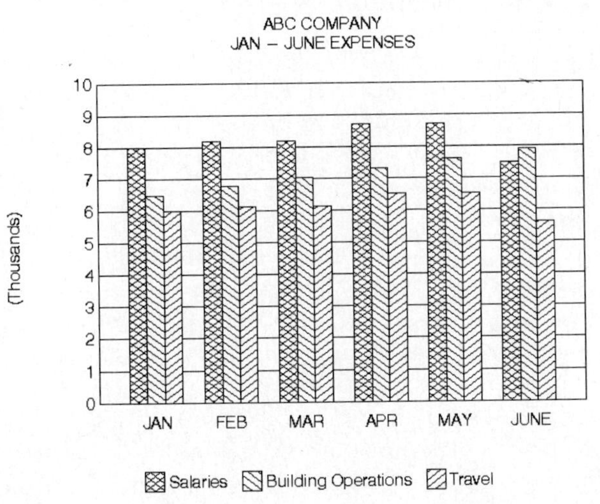

Figure 11-13.   *Horizontal grid lines*

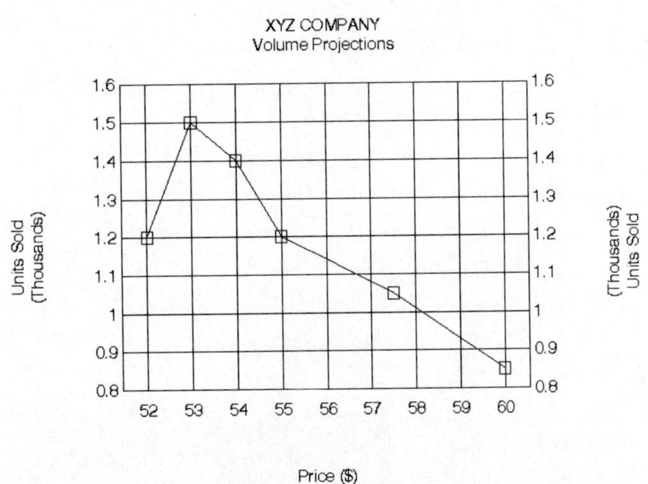

Figure 11-14.   *Grid lines in both directions*

Choosing Line and Symbol Options

1-2-3 allows you to show line graphs, XY, and lines in mixed graphs in a variety of formats by using the options under /Graph Options Format. You can show the graph as a smooth line connecting the points, as symbols marking the points with lines connecting them, or just as symbols. The selections made in this menu do not affect other graph types. Before you select a line and symbol option, you must first specify the range for the graph application as either Graph (all ranges in the graph) or one of the range letters, A through F. Once you select a graph series, you can select among Line, Symbols, Both, Neither, and Area. The last option was new with Release 2.3 and creates an area graph. You can also select the format of the series in Releases 2.3 and above by selecting a range to change under Format in the Graph Legends & Titles dialog box and then selecting one of the options from the pop-up dialog box.

The first Format option, Lines, connects the points for a data range with a line. The points are not marked by symbols when this option is chosen. The Symbols option omits the line and just marks the data points with one of the six different symbols that 1-2-3 provides. The third option, Both, provides both lines and symbols for your display. The Neither option may seem useless, since it means that neither lines nor symbols are shown. However, it can be used with the Data-Labels option (described later in this chapter) to mark the points with actual data values. The last option in Releases 2.3 and above, Area, creates *area graphs*. An area graph stacks the data ranges and fills the area between the data ranges with a hatch pattern. Figure 11-15 shows an area graph. The default setting for /Graph Options Format is Both.

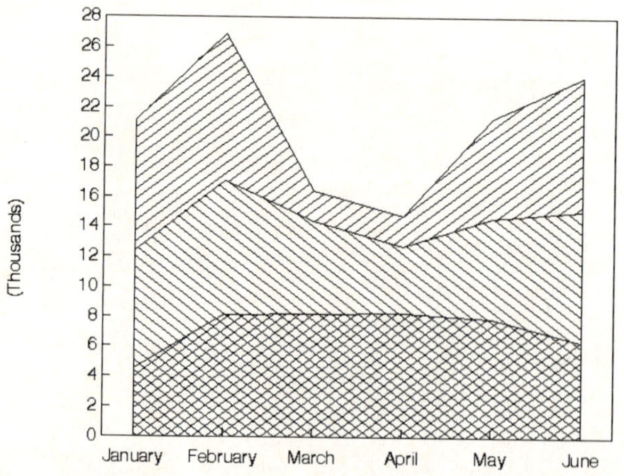

Figure 11-15.   *An area graph*

In a mixed graph, the series that is displayed as bars is customized with the same commands you use to customize bar and stacked bar graphs. The series that is displayed as lines is customized with the same commands you use to customize line and XY graphs. 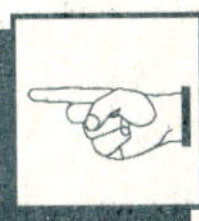

Choosing Color or Black-and-White

If you have a color monitor, 1-2-3 automatically displays the graphs in color. If you have a monochrome monitor, 1-2-3 automatically displays the graph in one color. You can change the way 1-2-3 displays your graph with /Graph Options Color and /Graph Options B&W. In Releases 2.3 and above, you can also display the graph in color by selecting the Colors on check box or in black-and-white by unmarking this check box in the Graph Settings dialog box.

When you save this image with /Graph Save for later printing on a printer that cannot print colors, you must change to /Graph Options B&W. This option distinguishes the different bars on your chart with hatch patterns when it prints.

The colors 1-2-3 uses depends on the monitor selected during the Install program. For example, if you are using a Color Graphic Adapter screen, 1-2-3 uses three colors. If you are using an Enhanced Graphic Adapter, 1-2-3 uses eight colors.

Selecting Scaling Options

1-2-3's scaling options let you override the scaling selections that 1-2-3 makes when constructing a graph. You always have the option of letting 1-2-3 make the decisions, and you seldom need to use the Scale option to improve upon the selections made by 1-2-3. You can use this command to change the scaling for the X- or Y-axis, or to specify a skip factor for X-axis data labels. The selections made for the X-axis only affect XY graphs. /Graph Options Scale Skip was discussed earlier in this chapter in the section called "Labeling the X-Axis."

Specify the scale to be changed by choosing /Graph Options Scale X-Axis or /Graph Options Scale Y-Axis. The menu presented for either of these selections looks like this:

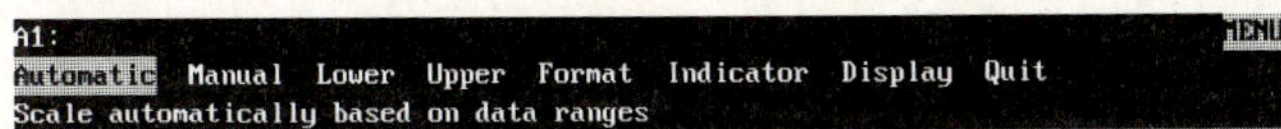

In Releases 2.3 and above, the menu under Y-axis also includes Display. When you are finished with this menu, select Quit to return to the Graph Options menu. All of the changes you make to the axis settings can be made in the Graph Scale Settings dialog box. This dialog box appears when you select Scale Options in the Graph Settings dialog box or when you select /Graph Options Scale.

The Automatic option is the default setting. It is also the method for returning to automatic scaling after requesting Manual. 1-2-3 remembers the settings you have made for a manual axis in case you decide to switch to a manual axis later.

Manual permits you to decide what the upper and lower limits of your scale are. If you choose this option, plan also to choose Upper and Lower to define the limits of your scale. To set the scale manually using the dialog box, unmark the Automatic check box so Manual is selected and then enter the low and high values the scale should use in the Lower Limit and Upper Limit text boxes. With a manual setting, 1-2-3 does not display values outside the established limits. In a bar or stacked bar graph, 1-2-3 displays a bar stretching the height of the graph for values over the established limits and an empty space for values under the established limits. In a line graph, the line connecting the points discontinues at the top or bottom of the graph to indicate values outside the established limits.

The Format option on the Scale menu allows you to use any of the numeric formats on the scale markers for the X- and Y-axis. When you select Format under X-axis or Y-axis in the Graph Scale Settings dialog box, 1-2-3 displays a pop-up dialog box so you can select from one of the available formats. You can format the numbers as Currency, Percent, or any of the other formats acceptable for the /Range Format command covered in Chapter 5.

The Indicator option permits you to turn off the label indicator that specifies size. As an example, say you are graphing sales in thousands of dollars, and 1-2-3 generates the label "Thousands" for use along the Y-axis. If you do not wish this to appear, select Indicator No. Yes is the default setting for this option and displays the indicator 1-2-3 creates. In Release 2.4, you can also add or remove the axis indicator by selecting to mark or unmark the Indicator on check box in the Graph Scale Settings dialog box.

The Display option sets which sides of the graph 1-2-3 displays the Y-axis labels. You can select Left, Right, Both, or None. To make this same change with the dialog box, mark or unmark the Labels on left and Labels on right check boxes under Y-axis to add or remove the Y-axis labels to the left or right side of the graph.

You will want to remove the indicator when a graph uses data that is already multiplied by a power of ten, such as financial data listed in the thousands. In this case, 1-2-3 will supply an incorrect indicator, such as thousands, when you want millions. Instead, include the indicator you want with the axis title such as "Sales (millions)."

Using Data to Label Your Graph

You can use the contents of worksheet cells to label the points or bars in a graph. 1-2-3 lets you assign data labels to any one of the data ranges involved in your graph.

Simply choose /Graph Options Data-Labels, and then enter the letter of your range choice (A through F). Alternatively, choose Group to enter the data labels for all the data ranges at once. In Releases 2.3 and above, you can also select data labels by selecting a series that you want to assign data labels to under Data labels in the Graph Legends & Titles dialog box that appears when you select the Legends & Titles command button from the Graph Settings dialog box. Then select a range containing the data labels. The range must contain as many cells as there are data points in the range or ranges to which you are assigning labels. The range can contain labels or values. The labels in the graph will have the same format the cell entries have in the worksheet. Enter the labels range by typing the range address or the range name or by pointing to the cells (from the dialog box press F4 (ABS) to enter the POINT mode). If you select Range, you must choose whether 1-2-3 divides the cells into the data labels for each data range according to columns or rows.

After entering the range of cells containing the labels, you must choose the location for the data labels relative to your data points. Your options are Center, Left, Above, Right, and Below. In the Graph Legends & Titles dialog box, select the label alignment by selecting the graph range under Alignment in the dialog box, and select the label position relative to the data points from the pop-up dialog box 1-2-3 displays. Figure 11-16 is a bar chart in which labels are shown above the data points to provide a clear description of the height of each bar. On graphs with bars, the Center, Left, and Right selections produce the same result as Above. On stacked bar graphs, 1-2-3 puts the data above the stacked bar regardless of the position selected.

To use data labels as the only marker on a graph, create a line graph. Then enter **/Graph Options Format Graph Neither**, which keeps lines and symbols from being displayed. Then center the data labels at each point on the chart with /Graph Options Data-Labels Center to create a display similar to Figure 11-17.

Resetting Graph Options

After specifying particular options for a graph, you might change your mind about some of them. Individual labels can be erased by reentering the appropriate command and deleting the label from the prompt. As an example, to remove the first-line

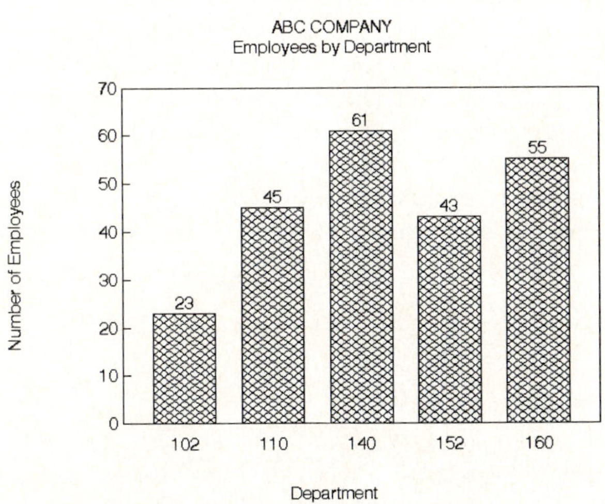

Figure 11-16.   *Data points marked with data labels*

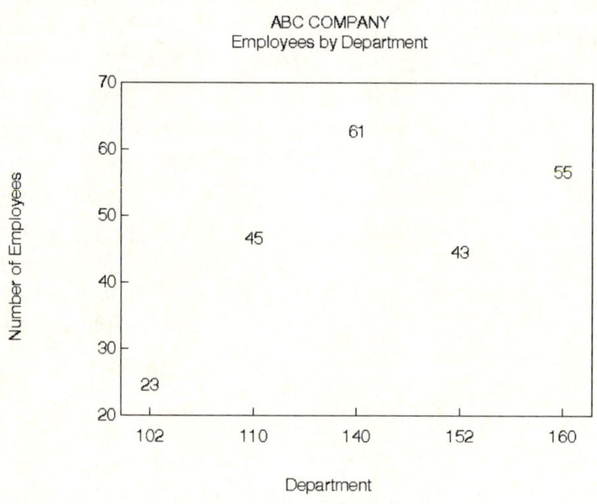

Figure 11-17.   *Data labels displayed without lines or symbols*

title of ABC COMPANY, enter **/Graph Options Title First** and delete the title ABC COMPANY from this entry. If a cell reference was used to supply the label, just delete the cell reference and backslash (\) from the entry.

If you want to eliminate all the graph settings, however, use /Graph Reset Graph. This command eliminates all graph settings, including ranges. It lets you redefine a new graph from the beginning.

The Reset command also allows you to remove just some of the graph settings. The Graph Reset menu provides a number of options for removing particular settings. You can remove the X data range by choosing X or any of the data ranges (A through F) by choosing the letter of the range you want to eliminate. You can remove all of the ranges by choosing Ranges. To delete the selections made with the Graph Options menu, choose Options.

Since the Reset menu remains displayed after you make a selection unless you select Graph, you must choose Quit or press ESC when you want to exit from this command.

Storing and Using Graphs

Each graph created up to this point has been the current graph for the worksheet. 1-2-3 limits the worksheet to having only one current graph at a time. To include several graphs in your worksheet you must name a current graph before you create a new one. Once a graph is named, it can become the current graph at a later point.

Another option for storing the graph once you create it is saving it to a file. 1-2-3 can save graphs to files that you can print with the PrintGraph program or to files used with other software packages such as WordPerfect and Lotus Manuscript, or you can use the graphs to add them to 1-2-3 worksheets with Wysiwyg.

Naming Graphs for Later Use

1-2-3 uses all the settings you enter for a graph to define the current graph. Since only one graph can be current at a time, you lose the original settings if you start choosing different ones for a new graph. If you want to retain the definition of the current graph while you begin a new graph, first save the current one with /Graph Name Create. When 1-2-3 prompts you for the name of the graph to create, you can enter any name up to 15 characters in length. To eliminate all of the settings after saving the graph, use /Graph Reset Graph. You can then start defining a new graph and, when the definition is complete, you can name it, too. When you save your worksheet, all the graph names and definitions are saved along with the other data.

A graph whose settings have been saved can be used again. To use the settings of a named graph, enter **/Graph Name Use** and specify the name you assigned previously with /Graph Name Create. The settings that were current at the time the graph was saved are activated, and 1-2-3 will display the named graph on your screen.

1-2-3's ability to name and save graphs lets you create a number of graphs on one worksheet. You can define and name all the graphs you need for a single application. Then, when you update your worksheet figures, you can create an up-to-date slide show of graphic results by using and viewing each of the named graphs. You need not re-create the graphs because their settings are saved with the worksheet.

Once you have created the graphs, you may need to list them. The /Graph Name Table command lists a worksheet's defined graphs in a table in the worksheet. When you execute this command, 1-2-3 prompts you for a location to start the graph name table. Specify an area three columns wide and with as many rows as the worksheet has named graphs. The table contains the graph names, the graph types, and the first-title line, if any. Figure 11-18 shows a graph name table.

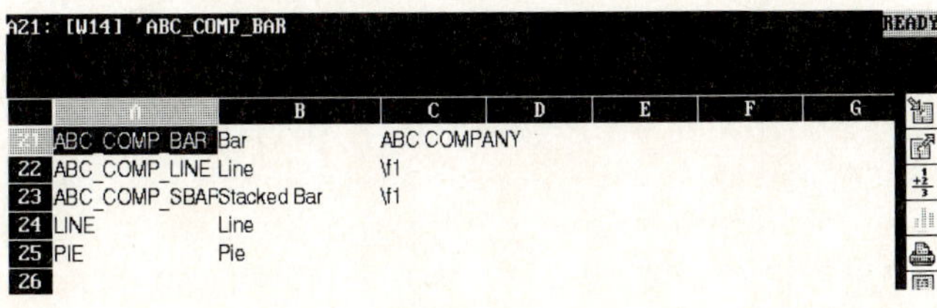

Figure 11-18.   *A table listing named graphs*

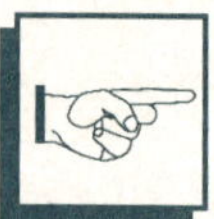

1-2-3 does not keep the setting and option changes that you make to a named graph unless you save it again with the /Graph Name Create command. This command saves the named graph settings with the other worksheet data. To use this graph in another 1-2-3 session, save the worksheet with /File Save.

Deleting Graphs

The /Graph Name Delete command permits you to eliminate stored graph settings that you no longer need. When you enter this command, 1-2-3 prompts you with a list of all existing graph names. Selecting a name from the list or typing in a name causes all the settings for that graph to be eliminated. If you change your mind and wish to reproduce the graph, you must reenter all the options, unless Undo is enabled. When you delete a named graph, you are only deleting the graph name and its related settings. The worksheet data the graph uses is not affected by creating and deleting named graphs.

1-2-3 also provides a quick delete feature. Use it with caution because it eliminates all saved graph names in the current worksheet. If you do want to eliminate all the current graph names and their associated settings, enter **/Graph Name Reset**. Since 1-2-3 does not provide a confirmation step for this command, be sure you do not accidentally type **R** while working with the /Graph Name menu.

Check the graphs in your worksheet before you reset them. Unless Undo is enabled, you cannot recover named graphs that you have reset. A good habit is to list the graphs in the current worksheet with the /Graph Name Table command before resetting them.

Saving Graphs to an External File

The graphs created in a worksheet are part of the worksheet file. The graphs in a worksheet cannot be printed directly from 1-2-3 or used in other programs, such as word processors. You can, however, extract a graph to an external file and use the external file in PrintGraph and other programs. For example, once you have saved a graph to a .PIC file, you can print it with PrintGraph, Allways, Wysiwyg, or incorporate it into a WordPerfect document.

You should be aware that you cannot save a graphic image with /File Save. This command can save only worksheet data, the current graph setting, and the graph settings stored with any graph names you have created. It creates a .WKS or .WK1 file, not the .PIC file that stores a graph's image. To create a .PIC file, you must first enter **/Graph Save**, and then you can provide a filename up to eight characters in length. 1-2-3 saves the current graph as a .PIC file. If you want to save a graph other than the current graph, you must first make the desired graph current with /Graph Name Use.

A graph that is saved to an external file cannot be read by a worksheet, but Allways and Wysiwyg can display the graph file in a worksheet range. Also, the external graphic image file contains the graph as it existed when you saved it. The graphic image file is not updated if you update the graph data.

Quitting the Graph Menu

The main Graph menu and several of its submenus remain on your screen until you choose the Quit option. Your other option for quitting is to press ESC the number of times required to return to READY mode.

Using the QuickGraph Icon

With Release 2.4 of 1-2-3, you have access to a shortcut for creating graphs. By using the QuickGraph icon (shown here) from the SmartIcons palettes, you can speed up the process of creating simple graphs.

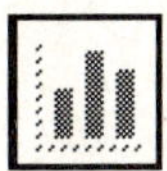

Before selecting the QuickGraph icon, you should select the range of cells that contain the data and the X-axis labels that you want to use in the graph. After selecting the range, select the QuickGraph icon from the SmartIcons palette. You can select this icon by clicking on it with the mouse, or by pressing ALT+F7 and moving to the icon using the arrow keys before pressing ENTER.

When you select the QuickGraph icon, the QuickGraph Settings dialog box opens, as shown in Figure 11-19. From this dialog box, you can select the graph type, whether the data series are in rows or columns, the orientation of the chart, and whether you are using colors or 3-D effects.

To select the type of graph, select one of the option buttons under Type in the QuickGraph Settings dialog box. To choose whether the data series are in rows or columns on the spreadsheet, select one of the option buttons under Data ranges in the dialog box. Select Vertical or Horizontal under Orientation to set the orientation of the graph.

If you would like to have 3-D effects with your graph, select the 3d-effect on check box. If you would like to use colors, instead of hatch marks, to indicate the separate data series, select the Colors on check box.

When you are finished selecting the settings for your graph, select the OK button or press ENTER. 1-2-3 shows you the current graph for the worksheet. Using the QuickGraph features is easier than using the 1-2-3 Graph menu commands. Use the QuickGraph icon to get graphs that you want to be able to review quickly, and save 1-2-3's Graph commands for custom graphs.

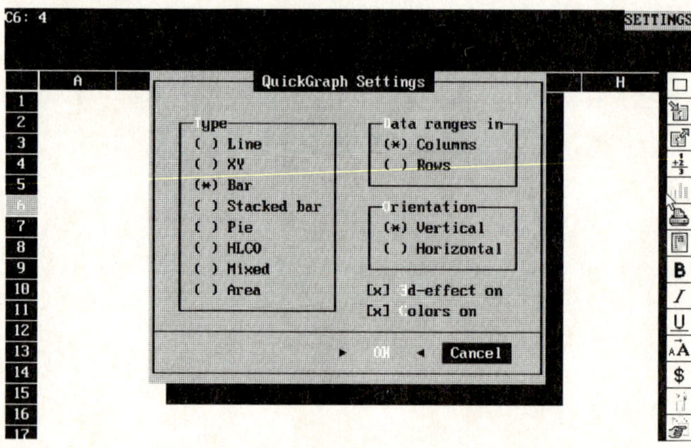

Figure 11-19.   *The QuickGraph Settings dialog box*

Wysiwyg Graph-Printing Features

Wysiwyg, the add-in that comes with 1-2-3 Releases 2.3 and above, makes printing and customizing graphs even easier. With Wysiwyg, you can customize a graph or graphic by including text and other shapes on it. Wysiwyg lets you add the graph to the current worksheet to print alongside the data it illustrates. Even more important, Wysiwyg makes printing graphs as easy as printing worksheet data with 1-2-3.

Before Wysiwyg can print a graph, it must be added to the worksheet. By adding the graph to the worksheet, you are creating a small version of the graph that is displayed on the worksheet as you work, and the graph can be printed from there.

When you select the :Graph Add command to add a graph to the worksheet, you are prompted to select one of four potential sources for the graph. You can select the current graph in 1-2-3 by selecting Current. If you want to select a named graph, select the menu option Named and choose the named graph you want to use. You can select PIC to choose from the graphs saved in a .PIC file. The other menu options have to do with Wysiwyg features, discussed in Chapter 15.

After you select the graph you want to add to your worksheet, you are asked to select the graph's display range. If you selected a range before selecting the :Graph Add command, that range is automatically selected as the graphic display range. When you specify the display range, Wysiwyg switches to WAIT mode. While you are waiting, Wysiwyg recalculates the graph to size it to the selected display range. When this is done, the graph appears on the worksheet, blocking any data underneath.

With Release 2.4, you can use the Add Graph icon to add the current graph to your worksheet. First select the range of cells in which you want the graph to appear. Then select the Add Graph icon. The current graph is added to the worksheet in those cells. This is a quick method of using Wysiwyg to enhance your worksheet. The Add Graph icon looks like this:

Customizing Your Graph with Wysiwyg

Wysiwyg offers a great many features for customizing the display of your graph. These customization features are discussed in Chapter 15. These features include making the chart transparent to the worksheet data beneath it, adding text and graphic images to the graphic, resizing and recoloring the graph, and other features that will help you create professional-looking graphs to accompany your reports.

Printing Your Graph with Wysiwyg

Printing the graph with Wysiwyg is as easy as printing worksheet information with 1-2-3, which you learned to do in Chapter 6. Once the graph is added to the worksheet, you merely need to include the entire display range for the graph in the print range, and then Wysiwyg prints the graph. If you do not include the entire display range, however, Wysiwyg only prints the portion of the graph that appears in the print range you selected. Before printing a graph with Wysiwyg, you may want to double-check the display range of any graphs, or you might be surprised.

As a review, these are the steps for printing with Wysiwyg:

1. Select :Print Range Set and select the range that you want to print from the worksheet.

2. Specify any of the printing customization features accessed through the :Print Settings or :Print Config menu. Make sure that you have the correct printer selected.

3. Select :Print Go to send the selected print range to the printer.

Printing Graphs with PrintGraph

1-2-3 has two ways of printing a graph either from within 1-2-3 or with a separate program. The first method covered in this chapter is to save the graph to a file, exit 1-2-3, and enter the PrintGraph program. The other option uses the Wysiwyg Add-In, covered in Chapters 6 and 15.

Although Wysiwyg allows you to print directly from the Wysiwyg menu, you may find PrintGraph a better choice in some situations. PrintGraph lets you print full-page graphs for your report. Since the PrintGraph program is separate from 1-2-3, Lotus was able to add many sophisticated print options beyond the standard features. The program has a menu structure similar to 1-2-3's. The main menu for PrintGraph is shown in Figure 11-20.

To print your graphs, leave the 1-2-3 menu to return to either the Access menu or DOS. If you are using Release 2 or above, you can enter **/System** to leave 1-2-3 temporarily, and type **Exit** when you want to return to 1-2-3. You can then choose the PrintGraph option from the Access menu or enter **Pgraph** at the DOS prompt. If you are using floppy disks, you must place the PrintGraph disk in your drive before finalizing the entry.

As previously noted, the Lotus PrintGraph program is the tool you usually use to obtain printed copies of your graphs. The program requires that the graph be saved on disk as a .PIC file. PrintGraph should have been configured for your system at the same time that 1-2-3 was configured. If it was not, you must return to Install to add the necessary drivers to the program.

This section discusses the options from Releases 2 and above of PrintGraph. The Release 1A options are similar, but the Settings option is divided between Options and Configure: Options gives you access to colors, paper size, and action settings, and Configure makes changes to hardware configurations such as directories and devices.

Selecting Graphics Files

If you choose Image-Select from the main PrintGraph menu, 1-2-3 displays the names of all the .PIC files from the disk listed under Graph Directory on the left side of the main PrintGraph screen, as shown in Figure 11-21. Simply follow the instructions on

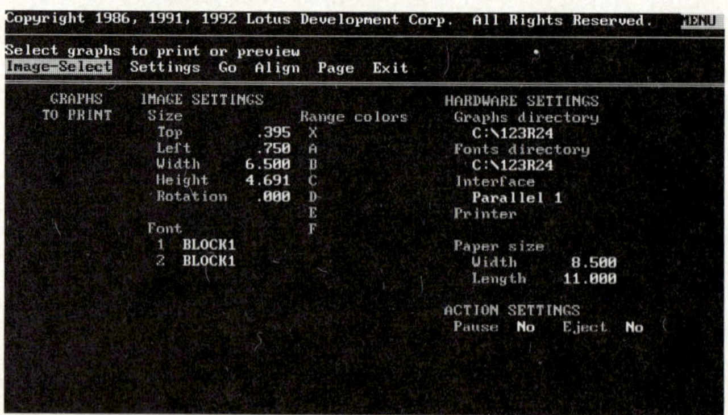

Figure 11-20.   The PrintGraph menu

```
Copyright 1986, 1991, 1992 Lotus Development Corp.  All Rights Reserved.  POINT

Select graphs to print


GRAPH FILE  DATE      TIME    SIZE
----------------------------------         Space bar marks or unmarks selection
23FG1121  02-10-91  13:23     1112         ENTER selects marked graphs
JANFIGS   04-24-92  14:29     1891         ESC exits, ignoring changes
PERSON3   04-24-92  14:31     1992         HOME moves to beginning of list
QTR2      04-24-92  14:32      986         END moves to end of list
                                           ↑ and ↓ move highlight
                                             List will scroll if highlight
                                             moved beyond top or bottom
                                           GRAPH (F10) previews marked graph
```

Figure 11-21.   *Selecting .PIC files to print*

the right side of the screen to use the different options. When you are finished, press
ENTER.

Making Setting Selections

The Settings menu provides access to all the options for PrintGraph, including
hardware and image settings. This menu includes Image, Hardware, Action, Save,
Reset, and Quit. When you want to return to the initial PrintGraph menu, select Quit.
Other menus contain Quit options so you can return to the previous menu.

Changing the Image Settings

The settings you select for the Image option apply to all the graphs selected for
printing. You can change the size of the printed graph, the fonts, and the range
colors.

Selecting Size   Select the Full option from the PrintGraph Settings Image Size
menu to print each graph on a full page. The chart shown in Figure 11-22 was printed
with this option. When 1-2-3 prints a full-page graph, it automatically rotates the
graph 90 degrees to a vertical orientation. This puts the X-axis along the longest side
of the page. You can also choose a half-page size by selecting Half. If neither of these
sizes meets your needs, you can create your own size by selecting Manual.

The Manual selection under Size presents a whole new submenu. From this menu
you can select settings for the top and bottom spacing to allow blank space at the top
and bottom of your page. There are also height and width settings to specify the
printed area of the graph. Because of the aspect ratio or size relationship between
the X- and Y-axis, it is easy to distort a graph when you select a new height and width.
A little experimentation should help you establish suitable settings for these values,
however. A good starting point is to try a ratio of 1 to 1.385 between the sizes of the
X- and Y-axis.

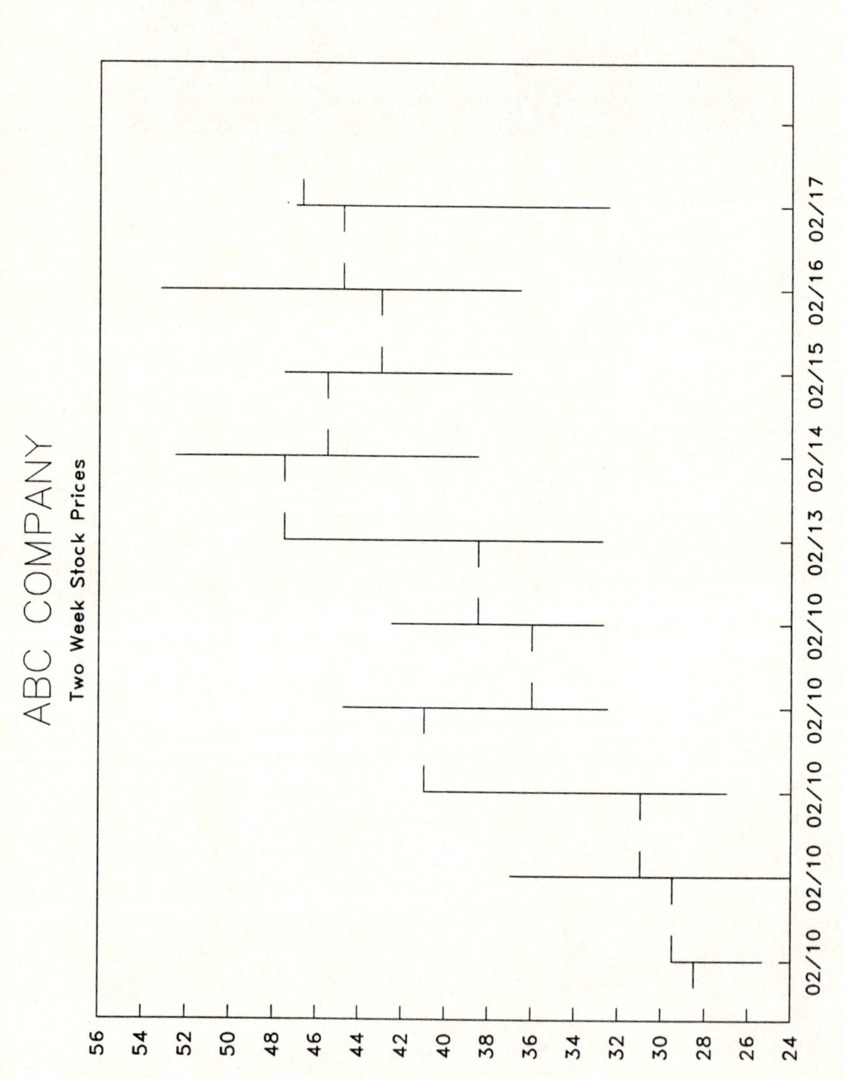

Figure 11-22.   A full-page graph

Rotation is the last size option. It permits rotation or turning of the graph as an alternative to changing its size. A rotation of 0 to 90 degrees can be specified.

Selecting a Font   You can choose a particular font for use with the PrintGraph program with Settings Image Font. The various fonts have characters with different sizes, shapes, and thicknesses. Your font selection affects the text printed on the graph for titles and legends, but not the graph itself. Options like Roman, Block, Script, and Italic are available. If you see a font name listed more than once, look at the number that follows each listing. This number determines how dark the font prints; high numbers print darker than low numbers. You have the option of choosing either one or two fonts. If only one is selected, it is used for the entire graph. If two fonts are specified, the first line of the graph title is printed with font 1 and the other text uses font 2.

Selecting Colors   PrintGraph assigns a default color of black to every range in the graph. With a single color printer, black is the only option. If you are printing on a color printer or plotter, PrintGraph allows you to set the colors for your various data ranges. After selecting Settings Image Range-Colors, you can choose from a list of colors that your output device supports.

When you select Range-Colors, PrintGraph asks you to select a range and provides X and A through F for choices. Once you specify the range, select one of the colors listed. With nine colors available, you may assign a different color to each range if you wish. When you print a graph, PrintGraph tells you which color pens should be loaded into the plotter.

Changing Hardware Settings

The Settings Hardware options establish the disk drive that is read by PrintGraph for the files it needs to print your graph. You also use the Hardware options to establish the printer to be used and the interface for the connection. The Hardware Settings menu remains on the screen until you choose Quit. The menu looks like this:

Changing the Directories for Graphs and Fonts   In Releases 2.3 and 2.4, PrintGraph looks for the .PIC files in the same location as the 1-2-3 files. In prior releases, PrintGraph looks for these files in drive A. You may want to change where PrintGraph looks for files to match where you save graphs with the 1-2-3 /Graph Save command.

To change the setting for the graph directory, enter **Settings Hardware Graphs-Directory**. You then need to enter the pathname for your files—for example, **C:\123R23\GRAPHS**—if you are using the default directory and 1-2-3 Release 2.3.

The pathname you enter is what PrintGraph uses when you choose Image-Select from the main PrintGraph menu.

To change the font directory, enter **Settings Hardware Fonts-Directory**. When prompted for the directory, enter the pathname that tells where the .FNT files are stored, for example, **C:\123R23**. When you choose the Go option from the main PrintGraph menu, 1-2-3 attempts to read the required fonts from the pathname you specified.

Choosing the Interface   With Releases 2 and above, you can choose up to eight different interface settings for your printer. You can access the various Interface options by entering **Settings Hardware Interface**. This command is identical to the 1-2-3 command /Worksheet Global Default Printer Interface and has the same selections. Like the 1-2-3 command, if you select a serial interface, you must also select a baud rate.

Selecting a Printer   You can use any of the graphics printers you have installed with the Install program while you are working with PrintGraph. To make your selection, enter **Settings Hardware Printer**. PrintGraph displays the names of the graphics printers you selected during installation and provides the options of high and low density for the different printers. High-density selections will produce better print quality but take longer to print. You can make a selection using the same keystrokes you used for selecting graphs (these are also listed on the screen).

Specifying Paper Size   You can take full advantage of printers that can print on different-sized paper. To use 14-inch paper, for example, use Settings Hardware Page-Size, leaving the length setting as it is and changing the width setting to 14.

Changing the Action Settings

The default action after printing one graph is to continue with the next one. The default setting is also not to advance the paper to the next page after printing. This allows you to print two half-page graphs on one sheet.

The three options for the PrintGraph Settings Action command are Pause, Eject, and Quit. Pause provides a choice of Yes or No. Choose Yes when you want a pause for changing the paper after each graph. Choose No when you are using continuous-form paper. The Eject option automatically pages between graphs if it is set to Yes. If you choose Eject No, 1-2-3 does not automatically page between graphs. Choosing Quit tells 1-2-3 that you do not need to make further changes to the Action settings.

Making Changes Permanent

All the changes you make to the PrintGraph program are temporary. Unless you save the new settings, they will revert to the defaults the next time you use PrintGraph. To make the current settings the new default values, use the Settings Save command. The new settings are saved to your PrintGraph disk in a file named PGRAPH.CNF.

Resetting the Settings Options

Choosing Reset from the Settings menu returns all the PrintGraph settings to their default values. The default values are the ones stored in the file PGRAPH.CNF.

Leaving the Settings Menu

The Quit option removes the Settings menu. It returns you to the main menu for PrintGraph.

Printing Selected Graphs

When you choose the Go option from the main PrintGraph menu, PrintGraph begins printing the graphs you listed under Image-Select. Refer back to Figure 11-22 for an example of a graph printed with PrintGraph. It uses the format settings established as it prints the graph. The CTRL-BREAK key provides a way to stop the printing if an emergency arises. (The stop will not take effect for a few seconds because information already sent to the printer must be processed.)

   If you are working with a one-drive system, you should have both the graph and the font directory set to drive A. You should have the PrintGraph disk in drive A when you initially request the program. After the fonts have been read into memory, you are prompted to insert the disk containing your data files. With a two-drive system or a hard drive, it is not necessary to transfer disks.

   Two options on the main PrintGraph menu allow you to affect the paper in your printer. The Page option advances the paper in your printer one full page. This option is useful for ejecting your paper after a graph is printed.

   The second option, Align, asks 1-2-3 to consider the current cursor location as the top of a form. It is your responsibility to have the paper positioned at the top of a form when you issue the Align command.

Ending Your PrintGraph Session

To end your PrintGraph session, select Exit from the main menu. Be sure to save configuration settings changes before leaving the program. Select Yes at the confirmation prompt.

Moving Beyond 1-2-3's Graph Features

With Release 2's many graphics features, you may not need any further enhancements. One enhancement you may want to consider is combining other graphics with the worksheet data they describe using the Wysiwyg Add-In covered in Chapter 15. For example, with Wysiwyg, you can add the current graph, named graphs, or images stored in .PIC and .CGM files and then add your own enhancements. Three other Lotus packages support 1-2-3's graph definitions and offer additional enhancements: Manuscript, Graphwriter II, and Freelance Plus.

Lotus Manuscript can print .PIC graphs, .WK1 data, and text in a single document. This package provides other features, although most of them are word-processing features.

Lotus Graphwriter II offers a production feature for graphs, allowing you to define each graph once and then produce it periodically as your 1-2-3 worksheets are updated for the current period. Although the package offers some additional graphic features, its greatest contribution is its ability to store information on all the graphs you need from many worksheets and to produce them for you automatically, grouping as many as 100 charts in one production run.

The Lotus Freelance Plus package provides graphics enhancements of a different sort. It lets you further customize graphs by using arrows or a corporate logo, or by tailoring the composite of any element of the graph. As an example, you can customize a corporate headcount report created with 1-2-3 by adding the company logo. You can also change the bars representing the headcount so they are composed of people figures stacked one on top of the other; the total number of people in the stack represents the relative size of the data entry.

GRAPHICS

Worksheet Range Copy Move File Print Graph Data System Add-In Quit
Type X ABCDEF Reset View Save Options Name Group Quit
Graph X ABCDEF Ranges Options Quit
Columnwise Rowwise
Line Bar XY Stack-Bar Pie HLCO Mixed Features
Use Create Delete Reset Table
Vertical Horizontal Stacked Frame 3-D Effect Quit
Legend Format Tiles Grid Scale Color B&W Data-Labels Quit
ABCDEF Range
ABCDEF Group Quit
Graph ABCDEF Quit
Y-Scale X-Scale Skip
Lines Symbols Both Neither Area
First Scond X-Axis Y-Axis
Horizontal Vertical Both Clear
Automatic Manual Lower Upper Form Indicator Display Quit

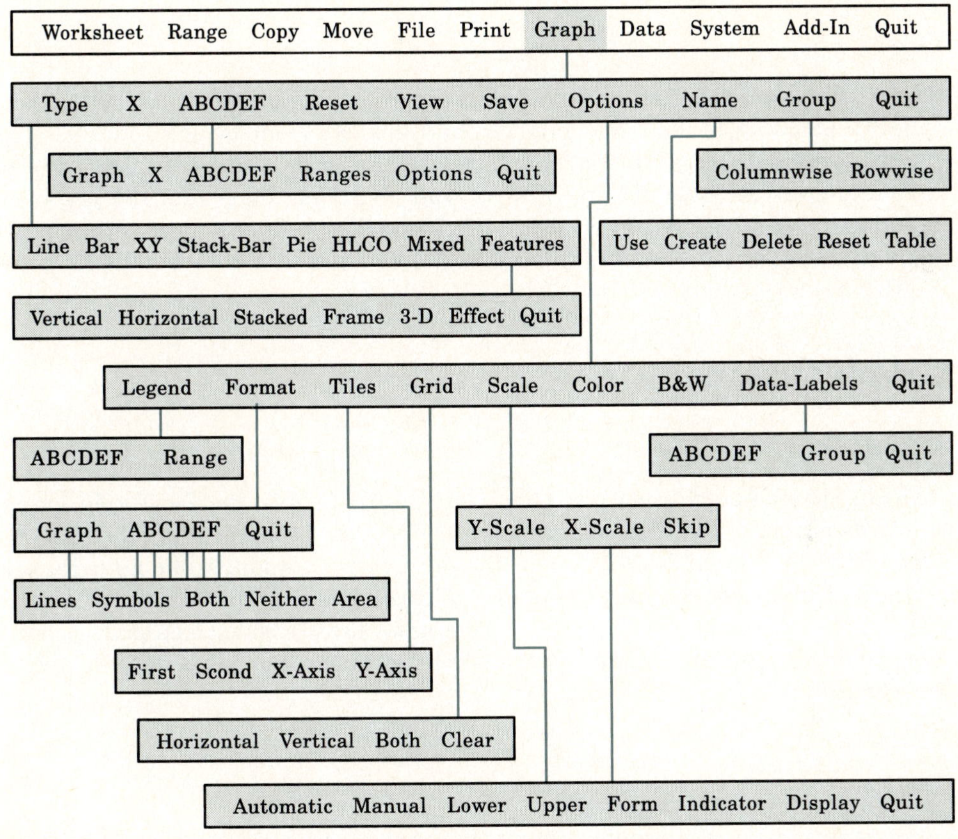

/Graph A B C D E F

Description

This is actually six different commands. Each one assigns one data range to be displayed on a graph. For instance, you would enter **/Graph A** and then specify the first graph data range by entering or pointing to the range or entering a range name.

Options

These commands use from one to six data ranges in your graph. To use all six data ranges, enter each of the range letters from A through F one by one and reference the data you want assigned to each one. Select a range by typing the range address or pointing. In Releases 2.3 and 2.4, you can also select ranges for the graph by entering the range address in the A through F text boxes under Ranges in the Graph Settings dialog box (remember to press F4 (ABS) if you want to select the range in POINT mode).

/Graph Group

Description

This command is used instead of /Graph A B C D E F X when the data for the graph is in adjacent cells. This command assigns the first row or column as the X range, the second row or column as the A range, the third row or column as the B range, and so forth until the command runs out of worksheet data or graph data range names. When this command is executed, 1-2-3 prompts for the worksheet data that you want divided into graph data ranges. You can enter the range addresses, a range name, or point to the cells you want to include.

Options

This command has two options, Columnwise and Rowwise, that determine whether the worksheet data is divided into graph data ranges according to columns or rows.

/Graph Name Create

Description

The /Graph Name Create command assigns a name to the current set of graph settings and stores them with your worksheet. If you want this name and its settings to be available during your next 1-2-3 session, be sure to save the worksheet with /File Save. This command is used for creating a new named graph and for saving the updates made to a named graph.

Options

Your only option for this command is the name you select. The name follows the rules for range names rather than filenames; you can use up to 15 characters.

Note

1-2-3 does not warn you if you select a name that has already been assigned to another graph. If you do this, it overwrites the existing settings with the current settings without asking you.

/Graph Name Delete

Description

The /Graph Name Delete command removes unneeded graph names one by one from the worksheet. Since this process frees up some memory space, it is wise to purge graph names and their associated settings when you no longer need them.

Options

Your only option for this command is the name you select to delete. 1-2-3 lists the current graph names below the prompt. You can select one of these names or type a name.

/Graph Name Reset

Description

This command removes all graph names and their settings from a worksheet. Since there is no cautionary prompt before the deletion, you risk losing all your graph definitions if you accidentally choose Reset from the Graph Name menu. Be careful not to accidentally type **R** when you are working within the /Graph Name command.

/Graph Name Table

Description

This command creates a worksheet table that lists the named graphs in the current worksheet. For each named graph it also lists the graph type and first-line title, if any.

Options

The only option for this command is the location of the table the command creates. When this command prompts you for a location for the graph name table, enter or point to any cell where you want the table to start. This command creates the table, starting at the selected cell, and writes over existing information.

/Graph Name Use

Description

The /Graph Name Use command chooses a graph name from the list associated with the current worksheet. The graph selected becomes the current graph and appears on the screen.

Options

You can either type the graph name or point to it in the list that 1-2-3 displays.

/Graph Options B&W

Description

This command displays graphs in one color. To differentiate between the bars on a bar chart, 1-2-3 automatically adds hatch mark patterns when the B&W option is in effect. This command must be executed before saving a graph to a .PIC file if you plan to print the graph using a monochrome printer. In Releases 2.3 and 2.4, this command is also selected when the Colors on check box in the Graph Settings dialog box is not selected.

/Graph Options Color

Description

This command displays your graphs in color. Only save a graph for printing with Color chosen if you have a color printer or a plotter. Choosing Color omits the hatch mark patterns that differentiate between parts of pie charts and bar graphs when you choose B&W. In Releases 2.3 and 2.4, this command is also selected when the Colors on check box in the Graph Settings dialog box is not selected.

/Graph Options Data-Labels

Description

The /Graph Options Data-Labels command adds specific labels to a range of data points. 1-2-3 obtains these data labels from the range of worksheet cells you specify.

Options

1-2-3 prompts for the name of the data range to which you want to assign labels; the range choices are A through F and Group. If Group is selected, this command assigns data labels one by one to data ranges A through F until the command runs out of label data or graph data ranges. When it prompts you to select between Columnwise and Rowwise, you are selecting how 1-2-3 divides the cells in the range into data labels for the graph data ranges. When you specify the data range, the labels range should contain the same number of cells as the data values selected for the graph data range. Next, select the labels' placement relative to the data point. For line graphs, the choices are Center, Left, Above, Right, and Below; for bar graphs, the choices are Above and Below. The other selections are equivalent to Above. When you are finished assigning data labels, select Quit to return to the Graph Options menu. In Releases 2.3 and 2.4, you can also select data labels using the Graph Legends & Titles dialog box that appears when you select the Legends & Titles command button from the Graph Settings dialog box. Under Data labels, enter the range address or point to the range containing the cell's entries to use as the data labels in the text box for the graph range you want to assign data labels. Under Alignment, select the graph range and the label position relative to the data points from the box 1-2-3 displays.

Note

In a line graph, you can use data labels as the only markers for your data points. To do this, choose /Graph Options Format Graph Neither to remove lines and symbols.

/Graph Options Format

Description

The /Graph Options Format command lets you select the type of line or XY graph you create. You can also choose whether data points are shown as symbols, are connected with a line, are marked with both symbols and a line, or neither. In Releases 2.3 and 2.4, you can also select graph series formats using the Graph Legends & Titles dialog box that appears when you select the Legends & Titles command from the Graph Settings dialog box. After selecting Format, select the graph range and the option described next from the box 1-2-3 displays.

Options

Your first choice is the range to which the format applies. Specify Graph as the range if you want your selection used for all ranges on the graph. Or select a specific data range by entering a letter from A through F. Then select one of the four options.

Lines

This option shows the data points connected by a line without marking the data points.

Symbols

This option shows only symbols, with no connecting line. (1-2-3 uses a different symbol for each of the ranges.)

Both

This option shows both the symbols and a connecting line.

Neither

This option shows neither lines nor symbols. Use this option in conjunction with the Data-Labels option to display no other markings on the graph except a centered data label that marks a point.

Area   This option creates the graph with lines. It fills the space between the lines (for each data range and the X-axis) with a different color or hatch pattern. If more than one graph range uses this format, 1-2-3 stacks the data—even if /Graph Type Features Stacked is set to No. An area graph treats negative numbers as 0.

/Graph Options Grid

Description

The /Graph Options Grid command adds vertical lines, horizontal lines, or both to a graph. These lines start at the markers on the X- or Y-axis and extend upward or to the right, depending on whether you choose Vertical, Horizontal, or Both. An additional option clears the existing grid lines. The lines can help interpret points on the graph. Grid lines are not used with pie charts.

Options

Horizontal   This option adds horizontal lines that extend across from the Y-axis. These lines are effective with bar graphs, since they help you interpret the value for the top of each bar.

Vertical   This option adds vertical lines that start at the X-axis and extend upward. They are most effective with an XY or line graph; they tend to detract from the clarity of a bar graph.

Both   This option adds lines in both directions at once. The lines form a grid pattern on the graph. Horizontal grid lines originate from the Y-axis. Vertical lines start at the X-axis.

Clear   This option eliminates any grid lines that you have added to a graph.

/Graph Options Legend

Description

This command displays legends at the bottom of your graph to describe the data represented by the different graph data ranges.

Options

You can choose any one of the ranges (A through F) each time you request this command. If you select Range, select the legends for all data ranges. You can either type in text or reference a cell address containing the legend you want to use. With the Range option, you must select a legend range containing up to six legends for the six data ranges. While this command has a 19-character limit for legends you enter directly, 1-2-3 does not limit the number of characters used for a legend in a referenced cell. The practical limit on the legend size is based on what 1-2-3 can fit in the graph. In Releases 2.3 and 2.4, you can also enter legends using the Graph Legends & Titles dialog box that appears when you select the Legends & Titles command button from the Graph Settings dialog box. Under Legends, enter the legend text or a backslash and the cell address next to the appropriate data range.

/Graph Options Quit

Description

The /Graph Options Quit command leaves the Graph Options sticky menu and returns to the Graph menu.

/Graph Options Scale Skip

Description

This command removes the congestion that can occur when you assign too many labels to be displayed along the X-axis. The skip factor you specify lets you use only some of the labels in the range. If you specify a skip factor of 3, for example, only every third label is used.

Options

You can specify any number from 1 to 8,192 for the skip factor. The default is 1, meaning that 1-2-3 uses every label in the range.

/Graph Options Scale X-Scale

Description

This command lets 1-2-3 choose the scale for the X-axis or, alternatively, lets you choose the scale yourself. These options only affect XY graphs. In Releases 2.3 and 2.4, you can also change the axis settings using the Graph Scale Settings dialog box that appears when you select the Scale Options command button from the Graph Settings dialog box. In the Graph Scale Settings dialog boxes, you can select and change all of the options described next.

Options

The /Graph Options Scale X-Scale command has seven options.

Automatic   This setting is the default. It lets 1-2-3 determine the proper scale.

Manual   This option informs 1-2-3 that you want to determine the scale range.

Lower   This is the lower limit or the smallest value that is shown on your scale. You define it when you select Manual.

Upper   This is the upper limit or the highest value that is shown on your scale. You define it when you select Manual.

Format   This option selects a display format (Currency, Percent, or the like) for the numeric values represented on the scale.

Indicator   This option turns on or off the size indicator for the scale. The default is Yes, allowing 1-2-3 to display indicators like "thousands." The other choice, No, hides the indicator.

Quit   This option returns you to the Graph Options menu.

/Graph Options Scale Y-Scale

Description

This command lets 1-2-3 choose the scale for the Y-axis or, alternatively, lets you choose the scale yourself.

Options

The /Graph Options Scale Y-Scale command has up to eight options. The first seven options, Automatic, Manual, Lower, Upper, Format, Indicator, and Quit, are identical to the options for the /Graph Options Scale X-Scale command. The last option, Display, is available only in Release 2.3 and above; it selects the side of the graph where 1-2-3 displays tick marks and labels for the Y-axis. You can select Left, Right, Both, or None for the location of the Y-axis tick marks and labels.

/Graph Options Titles

Description

This command adds titles to your graph to improve its clarity and readability. Your titles are limited to 39 characters if you type the titles at the prompt, but more characters are allowed if you use a cell reference. Referencing a stored title requires that you enter a backslash (\) and a cell address or range name containing the title.

In Releases 2.3 and 2.4, you can also enter titles using the Graph Legends & Titles dialog box that appears when you select the Legends & Titles command button from the Graph Settings dialog box. Under Titles, enter the title text or a backslash and the cell address in the First, Second, X-axis, or Y-axis text boxes.

Options

First   The label you enter after this choice is centered at the top of your graph.

Second   Your label entry for this option is centered and placed immediately below the first title.

X-Axis   This option places a title below the X-axis.

Y-Axis   This option places your entry vertically to the left of the Y-axis.

/Graph Quit

Description

This command exits the Graph menu and returns you to the worksheet READY mode.

/Graph Reset

Description

The /Graph Reset command cancels graph settings that you selected previously. You can choose to cancel all or some of the graph settings with the options for this command.

Options

Graph   This option cancels all graph settings and returns you to the Graph menu.

X   This option cancels the X data range.

A-F   Choosing one of this set of letter options cancels the data range for the letter selected.

Ranges   This option cancels the data ranges and data label settings for the X, A, B, C, D, E, and F data ranges.

Options   This option cancels the selections made with /Graph Options commands.

Quit   This option tells 1-2-3 that you have canceled all the settings you want to eliminate and returns you to the previous menu.

/Graph Save

Description

The /Graph Save command saves the current graph picture in a .PIC file separate from your worksheet. The file this command creates can be used by other programs such as PrintGraph, Wysiwyg, and Allways.

Options

After selecting this command, you have the choice of entering a filename or choosing one from the list that 1-2-3 presents. If you choose to use an existing .PIC filename, 1-2-3 prompts you either to confirm that you do want to reuse (and therefore overwrite) that file or to cancel your request.

/Graph Type

Description

The /Graph Type command picks from seven different formats for displaying your graph data. You can easily change from one format to another without any alterations other than selecting another type. If you do not select a graph type, 1-2-3 uses a line graph. You can select the graph type by selecting one of the option buttons under Type in the Graph Settings dialog box. This command has another option that changes how the basic graph formats display your data.

Options

Line   This graph plots the points of a data range and connects them with a line. The default is to use both symbols and a line on the graph. Symbols mark each point, and a line joins the data points. Up to six separate lines, displaying six data ranges, can be generated on one graph.

Bar   This graph uses up to six sets of vertical bars to represent the data ranges selected. 1-2-3 uses hatch mark patterns or colors to distinguish the different data ranges.

XY   This graph pairs X range values with values from the A through F data ranges. With this kind of graph, 1-2-3 generates a numeric scale for both the X- and Y-axis.

Stacked-Bar   For one data range, a stacked bar graph appears the same as an ordinary bar graph. Graphing several data ranges lets you compare them differently. Rather than adding the second set of bars to the right of the first, the stacked bar graph option stacks the second set on top of the first, the third on top of the second, and so on. The total height of a bar thus indicates the total of the values for that category. The different bars in a stack are distinguished by hatch patterns or colors.

Pie   A pie chart is used to compare the size of each of several categories relative to the whole. Each category shown in the pie is represented by a wedge whose size is proportional to its value compared with the values for the other categories in the chart. Only one set of data, the A range, can be shown. The B range can be used to indicate colors, hatch patterns, or wedges that are exploded.

HLCO   An HLCO, or High-Low-Close-Open graph in Releases 2.3 and 2.4 is used for financial commodities over time. For each set of data values, the HLCO has a line from the high to the low value. A projection to the left indicates the open value; a projection to the right indicates the close value. 1-2-3 uses the A data range as the high values, the B data range as the low values, the C data range as the close values, and the D data range as the open values. This graph type does not use the E and F data ranges.

Mixed   A mixed graph in Releases 2.3 and 2.4 displays the A, B, and C data ranges as bar graphs, and the D, E, and F data ranges as line graphs. The bars and lines can use the same formatting options that bar and line graphs can use.

Features   This option in Releases 2.3 and 2.4 is not a graph type and displays another menu of other options. Since the features available with this option are varied, they are described separately next.

/Graph Type Features

Description

This command creates variations of the other basic graph types. These options include axis orientation, stacking data ranges, adding frames, and adding a three-dimensional effect.

Options

Vertical   This option orients the graph axes so the X-axis is horizontal and the Y-axis is vertical; this is the default. You can also select this option by selecting the Vertical option button under Orientation in the Graph Settings dialog box.

Horizontal   This option rotates the axes so the X-axis is vertical and the Y-axis is horizontal. You can also select this option by selecting the Horizontal option button under Orientation in the Graph Settings dialog box.

Stacked   This option, if set to Yes, stacks the data ranges of line, bar, mixed, and XY graphs on top of each other; the default is No. You can also select this option by selecting the Stacked data ranges check box in the Graph Settings dialog box.

Frame   This option displays another menu that lets you select the frames your graph uses. 1-2-3 initially draws a frame around all four sides of the area in which it puts the graph data but you can select between All, Left, Right, Top, Bottom, and None to select where the frame is put. You can also select which sides of the data have frames using the Left, Right, Top, and Bottom check boxes under Frame in the Graph Settings dialog box. You can select Zero-Line, X-Axis or Y-Axis, and Yes to have the zero location marked with an additional line or No to remove it. You can also add or remove zero lines by selecting to mark or unmark the X-axis or Y-axis check box under Zero-line in the Graph Settings dialog box. The Margins option selects whether 1-2-3 leaves a blank area between the left and right edges of the graph and where the first data starts and the last data ends. You can select Yes (the default) or No. You can also add or remove margins to mark or unmark the Margins on check box in the Graph Settings dialog box. You can select Quit to return to the previous menu.

3D-Effect   This option adds a three-dimensional effect to bars in graphs when set to Yes; the default is No. You can also select this option by selecting the 3-D bars check box in the Graph Settings dialog box.

Quit   This option returns you to the Graph menu.

/Graph View

Description

The /Graph View command displays the graph that you have defined by selecting data ranges and a graph type. If a graph has not been defined, the screen appears blank when you select this command. To return to the Graph menu when you are through with the View option, press any key. You can also view the graph by pressing F10 (GRAPH). Using the F10 function key lets you see the graph when you are in the READY mode. Pressing any key returns you to the worksheet.

If you are using Release 2.3 or higher, you can press F10 (GRAPH) to display the current graph at any time—not only when 1-2-3 is in the READY mode. This means you can view a graph in the middle of another command. When you press a key, 1-2-3 returns to where it was before you pressed F10 (GRAPH).

Note

Your screen will appear blank when you try to display a graph if you have installed a different graphic screen than you are using or if your equipment does not support graphics. In both cases you can press any key to return to the Graph menu.

/Graph X

Description

The /Graph X command labels the points on the X-axis for a line or bar graph. For a pie chart the X values provide labels for the pie segments; for an XY chart they provide values to plot against the Y values. The labels assigned to the points must be stored in worksheet cells and specified with a range name or a range address or by pointing to the cells you want to use.

Options

There are no options for this command. If the labels you choose contain too many characters, 1-2-3 uses two rows to display the X labels, alternating the X labels between the rows. If the labels still have too many characters, 1-2-3 truncates the X labels. You can use /Graph Options Scale Skip to tell 1-2-3 not to use every label.

:Graph Add

Description

The :Graph Add command adds a graph created with 1-2-3 to a range of cells on the worksheet. The graph can be printed with Wysiwyg or viewed on the screen. You can add a current graph, a named graph, a graph saved in .PIC format, or a metafile graphic such as the SmartPics that come with Release 2.4. You can also create a blank graphic to modify.

Options

Current   This option adds the current graph to the worksheet.

Named   This option allows you to select a named graph to add to the worksheet.

PIC   This option allows you to select a graph saved in a .PIC file to add to the worksheet.

Metafile   This option allows you to select a graphic in the .CGM format to add to the worksheet.

Blank   This option adds a blank graphic to the worksheet.

:Print Range Set

Description

The :Print Range Set command sets the range of cells to be printed from the worksheet. See Chapter 6 for further information on Wysiwyg printing commands.

:Print Settings

Description

The :Print Settings command allows you to select from several options for customizing which pages of the print range will be printed and the appearance of the pages. See Chapter 6 for further information on Wysiwyg printing commands.

:Print Config

Description

The :Print Config command allows you to select from several options for configuring the printer or file to which you are printing. See Chapter 6 for further information on Wysiwyg printing commands.

PrintGraph Align

Description

The PrintGraph Align command tells 1-2-3 that you have your printer paper at the top of a form.

PrintGraph Exit

Description

This command exits the PrintGraph program.

PrintGraph Go

Description

This command prints the graphs chosen with Image-Select. The settings selected on the PrintGraph menu are used when printing the selected graphs. Pressing CTRL-BREAK stops the printing of a graph as soon as the printer buffer is empty. When a plotter is specified as the device, you receive a message prompting you to change plotter pens.

PrintGraph Image-Select

Description

This command selects the graph files to print.

Options

Image-Select presents a list of all the .PIC files in the directory established as the graphs directory. You can select files by pointing to them and pressing the spacebar to mark the filenames with a #. You can choose as many files as you wish. Your selection order controls the print order when Go is selected. If you press F10 (GRAPH) while pointing to a filename, 1-2-3 displays the graph on your screen. Press ENTER when you are finished.

PrintGraph Page

Description

This command advances the paper in your printer to the top of the next page.

PrintGraph Settings Action

Description

This command determines the actions PrintGraph takes after each graph is printed.

Options

Pause   When this option is set to Yes, PrintGraph pauses for a paper change between graphs. When it is set to No, PrintGraph expects continuous forms and continues printing graphs without pause.

Eject   When set to Yes, this option ejects the page after each graph is printed. When this option is set to No, PrintGraph prints the next graph on the same page if it fits.

Quit   The Quit option returns you to the Settings menu.

PrintGraph Settings Hardware

Description

The Settings Hardware option changes graph and font directories, the interface with the printer or plotter, the print device, and the paper size.

Options

Graphs-Directory   This option specifies the pathname for the .PIC files that you plan to print.

Fonts-Directory   This option specifies the pathname for the .FNT files that contain the fonts PrintGraph needs to produce your graphs.

Interface   This option defines the type of connection between your system and your printer or plotter (serial, parallel, or local area network device).

Printer   This option selects one of the graphics printers defined during installation.

Size-Paper   This option defines the length and width of the paper you are using.

Quit   This option returns you to the Settings menu.

PrintGraph Settings Image

Description

The Settings Image command determines the appearance of the graphics image. You can choose fonts, size, and range colors with this command.

Options

Size   This option permits the choice of a full-page graph, a half-page graph, and manual page-size definition. It also permits you to rotate the graph from 0 to 90 degrees before printing. The Manual option has a separate submenu.

Font   This option selects either one or two fonts from a list of fonts displayed by PrintGraph. Fonts with a 2 after the font name print darker than fonts with a 1. The first font you specify is used for the first title of the graph, and the second font is used for the remainder of the text.

Range-Colors   With this option you can choose ranges from A through F or X and select a color for each range by either highlighting the color name or typing the first character of the name. Naturally, this command is effective only if you have a color printer or a plotter.

Quit   This option returns you to the Settings menu.

PrintGraph Settings Quit

Description

This command returns you to the main PrintGraph menu.

PrintGraph Settings Reset

Description

The Settings Reset command returns your settings to the ones in the PGRAPH.CNF file (the default settings).

PrintGraph Settings Save

Description

This command saves the current settings in the PGRAPH.CNF file, making them the default settings for all subsequent sessions.

Part III

Enhancing and Expanding 1-2-3

Chapter **12**

Keyboard Macros

Many people are intimidated by macros because they have tried unsuccessfully to work with them. Macros, however, are a powerful and flexible feature of 1-2-3. They can be quite simple to master if you use a step-by-step approach and learn the most basic macros before attempting the more sophisticated variety. The Learn feature can record keystrokes to make the mastery of macros easier than ever. You also can improve your success ratio if you follow the procedures for creating macros outlined in this chapter and Chapter 13.

With 1-2-3 Release 2.4, you can assign macros to user icons. 1-2-3 provides 12 user icons that you can use in palette 7 or add to the custom palette. This feature gives you a quick way to access any macro with the SmartIcons palette.

Types of Macros

1-2-3's *keyboard alternative macros* can be used to automate printing, formatting, or any other task that is accomplished with menu selections. This type of macro provides an alternative to typing from the keyboard. Keyboard macros are good to begin with if you are new to macros, since they contain familiar keystroke commands. They can also provide a wealth of time-saving features. If you follow the instructions in this chapter, you can create keyboard alternative macros that are successful the first time you try them.

Some macros use commands that are available as keyword options from 1-2-3's advanced macro command language. With these *advanced command language macros*, you can read and write records to a file, create your own menus, utilize iterative loops, and alter the order in which commands are processed. 1-2-3's command language is a full programming language, and like other programming languages, it allows you to develop complete applications. With the Release 2.2 macro commands, you can control the appearance of the screen, including the frame at the top and side of the screen. Chapter 13 covers all the features of 1-2-3's advanced command language.

Both types of macros can be stored in the worksheet where they are used or in a separate file with the Macro Library Manager Add-In that comes with Releases 2.2 and above. With the Macro Library Manager, you can create a library of macros for use with many worksheets.

With Release 2.4, you can make macros even easier to use. You can assign macro code to a user icon while entering the keystrokes, or you can access code already stored on the worksheet.

Keyboard Macros

Like all macros, a keyboard alternative macro is nothing more than a column of label entries that have a name assigned to them. The contents of the labels are the sequence of keystrokes that you want 1-2-3 to execute for you. After all your label entries are stored in a column, you name the top cell in the column with the /Range Name Create command. You can use any name for a macro in Releases 2.2 and above, as long as it conforms to the rules of range names and falls within the 15-character limit. You should avoid using names that match existing range names, cell addresses, @function names, function key names, and advanced macro commands. Spaces and the period (.), the colon (:), and the comma (,) should be avoided. The special names consisting of a backslash (\) and a single letter that were required in earlier releases are still accepted. These special names allow you to execute a keyboard macro by pressing the ALT key in combination with the letter used as the macro's name, but these letters are not very descriptive.

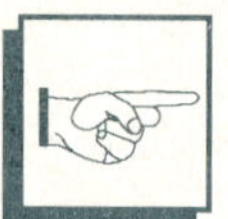

Start all macro names with the same letter. This makes it easier to locate macros in a list of range names. If you plan to create some macros with names like \A, use a backslash (\) to start longer name entries as well.

To execute a macro without the special backslash-letter combination name, press ALT-F3 and highlight the macro name in the list or type the name. You must press ENTER to start macro execution. The steps for creating and executing keyboard macros are summarized for you in the box entitled "The ABCs of Keyboard Macros."

Avoid macro names such as A10, @SUM, and any that duplicate cell addresses, existing range names, and 1-2-3's keywords. With so many other meaningful names from which to select, you can easily avoid names that can cause confusion.

Recording the Keystrokes

There are several options for storing macro keystrokes in Releases 2.2 and above. You can type them in a cell as label entries, or you can use the Learn feature to record them for you. The Learn feature is not automatic, as it is in Release 3; you must activate it before it records your entries. First consider the typing alternative. You need this technique to modify existing macros, and the procedure gives you an appreciation for the work that the new keystroke recorder does for you.

The ABCs of Keyboard Macros

1. Plan the task you want the macro to perform.

2. Use /Worksheet Learn to define a Learn range, and then position the cell pointer for beginning recording.

3. Press ALT-F5 (LEARN) to begin recording and perform all the steps in the macro.

4. Press ALT-F5 (LEARN) to stop recording. Steps 2 through 4 can be replaced by typing the macro entries directly into the macro cells as labels.

5. Edit the label entries in the macro column and make any required changes.

6. Record the macro name one cell to the left of the top cell in the macro column. Use the backslash key (\) and a single letter if you want to execute the macro with a single key combination. Or you can use any valid range name.

7. Use /Range Name Labels Right to apply the name to the macro.

8. Save the worksheet containing the macro.

9. Execute the macro using the ALT key plus the macro letter name, like S. If you used a range name, use ALT-F3 (RUN), highlight the name, and press ENTER.

Typing the Required Keystrokes

When you want to store a menu request in a macro, begin the sequence with a single quotation mark so it is treated as a label. This prevents 1-2-3 from executing a menu request immediately. Then enter the keystrokes. Indicate the request for a menu command with a slash, and record each of the menu commands by entering the first letter of the menu choice. For instance, to enter the keystrokes necessary to view a Worksheet Status screen, type '/ws or '/WS in the cell (case is not important).

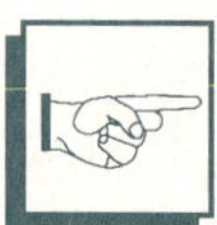

If you make a mistake repeatedly throughout a long macro, the quickest correction method is the Replace option of /Range Search.

In addition to specifying menu selections, you sometimes must indicate an ENTER keypress. The ENTER key is represented in a macro by the tilde mark (~).

Filenames or range names should be entered in full. As an example, to store the characters needed to retrieve a file named SALES from the default drive, enter '/FRSALES~ or '/FRsales~ in the macro cell. Although you can use all upper- or lowercase for the keystroke entries, a consistent combination can help to clarify range names, filenames, cell addresses, and menu selections.

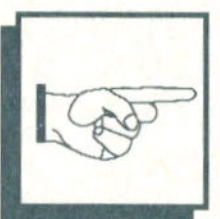

Beware of missing tildes. The single most frequent cause of mistakes in macros created by novice users is missing tildes. After recording the correct menu selections, it is easy to forget that you press ENTER at certain points when executing a command sequence from the keyboard. Even one missing tilde causes the macro to malfunction.

To correct a macro once it is entered, you can use the F2 (EDIT) key with the cell pointer on the cell containing the macro code. Since the macro code is nothing more than a label entry, special techniques are not required for making changes.

Recording Special Keys

There are a number of special keyboard keys, like the function keys and cell-pointer movement keys, that you will want to include in your macros. These keys and the macro keywords that stand for them are listed in the box called "Special Keys in Macro Commands." Note that all the keywords are enclosed in brackets ({}).

Whether you use the Learn feature to enter your macros or type them in, you must be familiar with the effect of each of these keys so that you can make intelligent modifications to existing macros. You should also be careful never to split these entries between cells. Opening and closing brackets, as well as everything in between, should be in the same cell.

There is no keyword for the NUM LOCK or SCROLL LOCK key, because it must be requested from outside a macro. CAPS LOCK is not represented either, since cell entries are typed right into a macro and you have your choice of typing either uppercase or lowercase letters. Case is also unimportant in operator entries made while a macro is executing, unless you are storing these entries on the worksheet and have prefer-

Special Keys in Macro Commands

1-2-3 has a macro keyword to represent each of the special keyboard keys, except for NUM LOCK, SCROLL LOCK, CAPS LOCK, ALT-F1 (COMPOSE), ALT-F2 (STEP), ALT-F3 (RUN), ALT-F4 (UNDO), ALT-F5 (LEARN), SHIFT, and PRTSC.

Cell Pointer Movement Key	Keyword
UP ARROW	{UP} or {U}
DOWN ARROW	{DOWN} or {D}
RIGHT ARROW	{RIGHT} or {R}
LEFT ARROW	{LEFT} or {L}
HOME	{HOME}
END	{END}
PGUP	{PGUP}
PGDN	{PGDN}
CTRL-RIGHT or TAB	{BIGRIGHT}
CTRL-LEFT or SHIFT-TAB	{BIGLEFT}

Editing Key	Keyword
DEL	{DELETE} or {DEL}
INS	{INSERT} or {INS}
ESC	{ESCAPE} or {ESC}
BACKSPACE	{BACKSPACE} or {BS}

Function Key	Keyword
F1 (HELP)	{HELP}
F2 (EDIT)	{EDIT}
F3 (NAME)	{NAME}
F4 (ABS)	{ABS}
F5 (GOTO)	{GOTO}
F6 (WINDOW)	{WINDOW}
F7 (QUERY)	{QUERY}
F8 (TABLE)	{TABLE}
F9 (CALC)	{CALC}

Special Keys in Macro Commands (continued)

F10 (GRAPH)	{GRAPH}
ALT-F7 (APP1)	{APP1}
ALT-F8 (APP2)	{APP2}
ALT-F9 (APP3)	{APP3}
ALT-F10 (APP4)	{APP4}

Special Key	**Keyword**
Input from keyboard during macro	{?}
ENTER key	~
Tilde (~)	{~}
{	{{}
}	{}}
/ or <	/,< , or {MENU}
CTRL-BREAK	{BREAK}

---

ence for the case of the entry. Other keys not supported are ALT-F1 (COMPOSE), PRTSC, ALT-F5 (LEARN), ALT-F2 (STEP), ALT-F3 (RUN), ALT-F4 (UNDO), and SHIFT.

Check the spelling of the special key names carefully. Your entries in a macro must be exact. A small mistake is just as serious as a large one, since 1-2-3 only recognizes entries that exactly match the defined set of options.

Cursor-Movement Keys

1-2-3 has macro commands for all of the different keystrokes you can use to move the cell pointer to any cell. You can also repeat keystrokes by either repeating the macro keyword as in {UP} {UP} {UP} or by using the repeat factor, which is a number in the keyword as in {UP 3} or {U 3}. All three representations have the same effect; they all move the cell pointer three cells above its current location.

The END and arrow key combination is supported in macros. You can enter {END} {RIGHT} to have the macro move the cell pointer to the last occupied cell entry on the right side of the worksheet.

Function Keys

With the exception of ALT-F1 (COMPOSE), ALT-F2 (STEP), ALT-F3 (RUN), ALT-F4 (UNDO), and ALT-F5 (LEARN), all the function keys can be represented by special macro keywords as listed in the box shown earlier, "Special Keys in Macro Commands."

Edit Keys

In addition to F2 (EDIT), which places you in the EDIT mode, there are several special keys that you use when correcting worksheet entries. When you are in EDIT mode, the macro commands for keys behave the same way when you press the keys in EDIT mode. You can use the {DEL} or {DELETE} and {BS} or {BACKSPACE} to remove one character at a time. You can include repeat factors such as {DELETE 4} just as you did with arrow keys. {ESC} or {ESCAPE} can remove an entry from a cell and delete a menu default, such as a previous setup string, so you can make a new entry.

Other Special Keys

As mentioned earlier, the tilde (~) represents ENTER. To use a macro to place an actual tilde in a cell, type {~}. To use a macro that places brackets in a cell, enter either {{} or {}}. These features can be useful in a macro that builds another macro.

Type {?} in a macro to let 1-2-3 know that you want the operator to input something from the keyboard. 1-2-3 then waits for you to make the entry and press ENTER. Chapter 13 covers two additional methods for indicating keyboard input that offer greater sophistication, in that they allow you to present a message to the operator regarding the data you wish to have entered.

Typing a Keyboard Macro

The following procedure for entering a macro is not the fastest way, but it should more than pay for itself in time savings during the testing and debugging phase when you are trying to get your macro to execute correctly.

- The first step in creating a keyboard macro is planning the task you want to accomplish. Without a plan, you are not likely to create a macro that is well organized and successful.

- After you have made your plan, test it by entering the proposed keystrokes for immediate execution by 1-2-3. As you enter each keystroke directly into the menus, record it on a sheet of paper. Later you will learn to capitalize on these written entries and actually turn them into the macro code. For now, you should type at least a few for a firsthand look at what each keystroke represents.

- If the menu selections handled your task correctly, use your sheet of paper as a script when you record the keystrokes as labels in the macro cells.

- Choose a location on your worksheet for recording your macro.

- Where possible, use range name references rather than cell addresses as you build your macro. 1-2-3 adjusts to a change in the range name location, but it does not adjust for changes in the location of cell addresses.

- You can record up to 240 keystrokes in one label cell, but it would not be advisable to do so because you could never read the entire entry at one time without editing the cell. At the other extreme, you can enter each single keystroke of the entry in a separate cell of the column. 1-2-3 reads down the column until it reaches a blank cell. However, this second approach is also not advisable because you would need so many cells to create even a short macro. The best approach is to select some reasonable upper limit for the number of characters to be entered in one macro cell and then, within that limit, move to a new cell whenever you reach a logical breaking place in your keystroke entries.

Keywords in a macro are easier to understand when they are spelled out. Use /Range Search with the Replace option to locate entries like {D} and change them to {DOWN}. You can even develop a macro that handles this task if you specify the search range it should use.

Remember to enter all your macro instructions as labels. Start them with a label indicator if the first character is a number or one of these characters: / \ + - @ # $ < .

Using the Learn Feature

The Learn feature can save you a significant amount of time in macro entry. It makes the creation of macros easy because you can execute a task without having to remember the representations for the special keys; 1-2-3 records the proper entries.

To start recording keystrokes, you must tell 1-2-3 where you want your keystrokes recorded and that you want 1-2-3 to start recording your keystrokes.

To tell 1-2-3 where you want the keystrokes recorded, you must enter **/Worksheet Learn** to display this menu:

Select Range to select the range that will contain the keystrokes. Select a range that contains one column and as many rows as you want the Learn range to occupy. To prevent the Learn range from becoming full, include more rows than you expect to use. If 1-2-3 displays the error message "Learn range is full," enter **/Worksheet Learn Range** and expand the existing Learn range. 1-2-3 continues storing keystrokes in the expanded Learn range. The Learn range should be in a place where it is not affected by the keystrokes you are performing. For example, you do not want the Learn range in a column you plan to delete or using rows you plan to delete. If you do so, 1-2-3 terminates recording the keystrokes when you delete the rows or column the Learn range uses.

To start recording the keystrokes, you must press ALT-F5 (LEARN). Once this key is pressed, the status line includes a LEARN indicator that tells you 1-2-3 is recording your keystrokes. All of the keystrokes that you press until the Learn feature is turned off are recorded in the Learn range. 1-2-3 stops recording keystrokes when you press ALT-F5 (LEARN), fill the Learn range, or delete the column or row that the Learn range uses.

The keystrokes are recorded in the Learn range using the same keywords that you would enter. 1-2-3 uses an abbreviation, such as {BS} for {BACKSPACE} in place of the lengthier keyword. 1-2-3 does not record any /Worksheet Learn commands, entries made in dialog boxes, or the following keystrokes: ALT-F1 (COMPOSE), ALT-F5 (LEARN), ALT-F4 (UNDO), SHIFT, NUM LOCK, or SCROLL LOCK.

If you change your mind or make a mistake while entering the keystrokes, you have two choices for the existing keystrokes stored in the Learn range. You can remove the existing recorded keystrokes with the /Worksheet Learn Erase command and start the keystrokes that you want to record from the beginning. An alternative is to continue recording the keystrokes and edit the keystrokes recorded in the Learn range.

Once you have finished recording the keystrokes, you can use them as a macro or part of one. To make the recorded keystrokes into a macro, you must name the first cell in the Learn range. If you want to further enhance the keystrokes into a more advanced macro, you can edit the labels containing the keystrokes. Figure 12-1 shows a large number of keystrokes entered with the Learn feature. Notice how the keystrokes are split up into manageable groups. You can use these keystrokes as a macro or add further enhancements such as using the macro commands discussed in Chapter 13.

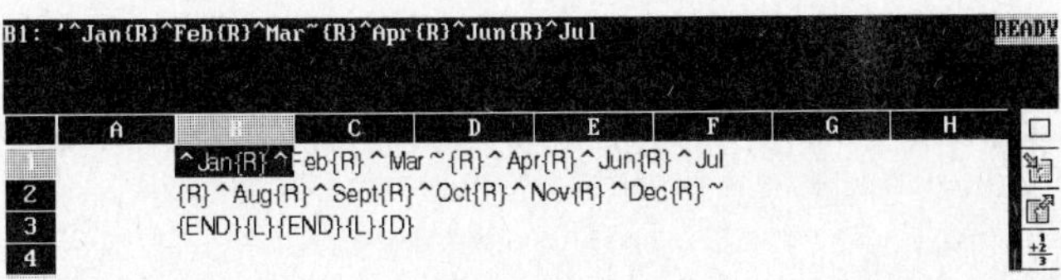

Figure 12-1.   *Keystrokes stored with the Learn feature*

After you record the keystrokes, you must enter the **/Worksheet Learn Cancel** command. This command removes the setting for the Learn range. If you do not enter this command and accidentally press ALT-F5 (LEARN), the keystrokes that you subsequently press record after the keystrokes that you have recorded.

Enter the keystrokes portion of a complex macro with the Learn feature so you will not accidentally forget a keyword. If you are developing a lengthy macro that uses the macro commands covered in Chapter 13 as well as keystroke macro keywords, use the Learn feature to record the keystroke portion of the macros. Then copy the recorded keystrokes to your macro.

Naming Your Macro

Once you have entered or copied all the macro keystrokes, you are ready to name your macro. Before doing this, position your cell pointer on the top cell in the macro, since this is the only cell that will be named. Then enter **/Range Name Create**. At the prompt for the range name, enter a backslash (\) and any single alphabetic character before pressing ENTER if you want to be able to execute the macro with a single key combination. An alternative is to type any valid range name and press ENTER to execute the macro with the ALT-F3 (RUN) option. Since you positioned your cell pointer before requesting the /Range command, simply press ENTER in response to the prompt for the range address. When you save the worksheet, the macro and its name are saved as well and are available whenever you retrieve the worksheet.

The naming conventions for 1-2-3's macros allow you to create an unlimited number of macros. You can also create 26 unique macro names using the backslash and the letters of the alphabet, such as \T. These macros can be executed with the ALT key in combination with the letter used in the macro name. 1-2-3 does not distinguish between upper- and lowercase characters in a macro name.

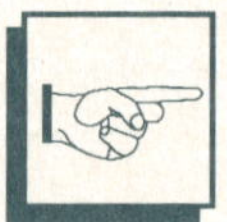

Choose a special character or letter as the first entry in all macro names. When you use F3 (RUN), 1-2-3 displays a list of all valid range names. To help distinguish macro names from other range names, start all of them with the same character. Using a special symbol like # will place them at the front of the list.

You can obtain a list of all your current macro names and the range addresses to which they are assigned with the /Range Name Table command. Enter **/Range Name Table**, and respond to 1-2-3's prompt for a table range by entering the address of the upper-left cell in any blank section of the worksheet where 1-2-3 can write the macro name assignments. This command is described more fully in Chapter 5.

Documenting Your Macro

As you create a macro, you are aware of the name you have assigned to it and the
function of each of its steps. A month from now, however, when you look again at the
macro cells, it may take some thought to remember what you were attempting to
accomplish. It is therefore a wise move to document information like the macro name
and the function of each step on the worksheet as you create the macro. The time
investment involved in this extra step more than pays for itself later on.

A good documentation strategy is placing the macro name in the cell immediately
to the left of the top macro cell. If the macro is named CURRENCY, type **CURRENCY**
in the cell immediately to the left of the top macro cell. If the macro is named \A,
you would enter '\A in the name cell. (The ' is needed to prevent 1-2-3 from
interpreting the backslash as the repeating label indicator and filling your cell with
the letter "A.")

The cell to the left of your top macro cell is an especially appropriate choice
because, if you have already placed the macro name there before actually naming
the macro range, you can use the /Range Name Labels Right command to name the
macro cell without typing the name in again. In other words, you can type the macro
steps, then type the macro name in the empty cell to the left of the macro, leave the
cell pointer on the name, enter **/Range Name Labels Right**, and press ENTER.

A good area to use for documenting macro instructions is a column of cells to the
right of the instructions. Depending on the length of your macro entries, you can
widen the column containing the macro instructions or move several cells to the right
of the macro column for the documentation entries. A brief description of every
command makes each step's function clearer and saves a significant amount from
the time you will spend later modifying the macro. Figure 12-2 shows a macro with
documentation entries for the individual macro instructions.

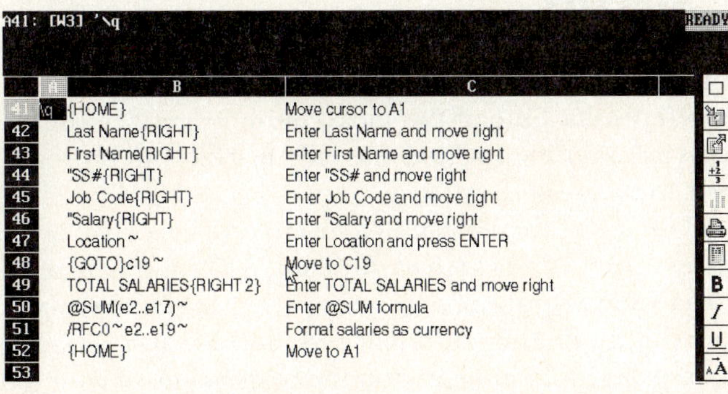

Figure 12-2.   A macro with documentation

Executing Your Macro

Once you have entered and named a macro, you can use it whenever you wish. Releases 2.2 and above support macro execution from READY mode or within a command. When used from within a command, macros can supply entries like graph titles or print headers. If your macro requires the cell pointer to be positioned in a certain cell, put the cell pointer there before executing the macro. The cell pointer does not need to be on the macro cell to execute the macro.

If the macro is named with a backslash-letter combination, you can execute the macro in several ways. The shortcut approach is to press the ALT key and, while the key is pressed, touch the letter key that you used in your macro name; then release both keys.

The other approach can be used regardless of the macro's name. Press the ALT-F3 (RUN) key or choose the Run icon, and 1-2-3 displays the names of all the range names in the current worksheet as well as any macros stored in any active macro library. (Macro libraries are discussed later in this chapter.) Highlight the name you want to use and press ENTER, or type the desired name.

Save the worksheet in which you recorded the macro before trying it. If the macro contains mistakes, saving it prevents you from losing your work if the macro writes over its own instructions or locks up your system. You might want to use the /File Save Backup command to maintain the integrity of the existing file until after macro testing.

Debugging Macros

The debugging process involves testing and correcting macros to ensure that you obtain the desired results. One of the most common mistakes made when creating keyboard macros is forgetting to enter the tilde mark (~) to represent each time the ENTER key needs to be pressed.

1-2-3 has a STEP mode that executes a macro one keystroke at a time so you can follow its progress and spot any area of difficulty. STEP mode is activated with ALT-F2 (STEP). Step is a toggle operation, so pressing ALT-F2 a second time turns STEP mode off again. When this mode is operational and you have not yet started debugging a macro, you can see the STEP indicator on the bottom line of your screen. In Release 2.4, you can use this SmartIcon to turn on STEP mode:

When the STEP indicator is on, any macro you invoke can be executed one instruction at a time. Press the spacebar whenever you are ready to move on to the next instruction. The cell address of the macro instruction that is executing is displayed at the bottom left of the screen along with the contents of this cell. A highlight marks the current instruction within this entry and scrolls to the right as you proceed step by step though the entry. Figure 12-3 shows the highlight within the line at the bottom of the screen.

While the macro is executing, SST will appear in place of STEP at the bottom of the screen anytime the macro pauses for user input.

To stop a malfunctioning macro, press the CTRL and BREAK keys simultaneously. This cancels macro operation immediately, and presents an ERROR indicator at the upper-right corner of the screen. Press ESC to return to READY mode so you can make corrections to your macro.

Once you develop a little experience with macros, you will probably find that you tend to make certain mistakes in your macros. Here are some common mistakes:

Misspelled keywords
Missing tildes (~)
Missing steps in menu selection sequences
Incorrect selections in menu selection sequences

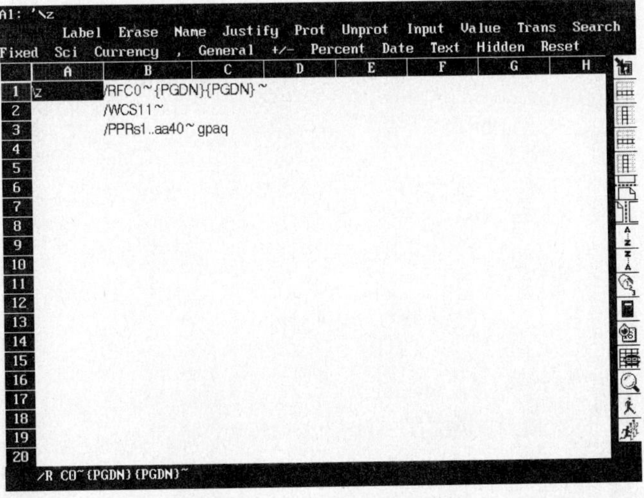

Figure 12-3.   *A macro in STEP mode*

Assigning Macros to User Icons

You can customize 1-2-3's SmartIcon palettes in two ways. In Chapter 14, you will learn how to change the icons that appear on the first palette. This procedure allows you to put all of the frequently used icons together on one palette. Another option is to assign macro instructions to any of the 12 user icons represented by U1 through U12. You can use this feature to store frequently needed text. This text is typed automatically when you select the icon. You can also use this feature to develop a custom formatting macro that meets your exact needs.

The Box titled "Assigning a Macro to a User Icon" summarizes the required steps, which are discussed in detail in the sections that follow. After assigning a macro to any of these user icons, you can use them just as you would any other icon, invoking the commands they represent or assigning one of them to your custom palette.

Defining a User Icon from the Keyboard

You can use the User icon on the second-to-last palette to define any of the 12 user icons labeled U1 through U12. After selecting the User icon, the User Icon Descriptions dialog box shown in Figure 12-4 appears. You need to decide which user icon you want to define and select that icon number.

Select Assign Macro to Icon to display a User-Defined Icon dialog box. You can supply a description of up to 72 characters in the Icon Description text box. Just as

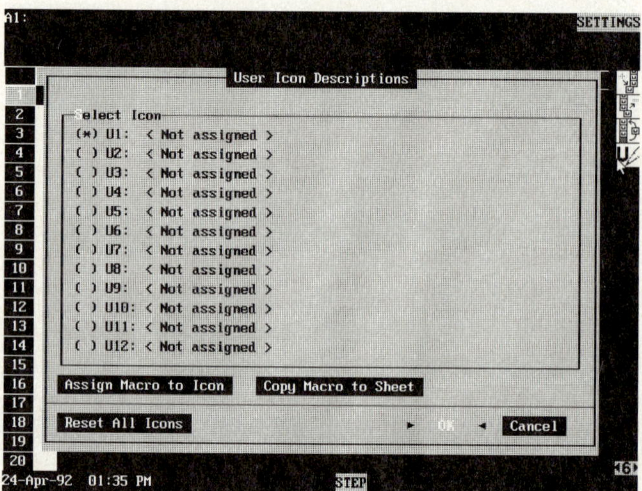

Figure 12-4.   *The User Icon Descriptions dialog box*

other icons display text in the control panel when they are highlighted, user icons will display whatever you enter as a description when they are highlighted.

Next, type the macro instructions in the Macro Text text box. You can use up to 240 characters to represent any menu command or keypress. The menu representations can be for 1-2-3 as well as Wysiwyg, so long as Wysiwyg will be attached when you use the macro. Defining user icons in this way does not change the appearance of the palette in which the macros appear, except that the description of the icon is displayed in the control panel when the description is highlighted. Figure 12-5 shows a definition for a macro that will format the selected range as currency with zero decimal places.

To complete the task, select OK. You can cancel the request by selecting Cancel. You can reset the current user icon definition by choosing Reset This Icon. You can also choose Reset This Icon if you need to reenter the text for a text box.

The Icons add-in would let you define additional icons at this point, or you can choose OK to return to 1-2-3's READY mode. Choosing Reset All Icons at this point resets all user icons so you can redefine them again. Your last option is Cancel, to eliminate any changes made in the Icons Description dialog box.

Defining a Macro with Stored Keystrokes

If you want to try a macro before assigning it to a user icon, or if you have an existing macro that you want to use with the user icons, 1-2-3 allows you to add the keystrokes with a reference to their location on the worksheet. Once added in this way, the keystrokes are added to the dialog box and will not be updated unless you edit the

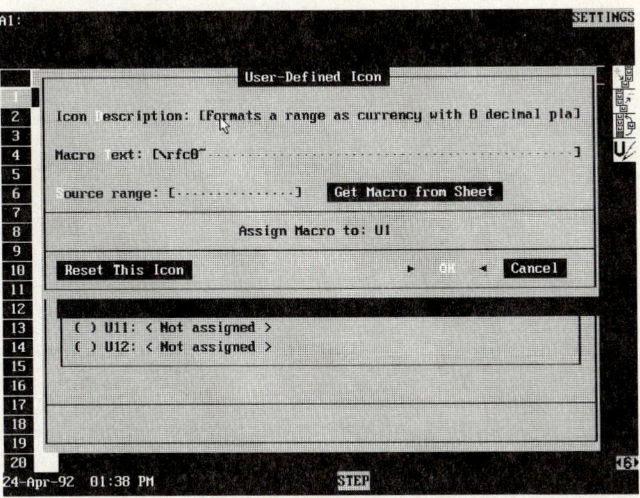

Figure 12-5.   *Screen providing a description and the icon text*

keystrokes with the Macro Text text box. In other words, you will not be able to revise the macro instructions on the worksheet or change the user icon definition once it is attached to the icon.

To obtain macro instruction from the worksheet, you define the user icon in the regular fashion until it is time to add the keystrokes. Rather than selecting the Macro Text text box, you select Source Range and specify the range containing the macro code or the name that you have assigned to the range. If you have stored macro instructions in F3..F6 and have named these instructions \c, you can enter either F3..F6 or \c as the range. Next, select Get Macro from Sheet to copy the entries to the sheet.

Modifying the Definition of a User Icon

Once you attach macro instructions to a user icon, you must use the same basic procedure to modify them as you did when you first defined them. These are steps that you must follow:

1. Select User Icon.

2. Select the user icon to modify.

3. Select Assign Macro to Icon.

4. Select the Macro Text text box.

5. Modify the text in the box to make any additions or corrections.

6. Select OK twice to return to 1-2-3's READY mode.

Assigning a Macro to a User Icon

1. Select User Icon from the SmartIcon palette.

2. Select the icon number that you want to define.

3. Select Assign Macro to Icon.

4. Type a description of up to 72 characters in the Icon Description text box.

5. In the Macro Text text box, type the macro instructions you want to attach, using up to 240 characters.

6. Select OK twice.

Debugging a Macro Assigned to a User Icon

If the macro that you attached to a user icon is not working the way you want, you will need to copy it to the worksheet in order to use the STEP mode to test it. The method you will use to complete the copy is as follows:

1. Select User Icon.

2. Select the user icon that you are having problems with.

3. Select Copy Macro to Sheet, specify an empty range on the worksheet, and then select OK.

Automatic Macros

1-2-3 has a unique feature that allows you to create an automatic macro for a worksheet. Every time a worksheet containing an automatic macro is retrieved, 1-2-3 immediately executes this macro. This feature has more application with the advanced macro commands discussed in Chapter 13. However, there may be situations where you want to execute, say, a /File Combine or a /Range Erase command as soon as a worksheet is retrieved. 1-2-3 also can suspend execution of automatic macros, so you should be familiar with this command, too.

Creating an Automatic Macro

The only difference between creating an automatic macro and a normal executable macro is in the macro name. There can be only one automatic macro on a worksheet, and it must have the name \0 (a backslash followed by zero).

Figure 12-6 shows an automatic macro designed to erase a range of input cells used by an @PMT function every time the worksheet is retrieved. This allows each new operator to enter new values for the principal, interest rate, and term.

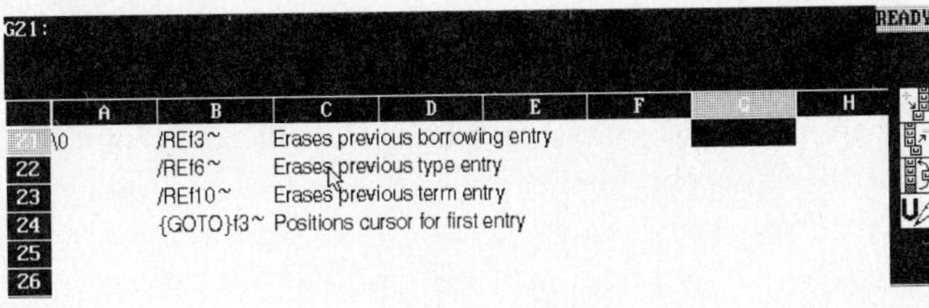

Figure 12-6.   A worksheet example with cells that the macro erases

To create this macro, place your instructions into a column of worksheet cells on the worksheet that triggers its execution and assigns the special \0 name to the name cell. Then save the worksheet with /File Save. The next time the worksheet is retrieved, the macro executes immediately.

If you are using macro libraries with \0 macros in memory rather than the worksheet, 1-2-3 can only execute one of these automatic macros. It chooses the one on the sheet before checking the libraries in memory. If there is more than one \0 macro in memory, 1-2-3 executes the one in the library that was loaded first. You can find more information on macro libraries at the end of this chapter.

Disabling Automatic Macros

If you change the setting for /Worksheet Global Default Autoexec to No, 1-2-3 does not execute automatic macros when you retrieve a file that contains one. When you first install 1-2-3, the default setting for this command is Yes. To make a permanent change to this setting, you have to use /Worksheet Global Default Update to save the change to the configuration file.

Ready-to-Use Macros

The macros in this section are ready to use; they are complete macros designed to perform the tasks described. Since it is likely your data are located in files or cells different from the data on the worksheets used to create these examples, you probably need to make minor modifications to the cell addresses referenced in the macros. Each macro description includes guidelines for its use and a section on potential modifications.

The same conventions have been used for all the macros. The name used for the macro is shown in the first column to the left of the top cell in the macro. The macro is written in the second column as labels. A description is placed in the third column. Uppercase characters are used for all the macro entries, including menu selections, responses to menu prompts, filenames, special key indicators such as {HOME} and {ESC}, and range names.

Worksheet Macros

Many repetitive worksheet tasks are candidates for macros. Examples are changing the global format, checking the worksheet status, and changing default settings like the printer interface. You can even have a macro do some of your typing in worksheet cells. For example, you can create a macro that enters the months for you. You can have a macro make changes to an entry to enhance it or to cover up existing errors.

A Macro to Display Formulas

1-2-3 prints the formulas behind your worksheet results when you specify /Print
Printer Options Other Cell-Formulas, but it creates one line of printed output per
cell. If you want to display or print out formulas while maintaining the integrity of
your worksheet design, you must change each formula cell to Text format. The steps
involved can be placed in a macro to simplify the task.

	A	B	C
1	FRMTTEXT	/WGFT	Request global format as text
2		/RFR	Request range format reset
3		A1..Z60~	Specify range as A1..Z60

The instructions in the first line request /Worksheet Global Format Text. Next, this
macro uses /Range Format Reset to make all the cells conform to the global format
setting of Text. It is followed by a range that contains all the entries on the worksheet
with which the macro is designed to work.

Guidelines for Use   It is important that you save your worksheet before executing this
macro. You should not save your worksheet afterward, since all your regular formats have
been superseded.

Modifying the Macro   You may want to add an instruction at the beginning to save
your worksheet so you do not lose your established formats. The only risk with this
addition is that you might execute the macro a second time and overlay your existing
file with the Text formatted version.

Another option is adding the commands necessary to print the file. These
instructions can be placed at the end of the macro. You can add a /Worksheet Erase
command after the /Print commands so that the formatted version is not saved to
disk after the macro ends. You also can add a command to increase the column width
so that complete formulas can display. You can alter the macro to select the range
with a specification of

```
{HOME}.{END}{HOME}
```

This approach selects A1 as the first cell in the range, and the last cell in the worksheet
is used as the last cell in the range.

A Macro to Insert Blank Rows

You can create macros that add and delete blank rows for you. When you use the
worksheet for calculations and printed reports, use the macro that inserts blank rows.

The macro that follows will insert blank rows:

	A	B	C
1	INSERT	/WI	Request worksheet insert
2		R	Specify rows
3		{DOWN 2}~	Move down to insert 2 rows

This macro adds three blank rows, but it can easily be modified to add any number you choose. The first macro instruction, in B1, requests a worksheet insert. The next instruction specifies that rows rather than columns should be inserted. The third instruction expands the insertion to three rows. You can use the shortcut approach for moving the cell pointer instead of writing this instruction as {DOWN} {DOWN}~.

Guidelines for Use   This macro requires that you place your cell pointer where you want to insert the blank rows, since they are added above the cell pointer. When you invoke the macro, the cell pointer row is shifted down to make room for the new rows. Just as with a keyboard entry of the same command, your formulas are adjusted to reflect the addition, but insertions at the top or bottom of a range do not expand the range.

Modifying the Macro   By changing the entry in B2, you can create a macro that inserts columns. You may also wish to modify the last instruction to allow for the addition of extra rows or columns. A third option is to end the macro after line 2 and allow the operator to specify the number of rows or columns to be added.

A Macro to Change the Global Default Directory

When you are working with completed worksheet models, you may want your directory set at drive C if all your completed models are stored on the hard drive. If you have a number of new models to create and want to store them on a floppy disk, you may want the directory set at drive B. You may also want to change the directory if you use 1-2-3 on two systems that have different configurations. Changing the drive with a macro eliminates the need for remembering the required command path.

You can change the existing directory to drive B:\ with the following macro:

	A	B	C
1	CHG_DIRB	/WG	Request worksheet global change
2		D	Specify a default change
3		D	Specify directory
4		{ESC}	Clears existing directory entry
5		B:\~	Sets new directory
6		Q	Quits default menu without saving

The first instruction requests a /Worksheet Global change. A default change and directory change are specified in the next two instructions. B4 causes the macro to remove the current global default directory setting. The instruction in B5 generates the new directory setting and finalizes it, and the last instruction leaves the Default menu and returns to READY mode.

Guidelines for Use   When you change the directory, both the old and the new directories must be available on the system you are using to change the settings. If you are changing the directory to a floppy drive, place a data disk in the drive before executing the macro, since 1-2-3 attempts to read the directory for the selected device. You can also use this macro to change the subdirectory for model storage and retrieval if you are using a hard disk.

Modifying the Macro   The instruction you are likely to want to modify in this macro is B5, which should contain the pathname of the device and directory you plan to use for data storage. As an example, if you are currently using drive A and want to change to a subdirectory that is on drive C, you might change this instruction to read C:\123\Dallas\Sales\~.

A Macro to Change the Global Printer Default Setup

When you install your 1-2-3 package, you have the option of installing more than one printer. You may have both a dot matrix and a letter-quality printer coupled to your system. You may want to use the letter-quality printer for printing most worksheets, and the dot matrix for printing graphs or quick drafts of a model.

If you want to change the default printer that 1-2-3 uses when you request /Print, but your second printer is cabled to another port, you must change both the printer requested and the interface. The printer is the device requested, and the interface specification tells 1-2-3 whether you have it cabled to a serial or parallel device or want to access one of the operating system devices on your local area network.

A macro for changing the default printer is as follows:

	A	B	C
1	CHG_DEF	/WG	Request worksheet global change
2		D	Specify default
3		P	Choose printer
4		I1	Set interface to parallel 1
5		N1	Set name to first printer installed
6		S\027\040\048\071~	Create default setup string
7		Q	Quit printer default menu
8		Q	Quit default menu

The first line requests a /Worksheet Global change. The next two lines tell 1-2-3 that you wish to use the Default Printer option. The instruction in B4 tells 1-2-3 to set the Interface option to the first parallel interface. The Name option is selected next, and the first name in the list of printers is specified. For this example, the printer selected is a Hewlett-Packard LaserJet II.

It is possible to change other default print settings at the same time you change the specified printer. Although you can now select many print options from 1-2-3's Print menus, whereas setup strings were required in earlier releases, many specialized setup strings still are not part of the menus. For instance, to have the default character set as HP German on the printer, you need a setup string. B6 contains this setup string of \027\040\048\071 on the Hewlett-Packard LaserJet II. This entry is correct for a first use of the setup string. However, if the worksheet already has a setup string, B6 in the macro should be changed to read S{ESC}\027\040\048\071~. The {ESC} instruction causes a problem if there is not a setup string already entered. The last two instructions quit the Default Printer submenu and the Default menu.

Guidelines for Use   Before creating this macro, you need to know the name and interface for the printer you want to use. The printer names you use in the macro depend on the options you selected during installation. You cannot access printer types that were not installed, because the necessary driver files are not available. If you plan to use a new printer device, you must go back to the installation program and add it there.

Modifying the Macro   If you planned to use a serial connection for your printer, modify B4 to I2 or I4. If you wanted a different setup string, modify the string in B6.

You can also expand this macro to include a change to the default settings for other print characteristics, such as margins and page length. If you want to have these new settings available the next time you use the package, add a command to select the Global Default Update option after exiting the Default Printer menu. Then you can save your changes to the file 123.CNF.

A Macro to Enter a Date in a Worksheet Cell

You have learned to enter dates in worksheet cells as values. If you enter a date as a label, you cannot use it in date arithmetic operations, unless you use @DATEVALUE to convert the string to a date serial number. Otherwise the cell does not have an internal serial date number behind the date displayed. Entering a date so you can use it in arithmetic formulas requires that you use the @DATE function, so a substantial number of additional keystrokes are required to enter many dates. A macro can solve this problem by making most of the entries for you, including @DATE, the parentheses, and the argument separators. The only entries you have to make are the year number, the month number, and the day number.

A macro to enter dates is shown in Figure 12-7. It is designed to make its entries in the current cell and begins by entering the keystrokes @DATE(. When the macro

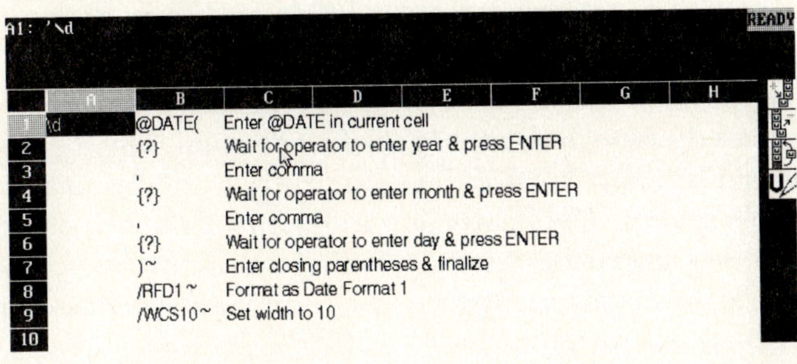

Figure 12-7.   A macro to enter dates

executes the first input instruction, {?}, it waits for you to make an entry and then stores your keystrokes in the cell. It then adds a comma to the cell and waits for additional input. Another comma is added next, after which the third input instruction is executed. The cell entry is completed with an entry of the closing parenthesis.

B8 contains the /Range Format Date 1 request for the cell in which the date entry was just made. The column that contains the cell is set to a width of 10 by a request for /Worksheet Column Set-Width 10.

Guidelines for Use   The {?} method of input does not provide a message prompt telling the operator what it is waiting for. It is important that the operator knows to enter the year number and press ENTER, the month number and press ENTER, and then the day number and press ENTER, since that is the argument order that the @DATE function requires. In Chapter 13 you learn how to use the {GETNUMBER} and {GETLABEL} macro commands to create prompts for the user.

Modifying the Macro   This macro can be modified to use any of 1-2-3's built-in @functions. Just begin the macro with a different keyword. The number of input statements depends on the number of arguments in the particular @function.

In Chapter 13, you learn how you can make a macro like this, which will display prompts as it fills a complete column of cells. As it exists now, you must move to another cell and reexecute the macro if you wish to enter additional dates.

A Macro to Handle Data Entry Errors

Macros can be used to correct a variety of data input errors. They are especially valuable since 1-2-3 gives you access to all the string functions.

For example, if you had employees' names entered in proper case in your database, as in Jeff Jones, only the first letter of each word is capitalized. Some string functions such as @EXACT, @HLOOKUP, and @VLOOKUP are case-sensitive, so if someone else updates your database and enters names such as BOB BROWN or bill smith, you are likely to have trouble with these functions. It could be time-consuming to make corrections so that all the entries match in format. However, you can create the macro shown in Figure 12-8 to change any entry into proper case.

The macro begins by preparing to edit the current cell. It then moves to the Home position and deletes the label indicator in the first position. The @PROPER function is entered, followed by (and ", since the string entry from the current cell must be enclosed in double quotes. The instruction in B4 moves the cell pointer to the end of the entry. The last instruction adds " at the end and follows it with). Before finalizing the entry, the macro recalculates the formula so it can be stored in the cell as a label rather than as a formula.

Guidelines for Use   This macro is position dependent. It will change only the label entry at the cell-pointer location to proper case. You must move the cell pointer and reexecute the macro to change additional cells.

Modifying the Macro   If you want your data in uppercase, you can use the @UPPER function in place of @PROPER. For lowercase, use @LOWER. You can also modify the macro to round numbers by changing @PROPER(" in B3 to @ROUND(and changing ") in B5 to ,0) which will round numbers to the nearest whole number.

A Macro to Enter a Worksheet Heading

If you need to create a whole series of worksheets that use the same heading, you can place the heading instructions in a macro and copy them into each worksheet. Since the macro is designed to begin the heading at the cell-pointer location, the headings need not start in the same position in each worksheet.

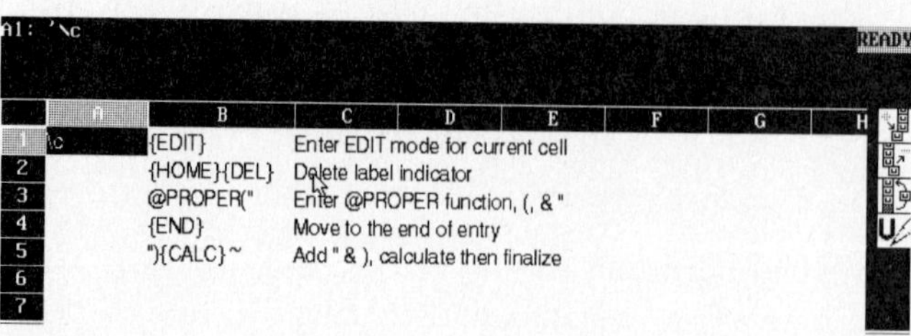

Figure 12-8.   *Proper case macro*

The following macro places headings for the quarters of the year across a worksheet:

	A	B	C
1	HEADING	^QTR1{RIGHT}	Enter QTR1 and move 1 cell right
2		^QTR2{RIGHT}	Enter QTR2 and move 1 cell right
3		^QTR3{RIGHT}	Enter QTR3 and move 1 cell right
4		^QTR4{RIGHT}	Enter QTR4 and move 1 cell right
5		^TOTAL~	Enter TOTAL and press ENTER
6		{END}{LEFT}	Move to the leftmost entry
7		{DOWN}	Move down 1 cell

Each of the first four macro instructions center-justifies one of the quarter headings in a worksheet cell and moves one cell to the right. The instruction in B5 places the heading TOTAL in a cell and finalizes the entry with ENTER. The cell pointer is then moved to the left of this section of the worksheet. It is on the first heading if the cell to its left is blank; otherwise it is in column A. The last instruction moves the cell pointer down one cell.

Guidelines for Use   The macro places the first heading at the cell-pointer location and moves to the right with subsequent entries, so it is important that you position your cell pointer before executing the macro.

Modifying the Macro   The macro can be modified to create any series of headings, like the months of the year, weeks of the month, multiple years, or account numbers. All you need to change are the headings themselves. You can easily modify the label prefix that begins each heading entry as well if you want different justification.

   This macro can be modified to create account names down a column. The only difference is that the cell pointer is moved down after each entry and the caret symbol (^) for center-justification would not be used.

Range Macros

You can create macros for all the /Range commands you use frequently. They can be either open-ended macros or closed ones. An open-ended macro is one that returns control to the operator before the range is selected. Closed macros are more limited in their application because they function only under one particular set of circumstances.

   If you are developing macros for yourself, open-ended macros add flexibility. If you are developing them for someone else and want to maintain as much control over the application as possible, try closed macros.

A Macro to Create a Range Name Table

The /Range Name Table command lists all the range names and their cell addresses in a table on your worksheet. This table is not updated automatically as you add new range names, however; you must execute the command sequence again to have 1-2-3 update the table. A macro can easily handle this task for you.

The short macro needed reads as follows:

	A	B	C
1	\T	{GOTO}G5~	Move cell pointer to table range
2		/RNT~	Request range name table at current location

The first instruction in the macro positions the cell pointer in the upper-left corner of the area where you want your table to appear—cell G5, in this example. The second instruction requests the /Range Name Table command.

Guidelines for Use   Before executing this macro, make sure the area to the right and below G5 (or wherever you send the cell pointer) is empty, since the macro overwrites any data that is stored there. If you plan to print the table of range names, you should always execute this macro before printing to ensure that your table of names is current.

File Macros

You can automate any of the /File commands with a macro. Although /File Save and /File Retrieve do not require a significant number of keystrokes, they are possible candidates for a macro because they are used so frequently. Other /File commands, such as Combine and Xtract, also can be automated. This may cut down on typing errors because the same keystrokes are executed each time.

A Macro to Save Files

/File Save does not require many keystrokes, but it should be done frequently so you do not risk the loss of your data. You can create a macro to save an existing file with one keystroke as follows:

	A	B	C
1	\S	/FS	Request file save
2		~	pecify existing filename
3		R	Replace file

The first line of the macro invokes the /File Save command. The tilde (~) in line 2 indicates that you want to retain the file's existing name. The final line tells 1-2-3 to replace the file on disk with the current contents of memory.

Guidelines for Use   This macro is designed to save a file that has been saved previously. It cannot be used if a file has never been saved to disk or if you want to use a new name for the file.

Modifying the Macro   This macro can easily be modified to allow you to input the filename. Simply use an input statement between lines 1 and 2 of the macro. If you prefer, a predetermined filename can be placed in the macro in the same location.

A Macro to Retrieve Files

The /File Retrieve macro that follows calls a new file into memory. The worksheet containing the macro is no longer resident in memory when the retrieve operation is completed. Such a macro is normally used as part of a larger macro that chooses the task you want to have performed and retrieves the appropriate file.

A retrieve macro might look like this:

	A	B	C
1	\R	/FR	Request file retrieve
2		SALES~	Specify SALES file

The first line of the macro issues the request to retrieve a file. The second line contains the filename and the tilde (~) to finalize the filename entry.

Guidelines for Use   This macro erases the worksheet containing the macro when it is executed. If you made changes to the current worksheet, you should save it before executing this macro.

Modifying the Macro   You can modify the macro to add a /File Save before the /File Retrieve. You can also change the name of the file being saved.

If you want, you can modify the macro so it has the name \0. This causes it to do an immediate retrieve of a second file as soon as the first one is retrieved. In this situation you probably want to add some other macro instructions at the beginning to perform a few tasks in the current file before retrieving the new file.

A Macro to Extract Files

The /File Xtract command is used to save a section of a worksheet in a separate worksheet. This process can be used, for example, to transfer end-of-period totals to a new worksheet for the next period. Although the new file-linking capability offers advantages when you need the data in one specific file, a macro to extract information to a separate worksheet makes it easily available from any worksheet. If you need to extract files frequently, consider the time-saving features of a macro that does the job.

Here is an extract macro:

	A	B	C
1	EXTRACT	/FXV	Request value extract
2		TOTALS~	Specify filename TOTALS
3		YEAR_END_TOTAL~	Enter range to extract
4		R	Specify replace

The first line contains a request to perform a /File Xtract Values operation to save the values from the original file. The next step contains the name of the file in which you want the new material saved. In this macro, the filename is TOTALS. The next instruction tells 1-2-3 what to place in the new file; you can specify a range address or a range name. This macro uses the range name called YEAR_END_TOTAL. The R that is in the last instruction tells 1-2-3 to replace the TOTALS file with the current contents of YEAR_END_TOTAL.

Guidelines for Use   This macro operates on two assumptions. First, it assumes that the range name YEAR_END_TOTAL has already been created. Second, it assumes that the file TOTALS has already been created, since it requests that 1-2-3 replace it.

Modifying the Macro   This macro can be modified easily to use a range address rather than a range name for the extract area. The filename used can also be modified. Either of these can be entered by the operator while the macro is executing if you use an input instruction.

A Macro to Combine Files

The /File Combine command allows you to add data from files on disk to the current worksheet without erasing the current worksheet as a /File Retrieve operation would do. Although establishing file links is the preferred approach in most cases, combining files allows you to retrieve the consolidating worksheet without updating any of the references to data in the other files. You could execute the macro when you decided that timing was appropriate for accessing the external data. A macro to handle the combining operation is shown in Figure 12-9. The final product of the macro is shown in Figure 12-10, where each figure represents the combined totals of each of the four company regions.

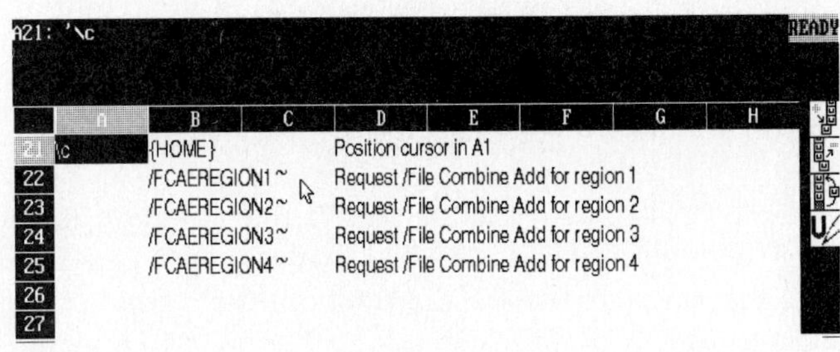

Figure 12-9.   A macro to combine files

Each of the detail worksheets contains the number 1 in column H in the row number that corresponds to the region number. After the macro has added all four regions to the consolidated company template, the four cells in column H should each contain the number 1, as they do in Figure 12-10. The 1 confirms that each detail worksheet has been combined with the total worksheet only once, since each detail worksheet has the number 1 in a different location. In addition to saving keystrokes, this macro ensures that the combining process is handled consistently and accurately. When you enter /File Combine commands from the keyboard to consolidate many worksheets, it is easy to forget which combining operations have been completed.

After moving to A1 to ensure correct cell-pointer placement, the macro executes the /File Combine instructions that follow. The four Combine instructions are the same, except for the filenames being combined. Each requests a /File Combine Add Entire-File operation for the appropriate region file.

Guidelines for Use   The region files are assumed to be in the current directory at the time you execute this macro. Each of the region files is also assumed to have a

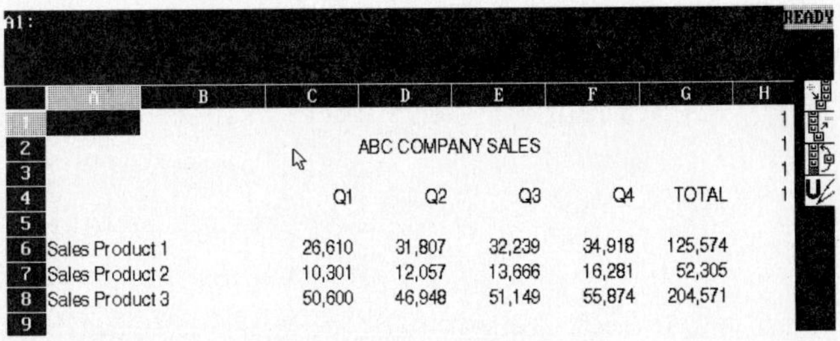

Figure 12-10.   The worksheet after combining files

format identical to that of the file in memory. The region file should contain the number 1 in column H in the row that corresponds to the region number (rows 1 through 4). As previously noted, these serve as flags to indicate that each region has been combined into the total worksheet. This is a good strategy to use with /Combine Add even when you are not using a macro.

Modifying the Macro   The macro can be modified to combine any number of files. Although each of the region files is combined with the Add option in this case, you can easily change the macro to use the Subtract option instead.

After you learn to add more sophistication to macros in Chapter 13, you may want to return to this macro and make it check for the 1's in column H using the {IF} and {BRANCH} instructions.

Print Macros

Since 1-2-3 can retain only one set of print specifications at a time, and since many worksheets contain more than one printed report, you may find that you are reentering print specifications each month as you print your worksheet reports. This wastes time and can lead to errors that might require the reprinting of a report.

You can avoid such problems by using macros to record the commands needed to print your reports. Once you have worked out the details, a macro can print as many reports as you like with one keystroke. Also, since the macro is tested, you will not have to reprint reports because of errors in print specifications.

A Macro to Create Printed Reports

Most of your reports are likely to be sent directly to the printer. It is possible that the margins, setup strings, header, and other specifications for the printed page may differ between two reports printed from the same worksheet. If you store the different print specifications in a macro, you need only position your paper at the top of a form and turn your printer on. 1-2-3 can handle everything else.

The macro shown here prints two different reports from one worksheet.

	A	B	C
1	\P	/PP	Request print
2		RA21..C35~	Specify range
3		OML20~	Set left margin to 20
4		MR55~	Request right margin of 55
5		MT15~	Request top margin of 15
6		H||Today's Date: @~	Create header with date
7		Q	Quit Options menu

8	G	Print
9	PA	Page & Align
10	RA51..H70~	Specify range
11	OML5~	Left margin 5
12	MR75~	Right margin 75
13	Q	Quit Options
14	G	Print
15	PA	Page & Align
17	Q	Quit print

The first instruction tells 1-2-3 that you want the /Print commands and would like your output sent directly to the printer. The first print range, A21..C35, is requested in B2.

The Options changes come next. The first request is to change the left margin to 20. Next, the right margin is set to 55. The top margin is set to 15. B6 specifies the header. There is no entry on the left or in the center of the header, so the line contains only two vertical bars to mark the positions. The rightmost portion of the header contains the constant "Today's Date:". It also contains @, which causes 1-2-3 to substitute the current date. Since this is the last change through the Options menu, Q is used to quit this menu. Printing is requested with G for Go in the next cell.

The Page and Align request is processed as soon as 1-2-3 finishes printing. This request causes 1-2-3 to page to the top of the next form and align its internal line count with the appropriate setting for a new page.

B10 contains the first instruction for the second report. Since the Print menu remains on the screen until you choose Quit, there is no need to make a new request for this menu. The first Options request for the second report is found in B11. The left margin is set at 5 and the right margin is set at 75.

B13 quits the Options menu. The second report is printed by G in B14. Page and Align are issued again to position the paper and 1-2-3's line count for your next Print request, and the Print menu is exited with Q in the last macro instruction.

Guidelines for Use   The critical factor for successful use of this macro is positioning your paper before turning your printer on. The position of your paper when you turn on your printer is where 1-2-3 assumes the top of the form to be. The macro assumes that the paper is at the top of a form when you start.

Modifying the Macro   You can modify this macro to conform to the specific ranges you need to print your report. These instructions are found in B2 and B10; they can be edited to supply a new range. Depending on the range you select and your exact printing requirements, you may need to modify Options parameters such as margins and setup strings. You may also want to add print options besides those listed in this macro. If you have additional reports to create, you can insert their specifications on new lines ahead of line 16. This way you can have one macro print all your reports.

You can also modify this macro to clear all the print options between reports, depending on how much your specifications change from report to report. If they stay almost the same, you might prefer to change just one or two options by including the appropriate commands and new values in your macro. On the other hand, if there are substantial changes, you might want to include /Print Printer Clear All in the macro. This can be accomplished by adding CA (for Clear All) after the G in B8.

A Macro to Store Print Output in a File

If you have never printed to a file, you may wonder why anyone would want to store printed output on a file. There are several good reasons. First, your printer may be out for repair, and you may want to save the printed output until later. Or you may simply want to continue with your current task and wait until later to print. Perhaps you are using a print utility that prints your output across the page sideways and you need to supply that program with print output stored in a .PRN file.

The macro presented here writes worksheet formulas to a file with one formula per line. The macro reads as follows:

	A	B	C
1	FORMULAS	/PF	Request print to file
2		FORMULAS~	Write to file FORMULAS
3		RA1..C20~	Specify range A1..C20
4		OO	Request Options Other
5		U	Request Unformatted
6		OC	Request Other Cell-Formulas
7		Q	Quit Options menu
8		G	Write requested file
9		CA	Clear all print specifications
10		Q	Quit Print menu

The first line in the macro requests the Print menu and selects File as the output destination. B2 contains the filename that is supplied in response to 1-2-3's prompt. The range to be printed is shown next and includes the cells in A1..C20.

The Options menu is requested next, and the Other selection from this menu is chosen. Unformatted output is requested to remove any formatting specifications in the current print settings. While still in the Options menu, the macro requests Other again, and Cell-Formulas is chosen to print each cell in the range on a line by itself and print the formulas. B7 contains a request to quit the Options menu, and the next instruction writes the output to disk. All print specifications are cleared with CA in B9, and the Print menu is exited via Q in B10.

Guidelines for Use   When your computer writes to disk files, it writes data to the disk in blocks. When you request Go, most of your print output is written to the disk. It is not until you request Quit from the Print menu that you can be sure that all of your output is written to the file, however. Also, the end-of-file indicator is not placed on the file until after you quit the Print menu. Be sure to leave your disk in the drive until after quitting to ensure that all your data is in the file.

Modifying the Macro   This macro works for any set of reports. You should eliminate the request for Other Cell-Formulas from B6 if you want the worksheet printed as displayed rather than as the formulas the macro requests. The range in B3 can be modified to print other reports.

If you want to print multiple reports to one file, you can begin the range specification process again after B8 or B9, depending on whether or not you want the existing print parameters cleared. If you want the output in a second file, place your second request after B10, and begin again with /Print File so you can request a new filename.

Graph Macros

Graphs normally require numerous settings. You have to add titles, data labels, grid lines, legends, and other options to create appealing graphs. You can save time and reduce errors by capturing the required keystrokes in a macro and making it available for use with departmental budgets or other worksheets in which the same formats are used by a number of managers.

A Macro to Create a Bar Graph   The following macro is designed to work with the sales worksheet used with the /File Combine macro shown earlier in Figure 12-10. It can be used for any of the regional budgets or the total company worksheet. The only change you may want to make is in the first line title.

The macro looks like this:

	A	B	C
1	GRAPH	/GRG	Request graph and reset all options
2		TB	Select bar type graph
3		XC4..F4~	X range for labels below x-axis points
4		AC6..F6~	First data range
5		BC7..F7~	Second data range
6		CC8..F8~	Third data range
7		OGH	Add horizontal grid lines

8	TF\D2~	First line title from D2
9	TY$ Sales~	Y-axis title
10	LAProduct 1~	Legend for first product
11	LBProduct 2~	Legend for second product
12	LCProduct 3~	Legend for third product
13	CQ	Request color and quit options
14	V	View graph

The macro begins in line 1 with a request for the Graph menu. This instruction also resets all the graph values. A bar graph is selected in the next instruction, after which the ranges for the different series used to create the graph are specified. The labels below the X-axis are the entries in cells C4..F4. The next three instructions assign values to data ranges A, B, and C.

The /Graph Options menu is requested next, and horizontal grid lines are added by the instruction in B7. The first line title is set to use the contents of cell D2. A Y-axis title of $ Sales is entered next. Legends for data ranges A, B, and C are then added. Color is requested as the last option, and the Options menu is exited. The graph is viewed with the V in B14.

Guidelines for Use   This macro can be used every time you update your worksheet. Of course, if you have just displayed a graph and simply want to see it again, the F10 (GRAPH) key is a quicker approach, since the graph specifications are not changed. This macro is useful when you are in a new 1-2-3 session and find that someone else has used the graphics features and deleted the definition of your graph.

Modifying the Macro   This macro can be modified to save the graph specifications under a graph name. A second, shorter macro can issue a /Graph Name Use command to make the specifications current at a later time.

A Macro to Use Different Graph Types

With the different choices 1-2-3 has for graph types, you may want to try each one to see which presents the data in the best format for your uses. The following macro displays the current graph data using each of the seven possible graph types:

	A	B	C
1	\G	/GTL	Display as a line graph
2		OTSLine Graph~QV	
3		TB	Display as a bar graph

4	OTSBar Graph~QV	
5	TX	Display as an XY graph
6	OTSXY Graph~QV	
7	TS	Display as a stacked bar graph
8	OTSStacked Bar Graph~QV	
9	TP	Display as a pie graph
10	OTSPie Graph~QV	
11	TH	Display as an HLCO graph
12	OTSHLCO Graph~QV	
13	TM	Display as a mixed graph
14	OTSMixed Graph~QVQ	

The odd lines in the macro set the graph type to different graph types and the even lines set the second title to the graph type. When you press ALT-G to execute this macro, the macro uses the current graph data. Each time the macro displays a graph it waits until you press a key to remove the graph before continuing with the other macro instructions.

Guidelines for Use

You would use this macro when you are building a graph and are not sure which graph type would best illustrate your data. A macro like this would be added to a macro library described later in this chapter since you might want to use this in multiple worksheets.

Modifying the Macro

Besides using a macro like this to try out the different graph types, you can also modify the macro to try other graphing features by changing the T and the letter after it in the odd lines in the macro. For example, you can use this macro as a basis for creating your own macro that tries out the different features available under the Release 2.4 /Graph Type Features command. You will want to change the second title in the graph to match the features you will invoke so as you view the graphs you can see the graph features they provide. If you are using a release prior to Release 2.3, omit the lines for the HLCO and mixed graph.

Data Macros

Macros can also save you time when used to automate functions in the data environment. Most of the /Data commands require that you make a number of selections before you complete your task. Some, like /Data Table, require that you complete preliminary steps before requesting the command. Also, since you must reissue the /Data commands if you want a sort, frequency analysis, regression analysis, /Data Table, or /Data Fill operation performed again, you could be executing them frequently. With the macro approach, you can enter them once, check their accuracy, and then store them in worksheet cells and use them as much as you want.

A Macro to Create a Data Table

A data table can perform a sensitivity analysis for you by systematically plugging values into your input variables. Before you ask 1-2-3 to perform this analysis, you must build a table shell on the worksheet. Since a macro to do this is a little more complicated than your other macros, you should take a look at the worksheet in Figure 12-11 before you study the next macro listing. Projections for Products A and B use the growth rates in C10 and C11 and the previous years' sales to project future periods. Product C is calculated as a percentage of Products A and B sales. The completed table is shown in Figure 12-12.

The rules for working with tables are found in Chapter 10; look at this chapter if you are not familiar with the /Data Table command. The table in your macro is calculated by having 1-2-3 substitute the values in column B for the growth of Product A in C10 each time the table performs a new calculation. The percentages in row 22 are substituted as new growth factors for Product B. The table contains the result of the formula in G7, which is the total sales in 1993.

The first macro instruction is found in J1, as shown here:

	I	J	K
1	\T	/DF	Request Data Fill
2		B23..B31~	Set fill range
3		.05~	Enter start value
4		.01~ ~	Enter increment & accept stop value
5		/DF	Request Data Fill
6		C22..H22~	Set fill range
7		.09~	Enter start value
8		.01~ ~	Enter increment & accept stop value
9		/DT2	Request Data Table 2
10		B22..H31~	Set range
11		C10~	Set input value 2
12		C11~	Set input value 1
13		{GOTO}A21	Move cell pointer to view table

	A	B	C	D	E	F	G	H
1			Sales Projections					
2								
3			1989	1990	1991	1992	1993	
4	Product A		1,000	1,080	1,166	1,260	1,360	
5	Product B		2,000	2,240	2,509	2,810	3,147	
6	Product C		700	780	869	969	1,080	
7	TOTAL		3,700	4,100	4,544	5,038	5,588	
8								
9								
10	% Growth A		8.00%					
11	% Growth B		12.00%					
12								

Figure 12-11.   *The worksheet for use with /Data Table*

This first instruction requests /Data Fill to start building the shell for the table. A fill range is established with the second instruction. Then a start value of .05 and an increment of .01 are specified. When the stop value prompt is displayed, the second tilde in J4 accepts the default, since it is greater than the stop value needed.

The second /Data Fill operation supplies the values across row 22. A start value of .09 is used, along with the same increment as the first range. The default stop value is accepted again.

The request for the /Data Table 2 command is made in J9. The table location is defined in B10 as B22..H31. The first input value is the value for the growth factor for Product A, stored in C10. The second input value is the growth factor for Product B, which is stored in C11. When this second input value is entered, the macro calculates the new values for G7 and places them in the table.

	A	B	C	D	E	F	G	H
21					PRODUCT B			
22		+G7	9.00%	10.00%	11.00%	12.00%	13.00%	14.00%
23	P	5.00%	5,119	5,224	5,332	5,443	5,557	5,674
24	R	6.00%	5,166	5,271	5,379	5,490	5,604	5,721
25	O	7.00%	5,214	5,319	5,427	5,538	5,652	5,769
26	D	8.00%	5,264	5,369	5,477	5,588	5,702	5,819
27	U	9.00%	5,315	5,420	5,528	5,639	5,753	5,870
28	C	10.00%	5,367	5,472	5,580	5,691	5,805	5,922
29	T	11.00%	5,421	5,526	5,634	5,745	5,859	5,976
30		12.00%	5,477	5,582	5,690	5,801	5,915	6,032
31	A	13.00%	5,534	5,639	5,747	5,858	5,972	6,089
32								

Figure 12-12.   *The completed table*

Guidelines for Use   This macro is designed to handle most of the table setup, as well as the call for /Data Table to do the calculations. The only tasks it does not perform are the entry of the formula in cell B22 and the formatting of the table cells. Be sure not to store information in the cells the table uses, since executing the macro would overlay these cells.

Modifying the Macro   This macro can be modified to create a table of a different size or with different input values generated by the /Data Fill operation. You can also modify the instructions in J3, J4, J7, and J8 to contain {?}, which allows the operator to enter the fill parameters, and therefore the input values, every time the macro is executed.

You can also modify the macro to handle the remaining preliminary steps for preparing the table. It is easy to include instructions for the entry of the formula in B22 and the /Range Format statements required to display the table as shown.

A Macro to Sort a Database

Sorting a database requires the definition of the data range. This does not have to be done every time you sort, but it must be done if you have added a new field or new records to your database. Since it is easy to forget to do this, you can have a macro handle this precautionary step to ensure that you do not sort just a section of your database.

The database this example uses is shown in Figure 12-13. The macro will sort the file into sequence by last name and uses the first name as a secondary key.

```
A1: [W12] 'Last Name                                                        READY
```

	A	B	C	D	E	F	G
1	Last Name	First Name	SS#	Job Code	Salary	Location	
2	Larson	Mary	543-98-9876	23	$12,000	2	
3	Campbell	David	213-76-9874	23	$23,000	10	
4	Campbell	Keith	569-89-7654	12	$32,000	2	
5	Stephens	Tom	219-78-8954	15	$17,800	2	
6	Caldor	Larry	459-34-0921	23	$32,500	4	
7	Lightnor	Peggy	560-55-4311	14	$23,500	10	
8	McCartin	John	817-66-1212	15	$54,600	2	
9	Justof	Jack	431-78-9963	17	$41,200	4	
10	Patterson	Lyle	212-11-9090	12	$21,500	10	
11	Miller	Lisa	214-89-6756	23	$18,700	2	
12	Hawkins	Mark	215-67-8973	21	$19,500	2	
13	Hartwick	Eileen	313-78-9090	15	$31,450	4	
14	Smythe	George	560-90-8645	15	$65,000	4	
15	Wilkes	Caitlin	124-67-7432	17	$15,500	2	
16	Deaver	Ken	198-98-6750	23	$24,600	10	
17	Kaylor	Sally	312-45-9862	12	$32,900	10	
18	Parker	Dee	659-11-3452	14	$19,800	4	
19	Preverson	Gary	670-90-1121	21	$27,600	4	
20	Samuelson	Paul	219-89-7080	23	$28,900	2	

```
24-Apr-92  01:43 PM                                    STEP
```

Figure 12-13.

The macro shown here begins in Y1 with a request for /Data Sort Reset:

	X	Y	Z
1	SORT	/DSR	Request Data Sort Reset
2		D	Select Data-Range
3		{HOME}{DOWN}	Set A2 as beginning of the range
4		.	Lock beginning or range
5		{END}{DOWN}	Move to last entry in first field
6		{END}{RIGHT}~	Move to last field on right
7		PA2~A~	Set Last Name as primary key
8		SB2~A~	Set First Name as secondary key
9		G	Complete sort
10		{HOME}	Move to A1 to view sorted records

Here the macro must be stored on a part of the worksheet away from the data. Since the range is set from the previous use, Reset is needed to unlock the beginning of the range. The cell pointer is moved to A2. This cell is locked in place as the beginning of the sort range by typing a period. The cell pointer is moved to the last entry in the column and then is moved across to the last column to complete the range specification.

A2 is defined as the primary key on which the records are to be sorted in ascending sequence. The secondary key is B2, which also is applied in ascending sequence. The G in B9 in the macro requests that the sort begin. The macro ends by moving to A1 so you can review your results.

Guidelines for Use   The macro assumes that the first and last data fields have values for every record. The instructions in B5 and B6 cannot work if some of the fields are blank.

Modifying the Macro   The macro can be modified to sort on any field. You can enter the range address for the macro, though this approach requires modification to the macro as the database expands.

The Macro Library Manager

You must add macros to each of your worksheets if you need different macros on each worksheet, but if you have a need for the same macro on multiple worksheets, you can use Macro Library Manager available in Releases 2.2 and above.

The Macro Library Manager allows you to save macros to the library that resides in a special area of memory and on disk. You can also invoke any macro previously saved to a library, as long as the library is loaded into memory. The Macro Library Manager can also store ranges of data that remain in memory as you save and retrieve files, so you can copy ranges from one worksheet to another. With the Macro Library Manager, you can develop your own set of accelerator keys for frequently used tasks by assigning a quick entry name to the set of commands with a range name like ALT-L.

To use the Macro Library Manager, you must use the Add-In features or Releases 2.2 and above. The Macro Library Manager is an Add-In that Lotus supplies with Release 2.2. You must add this program to memory with 1-2-3 before you can use the features the Macro Library Manager Add-In provides. While Chapter 14 contains a more complete description of using 1-2-3 Add-Ins, as a quick description you can use the Macro Library Manager Add-In by selecting /Add-In Attach, select MACROMGR.ADN, select a key such as 9 for ALT-F9, and select Quit to return to READY mode. When you want to use this Add-In, you can press the key combination you select (ALT-F9 in this example) or select /Add-In Invoke MACROMGR.

Using the Macro Library Manager

Once the Macro Manager Library is loaded and invoked, you can use its features to store and save worksheet ranges. You can execute any macro stored in a library in memory by executing it just as you would a macro on the worksheet, although a macro with the same name on the worksheet takes priority.

Both the worksheet and the macros stored by the Macro Library Manager occupy space in memory, but 1-2-3 allocates separate areas of memory to each. The Macro Library Manager can store up to ten libraries in memory at a time. Each library can store a maximum of 16,376 cells if you have sufficient memory. Unlike cells in a worksheet, you cannot see or edit these libraries unless you use the Edit feature of the Macro Library Manager to copy the cells onto the current worksheet. Also, these cells do not have the conventional cell address that 1-2-3 uses.

Each library contains a range copied from a worksheet that can contain as many macros as you want. Any range names including macro names are copied to the library. A macro library is like hidden columns in a worksheet that you can use but cannot directly modify.

When you save a macro library, a copy is saved to disk as well as memory by the Macro Library Manager. You can reference data from these libraries by loading a disk library into memory. Once the library is in memory, you can copy the library and make changes to the worksheet. When you save the worksheet range back to the library, the range disappears from the worksheet again and replaces the library in memory and on disk.

When you are finished with the Macro Library Manager menu, you can select Quit from the menu to return to 1-2-3. This leaves the Macro Library Manager Add-In still attached but inactive. You can reactivate this Add-In at any time.

Creating a Macro Library

Creating a macro library requires you to retrieve the worksheet containing the range you want to store in a library to the Macro Library Manager. Once you invoke the Macro Library Manager, select Save from the menu. The Macro Library Manager prompts for a filename and displays the existing libraries. You can select an existing filename or provide a new one. Do not include an extension since the Macro Library Manager adds an .MLB extension. You can make one library load every time you load the Macro Library Manager if you name the library file AUTOLOAD. If you select an existing library name, the Macro Library Manager prompts to determine if you want to replace the .MLB file. Selecting No cancels the command and returns you to the Macro Library Manager menu. Selecting Yes replaces the existing library file with the range you select.

After you specify the name of the library, the Macro Library Manager prompts for the worksheet range to put in the library unless you select a range beforehand. You select this range just as you select a range for any other 1-2-3 command since the Macro Library Manager returns control to the worksheet as it waits for you to select the worksheet range. Since a macro library does not store data as efficiently as 1-2-3 stores its worksheets, you want the range to have as few blank cells as possible. When you press ENTER to finalize the range, the Macro Library Manager prompt asks if you want the library protected with a password. Selecting No saves the new library to a file on disk without password protecting the library. If you select Yes, you are prompted for a password of up to 80 characters. Like the password for worksheets, the password for a library is case-sensitive, so you must remember the case of the characters that you enter.

When you save a worksheet, the worksheet remains in memory after the save operation, but saving a range for a library works differently. Saving a macro library is like moving a range from the worksheet to the library, because the range that you save as the library is removed from the worksheet. Any references within the worksheet to these cells are now references to blank cells. If you want to save data to a library and continue to work with it on the worksheet, you must save the range and then use the Edit menu option to copy the data from the library back to the worksheet. Another option is to save the worksheet file, since this also prevents the accidental loss of any worksheet entries.

Looking at an example will help to clarify how this works. Figure 12-14 contains a few macros that have been entered on the worksheet and named with the entries in column A. To save these macros as a library that can be executed from other worksheets, use /Add-In Invoke, select MACROMGR, and press ENTER. An alternative to invoking the Macro Library Manager is pressing the ALT key sequence assigned to the Macro Library Manager when you initially attached it. Select Save from the menu displayed. Type the name that you want to use for the library file using the rules that you use for other filenames, and then press ENTER. Highlight A1..B10 (the cells containing macro names and instructions). When you press ENTER, a copy of

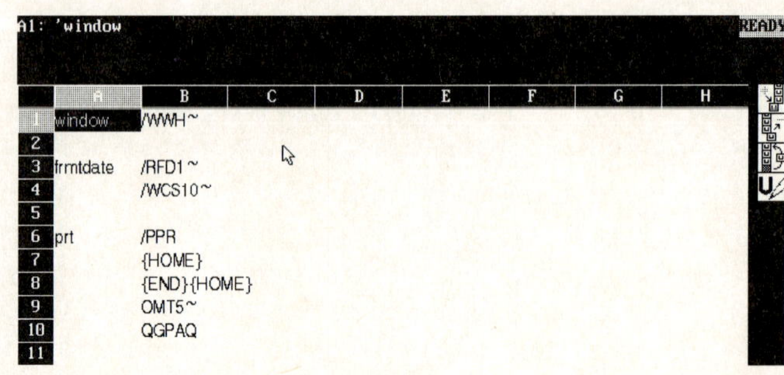

Figure 12-14. *The macro entries before saving them to a library*

the macros is stored to a file with the name that you specified and an .MLB extension. The macros are removed from the current worksheet, but are still available in memory in an area frequently referred to as *hyperspace.* There is no way to see these entries without using the Edit feature of the Macro Library Manager to bring them onto the worksheet for review and changes. You can still execute them as if they were a part of the worksheet.

Protecting a Macro Library

Protecting a library with a password does not prevent other people from using the data in the library, it only prevents them from changing it. You should protect a library with a password if you plan to use the library on a network, although this does not limit network access. You must do that by controlling who has the password for the file.

The Macro Library Manager does not prevent multiple users from changing data in a library at the same time. This means that the changes made by the last user to save data eliminate the effect of the changes made by the other user. Protecting a library with a password reduces the chance that more than one person will edit the library at a time, since you can choose to provide the password to only one user.

Loading a Macro Library

When you select Save from the Macro Library Manager, an external .MLB file is created. This copy of the range remains in memory for the current session but is not available in your next session unless you attach the Macro Library Manager and load the macro back into this special area of memory.

You can load a library that you have created from another session to use in this session. To load a library, select Load from the Macro Library Manager menu and select the library filename. If a library is already loaded with the same name, you have the option of having the library that you want to load replace the one in memory with the same name (the Yes option) or canceling the command (the No option).

If you plan to load several macro libraries, the order in which they are loaded affects the macro executed when more than one contains a macro with the same name. In other words, if two macro libraries contain a macro named WINDOW, the WINDOW macro in the library loaded first is executed.

Copying Data from the Macro Library to the Worksheet

The information a library contains is not readily visible since the Macro Library Manager does not let you see or edit the library data directly. Instead, you can see the data by copying the library to a worksheet range. After you edit the library data in the worksheet, you can save the macro library again so the library contains the newest changes. To copy a library to the worksheet, select Edit from the Macro Library Manager. Then select the library whose contents you want to copy to the current worksheet. If the macro library is protected with a password, you must enter the password when the Macro Library Manager prompts for it. Then the Macro Library Manager prompts you for what action to take when the macro library contains some of the same range names that the worksheet has. If you select Ignore, the range names in the worksheet have priority over the range names in the library. If you select Overwrite, the range names in the library have priority over the range names in the worksheet. When the Macro Library Manager prompts for a range for the library contents, enter the first cell in which to place the library contents. The library will overwrite any worksheet contents beginning at the cell you selected.

This command is used for both editing a library's contents and for copying information from one worksheet to another. If you are editing a library's contents, you must use the Save command to replace the old library contents with the new library contents. For example, you can use the Edit command to copy the MACROLIB macro library to the current worksheet beginning at cell C1. After you have edited the cells using the same keystrokes and commands that you use to edit any 1-2-3 cells, you invoke the Macro Library Manager Add-In again, select Save, highlight the MACROLIB library name in the list and press ENTER. After selecting Yes to confirm that you wanted to overwrite the current library's contents, you select all the cells that you wanted in the library.

As an example of using a macro library to copy data between worksheets, suppose you have the months spelled out in cells A3..A14 in the BUDGET worksheet. You want to copy this data to the SALES worksheet starting at B5. First, retrieve the BUDGET worksheet. Then invoke the Macro Library Manager and select Save. Next enter **MONTHS** for the macro library name, select A3..A14 as the range that you want to move from the current worksheet, and select No for the password. To change the worksheet, you enter **Quit** to return to 1-2-3, and then enter **/File Retrieve** and select SALES to retrieve. You would not want to save the BUDGET file since it would save the file without the months. When the SALES file appears, you invoke the Macro Library Manager and select Load and then the MONTHS macro file. Next select Edit to copy the macro library to the SALES file and MONTHS as the file to copy. Then select Ignore and point to B5 as the cell to which to copy the macro library before pressing ENTER. Now both of the worksheets have the months, but you only typed them once.

Using Range Names in a Macro Library

Since a macro library does not have cell addresses even though it saves cells, the macro library uses range names to specify all references. These range names are used with the macro commands covered in the next chapter. The libraries also use range names to name macros since one library can contain an unlimited number of macros. Each macro must be referenced by its range name instead of an address. Range names that a library uses must be assigned when the range containing the contents for the library is still in a worksheet.

Listing Range Names in a Macro Library   Since range names are so important to a macro library, you should know what they are. To list the range names that a loaded macro library uses, select Name-List from the Macro Library Manager menu. Then select the library from which you want the list of names. When the Macro Library Manager prompts for the range for the list, select the cell in which you want the list to start. The list uses one column and as many rows as the macro library has range names.

Running a Macro from a Macro Library

While a macro library can copy data between worksheets, it can also store macros and run them in any worksheet. A macro run from a macro library executes using the current worksheet. The macro must be named to run from a macro library.

You can execute a macro from a macro library the same way you execute a macro from the current worksheet. You can either press ALT and the single letter of the macro's name, or you can press ALT-F3 (RUN) and highlight or type the name and press ENTER. When you press F3 (NAME) for a full screen display of range names and point to a macro name from a macro library, the macro library name appears in place of the range address. Also, the range names are in the order that the macro libraries are loaded.

When you execute a macro, 1-2-3 first looks at the current worksheet. If the worksheet does not have a macro with that name, it looks through the macro libraries in the order they are loaded or saved. The first macro library that contains the macro that 1-2-3 is looking for will be the copy of the macro that 1-2-3 will execute. Therefore if macros in two separate macro libraries have the same macro name of \A, 1-2-3 executes the macro in the macro library that is loaded or saved first. Also, because macro commands cannot use cell addresses in the macro library, you must use a range name.

Removing a Library from Memory

The memory a library uses decreases the memory available for other purposes, including storing the current worksheet. When you have finished using a macro library, you should remove it from memory so the memory can be used elsewhere. To do this, select Remove from the Macro Library Manager menu. The Macro Library Manager lists the libraries in the order they were created or loaded. Highlight one from the list and press ENTER. The library is still saved on disk so you can load it again if you want. To remove the library from the disk, you must use the /File Erase Other command. To limit the files list to include only the macro library files, select *.MLB, and press ENTER.

Advanced Options Used with Advanced Macro Commands

In the next chapter you will examine all the options pertaining to advanced macro commands. These commands function as a programming language that offers you more sophisticated choices in your work with macros. Although you do not as yet understand the features offered by these commands, there are a few important points to note before you start building macros with them for storage in the Macro Library Manager libraries.

- Subroutines are separate sections of macro code that can be executed from within a macro to change the execution flow of an entire macro. Subroutines can be in the current worksheet or a macro library file currently stored in memory.

- Any advanced macro command that expects a range to reference data can reference this data when it is stored in a library or the worksheet. To use a range in a macro library, the advanced macro command must use a range name. Naturally, 1-2-3 first searches the current worksheet for the named range and then proceeds to look through the libraries in the order in which they were loaded.

- Formulas in a library must either reference cells in the same library or cells in the current worksheet. If a formula contains an external file link to another worksheet, the Macro Library Manager prohibits your saving the range to a library until you remove the external file link. The Macro Library Manager also prohibits formulas from referencing cells in another library.

- A formula in a library that references other cells in the library continues to reference the same cells even though the library does not use cell addresses. These formulas are recalculated when the library is saved, when a cell in the library changes from a macro instruction, or when the {RECALC} or {RECALCCOL} command recalculates a range in the macro library (these commands are also discussed in Chapter 13). Formulas in the worksheet cannot reference cells in a library.

MACROS

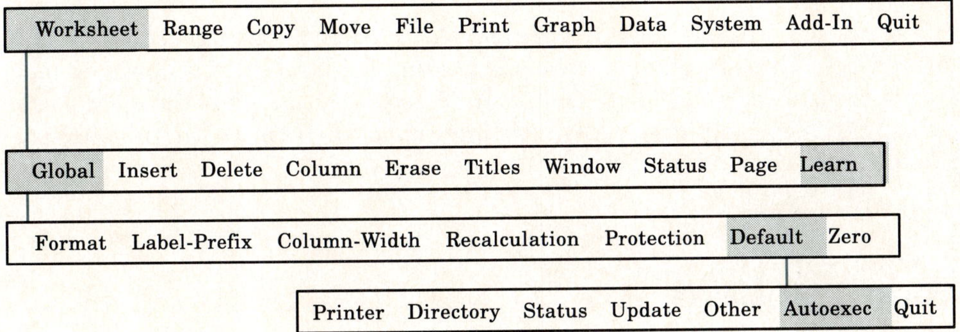

/Worksheet Global Default Autoexec

Description

This command determines whether or not 1-2-3 executes \0 macros in files when they are retrieved.

Options

This command provides options of Yes and No. A selection of Yes is the default and causes 1-2-3 to execute all \0 macros. A selection of No causes 1-2-3 not to execute these automatic macros. In Releases 2.3 and 2.4, you can also make these automatic macros execute or not execute by selecting to mark or unmark the Auto-execute Macros on check box in the Default Settings dialog box.

/Worksheet Learn

Description

This command records macro entries on the worksheet. You can use this command to establish a recording range, to cancel a range specification, or to erase a range.

Options

Cancel   This option cancels a Learn range specification. It is best to cancel a Learn range that is specified if you no longer plan to use it. Once it is canceled, accidentally pressing ALT-F5 does not add new entries in this range. Before you can record entries, a new range must be specified with /Worksheet Learn Range.

Erase   This option erases the current contents of the Learn range, but does not cancel the currently specified range.

Range   This option specifies a range where 1-2-3 can record keystrokes when you invoke Learn with ALT-F5 (LEARN). You should specify a single column of cell entries as the range. If you specify a multiple column range, 1-2-3 can use only the leftmost column in the range since a macro must consist of label entries within a column.

Note

If you fill the Learn range after you start recording, 1-2-3 displays a message indicating that the Learn range is full. You can press ESC, then select /Worksheet Learn Range, and expand the range. 1-2-3 then allows you to expand the range without erasing your previous keystrokes.

Edit

Description

The Edit command copies a macro library file to a worksheet for editing. If the file is password protected you must provide the correct password.

Options

You can select the name of the .MLB file to use, and then you can choose Ignore or Overwrite from a menu. Ignore uses range names in the worksheet where there are duplicates, and Overwrite uses the range names from the library. Select the first cell where the Macro Library Manager should start copying the macro library's contents to the worksheet. 1-2-3 overwrites worksheet data with the contents of the .MLB file.

Load

Description

This command copies data from a library file into memory.

Options

You can select from the .MLB files presented from the current directory or press ESC and edit the drive and directory specification. If there is already a library with the selected name in memory, the options Yes and No are presented. Yes overwrites the old macro library with the new one, and No retains the old library.

Name-List

Description

This command creates a list of range names contained in a loaded macro library. You can compare this list against range names in the current worksheet.

Options

You can select which macro library you want to use when listing names.

Quit

Description

This command exits the Macro Library Manager menu but leaves the Macro Library Manager attached.

Remove

Description

This command removes a macro library from memory. It does not remove the file from disk. Removing a file from disk must be handled with /File Erase Other or the DOS ERASE command.

Save

Description

This command moves a range on the worksheet to a macro library file (.MLB file) and retains the macro library file in memory independent of the worksheet. To move the range to a file that loads automatically when you start the Macro Library Manager, name the file AUTOLOAD.MLB.

Options

First, enter the name of the file to contain the macro library (the Macro Library Manager will add an .MLB extension). If the filename you select exists, select Yes to overwrite the file or No to retain the existing file. Next, select No if you do not want the macro library password protected or Yes if you do, and then enter the password as you would for the /File Save command.

Chapter **13**

Command Language
Macros

Command language macros are even more powerful than the keyboard alternative macros described in the last chapter. Command language macros allow you to perform repetitive tasks with ease and to automate applications so that even novice users can handle complex worksheet tasks. They also allow you to use features that are not part of the 1-2-3 menu structure.

Although the Release 1A /X macro commands are still supported for compatibility, you should not use the /X commands because 1-2-3 has macro commands that perform the same function and are more descriptive. Each /X command has a replacement command in Releases 2.2 and above.

Macro commands are very powerful and provide options beyond menu selections. You can alter the execution flow of a macro by branching to a new location. You can also create your own custom menus patterned after 1-2-3's.

Command language macros are not for everyone, however. They are built with 1-2-3's command language, which is essentially a programming language. As with any programming language, you are likely to have moments of frustration and exasperation as you strive to make 1-2-3 understand your needs. To succeed in creating command language macros, you must define your needs exactly. You need blocks of uninterrupted time so you can concentrate fully on the details this demands. Finally, you need persistence to stick with the task until the macro works correctly. Given these efforts, you can learn to create macros you are proud of.

You can use the techniques discussed in Chapter 12 to create a macro that contains a {BRANCH} command to change the flow of macro execution, yet still attach this macro to a user icon. You will use the same User icon for defining what these custom icons do, although you will need to store the keystrokes in the worksheet first. Remember: You are limited to 240 keystrokes for each user icon.

565

This chapter is designed to provide strategies for creating command language macros as painlessly as possible. The first part of this chapter explores the differences between command language and keyboard macros. The second part offers some general strategies for creating macros and discusses specific techniques used by programmers working in other programming languages to ensure the correct operation of their programs. Since the 1-2-3 macro command language is also a programming language, you are likely to find some of these techniques helpful when writing your macros. The third section of this chapter describes each macro command separately. It provides a description and a working example that incorporates the macro command.

Differences Between Command Language Macros and Keyboard Macros

Command language macros are entered in the same way as the keyboard variety covered in Chapter 12. Like keyboard macros, they are label entries stored in a column of worksheet cells. Just as you needed to follow rigid rules when entering a keyboard menu selection sequence, you also have to follow rules when entering instructions from 1-2-3's macro command language. The command keyword and any arguments it requires must always be enclosed in brackets ({ }), for example, {BRANCH A9}. Arguments must always be entered in the prescribed order.

How do you know when to use command language macros and when to use keyboard macros? It is really quite easy. When a keyboard macro works, use it. When you want to accomplish things that menu commands cannot handle, it is time to use a command language macro.

Your first command language macros may use only a few statements. The following macro enters a date in five cells in a column:

1	\D	{LET z1,0}
2	top	{IF z1=5}{BRANCH finish}
3		@DATE(
4		{?}
5		,
6		{?}
7		,
8		{?}
9		)~
10		{DOWN}
11		{LET z1,z1+1}
12		{BRANCH top}
13	finish	{QUIT}

After you master the simpler variety of command language macro, you can begin to think of more sophisticated tasks you would like to delegate to 1-2-3. Many of these require the use of command language instructions, but they are likely to employ the familiar built-in functions, formulas, and menu options, as well.

Release 2.4 has all the power needed, especially with its ability to process the arguments you use within a macro instruction before executing the commands. As long as you are working with the 1-2-3 package, you want all its features at your disposal.

Constructing and Using Command Language Macros

A command language macro normally consists of a number of detailed steps that must be executed in a logical order. When you communicate instructions to another person, you can often be less than fully specific and still get the desired results. That is because human beings can interpret directions and make assumptions about the exact way a task should be performed. If people know your way of doing business and have worked for you in the past, their interpretations and assumptions about the way you want a particular task done are likely to be correct.

When you ask a computer to do your bidding, however, there are no interpretations and no assumptions. You get exactly what you ask for, whether or not it is what you want. If you leave out a step or provide the steps in the wrong sequence, you get results different from what you expect.

Since you can't change the way computers do their processing, you must learn to set up tasks in a way that a computer can handle. You need to create a road map showing what you want the computer to do for you. If you create this road map on paper, it is easy to separate logic and syntax. *Logic* refers to the steps in the task you want the computer to perform, and *syntax* refers to the detailed instructions in the 1-2-3 macro command language and the arguments they need to execute successfully. If you do not have all the logic of your macro worked out, you can never solve the problem by entering specific instructions. You need to know where you are going and the general route you plan to follow before you start.

Planning Command Language Macros

You can use a variety of techniques to map out your logic flow. The following subsections describe these techniques in more detail. You can use one of them, or you can develop your own technique. The important thing is to completely think through the steps needed to complete your tasks before you get involved with the command language syntax. If you attempt to tackle both logic and syntax at once, and your macro does not work, you cannot know where to begin the correction process.

Flowcharts

Flowcharts are diagrams of the detailed logic in a macro or other program; they are constructed with special symbols. These symbols are joined with lines to form a pictorial representation of the logic flow. A standard set of symbols is used so that any programmer can understand a flowchart created by another individual. In fact, a programmer often asks another programmer to review the flowchart of a problem solution before it is coded to help identify logic errors early in the testing process.

In most flowcharts, the diamond represents a decision to be made, the small circle is a connector, the parallelogram marks input and output operations, and the rectangle indicates arithmetic operations and other processes. Figure 13-1 shows a flowchart using these symbols. It describes the logic required to combine a variable number of region files into one worksheet. This allows someone to create division or total company reports with one worksheet. Ctr1 and Ctr2 are counters.

If you use flowcharts for mapping your program logic, there is no need to buy a special flowchart template to create the special symbols. Drawing them by hand is just as effective. You can even use a different set of symbols if you prefer.

Pseudocode

Pseudocode consists of statements written in something like computer code but without concern for precise syntax. It is a shortcut method of documenting your logic with everyday English words. It is quicker to use than flowcharts because there are no figures to be drawn, and it is closer to the final form of program code that you use. When writing pseudocode, don't concern yourself with spelling, grammar, or complete sentences; in fact, phrases are best, as long as they are clear.

The following lines of pseudocode describe the same process that was pictured in the flowchart in Figure 13-1. The first column represents labels that the macro uses to branch to. The second column shows the steps the macro performs.

	Initialize Ctr2 to 1
	Position cell pointer
	Enter number of regions to combine
	Set Ctr1 = # regions
Combine	Use /File Combine Add
	If Ctr1 = Ctr2 branch to End
	Add 1 to Ctr2
	Branch to Combine
End	Quit

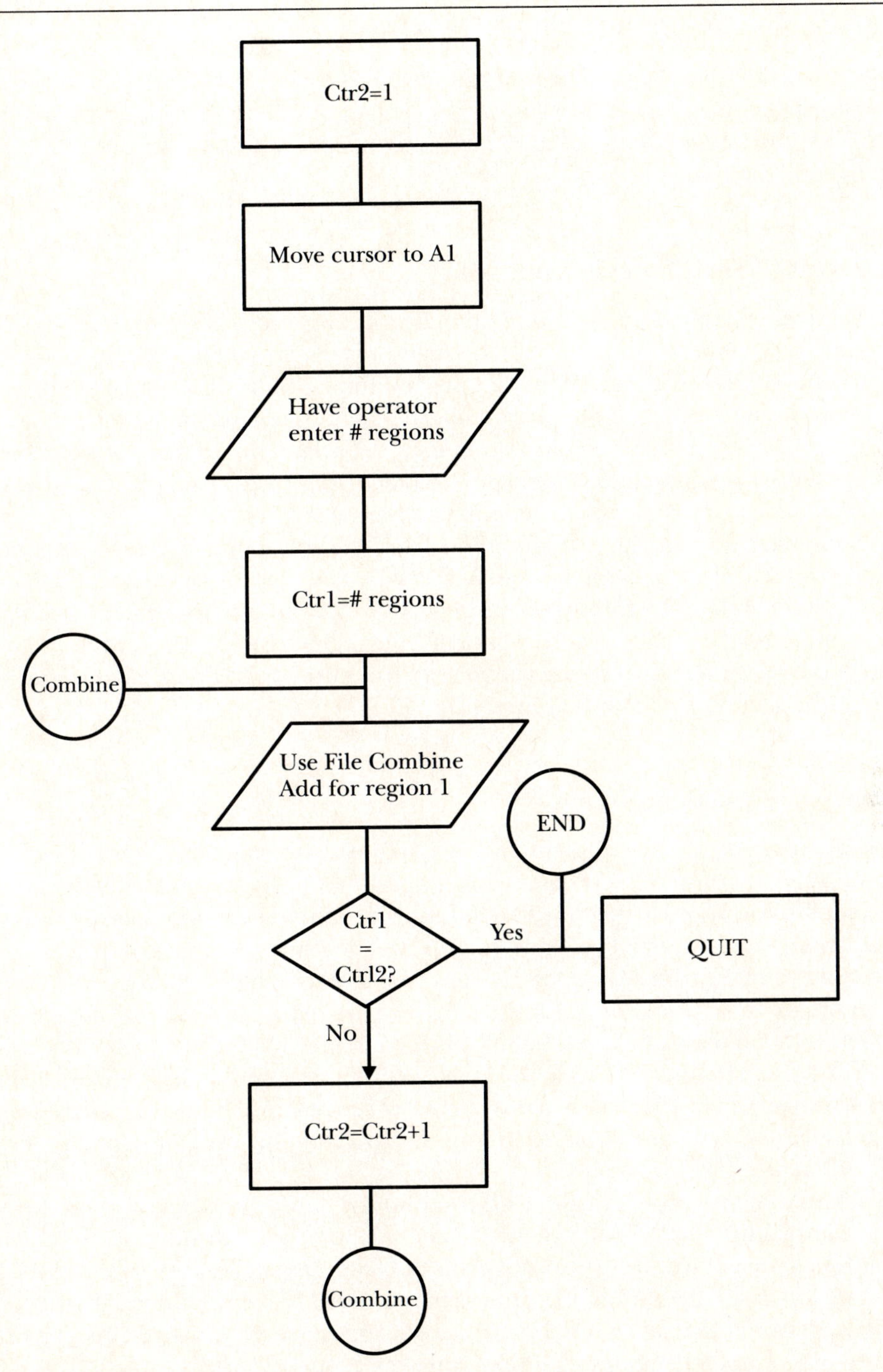

Figure 13-1. *A flowchart for combining files*

Strategies for Designing Complex Macros

A three- or four-line command language macro is no more difficult to create than a keyboard macro. It is so small that you can keep track of its entire logic flow mentally. More sophisticated command language macros, however, need more careful structuring and planning.

Branching Versus Straight-Line Code

It is easy to create macro code that branches all over the place; programmers refer to this as "spaghetti bowl" code. It usually results from lack of planning. New instructions are simply added as the programmer thinks of them. If there is not enough room to insert all the instructions needed, the program branches away to a blank location and then branches back again to execute the remaining instructions. The result is confusion. It may be faster to code a program or a macro in this fashion, but making it work correctly is something else again.

Straight-line code is at the opposite end of the spectrum. Wherever possible, it proceeds from the top to the bottom of the logic flow without branching. Of course, branching need not be forbidden entirely. A little common sense can go a long way in creating macros that are both workable and correct. Straight-line code, however, offers the advantage of allowing you to read from the top to the bottom of the code and get a picture of what it is accomplishing.

Main Code and Subroutines

You can write a large macro that contains, say, 400 instructions and list them consecutively down a column on your worksheet. To get a picture of what this macro is designed to accomplish you would have to read all 400 lines of code. A better approach is to separate your macros into a mainline code section and subroutines. Properly planned, this structure combines the advantages of branching and straight-line code.

A manageable upper limit for the length of the main section is considered to be 50 lines. Detail tasks are taken out of this section and placed in subroutines, which are referenced by instructions in the main section. Because the main section is short, it can be scanned quickly to learn the essence of the macro. This form of organization also makes it easier to test the macro one section at a time and thereby trace errors to particular sections of code.

When a main program calls a subroutine, the subroutine instructions are executed until a {RETURN} is encountered or the end of the subroutine is reached. At that time, control will return to the main program that called the subroutine. The instruction immediately following the subroutine call is executed next. A subroutine call is always indicated by enclosing the subroutine name in brackets. To call a subroutine named Print, for example, you would enter {Print}.

The following example shows how a main program and its subroutines might be structured:

```
Main Routine

        ...

        ...

        {update}

        {print}


Subroutines
update      ...

        ...

        ...

        {RETURN}


print       ...

        ...

        {RETURN}
```

The ellipsis (...) entries represent macro instructions appropriate for the routines. Note that with this structure, you can read down the main code and see that an update operation will be performed, followed by a print operation. You need not read the precise instructions in either subroutine to understand the program's basic structure.

When you call a subroutine, you can pass arguments to it. This allows you to tailor the routine to each particular situation. Passing arguments to a subroutine requires that the arguments be included in the instruction that calls the subroutine. In addition, the subroutine must contain a {DEFINE} instruction that provides a storage location for each argument passed to it. Releases 2.2 and above support a maximum of 31 arguments for each subroutine. This maximum number of arguments can only be used when the arguments are listed without type declaration. If each argument has a type declaration, like :string or :value, the argument limit is 15 because each type declaration uses the space of an argument.

When it encounters a {RETURN} statement, 1-2-3 returns to the subroutine calling location and executes the instruction immediately following the subroutine call. If 1-2-3 encounters a second subroutine call before a {RETURN} instruction, it begins executing the code in the second subroutine. Adding various levels of subroutine calls within a macro is referred to as *stacking* or *nesting* subroutine calls. The number of levels of stacked subroutines that you can use is limited by available memory, although you may reach a practical limit well before you run out of memory.

Limit nested subroutines to three levels. It can be difficult to decipher the logic of a program when it contains nesting of subroutines that exceed three levels.

You can have a main program that calls the same subroutine multiple times and passes different arguments to it each time. For example, you might want to print your worksheet with three different setup strings, using an argument to pass a setup string to the print subroutine. Your main program might appear as follows:

```
{print k1}
{print k2}
{print k3}
```

Each time a call is executed, whatever is stored in the specified cell (that is, K1, K2, or K3) is passed to the subroutine.

The print subroutine would require a storage place for only one argument, since only one argument is passed to it each time it is executed. Assuming Setup was defined as a range name, the print subroutine might appear like this:

```
print      {DEFINE Setup:string}

           ...

           ...

           {RETURN}
```

Setup is defined as a string argument; it contains the value of K1, K2, and K3 from each execution of the Print routine. You must include a location argument in the {DEFINE} command for each argument passed by the subroutine call.

The location arguments in a {DEFINE} command support the addition of *:string* or *:value*. If you use *:string*, 1-2-3 stores the argument that is passed to the location argument as a left-aligned label. When *:value* is used, 1-2-3 stores the entry if it is a number or evaluates the argument if it is a formula. When a cell address or range name is supplied as an argument, 1-2-3 evaluates the cell reference and stores the contents based on the type of entry it finds. The way the result is stored depends on the type of formula evaluated. String formulas return labels, and numeric formulas return numbers. If you omit the argument, 1-2-3 uses *:string*.

Entering Command Language Macros

Having mapped out a plan for your macro, you are ready to begin entering actual code. Command language macros are entered in the same manner as keyboard alternative macros. As with keyboard macros, you can use the Macro Library Manager in Releases 2.2 and above to enter a macro in a macro library or as part of a file that contains worksheet or data management entries. If you enter them within an existing file, use an area of the worksheet away from other entries and calculations. Choose an out-of-the-way location that has room for a blank column on both sides of the macro instructions column. Then you can use the column to the left of the macro for the macro name and any range names you might assign to different sections of the macro. You might want to consider a location diagonally opposite from your data. This way, if you insert rows or columns in the data portion of the worksheet, the macro is not affected.

You can use either upper- or lowercase for macro commands, argument names, cell address references, keyboard commands, and macro names. You must follow the command syntax exactly, using the brackets ({ }) around each command entry, and the exact spelling for each command keyword.

As you enter each of the macro commands, you must supply the proper type of data for each type of argument. Although you can use the specified type of entry within the macro, you can also use range names, cell addresses, or an appropriate formula to supply the necessary argument information. Commas or semicolons may separate the arguments. A closing bracket follows the last argument entry.

Arguments that are literal strings sometimes require quotation marks around them. Quotation marks are needed when the string contains 1-2-3's separator characters (a comma, a semicolon, a colon, or a period).

Each cell in the column where you make your macro entries can contain up to 240 characters, since each macro instruction is entered as a label. It is not recommended that you use entries that even approach this upper limit, however. Forty or fifty characters is a reasonable upper limit if you want your macros to be readable. You must complete each macro instruction in the same cell where you begin entering it.

Naming Command Language Macros

Command language macros are named in the same fashion as keyboard macros. You can name the macros either using a backslash and a letter or a range name. The first cell of the macro is named with the /Range Name Create or /Range Name Labels Right command. 1-2-3 will execute all of the macro instructions until 1-2-3 encounters a {QUIT} command or a nonlabel cell.

Creating a Macro Shell

If you like, you can code all your macro instructions at once. It often works better, however, to code just the major instructions first. As an example, if you have a macro that branches to one of four principal subroutines that depends on operator input, first code only the instructions to process the operator's input and the beginning instructions for each of the four subroutines. At the beginning of each subroutine, place an instruction that informs you that you have reached that particular routine. In this manner you can check out the upper-level logic of your macro without investing time in creating detailed code. This kind of "framework" code is called a *macro shell.*

This approach to program construction is referred to as *topdown programming.* It can save considerable time by allowing you to detect major logic problems before you proceed with detailed coding. If a problem occurs, there are far fewer instructions at this point to change or move.

For example, you might construct a shell that consists of little more than subroutine calls and instructions to display messages. You can use a "dummy" input statement with the {GETNUMBER} or {GETLABEL} command solely to display a message on the screen. The {INDICATE} instruction is another option to inform you of a macro's progress.

This method speeds up your testing process significantly, because you can test the program's basic logic by invoking each subroutine and checking the special message it displays. Once you check the execution flow, you can add the detailed code needed to complete the subroutines.

Figure 13-2 provides an example of this shell structure. Here, each subroutine contains only an instruction to let you know that you have arrived at that location in the macro. Once this program pattern checks out correctly, you can add instructions for each routine.

Creating Interactive Macros

Interactive macros are macros that change as they are executed. They can change logic flow in response to entries by the operator. They can even change entries in instructions, such as filenames.

Macros that Respond to Operator Input

As you look through the various macro commands in this chapter, you can find several that accept operator input. These include {?}, {GETLABEL}, {GETNUMBER}, {GET}, and {LOOK}. You can use the information obtained from these entries to control

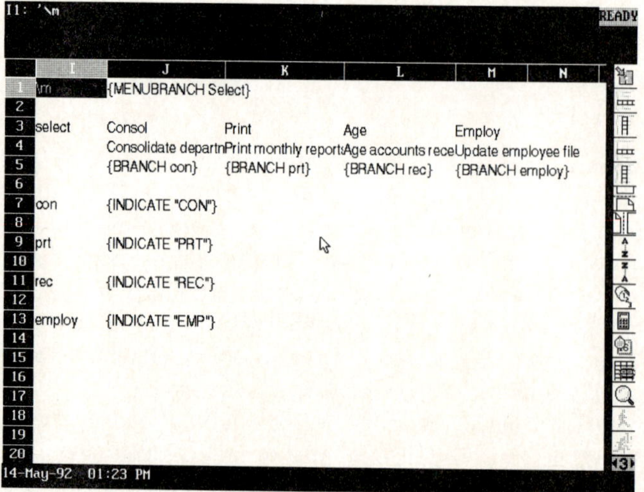

Figure 13-2.   *A macro shell for a menu*

{BRANCH} instructions and subroutine calls, as well as other processing within the macro.

Dynamically Altered Macros

Dynamically altered macros store information that is input or calculated during execution as part of the macro itself.

For example, in a file retrieve instruction, you might want to change the file retrieved depending on the application you are working on. To do this, use a menu selection to determine the application and have this instruction alter the following macro instruction sequence:

```
/fr
blank

~
```

The macro cell that contains the word "blank" is actually an empty cell. You want to have the macro make an appropriate entry in this cell, using either a {PUT} or a {LET} instruction. Thus the macro alters itself to perform the exact action you want.

A simpler form of this dynamic alteration can be seen in the example of the {GETNUMBER} command, where dates are being temporarily entered in macro cells for later storage in a different area of the worksheet. Depending on your entries, the macro is altered to create a variety of date entries.

Releases 2.2 and above offer a more sophisticated way to handle dynamic changes now that they process all the arguments within instructions. You can have a GETLABEL instruction store a filename in a range name and then use the range name in a file retrieve instruction. Your worksheet entries might look something like this,

```
\T          {GETLABEL "Enter the file name to retrieve :",F_NAME}
            /fr{F_NAME}~

            ...

            ...

            ...
      F_NAME
```

where F_NAME and \T are range names for the cells to the right.

Documenting Command Language Macros

Macro documentation consists of comments added to the worksheet to explain the macro. Its main purpose is to make each macro step clear to someone who was not involved in the macro's creation. However, you also are likely to find it helpful when you look back at a macro you wrote, say, three months previously. All of the examples in this chapter add documentation to the right of the macro instructions. Be as brief as possible, but make sure you clearly describe all formulas or other entries that might not be clear at a later time.

Variables in a macro should be given meaningful names. This minimizes the need for supplemental documentation and makes formulas in the macro easier to read.

If you are like most people, you probably do not want to bother with the documentation step. Learn to think of documentation as a worthwhile investment that can save you time in the future and make it possible to delegate the maintenance of your applications to others as you move on to new responsibilities. A few extra minutes spent documenting a macro when you have just finished creating it can pay off in hours of time saved later.

Testing Command Language Macros

Do not assume that a macro works correctly unless you have tested it. A multiple-step testing process is the most efficient and ensures that your macro works under all conditions. Here are the steps to macro testing:

1. Your first test should be an easy one. If the macro performs calculations, use even numbers so you can check its answers mentally. If you choose a complicated number, you might make arithmetic mistakes yourself while testing it.

2. If your macro is an *iterative* one (one that is executed numerous times), test only two or three iterations of its cycle. This saves time and makes it easier to check results.

3. Next, try to see what the macro does with exceptions or unusual conditions that occur only sporadically.

4. Check for error conditions next. If the macro prompts you for the number of times you want to execute a certain routine, enter **−25**. If it asks for a number of vacation days, respond with **560**. If it asks for a salary increase, enter **1500%** See whether it responds to the error conditions as you would expect.

5. If your macro fails at any step along the way, correct the error condition and go back to the first step for a quick recheck after the change. Never assume that a change to one part of a macro does not affect another part. It often does, and the only way you can know for sure is to test the entire macro.

6. If your macro is used by others, involve them in the testing process. No one knows better the type of data that is entered into the macro than the person who uses the program every day. This approach also helps you discover if you have to change the macro because you have misinterpreted the user's needs. For instance, you may have allowed for the entry of an invoice amount, whereas the user expected the macro to compute a total invoice amount based on entry of detail figures.

7. If you are designing a macro to work in a number of worksheet applications, you must test its operation in more than one worksheet.

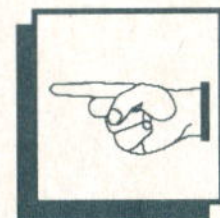

Turn on the Undo feature with /Worksheet Global Default Other Undo Enable before starting to create macros. Then you can press ALT-F4 *(UNDO) to eliminate all the effects of the macro if it causes errors in the worksheet.*

Executing Command Language Macros

Executing a completed command language macro is easy. Just as you did with a keyboard macro, you simply press the ALT key and the letter key of the macro's name simultaneously. An alternative is to press ALT-F3 (RUN) and select the name of the macro you want to execute. There are several other things you should be aware of before executing a macro, however.

Using Undo While Running Macros

As previously stated, if you run a macro with Undo enabled, you can press ALT-F4 (UNDO) to cancel all the effects of the macro on the worksheet. 1-2-3's Undo feature eliminates the effect of menu selections and macro commands within the normal scope of its capabilities; that is, the action of Undo is confined to the worksheet and cannot eliminate /File Save and print operations that have been completed. If 1-2-3 does not have sufficient memory to run the macro with Undo turned on, it prompts you before turning Undo off.

Updating the Worksheet

As you begin using macros, you will find that some of the macro commands update worksheet cells. They do not always update these cells immediately, and sometimes the worksheet must be recalculated before the update takes place. For some commands, pressing the ENTER key may be sufficient to cause the updating. You should follow these commands with a tilde (~) if immediate update is critical to the successful execution of the macro. Other commands require that the worksheet be recalculated.

The following commands update the worksheet if you follow them with a tilde (~) or {CALC}:

{CONTENTS}	{LET}
{DEFINE}	{LOOK}
{FILESIZE}	{ONERROR}
{FOR}	{PUT}
{GET}	{READ}

{GETLABEL}	{READLN}
{GETNUMBER}	/XI.
{GETPOS}	/XN

Stopping a Macro

Unless you have disabled the BREAK key by including {BREAKOFF} in your macro, you can interrupt a macro in midstream simply by pressing CTRL-BREAK. This displays an ERROR indicator on the screen. If you then press ESC, you can leave the macro and return to READY mode. {BREAKOFF} is described in the "Macro Commands" section next in this chapter. You can also now include {BREAK} within a macro. This allows you to return to READY mode from within a menu.

Macro Commands

Syntax of Macro Commands

1-2-3's command language has two separate types of macro commands: commands without arguments and commands with arguments. Both types include a keyword in brackets. Subroutine calls are exceptions to these rules. "The Macro Language Commands" box lists macro commands and their functions.

The format of a command without arguments is nothing more than a keyword enclosed in brackets. Examples are {RETURN}, {RESTART}, and {QUIT}.

The format of a command with arguments consists of the keyword followed by a blank space and a list of arguments separated by commas or semicolons. As with @function arguments, no spaces are allowed between or within arguments except for the space after the macro command name. The entire entry is enclosed in brackets. Here are two examples:

    {GETLABEL "Enter your name :",A2}
    {FOR Counter,1,20,1,Loop}

The following section describes all the arguments for each command and specifies which of the arguments are optional.

Conventions for Macros in this Chapter

The same conventions have been used for all the example macros whenever possible. The macro name and subroutine name are shown in the first column to the left of the top cell in the macro. The macro instructions are written in the second column

The Macro Language Commands

Macro Command	Function	Type of Macro
{?}	Accepts keyboard input	Interactive
{BEEP}	Sounds bell	Screen
{BLANK}	Erases cell or range	Data
{BORDERSOFF}	Turns off the worksheet frame—identical to {FRAMEOFF}	Screen
{BORDERSON}	Restores the worksheet frame—identical to {FRAMEON}	Screen
{BRANCH}	Changes execution flow to a new routine	Flow
{BREAKOFF}	Disables BREAK key	Interactive
{BREAKON}	Restores BREAK key function	Interactive
{CLOSE}	Closes an open file	File
{CONTENTS}	Stores the numeric contents of a cell as a label in another cell	Data
{DEFINE}	Specifies location and type of arguments for a subroutine cell	Flow
{DISPATCH}	Branches to a new location indirectly	Flow
{FILESIZE}	Determines number of bytes in a file	File
{FOR}	Loops through a macro subroutine multiple times	Flow
{FORBREAK}	Cancels current {FOR} instruction	Flow
{FRAMEOFF}	Turns off the worksheet frame	Screen
{GET}	Halts macro to allow single-keystroke entry	Interactive
{GETLABEL}	Halts macro to allow label entry	Interactive
{GETNUMBER}	Halts macro to allow number entry	Interactive
{GETPOS}	Returns to pointer position in a file	File

Macro Command	Function	Type of Macro
{GRAPHOFF}	Restores graph settings to before {GRAPHON}	Screen
{GRAPHON}	Displays a graph or makes a set of graph settings active	Screen
{IF}	Causes conditional execution of command that follows	Flow
{INDICATE}	Changes mode indicator	Screen
{LET}	Stores a number or label in a cell	Data
{LOOK}	Checks to see if keyboard entry has been made	Interactive
{MENUBRANCH}	Allows the construction of a custom menu	Keyboard
{MENUCALL}	Executes a custom menu as a subroutine	Interactive
{ONERROR}	Branches to an error-processing routine	Flow
{OPEN}	Opens a file for read or write access	File
{PANELOFF}	Eliminates control panel updating	Screen
{PANELON}	Restores control panel updating	Screen
{PUT}	Stores a number or label in one cell of a range	Data
{QUIT}	Ends the macro and returns to READY mode	Flow
{READ}	Reads characters from file into cell	File
{READLN}	Reads a line of characters from a file	File
{RECALC}	Recalculates formulas in a range row by row	Data
{RECALCCOL}	Recalculates formulas in a range column by column	Data
{RESTART}	Clears subroutine pointers	Flow

Macro Command	Function	Type of Macro
{RETURN}	Returns to the instruction after the last subroutine call or {MENUCALL}	Flow
{*routine*}	Calls the subroutine specified by *routine*	Flow
{SETPOS}	Moves file pointer to a new location in the file	File
{SYSTEM}	Executes an operating system command	
{WAIT}	Waits until a specified time	Keyboard
{WINDOWSOFF}	Suppresses window updating	Screen
{WINDOWSON}	Restores window updating	Screen
{WRITE}	Places data in a file	File
{WRITELN}	Places data in a file and adds a carriage return/line feed at the end	File
/XC	Calls a subroutine	/X
/XG	Branches to a new location	/X
/XI	Tests a logical condition	/X
/XL	Gets a label entry from the keyboard	/X
/XM	Creates a user-defined menu	/X
/XN	Gets a number from the keyboard	/X
/XQ	Quits the macro	/X
/XR	Returns control to the main macro code from a subroutine	/X

as labels, except for menu macros, which extend to the right into additional columns. The columns on the worksheets where the macros were entered were widened to allow for the complete entry of each element. When possible, documentation has been placed in the third column.

In the following sections, lowercase characters are used for menu selections and responses to menu prompts. Filenames, command keywords, and special key indicators, such as {HOME}, {ESC}, {IF}, and {MENUBRANCH}, are shown in uppercase.

Range names, which also serve as subroutine names, are shown in lowercase. When used within the text, these names are boldfaced to indicate their special use. Arguments in the text appear in italics.

The macro commands in the sections that follow are grouped according to the categories in which they are placed in your 1-2-3 manual: commands that affect the screen, commands that interact with the keyboard operator, commands that control the flow of execution within a macro, commands that affect data entry, and commands that access file data. For each command you will find a description, format rules, descriptions of arguments (if any), suggestions for use, and an example. Special setup procedures, if any, are also described.

Macro Commands that Affect the Screen

Macro commands that affect your screen can handle such tasks as updating the Window option and control panel. If the macro commands display as they execute, you have an indication of where the macro is at any particular moment. But the macro's quick progress can cause a flicker as the screen is updated. These macros also give you the ability to create your own mode indicator and to sound your computer's bell to get the operator's attention.

{BEEP}

The {BEEP} command sounds your computer's bell.

Format   The format for the {BEEP} command is

    {BEEP *number*}

where *number* is an optional argument to set the tone of the bell. The *number* argument can have any value from 1 to 4; 1 is the default when no number is specified.

Use   You can use the beep to alert the operator to an error, indicate that you expect input, show periodically that a long-running macro is still functioning, or signify the conclusion of a step.

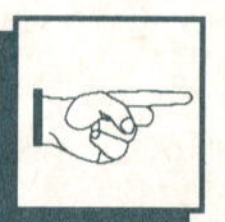

Switching the beep tone off with /Worksheet Global Default Other Beep No causes this macro instruction to have no audible effect.

Example   In this example, {BEEP} is used to indicate that an input instruction follows.

    {BEEP 3}
    {GETNUMBER "Enter your account number",F2}

This {BEEP} instruction causes the computer's bell to ring with tone 3 right before the input message is displayed.

Note   When you use a tone argument other than 1 through 4, 1-2-3 divides the number by 4 and uses the remainder for the tone value.

{FRAMEOFF}

The {FRAMEOFF} command turns off the display of the worksheet frame.

Format   The format for the {FRAMEOFF} command is

    {FRAMEOFF}

This command has no arguments.

Use   This command allows you to create a help display or data entry form without the distraction of the frames containing column letters and row numbers. The frame will not be restored to the display until a {FRAMEON} instruction is encountered or the macro ends.

Example   The screen in Figure 13-3 is created with text entries and format commands. If the {FRAMEOFF} command is added to the macro code as the first macro instruction, the row and column headings are eliminated and the screen will look like Figure 13-4.

Note   This command is equivalent to {BORDERSOFF}.

If Wysiwyg is attached {FRAMEOFF} will have no effect. You must use :Display Options Frame.

{FRAMEON}

The {FRAMEON} command restores the display of the worksheet row and column frame after it has been disabled with {FRAMEOFF}.

Format   The format of the command is

    {FRAMEON}

This command has no arguments.

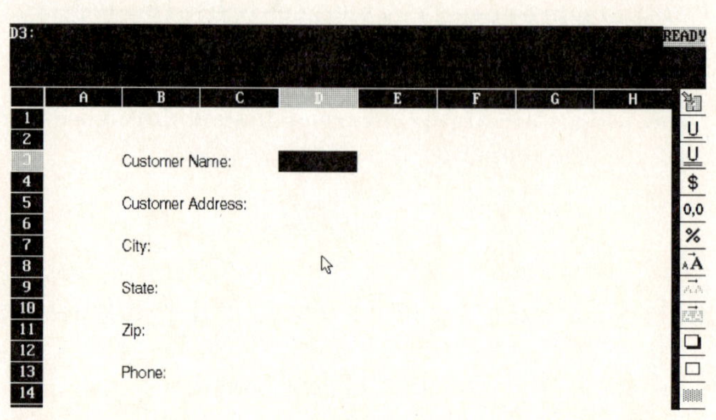

Figure 13-3. *The data entry form with a frame*

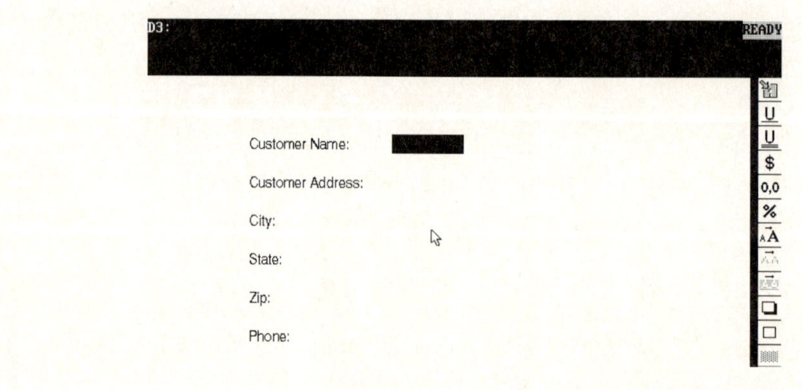

Figure 13-4. *The data entry form after {FRAMEOFF} is executed*

Use You can use the {FRAMEON} command to restore the display of the frame when a task requiring cell-pointer positioning is required. You might remove the frame to display a help screen or a data entry form. If the next required task is completing data entry in a group of cells, you might want to restore the frame.

Example The following code illustrates the restoration of the frame after executing macro commands:

```
1          customer        {FRAMEOFF}          Eliminate frame
```

	...	
	...	
10	{FRAMEON}	Restore frame

Setup   You must create the range name **customer** before invoking this macro.

Note   This command is equivalent to {BORDERSON}.

{GRAPHOFF}

The {GRAPHOFF} command removes a graph displayed with the {GRAPHON} command.

Format   The format of the command is

    {GRAPHOFF}

The command has no arguments.

Use   You can use this command after using a {GRAPHON} command that you executed. You may display a graph with {GRAPHON} for a fixed amount of time or allow the user to make an entry that removes it. Either way, when you want the graph eliminated from the screen, use {GRAPHOFF}.

Example   The following macro code displays and removes a graph:

1	dispgrph	{GRAPHON pie1}	Display pie graph
2		{WAIT @NOW+@TIME(0,0,20)}	Wait 20 seconds
3		{GRAPHOFF}	

The graph remains on the display for the 20 seconds generated by the {WAIT} instruction. Next it is removed with the {GRAPHOFF} command.

{GRAPHON}

The {GRAPHON} command makes a specific graph current and displays this graph on the screen.

Format   The format of this command depends on the specific action desired. {GRAPHON} with no arguments displays the current graph on the screen. To make another graph current and display it on the screen, the format of the command is

{GRAPHON *named-graph*}

where *named-graph* is a set of graph definitions. Another format of this command is

{GRAPHON *named-graph*,no display}

Although the named graph is still made current, it is not displayed on the screen.

Use   You can use this command to display a graph on the screen for the user. Since the macro continues to process commands, you can make customization changes available without the user needing to know the commands required to make enhancements to the graph. Since the graph remains on the screen, you can perform other macro instructions in the background.

You can also use this command to make a set of graph specifications current, yet not display them immediately. This allows you to provide a menu of options for the user that affect the graph. When the selections are made, you can issue the {GRAPHON} command again without the no display argument, and the graph displays with the changes made from the user's selections.

Example   You can use this command to create a slide show of graphs. The following example displays four graphs for 30 seconds each:

1	slides	{GRAPHON pie1}	Display graph pie1
2		{WAIT @NOW+@TIME (0,0,30)}	Wait 30 seconds
3		{GRAPHON bar1}	Display graph bar1
4		{WAIT @NOW+@TIME (0,0,30)}	Wait 30 seconds
5		{GRAPHON pie2}	Display graph pie2
6		{WAIT @NOW+@TIME (0,0,30)}	Wait 30 seconds
7		{GRAPHON bar2}	Display graph bar2
8		{WAIT @NOW+@TIME (0,0,30)}	Wait 30 seconds

The graphs continue to appear until a {GRAPHOFF}, another {GRAPHON}, a {?}, an {INDICATE}, or other macro command displays a prompt or menu in the control panel (like {GETLABEL}, {GETNUMBER}, {MENUCALL}, {MENUBRANCH}, /XL, /XM, or /XN).

{INDICATE}

The {INDICATE} command provides the ability to customize the mode indicator in the upper-right corner of the screen.

Format   The format of the {INDICATE} command is

{INDICATE *string*}

where *string* is any character string. The string is displayed in place of 1-2-3's regular indicator. Using the empty string {INDICATE " "} removes the indicator light from the control panel. Using no string, that is, {INDICATE}, returns the indicator to the default. The mode indicators in Release 2.01 are limited to five characters, and in Releases 2.2 and above, your only limit is the number of characters that fits in the control panel.

Use   The indicator you select with this command remains until you use the command again to establish a new setting. The setting continues beyond the execution of the macro. If you set the indicator to FILE, FILE remains on the screen even if you are in READY mode. Remember to include {INDICATE} without an argument at the end of any macro that has used this instruction. Doing so restores 1-2-3's normal indicator display at the conclusion of the macro.

The {INDICATE} command is useful when you are designing automated applications. If you have a series of menu selections for the operator to use, you can have an {INDICATE} instruction for each path that supplies a string related to the selection the operator has made. This command is also useful in testing macro shells. Each subroutine can be represented initially by nothing more than an {INDICATE} with a suitable character string. This allows you to check the logic flow. If you have a budget subroutine, for example, you might represent it in your shell with {INDICATE "budget subroutine"}.

Example   The macro shown here changes the mode indicator several times:

1	\I	{INDICATE "SETUP"}	Change indicator to SETUP
2		/wcs15~	Change column width to 15
3		/rfc0~{DOWN 5}~	Format as currency 0 decimals
4		{INDICATE "SPLIT"}	Change indicator to SPLIT
5		{DOWN 5}	Move down 5 cells
6		/wwh	Create horizontal window
7		{INDICATE}	Eliminate indicator setting

The first step in the macro changes the indicator to SETUP. The macro then performs worksheet commands to set up the worksheet with a new column width adjustment and Currency format.

The instruction in B4 changes the indicator to SPLIT. A horizontal second window is then created. Finally, the {INDICATE} command is used without an argument to return to the default setting of READY mode when the macro ends. Without this last instruction, the mode indicator would still read SPLIT after the macro executed.

You may want to try this macro in STEP mode, since it does not remain in any one mode for very long. You can see just the indicators flash on the screen briefly, unless you slow the macro down.

{PANELOFF}

The {PANELOFF} command prevents 1-2-3 from redrawing the control panel while the command is in effect.

Format   The format for the {PANELOFF} command is

{PANELOFF} or {PANELOFF clear}

When the second form is used, the control panel and status line are cleared before freezing it.

Use   This command reduces the flicker that can occur when macro instructions are executed. It is also useful if you do not want the operator to be aware of the exact instructions being executed. Even if the operator turns the STEP mode on to slow down the operation of the instructions so they can be read, the control panel and status line are not updated while {PANELOFF} is in effect. This command affects only the execution of menu commands, since 1-2-3 does not use the control panel for advanced macro commands like {BRANCH} and {IF}. Control panel and status line updating start when 1-2-3 performs a {PANELON} command or when the macro ends.

Example   The following macro lets you determine whether you want the control panel updated as you execute the macro:

1	\P	GETLABEL "Update Control Panel?",update}
2		{IF update="Y"}{BRANCH yes}
3		{PANELOFF}
4		{BRANCH finish}
5	yes	{PANELON}
6	finish	{GOTO}d1~
7		/rfc2~~
8		/wcs12~
9		{GOTO}f3~
10		/rfp3~{DOWN 3}~

This macro lets you see the effect of updating the panel instead of disabling it. The first instruction expects a Y if you want to update the control panel and an N if you do not. The entry you make is stored in a range (cell) called **update**, which is checked by the {IF} statement in B2. If the entry in **update** is a Y, control passes to B5. If it is any other value, control passes to B3, where {PANELOFF} disables updating of the control panel. B4 branches to the subroutine called **finish** to bypass the instruction that turns the control panel on. The remainder of the macro moves the cell pointer to D1 and then invokes a /Range Format and a /Worksheet Column Set-Width command. The cell pointer is moved to F3, and another format instruction is issued before the macro ends.

Setup   In addition to entering the macro instructions and naming the macro \P, you must select a cell to contain the response to the {GETLABEL} instruction. This cell should be assigned the range name **update**. Range names must also be assigned to two sections of the macro. B5 is assigned the range name **yes**, and B6 is assigned the range name **finish**. You may wish to enter these labels in the first column as documentation and assign the names with /Range Name Labels Right.

{PANELON}

The {PANELON} command restores the default setting of having 1-2-3 update the control panel with each instruction executed.

Format   The format for the {PANELON} command is

    {PANELON}

This command has no arguments.

Use   This command is useful when you want to reactivate control panel updating in the middle of a macro.

Example   The example for the {PANELOFF} instruction shows the effect of both {PANELOFF} and {PANELON} on the control panel.

{WINDOWSOFF}

The {WINDOWSOFF} command freezes the entire screen, with the exception of the control panel and status line until 1-2-3 performs a {WINDOWSON} command or the macro ends.

Format   The format for the {WINDOWSOFF} command is

{WINDOWSOFF}

The command has no arguments.

Use   Using this command reduces the flicker that occurs on the screen with each new macro instruction executed. Without this command, you see the screen flicker as ranges are selected, the cell pointer is moved, and entries are generated for worksheet cells. This flicker can be annoying to the operator and is best eliminated. Eliminating window updating also reduces execution time for long macros, since it means that 1-2-3 does not have to redraw the screen every time you move the cell pointer or manipulate data.

Like {PANELOFF}, {WINDOWSOFF} is also useful when you do not want the operator to be aware of each activity performed. You can change the mode indicator to WAIT and resume window updating (with {WINDOWSON}) at an appropriate point in the macro. These commands also speed up the execution of the macro since 1-2-3 does not need to update the screen.

Example   The following macro allows you to monitor the effects of updating the window or freezing it during the execution of the macro:

1	\W	{GETLABEL "Do you want the window updated?",update}
2		{IF update="Y"}{BRANCH yes}
3		{WINDOWSOFF}
4		{BRANCH finish}
5	yes	{WINDOWSON}
6	finish	{GOTO}d1~
7		/rfc2~~
8		/wcs12~
9		{GOTO}f3~
10		/rfp3~{DOWN 3}~

With just one entry in response to a prompt message, you can change the window updating option. This lets you see the difference between updating and freezing.

The first instruction expects a Y if you want to update the screen while the macro executes and an N if you do not. The entry you make is stored in the cell range **update**, which is checked by the {IF} statement in B2. If the entry is a Y, control passes to B5, where {WINDOWSON} is executed. If it is any other value, control passes to B3, where {WINDOWSOFF} disables updating of the window portion of the screen. B4 branches to the subroutine called **finish** to bypass the instruction that turns window updating on. The remainder of the macro moves the cell pointer to D1 and then invokes a /Range Format and a /Worksheet Column Set-Width command. The cell pointer is moved to F3, and another format instruction is issued.

Using this macro with the two alternative responses shows you what both ways look like to the user. You can then select the approach you think would be most appropriate for your application.

Setup   In addition to entering the macro instructions and naming the macro \W, you must select a cell to contain the response to the {GETLABEL} instruction. This cell should be assigned the range name **update**. Range names must also be assigned to two sections of the macro. B5 is assigned the range name **yes**, and B6 is assigned the range name **finish**. You may wish to enter these labels in the first column as documentation and assign the names with /Range Name Labels Right.

{WINDOWSON}

The {WINDOWSON} instruction returns to the default setting of having the screen updated with each instruction.

Format   The format of the {WINDOWSON} command is

    {WINDOWSON}

This command has no arguments.

Use   Use this command when you want to reactivate screen updating. It could be inserted near the end of a macro to have the screen updated with the current results.

Example   The example found under {WINDOWSOFF} provides a look at the {WINDOWSON} command.

Interactive Macro Commands

{?}

The {?} command is actually an advanced macro instruction, although it was introduced in Chapter 12. As you know, it allows the operator to enter information from the keyboard.

Format   The format for the {?} command is

    {?}

This command has no arguments.

Use   Use the {?} command when you need to obtain just a few pieces of information from the operator. If you have more extensive needs, {GETNUMBER} and {GETLABEL} are more useful, because they allow you to supply prompts as part of the instruction to clarify the exact information you want.

If you do use the {?} instruction, you can precede it with an instruction to place a prompt message in the current cell, as follows:

```
Enter your department number~
{?}
```

The number entered by the operator would replace the message placed in the current cell by the previous instruction.

Example   You can use the {?} macro command to enter a series of values, such as the entries needed for the @DATE function. You can add a loop to add several @DATE formulas. The macro would appear as follows:

1	\D	{LET a1,0}{QUIT}	Initialize A1 to 0
2	top	{IF a1=10}	Check for max value in counter
3		{LET a1,a1+1}	Increment counter
4		@DATE(	Enter first part of function
5		{?}	Pause for the entry of year
6			Generate comma separator
7		{?}	Pause for the entry of month
8			Generate comma separator
9		{?}	Pause for the entry of day
10		)~	Generate close and finalize
11		{DOWN}	Move cursor down 1 cell
12		{BRANCH top}	Begin loop again

This macro shows how the {?} can be enhanced with the use of other instructions to produce multiple dates rather than a single entry.

Setup   In addition to entering the macro instructions and a macro name assignment of \D, you must assign the range name **top** to the macro.

{BREAKOFF}

The {BREAKOFF} command is used to disable the BREAK key function, thereby preventing the interruption of a macro.

Format   The format of the {BREAKOFF} command is

{BREAKOFF}

This command has no arguments.

Use   Normally CTRL-BREAK can be used to stop a macro. It displays ERROR as a mode indicator. When you press ESC, you can proceed to make changes to the worksheet from READY mode. However, when you have designed an automated application and want to ensure its integrity by maintaining control throughout the operator's use of the worksheet, you can disable the Break feature by placing {BREAKOFF} in your macro. Be sure you have tested the macro before doing this, because a macro that contains an infinite loop and {BREAKOFF} can be stopped only by turning off the machine.

Example   Since the {BREAKOFF} command disables the ability of the CTRL-BREAK sequence to stop a runaway macro, it can be dangerous. It is even more dangerous in a \0 macro that executes automatically, since there is then no way to interrupt the macro.

This may be exactly what you want if you have enabled the Protection feature and wish to ensure that the operator's entries are restricted to the cells you choose. With Worksheet Protection, you can prevent accidental destruction to the contents of cells, but you cannot prevent malicious destruction, since an operator can turn Protection off. However, if you allow worksheet updating only through a controlled access macro with /Range Input statements, disable Break, and save the file at the end before erasing the worksheet, the operator cannot do anything other than what you have established. The only problem is that *your* access also is limited. A solution to this problem is presented later in this chapter, after a discussion of what is needed to prevent an operator from making illegal changes.

The macro reads as follows:

1	\0	{BREAKOFF}
2		{GETLABEL "Update employee names?",r1}
3		{IF r1<>"Y"}{BRANCH address}
4		/ria2..b20~
5	address	{GETLABEL "Update employee addresses?",r2}
6		{IF r2<>"Y"}{BRANCH phone}
7		/ric2..f 20~
8	phone	{GETLABEL "Update employee phone numbers?",r3}
9		{IF r3<>"Y"}{BRANCH salary}
10		/rig2..g20~

11	salary	{GETLABEL "Enter password to update salaries",r4}
12		{IF r4=z1}{BRANCH update}
13	end	{BREAKON}
14		
15	update	/rih2..h20~
16		{BREAKON}

The first instruction contains {BREAKOFF}, but you should not add this until you have tested the macro. From here the macro controls the updating of various sections of an employee database. Certain fields cannot be changed, others can be changed as desired, and salaries are updatable only with the correct password.

The first {GETLABEL} instruction checks to see if the operator wants to update the section of the database that includes employee names. If the response is Y, the macro proceeds to the /Range Input instruction. The names in the database for our example are located in the first and second worksheet columns A and B, and this instruction allows the operator to change any of them.

If the operator does not want to alter any names and responds with N, the **address** section of the macro is executed next. Again, the operator responds to the {GETLABEL} prompt, and if updates are needed, a new Range Input instruction is established.

The next section is **phone**, which allows the updating of phone numbers in the same manner. When the operator is finished with this section, **salary** is next. This section functions a little differently in that the {GETLABEL} instruction expects a password. This password must match the one stored in cell Z1. Since Break is disabled, the operator must know the password, because it is impossible to interrupt the macro to look at the contents of Z1. If the operator's entry matches Z1, the macro branches to **update** and allows updates to the section of the worksheet where salaries are stored. In our example, this is H2..H20, but of course it could be changed to any appropriate range.

{BREAKOFF} is then canceled with {BREAKON} before the macro ends, although this is not mandatory because ending a macro automatically disables {BREAKOFF}. This macro leaves the worksheet vulnerable to unauthorized changes after the update is completed, because the worksheet is still on the screen. To prevent this, the {BREAKON} instruction can be replaced with /fsemploy~r/wey to both save the worksheet and erase memory. If you do this, you have forever locked both the operator and yourself out of this worksheet unless Undo is enabled.

A fix for this problem is to store another password in a different cell and request the password right before the /File Save. If the password is entered correctly, {BREAKON} is executed and another instruction asks if you have further changes.

Setup   You must complete a number of steps in addition to the entry and naming of the macro.

- The cells in which you allow entries must be unprotected with /Range Unprot.

- Range names of **/0**, **address**, **phone**, **salary**, **end**, and **update** must be assigned to the macro instructions in rows 1, 5, 8, 11, 13, and 15, respectively.

- The password to allow salary updates must be stored in Z1.

{BREAKON}

The {BREAKON} command restores the BREAK key function so that you can press CTRL-BREAK to interrupt a macro.

Format   The format of the {BREAKON} command is

    {BREAKON}

This command has no arguments.

Use   You may elect to disable the Break feature during part of a macro and then restore its operation for a later section, for printing or data entry. Break is always restored at the end of a macro.

Example   The example found under {BREAKOFF} contains an explanation and example of the {BREAKON} instruction. {BREAKON} is the default setting and is needed only to restore the default after using {BREAKOFF}.

{GET}

The {GET} command is designed to accept the entry of a single character from the keyboard.

Format   The format of the {GET} command is

    {GET *location*}

where *location* is the storage location for the single character you enter from the keyboard. Your entry can be an alphabetic character, a numeric digit, or any other key, including one of the special function keys such as F9 (CALC) or F2 (EDIT).

Use   This command provides another option for keyboard input. The command offers an advantage over commands like {?}, {GETLABEL}, and {GETNUMBER} in that it can restrict the keyboard response to a single character. However, it lacks the ability to display a prompt message as the commands {GETNUMBER} and

{GETLABEL} can. {GET} is the ideal solution for situations where you want to build your own full-screen menu and expect a one-letter code for each selection.

Example   The screen in Figure 13-5 presents a full-screen menu that offers selections in Smith Company's accounting application. Letter selections represent a budget update, aging of receivables, and other accounting functions. Instructions at the bottom of the screen tell the operator to enter the letter representing a menu choice.

The following macro works with this menu:

1	\G	{BLANK a20}
2		{INDICATE}
3		{GOTO}a1~
4		{GET choice}
5		{IF choice="B"}{BRANCH budget}
6		{IF choice="R"}{BRANCH rec}
7		{IF choice="I"}{BRANCH inv}
8		{IF choice="U"}{BRANCH payroll}
9		{IF choice="P"}{BRANCH report}
10		{INDICATE "ERROR"}
11		{LET a20,"Incorrect entry re-execute macro"}{CALC}
12		
13	budget	{GOTO}q1~
14		{GETLABEL "Budget routine",z1}
15		{CALC}

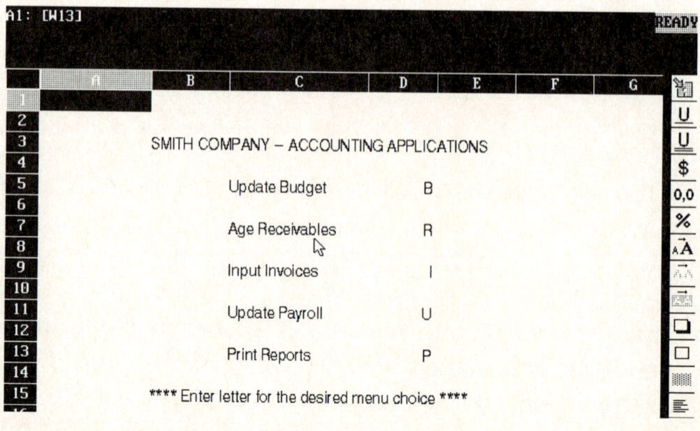

Figure 13-5.   The menu for {GET} example

The macro begins with a {BLANK} instruction to make sure A20 has been erased. This cell must be erased because it is used to present an error message to the operator when incorrect entries have been made.

The {INDICATE} instruction in line 2 ensures that the mode indicator is in its default state, without any previous displays in this area of the screen. Again, this is necessary so that the mode indicator can be set to ERROR if an incorrect response is made.

The cell pointer is next moved to A1 to display the entire menu. The {GET} instruction accepts a single-character response and stores it in a cell that has previously been assigned the range name **choice**.

The next five instructions check the value of **choice** and then branch to appropriate subroutines. Only one subroutine is shown in the listing, but they all follow the same pattern. **Budget** is a shell routine that does nothing more than move the cell pointer and display a message letting the operator know what routine has been reached. This shell can be expanded later to include a full set of instructions to do the appropriate processing.

If none of the branches is taken, this means that the operator entered an unacceptable character. When this happens, the mode indicator is set to ERROR in line 10, and an error message is placed in A20 with the {LET} instruction, which assigns a string value to A20.

{GETLABEL}

The {GETLABEL} command permits the entry of a character string from the keyboard in response to a prompt message.

Format   The format for the {GETLABEL} command is

{GETLABEL *prompt message, location*}

The argument *prompt message* is a string that must be enclosed in double quotation marks if it contains a character that can be used as an argument separator (a comma, colon, semicolon, or period), or a cell reference, range name, or formula that produces a string. The string displays in the control panel. Its length is limited to the 72 characters at the top of the control panel. If you supply a longer string, it scrolls off the screen.

The argument *location* is a reference to a cell or range name where the information entered from the keyboard is stored. Up to 80 characters will be accepted as input. If a range is supplied for the argument, the character string entered is stored in the upper-left cell of the range.

Use   The {GETLABEL} command stores your entry as a left-justified label in the location specified. This feature also makes the command appropriate for numeric entries when you want them placed at the left edge of the cell so they can be read as macro keystrokes.

Example   Figure 13-6 shows a screen that might be used to capture data-entry information. The following instructions are an extract from a macro that might be used with this data-entry screen:

```
1    \E      {GOTO}c3~
2            {GETLABEL "Enter Name (Last, First)",c3}
3            {GOTO}c5~
4            {GETLABEL "Enter Street Address",c5}
5            {GOTO}c7~
6            {GETLABEL "Enter City",c7}
7            {GOTO}c9~
8            {GETLABEL "Enter State",c9}
9            {GOTO}c11~
10           {GETLABEL "Enter Zip",c11}~
```

The first macro instruction moves the cursor to C3. Then the {GETLABEL} instruction presents a prompt and stores the response in C3. The cell address was added for clarity. The remaining instructions all follow the same pattern, providing a prompt for each new piece of information required and storing it in the current cell. At the end of these instructions, you might wish to add further instructions to move this data to the next available database record within the worksheet or perform some additional manipulations with the data.

Setup   The macro example requires a predefined menu. The macro also assumes that the cell pointer is positioned in A1 before the macro begins. You could add a {HOME} instruction at the top of the macro to eliminate this assumption if you choose.

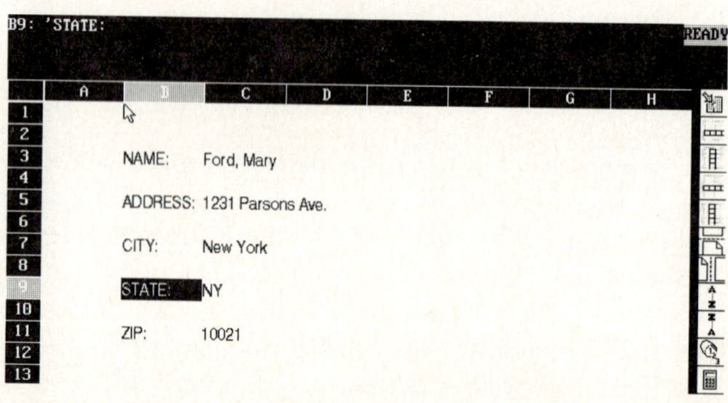

Figure 13-6.   *The data entry screen for {GETLABEL} example*

Note   {GETLABEL} is equivalent to the Release 1A /XL command. To use the /XL command, enter */XLprompt~location~* where *prompt* is the message displayed in the control panel and *location* is the cell address or range name where the entry is stored.

{GETNUMBER}

The {GETNUMBER} command permits the entry of numeric information from the keyboard in response to a prompt message.

Format   The format for the {GETNUMBER} command is

    {GETNUMBER *prompt message, location*}

The argument *prompt message* is a string that must be enclosed in double quotation marks if it contains a character that can be used as an argument separator (a comma, colon, semicolon, or period) or a cell reference, range name, or formula that produces a string. The string displays in the control panel. Its length is limited to the 72 characters at the top of the control panel. If you supply a longer string, it scrolls off the screen.

    The argument *location* is a reference to a cell, range, or range name where the information entered from the keyboard is stored. A numeric value, formula, or range name referencing a numeric value can be entered. If a range is supplied for the argument, the numeric value entered is stored in the upper-left cell of the range.

Use   You can use the {GETNUMBER} command to store an entry as a value rather than as the label that the {GETLABEL} stores.

Example   The {GETNUMBER} command can be used when you want a number from the operator such as the number of times a set of macro instructions should be executed, as in this macro.

1	\L	{LET p1,0}
2		{GETNUMBER "Number of dates to enter?",p2}
3	begin	{IF p1=p2}{QUIT}
4		{LET p1,p1+1}
5		{GETLABEL "Enter month number",month}
6		{GETLABEL "Enter day number",day}
7		{GETLABEL "Enter year number,e.g. 91",year}
8		@DATE(
9	year	91

10		,
11	month	1
12		,
13	day	12
14		)~
15		{DOWN}
16		{BRANCH begin}

The first instruction initializes a counter to zero. The next instruction, {GETNUM-BER}, asks how many dates you want to enter. The response you make controls the number of iterations performed by the macro. As soon as the counter is equal to the number of iterations you have requested, the {IF} instruction in the third line stops the macro execution.

Until then, each cycle increments the counter by one. The cycle includes three {GETLABEL} instructions that you can use to obtain the date components in a convenient sequence. Since you are storing these components in worksheet cells, you are not restricted to the year, month, and day sequence required by the @DATE function. The current instructions obtain month, day, and year, respectively. These pieces of information are stored in a different sequence from how they are entered, so they are in the correct order for the @DATE function. The macro then enters a date into a cell. The **year, month,** and **day** range names in the macro show the year, month, and day number from the last time the macro was executed.

After the date entry is finalized, the cell pointer is moved down one cell, and control branches to the top of the loop, which is named **begin**. The macro ends when the {IF} instruction at the top of the loop encounters the equal condition and executes {QUIT}.

Setup   The macro requires that range names be established for **begin, month, day,** and **year** before the macro is executed.

Note   {GETNUMBER} is equivalent to the Release 1A /XN command. To use the /XN command, enter /XN *prompt~location~* where *prompt* is the message displayed in the control panel and *location* is the cell address or range name where the entry is stored.

{LOOK}

The {LOOK} command checks the keyboard buffer for characters and places the first character in this buffer as an entry in the range identified by the *location* argument. It is similar to {GET}, except that with {LOOK} the operator can type the entry ahead and the macro still finds it.

Format   The format of the {LOOK} command is

{LOOK *location*}

where *location* is a cell address or range name used to store the character from the type-ahead buffer. If {LOOK} finds the buffer blank, it erases *location*.

Use   {LOOK} does not suspend macro execution while waiting for an entry, as the {GET} instruction does. Normally you use {LOOK} within a loop, allowing a certain amount of time for an entry before canceling the instruction. You may or may not want to update the file before canceling.

Example   The following macro uses the {LOOK} instruction to process a menu request from the same application designed for {GET} earlier in this section:

1	\L	{INDICATE}{HOME}
2		{LET time,@NOW}
3	keep	{LOOK selection}
4		{IF selection<>""}{BRANCH process}
5		{IF @NOW<(time+@TIME(0,10,0))}{BRANCH keep}
6		{INDICATE "ERROR"}
7		{LET a20, "No selection mode—Reexecute macro"}
8		
9	process	Macro instructions to process menu selection

Unlike the example with {GET}, this macro does not wait beyond a specific amount of time. It uses a loop to control the time it waits if the selection is not in the type-ahead buffer.

The macro begins by setting the indicator to its default setting and moving the cursor to A1. It then places the current date and time in a cell named **time**.

The next instruction begins the loop for checking the type-ahead buffer. {LOOK} is executed and stores the first character from the type-ahead buffer, if present, in **selection**. The next instruction, in line 4, checks to see if anything has been placed in **selection**. If anything is stored there, the macro branches to **process**. If the cell is empty, the macro continues to the {IF} instruction in line 5. This {IF} instruction compares the current time against the time stored at the beginning (in **time**) plus an acceptable wait interval. For this example, the wait time was set at 10 minutes. If the current time is less than 10 minutes after the beginning time, the macro continues to look for an entry by branching to the **keep** subroutine. If the chosen time interval has elapsed, the macro sets the indicator to **ERROR** and displays an error message in A20. Alternative strategies might be to save the file, clear memory, and quit 1-2-3.

The **process** section of this macro is not shown, but it contains instructions similar to those in the {GET} example shown earlier.

Setup   The example macro requires that cells for the storage of variables be named **time** and **selection**. The range names **keep** and **process** must be assigned to locations in the macro as shown.

{MENUBRANCH}

The {MENUBRANCH} command allows you to branch to a location containing information required to build a customized menu. Once this branch occurs, the macro executes instructions based on your menu selections.

Format   The format of the {MENUBRANCH} command is

    {MENUBRANCH *location*}

where *location* is a cell address or range name that represents the upper-left cell in the area for menu storage. This area must be a minimum of three rows deep and two columns wide. You may have up to eight columns of menu information.

Use   Information for the customized menu must be organized according to the following rules:

- The top row of the menu area contains the menu selection words that you want to use. Each of these words should begin with a different character, just as in 1-2-3's menus. This allows the operator to enter the first letter of an option to represent its selection or to point to the option. Menu selection words are entered one to a cell. You may use up to eight cells across, providing eight menu options.

- The second row of the menu area contains the expanded description for each menu choice that is displayed when you point to the menu selection. As you make one label entry in each cell and move across, it is likely that the entries appear truncated, since they are long labels. Although you should keep your descriptions brief, do not be concerned about this apparent overlap. Place the description in the appropriate column for the menu choice.

- Place the remainder of the macro instructions appropriate for each choice in the column with the menu item and expanded description. Begin these instructions in the cell immediately under the expanded description, and extend as far down the column as you need. You may include a branch to a subroutine.

Example   {MENUBRANCH} can be used to create a menu with four different selections, as shown here:

The macro that created this custom menu is shown in Figure 13-7. The macro begins with the {MENUBRANCH} instruction and has all the menu options stored at a location named **select**. The cell J3 is the one to which this name was attached, although the menu selections and descriptions extend down from there and to the right.

The menu selections shown in J3..M3 are the words "Consol," "Print," "Age," and "Employ." As required, each word begins with a different letter. The expanded descriptions appear in cells J4..N4. They are as follows:

J4	Consolidate department budgets
K4	Print monthly reports
L4	Age accounts receivable
M4	Update employee file

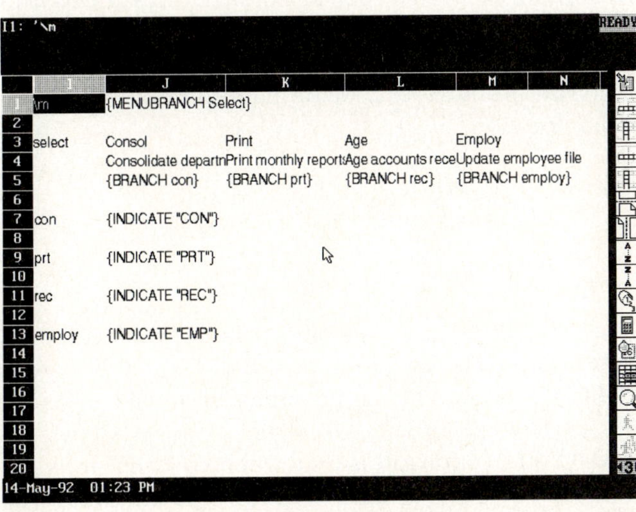

Figure 13-7.   *The macro for creation of a custom menu*

As you enter the second through the fourth descriptions, it appears that you are writing on top of previous ones, but you need not be concerned. Each description is stored as a label in the appropriate cell.

The last step in creating a menu macro is to fill in the cells underneath the descriptions with all the instructions for each choice. In our example, these instructions occupy only row 5, but internally the entries could extend down in the columns to row 50 or longer.

In this macro, each option has a branch to a different subroutine. At this point the routines are simply shells to allow you to check the logic. The only action taken in each shell is to change the indicator to the entry specified.

Setup   The entire menu section must be entered before a macro like this can be tested. It is the only example of a macro that can extend across as many as eight columns. Actually, it is eight individual macros in adjacent columns.

All the names listed in column I must be assigned to the respective cells in column J. /Range Name Labels Right is the easiest way to handle this task.

Note   {MENUBRANCH} is equivalent to the Release 1A /XM command. To use the /XM command, enter /XM*location~* where *location* is the cell address or range name where the menu starts.

{MENUCALL}

The {MENUCALL} command displays a custom menu as does {MENUBRANCH}, but it executes the menu as a call rather than as a branch. This affects the execution flow at the end of the menu processing. With {MENUBRANCH}, the macro ends when the code for the selected option completes. With {MENUCALL}, control returns to the statement following {MENUCALL} in the main code for the macro, and execution begins again at that location.

Format   The format of the {MENUCALL} command is

    {MENUCALL *location*}

where *location* is a cell address or range name that represents the upper-left cell in the area for menu storage. This area must be a minimum of three rows deep and two columns wide. You may have up to eight columns of menu information.

Use   The {MENUCALL} command is used when you want to continue executing the macro instructions directly beneath the {MENUCALL} macro instruction. The structure of the menu and the rules it must follow are identical to the structure and rules described for the {MENUBRANCH} command.

Example   An example of {MENUCALL} is exactly the same as the one for {MENUBRANCH}, except that you expect to see statements after {MENUCALL} in the main code. These are executed after the menu processing has completed.

{WAIT}

The {WAIT} command halts the execution of a macro until a specified time.

Format   The format of the {WAIT} command is

> {WAIT *time-serial-number*}

where *time-serial-number* is a decimal value that represents the serial time number for the time of day when you want execution to continue.

Example   You can use the {WAIT} command to delay a macro's execution for several seconds or minutes. To do this, the time-serial-number used by {WAIT} can be computed by adding a time value to the value computed with @NOW to create a fixed delay. You may, for example, want to display information on the screen for 30 seconds to allow time for it to be read, like this:

> {WAIT @NOW+@TIME(0,0,30)}

This adds 30 seconds to the current time and waits until that time is reached before continuing execution. While 1-2-3 is waiting, the mode indicator says WAIT. The macro shown as an example for the {LOOK} command also uses the {WAIT} command to delay macro execution.

Macro Commands that Affect the Flow of Execution

{BRANCH}

The {BRANCH} command moves the flow of execution in your macro to a new location.

Format   The format of the {BRANCH} command is

> {BRANCH *location*}

where *location* is a cell address or a range name that tells 1-2-3 the location of the next keystroke to be executed. If you specify a range name that refers to a range of cells, 1-2-3 begins execution with the keystrokes in the upper-left cell of the range.

Use   {BRANCH} is frequently used with a condition test to change the flow of execution. As an example, you might have the following entry in your macro:

>   {IF A1>10}{BRANCH end}
>
>   ...
>
>   ...
>
> end   {QUIT}

In this case you may have been using A1 as a counter, and when A1 exceeds 10 your task is finished. This sequence of instructions would then branch to **end** and execute the {QUIT} instruction stored there.

Example   The following listing is an excerpt from a macro that combines the data in four files:

1	\C	{GETLABEL "Begin combine?",h21}
2		{IF h21<>"Y"}{BRANCH stop}
3		{HOME}
4		/fcaeREGION1~
5		/fcaeREGION2~
6		/fcaeREGION3~
7		/fcaeREGION4~
8	stop	{CALC}

The excerpt begins by asking the operator whether to proceed with the consolidation. The logical {IF} in the next line checks for any value other than Y and uses the {BRANCH} instruction to alter the execution flow to **stop** if such a value is found. **Stop**   calculates the worksheet and ends the macro.

Assuming a Y was entered, the cursor is moved to A1 and the four files are combined with the /File Combine Add Entire-File command. The worksheet is then recalculated, and the macro ends.

Note   This is equivalent to the Release 1A /XG command. To use the /XG command, enter /XG*location*~ where *location* is the cell address or range name of the next macro instruction to execute.

{BRANCH} is frequently confused with {GOTO}, but they are not the same. {GOTO} repositions the cell pointer without affecting the execution of the macro. {BRANCH} alters the macro's execution flow but does not move the cell pointer.

{DEFINE}

The {DEFINE} command allocates space for arguments to be passed to subroutines and establishes the type of information they contain.

Format   The format of the {DEFINE} command is

{DEFINE *location*1:*type*1,*location*2:*type*2,...*location*n:*type*n}

The argument *location* is a cell where the value being passed to the subroutine is to be stored. This cell can be specified with a cell address or a range name. If you specify a range name that references a group of cells, the upper-left cell in the range is used for storage.

The argument *type* tells 1-2-3 whether value or string data is to be passed to the subroutine. *Type* may be entered as either a value or string, like this:

{DEFINE price:value,supplier:string}

where **price** and **supplier** are range names that are used for passing the arguments to the subroutine. **Price** contains value data, and **supplier** contains strings. String is the type default.

Example   Examples of the {DEFINE} command are included in the "Main Code and Subroutines" section at the beginning of the chapter and also later in the chapter under the {*routine*} macro command.

{DISPATCH}

The {DISPATCH} command allows you to use the contents of a cell to determine the branch location.

Format   The format of the {DISPATCH} command is

{DISPATCH *location*}

where *location* is a cell address or a range name that refers to a single cell. This cell in turn must contain a cell address or a range name of another cell. {DISPATCH} reads this information from the cell and branch to the location represented by its contents.

Use   This command is useful when you need to set up a variable branching situation based on the contents of data fields or other worksheet results. It differs from the

{BRANCH} command in that {BRANCH} immediately executes the instructions in the cells beginning at *location*, whereas {DISPATCH} first reads *location* to determine the final branch location at which it executes instructions.

Example   The macro shown here provides an example of {DISPATCH}:

1	\D	{IF due_date>@NOW}{LET routine,"not_due"}
2		{IF due_date<=@NOW}{LET routine,"over_due"}
3		{CALC}{DISPATCH routine}
4		
5	not_due	{LET A18, "Account not yet due"}
6		
7	not_due	{LET A18, "*** Account Overdue***"}

This macro is designed to take two different paths, depending on whether the date in **due_date** is greater than today's date. The first instruction checks **due_date** against @NOW. If **due_date** is greater, it places the value **not_due** in the cell named **routine**. If the opposite condition is true, the value **over_due** is placed in **routine**.

The worksheet is calculated to place these values in **routine**, so you can see them displayed if you use the STEP mode for this macro. {DISPATCH} is the next instruction. It reads the entry in **routine** and then branches to the appropriate location. Again the two subroutines have been set up in the example as shells, but they can be expanded easily to handle whatever tasks you require.

{FOR}

The {FOR} command executes the code at a given location numerous times through a loop that it establishes.

Format   The format of the {FOR} command is

{FOR *counter,start,stop,increment,starting-location*}

The argument *counter* is a location within the worksheet that the {FOR} instruction can use to count the number of iterations performed. {FOR} initializes this location with the value you specify for *start*.

The argument *start* is the initial value for *counter*.

The argument *stop* is the end value for *counter*, which never exceeds this value.

The argument *increment* is the amount that should be added to *counter* for each iteration of the loop.

The argument *starting-location* is a cell address or range name that specifies the location of the routine to be executed repetitively.

None of these values should be altered from within the subroutine. *Start, stop,* and *increment* are maintained internally by 1-2-3.

Use   You have seen examples earlier in this chapter of loops created without the {FOR} statement. Using {FOR} can make looping tasks easier, since it automatically handles initialization of the counter, increments it with each iteration, and checks for the last execution of the loop. When you create an iterative process outside of {FOR}, you must manage these tasks yourself.

The rules used by {FOR} in processing a loop are as follows:

- Before each pass through the loop, {FOR} compares *counter* and *stop.* If *counter* is less than or equal to *stop,* the loop is processed. If *counter* is greater than *stop,* control passes to the instruction following {FOR}.

- At the end of the *start* routine or at a {RETURN}, control passes to the top of the loop. At this time, *counter* is increased by *increment.*

- If *stop* is less than *start,* the loop is not executed. A loop with an *increment* of 0 is an infinite loop; it can be stopped only by pressing CTRL-BREAK.

- If {QUIT} or {FORBREAK} is used at the end of the loop rather than {RETURN}, the loop ends.

Example   The following macro is designed to enter a column of numbers from the numeric keypad and to sum the numbers once they are entered. An arbitrary limit of 20 numbers was established, but if you want to stop sooner, enter **z.**

The macro instructions are as follows:

```
1       \F              {FOR counter,1,20,1,numbers}

2                       /re~

3                       @SUM(

4                       {UP}.{END}{UP}

5                       )~

6

7       numbers         {?}~

8                       {IF @CELLPOINTER("contents")="z"}{FORBREAK}

9                       {DOWN}
```

The first instruction sets up the loop with an initial value of 1, an *increment* of 1, and a *stop* value of 20. A cell named **counter** is used to store the number of iterations performed, and **numbers** is the location of the code that begins the loop.

Numbers is executed next. In every iteration, it expects you to enter a value. You may use the numeric keypad if you disable the movement keys with NUM LOCK.

The next instruction checks to see whether the current cell contains z. If it does, the {FOR} loop ends (via {FORBREAK}), regardless of the number of iterations completed, and control returns to line 2. If z was not entered, the cell pointer moves down one cell. The **counter** is incremented by 1, and the loop begins again.

When control returns to the macro instruction after the {FOR} command, the current cell is erased. It is either blank already or contains z, depending on how the loop ended. The @SUM instruction is added to this cell. The complete list of numbers you entered is added then, and the @SUM function is finalized.

Setup   The range name **numbers** must be assigned to the macro instruction in line 7. You must also assign a range name to **counter**. Before executing the macro, position your cell pointer in the desired location for the column of numbers to be entered, and turn on NUM LOCK, since this cannot be done from the macro.

{FORBREAK}

The {FORBREAK} command cancels processing of a {FOR} loop before the stop value is reached. When the {FORBREAK} command is executed, 1-2-3 continues executing the next macro instruction in the cell below the {FOR} command.

Format   The format of the {FORBREAK} command is

    {FORBREAK}

This command has no arguments.

Use   Normally {FORBREAK} is used in conjunction with an {IF} statement that checks the value of a variable and, on a certain condition, exits the loop. As an example, if you want to process a loop 20 times or until the account balance is zero, {FORBREAK} can be executed based on a test of the account balance.

Example   The {FOR} example also contains an example of a {FORBREAK} instruction that can end the loop early, based on the contents of a cell.

{IF}

The {IF} command will conditionally execute the command on the same line with {IF}.

Format   The format of the {IF} command is

    {IF *condition*}

where *condition* is any expression with either a numeric or a string value.

Use   The statement on the same line as the {IF} statement is treated as a THEN clause: "IF the expression is true, THEN the instruction following is executed." Any numeric expression is considered true as long as it is not the numeric value 0. A false condition, blank cells, NA, and string values all will evaluate as 0.

The instructions on the line after {IF} are regarded as the ELSE clause. Normally the THEN clause contains a {BRANCH}; otherwise, the macro executes the instructions in the ELSE clause after completing the THEN instructions.

Example   The macro shown here provides an example of the {IF} command:

1	\H	{GOTO}i1~	Move cursor to read directions
2		{GET k1}	Get type
3		{IF k1="C"}{LET c15,i20}	Check Budget Year/Set heading
4		{IF k1="P"}{LET c15,i19}	Set heading for previous year
5		{GOTO}b16	Move cursor to B16
6		^QTR 1	Enter ^QTR 1
7		{RIGHT}^QTR 2	Move cursor right and enter ^QTR 2
8		{RIGHT}^QTR 3	Move cursor right and enter ^QTR 3
9		{RIGHT}^QTR 4	Move cursor right and enter ^QTR 4
10		{RIGHT}^TOTAL	Move cursor right and enter ^TOTAL
11		{END}{LEFT}	Move to end on left (B16)
12		{DOWN}	Move down 1 cell

This macro establishes a heading for a budget report and uses the {IF} command to determine which budget year to print at the top of the report.

At the beginning of the macro the cell pointer is moved to cell I1, where directions are displayed. Then {GET} waits for a single-character entry of C for current or P for previous.

The {IF} statements in lines 3 and 4 check the character entered to determine the proper heading to use; then it is placed in C15. The statement following each {IF} on the same line is executed only if the condition shown for that {IF} is true.

The macro then proceeds to complete the remainder of the heading after the year is entered. The year is selected by the {IF} command as described in the previous paragraph. At the end of the macro, the cell pointer is positioned immediately beneath the first-quarter heading to be ready for the operator's first entry.

Setup   The macro expects to find headings for the previous and current budget years in I19 and I20, respectively.

Note   {IF} is equivalent to the Release 1A /XI command. To use the /XI command, enter /XI *condition~keystrokes for true condition. Condition* is the condition to evaluate and *keystrokes for true condition* are the keystrokes to execute if the condition is true.

{ONERROR}

The {ONERROR} command allows you to intercept errors or process them yourself during macro execution.

Format   The format of the {ONERROR} command is

{ONERROR *location,message-location*}

The argument *location* is the location to which 1-2-3 branches for error processing when an error is encountered.

The argument *message-location* is a cell containing the message that 1-2-3 displays at the bottom of the screen when an error occurs.

This argument is optional, but if you do not supply it, you will not be able to determine what type of error occurred.

Use   Since the {ONERROR} command is not effective until 1-2-3 has executed it within the flow of the macro, you should place it near the beginning of your macro. It remains in effect until either another {ONERROR} command is executed, an error is encountered, CTRL-BREAK is pressed, or the macro ends. Since CTRL-BREAK registers as an error, you can use {ONERROR} to intercept Break requests without using {BREAKOFF}. Once {ONERROR} is used to intercept an error, it normally is not available again in the same macro. If you want to reinstate {ONERROR} after using it, the routine at *location* should contain another {ONERROR} command.

Example   The following macro shows the macro and message 1-2-3 uses when an error occurs:

1	\0	{ONERROR start_over,message}	If error restart
2		{update_pay}	Update payroll
3		/fs~r	Saves results
4			
5	start_over	{WAIT @NOW+@TIME(0,0,10)}	Display message
6		/frPAYROLL~	Retrieve and restart
7			
8	message	Unable to complete process starting over	

This macro automatically executes when the file is retrieved. The {ONERROR} command directs 1-2-3 to execute the macro starting at the cell called **start_over** if an error occurs while 1-2-3 executes the UPDATE_PAY macro. If an error occurs, 1-2-3 displays the message in the cell labeled **message** for ten seconds before retrieving the file again so you can start over. This type of error processing would occur when you want an all or none transaction processing. If the macro cannot perform all of the changes and save the modified file, it does not save any changes. In a payroll example, you would not want to perform payroll computations for only half of your employees. You would want to make the computations for all of them or none of them.

{QUIT}

The {QUIT} command terminates a macro.

Format   The format of the {QUIT} command is

    {QUIT}

This command has no arguments.

Use   The {QUIT} command can be used as a value at the end of a condition test, for example, {IF a1>10}{QUIT}. When the condition evaluates as true, the macro and all its subroutines end.

Note   {QUIT} is equivalent to the Release 1A /XQ command. To use the /XQ command, enter /**XQ**.

{RESTART}

The {RESTART} command cancels the execution of the current subroutine and eliminates all pointers to routines that called it so it cannot return.

Format   The format of the {RESTART} command is

    {RESTART}

This command has no arguments.

Use   When you include this command anywhere within a called subroutine, it will immediately cancel the call, complete the routine, and continue executing from that point downward. All upward pointers to higher-level routines are canceled.

{RETURN}

The {RETURN} command is used to return from a subroutine to the calling routine. It is used in conjunction with {MENUCALL} and {*routine*}. A blank cell or one containing a numeric value has the same effect as {RETURN} when it is encountered in a subroutine.

Format   The format for the {RETURN} command is

    {RETURN}

This command has no arguments.

Use   Placing {RETURN} anywhere in a called subroutine sends the flow of control back to the instruction following the one that called the subroutine. Unlike {RE-START}, {RETURN} does not cancel upward pointers. Check the example under the {*routine*} command for further information on the use of {RETURN}.

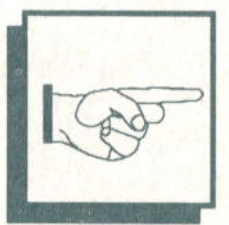

Do not confuse {RETURN} with {QUIT}. {RETURN} continues processing after returning to the calling routine. {QUIT} ends the macro. With {QUIT}, no further instructions are processed.

Note   {RETURN} is equivalent to the Release 1A /XR command. To use the /XR command, enter **/XR**.

{*routine*}

This command calls the subroutine it specifies. Its format is different from that of all the other macro commands; it contains no keyword, only the argument *routine* and any optional value arguments you may choose to use.

Format   The format of the {*routine*} command is

    {*routine argument1,argument2,...argumentn*}

The *routine* is a range name assigned to a single cell. This name must not be the same as any of the function key or cursor movement key names, such as {UP}, {EDIT}, or {CALC}.
    The *arguments* are optional values or strings passed to the subroutine. They must have corresponding entries in a {DEFINE} statement.

Example   The following macro provides an example of the use of a subroutine call:

1	\R	{GETNUMBER "How many items did you buy?",k1}
2		{LET counter,0}
3		{LET k5,0}{LET k6,0}
4		{purchase k1}
5		{INDICATE "DONE"}
6		{GOTO}q1~The total purchased is :~
7		{RIGHT 3}+k6~/rfc2~~
8		{QUIT}
9		
10	purchase	{DEFINE k2:value}
11		{IF counter=k2}{BRANCH end}
12		{GETNUMBER "Enter Purchase Amount"}
13		{LET k6,k6+k5}
14		{LET counter,counter+1}
15		{BRANCH purchase}
16	end	{RETURN}

This macro allows you to enter as many purchase amounts as you wish, and totals them for you.

The first instruction prompts you for the number of items purchased. This number is stored in cell K1. The next two instructions do some housekeeping by zeroing counters that the macro will use.

The subroutine call is in line 4. Notice that the optional argument is used to pass the value in K1 to the subroutine.

The subroutine that begins in line 10 first uses a {DEFINE} statement to set aside K2 for the information passed to it and declares this information to be a numeric variable. It uses **counter** to loop within the subroutine until **counter** is equal to the number of purchases specified. Until that time, it increments cell K6 by the purchase amount each time, increments **counter** by 1, and then branches back to the top of the subroutine.

When all purchases are processed, the subroutine branches to **end**, where a {RETURN} statement is located. This statement returns control to line 5 in the main routine. The mode indicator is then changed to DONE, and the total amount purchased is displayed.

Note   This is equivalent to the Release 1A /XC command. To use the /XC command, enter /**XC***location*~where *location* is the cell address or range name of the routine to execute.

{SYSTEM}

The {SYSTEM} command in Releases 2.2 and above temporarily suspends 1-2-3 and executes an operating system command. You do not need to enter **EXIT** at the end, as you do when /System is executed outside a macro, because 1-2-3 is automatically resumed. The command you enter after SYSTEM cannot exceed 125 characters and must be enclosed in quotes as in {SYSTEM "DIR"}. To suspend 1-2-3 without executing an operating system command, you must use /S.

Format   The format of the {SYSTEM} command is

    {SYSTEM *command*}

where *command* is any operating system command including the name of a batch file as long as the command is not longer than 125 characters.

Example   The following code provides an example of the use of {SYSTEM} for several operating system tasks:

    ...
    {SYSTEM "COPY BUDGET.WK1 A:"}
    {SYSTEM "COPY SALES.WK1 A:"}
    ...

Note   Do not attempt to execute TSR's or any other program that stay resident in memory with {SYSTEM}.

Macro Commands that Manipulate Data

The macro commands in this section allow you to manipulate values and strings stored in worksheet cells. You can use these commands to blank out a section of the worksheet or store a value or string in a cell. Commands from this section can also be used to recalculate the worksheet in row or column order.

{BLANK}

The {BLANK} command is functionally equivalent to /Range Erase; it erases a range of cells on the worksheet.

Format   The format of the {BLANK} command is

    {BLANK *location*}

where *location* is a range of cell addresses or a range name associated with one or more worksheet cells.

Use   This command can be used to clear data from previous uses of the worksheet. You might want to clear a data-entry area with this command. The difference between the {BLANK} command and /Range Erase is that the {BLANK} command does not have to be started from READY mode so you can use it while you are doing something else.

Example   Figure 13-8 presents a data-entry screen to be used with a macro. The screen shown contains the data from the previous entry, which may confuse an operator ready to enter a new record. To clear the screen, add the following lines of code to an existing macro, placing them so they are executed following the processing of the current record:

| 1 | \B | {BLANK c3..c11} |
| 2 | | {CALC} |

The lines are shown with a macro name, so they could be executed from the keyboard without incorporating them into another macro if desired. The first line requests that the range C3..C11 be erased. The second line calculates the worksheet to ensure that these cells are blanked immediately.

{CONTENTS}

The {CONTENTS} command stores a numeric value in a cell as a label with a specified format.

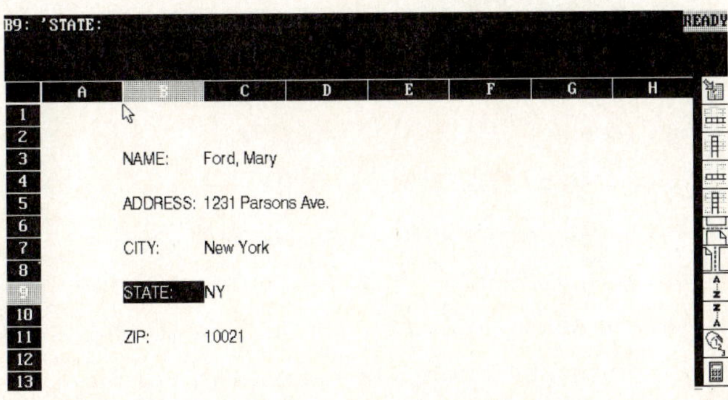

Figure 13-8.   *A data-entry screen containing old data*

Format   The format for {CONTENTS} is

{CONTENTS *destination,source,width,format*}

The argument *destination* is the location where you want the label stored. You may specify it as a cell address or a range name.

The argument *source* is the location of the value entry you want stored in *destination* as a string (label). You may specify this location as a cell address or a range name.

The argument *width* is an optional argument unless you choose to specify *format*, in which case *width* is required. *Width* determines the width of the string entry. If you do not specify width, it is obtained from the *source* location.

The argument *format* is an optional argument that allows you to determine the exact manner in which the *source* value is formatted in the destination string. Table 13-1 shows a list of the values you may select for this argument.

0 to 15	Fixed format with 0 to 15 decimal places, depending on the number. 0 means zero decimal places and 15 means 15
16 to 32	Scientific format with 0 to 15 decimal places
33 to 47	Currency ($) format with 0 to 15 decimal places
48 to 63	Percent (%) format with 0 to 15 decimal places
64 to 79	Comma (,) format with 0 to 15 decimal places
112	+/− format
113	General format
114	Date format 1 (DD-MM-YY)
115	Date format 2 (DD-MMM)
116	Date format 3 (MMM-YY)
117	Text display
118	Hidden
119	Date format 6 (HH:MM:SS AM/PM)
120	Date format 7 (HH:MM AM/PM)
121	Date format 4 – Full International date display
122	Date format 5 – Short International date display
123	Date format 8 – Full International time display
124	Date format 9 – Short International time display
127	Default Numeric display format for the worksheet

Table 13-1.   *Codes and Associated Formats for the {CONTENTS} Command*

Example   If you ever want to display the formula behind a cell at a given location, the {CONTENTS} command allows you to do this. Let's say that the *source* location is D1 and it contains the formula +Z1*Z3, although the number 30 displays in the cell. The formula behind D1 can be displayed in D5 with the following macro statement:

> {CONTENTS D5,D1,9,117}~

In this statement, D5 represents the *destination* location and D1 represents the *source*. A *width* of 9 is established, and the *format* represented by 117 is selected. The number 117 specifies Text display, so the formula behind D1 will display in D5. Remember that it is no longer a formula but a label once it is stored in the *destination* location.

{LET}

The {LET} command permits the assignment of a number or string to a location on the worksheet.

Format   The formats for the {LET} command are

> {LET *location,number*} or {LET *location,string*}

The argument *location* is the address or range name of the cell in which you want to store the value or label. If you specify *location* as a range, only the upper-left cell in the range is used.

The argument *number* is a numeric value or a formula that evaluates to a numeric value. The argument *string* is a string or a string formula.

Use   This command is useful whenever you wish to control the value in a worksheet cell. It can be used with a loop to increment a counter. Since it can be used with either strings or values, it is extremely flexible. Here are several examples:

{LET a1,10}~	Stores 10 in cell A1
{LET a1,a1+1}~	Increments cell A1 by 1
{LET a1,"ABC"&"COMPANY"}~	Places ABC COMPANY in cell A1

You can even use {LET} to equate a cell to the value in a cell in an external file with a link. For example, you might enter:

> {LET A1,<<SALES.WK1>>TOT_SALES}~

The tildes following these commands cause 1-2-3 to update the worksheet immediately.

You also have the option of using an indicator for numeric values that tells 1-2-3 whether you wish them treated as numbers (values) or as strings. The examples that follow show the proper format:

{LET a1,5+1:value}	Places a 6 in cell A1
{LET a1,5+1:string}	Places '5+1 in cell A1

Example   The {LET} command can be used to initialize and increment a counter when you want to set up your own loops. The following shell shows the format of a loop using {LET} in this way:

1	\S	{LET counter,1}
2	top_loop	{IF counter>stop}{BRANCH end_loop}
		...
		...
		...
8		{LET counter,counter+1}
9		{BRANCH top_loop}
10	end_loop	{QUIT}

If you choose to build your own loop rather than use the {FOR} instruction, you must always initialize your counter, increment it, and test it to see that it is within an acceptable range. In this example, **stop** is a range name used to contain the ending value for this range.

{PUT}

The {PUT} command puts a value in a location within a range. Unlike {LET}, which accepts only a cell address, {PUT} lets you select a row and column offset within a range.

Format   The formats for the {PUT} command are

{PUT *location,column,row,number*}

or

{PUT *location,column,row,string*}

The argument *location* is a range of cells identified by cell addresses or a range name.

The argument *column* is the column number within the *location* range. The first column in the range is column 0.

The argument *row* is the row number within the *location* range. The first row in the range is row 0.

The argument *number* is the value to be stored at the specified *location*.

The argument *string* is the string to be stored in the specified *location*.

Use   This command is similar to {LET}, but it has additional flexibility because it lets you store values within a range. A few examples and their results follow:

{PUT a1..b5,0,3,4} places a 4 in cell A4
{PUT a1..b5,1,0,3} places a 3 in cell B1
{PUT a1..b5,0,15,0} causes an error, because a row number of 15 is not within the range specified

Example   This command could be used to supply the values for a table. You might have entries like this in your macro:

{PUT table,0,0,100}~
{PUT table,0,1,d5/2}~

The tilde (~) at the end of each instruction causes the table entry to be updated immediately.

Note   The row and column offsets must be within the range you establish with the location argument. When they are not, an error occurs. This error cannot be processed with {ONERROR}.

{RECALC}

The {RECALC} command recalculates the formulas within the range you specify, proceeding row by row within this range.

Format   The format for the {RECALC} command is

{RECALC *location,condition,iteration*}

The argument *location* is the range of the worksheet that you want to have recalculated.

The optional argument *condition* specifies a condition that must be true before the *location* range selected is no longer recalculated. As long as *condition* is false, 1-2-3 continues to recalculate the worksheet. This argument is used in conjunction with the optional argument *iteration,* which specifies the number of times that formulas within the location range are recalculated as long as *condition* is false. When *condition* is true, recalculation stops, even though you may not have used all the iterations. With each iteration the count is reduced by 1. When it is zero, no further recalculation occurs.

Use   When you use {CALC}, the entire worksheet is recalculated. This can be unnecessarily time-consuming if you need just a section of it recalculated. The {RECALC} and {RECALCCOL} commands are designed for this purpose. Use {RECALC} when the area you are recalculating is below and to the left of the cells referenced by the formulas in this area. Use {RECALCCOL} when the area you are recalculating is above and to the right of the cells referenced by the formulas in this area. If the formula is *both* above and to the left of cells with new values, you must use {CALC} and recalculate the entire worksheet.

Example   If you have a macro that changes the value of cell AB10 and you are interested in the value of cell Z12, which is affected by AB10, you can use a {RECALC} instruction in your macro, as follows:

    {RECALC z1..ab12}

1-2-3 recalculates row by row to obtain the correct result of AB10 and thus for Z12. You can also add a condition and iteration count to this instruction:

    {RECALC z1..ab12,z3>20,10}

The recalculation of the specified range now continues until either Z3 is greater than 20 or 10 iterations are performed.

{RECALCCOL}

The {RECALCCOL} command recalculates the formulas within the range you specify, proceeding column by column within this range.

Format   The format for the {RECALCCOL} command is

    {RECALCCOL *location,condition,iteration*}

The argument *location* is the range of the worksheet that you want to have recalculated.
    The optional argument *condition* specifies a condition that must be true before the *location* range selected is no longer recalculated. As long as *condition* is false, 1-2-3

continues to recalculate the worksheet. This argument is used in conjunction with the optional argument *iteration,* which specifies the number of times that formulas within the location range are recalculated as long as *condition* is false. When *condition* is true, recalculation stops, even though you may not have used all the iterations. With each iteration the count is reduced by 1. When it is zero, no further recalculations will occur.

Use   Use {RECALCCOL} when the area you are recalculating is above and to the right of the cells referenced by the formulas in this area. If the formula is *both* above and to the left of cells with new values, you must use {CALC} and recalculate the entire worksheet.

Example   {RECALCCOL} follows the same syntax rules as {RECALC}. Select one or the other depending on whether a row or a column order of recalculation fits best with your application. Refer to the example under {RECALC} for additional information.

Macro Commands that Handle Files

The file macro commands provide sequential file-handling capabilities equivalent to the ones you find in the BASIC programming language. You can use these commands in macros to read and write records to text files. If you have never worked with files, you will want to review a section from a data processing text that overviews records, file size concepts, file input and output procedures, and other basic terminology connected with the use of files before you try to use these macros.

The commands in this section are interdependent. For example, it is not possible to use {READLN}, {READ}, {WRITE}, or {WRITELN} unless you have first opened the file with {OPEN}. Short examples dealing with the syntax are provided with each command. Examples showing commands used in context with other required commands are found under {FILESIZE}, {READ}, {READLN}, {WRITE}, and {WRITELN}.

{CLOSE}

The {CLOSE} command closes the file you opened with the {OPEN} command. You must close one file before opening a second one. If you use this command when there are no open files, 1-2-3 ignores it.

Format   The format for the {CLOSE} command is

    {CLOSE}

This command has no arguments.

Use   You must use this command when you are finished working with a text file.
You can look under the {READ} command for an example of using this command.

{FILESIZE}

This command allows you to determine the number of bytes or characters in your
file.

Format   The format for the {FILESIZE} command is

{FILESIZE *location*}

where *location* is the cell address or range name of the cell where you want 1-2-3 to
store the number representing the length of your file.

Use   The file must be open before you use this command. Remember, too, that the
character for the end-of-file condition is included in the count for {FILESIZE}. If you
know the length of the records on the file, you can use {FILESIZE} to determine how
many records the file contains.

Example   The following macro uses the {FILESIZE} command:

1	\F	{OPEN "B:TEST.PRN",R}	Open a file for reading
2		{FILESIZE g21}	Determine its size
3		{CALC}	Update worksheet
4		{CLOSE}	Close file

The first step in the macro is to open the file, since a file must be opened before
{FILESIZE} can be used. The entry in line 2 determines the number of bytes in the
file and places this number in cell G21. {CALC} is included to update the worksheet
cell immediately, after which the file is closed.

{GETPOS}

The {GETPOS} command determines the current position in a file.

Format   The format for the {GETPOS} command is

{GETPOS *location*}

where *location* is the address or range name of the cell where you want the current position number stored. Remember that the first character in a file is considered position 0.

Example   You can use this command to monitor your progress through a file, comparing the current position to the file size so that you do not attempt to read beyond the end of the file. After reading a record, you might include a {GETPOS} instruction, like this:

```
{READLN a10}
{GETPOS current}
```

You could then compare **current** and the result from the {FILESIZE} command and determine the number of records yet to read.

{OPEN}

The {OPEN} command allows you to open a file and specify whether you plan to read the file, write to it, or do both.

Format   The format for the {OPEN} command is

```
{OPEN file,access}
```

The argument *file* is a string or range name referring to a single cell that contains a string or string formula that references the name of the file you want to open. The cell string has an upper limit of 64 characters and can include the entire pathname and subdirectory, as well as the filename extension.

The argument *access* is a single character that controls the type of access you have to the file. The possible code characters are as follows:

- R means read-only. You cannot write to the file if your access mode is R.

- W means write-only. This argument opens a new file or re-creates an existing file. You cannot read from the file if your access mode is W.

- M allows modifications to the file, permitting both read and write access. It can be used only on existing files.

- A means append. This argument opens the existing file and adds data written to it at the end of the file. You can both read and write data.

Use   If you want to use an error routine in the event {OPEN} fails, you can place it on the same line as {OPEN} as a subroutine call; for example, {OPEN SALES,R}{fix_err}.

{READ}

The {READ} command reads the number of characters specified into the location you define, starting at the file pointer's present location.

Format   The format for the {READ} command is

{READ *byte-count, location*}

The argument *byte-count* is the number of characters you want to have read from the file, beginning at the current position in the file. If the number of bytes is larger than the number of remaining characters in the file, {READ} takes the amount of data remaining. *Byte-count* must be a numeric value or an expression that evaluates to one. The number should be between 0 and 512.

The argument *location* is the address or range name for the cell where you want the string of characters to be stored. The data is stored in this location as a left-justified label.

Example   The following macro shows the use of the {READ} instruction:

1	\R	{OPEN "B:TEST.PRN",R}	Open file for reading
2		{SETPOS 6}	Move file pointer
3		{READ 9,g22}	Read nine characters
4		{CALC}	Update worksheet
5		{CLOSE}	Close file

The file is opened for reading in the first instruction. The file pointer is then set at 6, which is the seventh character in the file. Nine bytes (characters) are read from the file and stored in cell G22. The worksheet is recalculated immediately to show this entry, after which the file is closed.

{READLN}

The {READLN} command copies a line of characters (a record) from a file and places it at the location specified.

Format   The format for the {READLN} command is

{READLN *location*}

where *location* is the cell address or range name that specifies the cell where you want the line of data stored.

Use   The function of the {READ} command depends on the number of bytes. {READLN}, by contrast, looks for a carriage return/line feed to know how many characters to read. Like {READ}, it uses the current file-pointer position as the starting point and can be used with {SETPOS}.

Example   The following macro reads one line from a text file:

1	\Z	{OPEN "B:TEST.PRN",R}	Open file for reading
2		{READLN place}	Read one line from file
3		~	Update worksheet
4		{RIGHT}	Move cell pointer
5		{CLOSE}	Close file

The file is first opened. {READLN} then reads the first line from the file and places these characters in **place**. A tilde (~) rather than {CALC} is used to update the worksheet, since the tilde is just as effective and more efficient. The cell pointer is moved to the right, and the file is closed.

{SETPOS}

The {SETPOS} command positions the file pointer at the location you specify.

Format   The format for the {SETPOS} command is

{SETPOS *number*}

where *number* is a numeric value or an expression that results in a numeric value that tells 1-2-3 which character you want the pointer set on. Remember that the first character in the file is considered to be position 0.

Use   1-2-3 does not prevent you from setting the pointer at a location beyond the end of the file. You should always use {FILESIZE} to ensure that this does not occur.

Example   Given the following information stored in a file,

ABC Company, LaCrosse, MI

setting the pointer to 4 would place it on the C in "Company."

{WRITE}

The {WRITE} command places a set of characters in a file that you have opened.

Format   The format for the {WRITE} command is

{WRITE *string*}

where *string* is a character string, an expression evaluating to a character string, or a range name assigned to a single cell that contains a string.

Use   When you use this command, 1-2-3 writes a string to the file at the current location of the file pointer. It then moves the pointer to the end of this entry to place it in position for writing the next set of characters.

Example   If you have a column of worksheet cells that contains the days of the week, use this command to write this list of names to a file. If you use {WRITE}, they will all be in one line (record) of the file.

Assuming that you position your cell pointer at the top of the list, the macro that follows writes all seven names for you:

1	\Z	{OPEN "B:TOGETH.PRN",W}
2		{LET ctr,1}
3	top	{IF ctr>7}{BRANCH end}
4		{WRITE @CELLPOINTER("contents")}
5		{DOWN}
6		{Let ctr,ctr+1}
7		{BRANCH top}
8	end	{CLOSE}

The file is opened for write access in the first instruction. A counter is initialized in line 2. The first statement in the iterative loop of the macro checks the counter to see whether it is greater than 7. If it is, the macro ends by closing the file.

If the counter is not greater than 7, the loop continues. The contents of the current cell are written to the file using the built-in function @CELLPOINTER. The pointer is moved down, and **ctr** is incremented. The execution flow then branches to the top of the loop. The macro continues in this cycle until it has written all seven entries to the file.

Since entries are written sequentially on the same line, the result of using this macro is

MondayTuesdayWednesdayThursdayFridaySaturdaySunday

assuming the first cell contained Monday and the days proceeded in order throughout the week as you moved down the column.

Setup   The macro requires that the range names **top**, **end**, and **ctr** be assigned to
appropriate cells. Also, the days of the week must already be in the worksheet, and
your cell pointer must be positioned on the first one before you execute the macro.

{WRITELN}

The {WRITELN} command places characters in an open file. In contrast to {WRITE},
it adds a carriage return or line feed to the end of each character string written, so
a new line or record is created in the file each time the command is used.

Format   The format for the {WRITELN} command is

    {WRITELN *string*}

where *string* is a character string, an expression evaluating to a character string, or a
range name assigned to a single cell that contains a string.

Use   When you use this command, 1-2-3 writes a string to the file at the current
location of the file pointer. It then moves the pointer to the beginning of the next
line to place it in position for writing the next set of characters.

    Using {WRITELN ""} generates a carriage return or line feed at the current
position in the file. You might want to build a record with a series of {WRITE}
commands, and then use {WRITELN} to add a line feed before beginning the next
record.

Example   This macro writes a series of string literals to a file named DAYS. It reads
as follows:

1	\Z	{OPEN "B:DAYS",W}
2		{WRITELN "Monday"}
3		{WRITELN "Tuesday"}
4		{WRITELN "Wednesday"}
5		{WRITELN "Thursday"}
6		{WRITELN "Friday"}
7		{WRITELN "Saturday"}
8		{WRITELN "Sunday"}
9		{CLOSE}

The file is first opened. Seven individual {WRITELN} statements are then used to write character strings to the file, after which the file is closed.

If you import the text file created with this macro into the worksheet with your cell pointer in Z1, Z1..Z7 will contain the following:

    Monday
    Tuesday
    Wednesday
    Thursday
    Friday
    Saturday
    Sunday

Since each day was written to a separate line when the file was imported, each record is written to a different cell.

Chapter **14**

Using 1-2-3's Built-In Add-Ins

You can give 1-2-3 additional features using add-ins. Add-ins are products provided by Lotus or other manufacturers that can provide additional functions to the 1-2-3 worksheet, macro commands, and special features such as spreadsheet publishing. Since 1-2-3 is loaded when you use them, these products add onto the features 1-2-3 provides.

Release 2.4 includes seven add-ins: Viewer, Macro Library Manager, SmartIcons, Tutorial, BackSolver, Auditor, and Wysiwyg. The Viewer add-in, described in Chapter 8, lets you look at files to select which worksheet to retrieve or which file to view, or lets you just browse through available files. The Macro Library Manager add-in, described in Chapter 12, lets you store worksheet data so you can transfer data between worksheets or use macros in multiple worksheets. The Auditor add-in provides worksheet auditing features such as following the path of cell values used in other formulas and finding other cells that are used by a formula. The Tutorial add-in, which leads you to 1-2-3 Go!, guides you through learning 1-2-3 features. The Wysiwyg add-in provides advanced spreadsheet publishing features. You may have already used some of the Wysiwyg features mentioned earlier in this book, and you can learn all about Wysiwyg in Chapter 15, "Using Wysiwyg."

Release 2.2 only included the Macro Library Manager and the Allways add-ins. The Allways add-in provided many of the same features available in Wysiwyg. Release 2.01 did not include any add-ins.

Most add-ins are made by other manufacturers, and are compatible, which means that as you upgrade to Release 2.4, you should be able to use most of the add-ins you have acquired for prior releases. With some add-ins, you may need to contact the

631

add-in manufacturer and acquire an updated version of the program if it does not run with Releases 2.2 and above.

This chapter covers how you use 1-2-3 add-ins and the built-in add-ins of Release 2.4. (Remember that Viewer, the Macro Library Manager, and Wysiwyg are covered in Chapters 8, 12, and 15, respectively.) Add-ins use the Add-In Manager, which is part of the 1-2-3 menu of Releases 2.2 and above, but can also be accessed by pressing ALT-F10. Before you can use an add-in, you must install it according to its accompanying directions. The add-ins that accompany Releases 2.2 and above are installed as part of 1-2-3's installation process, described in Appendix A.

Activating the Add-In Menu

The Add-In menu allows you to work with one or more separate add-in programs. You can activate the Add-In menu by selecting /Add-In or by pressing ALT-F10 (ADDIN) to display the menu shown here:

These commands are used to attach, detach, and invoke add-in programs. Attaching an add-in is the first step, since it places the add-in in memory and makes it available to 1-2-3. After selecting Attach, select the add-in either from a list of current directory files with an .ADN extension or from another directory. For example, to load BackSolver, select BSOLVER.ADN. You are asked whether you want to assign the add-in to a function key. With Release 2.4, two add-ins are auto-attached so that they automatically load into memory each time you start 1-2-3. These are the SmartIcons add-in and the Wysiwyg add-in.

For add-ins with menus, assigning a key allows you to invoke the Add-In menu quickly. You can select No-Key, 7, 8, 9, or 10. With Release 2.4, 7 is assigned to the SmartIcons add-in, which is auto-attached. The last four options represent the key combinations ALT-F7, ALT-F8, ALT-F9, and ALT-F10, respectively. Usually, add-ins without menus—such as the ones that provide additional functions and macro commands—use the No-Key selection. For instance, since the colon is preassigned to invoke the Wysiwyg menu, you will want to select No-Key. Once you select how to invoke the add-in, 1-2-3 returns to the Add-In menu. The screen will change with some add-ins but not with others. To return to READY mode, select Quit.

Other Add-In Menu Commands

Although Attach and Quit may be the only add-in commands you need to use for add-ins with 1-2-3, you will want to learn how you can use the other commands on the Add-In menu. You can remove add-ins from memory or activate add-ins. To invoke or activate an add-in program, select Invoke from the Add-In menu and then the name of the add-in. If you selected 7, 8, 9, or 10 instead of No-Key when you loaded the add-in, you can also invoke the Add-In menu by pressing ALT-F7, ALT-F8, ALT-F9, or ALT-F10. Each add-in uses part of your computer's memory. When you are using large worksheets, you may want to remove one or more add-ins from memory to leave more room for your worksheet files. To remove one add-in from memory, select Detach from the Add-In menu and then the add-in you want to remove from the list 1-2-3 presents. To remove all add-ins from memory, select Clear from the Add-In menu. You do not want to remove an add-in from memory if you are using it. For example, removing Wysiwyg from memory removes all of the Wysiwyg formats from the worksheet display (if you have not saved the file, these formats are lost permanently). Also, any changes you make to the worksheet, such as inserting a column or row, will not be reflected in the Wysiwyg format file that stores the formatting information for the worksheet.

Changing 1-2-3's Defaults for Add-Ins

Just as you can set 1-2-3 to use a different directory automatically by changing its default settings, you can also set 1-2-3 to load add-ins. The /Worksheet Global Default Other Add-In command sets the add-ins loaded when 1-2-3 is loaded and determines whether any add-ins are activated when they are loaded. To have 1-2-3 automatically load an add-in, enter /Worksheet Global Default Other Add-In Set followed by a number, 1 through 8. Then select the name of the add-in file you want to load and the key you want to assign to the add-in. Like the /Add-In Attach command, 1-2-3 only shows the keys that you have not already assigned. Release 2.4 provides you with two add-ins that load into memory with 1-2-3: Wysiwyg and SmartIcons.

Next, 1-2-3 asks if you want the add-in activated or invoked after the add-ins are loaded. You can select Yes or No. Only one add-in can be automatically invoked. If you change your mind, you can remove one of the add-ins from automatically loading by selecting Cancel and the number assigned to the add-in (not the key). When you are finished with the menu, you can select Quit to return to the Worksheet Global Default menu. From this menu, you can select Update so that 1-2-3 will automatically load the add-ins in the next session.

The Auditor Add-In

The Auditor add-in lets you follow the path of cells that formulas use and the path of formulas that 1-2-3 recalculates. Specifically, with the Auditor add-in, you can use the following features:

- Find cells that are used by another cell's formulas (precedents)

- Find cells that use another cell in their formulas (dependents)

- Find formulas in a range

- Find formulas in the order in which 1-2-3 recalculates them

- Find cells that are part of a circular reference

- Select whether the add-in lists the cell in the worksheet, highlights it, or moves to the cell that it finds

Like other add-ins, you must attach the Auditor add-in before you can use it. When you add the Auditor add-in, you will select the file AUDITOR.ADN. After you attach the add-in, you can invoke it to display the menu that is shown here:

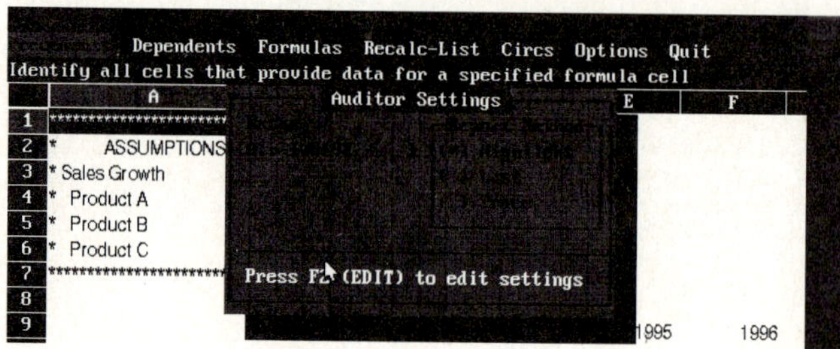

Using the Auditor Add-In

To use the Auditor add-in, you must make three decisions. First, you must select how you want the Auditor add-in to indicate the cells that you want it to find. Second, you want to select the range of cells that you want the Auditor to search through for the cells you want it to find. Last, you must select the cells you want the add-in to find. Besides using the Auditor Add-In menu, you can also use the dialog box for the first two decision processes.

The first decision to make when you use the Auditor is how you want the add-in to display the information it finds for you. You have three choices: Highlight, List, or Trace. Selecting Options from the initial Auditor Add-In menu allows you to select one of the three. You can also select an option button in the Auditor Settings dialog box under Report Method.

The Highlight option changes the cells that you select to a different color. If you are using other add-ins that control how the worksheet is displayed (such as Wysiwyg), the difference may not appear. The cells you select remain highlighted until you select Reset Highlight from the Options menu.

The List option lists the cell addresses and their contents in a worksheet range. If you select this option, after selecting an Auditor add-in command to select a group of cells, you will need to select a range where the add-in can write the information. Like the 1-2-3 /Range Justify command, this can either be a single cell that lets 1-2-3 write over any cells between the selected cell and the bottom of the worksheet or it can be a complete range that limits the Auditor add-in to using only the selected cells before it displays a message that the range is full.

The third choice, Trace, lets you move from one selected cell to another using the arrow keys—much like when you use the 1-2-3 /Range Input command to move between unprotected cells in a range.

The second decision to make is which cells you want to include in the search. Initially, the Auditor add-in is set to use the entire worksheet, but you can limit the worksheet range the Auditor uses by selecting Options Audit-Range and selecting a specific range to narrow the search. You can also select the range by entering the range in the Range text box in the Auditor Settings dialog box. If you use this method to specify which range to use, press F4 (ABS) to switch 1-2-3 into the POINT mode so you can visually see the cells you will select. If you later change your mind, you can select Options Reset Options to make the Auditor return to using the entire worksheet for the audit range, and you can choose the highlighting for how the cells found should be indicated.

The third decision you will make with the Auditor add-in involves which cells you want it to find. The menu option you select (other than Quit and Options) selects the cells the add-in finds. You only have to select the audit range and how you want any cells found to be indicated once because these settings are retained until you unload the add-in or the worksheet. This is like the 1-2-3 Data Query menu, which only requires you to select input, criteria, and output ranges once; after you select those, you can make other selections from the menu to select the database records you want. To select the cells you want the Auditor add-in to find, select Precedents, Dependents, Formulas, Recalc-List, or Circs.

Finding Cells Used in a Formula

Finding the cells a formula uses can be made easier using the Auditor because it can highlight these cells, move to the cells, or list the cells in the worksheet. To find these cells, select Precedents. For example, using Figure 14-1, you can find the cells that are used in the formula in D11. (Figure 14-2 shows the same worksheet as Figure 14-1 formatted as text.) After you select Precedents, you must select the cell or range of cells containing the formulas (to limit the Auditor's search for the cells these formulas use).

The next step depends on how the Auditor indicates the cells it finds. If the Auditor highlights the cells it finds, the main Auditor menu is displayed after the cells are highlighted. If the Auditor moves to the cells it finds, the Auditor simply moves to the first cell it finds. Then the Auditor displays a menu containing Forward, Backward, and Quit. Select Forward to move to the next cell the Auditor finds, select Backward to move to the previous cell, or select Quit to return to the Auditor menu.

If the Auditor lists the cells it finds, the Auditor prompts you for where you want the list. Select a cell or range where the Auditor can list the cells it finds. 1-2-3 erases everything from the cell to the bottom of the worksheet in the same column before

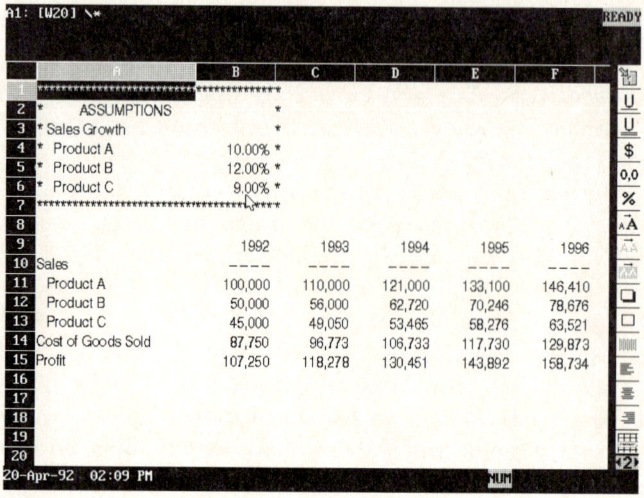

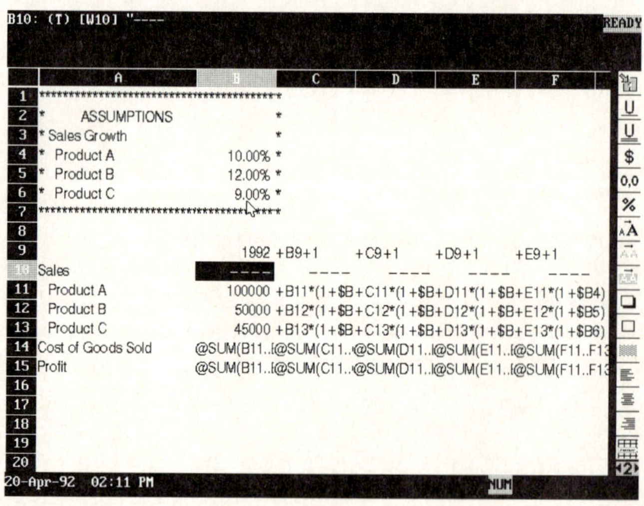

Figure 14-1.   *Worksheet for use with Auditor examples*

Figure 14-2.   *Worksheet in Figure 14-1 formatted as text*

it writes the cells to the list. The list is one column wide and as many rows long as necessary. The list contains the cell addresses and the contents of the cells the Auditor finds. The first cell of the list describes the contents below it.

Using Figure 14-1 as an example, if you select D11 as the cell that you want to find the precedents, the Auditor will find B4, B11, and C11.

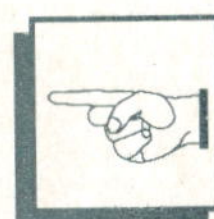

You can limit the range that the Auditor uses to list the cells it finds by selecting a range. Then the Auditor will only erase the selected range before listing the cells it finds if the range is big enough. If the range is not large enough, the Auditor will display an error message. Also, the range you select should not contain any preexisting entries since the Auditor will not write over the range until you remove the previous entries. The only exception is when the range contains the list from a previous use of the Auditor to list cells.

Finding Formulas Used by a Cell

Finding formulas that use a cell as part of the formula can be difficult. Without the Auditor add-in, you must use the /Range Search command to find these cells. You can find the formulas that depend on another cell so if you are planning to delete it, you will know which cells are affected. For example, you can use the Auditor to find which cells will be affected if you change Product A's growth in B4 of Figure 14-1 to 15 percent. To find these cells, select Dependents. Next, you must select the cell or range of cells containing the values for which the Auditor finds formulas that use these values.

Like finding formula dependents, the Auditor will highlight the cells, move to them (with the Forward and Backward menu options), or list them on the worksheet after you select a cell or range to put the list. If you use B4 as the cell you select after selecting Precedents, the Auditor will find C11..F11 and C14..F15.

Finding Formulas in a Range

Besides listing formulas using the /Print Printer Options Other Cell-Formulas command, you can also find them using the Auditor. You can use the Auditor when you are checking a worksheet to ensure that the cells you expect to contain formulas actually do. To find the cells that contain formulas, select Formulas. The Auditor will find the formulas in the Audit range and highlight them, move to them, or list them on the worksheet as the Auditor does for the Precedents and Dependents options.

For example, you can use the Auditor to list the formulas in the worksheet in Figure 14-1. When you select Formulas and select A21 for where the formulas will be listed, the results shown in Figure 14-3 will display.

Finding Formulas in the Order They Are Recalculated

If you are developing a complex model, you may want to know the order in which 1-2-3 recalculates the formulas. You can list formulas in the order 1-2-3 recalculates them using the Auditor by selecting Recalc-List. Depending on the selection for how

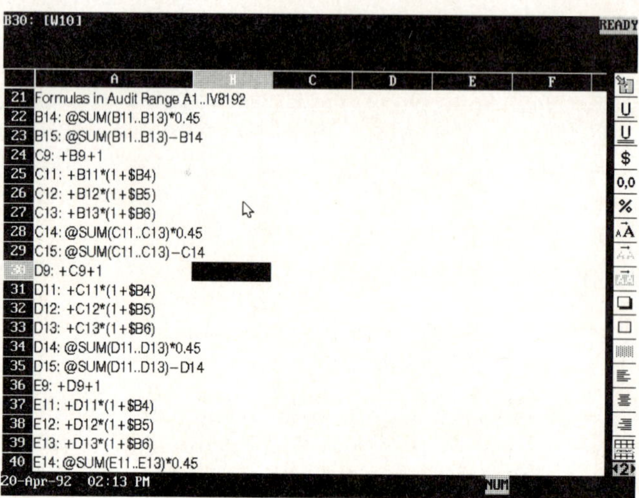

Figure 14-3.   *Auditor's list of formulas*

the Auditor indicates the cells it finds, the worksheet cells will be either highlighted, traced, or listed. If you are listing cells, the first cell of the list describes recalculation order as well.

Finding Cells Used in Circular References

Besides using /Worksheet Status to find a circular reference, you can also use the Auditor to find these cells. Unlike /Worksheet Status, using the Auditor shows all of the cell entries that are part of the circular reference. You find the cells that are part of a circular reference by selecting Circs. Depending on the selection for how the Auditor indicates the cells it finds, the worksheet cells will be either highlighted, traced, or listed.

The Backsolver Add-In

The Backsolver add-in can solve backward from the answer to the value or values that you need to achieve a specific result. You may often want to proceed backward from the final result to find the value that you need to achieve a known result. For example, given an affordable monthly payment, Backsolver can tell you the price of the house you can buy and still meet this payment. Given that your goal is to break even, Backsolver can tell you how many units you must sell to achieve this aim.

You enter Backsolver problems directly on the worksheet, without special techniques. After you invoke Backsolver, the location of the required information is defined, and Backsolver goes to work.

When you invoke Backsolver, a menu appears in the control panel, as shown in Figure 14-4. You need to specify two locations and a setting before asking for a solution. In Figure 14-4, the formula calculates the monthly payment, depending on how large a mortgage you are taking on and how many total payments you are going to make. If you have a good idea what you can afford to pay each month, you can calculate the maximum price of the house you can afford to buy.

In this example, you would first create the model shown in Figure 14-4, setting up the formula and data that Backsolver is going to work with. Then you would attach and invoke Backsolver.

1. Select Formula-Cell from the Backsolver menu and specify C2 as the cell containing the formula.

2. Select Value and enter **550** as the amount you are willing to pay each month toward your rent.

3. Select Adjustable and enter **C3**, the total loan amount, as the value in the formula that can be adjusted.

4. Select Solve. Backsolver will calculate that if you can pay $550 a month toward a 30-year mortgage at 8 percent annual interest, you can afford a total mortgage of $74,956. Now you know what price range of houses you should be looking at.

Formula Cell	The address of the formula you want to evaluate to find a specific value. You can specify the formula cell either by entering the name or range address of the cell or by pointing to the cell using either the keyboard or a mouse. The formula cell must be affected by the cell or cells specified as adjustable.
Value	The value you want the formula-cell to equal.
Adjustable	The cell or range of cells you want to vary in order to produce the specified value in the formula-cell. (These do not need to include all the cells that are referenced or that affect the formula—only the ones you want to vary.)

After specifying these cells and values, select Solve. If the Backsolver succeeds in finding values for the adjustable cells that result in the specified value in the formula cell, the values are substituted into the appropriate cells on the worksheets.

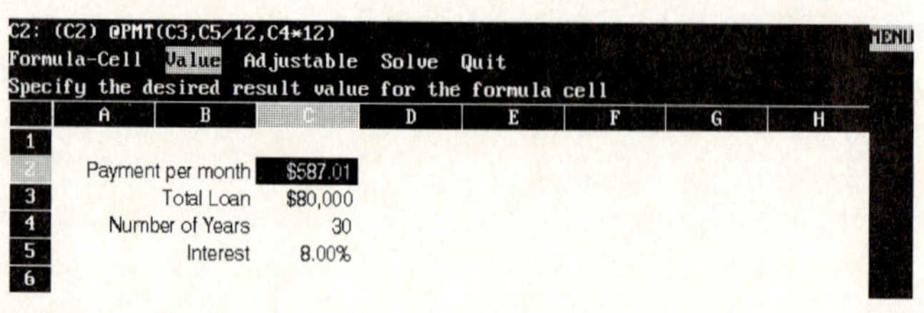

Figure 14-4.   *Model with BackSolver menu*

The SmartIcons Add-In

The SmartIcons add-in is new with Release 2.4. The SmartIcons add-in is autoloaded with 1-2-3, which means that it is automatically attached each time you start 1-2-3. This add-in provides you with several palettes of icons that represent various things you can do with 1-2-3. Select an icon, using either the mouse or the keyboard, to carry out these options. The icons can apply formatting to a range of cells, quickly create a graph, delete rows or columns, and much more. The icons serve as a shortcut you can use to bypass the menu system, and they carry out certain procedures quickly.

The icons appear on the icon palette displayed at the right edge of the screen, as you can see in Figure 14-5. When Wysiwyg is attached, the icons have a graphic representation. When Wysiwyg is not attached, the icons are displayed using characters. Some of the icons are used specifically to access Wysiwyg features and will not function when Wysiwyg is not attached. The icons that access 1-2-3's features function regardless of whether Wysiwyg is attached, although the icons look different.

Only a few of the icons appear on any one icon palette. The number of palettes you have depends on your monitor and whether or not Wysiwyg is attached. For example, with a VGA monitor and Wysiwyg attached, you will have seven icon palettes. Beneath the icon palette, you can see the palette number, flanked by two arrows. The first icon palette is the custom palette. You can remove and add icons to this palette and move the icons around on the palette. The other palettes are set and cannot be altered.

Using the SmartIcons

You can use the icon palette with either the mouse or the keyboard. The icon palette is easier to use with the mouse, but the keyboard methods are still simple. To select a particular icon with the mouse, simply point the mouse pointer at the desired icon and click the left mouse button once. The icon is activated, and the assigned activity

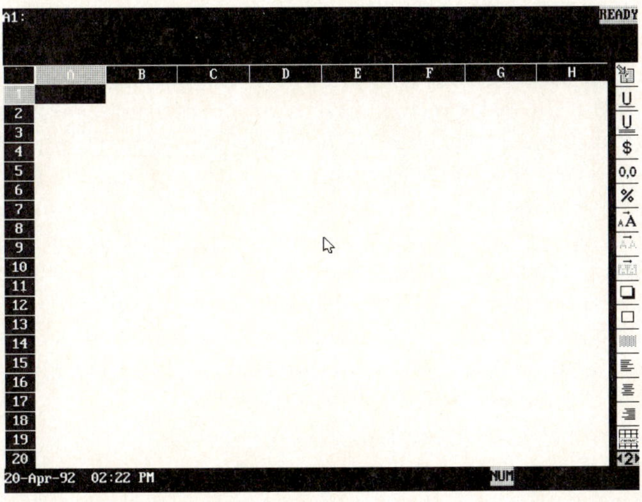

Figure 14-5.   SmartIcon palette

is carried out. To switch to another icon palette, click the left mouse button once on the arrows on either side of the icon palette number beneath the icon palette.

To use the keyboard, you have to invoke the add-in and then use the arrow keys to select the desired icon. Since the SmartIcons add-in is auto-attaching, you do not need to attach it each time you want to use it. The only circumstance under which you would have to attach this add-in is when you have previously detached it yourself. Unless you specify otherwise, SmartIcons will always load into memory with 1-2-3 and be available for use.

To invoke the SmartIcons add-in, you can use either the menu or the shortcut key combination. The shortcut key assigned to SmartIcons when it auto-attaches is ALT-F7. If you prefer to use the menu, select /Add-In Invoke, highlight the name ICONS, and press ENTER. After invoking the add-in, you can select an icon by moving to it using the UP ARROW and DOWN ARROW keys and pressing ENTER. When you want to move from one palette to the next, use the LEFT ARROW and RIGHT ARROW keys.

Modifying the Custom Palette

Only the first palette, called the custom palette, can be customized. The other palettes are all set, both in contents and in order. You can remove or add icons to the custom palette and also move the icons around. You customize the custom palette using three other icons, which appear on the second-to-last palette.

Removing an Icon

Since the custom palette is full, you need to remove icons before you add any. Removing an icon from the custom palette is as easy as selecting an icon to use. The first step is to select the Remove Icon icon from the second-to-last palette. This icon always appears on the second-to-last icon palette, no matter how many palettes you have. When you select this icon, the custom palette appears, and you are prompted to select the icon you want to remove. Select the icon as you normally would, either by clicking it with the mouse or by highlighting it with the UP ARROW and DOWN ARROW keys and pressing ENTER. The icon is then removed from the custom palette. Since all of the icons on the custom palette also appear on one of the other palettes, you can always replace any icons you remove from the custom palette.

For example, if you wanted to remove the Data Sort Descending SmartIcon from the Custom Palette, you would follow these steps:

1. Click with the mouse on the palette number box beneath the icons until the second-to-last palette is displayed (the number of this palette will depend on your monitor and whether or not Wysiwyg is attached). If you are not using a mouse, press ALT-F7 to activate the SmartIcons add-in. Then press the RIGHT ARROW or LEFT ARROW keys until the second-to-last palette is displayed.

2. Select the Remove Icon icon from the palette. You can do this by clicking on the icon with your mouse or by moving to it using the UP ARROW and DOWN ARROW keys and pressing ENTER.

3. Select the Data Sort Descending icon from the custom palette when it appears. The Data Sort Descending icon (on a VGA monitor and with Wysiwyg attached) is the last icon on the custom palette. You can select the Data Sort Descending icon with either the mouse or the keyboard.

When you select the icon, it is removed from the custom palette.

Adding an Icon

Adding an icon is just as easy as deleting one. You use the Add Icon icon from the second-to-last palette. The Add Icon icon is the first of the icons on this palette. To add an icon to the Custom Palette, select the Add Icon icon. You are then prompted to select the icon you want to add to the Custom Palette. Select the icon as you normally would, by clicking it with the mouse or by using the Arrow keys to highlight it and then pressing ENTER. When you select the icon, a copy of it appears at the bottom of the custom palette.

For example, you may want to move the Outline icon to the custom palette. This icon uses Wysiwyg to create a line around the outside of the range selected. To add this icon to the Custom Palette, follow these steps:

1. Move to the second to last icon palette, as previously described.

2. Select the Add Icon icon using either the mouse or the keyboard.

3. Move to the palette on which the Outline icon appears and select it using either the keyboard or the mouse. In Figure 14-6, you can see the result.

Moving Icons

You may want to move icons on the custom palette to make their placement more logical or to keep related icons together. When you want to move an icon, select the Move Icon icon from the second-to-last menu. The custom palette appears, and you are prompted to select the icon you want to move. Do so in the usual fashion. Then you are prompted to choose the place to which you want to move the icon. Do so by selecting the icon currently in the position where you want the selected icon to be. The icon you first selected appears in that position, and the icon you selected second and those beneath it move down one place to make room for it.

If you wanted to move the Outline icon to the top of the Custom Palette, you would follow these steps:

1. Go to the second-to-last palette and select the Move Icon icon.

2. Select the Outline icon on the custom palette when it appears.

3. Select the top icon in the custom palette, which should be the File Save icon.

Figure 14-6.   *Custom palette with Outline icon added*

As you can see in Figure 14-7, the Outline icon takes the place of the File Save icon, and the other icons all move down one space to make room.

User Icons

The last palette that appears contains 12 user icons. You can assign macros to these icons. These macros are activated and perform their operations when the user icon is selected. The last icon on the second-to-last palette is the User Icon icon, which allows you to add the correct information to the icon palette. This icon assigns a macro to one of the 12 user icons that appear on your last palette. You can create the macro to be assigned to an icon on a worksheet, or you can enter the macro from the keyboard. The icon can use a macro created on a worksheet even if that worksheet has been deleted.

To assign a macro to a user icon, select the User Icon icon; the User Icon Descriptions dialog box shown in Figure 14-8 appears. Then select the user icon to which you want to assign the macro. When you have selected a user icon to define, select the Assign Macro to Icon button, opening the User-Defined Icon dialog box shown in Figure 14-9.

Enter up to 72 characters in the Icon Description text box to provide a description of the macro. This description is shown in the User Icons Descriptions dialog box

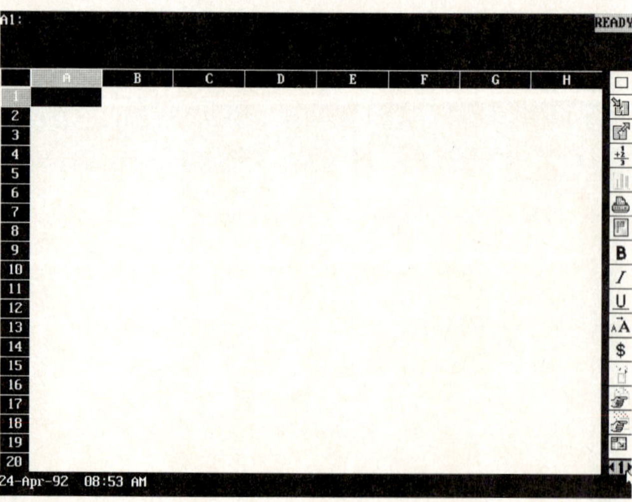

Figure 14-7.   *Outline icon moved to the top of the palette*

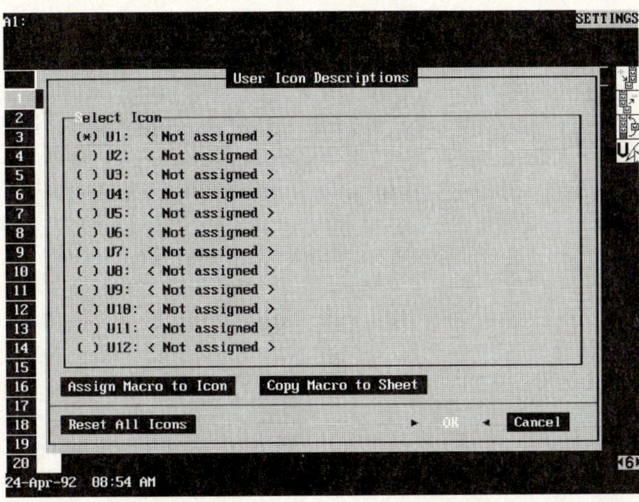

Figure 14-8.   *User Icon Descriptions dialog box*

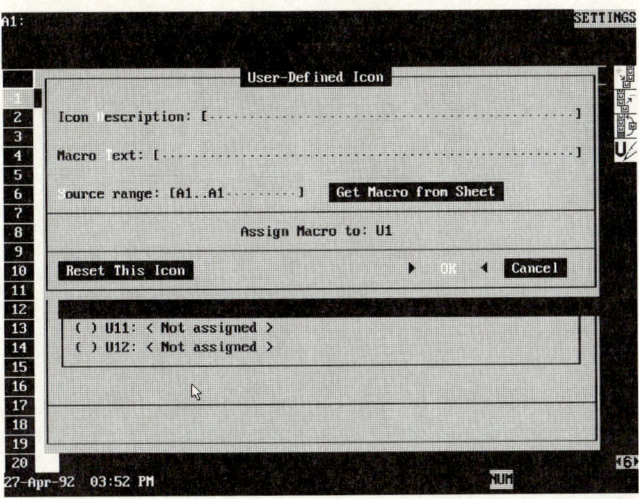

Figure 14-9.   *User-Defined Icon dialog box*

and appears on the control panel when the icon is highlighted or when you point at the icon and press the right mouse button.

Either type the macro in the Macro Text text box or specify the range in which the macro is entered on the current worksheet in the Source Range text box. If you are copying the macro from the worksheet to the icon, you need to select the Get Macro from Sheet button after entering the range in the Source Range text box. You can specify the range either by entering a range address or by entering a range name.

When you are finished defining the macro, select the OK button to return to the User Icon Descriptions dialog box. If at any point in the process of creating the user icon you want to erase all of the definition you have created, you can select the Reset This Icon button to delete all of the entries you have made in the User-Defined Icon dialog box.

If you wish to clear the definition of all of the icons, select the Reset All Icons button in the User Icon Descriptions dialog box. This removes the definitions of all of the defined user icons. When you are finished with the User Icon Definitions dialog box, select the OK button.

You might want to create a user icon that would format a selected range with a currency format, but without any numbers after the decimal place. To do this, you would follow these steps:

1. Click with your mouse on the palette number box beneath the icons until the second-to-last palette is displayed. If you are not using a mouse, press ALT-F7 to activate the SmartIcons add-in. Then press the RIGHT ARROW or LEFT ARROW keys until the second-to-last palette is displayed.

2. Select the User Icon icon by clicking on it with the mouse or by pressing the UP ARROW and DOWN ARROW keys until the icon is highlighted and then pressing ENTER.

3. When the User Icon Descriptions dialog box appears, select the second icon by pressing **S** and **2** or by clicking the option button with the mouse.

4. Select the Assign Macro to Icon command button either by pressing A or by clicking it with the mouse. This opens the User-Defined icon dialog box.

5. Press **D** or click on the Icon Description text box to activate it.

6. Type the following into the Icon Description text box: **Formats a range with the currency format and no decimal places.** Then press ENTER.

7. Activate the Macro Text text box by pressing **T** or by clicking it with the mouse.

8. Enter the macro commands. For this macro, you would enter **\RFC0~** in the Macro Text box and then press ENTER. The User-Defined Icon dialog box looks like Figure 14-10.

9. Select the OK command button or press ENTER to return to the User Icon Descriptions dialog box.

10. Select the OK command button or press ENTER to return to 1-2-3.

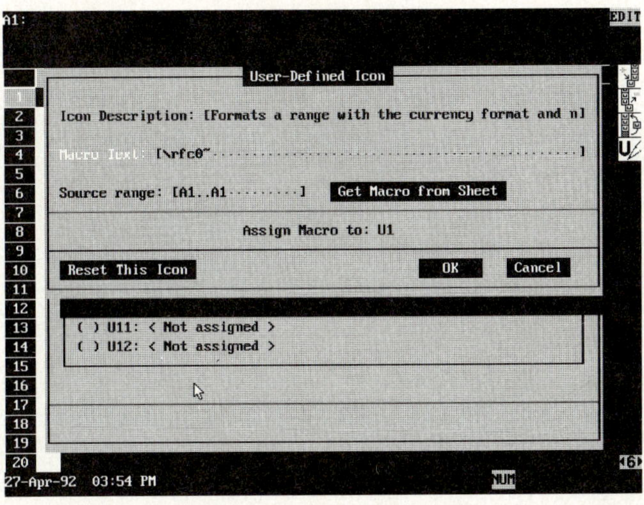

Figure 14-10.   *User-Defined Icon dialog box after defining a user icon*

The SmartIcons

SmartIcons has 77 icons, each with a different purpose. Table 14-1 lists these icons
in the order in which they appear. Which palette each icon appears on and how many
palettes you have depends on your monitor or graphics card and whether or not you
have Wysiwyg attached.

Saves the worksheet to disk

Retrieves a worksheet from a disk

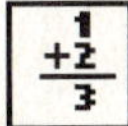
Adds the sum function to empty cells at the bottom or right of the
selected range, summing the values in the range. If the selected range
has no values, inserts a function in the selected range summing the
values in the nearest data.

Displays the current range as a graph

Table 14-1.   *The SmartIcons*

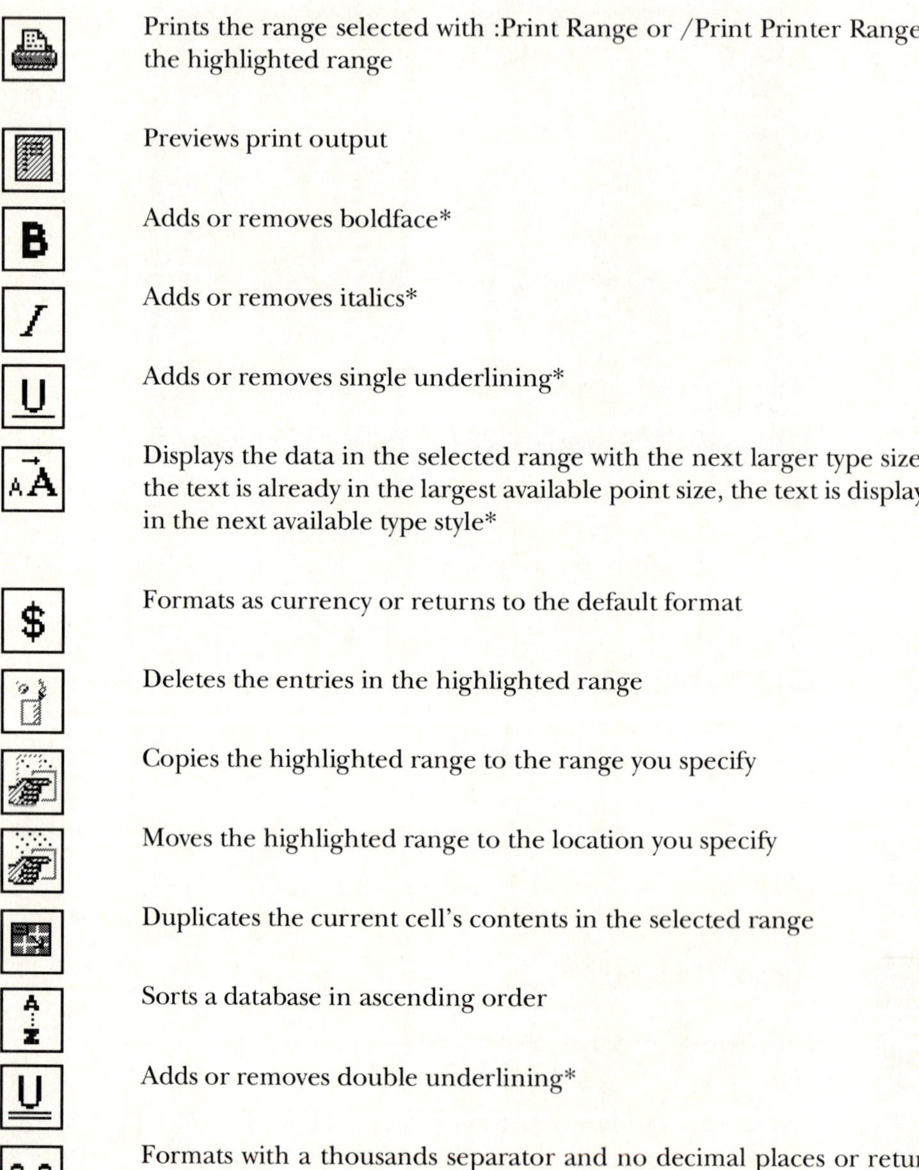

	Prints the range selected with :Print Range or /Print Printer Range or the highlighted range
	Previews print output
	Adds or removes boldface*
	Adds or removes italics*
	Adds or removes single underlining*
	Displays the data in the selected range with the next larger type size. If the text is already in the largest available point size, the text is displayed in the next available type style*
	Formats as currency or returns to the default format
	Deletes the entries in the highlighted range
	Copies the highlighted range to the range you specify
	Moves the highlighted range to the location you specify
	Duplicates the current cell's contents in the selected range
	Sorts a database in ascending order
	Adds or removes double underlining*
	Formats with a thousands separator and no decimal places or returns the format to the default
	Formats as a percentage using two decimal places or restores the default format

Table 14-1.   *The SmartIcons* (continued)

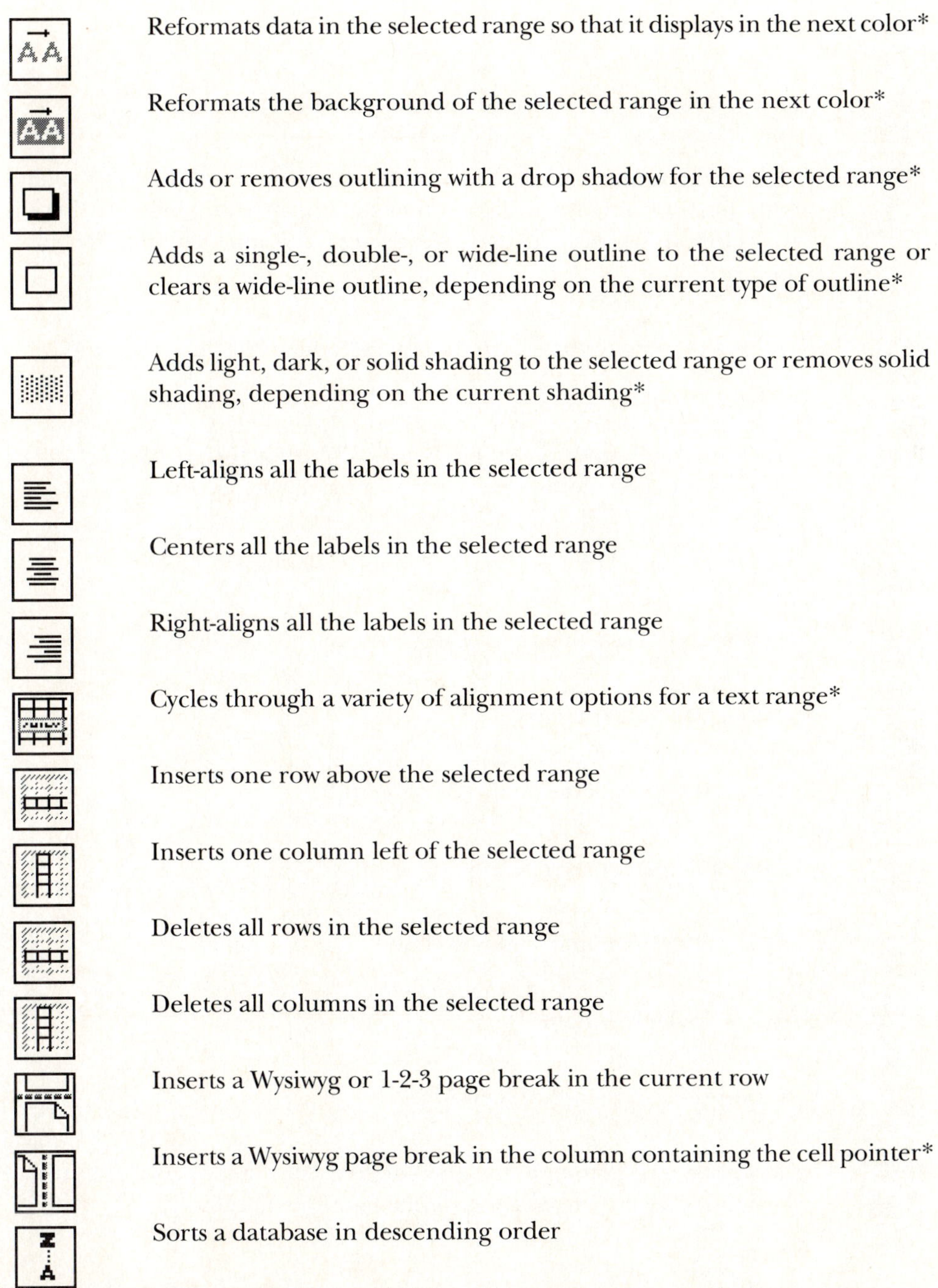

Reformats data in the selected range so that it displays in the next color*

Reformats the background of the selected range in the next color*

Adds or removes outlining with a drop shadow for the selected range*

Adds a single-, double-, or wide-line outline to the selected range or clears a wide-line outline, depending on the current type of outline*

Adds light, dark, or solid shading to the selected range or removes solid shading, depending on the current shading*

Left-aligns all the labels in the selected range

Centers all the labels in the selected range

Right-aligns all the labels in the selected range

Cycles through a variety of alignment options for a text range*

Inserts one row above the selected range

Inserts one column left of the selected range

Deletes all rows in the selected range

Deletes all columns in the selected range

Inserts a Wysiwyg or 1-2-3 page break in the current row

Inserts a Wysiwyg page break in the column containing the cell pointer*

Sorts a database in descending order

Table 14-1. *The SmartIcons (continued)*

Fills the selected range with a series of values

Recalculates all of the formulas in the worksheet

Enters the number that indicates the current date and time and applies the default date format, if no other date format is applied. If there is either a date or time format already applied to the cell, that format is used

Adds a graphic to the selected range, which circles the data*

Changes the displayed size of the worksheet, enlarging the display by 125% or 150%, reducing it by 63% or 87%, or returning to the normal display size, depending on the current display size setting*

Turns on the STEP mode used for macro debugging

Lets you choose a macro to run

Moves the cell pointer one cell to the left

Moves the cell pointer one cell to the right

Moves the cell pointer one cell up

Moves the cell pointer one cell down

Starts the Help system

Moves the cell pointer to cell A1

Moves the cell pointer to the lower-right corner of the active area, which is defined by the intersection of filled and blank cells

Table 14-1.   *The SmartIcons* (continued)

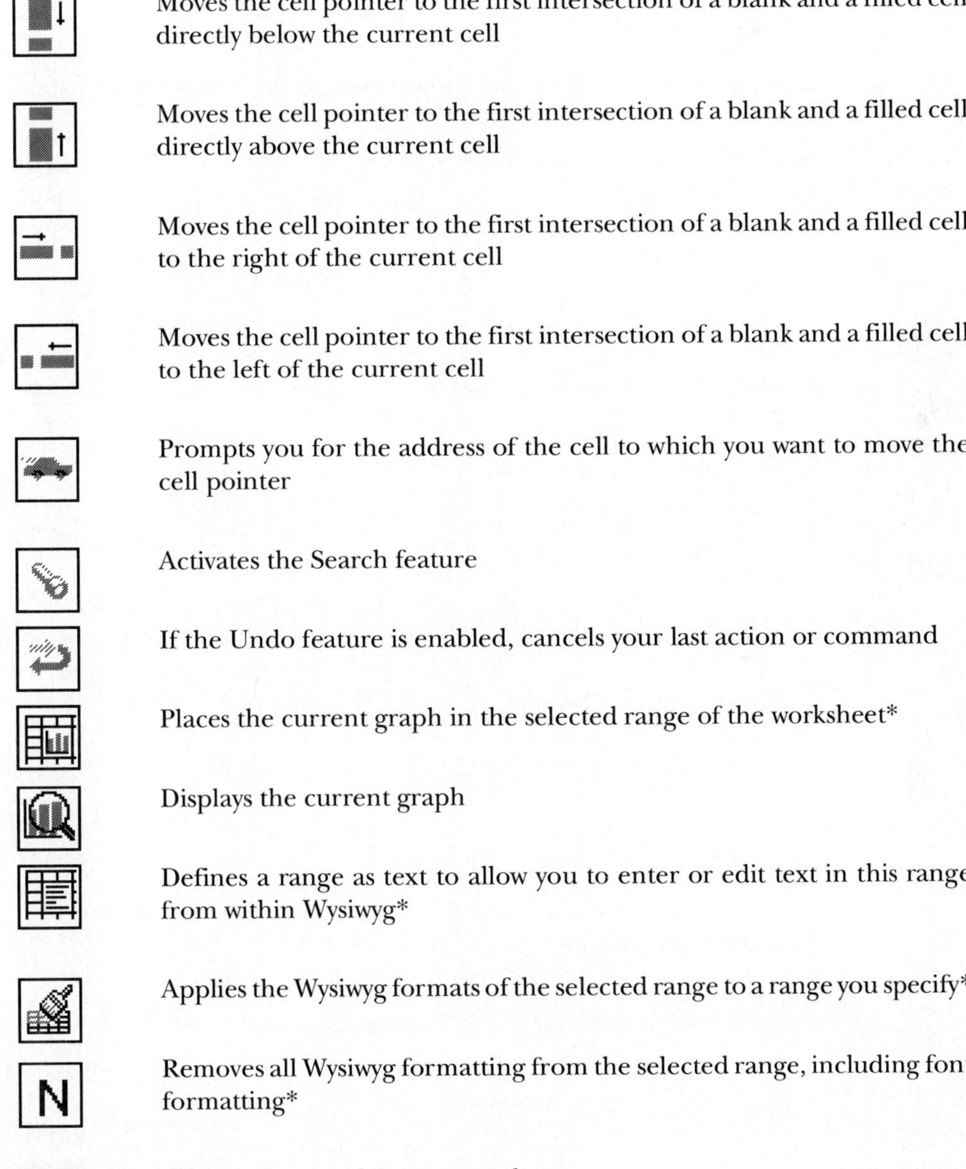

Moves the cell pointer to the first intersection of a blank and a filled cell directly below the current cell

Moves the cell pointer to the first intersection of a blank and a filled cell directly above the current cell

Moves the cell pointer to the first intersection of a blank and a filled cell to the right of the current cell

Moves the cell pointer to the first intersection of a blank and a filled cell to the left of the current cell

Prompts you for the address of the cell to which you want to move the cell pointer

Activates the Search feature

If the Undo feature is enabled, cancels your last action or command

Places the current graph in the selected range of the worksheet*

Displays the current graph

Defines a range as text to allow you to enter or edit text in this range from within Wysiwyg*

Applies the Wysiwyg formats of the selected range to a range you specify*

Removes all Wysiwyg formatting from the selected range, including font formatting*

Adds an icon to the custom palette

Table 14-1.   *The SmartIcons* (continued)

Removes an icon from your custom palette

Moves an icon on your custom palette to another location on the palette

Displays the descriptions of user icons U1 through U12, lets you assign macros and descriptions to those icons, and lets you copy the text of one of those icons to the worksheet for debugging

Runs the macro assigned to U1 icon

Runs the macro assigned to U2 icon

Runs the macro assigned to U3 icon

Runs the macro assigned to U4 icon

Runs the macro assigned to U5 icon

Runs the macro assigned to U6 icon

Runs the macro assigned to U7 icon

Runs the macro assigned to U8 icon

Runs the macro assigned to U9 icon

Runs the macro assigned to U10 icon

Runs the macro assigned to U11 icon

Runs the macro assigned to U12 icon

Note: Asterisks (*) indicate icons that invoke Wysiwyg-specific features.

Table 14-1.   *The SmartIcons* (continued)

The Tutorial Add-In

Besides learning about 1-2-3 as you build your models, you can also learn 1-2-3 features by reviewing the Tutor add-in. The Tutor add-in guides you through the basics of 1-2-3's features. It also includes a glossary so you can learn the meaning of 1-2-3 terms.

Like other add-ins, you must attach the Tutor add-in before you can use it. Unlike other add-ins, you must detach all other add-ins first. You will also want to save the current worksheet before invoking the Tutor because the Tutor will put its own entries in the worksheet and erase yours. When you attach the Tutor add-in, you will select the TUTOR.ADN file.

Once the Tutor add-in is invoked, you can select one of the topics from the menu. Selections are made by pressing the arrow keys to move through the list and then pressing ENTER to select the one you want. You can also move one screen at a time by pressing PGDN and PGUP. Other keys you may want to use include HOME and END to move to the first and last items in a list and INS to fill in an entry when Tutor prompts you to enter data that the tutorial uses. You can use ESC to leave the tutorial when you are finished.

To use the glossary that is part of the Tutor add-in, press ALT-G. The Tutor add-in displays a list of terms that 1-2-3 uses. Selecting one displays a brief definition of the term.

The Tutor add-in takes about 1MB of space. If you need the space and your 1-2-3 skills *have progressed beyond the lessons the Tutor add-in provides, you may want to remove the* *Tutor add-in from your hard disk by deleting the contents of the TUTOR subdirectory,* *removing the TUTOR subdirectory, and deleting the file TUTOR.ADN.*

Using Macros with 1-2-3 Add-Ins

Just as you can create macros within 1-2-3, you can create macros that load and use your 1-2-3 add-ins, such as Wysiwyg. Some add-ins can be used with macros while others cannot. The Allways add-in cannot be used with macros, but you can create macros to load and use the add-ins that come with 1-2-3 Releases 2.3 and above. You must try other add-ins to find out whether they work with macros. Just as you use keystrokes for 1-2-3 instructions, you can use the same method of storing keystrokes in 1-2-3 cells to run as macros. With Releases 2.3 and above, you can also use the /Worksheet Learn command to record the keystrokes you want in a macro. Figure 14-11 shows a macro that loads and adds add-ins. A macro like this would be in a worksheet called AUTO123.WK1 and it would load every time you use the macro.

If you want to invoke an add-in within a macro, you can use {APP1}, {APP2}, {APP3}, and {APP4} for the ALT-F7, ALT-F8, ALT-F9, and ALT-F10 key combinations to invoke an add-in.

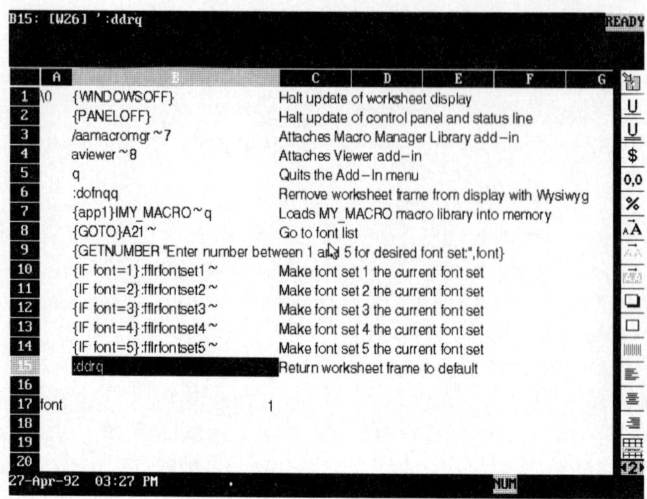

Figure 14-11.   *A macro to attach and use several add-ins*

ADD-IN AND AUDITOR MENU

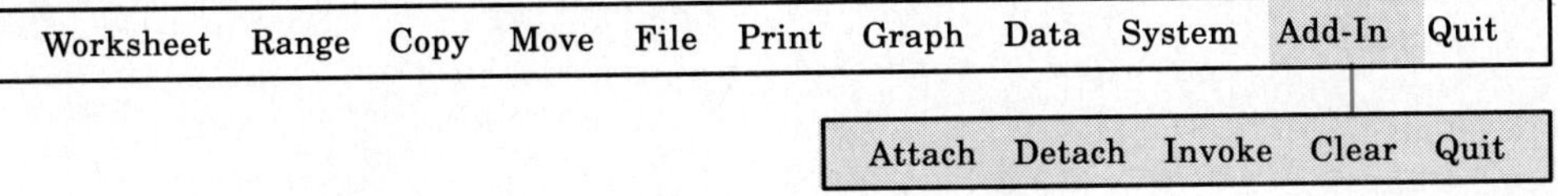

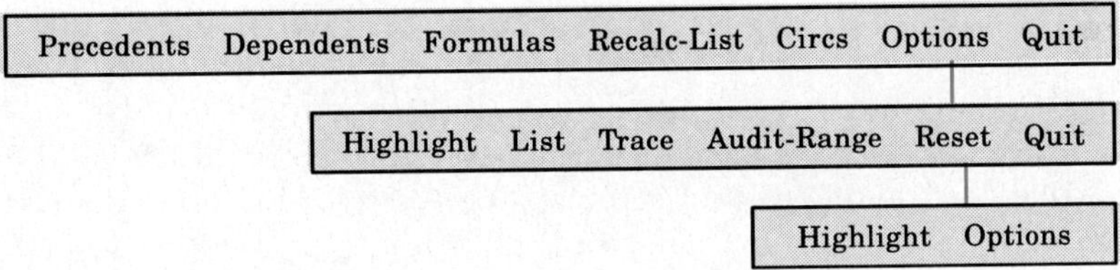

BACKSOLVER ADD-IN MENU

The Add-In Menu

The Add-In menu allows you to attach and invoke programs designed to run when
1-2-3 is active.

/Add-In Attach

Description

This command attaches add-in programs to use with 1-2-3. Add-ins extend the basic
functionality of 1-2-3. A loaded add-in remains in memory until you remove it or end
your 1-2-3 session.

Options

The options for this command are to select the add-in to load and the key to use to
invoke the add-in. For the second set of options, you can choose No-Key to invoke
the add-in with /Add-In Invoke, or you can select 7, 8, 9, or 10, assigning ALT-F7, ALT-F8,
ALT-F9, or ALT-F10 to be used to invoke the add-in.

/Add-In Clear

Description

This command frees all loaded add-ins from memory.

/Add-In Detach

Description

This command frees a specific add-in from memory. If you have assigned the add-in
to a function key, it is also freed and available for assignment to another add-in.

Options

The only option is to select the add-in to remove from memory.

/Add-In Invoke

Description

This command activates the menu commands or functions of an add-in that you have loaded into memory. If an add-in is not loaded, you cannot invoke it. Because Wysiwyg uses the colon to activate its menu, you do not need this command to invoke Wysiwyg.

Options

The options for this command let you select the add-in to invoke.

Note

If you assigned a function key to an add-in, you can invoke the add-in with the function key as well as the menu.

/Add-In Quit

Description

This command leaves the Add-In menu and returns you to READY mode.

/Worksheet Global Default Other Add-In

This command specifies up to eight add-in programs to attach when you start 1-2-3. You have the option of automatically invoking one of these eight add-ins. This command also allows you to assign function keys ALT-F7 through ALT-F10 to an add-in that is automatically attached. With Release 2.4, two add-ins are ready to load into memory on 1-2-3: SmartIcons and Wysiwyg.

Set   This option allows you to specify an add-in that should be attached in each session. You are asked to select a number from 1 through 8 to establish which add-in slot is being used. You select an .ADN file from the list of .ADN entries in the current directory. Then you can assign the add-in to any of the keys from ALT-F7 through ALT-F10, if they have not already been assigned. 1-2-3 then asks you to select whether or not to automatically invoke the add-in. (Note that you can only specify Yes for one add-in.)

Cancel   This option detaches the attached add-in specified and cancels its attachment in future sessions.

Quit   This option returns you to the previous menu, which is /Worksheet Global Default Other.

Note   You must remember to save your changes after returning to the /Worksheet Global Default menu by selecting Update. If you forget this step, 1-2-3 does not update the 123.CNF file and your changes do not affect your next 1-2-3 session.

Auditor Add-In Commands

The Auditor add-in is new to 1-2-3 Releases 2.3 and above. It provides commands that allow you to quickly identify potential problems in your worksheets.

Circs

Description

This command finds cells in the audit range that are part of a circular reference.

Options

The only option for this command is tracing through cells it finds or selecting where this add-in places the list of cells on the worksheet.

Dependents

Description

This command finds cells in the audit range that contain formulas that reference cells in a range you select. These are the formulas that depend on cells in the selected range.

Option

After selecting this command, you must select the range of cells for which you want to find formulas that use the selected cells. Next, the add-in highlights the cells, traces through the cells, or puts the list of cells on the worksheet after you select where you want the list placed.

Formulas

Description

This command finds formulas in the audit range.

Option

The only option for this command is tracing through cells containing formulas or selecting where this add-in places the list of cells and their formulas on the worksheet.

Options

Description

This command performs three functions. First, it sets how cells selected with other Auditor add-in commands are indicated. Second, this command sets the worksheet range the other Auditor add-in commands use. Third, this command returns the Auditor add-in settings to their defaults.

Options

Highlight   This option displays the cells that the Circs, Dependents, Formulas, Precedents, and Recalc-List commands find in a different color or boldface. You can also select this option by marking the Highlight option button in the Auditor Settings dialog box. When the Auditor add-in marks cells it finds this way, the cells remain highlighted until you select the Options Reset Highlight command. Each time you use a new command, the cells the Auditor finds are highlighted in addition to the cells the Auditor has found from previous commands.

List   This option lists the cells that the Circs, Dependents, Formulas, Precedents, and Recalc-List commands find in a worksheet range. You can also select this option by marking the List option button in the Auditor Settings dialog box. When you select the Circs, Dependents, Formulas, Precedents, or Recalc-List command, you must select where you want the Auditor add-in to list the cells it finds in the worksheet. You can select a cell and the Auditor will use from that cell to the bottom of the worksheet. The Auditor will not put anything in this range if it contains any entries unless the entries are the result of a previous Auditor command. The list this command creates will contain the cell addresses of the cells it finds followed by their formulas. The first cell in the list will describe the Auditor command used and the audit range. If you use the Recalc-List command, it will display the current worksheet recalculation mode.

Trace   This option moves to the cells that the Circs, Dependents, Formulas, Precedents, and Recalc-List commands find in a worksheet range. You can also select this option by marking the Trace option button in the Auditor Settings dialog box. When you select one of the other Auditor commands, the Auditor will display a menu containing Forward, Backward, and Quit. Select Forward to move to the next cell the Auditor finds, select Backward to move to the previous cell the Auditor finds, and select Quit to return to the Auditor menu.

Audit-Range   This option selects the range that the Circs, Dependents, Formulas, Precedents, and Recalc-List commands use to find cells. Select a range in the current worksheet to use. By default the Auditor add-in will use the entire worksheet (A1..IV8192). You can also select an audit range by entering a range address in the Range text box in the Auditor Settings dialog box.

Reset   This option resets the highlight or the options displayed in the Auditor Settings dialog box. After selecting Reset, you can select Highlight to return all of the cells the Auditor add-in has highlighted to their original display. You can also select Options to return the report mode to Highlight and the audit range to A1..IV8192.

Quit   This option returns to the Auditor add-in's initial menu.

Precedents

Description

This command finds cells in the audit range that are used by formulas in a range you select. These are the cells that the formulas in the selected range depend on.

Options

After selecting this command, you must select the range of cells containing the formulas for which you want to find the precedents. Next, the add-in highlights the cells, traces through the cells, or puts the list of cells on the worksheet after you select where you want the list placed.

Quit

Description

This command leaves the Auditor add-in and returns to 1-2-3 READY mode. Any cells highlighted by the Auditor will continue to be highlighted because any cells listed in the worksheet are still there.

Recalc-List

Description

This command finds formulas in the audit range in the order 1-2-3 recalculates them. This command takes into account the recalculation order selected with the 1-2-3 /Worksheet Global Recalculation command.

Option

The only option for this command is tracing through cells in the order 1-2-3 will recalculate them or selecting where this add-in places the list of cells and their formulas on the worksheet.

Backsolver Add-In Commands

Formula_Cell

Description

This command specifies the cell containing the formula that Backsolver is to use.

Options

Specifies the cell that contains the formula.

Value

Description

This command specifies the value that you want the formula to calculate.

Options

You may specify the value you want the formula to calculate.

Adjustable

Description

This command specifies the range of cells that contain values that can be adjusted to result in the value specified.

Solve

Description

This command starts the Backsolver calculating the values needed in the adjustable cells for the formula in the formula cell to result in the specified value.

Quit

This command quits the Backsolver add-in.

The Smarticons Add-In Command Icons

Add Icon

 Adds an icon to the custom palette. First select this icon. Then select the icon you wish to add to the custom palette. The icon appears at the bottom of the custom palette. If the custom palette is full, the last icon is deleted when the icon you select is added.

Remove Icon

 Removes an icon from your custom palette. First select this icon. Then select the icon on the custom palette that you wish to remove. When the icon is deleted, the icons beneath it move up to fill in the space it occupied.

Move Icon

 Moves an icon on your custom palette to another location on the palette. First select this icon. Then select the icon you want to move. Last, select the icon in the position to which you want to move the first icon.

User Icon

 Displays the descriptions of user icons U1 through U12. Lets you assign macros and descriptions to those icons and lets you copy the text of one of those icons to the worksheets for debugging. First select this icon. Select the option button for the icon you want to work with. If you want to copy the assigned macro to the worksheet, select the Copy Macro to Sheet button. The macro is copied to the range you selected before selecting the user icon. If you want to assign or edit the macro or the description of the user icon, select the Assign Macro to Icon command button. Use the Icon Description text box to enter the description of the icon's macro. Use the Macro Text text box to enter the macro or enter the range in the Source Range text box and select the Get Macro from Sheet command button to copy a macro from the current worksheet to the user icon.

Chapter 15

The Wysiwyg Add-In

Wysiwyg is an acronym that stands for "what you see is what you get." 1-2-3 Release 2.4's Wysiwyg is a spreadsheet publishing package that provides a completely new way to work with your spreadsheet information that is automatically available when you start 1-2-3. (With Release 2.3, you must attach the add-in before using its features.) Wysiwyg's features can significantly enhance the output that you produce with 1-2-3 as you have seen in examples in earlier chapters. You can add graphs to a worksheet range so that when you print the worksheet range you will print both the graph and the surrounding worksheet data. You can also use Wysiwyg to change the appearance of the worksheet data by adding features such as lines, boxes, boldface, italics, and different fonts. Wysiwyg not only uses the features of the printer to print your worksheet but also displays the worksheet as it will appear when printed.

Although Wysiwyg and 1-2-3 are separate products, the menu interface to the two is so similar that you will quickly learn how to use the Wysiwyg commands you want. The Wysiwyg menus and the 1-2-3 menus are available at the same time. This means that you can switch between altering the worksheet data with 1-2-3 and altering the worksheet data with Wysiwyg. This chapter expands on the basic Wysiwyg features you've seen in earlier chapters and provides a one-stop look at all that Wysiwyg offers.

The Wysiwyg Interface

When Wysiwyg is loaded, the appearance of the screen changes to look exactly like the output that will be produced when you print the worksheet. When Wysiwyg is loaded, the control panel describes the special attributes added by Wysiwyg to the current cell after the cell address and before the 1-2-3 formatting information—attributes such as cell protection, cell format, and column width. Figure 15-1 provides a look at a screen after Wysiwyg is loaded and before Wysiwyg formatting changes are made to the worksheet. You will notice that the font appears different from the font in the normal 1-2-3 display.

While the Wysiwyg screen is attached, you can continue using 1-2-3 just as you did before you attached Wysiwyg. When you type a slash, you will see the 1-2-3 menu and you can continue working with the 1-2-3 commands. The Wysiwyg menu commands are available by typing a colon. Several Wysiwyg commands use dialog boxes that you can use in place of menu selections just like 1-2-3 commands.

The Wysiwyg commands let you change the appearance of the worksheet. These changes are not stored as part of the worksheet file but in a separate file with the same filename as the worksheet but with an .FMT extension. When you retrieve a worksheet while Wysiwyg is loaded, Wysiwyg looks for a file with the same filename as the worksheet and an .FMT extension to use for the Wysiwyg formatting information. When you save a file in 1-2-3, Wysiwyg also saves the Wysiwyg formatting in the file with the same filename and an .FMT extension.

Just as in 1-2-3, the control panel comprises the top three lines of the screen. The only difference in the information displayed when Wysiwyg is loaded and when it is not loaded is that Wysiwyg displays descriptions about the Wysiwyg formats of the

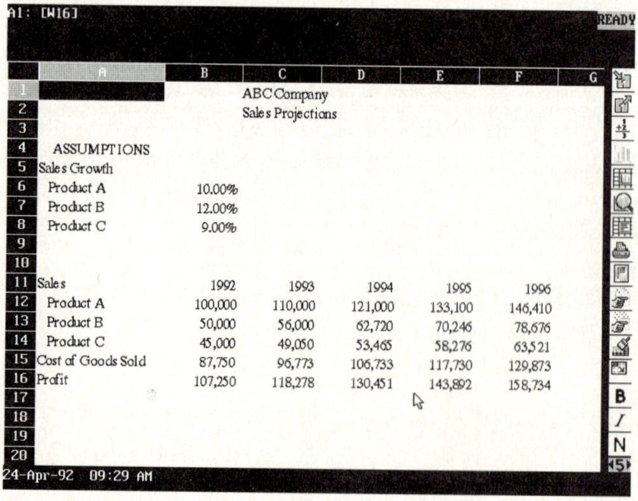

Figure 15-1.   A Wysiwyg screen with a 1-2-3 worksheet

current cell next to the cell address. The formatting descriptions Wysiwyg will display may look something like this:

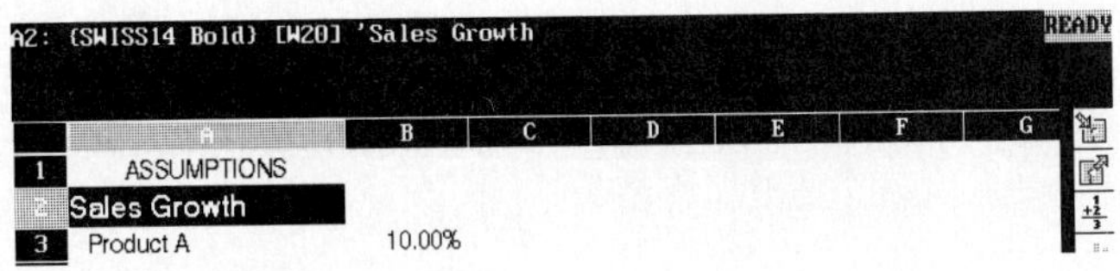

Information about the Wysiwyg formats is listed between the curly braces. As you can see in the example, the entry is boldfaced, and uses the Swiss 14-point font. A list of the format descriptions you may see is provided in Table 15-1.

Descriptions	Meaning
Bold	Cell's contents are boldfaced.
color1/color2	Color of text appears before the slash and background color is shown after the slash. If one of these two color choices uses the defaults, that part of the formatting description does not appear.
font	Font of cell is described in text. Examples are SWISS12, DUTCH14, and COURIER10.
Italics	Cell's contents are italicized.
LRTB	Lines appear on sides of cell. L indicates Left, R indicates Right, T indicates Top, and B indicates Bottom. These letters are combined to show which sides of the cells have lines; for example, TL indicates a cell with a line at the top and left side.
S1, S2, or S3	Cell has light (S1), medium (S2), or dark (S3) shading.
U1, U2, or U3	Cell has single (U1), double (U2), or wide (U3) underlining.
Graph *name*	Cell is used by graph indicated by name.
Text	Cell is part of a text range.
MPage	Cell is at a manual page break.
Page	Cell is at an automatic page break.
H*points*	Height of row is set by the number of points.
Shadow	Cell is part of a range that has a shadow box drawn around it.
–	Negative numbers in the cell are shown in red.
named_style:	Cell uses named style format described by named_style.

Table 15-1.   *Wysiwyg Format Descriptions*

You can invoke the Wysiwyg menu by typing a colon (:). Once the menu is on the screen, you can make a selection using the same methods you use for selecting 1-2-3 menu items. Just as in 1-2-3, pressing ESC backs you out of the current activity by one menu level and CTRL-BREAK returns you to the READY mode.

Function keys work in the same way as they do with 1-2-3 alone. The only difference is F1 (HELP). Pressing F1 (HELP) displays help for Wysiwyg when the Wysiwyg menu displays and help for 1-2-3 at other times.

Using Different Fonts

A *font* is a typeface or character design of a particular style and size. Each typeface you select has an appearance that is different from other typefaces. The characters may be plain or may have many embellishments. Fonts without embellishments are referred to as *sans serif* fonts. Fonts with embellishments on the characters are referred to as *serif* fonts. Figure 15-2 shows the Dutch typeface, which is a serif font; the Swiss typeface, which is sans serif; and the Xsymbol font, which creates many characters that are not part of the standard character set. The Xsymbol characters are shown in a column in Appendix B, "LICS Codes." Wysiwyg also has a Courier typeface, which is similar to the style that typewriters use. Depending on the printer you selected during installation, you may have other print styles supplied by your printer. You may also have fonts provided by other software giving you even more typefaces from which you can choose.

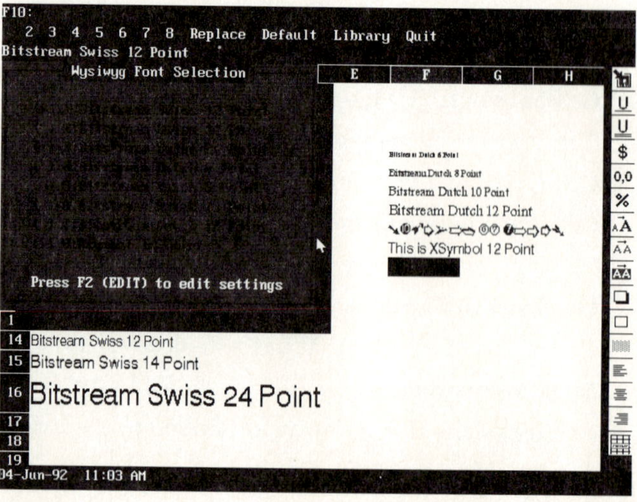

Figure 15-2.   *The default font set*

The size of a font is measured in points; each point is 1/72 of an inch. For example, a point size of 24 indicates that a character is one-third of an inch tall. You can use point sizes between 3 and 72 points. Most users select 10 point for regular text, 5 point for fine print, and around 20 point for headings.

Choosing a Font Set

Each worksheet can use up to eight different fonts. You can use the eight default fonts that Wysiwyg initially provides or change them to other fonts. To see the current fonts, type **:FF** to select :Format Font. These eight fonts are assigned the numbers 1 through 8 and are shown in Figure 15-2 with examples of the different fonts. To leave this menu, you must assign a font to a range or select Quit.

By default, all of the worksheet cells use font 1. You can use another font by selecting another font choice and telling Wysiwyg the ranges for applying the different font. To change the font used by a range to another font in the selected font set, select :Format Font and the number of the font you want to use. For example, to change the font of C1 in Figure 15-1 to Swiss 24 point, move the cell pointer to C1, type **:FF** (the colon for the Wysiwyg menu, and F twice to select Format and Font); then type **3** to select the third font. Wysiwyg prompts for the range to use with the font; press ENTER to select the current cell.

With Release 2.4, you can select the Font icon to change the Font used for the text in the selected range. To do so, select the range in which you want to use a different font. Then select the Font icon (shown here). The range is now formatted with the next font from the current font library. The appearance of the entries depends on which font was current when you selected the Font icon.

You can use all eight fonts on a worksheet although this approach is not recommended. Too many fonts on one page distract the reader from the information presented. It creates a busy effect and detracts from the successful communication of information. Three different font sizes on one worksheet is a good guideline that should not normally be exceeded. You might use all eight fonts when you have several reports on the same worksheet and each report uses different fonts.

Changing the Available Fonts

While you can have only eight fonts in a worksheet, you can define which eight fonts the worksheet will use. You must give up the use of one of the existing fonts when you select a new font for the current set since there can never be any more than eight fonts in one set. You can select Format Font Replace from the Wysiwyg menu and select the number of the font you wish to replace. Wysiwyg presents a list of all the typefaces—such as Swiss, Dutch, Courier, Xsymbol, or Other. If you select Other, you must select one of the typefaces in the list that Wysiwyg displays. Next, select the point size that you want by typing a number between 3 and 72. This updates the font listed below the Format Font menu. If you replace one of the fonts assigned to the worksheet, cells assigned to that font number will use its replacement. For example, you can change the font that most cells in Figure 15-1 will use to Dutch 12 point by selecting :Format Font Replace 1 Dutch and pressing ENTER to select the default size of 12 points. When you select Quit twice to return to READY mode, you can see that all of the worksheet except C1 uses Dutch 12 point.

When you change the current font set, the change is effective immediately and stays in effect until you make another change or end the current session. The font settings are saved with the worksheet files that you use with them. If you want to change the default font set that is loaded at the beginning of each new Wysiwyg session you must select Default and Update to make the current font selections the defaults. At any time you can also replace the current font set with the default font set by selecting :Format Font Default Restore.

Creating a Library of Font Sets

Since each application may require a unique combination of fonts, Wysiwyg allows you to create a library of named font sets and retrieve any font set from this library. The library can consist of as many font sets as you need to meet a variety of printing needs. To make the current font set a library font file, enter : and select Format Font Library Save and a valid filename. These files have an .AFS extension. When you want to make the fonts in a library font file the current font set, select :Format Font Library Retrieve and the name of the library font file. To remove a font set you no longer need, you can select :Format Font Library Erase and specify the name of a library font file.

Adding Boldface

If you want to highlight text in certain cells, you can boldface the contents of these cells with the :Format Bold command. You can select the range to boldface before or after selecting the :Format Bold command. Selecting Set after :Format Bold adds boldface to the text in the range, and selecting Clear removes boldface from the text in the range. Figure 15-3 shows boldface added to B11..F11 and A16..F16.

With Release 2.4, instead of using the :Format Bold command, you can use the Bold icon from the SmartIcons icon palette. First, select the range containing the text you want to boldface. Next, select the Bold icon. If the text is already formatted

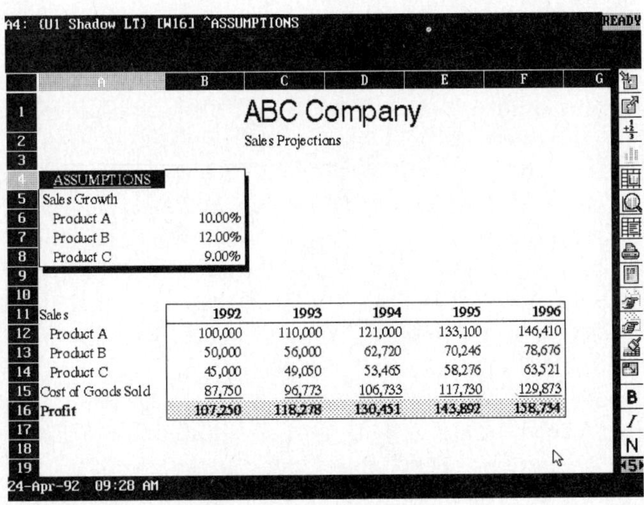

Figure 15-3.   The worksheet after adding different formats

as bold, then selecting the icon removes bold from the selected range. The Bold icon looks like this:

Adding Italics

If you want to emphasize the text in certain cells, you can italicize the contents of those cells with Wysiwyg. To do this, select the :Format Italics command. You can select the range to italicize before or after selecting this command. If you select Clear, you remove the italics from the selected cells.

If you are using Release 2.4, you can use the Italics icon from the SmartIcons palette instead of selecting the :Format Italics command. To use this icon, first select the range of cells you want to italicize. Select the Italics icon (shown here). If the text is already italicized, this removes the italics from the contents of the range.

Adding Underlining

Wysiwyg also allows you to add three styles of underlining to cells. Wysiwyg underlines only the text within a selected range; it does not place the underline marks under blank areas in the selected cells. To add underlining, select :Format Underline; then select Single, Double, Wide, or Clear. Single adds a narrow line below cell entries; Double adds two narrow lines below cell entries; Wide adds a wide line below cell entries; and Clear removes any underlining added with the three other options. Like other :Format commands, you can select the range to use with this command before you activate the menu to select :Format Underline or after you select Single, Double, Wide, or Clear. Figure 15-3 shows the Wysiwyg screen after single underlining was added to A4 and to B15..F15.

You can also use two of the SmartIcons with Release 2.4 as a shortcut when you are underlining text in a range. Select the range that includes the text you want to underline. Then select either the Single Underline or the Double Underline icon, as appropriate. Both icons are shown here. If you choose one of these two icons and the range is already formatted for that feature, the formatting is removed.

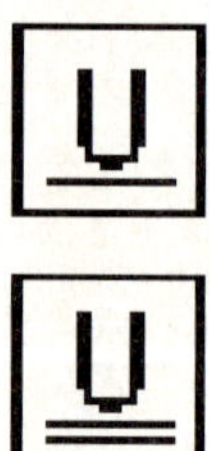

Adding Lines

Lines and boxes can help set off information in the worksheet from other entries. Wysiwyg has several different options for adding lines to a worksheet. Figure 15-3 shows a worksheet where different types of lines are used. These lines include the outline around A4..B8 and B11..F16 and the line on the bottom of B11..F11. These lines are added by selecting :Format Lines and one of the options. Like other :Format commands, you can select the range to work with either before you select :Format or after you select one of the options for the lines to add.

The Top, Bottom, Left, and Right options add lines to the top, bottom, left, and right sides of cells. Adding a line to the top of a cell is the same as adding it to the bottom of the cell above it. Adding a line to the right edge of a cell is the same as adding a line to the left edge of the cell in the next column. Selecting All adds lines to all four sides of the cells. Selecting Outline adds lines to the edge of the range selected. Each of these six options draws a single narrow line. The Double and Wide options draw double lines and wide lines. If you select Double or Wide, you must also select from Top, Bottom, Left, Right, All, or Outline to indicate where you want the double or wide lines placed. You can remove some or all of the lines added with any of these options by selecting Clear and then Top, Bottom, Left, Right, All, or Outline to select the lines to clear. The last option, Shadow, draws a box with a shadow around a range (see the shadow box around A4..B8 of Figure 15-3). This box is added by selecting Set after selecting Shadow. To remove a shadow box, select :Format Lines Shadow Clear.

If you are using Release 2.4, you will find two SmartIcons that can help you add lines to your worksheet. One is the Shadow icon and the other is the Outline icon. To use these, you need to select the range you want to affect and then select the icon. When you select the Shadow icon, the selected range is outlined, and a drop-shadow appears at the bottom and right side of the outline. When you select the Outline icon, the entire range is outlined with a single line, a double line, a wide line, or no line, depending on whether there was any outline formatting applied to that range previously. Continued clicking of the Outline icon cycles through all of the options. The Shadow and Outline icons look like this:

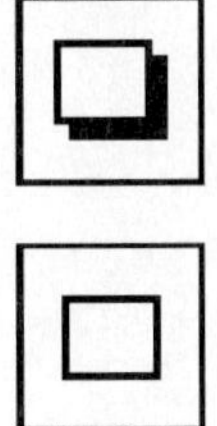

Adding Color

You can add color to your output if you have a printer or screen that supports colors. In addition you can also display negative numbers in a different color. You can use colors to emphasize information that needs more attention.

To set the color of a range, use the :Format Colors command. By selecting the Text option, you are changing the color of the text that is stored in the selected range (even if the text extends into the display space of other cells). If you select the Background option, you are changing the background color of the cells (rather than the background color of the text). For these two options, your choices are Normal, Red, Green, Dark-Blue, Cyan, Magenta, and Yellow. Another option is to select Reverse, which switches the colors for the text and background. By selecting Negative, you can select Normal (which displays negative numbers using the normal color) or Red (which displays negative numbers in red). The final option, Quit, returns you to the READY mode.

If you are using Release 2.4, you can also change text and background color using icons from the SmartIcons palettes. You need to select the range to be affected by this formatting first. Then select either the Color Text or Color Background icon, which are illustrated below. When you select one of these icons, the color of either the text or the cell, depending on which icon you selected, changes to the next color on the list. Continued selection of the icon cycles through the other options.

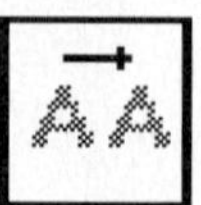

Adding Shading

Shading can be used to create a backdrop for a graph or can be added to information enclosed within boxes. You can choose light, dark, or solid shading. In most cases light shading is more effective when the cells to be shaded contain data. It is much easier to read the text in the file when the shading is light. Figure 15-3 shows a worksheet that uses light shading to emphasize a range of data. To add shading, select :Format Shade and choose Light, Dark, Solid, or Clear to add or remove shading to or from a range. Select the range either before selecting :Format or after selecting one of the four options.

With Release 2.4, you can add shading using the Shade icon from the SmartIcons palette. To add shading using this icon, select the range that you want to shade first and then select the Shade icon. When you select this icon, the selected range is shaded light, dark, solid, or not at all, depending on how the range was shaded before you selected the icon. The Shade icon looks like this:

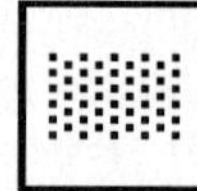

Removing Formats

Most of the format options that you select in Wysiwyg can be undone by the same command that added the format but by selecting a different option. If you have several formats that you want to remove, you may want to use the :Format Reset command and select a range to reset all Wysiwyg formats (unless you select a range before selecting :Format Reset). This command removes all Wysiwyg format enhancements and returns the font of the selected range to font 1. This command does not affect 1-2-3 formats and formats that are entered directly into a cell (more on this later in the chapter).

If you are using Release 2.4, you can use the Normal icon as a shortcut for removing all Wysiwyg formatting from a cell. Simply select the range of cells from which you want to remove all Wysiwyg formatting. Then select the Normal icon (shown below). All Wysiwyg formatting is removed from the selected range. Any formatting that is typed directly into the cell, such as the codes for bold and other formats described in the section "Adding Formats to Text in Entries," and any 1-2-3 formatting codes are not removed by the Normal icon.

Using Named Format Styles

Besides adding each format you want individually, you can group a set of formats into a named style and apply the named style to a range, rather than applying the :Format commands that produce the formatting represented. As an example, suppose you are setting several ranges to use boldface and the sixth font. You can use the :Format Bold and :Format Font 6 commands to add the formatting to one range and use a cell from the range to define the named style. The next time you want to boldface and set the font to font 6 for a range, you can apply the named range and both formats will be applied automatically.

To define a named style, move the cell pointer to a cell containing the formats you want associated with a named style. Select :Named-Style Define and a number between 1 and 8 as the number you want to define. When Wysiwyg prompts for a cell to use for the definition, press ENTER to select the current cell, or select another cell to use. If you selected a range before selecting :Named-Style, Wysiwyg uses the first cell of the selected range. Next, type up to six characters for the name of the named style and press ENTER; then type up to 37 characters for a description and press ENTER.

To use a named style, move the cell pointer to the first cell where you want to apply it. Select :Named-Style and the number (1 through 8) of the named style you want to apply. The description of each format appears on the third line of the control panel screen. Finally, select the range that will use the named style (unless you selected a range before you selected :Named-Style).

As an example, you can define a named style that boldfaces and underlines text. First, go to a cell and press F4 (ABS), then select **:Format Bold Set** and **:Format Underline Single**. Next, select **:Named-Style Define 1** to change the first named style. Press ESC to remove Normal; type **B&U** for the style name; press ENTER; type **Boldface and underline** for the description; and press ENTER again. To use this style, move the cell pointer to the first cell to use these two formats and select :Named-Style 1:B&U. Then select the range that you want to boldface and underline.

Using Text Ranges and Adding Formats to Text

With Wysiwyg you can treat a worksheet range as a text range, which allows you to use the range as if you are using a word processor. When you use text ranges, you can enter the text directly onto the worksheet and see how it will appear within the selected range. You can also use the text alignment options to alter the alignment of the text within the range. Another command you can use while working with text ranges lets you reformat the range, which is like reformatting a paragraph in a word processor. Other features of Wysiwyg that make it similar to a word processor are the formatting features described earlier for text within a label entry. For example, you can boldface and italicize parts of an entry.

Entering and Editing a Text Range

Creating and using a text range is as simple as selecting the range to treat as text, and entering or editing the text in the range. To select the range to use as a text range, select :Text Set and the range. With Release 2.4, select the range and then select the Text Set icon from the SmartIcons palettes as a shortcut for setting the text range. The range should be as wide as you want the labels to extend in each line. You may also want to include additional rows so that the text has room to expand if needed. If the range you select is too small for the text you enter, you will see an error message, indicating that the text range is full. The text is actually stored in the first column of the range although the entries use the entire range to display. If the range already has entries, the entries will use the alignment of the first label in the range. When you are ready to enter or edit text in the range, select :Text Edit. You can also edit a text range with a mouse by double clicking one of the cells in the text range with the left mouse button. Wysiwyg will suggest the text range that contains the cell pointer or the last text range edited. You can either accept this range or select a different range. When you are editing the text, your entries are made directly to the worksheet rather than in the control panel, as shown here:

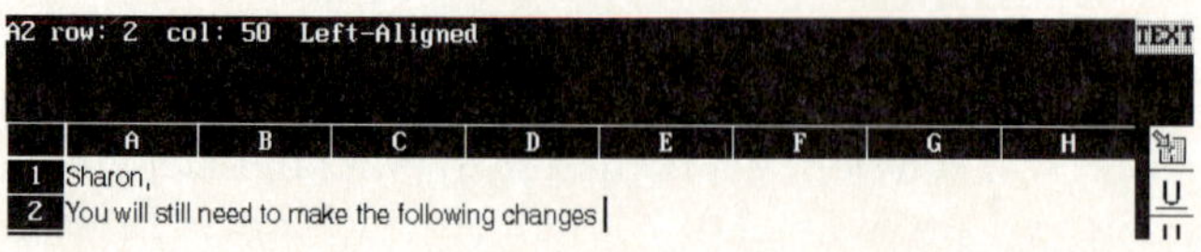

This means that if you make a mistake while entering text, you cannot press ESC to start over. Wysiwyg also handles word wrapping, which moves the cursor to the next line when the current line is full. While you are editing the text, the editing keys behave more like they do in a word processing package. Table 15-2 lists the editing keys you can use while editing a text range. Figure 15-4 shows a text range. Notice how the control panel displays {Text} to indicate that the cell pointer is on a cell that is part of a text range. Also, the paragraph symbol, which indicates where a paragraph ends, will appear in the control panel but does not appear in the worksheet display. Later, when you learn how to add graphs to a worksheet range, you will find that the graphs change into shaded areas during editing, and Wysiwyg wraps the text around the graph.

Key	Effect
LEFT ARROW	Moves cursor one character left
RIGHT ARROW	Moves cursor one character right
DOWN ARROW	Moves cursor one line down
UP ARROW	Moves cursor one line up
CTRL-LEFT ARROW	Moves cursor to beginning of previous word
CTRL-RIGHT ARROW	Moves cursor to beginning of next word
CTRL-ENTER	Ends current paragraph (with a paragraph symbol) and starts a new one
DEL	Deletes character to the right of cursor
END	Moves cursor to the end of the line when pressed once and moves cursor to the end of the paragraph when pressed again
ENTER	Moves cursor to the next line
ESC	Stops editing text range and returns to READY mode
F3	Displays menu to add formats to a text range
HOME	Moves cursor to the beginning of the line when pressed once and moves cursor to the beginning of the paragraph when pressed again
INS	Switches between insert and overstrike mode
PGDN	Moves to bottom or next screen of text range
PGUP	Move to top or upper screen of text range

Table 15-2.   Editing Keys for Editing a Text Range

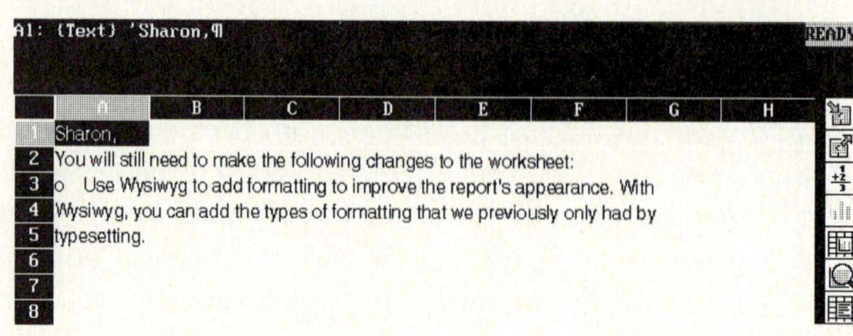

Figure 15-4.   *Using a text range*

Changing the Alignment of a Text Range

After you have entered the text range, you may want to try some of the different alignments that Wysiwyg provides for text ranges. Unlike label prefixes, text range prefixes align the entries in a range rather than in a cell. To change the alignment of a text range, select :Text Align and then Left, Right, Center, or Even. The Left, Right, and Center options are like 1-2-3's alignment choices, enabling you to left justify, right justify, and center labels. The Even option adds spaces between words in the labels so that both the left and right sides are aligned for all lines except the last (like the paragraphs in this book). After choosing one of the options, select the range of text to align. Figure 15-5 shows text ranges that use the different alignments.

You can create a Wysiwyg text range or change the alignment of a text range by using the Text icon. Before selecting this icon, either select a range of cells in which you want to create a text range, or one in which are the cells already formatted as

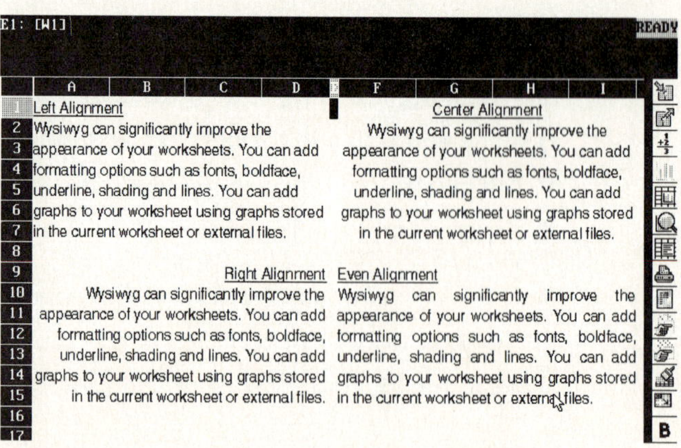

Figure 15-5.   *Different types of alignment for text ranges*

text. If the cell or range of cells you select is not formatted for text, then selecting this icon formats them as text. If the cell is formatted as text but is empty, the text format is removed. If the cell is formatted for text and contains an entry, then the alignment of the text changes. The Text icon looks like this:

Reformatting a Text Range

As you edit a text range, you may want to rearrange the text in it. This is often the case when you are making an existing range of labels into a text range and you want to rearrange the labels to look like a paragraph. Also, as you edit the text in a text range, the text will no longer fit into each cell; you will want to readjust the text that appears in each label. A third use is if you use F2 (EDIT) to alter an entry in a text range. The :Text Reformat command reformats the text in a text range to use the worksheet area you select. After selecting :Text Reformat, select the range. For example, to reformat the text in Figure 15-4, you would select A1..G5. Unlike the 1-2-3 /Range Justify command, you must select all the rows you want to reformat as well as the columns the text should be distributed over (assuming that the total width is less than 512 characters). Also unlike the /Range Justify command, the :Text Reformat command maintains your separate paragraphs.

Paragraphs are indicated by the paragraph symbol, which you add by pressing CTRL-ENTER to start a new paragraph, a blank line separating paragraphs, or a line that starts with a space. The :Text Reformat command also provides different results from the /Range Justify command since the :Text Reformat command takes into account the font size of the characters and any special formatting you add to the text (as described in the next section).

Adding Formats to Text in Entries

Besides using formatting such as fonts, boldface, and italics with :Format commands that apply to entire cells, you can also use these formats within a cell entry. While these examples use text ranges, you can add formatting to text in text ranges or labels although the steps are slightly different.

To add formatting to text in a text range, position the cursor before the character where you want the format to begin and press F3. This displays a menu containing Font, Bold, Italics, Underline, Color, + (for superscript), – (for subscript), Outline, and Normal. To add one of these formatting options, select the format to add.

If you select Font, you must also select a number between 1 and 8 that represents the font you want to use. If you select Color, you must then select from Normal, Red,

Green, Dark-Blue, Cyan, Yellow, or Magenta. When you change a format option, Wysiwyg adds a formatting sequence that will appear in the control panel during READY mode when the cell is highlighted. The format you select lasts until the end of the text you are entering or the end of the cell (whichever is farther away). You may later see Wysiwyg adding a formatting sequence to end the formatting feature if you reformat the text. Of course you can also end a format before the end of a cell, move the cursor to where you want the format to end, press F3, and select Normal.

The other method of adding formatting to text in a label lets you directly enter the formatting sequences. This can be done either in a text range or when entering a label in EDIT or LABEL mode. To enter a formatting sequence, press CTRL-A and type one of the codes listed in Table 15-3. These codes are case-sensitive, so you must use the same case that appears in the table. You can press CTRL-E and the code to stop the effects of the formatting sequences, or CTRL-N to stop them all.

Code	Format Added
b	Boldface
d	Subscript
f	Flashing
i	Italics
u	Superscript
x	Text is backwards (flipped on its x-axis)
y	Text is upside down (flipped on its y-axis)
1_	Single underlining
2_	Double underlining
3_	Wide underlining
4_	Outline around characters
5_	Strike through characters
1c to 8c	Text is in a different color; the number 1 through 8 represent the colors Normal (set with :Display Colors Text), Red, Green, Dark-Blue, Cyan, Yellow, and Magenta
1F to 8F	Font selected; the numbers 1 through 8 represent the eight fonts available with :Format Font
1o to 255o	Outline of characters; the higher the number, the greater the distance between the sets of lines in the outline

Table 15-3.   *Formatting Sequences*

For example, suppose you want to boldface and underline "twenty percent" in "This report assumes twenty percent growth." First, move the cursor to the first "t" in "twenty." Press CTRL-A and type **b** to add boldface, and then press CTRL-A and type **1_** to add underlining. Next, move to after the "t" in "percent" and press CTRL-N. The final result looks like this:

This report assumes **<u>twenty percent</u>** growth.

When you edit the text, this appears in the control panel:

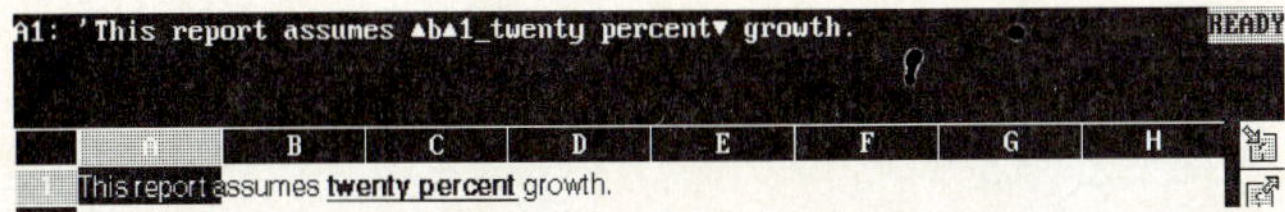

The ▲b, ▲1_, and ▼0 are the formatting sequences that indicate when the formats should start and stop. You can remove formatting sequences by deleting them just as you delete other characters in an entry. Since these formatting sequences are part of the entry, you do not want to use cells containing them with the /Range Name Labels command or as part of a range you are sorting with the /Data Sort command.

Removing a Text Range

As you work with a worksheet that includes text ranges, you may need to remove some of them. For example, if a paragraph you added to the end of a report no longer applies, you may want to use /Range Erase to erase the entries and then tell Wysiwyg that you no longer want to use the range as a text range. To stop using a range as a text range, select :Text Clear and the range to clear. The :Text Clear command does not erase any worksheet data (including the text stored in each cell) or any formatting you have added to the labels. Once you use the :Text Clear command, any alignment set with :Text Align disappears and the labels in the range use the default alignment within a cell.

Copying, Moving, and Importing Formats

Besides adding Wysiwyg formats to worksheet cells, you can also copy and move them to new locations. The 1-2-3 /Copy and /Move commands will copy both the data and the Wysiwyg formats to a new location. Wysiwyg has :Special Copy and :Special Move commands with which you can copy and move Wysiwyg formats to new locations without copying or moving the worksheet data. These two Wysiwyg commands copy only Wysiwyg formats; they will not copy 1-2-3 formats, graphics (described later), or worksheet data. Wysiwyg also has commands that let you export and import Wysiwyg formats to and from format files. These commands let you apply formats from one range to other ranges.

The :Special Copy and :Special Move commands are similar to the 1-2-3 /Copy and /Move commands. After selecting either :Special Copy or :Special Move, select the range containing the Wysiwyg formats you want to copy or move. If you select a range before activating the Wysiwyg menu, Wysiwyg will use this range as the from range. Next, select the first cell of the range where you want the formats copied or moved. With :Special Copy, you can select a range as the to range when you want to make several copies of the formats. As an example of the :Special Copy command, suppose you want to copy the font, boldface, and underlining in C1 of this worksheet:

To copy this format to C2, select :Special Copy, press ENTER to use C1 as the from range, press the DOWN ARROW, and press ENTER to use C2 as the to range. The resulting worksheet looks like this:

Another method of transferring Wysiwyg formats is to export them to another format file or import them from another format file. The format files are the files with the .FMT extension that Wysiwyg uses to store formatting descriptions for a worksheet. As an example, suppose you have two worksheet files that use the same formats. If you want to make the same changes to the formats in each file, you have to repeat the Wysiwyg commands twice. Another option is to make the changes in one of the two files. Once the changes are made, you can export the changed format file to the unchanged one or import the changed format file into the unchanged one.

To see how importing and exporting works, suppose you have the DIV_SALE worksheet shown in Figure 15-6 and you want to apply the Wysiwyg formats from the SALEPROJ worksheet shown in Figure 15-3 to the DIV_SALE worksheet. Switch to the SALEPROJ worksheet in Figure 15-3, select :Special Export, and type **DIV_SALE** as the name of the format file to export. The format file has the same name as the

A4: [W16] 'Divisions: READY

	A	B	C	D	E	F	G
1			ABC Company				
2			4th Quarter Sales Report				
3							
4	Divisions:	# of Stores					
5	Northeast	578					
6	Southwest	247					
7	Southeast	378					
8	Northwest	347					
9							
10							
11	Sales	1st	2nd	3rd	4th	Total	
12	Northeast	812,934	844,296	886,527	847,608	3,391,365	
13	Southwest	293,847	262,244	285,190	306,225	1,147,506	
14	Southeast	376,193	409,293	444,317	492,470	1,722,273	
15	Northwest	583,917	592,289	561,944	560,033	2,298,184	
16	Profit	2,066,891	2,108,122	2,177,978	2,206,336	8,559,328	
17							

Figure 15-6.   *The worksheet before adopting formats from another worksheet*

worksheet to which the formats apply. You may also need to select Replace if the worksheet already has a format file. When you select /File Retrieve DIV_SALE, the worksheet will use the exported Wysiwyg formats from the SALEPROJ worksheet. Another option is to switch to the DIV_SALE worksheet and select the :Special Import All command and SALEPROJ.FMT as the format file to import. The result is shown in Figure 15-7.

When you import a format file, before you select the format file you can select whether you want to import all the Wysiwyg formats, fonts, and graphs (All), just the

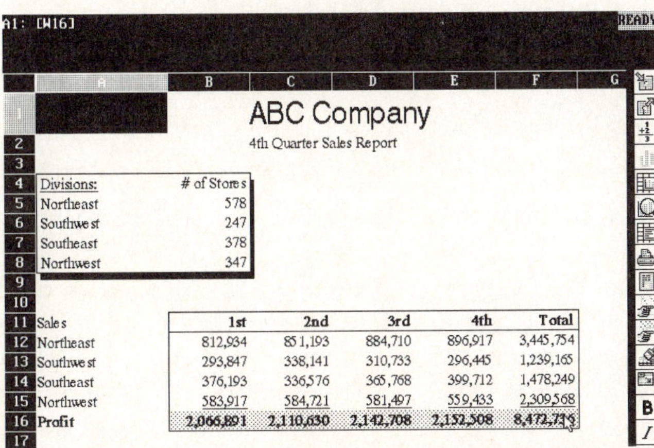

A1: [W16]   READY

	A	B	C	D	E	F	G
1			ABC Company				
2			4th Quarter Sales Report				
3							
4	Divisions:	# of Stores					
5	Northeast	578					
6	Southwest	247					
7	Southeast	378					
8	Northwest	347					
9							
10							
11	Sales	1st	2nd	3rd	4th	Total	
12	Northeast	812,934	851,193	884,710	896,917	3,445,754	
13	Southwest	293,847	338,141	310,733	296,445	1,239,165	
14	Southeast	376,193	336,576	365,768	399,712	1,478,249	
15	Northwest	583,917	584,721	581,497	559,433	2,309,568	
16	Profit	2,066,891	2,110,630	2,142,708	2,152,508	8,472,735	
17							

Figure 15-7.   *The worksheet after importing formats*

named styles (Named-Styles), the font set (Fonts), or the graphs added to the worksheet (Graphs). The last option adds the graphs in the format file to the current worksheet rather than replacing the graphs in the current worksheet with the graphs in the imported format file. When you import and export graphs, the current graph in the worksheet and named graphs in the worksheet are not transferred but their position and any enhancements are transferred. (Using Wysiwyg with graphs is covered later in the chapter.) When importing and exporting formats, the two worksheet files involved should have the same design, since the location of the imported or exported format is the same in both worksheets. If the design of the worksheet is different, you may have the formats applied to different cells from those you intended.

These two commands can also use format files in other formats. This allows you to import and export formatting with other Add-Ins such as Allways. While omitting a file extension in the filename defaults to using .FMT, you can also use .ALL to use an Allways format file. When you use Allways format files, you can only import and export formatting features that are common between Wysiwyg and Allways. For example, if you export the formats to an Allways format file, you will notice these changes:

- Changes made with :Format Color Background, :Format Lines Shadow, :Display Colors, :Graph Settings Opaque, :Print Layout Compression, and :Print Settings Frame have no effect.

- Lines added with :Format Lines Double (Left, Right, and Top) and :Format Lines Wide are saved as single lines while lines added with :Format Lines Double Bottom are saved as double underlining.

- Named styles are lost.

- Only .PIC graphs added to a worksheet are recorded in the Allways format file.

- Graph enhancements made with :Graph Edit are removed.

- Text ranges are treated as labels.

Changing Column Widths and Row Heights

Column widths and row heights can be set in either of two ways. Column widths can be set with the 1-2-3 /Worksheet Column commands or the Wysiwyg :Worksheet Column command. The :Worksheet Column command is just like the /Worksheet Column Column-Range command. When you select :Worksheet Column Set-Width, select the range of columns to change and then enter the number of characters wide you want the columns. The column widths are the number of characters wide (between 0 and 240), using the width of the characters of font 1 rather than the fonts that the entries in the columns use. The :Worksheet Column Reset-Width command returns a range of columns that you select to the global column width set by the /Worksheet Global Column-Width command.

Row heights are either set automatically by Wysiwyg to match the height of the text in the row using the fonts you select or by the :Worksheet Row command. When you select :Worksheet Row Set-Width, select the range containing the rows to change and enter the number of points for the new row height. You can also use the UP ARROW and DOWN ARROW to increment the row heights a point at a time. To use Wysiwyg's default row heights, which are based on the height of the fonts used in the row, select :Worksheet Row Auto and the range containing the rows to let Wysiwyg set the height.

You can also use the mouse for changing row height and column width in Wysiwyg. Simply point the mouse at the line dividing the columns or rows. Clicking and dragging the mouse, will drag the line. When you release the mouse, the row or column adjusts to fit where you moved the separation line.

Changing the Wysiwyg Display

Wysiwyg provides a number of options for altering the appearance of the display. These options change how 1-2-3 and Wysiwyg appear on the screen but do not change the appearance of the worksheet in the way that the :Format commands do. The options affecting the display can be found under the menu option :Display. The options you select with the :Display commands do not affect your print output. They are designed to allow you to customize the presentation of information on the screen to meet your needs. When you are ready to leave the :Display menu to return to READY mode you can select Quit.

Graphics Versus Text Mode

A big advantage of Wysiwyg is that it displays your spreadsheet as it will appear when you use Wysiwyg to print. This feature requires that your computer and monitor are capable of displaying graphics. Some monitors can display only text, which means that although you can alter the worksheet format and print it using Wysiwyg's features, the worksheet on the screen looks like the standard 1-2-3 screen.

If you have a graphics monitor, you can choose how you want your worksheets displayed. You can display it in text mode, which means that 1-2-3 is faster and the worksheet does not appear as it will print. The text mode uses the standard 1-2-3 fonts, attributes such as boldface and underlining will not appear, and added graphs do not appear on the worksheet display. The control panel will continue to display the format descriptions of the formats that are applied to the cell. To use the text mode, select :Display Mode Text. To display Wysiwyg using the default graphics mode, select :Display Mode Graphics and the worksheet will appear as it will be printed.

For graphics display modes, you have two choices: you can display the worksheet using colors or using only black and white. To use colors, select :Display Mode Color. To use only black and white, select :Display Mode B&W.

Changing Colors

If you are using a color monitor with Wysiwyg, you can select from a rainbow of colors for your display. You can set the color of the various worksheet components with the :Display Colors commands. Unlike the :Format Color command, the :Display Colors command only changes colors of different parts of the Wysiwyg display rather than changing the colors of ranges in the worksheet. These options let you select the color for the background, the text, the unprotected cells, the cell pointer, the grid, the frame (the border of row numbers and column letters), negative numbers, the lines that you add with :Format Lines, and the drop shadow added with :Format Lines Shadow. To change the colors used by the worksheet, select :Display Colors and an option from Background, Text, Unprot, Cell-Pointer, Grid, Frame, Neg, Lines, or Shadow. For these nine options you can select from Black, White, Red, Green, Dark-Blue, Cyan, Yellow, or Magenta. The Neg option only changes the color of the negative numbers that appear on the screen. The :Format Color Negative command changes the color used to display and print negative numbers. You can also change the eight colors. For example, you may want to use a lighter blue for the Dark-Blue selection. To change the colors that the eight color selections represent, select Replace and the color you want to change. Wysiwyg displays the color number of the current color, which is a number between 0 and 63. You can type the number of the color you want. When you finish, select Quit to return to the :Display Colors menu.

Zooming In and Out

Wysiwyg has several different display sizes. You can zoom in to your worksheet to see the cells up close. You can zoom out to see how the worksheet appears without printing it. Like the other :Display menu commands, zooming in or out does not affect the printed output.

When you select :Display Zoom, you can choose from the options of Tiny, Small, Normal, Large, Huge, or Manual. Tiny displays the worksheet at 63 percent of its normal size; Small displays it at 87 percent of its normal size; Normal displays it at its normal size; Large displays it at 125 percent of normal size; and Huge displays it at 150 percent of its normal size. With Manual, you can enter a number representing the percentage of its normal size at which you want to view the worksheet. Enter a number between 25 and 400, where numbers below 100 display the worksheet entries smaller than their actual size and numbers above 100 display the worksheet entries larger than their actual size.

With Release 2.4, you can select the Zoom icon from the SmartIcons palette to invoke the :Display Zoom command. When you do so, the display changes to the next zoom setting, depending on how it is currently formatted. This means it will move from normal to large, from huge to tiny, or from small to normal. You do not have the option of setting the percentage of zoom manually when you use the Zoom icon, shown here.

Another option for setting the size of the cell entries that appear on your screen is to set the number of rows that appear on the screen. When you change the number of rows that appear on your screen, you are changing the height of the displayed entries without changing the height Wysiwyg actually uses for the rows. To set the number of worksheet rows that Wysiwyg displays, select :Display Rows and enter a number between 16 and 60 for the number of rows to display. Wysiwyg may actually display more or less depending on the graphics display card and the size of the default font.

Setting the Appearance of the Cell Pointer

Wysiwyg has two ways to indicate the cell pointer. The default is a solid rectangle, like the cell pointer in C2 shown in Figure 15-8. To change the cell pointer's appearance, select :Display Options Cell-Pointer and then select Outline to display the cell pointer as an outline around the current cell.

Setting the Appearance of the Worksheet Frame

Another change you can make to the Wysiwyg display is to change how the worksheet frame appears. The worksheet frame is the bar with the column letters and row numbers at the top and left of the worksheet. Wysiwyg has several options for how

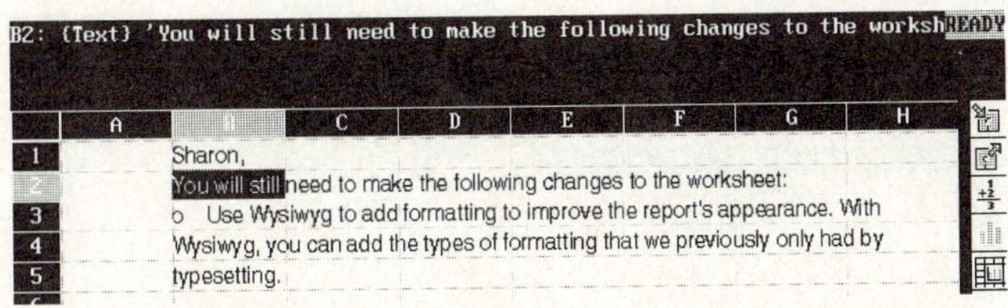

Figure 15-8.   *The cell pointer appears as a solid rectangle*

this frame will appear. To try the other frame display options, select :Display Options Frame. This command has five options: 1-2-3, Enhanced, Relief, Special, and None. 1-2-3 displays a frame similar to the 1-2-3 frame when Wysiwyg is not loaded, where there are no lines indicating where each column or row begins or ends. Enhanced is the default Wysiwyg frame that you see in many of this chapter's figures (such as Figure 15-7). The Relief option displays a frame that has a three-dimensional look as well as changing the cyan (light blue) on the screen to gray.

The Special option creates a frame that measures distances in terms of inches, centimeters, characters, or points and picas. If you select Special, you must select Characters, Inches, Metric, or Points/Picas. Selecting Characters creates a frame that indicates the number of characters across and lines down. Selecting Inches creates a frame that indicates the number of inches across and down. Selecting Metric creates a frame that indicates the number of centimeters across and down. Selecting Points/Picas creates a frame that indicates the number of points across and down. You can use the Inches and Metric options to determine how the worksheet will be placed on the page since Wysiwyg keeps track of the width of each column and the height of each row. Finally, None removes any frame created by another option. Figure 15-9 shows some frames created by the different options.

Showing Grid Lines

In 1-2-3 the cells are divided into columns and rows, although 1-2-3 does not draw lines indicating the separate columns and rows. In Wysiwyg, you can use the default

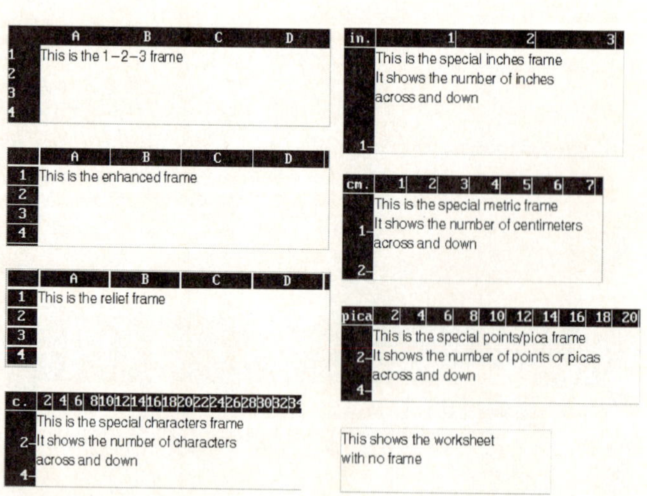

Figure 15-9.   *Different frame options*

of not displaying lines to divide the columns and rows or you can add lines by selecting :Display Options Grid Yes. This adds grid lines that separate the cells on a 1-2-3 spreadsheet (as shown in Figure 15-8). If you later want to remove these lines, select :Display Options Grid No.

Showing Page Breaks

When you select a range to print, Wysiwyg draws dotted lines indicating how the range will be broken into pages. While you can use these dotted lines to guide you so that you have the desired information on each page, they can also be distracting. If you want to remove these dotted lines, select :Display Options Page-Breaks No. If you later want to display these page breaks again, select :Display Options Page-Breaks Yes.

Setting the Display Intensity

Wysiwyg can also display your worksheet at a higher level of brightness. To use a brighter display, select :Display Options Intensity High. This changes Wysiwyg to use brighter versions of the display colors. When you want to return to the normal intensity, select :Display Options Intensity Normal. Some monitors have their own controls for making the display more or less bright. You may want to use the monitor knobs instead of these commands.

Setting the Directory Containing Font Files

Wysiwyg uses font files that are normally stored in the Wysiwyg subdirectory. For Wysiwyg and 1-2-3 to display and print the worksheet with the correct fonts, it is important for Wysiwyg to know where the files are contained. If Wysiwyg cannot find the font files, it uses the 1-2-3 system font. To set where Wysiwyg can find these files, select :Display Font-Directory and enter the directory containing the font files.

Setting the Display Adapter

Wysiwyg is designed to display its graphic display of the worksheet using a variety of hardware for monitors and display adapter cards. You can change the display adapter if Wysiwyg is not using the best one for your system or if you want to see how the Wysiwyg screen will appear on other monitors. To select the display adapter Wysiwyg uses for displaying your worksheet, select :Display Options Adapter and one of the options. The default, Auto, uses the graphics display adapter selected with the 1-2-3 Install program. The other choices are labeled 1 through 9 and have descriptions below them. You can select the one you want to use. Wysiwyg will not let you select options your hardware will not support. You can also select Blink and then Yes to allow 1-2-3 and Wysiwyg to make entries blink or No to prevent Wysiwyg and 1-2-3 from blinking.

Setting the Display Default

If you are frequently making the same changes to the Wysiwyg display, you will want to make these settings the defaults. You can use default settings to return all of the :Display command settings to their defaults after you have made numerous changes. To make the current display choices the new defaults, select :Display Default Update. If you want to replace the current display settings with the defaults, select :Display Default Restore. The default display settings are stored in the file called WYSIWYG.CNF.

Using Wysiwyg for Your Graphs

Wysiwyg lets you work with graphs in your worksheet. You can use graphs saved in .PIC or .CGM files, graphs created with the /Graph commands, or empty graphs to which you can add your own enhancements. With Wysiwyg you can add the graphs directly into a worksheet. By including a graph in the print range when you print with Wysiwyg, you can print the graph in the location where it appears on the worksheet. You can print your graphs on the same sheet of paper with text entries from the worksheet and choose exactly where the graph is placed on the page. Additional graphics features with Wysiwyg allow you to take these graphs (stored in separate files or in worksheets) and add enhancements. You can add text, lines, and freehand drawing. Unlike the :Format commands, the :Graph commands you use to work with graphics have sticky menus; you must select Quit to return to READY mode or the previous menu level.

Adding and Removing Graphs

The :Graph Add command is used to add graphs to a worksheet. Graphs are attached to a range of the worksheet and occupy space on the worksheet display. You can continue to make entries in these cells but unless you set the graph to display the contents beneath it, these entries will appear hidden.

Once you select :Graph Add, you must select the type of graph you are adding. You can select Current, Named, PIC, Metafile, or Blank. If you select Current, you will add the current graph (the one you see when you press F10 (GRAPH)). If you select Named and one of the named graphs in the current worksheet, you will add the selected named graph. If you select PIC and one of the graph image files saved with a .PIC extension, you will add a graph that is saved in a .PIC file. If you select Metafile and one of the graphic image files saved with a .CGM extension, you will add a graph that is saved in a Metafile format. Metafiles are graphic image files that can be created from a variety of programs. 1-2-3 includes a variety of .CGM files in the directory containing the program files that you can include in your worksheets. If you select Blank, you will add an empty graph. This lets you start from scratch to create your own graphics.

With Release 2.4, you can select the Add Graph icon from the SmartIcons palette as a shortcut for adding the current graph to the worksheet. Before selecting this icon, select the range where you want the graph to appear. Then select the icon. The current graph appears in the selected range of the worksheet. The Add Graph icon is shown here:

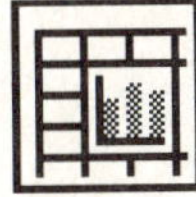

You can specify the range for the graph by typing the range address or name or by highlighting the cells. Like the :Format commands, you can select the range before selecting :Graph Add, and Wysiwyg will use the selected range. Highlighting is the preferred approach since it lets you view the area the graph will occupy on the spreadsheet. Wysiwyg uses the range you select to determine the size and placement of the graph. The graph is expanded or contracted to fit into the selected range. Figure 15-10 shows two graphs that were added to ranges on the Wysiwyg screen.

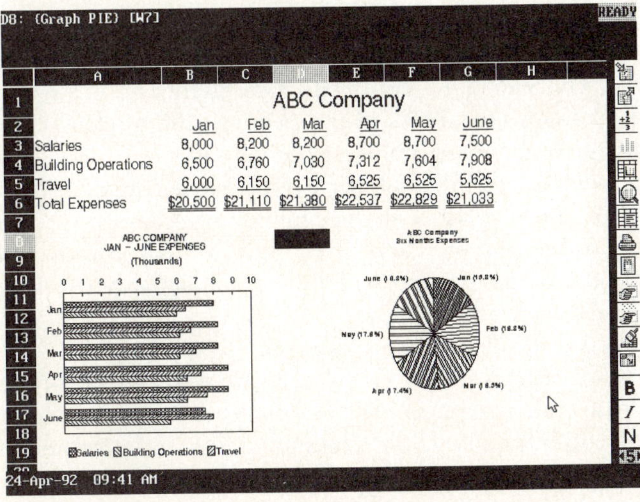

Figure 15-10.   *Two graphs added to a worksheet*

You can remove a graph from the worksheet with the :Graph Remove command. After selecting this command, you must select a cell or range containing the graph to remove from the worksheet, or press F3 (NAME) and select the name of the graph you want to remove from the list Wysiwyg provides. You can also remove more than one graph by including more than one graph in the range you select for this command. Removing a .PIC or .CGM graph from a worksheet does not affect the copy of the graph stored on disk. Also, named graphs and the current graphs on the worksheet are still stored as part of the worksheet so that you can access them with the /Graph commands. Any worksheet data that is beneath a graph is untouched by this command; worksheet data that was hidden by a deleted graph will reappear. If you make any enhancements to the graph as described in the next section, these enhancements will be lost.

If you want to locate a graph quickly to check it before removing it or changing its settings you can use the :Graph Goto command. After selecting this command, select the name of the graph and press ENTER. This command moves you to the first cell that the graphic uses.

Changing the Graph Settings

Once you add a graph to a worksheet, the :Graph menu has several commands that let you alter the appearance of the graph. You can change the graph's position and size, change the graph that appears, make worksheet data display through the graph, and set when graphs will be updated.

Changing the Graphic's Location and Size

Unlike the formatting added with the :Format commands—which can be moved with 1-2-3 commands such as /Move—graphics do not change their size or location with 1-2-3 commands. The only 1-2-3 command that changes a graphic is /Worksheet Column, which changes the widths of the columns the graphic uses. Wysiwyg has several commands to change a graphic's location and size.

If you want to move a graphic, use the :Graph Move command. When you select this command, you must select which graphic to move, unless you selected a range containing the graphic to move before you started this command. You can either select a cell from the range that the graphic uses to display or press F3 (NAME) and select the name of the graphic to move.

Next, Wysiwyg prompts for the new location. As with the /Move command, move the cell pointer to the first cell that you want for the new location of the graphic. The moved graphic uses the same number of columns and rows as the original, so the graph may be a different size if the column widths and row heights of the new worksheet area are different.

If you want to change the size of a graphic as well as changing the position, use the :Graph Settings Range command. When you select this command you must select which graphic to alter, unless you selected a range containing the graphic before you selected this command. You can either select a cell from the range that the graphic uses to display or press F3 (NAME) and select the name of the graphic. Wysiwyg displays the current selected range of the graphic. Like other 1-2-3 commands that prompt you with a range, you can expand or contract the range the graphic uses with the arrow keys. You can type a period to change which corner of the range is anchored. You can also press ESC or BACKSPACE to convert the range address to a single-cell address. Once you have a single-cell address, you can move to a new location and define another range for the graphic. When the range you want is highlighted, press ENTER to use the new range.

Other Graph Settings

The :Graph Settings command has several options for changing the appearance of a graphic. You can change the graph that appears in a graphic, and you can select whether underlying worksheet data appears, whether graphs appear on the work- sheet, and when a graph is updated.

To display a different graph in the range established, use the :Graph Settings Graph command and select from Current, Named, PIC, Metafile, or Blank to select the graphic you want to appear in the window. If you select an option like PIC or Metafile, you must also specify the name of a new file. If you select Named, you must select the name of the graph to display.

The :Graph Settings Display and :Graph Settings Opaque commands control the appearance of graphics. When you select :Graph Settings Display and select Yes or No, you are selecting whether a graphic in the worksheet appears on the screen as the graphic or as a shaded rectangle. Displaying a graphic as a shaded rectangle can make 1-2-3 and Wysiwyg run noticeably faster, since Wysiwyg does not constantly update the screen to draw the graphic.

Selecting :Graph Settings Opaque selects whether worksheet data in the range a graphic uses to display shows through the graphic. Selecting Yes hides underlying worksheet data and selecting No displays the worksheet data. For both the :Graph Settings Display and :Graph Settings Opaque commands, you must select the range containing at least one cell from the graphic you want to change or press F3 (NAME) and select the name of the graphic.

When you add the current graph or a named graph to the worksheet, every time the current or named graph changes, Wysiwyg changes the graph in the worksheet. You can change when the graphs on the worksheet are updated with the :Graph Settings Sync command. When you select Yes, the default, Wysiwyg constantly updates the current and named graphs on the worksheet. When you select No, Wysiwyg updates a graph only when you retrieve the file or use the :Graph Compute com- mand. The exception to retrieving the file is when recalculation is set to Manual, which means you must press F9 (CALC) to update the graph. After selecting one of the two options, you must select a cell from the graphic or press F3 (NAME) and select the name of the graphic. You can also change several graphics by including multiple graphics in the range you select for this command. If you select a range with one or more graphics before you select :Graph Settings Sync, Wysiwyg uses the graphics in the range for the command.

The :Graph Compute command tells Wysiwyg to update every graphic in the worksheet. Any current or named graphs are updated. All graphics from .PIC or .CGM files are reread into memory and updated on the worksheet.

Viewing Graphs

Wysiwyg has several options for looking at graphs besides adding them to a worksheet. You can use Wysiwyg to display a graph saved in a .PIC or .CGM file. You can also use Wysiwyg to display one of the graphics on the worksheet using the full screen.

To display one of the graphics in the current worksheet using the entire screen, select :Graph Zoom. Next, either select a cell from the range the graphic uses or press F3 (NAME) and select the name of the graphic from the list 1-2-3 provides. (You can also select a range containing the graphic before you select :Graph Zoom.) After viewing the graphic, press a key to remove the graphic and return to the :Graph menu.

To display a graphic stored in a .PIC or .CGM file, select :Graph View. Next, select PIC to view a file with a .PIC extension or Metafile to view a file with a .CGM extension, and then select the file to display. After viewing the graphic, press a key to remove the graphic and return to the :Graph menu.

Making Enhancements to Graphics

Wysiwyg includes a graphics editing window that you can use to edit and enhance graphics. You can use this to create drawings in blank graphs as well as to annotate existing graphs. The graphics editing window provides many of the graph features you expect in a full-blown graphics package. With Wysiwyg, as well as many other graphics packages, you will find it easier to edit graphics using a mouse, since it is easier to point to what you want in a graph with a mouse than to continually press the arrow keys.

The graphics editing window is accessed by selecting :Graph Edit and the graph you wish to alter (unless you select a range containing the graph to alter before selecting :Graph Edit). With a mouse, you can also double-click a cell that the graphic uses to display and Wysiwyg will display the graphic in the graphics editing window. Once you are in the graphics editing window, you can only exit the menu by selecting Quit. This means that if you are backing out of a command in the graphics editing window by pressing ESC you do not have to worry that you may press ESC too many times.

When you are in a graphics editing window, your screen looks like Figure 15-11. As this figure shows, Wysiwyg displays the graph on the screen with lines at the top

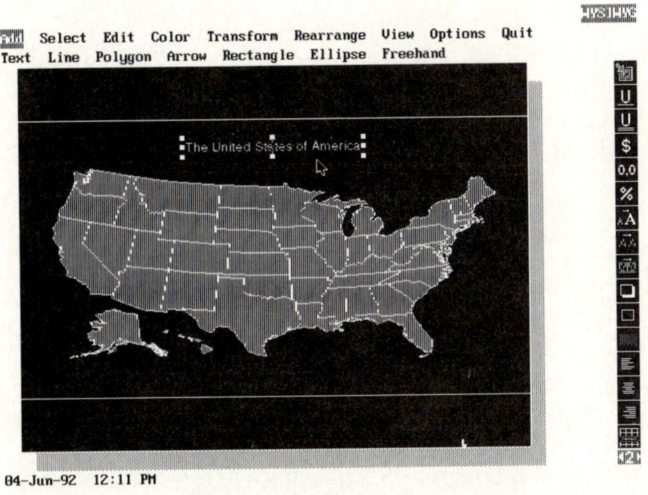

Figure 15-11.   *The graphics editing window*

and bottom indicating the limits of the graph size. This means that the lines will be different for each graphic you edit based on their relative size.

In the graphics editing window, each item you can manipulate is called an *object.* A current graph, named graph, or image from a .PIC or .CGM file is considered a single object, although a graph has different pieces such as titles, axes, and data labels. If you want to change these components of the graph, you must use the 1-2-3 Graph menu.

A graphics editing window also includes a *bounding box* when you move or change the size of an object. It outlines the object you are changing to show you where the object will be moved or the new size of the object. When you are pointing to something in the bounding box, the plus sign that indicates your current position is called the *cursor.* When you work with objects, you must select them to let Wysiwyg know which object you want to change. An object is selected when it is marked with selection indicators like the selection indicators on the text in Figure 15-11. Most of the objects you will work with are the graphic objects you add yourself such as text or freehand drawings. You can also select the underlying graphic, which is the 1-2-3 graph or image in a .CGM file. Many of the :Graph Edit commands do not work with the underlying graphic although you can use :Graph Edit commands to change the colors and some other attributes.

Selecting Objects

There are several methods for selecting objects in the graphics editing window. The method you will choose depends on whether you are using a mouse and on the number of objects you want to select. With a mouse you can move the cursor to an object and click on the object. Selecting an object in this way deselects any previously selected objects. You can also deselect an object by clicking on a selected object. If you want to select multiple objects, move to the first corner of a box that you will draw to contain all of the objects to select. Then drag the mouse to draw a box containing all of the objects you want to select. When you release the mouse, the objects that are in the box you drew are selected. You can also select or deselect an object without affecting other selected objects by pressing SHIFT as you select or deselect an object.

Another method of selecting objects is to choose Select from the :Graph Edit menu. This displays another menu with the selections One, All, None, More/Less, Cycle, Graph, and Quit. Selecting One and then selecting an object deselects any other selected objects. You can use this option to select the underlying graphic (the current or named graph, or the image from the .PIC or .CGM file). Choosing All adds the selection indicators to all the objects except the underlying graphic in the graph. Choosing None deselects any selected objects. Choosing More/Less lets you select or deselect objects while keeping other objects selected or deselected. After selecting More/Less, point to an object to select or deselect and press the spacebar. When all of the objects you want to use are selected, press ENTER. Choosing Cycle proceeds through all of the objects in the graphic each time you press a pointer movement key to change the object marked with outlines or selection indicators. To select or deselect the object with the outlines or selection indicators, press the spacebar. You can stop cycling through the objects by pressing ENTER. Choosing Graph selects the underlying graphic and deselects other objects.

Adding Objects to a Graphic

The graphics editing window lets you add several types of objects to a graphic. You can add arrows, ellipses, lines, polygons, rectangles, text, and freehand drawing. To add one of these items, select Add in the graphics editing window and the type of object you want to add. The type of object you add determines the information you must provide. These are the objects you can add and the information you must provide for each object:

Arrow

Move the cursor to where you want the arrow to start and click the left mouse button or press the spacebar. Move to the next point on the line that makes up the arrow and click the left mouse button or press the spacebar. Finally, move to where you want the arrow to end and double-click the left mouse button or press ENTER.

Ellipse

Move the cursor to where you want the corner of the box that will define the ellipse. Next, move to draw the bounding box so that the ellipse can just fit inside it and press ENTER.

Freehand

Move to where you want the freehand drawing to begin. Press the left mouse button and drag it to where you want the lines to be drawn. When you release the left mouse button you can draw another freehand line or double-click the mouse to finish drawing.

Line

Move the cursor to where you want the line to start and click the left mouse button or press the spacebar. Move to the next point on the line and click the left mouse button or press the spacebar. Finally, move to where you want the line to end and double-click the left mouse button or press ENTER.

Polygon

Move the cursor to where you want one corner of the polygon and click the left mouse button or press the spacebar. Next, move to each corner of the polygon and click the left mouse button or press the spacebar. Finally, move to the last corner of the polygon and double-click the left mouse button or press ENTER. Wysiwyg draws a line between the first corner and the last corner of the polygon.

Rectangle

Move the cursor to where you want one corner of the rectangle. Move to draw the bounding box so that it is the size of the rectangle and press ENTER.

Text

Type the text you want to add, using formatting sequences if you want to add formatting to the text. You can also use the contents of a cell by typing a backslash and the cell address containing the text you want to use. After pressing ENTER, move to where you want the text and press ENTER or click the left mouse button.

You can add as many of each of the types of objects as you want. Wysiwyg also has a few features for adding objects. By pressing SHIFT as you select positions for the objects, you can change ellipses to circles and rectangles to squares, and make lines using only 45-degree-angle increments. (In other words, use SHIFT to make sure that your lines are straight.)

Another special feature is available when you must select a position for an object. Besides moving the cursor with the mouse or the arrow keys, you can also type the x- and y-coordinates separated by a comma, as in 400,1600. X- and y-coordinates can range between 0 and 4095 with 0,0 representing the lower-left corner. You can use this feature to ensure that objects you are adding are aligned.

Changing the Appearance of Objects

Once you have added an object, you can make several changes to the object. You can change the colors it uses. For objects with lines, you can change the line width and style. For text objects, you can change the text, font, alignment, and magnification.

Changing the Color of Objects

By selecting Color in the graphics editing window, you can change the colors that the object uses. With graphs you have more color selections than with :Format Color. You can select Lines to change the color of the lines and the outlines in objects like rectangles and freehand drawings. For this option you can select from Black, White, Red, Green, Dark-Blue, Cyan, Yellow, Magenta, and Hidden. You can select Inside and then choose one of the many colors from the palette that Wysiwyg displays to change the inside color of solid objects like rectangles. You can select Map to change up to eight of the colors the underlying graphic uses. Select one of these letters or numbers and select a color to use. This option lets you change the colors of the underlying graphic without using the /Graph commands or needing to create the .PIC or .CGM files with different colors. You can use this command to change the colors of the .CGM files 1-2-3 provides. You can select Background and then select one of the colors from the palette to change the color that is behind an object, such as the background behind text.

Changing the Appearance of Lines

You can make four types of changes to lines. You can change the line width, the line style, the arrowhead style for arrows, and the line smoothing. With these commands, you may select the objects to change before or after entering the command.

To change the line width, select Edit Width and the description of the line width you want. To change the line style, select Edit Line-Style and the description of the line style you want. Initially, lines use the Very Narrow line width and a solid line.

You can also change the arrowheads on arrows. By selecting Edit Arrowheads, you can choose between Switch, One, Two, and None. Switch changes the end of the line where the arrowhead appears. One adds one arrowhead at one end of the line. Two adds arrowheads at both ends of the line. None uses no arrowheads so that the arrows look like regular lines.

With solid objects such as rectangles, polygons, some freehand drawings, and connected lines, you can smooth the lines so that curves rather than angles connect the lines of an object. To change the smoothing, select Edit Smoothing and then None, Tight, or Medium. None, the default, does not use any smoothing, Tight uses the smallest amount, and Medium uses the largest amount of smoothing. Figure 15-12 shows some objects that have different amounts of smoothing.

Changing Text Objects

Wysiwyg has four commands for altering text objects that are not part of the underlying graphic. You can change the text in the text object, the alignment, the font, and the size. By selecting Edit Text, you can alter the text that is in the selected text object and press ENTER when you are finished. By selecting Edit Font, you can alter the font a text object uses from the default (font 1) to one of the eight fonts that are part of the current font set. By selecting Edit Centering, the text is aligned relative to the line area the text occupied when it was originally entered. By selecting Options Font-Magnification and a number between 1 and 1000, which represents the percentage of the text's normal size, you can expand or contract the size of all text in a graphic (including the text in the underlying graphic). By entering a number less than 100 you will shrink the text, and by entering a number greater than 100 you will expand the text. You can also enter 0, which displays the text in the graphic using

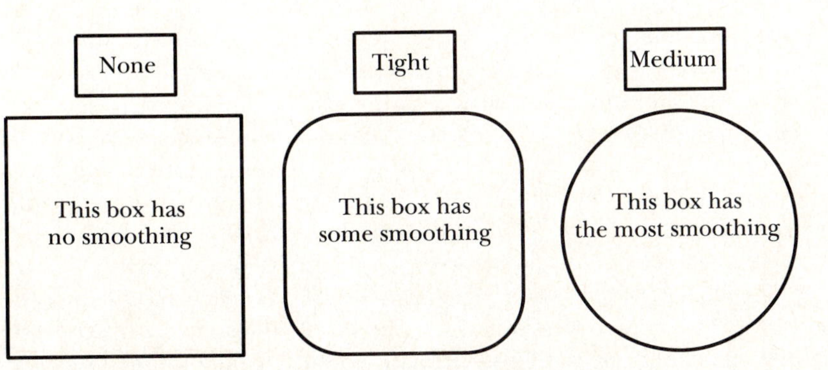

Figure 15-12.   *Different smoothing levels on boxes*

the original point size rather than the default Wysiwyg scaling. With each of the :Graph Edit commands (except Options Font-Magnification), you can either select the objects to change before or after entering the command.

Changing the Graphics Editing Screen

Wysiwyg has two commands that change the appearance of the graphics editing screen without changing the graphic on the screen. You can add grid lines that indicate the cells by selecting Options Grid Yes. The resulting lines indicate the boundaries of each cell used to display the graph. You can hide these lines by selecting Options Grid No. You can also change the cursor to a larger cross or plus sign by selecting Options Cursor Big. By selecting Options Cursor Small, the cursor is returned to its default size.

Rearranging Graph Objects

Wysiwyg has many commands to help you change the position, size, and appearance of objects on the graph to customize the graph to look exactly as you want. With these commands, you can select the objects to change before or after entering the command.

If you want to prevent an object from changing, select the object and then Rearrange Lock. Once an object is locked, it cannot be changed until you select Rearrange Unlock.

To move an object, you can select Rearrange Move. Wysiwyg draws a boundary box around the selected object that you can move. You can also move an object by selecting it and dragging the mouse from the initial location to where you want the object moved. If you press SHIFT while you move the object, you will only move the object in 45-degree increments. You can use this when you want to move an object up or down without moving it sideways.

You can also change the size of objects. To alter the size of an object, select Transform Size. Wysiwyg draws a boundary box around the selected object that you are resizing. You can move the lower right corner of the box to a new location to expand or contract the size of the selected object. The new size of the boundary box sets the size of the object in it. By pressing SHIFT while you change the object's opposite corner, the resized object will have the same height-to-width proportion as the original.

To copy an object, select Rearrange Copy and Wysiwyg creates a copy of the selected object next to the original. You can also copy objects by selecting them and pressing INS. The copied version of an object becomes the only selected object. Therefore, you can immediately use Rearrange Move to move it to a new location.

To delete an object, select Rearrange Delete. You can also delete objects by selecting the objects and pressing DEL. If you discover that you deleted the wrong object, select Rearrange Restore and the last object (or group of objects) is returned to the graphic.

As you add more objects, the overlaying objects are placed on top of each other. You can change which objects are on the top and bottom. To place an object to display on top of other overlaying ones, select the object and Rearrange Front. To move a selected object to the bottom, select Rearrange Back.

Wysiwyg has several commands that rotate and flip objects. To turn an object 90 degrees counterclockwise, select Transform Quarter-Turn. Each time you use this command the selected objects are rotated an additional 90 degrees. If you want to rotate an object by a different increment, select Transform Rotate and move the cursor in the direction you want the object rotated or type the number of degrees you want the object rotated. To flip an object so that it is backwards, select Transform X-Flip. To flip an object so that it is upside down, select Transform Y-Flip.

Another variation of rotating is *skewing* the object one way or another. You can change the vertical slant of an object by selecting Transform Vertical. This shifts the vertical sides of an object in different directions. You can change the horizontal slant of an object by selecting Transform Horizontal. This shifts the horizontal sides of an object in different directions. Figure 15-13 shows both types of skewing added to objects. You cannot use this feature with the underlying graphic. Also, selecting Transform Vertical for text changes the vertical position where each letter starts without changing the slant of the letters. Horizontal skewing has no effect. If you make changes with the Transform menu that you do not like, you can remove the effect of all Transform commands made while the same objects were selected by selecting Transform Clear.

Changing How Graphics Appear in the Graphics Editing Window

Wysiwyg has several commands that let you change the amount of the graphic that appears in the graphics editing window. You can use these commands to look at the

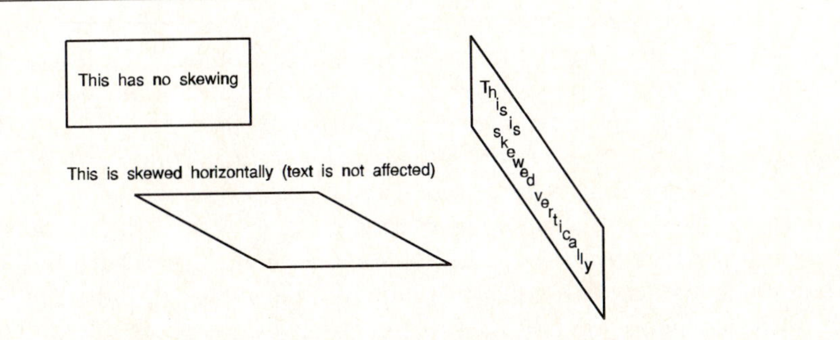

Figure 15-13.   *The skewing boxes and text*

graphic in greater detail. To look at the graph closer up, you can type + or select View +. Each time you type + or select View +, Wysiwyg expands the graphic that appears in the graphics window. You can expand the graphic five times with + or View + as well as contract it by typing − or selecting View −.

Another method of zooming into the graphic is the View In command. When you select the View In command, you must select a rectangle in the graphic that you want to see in greater detail. Wysiwyg blows up this selected area so that it is larger. You can return to displaying the entire graphic by typing + or selecting View + several times or by using the View Full command once.

When you are looking at a graphic closely, you may want to change the part of the graphic that appears in the graphics editing window. When you select View and then Up, Down, Left, or Right, Wysiwyg shifts the graphic a half screen in the direction you select. If you expect to move the graphic around in the graphics editing window frequently, you may want to use the View Pan command. When you select View Pan, you can utilize the View commands also available through the other View menu choices. You can type + and − to expand and contract the graphic and use the arrow keys to shift the part of the graphic that appears in the graphics editing window until you press ENTER to return to the main graphics editing window menu.

Printing with Wysiwyg

Wysiwyg offers more print options than are available with 1-2-3. Wysiwyg can print with the additional formatting available through Wysiwyg's menu commands and formatting sequences, which exceed 1-2-3's Print menu commands. Also, Wysiwyg can maintain a library of layout sheets that are definition templates for a report or group of reports. By using Wysiwyg to print, you can also alter many of the configuration options and settings directly from the :Print menu. With its preview feature Wysiwyg can also show you how the output will appear.

As you use Wysiwyg's :Print menus, a dialog box displays many of the print settings. Figure 15-14 shows the :Print menu and the dialog box. You can always remove the dialog box and display the worksheet below by selecting Info. Some of the commands like Go, File, and Range should already be familiar since 1-2-3 has similar options. Range allows you to define the area of the worksheet to be printed. Printing does not take place until you have selected a print range with Range and started the print operation with the menu command Go, File, or Background. The File selection tells Wysiwyg that you want your output directed to an encoded file. This feature works similarly to the /Print Encoded command in 1-2-3. The Background selection is just like /Print Background for printing worksheets in the background. Other options that you select from the :Print menu will affect the printout. You will find other familiar options in some of the second-level print selections.

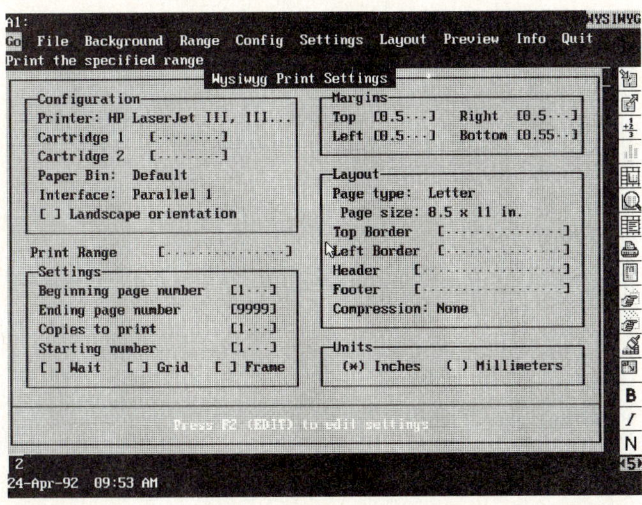

Figure 15-14.   *The Wysiwyg Print Settings dialog box*

Wysiwyg formats will print only if you print with Wysiwyg, not 1-2-3. If you print a range with 1-2-3 that contains Wysiwyg formatting sequences, they will not print as planned.

The Basic Print Process

Printing in Wysiwyg can be easy if you want to use Wysiwyg's defaults. To print a worksheet with Wysiwyg, select :Print Range Set. This command selects the range to print. Like printing in 1-2-3, any hidden columns are not printed. You can, however, print a worksheet range that has a graph added with the :Graph Add command to print the graph. Once you select the range to print, Wysiwyg adds dashed lines to the worksheet area, indicating where it will break the output into pages.

Wysiwyg displays in the control panel the {Page} Wysiwyg format indicator when the cell pointer is on a cell where the range is divided into pages. You can use these page indicators to determine whether you want to add your own page breaks or to change the worksheet so that more worksheet data will fit on each page. If you want to remove the setting for the ranges to print, select :Print Range Clear. You will probably use the :Print Quit command to return to the READY mode and make final modifications to the worksheet range you want to print.

Once the range to print is selected, you can print the worksheet with Wysiwyg by selecting :Print Go. This command prints the worksheet to the printer. If you want to print the worksheet to a file, select :Print File and type the name of the file in which

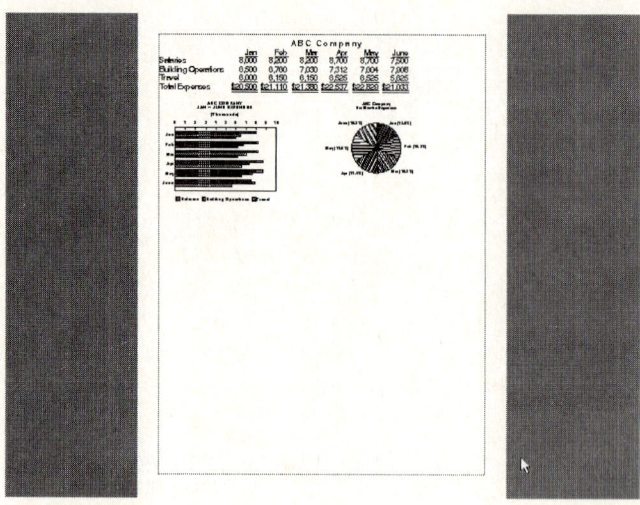

Figure 15-15.   *Previewing a worksheet to print*

you want the output saved. This file will have an .ENC extension and will contain all of the information the installed printer needs to print the output as desired. Unlike 1-2-3, Wysiwyg will print to a file as soon as you select File, provide a filename, and press ENTER. Since Wysiwyg uses more graphics features than 1-2-3, these .ENC files will be much larger than the .ENC files you create with /Print Encoded. A file created with the :Print File command should only be printed to the same type of printer that is listed in the status screen, since each type of printer uses different printer codes.

Like 1-2-3 you can also print in the background with Wysiwyg by selecting Background and the name of the temporary file where Wysiwyg will write the information it will send to the printer. Like background printing in 1-2-3, you must load BPRINT at the DOS prompt before you use :Print Background. Like printing to a file, background printing starts once you select Background and provide the name of the file to use.

If you want to see how your selected print range will look when it is printed, select Preview. This displays your worksheet as it will appear when printed, as shown in Figure 15-15. When the output prints on several pages, pressing any key except ESC displays the next page. Pressing ESC or pressing any key when you are viewing the last page returns you to the :Print menu.

With Release 2.4, you can select the Page Preview icon from the SmartIcons palette as a shortcut for both setting a print range and previewing how the range will print. First, highlight the range you wish to print or preview. Then select the Page Preview icon (shown below). You can view how the selected range will print just as if you had selected Preview from the menu. Press any key to return to the worksheet. The range you selected is now set as a print range.

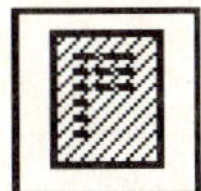

Adding Page Breaks

If you are not happy with the page breaks inserted by Wysiwyg, you can set your own manual page breaks. The page breaks that you set with Wysiwyg are different from the page breaks you set with 1-2-3. These page breaks are not interchangeable. Also, you can add both column and row page breaks, unlike 1-2-3. To add a page break, move the cell pointer to the cell in the first column or row that you want on the next page. Select :Worksheet Page. To add a page break so that the current column is the first column on the new page, select Column. To add a page break so that the current row is the first row on the new page, select Row. When you add a page break, Wysiwyg displays a dashed line where the page break is located. When you have finished adding page breaks, select Quit to return to the READY mode. You can delete the page breaks by selecting :Worksheet Page Delete. When your cell pointer is positioned at the location of a page break, this command deletes page breaks at the current column and row. If you do not want to see the dashed lines representing page breaks, select :Display Options Page-Breaks No.

With Release 2.4, you can select one of two icons from the SmartIcons palette to insert Wysiwyg page breaks. One icon inserts horizontal page breaks, the other vertical page breaks. To insert a page break using the icons, position the cell pointer in a cell in the row that you want to be the first row of the new page or in the column that you want to be the first column on a new page. Then select the appropriate icon. A dashed line will appear, indicating where the page break falls. the Page Break icons are shown here:

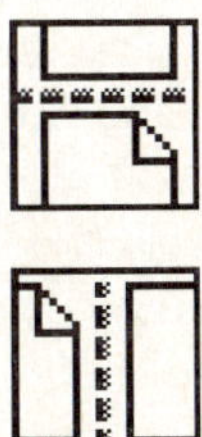

Layout Options

The :Print Layout commands control the page layout. These commands are similar to the commands found in 1-2-3's Print Options menu although there are a number of new additions. The :Print Layout menu is a sticky menu; you can select Quit or press ESC when you want to return to the :Print menu.

Setting the Page Size

Wysiwyg can print on any page size that your printer supports. You can select the page size with the :Print Layout Page-Size command. Your choices are 1:Letter (8 1/2" x 11"), 2:A4 (8.268" x 11.693"), 3:80x66 (8 1/2" x 11" fanfold), 4:132x66 (14" x 11" fanfold), 5:80x72 (8 1/2" x 12" fanfold), 6:Legal (8 1/2" x 14"), 7:B5 (6.929" x 9.843"), and Custom. If you select Custom, type the length and the width followed by "in" for inches, "mm" for millimeters, or "cm" for centimeters.

Setting Margins

By default Wysiwyg uses .5 inch for the top, left, and right margins and .55 for the bottom margin. You can change these margins by selecting :Print Layout Margins. For the four options Left, Right, Top, and Bottom, select the option to change and type the new margin followed by "in" for inches, "mm" for millimeters, or "cm" for centimeters. After setting the margins, select Quit to return to the :Print Layout menu. The total of the left and right margins must be less than the page width and the total of the top and bottom margins must be less than the page height.

Adding a Header or Footer

Just as in 1-2-3, you can add headers and footers to the page layout. To add a header or footer select :Print Layout Titles and either Header or Footer. The header and footer must follow the same rules as in 1-2-3, which means that you can have up to 240 characters and you can use special characters such as #, @, |, and \. (The rules and examples for headers and footers are provided in Chapter 6.)

You can use formatting sequences to add formatting to a header or footer. The 240-character limit includes formatting sequences and special characters created with ALT-F1, which may use more than one character of memory. The header and footer in Wysiwyg are separate from the header and footer in 1-2-3. Therefore, when you first select :Print Layout Titles Header or Footer, you will not see any header or footer entered with the /Print Printer Options Header or Footer command. When you use a header or footer, Wysiwyg skips two lines between the header or footer and the worksheet data. To remove a header or footer, select Clear and then Header, Footer, or Both. You will also need to select Quit when you are finished with the :Print Layout Titles menu.

Border Options

Wysiwyg can also have border columns and rows that print on every page just like the 1-2-3 /Print Printer Borders command. This lets you maintain column and row headings on long and wide worksheets. To add borders select :Print Layout Borders. To add rows at the top of every page, select Top and a range containing cells from the rows you want to use. To add columns on the left of every page, select Left and a range containing cells from the columns you want to use. If you later decide that you do not want these border columns or rows, select Clear and then Top, Left, or All to select the borders to remove. When you have finished selecting the border columns and/or rows, select Quit to return to the :Print Layout menu. As with 1-2-3, you do not want to include the same columns and rows in the print range that you are using in the border because if you do they will print twice. Since the Borders option works the same as in 1-2-3 you may want to look at the examples in Chapter 6.

Compressing the Layout

One of Wysiwyg's unique features is the ability to compress or expand the printed output. You can compress the output to fit on one page or tell Wysiwyg by how much you want the output expanded or contracted. To change the compression of the output, select :Print Layout Compression. If you select Automatic, Wysiwyg will compress the output so that it fits on one page. If the output range contains manual page breaks that you added with the :Worksheet Page command, Wysiwyg uses these page breaks to determine how each page should be compressed. You can also select Manual. If you select Manual, you must enter the percentage by which you want the output compressed as a number between 15 and 1000. Numbers less than 100 compress the output and numbers greater than 100 expand the output. For example, a Manual compression of 50 compresses the output to 50 percent of its original size while a compression of 500 expands the output to five times (500 percent) its original size. The third choice is None, which does not compress or expand the output. None is the default.

Creating a Library of Page Layouts

Wysiwyg allows you to create and maintain a library of page layouts. You can retrieve any layout and use it in your next print request. The :Print Layout Library commands are Erase, Retrieve, and Save.

Like other Erase commands, this Erase option eliminates a page layout library file on disk. The Save option allows you to specify a name for the current layout and save it to disk for later use. The Retrieve option reads the specified page layout from disk, making it the current layout. Its settings are used to define the print settings for the :Print Go command. Wysiwyg page layout libraries are stored in files with .ALS extensions.

Setting the Page Layout Default

If you frequently use the same settings for the page layout, you will want to make these settings the defaults. Another use of a page layout default is to replace the current page settings with the page layout defaults that Wysiwyg has saved as part of its configuration file. To make the current page layout become the new default page layout, select :Print Layout Default Update. If you want to make the default page layout replace the current page layout settings, select :Print Layout Default Restore. The default page layout is stored in the file called LAYOUT.CNF.

Changing Print Configuration Options

You can change your print configuration from the Wysiwyg :Print menu with the :Print Config command. These configuration settings include font cartridges, printer interface, print bin, and orientation. When you are finished with the :Print Config menu, select Quit to return to the :Print menu.

The Printer option selects the printer to use from a list of printers installed during 1-2-3 installation. The Interface option selects the connection between your computer and your printer. You can select from Parallel 1, Serial 1, Parallel 2, Serial 2, or the DOS devices LPT1, LPT2, LPT3, COM1, or COM2. This option presents the same settings as the 1-2-3 /Worksheet Global Default Printer Interface command.

The Orientation options let you change the direction of print on the output page. Portrait output is standard with the lines of print running across the 8 1/2-inch sheet of paper. Landscape output uses the paper sideways and prints lines across the 11-inch width. By selecting Landscape, you can print your output sideways if your printer supports this.

If you are using a printer that supports font cartridges or font cards, you can tell Wysiwyg which cartridges are installed so that you can use these fonts in Wysiwyg. By selecting 1st-Cart or 2nd-Cart and one of the font-cartridge or font-card files, the fonts will become available with the :Format Font Replace command. It is important that you select the correct font cartridge or font card files to get the results you want.

If your printer has multiple paper feeding options, you can select how paper is fed to the printer by selecting Bin. The Bin option has five choices: Reset, Single-Sheet, Manual, Upper-Tray, and Lower-Tray. Upper-Tray and Lower-Tray select which of two trays the printer takes paper from if the printer has two paper trays. Single-Sheet uses the printer's single-sheet feeder and Manual uses the printer's manual paper-feed option. Reset removes the setting made by one of the other four choices.

Altering Print Settings

The :Print Settings command lets you choose options for how Wysiwyg will print the range you select. This command has the options Begin, End, Start-Number, Copies, Wait, Grid, Frame, Reset, and Quit. The Reset option returns all settings for the other options to the default setup and Quit returns to the :Print menu.

If you are printing a report that you want to combine with other documents, you may want the page number to start with a different number than 1. By selecting Start-Number and typing a new number, you set the page number of the first page of the output to whatever number you type.

After selecting a print range you may decide that you do not want to print the entire range. This is especially true if you made a correction to the worksheet and you need to reprint only one page. Rather than redefining the print range, you can select :Print Settings Begin and type the number of the first page of the selected range to print. Next, select End and type the number of the last page of the selected range to print. These two options depend on the Start-Number option. For example, if you use 3 and 4 for the Begin and End options and start numbering pages with 3, Wysiwyg will print the first two pages of the selected range because these pages have page numbers that start with 3 and end with 4.

The Copies option lets you print more than one copy by entering a number other than 1. The Wait option is used for situations when you need to hand-feed sheets into your printer. Selecting Wait Yes causes Wysiwyg to wait until you insert a sheet of paper before continuing printing the next sheet.

The Frame and Grid options select whether Wysiwyg will print the worksheet frame and the grid. Selecting Yes for either of these options prints the selected option and selecting No (the default) omits the option. Unlike the other options for the settings commands, the settings for these two options are saved with the format file. The settings chosen for the other options are only in effect for the current session.

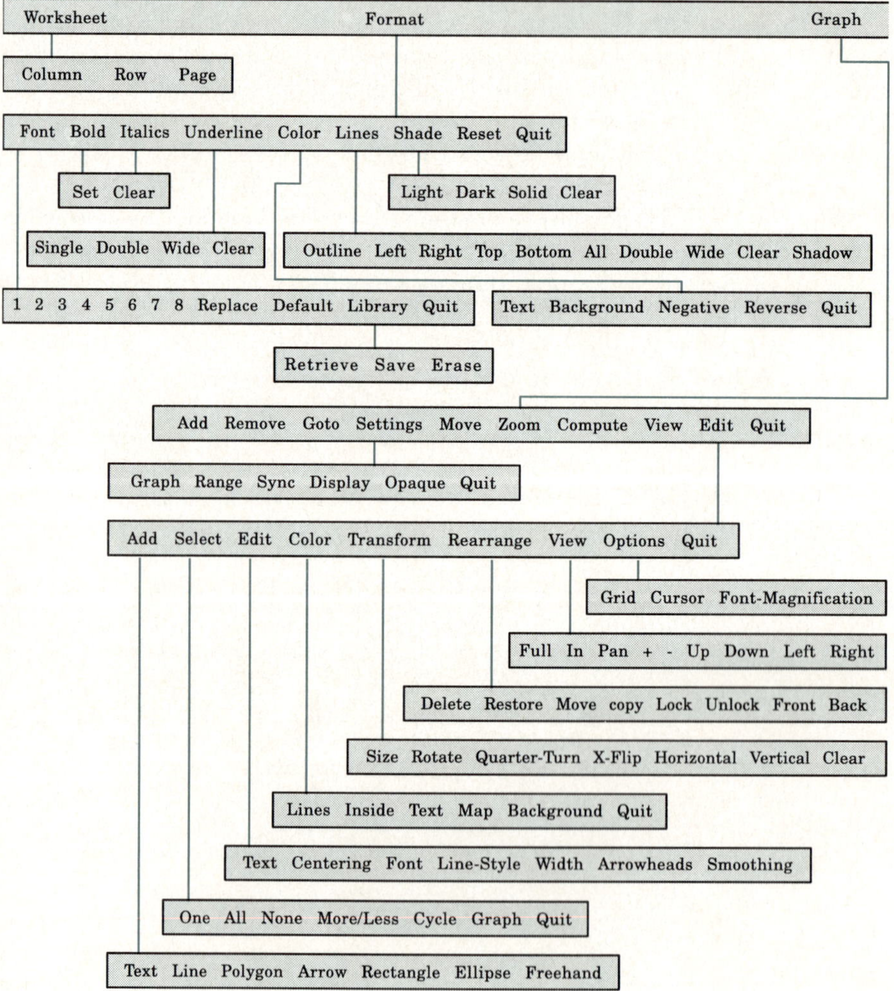

Worksheet   Format   Graph
Column   Row   Page
Font Bold Italics Underline Color Lines Shade Reset Quit
Set Clear
Light Dark Solid Clear
Single Double Wide Clear
Outline Left Right Top Bottom All Double Wide Clear Shadow
1 2 3 4 5 6 7 8 Replace Default Library Quit
Text Background Negative Reverse Quit
Retrieve Save Erase
Add Remove Goto Settings Move Zoom Compute View Edit Quit
Graph Range Sync Display Opaque Quit
Add Select Edit Color Transform Rearrange View Options Quit
Grid Cursor Font-Magnification
Full In Pan + - Up Down Left Right
Delete Restore Move copy Lock Unlock Front Back
Size Rotate Quarter-Turn X-Flip Horizontal Vertical Clear
Lines Inside Text Map Background Quit
Text Centering Font Line-Style Width Arrowheads Smoothing
One All None More/Less Cycle Graph Quit
Text Line Polygon Arrow Rectangle Ellipse Freehand

WYSIWYG

Print   Display   Special   Text   Named-Style   Quit
Copy Move Import Export
1 2 3 4 5 6 7 8 Define
Edit Align Reformat Set Clear
Mode Zoom Colors Options Font-Directory Rows Default Quit
Restore Update
Graphics Text B&W Color
Tiny Small Normal Large Huge Manual
Frame Grid Page-Breaks Cell-Pointer Intensity Adapter Quit
1-2-3 Enhanced Relief Special None
Background Text Unprot Cell-Pointer Grid Frame Neg Lines Shadow Replace Quit
Go file Backround Range Config Settings Layout Preview Info Quit
Set Clear
Page-Size Margins Titles Borders Compression Default Library Quit
Left Right Top Bottom Quit
Top Left Clear Quit
Retrieve Save Erase
Header Footer Clear Quit
None Manual Automatic
Restore Update
Begin End Start-Number Copies Wait Grid Frame Reset Quit
Printer Interface 1st-Cart 2nd-Cart Orientation Bin Quit

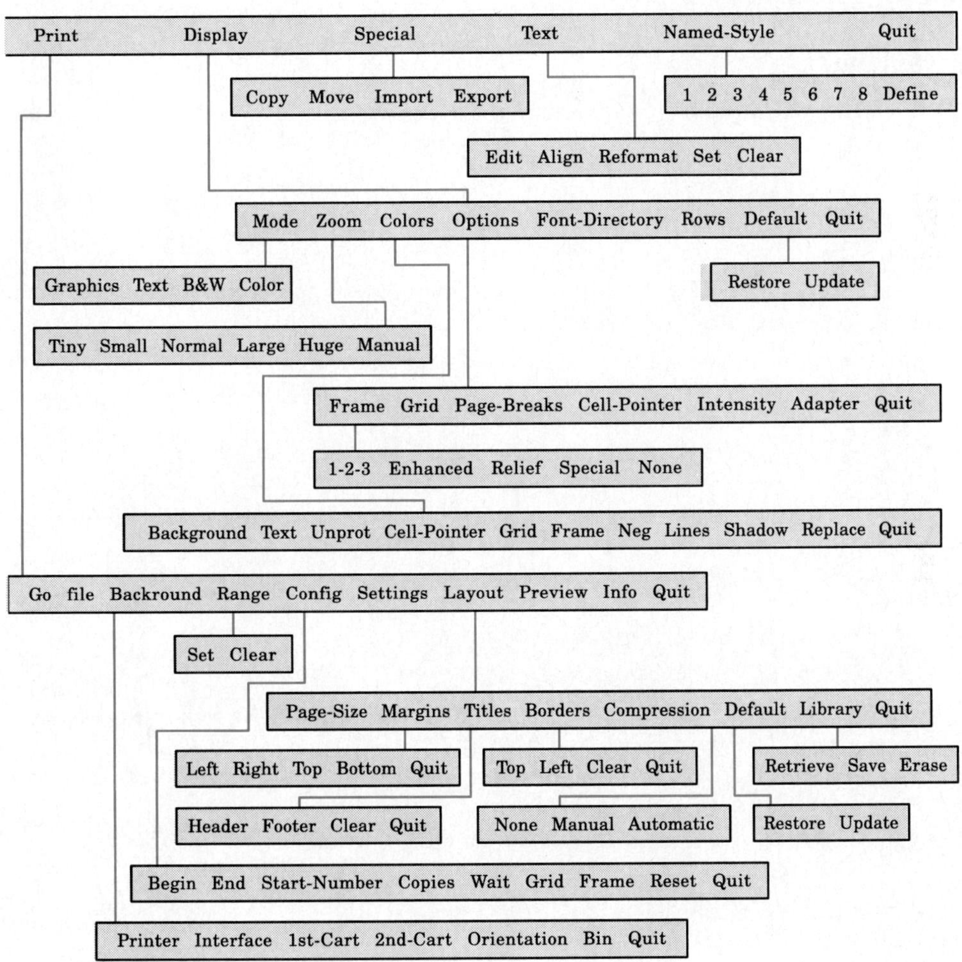

Wysiwyg Commands

Wysiwyg is an Add-In for 1-2-3 Releases 2.3 and above. It adds spreadsheet publishing features to 1-2-3.

:Display Colors

Description

The :Display Colors command customizes the Wysiwyg display if you have a color monitor.

Options

This command has 11 different options. The eight default colors to choose from are black, white, red, green, dark-blue, cyan, yellow, and magenta.

Background   This option selects the color for the background.

Text   This option selects the color for the text.

Unprot   This option selects the color for the text of unprotected cells.

Cell-Pointer   This option selects the color for the cell pointer.

Grid   This option selects the color for the grid lines.

Frame   This option selects the color for the worksheet frame.

Neg   This option selects the color for negative values in the worksheet.

Lines   This option selects the color for the cell borders.

Shadow   This option selects the color for drop shadows.

Replace   This option selects the eight colors used by the other options. Select the color to change and type a number between 0 and 63 to adjust the color.

Quit   This option returns you to the :Display menu.

:Display Default

Description

This command replaces the current display settings with the default settings or creates new default settings. The default settings are those used by Wysiwyg when you load it. This includes most of the settings made through :Display.

Options

Restore   This option replaces the current display settings with the default settings.

Update   This option replaces the default display settings with the current display settings.

:Display Font-Directory

Description

This command chooses the directory that contains the Wysiwyg fonts.

Options

Your only option with this command is which directory to use.

:Display Mode

Description

This command selects between text and graphics modes, assuming your monitor can support both modes. In graphics mode you can see the output on the screen exactly as it prints. In text mode your display looks like the 1-2-3 display. The Wysiwyg features selected still print but do not affect the appearance of the 1-2-3 display.

Options

Graphics   This option displays the worksheet as it will look when printed.

Text   This option displays the worksheet as it appears in 1-2-3 without Wysiwyg loaded.

B&W   This option sets the worksheet display to black-and-white graphics mode.

Color   This option sets the worksheet display to color graphics mode.

:Display Options Adapter

Description

This command sets the display adapter Wysiwyg uses to display your worksheet in graphics mode.

Options

Your choices for this command are Auto, which uses the monitor and display selection made in 1-2-3's Install program; the numbers 1 through 9, which display your worksheet using different display types as described in the line below the menu; and Blink, which determines how Wysiwyg uses the blinking attribute. 1-2-3 will not let you select one of the options if it is not appropriate for your system.

:Display Options Cell Pointer

Description

This command chooses the appearance of the cell pointer.

Options

Solid   This option displays the cell pointer as a solid rectangle.

Outline   This option displays the cell pointer as an outline.

:Display Options Frame

Description

This command chooses how the worksheet frame appears. Changing the frame does not change the column and row orientation of 1-2-3.

Options

1-2-3　This option displays the standard 1-2-3 worksheet frame, which has no lines separating the column and row headings.

Enhanced　This option displays the default Wysiwyg worksheet frame, which has lines separating the column and row headings.

Relief　This option makes the worksheet frame appear as three-dimensional.

Special　This option causes the worksheet frame to appear as a ruler indicating characters, inches, centimeters, or points/picas. Select Characters, Inches, Metric, or Points/Picas to select the type of ruler you want.

None　This option hides the worksheet frame. Your screen will have no row and column headings.

:Display Options Grid

Description

This command makes the grid lines that mark the boundaries of each cell appear or disappear.

Options

The only options for this command are Yes and No. Yes displays the grid lines, while No hides the grid lines.

:Display Options Intensity

Description

This command determines the brightness level of the display screen.

Options

Normal　This option causes the screen to have normal brightness.

High　This option causes the screen to have a high brightness level.

:Display Options Page-Breaks

Description

This command sets whether page breaks are displayed in the worksheet.

Options

This command has the options of Yes and No. Choosing Yes displays the page breaks, while choosing No hides the page breaks.

:Display Options Quit

Description

This command returns to the :Display menu.

:Display Quit

Description

This command leaves the :Display menu and returns to the READY mode.

:Display Rows

Description

This command chooses how many rows appear on the screen.

Option

The only option is the number of rows to display on the screen (between 16 and 60). The higher the number you choose, the smaller the size of the rows displayed.

:Display Zoom

Description

 This command is used in graphics mode to change the size of the cells in the worksheet display. It makes the normal cell size either larger or smaller.

Options

Tiny   This option displays cells at 63 percent of normal size.

Small   This option displays cells at 87 percent of normal size.

Normal   This option displays the cells in their actual size.

Large   This option displays the cells at 125 percent of normal size.

Huge   This option displays the cells at 150 percent of normal size.

Manual   This option manually reduces or enlarges the cell size. You can choose a number from 25 to 400, where 400 is the largest cell size (400 percent of normal size).

:Format Bold

Description

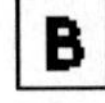 This command either sets or removes boldface for a range of cells. To use this format while editing text press CTRL-A, type b, type the text you want to boldface, press CTRL-E, and type b. You can select the range for the format either before selecting :Format Bold or after selecting an option.

Options

Set   This option adds boldface to the selected range.

Clear   This option eliminates any boldface from the range.

:Format Color

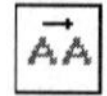

Description

This command specifies the colors of a range for both displaying and printing (if you have a color printer). To use this format within a cell, press CTRL-A and type **1c** (default color), **2c** (red), **3c** (green) **4c** (dark- blue), **5c** (cyan), **6c** (yellow), **7c** (magenta), or **8c** (reversed colors). When you are finished, press CTRL-E and type the same formatting sequence.

Options

Text   This option selects the color of a range of cells. You can choose from Normal (the default color), Red, Green, Dark-Blue, Cyan, Yellow, and Red.

Background   This option chooses the color of the background of a range of cells. You can choose from Normal (the default color), Red, Green, Dark-Blue, Cyan, Yellow, and Magenta.

Negative   This option chooses the color of negative values in a range of cells. You can select Normal (the default color) or Red as the color for these cells.

Reverse   This option reverses the colors of the text and background of cells in the chosen range.

Quit   This option leaves the menu and returns you to the READY mode.

:Format Font

Description

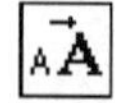

The :Format Font command allows you to assign fonts to ranges and select the fonts that are part of the current font set. When you select this command, a list of the eight current fonts appears on the screen. To use this format within a cell press CTRL-A and type **1F** (font 1), **2F** (font 2), **3F** (font 3), **4F** (font 4), **5F** (font 5), **6F** (font 6), **7F** (font 7), or **8F** (font 8). Press CTRL-E and type the same formatting code when you are finished. You can also press CTRL-A and type **d** (subscript) or **u** (superscript) for other formats.

Options

1 Through 8   This option assigns the selected font to a range that you select before entering the :Font Format command or after selecting a number between 1 and 8.

Replace   This option replaces one of the fonts in the current font set with the fonts from the master directory. Select the number of the font to replace and the style desired; then type the point size and press ENTER.

Default   This option replaces the current font set with the default font set or saves the current font set as the default. When you choose this option, you must choose Restore (which replaces the current font set with the default), or Update (which replaces the default font set with the current font set).

Library   This option maintains the font libraries. It gives you three choices. Select Retrieve and a font library file with an .AFS extension to replace the currently selected fonts with the fonts in the font library file. Select Save and enter a filename to save the current set of fonts as a font library file. Select Erase and a font library file to remove the file from the disk.

Quit   This option returns you to the READY mode.

:Format Italics

Description

I   This command adds or removes italics from a range of cells. To use this format within a cell, press CTRL-A, type i type the text to italicize, press CTRL-E, and type i again. You can select the range for this command before entering the command or after selecting an option.

Options

Set   This option adds italics to a range of cells.

Clear   This option removes italics from a range of cells.

:Format Lines

Description

This command creates lines, boxes, or outlining around cells. You can use this command to create a box around a range of worksheet cells or to draw lines anywhere on the output. You can select the range this command uses before selecting :Format Lines or after selecting one of the options.

Options

Outline   This option draws an outline around the range of cells.

Left   This option draws lines at the left edge of the cells in the range.

Right   This option draws lines at the right edge of the cells in the range.

Top   This option draws lines at the top of the cells in the range.

Bottom   This option draws lines at the bottom of the cells in the range.

All   This option draws a box around each cell in the range.

Double   This option adds double lines. Choose from Outline, Left, Right, Top, Bottom, or All for the location to draw the lines.

Wide   This option draws wide lines. Choose from Outline, Left, Right, Top, Bottom, or All for the location to draw the lines.

Clear   This option removes any lines assigned to cells in the range. Choose Outline, Left, Right, Top, Bottom, or All to select the location of the lines to remove.

Shadow   This option adds (Set) or removes (Clear) a shadow from a range. A shadow is dark shading added to the bottom and right side of the range.

:Format Quit

Description

This command returns you to the READY mode.

:Format Reset

Description

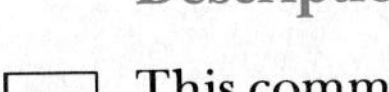

This command removes all the formatting applied to a cell or range in one easy step. It removes boldface, underlining, shading, and lines. It establishes font 1 for the cell with the default display color.

Options

The only option for this command is the range you select to reset.

:Format Shade

Description

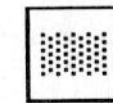

This command adds contrast to your display and printouts through the addition or removal of shaded backgrounds on any range of cells. You can select the range this command alters either before you select :Format Shade or after you select one of the options.

Options

Light   This option adds light shading to the range.

Dark   This option adds dark shading to the range.

Solid   This option adds solid shading to the range.

Clear   This option removes any shading already assigned to a range of cells.

:Format Underline

Description

This command adds different kinds of underlining to one or more cells. To use this format within a cell press CTRL-A and type 1_ (single underlining), 2_ (double underlining), or **3_** (wide underlining). Press CTRL-E and type 1_, **2_**, or 3_ when you are finished. You can select the range this command affects either before you select :Format Underline or after you select one of these options.

Options

Single   This option adds a single underline under all the text in the range selected.

Double   This option adds a double underline under all the text in the range.

Wide   This option adds a wide underline under all the text in the range.

Clear   This option removes any underlining currently used in the specified range.

:Graph Add

Description

 This command adds graphs to the worksheet. Wysiwyg sizes the graph to fit within the range that you specify. You can also change the range for the graph once it is placed to alter its size.

Options

After selecting one of these options and any graph or filename the option requires, you must select the worksheet range where Wysiwyg will display the graph.

Current   This option adds the current graph to the worksheet.

Named   This option adds a named graph to the worksheet. Select a named graph from the list Wysiwyg provides.

PIC   This option adds a graph in a .PIC file to the worksheet. Select a .PIC file to add.

Metafile   This option adds a graphic image in a .CGM file to the worksheet. Select a .CGM file to add.

Blank   This option marks a worksheet range where you will eventually place a graph or create your own graphic image.

Note

Changing the row height and the column width of the cells within the range used by the graph alters its size as well.

:Graph Compute

Description

This command updates all graphs added to active worksheet files. This means that .PIC and .CGM graph files are read into the worksheet and 1-2-3 updates the current and named graphs to reflect changes in the graph settings or worksheet data.

:Graph Edit Add

Description

This command adds various items to a graph. You must select the graph to alter at Wysiwyg's prompt (you can press F3 (NAME) to list the graph names) or select a cell from the range used to display the graph you want to alter.

Options

Text   This option adds text to this graph. Type the text you want to add (or type a \ and the address or range name of the cell containing the content you want to use), press ENTER, move the text to where you want it to appear, and press ENTER again. You can use CTRL-A formatting sequences to add formatting to the text.

Line   This option adds a line to the graph. Move to the first point on the line, press the spacebar, move to the ending position of the line, and press ENTER.

Polygon   This option adds a polygon to the graph. Move to where you want a corner of the polygon and press the spacebar. Continue moving to each corner and pressing the spacebar. When you move to the last corner of the polygon press ENTER. Wysiwyg will draw the line for the last side of the polygon.

Arrow   This option adds an arrow to the graph. Move to the beginning point of the arrow, press the spacebar, move to the ending position for the arrow, and press ENTER.

Rectangle   This option adds a rectangle to the graph. Move to where you want the first corner of the box, press the spacebar, move to the opposite corner of the box, and press ENTER.

Ellipse   This option adds an ellipse or a circle to the graph. Move to where you want the first corner of the box that defines the ellipse's size, press the spacebar, move to the opposite corner of the box, and press ENTER.

Freehand   This option draws freehand lines on the graph. Move to the first point where you want to start drawing lines and press the spacebar. As you move on the graph, Wysiwyg draws lines that follow your movements until you press ENTER.

Note

By pressing SHIFT as you move on the graph, you can adjust the object you are drawing so that a rectangle becomes a square, an ellipse becomes a circle, and lines are drawn at 45-degree increments.

:Graph Edit Color

Description

This command chooses from numerous colors for the graph and objects that have been added to the graph.

Options

The options for this command select the color used by a graph object or the entire graph. When using this command, you can either select the object before you select the command or after you select the color to be used by the object.

Lines   This option selects the color for specific lines and outlines.

Inside   This option selects the color to use to fill a specific object of the graph.

Text   This option chooses a color for specific text.

Map   This option changes the graph's colors to different colors.

Background   This option selects the color for the background of the graph.

:Graph Edit Edit

Description

This command manipulates objects that are added to the graph. You can either select the object to edit before selecting this command or after making the choices for the selected option.

Options

Text   This option edits text that has been added to the graph. Edit the text and press ENTER when you are finished.

Centering   This option chooses the alignment for text that is added to the graph— either left, center, or right.

Font   This option changes the font of text in an object to one of the eight font choices given with the :Format Font command.

Line-Style   This option changes the type of lines used by an object. Select from 1:Solid, 2:Dashed, 3:Dotted, 4:Long-Dashed, 5:Chain-Dotted, 6:Chain-Dashed, and 7:Hidden.

Width   This option changes the width of the lines used by an object. Select from 1:Very-Narrow, 2:Narrow, 3:Medium, 4:Wide, and 5:Very-Wide.

Arrowheads   This option alters the direction that the arrow points (Switch), adds an arrowhead to a line (One), adds arrowheads to both ends of the line (Two), and removes arrowheads from lines (None).

Smoothing   This option takes an object and replaces its angles with curves. The choices for this option vary the degree of smoothing. Select from None (objects appear without smoothing), Tight (some smoothing is present), and Medium (objects appear with the most smoothing possible). (Refer back to Figure 15-12.)

:Graph Edit Options

Description

This command changes the size of all of the text in a graph, changes the cursor size, or adds or removes grid lines in the graph.

Options

Grid   This option adds (Yes) or removes (No) grid lines that indicate cell boundaries in the graph.

Cursor   This option changes the size of the graphics editing window cursor. The cursor either appears as a small cross (if you choose Small) or a large cross (if you choose Big).

Font-Magnification   This option changes the text size of all of the text in a graph. You can choose a number between 0 and 1000 for the scaling factor. Numbers less than 100 decrease the font size, and numbers greater than 100 increase the font size. Zero uses the point size chosen for the text without adjusting it for the graph size.

:Graph Edit Quit

Description

This command returns you to the READY mode in 1-2-3. This is the only way you can leave the :Graph Edit menu.

:Graph Edit Rearrange

Description

This command rearranges objects in a graph. For all of the options except Restore, you can select the object before or after selecting the command.

Options

Delete   This option removes objects from the graph. You can also delete selected objects by pressing the DEL key.

Restore   This option restores the object that was last deleted.

Move   This option moves objects to a new location. Simply move the object to the new location and press ENTER.

Copy   This option copies objects in your graph next to the original. You can also copy objects by pressing the INS key.

Lock   This option locks objects so that they cannot be altered.

Unlock   This option enables locked objects to be altered.

Front   This option places selected objects in front of other objects.

Back   This option places selected objects behind other objects.

:Graph Edit Select

Description

This command selects objects to use with the :Graph Edit commands.

Options

One   This option selects one object to edit.

All   This option selects all the objects to edit except the underlying graph.

None   This option deselects all objects.

More/Less   This option selects more or fewer objects to edit. Selecting an unselected object adds the object to the current selection. Selecting a selected object removes the object from the current selection.

Cycle   This option selects objects to edit by cycling through all of the objects. Press the arrow keys to cycle through the objects. Press the spacebar to select the object and ENTER when you're finished selecting objects.

Graph   This option selects the underlying graph but not the objects added to it.

Quit   This option returns you to the :Graph Edit menu.

:Graph Edit Transform

Description

This command changes the size and orientation of the selected objects. You can select the object to change either before or after selecting the command and one of its options.

Options

Size   This option alters the size of the object.

Rotate   This option rotates an object around its axis.

Quarter-Turn   This option rotates the selected object by 90 degrees.

X-Flip   This option vertically flips the selected object.

Y-Flip   This option horizontally flips the selected object.

Horizontal   This option changes the size and slant of the object by changing its width.

Vertical   This option changes the size and slant of the object by changing the height of the object.

Clear   This option cancels the :Graph Edit Transform commands performed on the selected objects.

:Graph Edit View

Description

This command changes what portions of the graph you view.

Options

Full   This option displays the graph in its normal size.

In   This option enlarges a portion of the graph so that it occupies all of the window. Select the two corners of a box containing the area of the graph you want to appear in the window.

Pan   This option displays selected sections of the graph by moving with the arrow keys to select the parts of the graph that appear.

+   This option displays the graph larger in the window.

-   This option displays the graph smaller in the window.

Up   This option shifts the graph upward.

Down   This option shifts the graph downward.

Left   This option shifts the graph to the left.

Right   This option shifts the graph to the right.

:Graph Goto

Description

This command moves the cell pointer to the first cell on a worksheet that contains a graph.

Options

The only option for this command is to select the graph to go to from the list Wysiwyg provides.

:Graph Move

Description

This command moves any graph on the worksheet to a new location.

Options

The options for this command select the graph to move and the cell to contain the upper-left corner of the graph.

Note

The 1-2-3 /Move, /Worksheet Insert, and /Worksheet Delete commands have no effect on the graph's position. The /Worksheet Column Width command will change the width of the columns Wysiwyg uses to display the graph.

:Graph Quit

Description

This command returns you to the READY mode.

:Graph Remove

Description

This command removes graphs that are on the worksheet. It does not affect any graph files on disk.

Option

The only option for this command is to select which graph to remove.

:Graph Settings

Description

This command alters several settings for a graph. You can select the graph to alter by moving the cell pointer to any cell the graph uses or by entering the graph name.

Options

Graph   This option replaces a graphic with a different one. Select Current, Named, PIC, Metafile, or Blank and the graph name or filename if necessary.

Range   This option changes the size of the range the graphic uses.

Sync   This option selects whether graphics are recalculated automatically. Select Yes or No.

Display   This option displays the graphics (Yes) or displays them as shaded ranges (No).

Opaque   This option hides the worksheet entries under the graph (Yes) or makes them visible (No).

Quit   This option returns you to the READY mode.

:Graph View

Description

This command displays a graph that is saved as a .PIC file or .CGM file.

Options

PIC   This option displays a .PIC file for viewing. Select the .PIC file to view.

Metafile   This option displays a .CGM file for viewing. Select the .CGM file to view.

:Graph Zoom

Description

This command displays any graph in the current worksheet on the full screen.

Option

Your only option is to select a graph from the current worksheet.

:Named-Style

Description

This command formats a range by using a named-style format. Wysiwyg named-style formats are applied to a cell and have been assigned a name with which to format a range.

Options

1 Through 8   These options assign the format of a named style to a range. Select the range to apply the format.

Define   This option defines the eight named styles. Select the named style to change, select the cell containing the format that the named style represents, edit the six characters that will appear next to the number, and enter the style description that will appear in the control panel when the named style is highlighted.

:Print Background

Description

This command prints your Wysiwyg output in the background so you can continue to work on other tasks. When you print in the background, Wysiwyg stores the printed information temporarily in a file. Before you can use this command you must execute the BPRINT program from DOS.

Option

Your only option for this command is the filename you enter where Wysiwyg temporarily stores the information to be printed. Wysiwyg will add a .ENC extension. If you specify an existing filename, you must select between Cancel and Replace. After you select the name of the file, Wysiwyg will start sending the information to the file. When Wysiwyg has sent all of the information in the file to the printer, Wysiwyg deletes the temporary file.

:Print Config

Description

This command changes print configuration options like font cartridges, printer interface, print bin used, and the print orientation.

Options

Printer   This option selects a printer to use from the list of printers chosen during installation.

Interface   This option selects the connection between the computer and the printer. Select a number between 1 and 9, representing Parallel 1, Serial 1, Parallel 2, Serial 2, LPT1, LPT2, LPT3, COM1, or COM2.

1st-Cart   This option chooses the first font cartridge.

2nd-Cart   This option chooses the second font cartridge.

Orientation   This option selects whether the printer prints in Portrait mode, which is standard, or Landscape mode, which rotates your print output 90 degrees to print it sideways.

Bin   This option selects the bin the printer retrieves the paper from for printers with multiple-sheet feed options.

Quit   Returns you to the :Print menu.

:Print File

Description

This command prints your Wysiwyg output to disk rather than to the printer. To print the resulting file, use the DOS COPY command. You do not need 1-2-3 or Wysiwyg to handle printing from disk.

Option

The only option for this command is the filename you enter. Wysiwyg adds .ENC as the extension for the file. If you specify the name of an existing file, you must select from Cancel or Replace. Once you select the name of the file, Wysiwyg starts sending information to the file; you do not need to select Go as you do when printing with 1-2-3.

:Print Go

Description

This command tells Wysiwyg to start printing to the printer.

:Print Info

Description

This command removes or displays the Wysiwyg Print Settings dialog box.

:Print Layout Borders

Description

This command changes the border columns and border rows. These columns and rows will appear on each page printed.

Options

Top   This option chooses border rows for the top of the printed pages. Select a range containing the rows to use.

Left   This option chooses border columns for the left of the printed pages. Select a range containing the columns to use.

Clear   This option removes existing border columns and rows.

Quit   This option returns you to the :Print Layout menu.

:Print Layout Compression

Description

This command sets whether or not to compress the output when it is printed.

Options

None   This option prints with no compression.

Manual   This option lets you manually define the extent of expansion or compression. Enter a number less than 100 to compress the output, or a number greater than 100 to expand the output.

Automatic   This option compresses the output to fit an entire print range on a page. It uses manual page breaks to determine how much data fits on each page.

:Print Layout Default

Description

This command changes the current page layout or default page layout.

Options

Restore   This option replaces the current settings with the default ones.

Update   This option replaces the default settings with the current ones.

:Print Layout Library

Description

This command maintains a library of page layouts on disk. This allows you to use the same page layout in several worksheets.

Options

Retrieve   This option replaces the current page layout with a layout saved to disk. Select a page layout library.

Save   This option stores the current layout in a file. Enter a name for the page layout library. If the name you specify already exists, you must choose Cancel or Replace to specify if you want to replace the existing file with the current layout.

Erase   This option permanently removes a layout from the library.

:Print Layout Margins

Description

This command changes any of the margins on the page layout.

Options

You can specify which of the margins you want to change by selecting Left, Right, Top, or Bottom and then entering the distance you want for the margin. You can also choose Quit to return to the Layout menu.

:Print Layout Page-Size

Description

This command specifies the dimensions of the paper you will use for output.

Options

1 Through 7   These options select the following predefined page sizes:

Letter size (8 1/2 x 11 inches)
International A4 size (8 1/4 x 11 11/16 inches)
80 column by 66 line listing size (8 1/2 x 11 inches)
132 column by 66 line listing size (14 x 11 inches)
80 column by 72 line listing size (8 1/2 x 12 inches)
Legal size (8 1/2 x 14 inches)
International B5 size (6 11/16 x 9 27/32 inches)

Custom   This option defines a custom page size. Enter the length and width followed by "in" for inches, "mm" for millimeters, or "cm" for centimeters.

:Print Layout Titles

Description

This command creates or removes a header or footer for the top or bottom of every page of output.

Options

Header   This option supplies the header that appears at the top of every page. Enter the header using the same rules as for headers in 1-2-3.

Footer   This option supplies the footer that appears at the bottom of every page. Enter the footer using the same rules as for footers in 1-2-3.

Clear   This option removes an existing header or footer or both.

Quit   This option returns you to the :Print Layout menu.

:Print Preview

Description

 This command previews how the print range will appear when printed. After viewing the preview, press any key to display the next page or, on the last page, return to the :Print menu.

:Print Quit

Description

This command returns you to the READY mode.

:Print Range

Description

This command clears or sets a range for printing.

Options

Set   This option selects the print range. Select any range to print.

Clear   This option eliminates the setting of the range to print.

:Print Settings

Description

This command controls how Wysiwyg prints the print range.

Options

Begin   This option specifies the first page to print.

End   This option specifies the last page to print.

Start-Number   This option specifies which page number to use on the first page.

Copies   This option specifies the number of copies to print.

Wait   This option pauses the printer before pages (Yes) or restores continuous printing (No).

Grid   This option chooses whether grid lines that indicate cell boundaries are printed (Yes) or omitted (No).

Frame   This option decides whether to print the frame of the worksheet (Yes) or not to (No).

Reset   This option restores the default print settings.

Quit   This option returns you to the :Print menu.

:Quit

Description

This command returns you to the READY mode.

:Special Copy

Description

This command copies any format options added to a range with Wysiwyg to another range.

Options

The options to copy work the same as 1-2-3's /Copy command options. They are not menu selections but selections of the size of the range you define for the from and to ranges. You can copy one cell to one cell, one cell to many cells, or many cells to many other cells.

:Special Export

Description

This command saves the formatting of the current worksheet to a file with an .FMT (Wysiwyg) or .ALL (Allways) extension.

Option

Your only option with this command is what to call the file. (If you name it after an existing file, you can either Cancel the request or Replace the existing file.) The extension of the file determines the format of the file this command creates. If you do not supply an extension, Wysiwyg uses .FMT.

:Special Import

Description

This command imports the worksheet format stored in a file with an .FMT extension to the current worksheet. The imported format replaces all Wysiwyg formatting added to the current worksheet.

Options

After selecting one of these options you must select the name of the format file that you want to import.

All   This option replaces all formats, named styles, and graphics with the formats, named styles, and graphics in the file you select.

Named-Styles   This option replaces the named styles with the named styles in the file you select.

Fonts   This option replaces the font set with the font set in the file you select.

Graphs   This option adds the graphics from the file you select to the current worksheet file.

:Special Move

Description

The :Special Move command moves formats assigned to a cell or range to another cell or range. The destination range adopts the formats of the source range and the source range formats are reset to the default format.

Options

You can specify any from and to ranges that you want to receive all of the Wysiwyg format options.

:Text

Description

 This command works with worksheet ranges as text paragraphs.

Options

Edit   This option lets you edit text in a text range as if you were using a word processor. Enter or edit the text and press ESC when finished.

Align   This option changes the alignment of text in a text range to Left, Right, Center, or Even (both sides of each line are aligned).

Reformat   This option moves text from one cell to another in a text range so that the resulting range fits in the boundaries of the text range. Select the text range to reformat.

Set   This option chooses a worksheet range to be a text range. Select the range to be part of a text range.

Clear   This option stops treating a worksheet range as a text range. Select the range from which to remove the text range attribute.

:Worksheet Column

Description

This command changes the column width or resets the column to the global column width.

Options

Reset-Width   This option returns the column width to the global column width set by 1-2-3. Select a range containing the columns to reset.

Set-Width   This option sets the column width. Select a range containing the columns to change and enter the new column width.

:Worksheet Page

Description

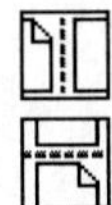

This command specifies the exact location for a page break. Otherwise, Wysiwyg breaks output into pages when pages become full.

Options

Row   This option ends a page at the current row.

Column   This option ends the page at the current column.

Delete   This option removes the page break previously inserted at the current location.

Quit   This option returns you to the READY mode.

:Worksheet Row

Description

This command sets the row height of any row within Wysiwyg. You can either allow Wysiwyg to make changes automatically based on font sizes of text or provide a specific height setting.

Options

Set-Height   This option sets the row height. Select a range containing the rows to change and enter a new row height in points.

Auto   This option sets the row height to fit the largest text in the row. Select a range containing the rows to change.

Part **IV**

Appendixes

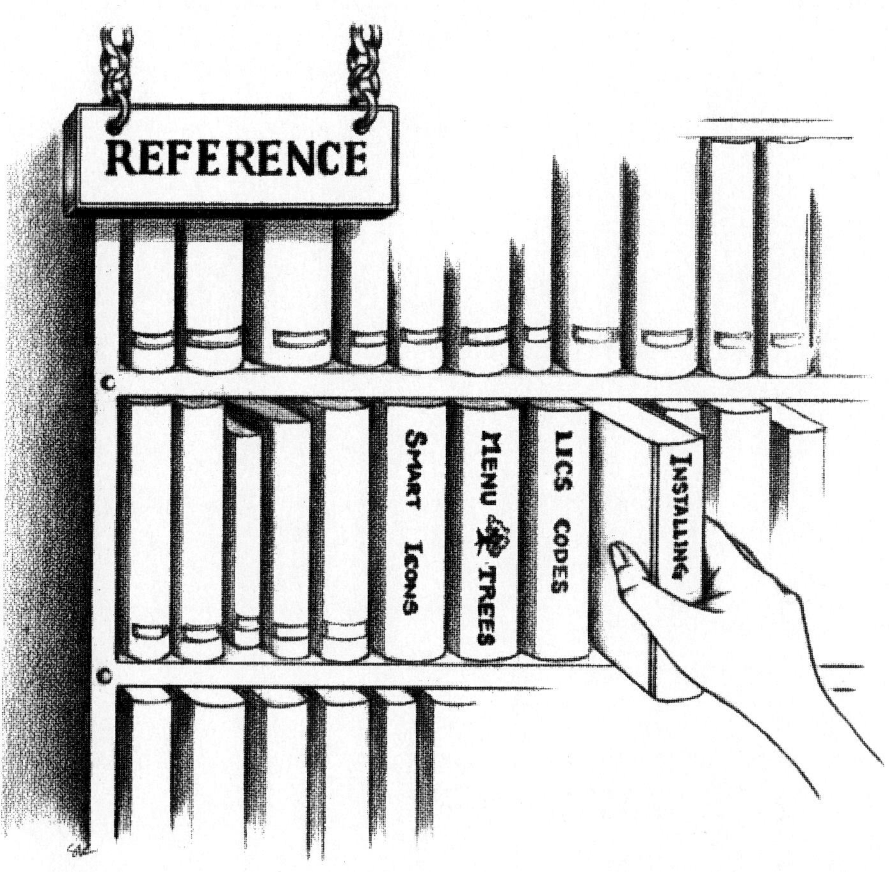

Appendix **A**

Installing 1-2-3

This appendix is an introduction to installing Lotus 1-2-3 and its accessory programs on your system. It discusses 1-2-3 installation on various types of equipment. You will find detailed instructions to ensure that the installation process proceeds smoothly.

If your copy of 1-2-3 has already been installed by your computer dealer or someone else, you do not need to read this appendix. If your copy of 1-2-3 is still covered in shrink-wrap packaging, you need to install the package. You will find this appendix a valuable reference describing the steps that you must take. It also provides some information on various equipment options to help you make informed selections during the installation process.

Before going into specifics, this appendix introduces the hardware options and the various system components. You cannot install 1-2-3 if you do not have at least some general knowledge about the system you are using. For the Install program to configure your copy of 1-2-3 to run with your specific hardware components, you must be able to tell the program what those components are.

Your Equipment

1-2-3 is designed to run on a personal computer or on one of the newer 80286- or 80386-based machines such as an AT or a PS/2 from IBM, or a compatible computer.

Because the compatibles market is constantly changing, you need to check with your dealer for the most up-to-date list of certified compatibles. In case of doubt, have the dealer demonstrate 1-2-3 on the machine you are considering. This appendix assumes that you have an IBM PC, XT, AT, or PS/2, or a system compatible with one of these. You must also have a keyboard and a monochrome or color monitor. With Releases 2.3 and 2.4, you can also use a mouse or another tracking device.

745

Minimum Configuration

The minimum system configurations required for the different releases of 1-2-3 are listed in Table A-1. Notice the differences in memory and disk drive support among the different versions. The table shows only the minimums; you should have RAM and storage space beyond the amounts listed to efficiently use 1-2-3. If you are using Add-Ins with 1-2-3, you will need more memory and disk space than the minimum given in the table.

Adding Memory

The models you create are limited by the amount of memory on your system. You can use all of the package features even if you are operating 1-2-3 at the lowest memory level possible, but you will be restricted in the size of your data files, the size of your spreadsheet applications, and the number of Add-Ins you can have in memory. If you plan to build large models, you should consider expanding the memory of your machine. Network and terminate and stay resident (TSR) software can still be used with 1-2-3, but these programs further limit the size of your worksheets. If you are using Add-Ins with 1-2-3, you may want to disable Undo so that your worksheets do not run out of memory.

With Release 2, you also have the option of expanding memory beyond the standard 640K. To do this, select a card that conforms to the Lotus/Intel/Microsoft Expanded Memory Specification 2.2, such as the AboveBoard card. With these cards, 1-2-3 can use up to 4MB of memory (approximately 4,000,000 characters) above the 640K memory limit. This expanded memory allows you to build large data files and spreadsheets with the 1-2-3 program. You need to run the expanded-memory management software that comes with your card before 1-2-3 can access this additional memory.

Release 1A	192K RAM, 2 double-sided/double-density (DS/DD) disks or one hard disk and one DS/DD disk
Release 2	256K RAM, one DS/DD disk or one hard disk
Release 2.2	384K RAM, one DS/DD disk or one hard disk with 1.7MB free
Release 2.3	384K RAM, one hard disk with 1.7-6MB free
Release 2.4	512K RAM, one hard disk with 1.7-6MB free

Table A-1.   Minimum Configurations

Releases 2 and above also support the addition of a math coprocessor. The 8087, 80387, and 80287 coprocessor chips are supported and are automatically recognized once they are installed. Spreadsheet models with a significant number of calculations will be computed much faster if you add one of these chips to the motherboard of your machine.

The Keyboard

You will begin using the keyboard in this appendix as you work with the Install program. Any directions given refer to key names on the regular or enhanced keyboard. The enhanced keyboard offers a second set of movement keys as well as the numeric keypad so that you can use the numeric keypad for numbers while you use the second set of movement keys for moving in 1-2-3. Pressing the key labeled NUM LOCK toggles the numeric keypad between movement keys and number keys. Other keyboard types usually have the same keys, but you must look to see where these keys are located.

Monitors

Monitors can be described using two features. The first feature is whether the monitor can display multiple colors. Monitors come in two basic varieties: color and monochrome (one color).

The second feature of a monitor is the resolution, or how many dots of light your monitor can display across the screen—the more dots your monitor uses to fill the screen, the sharper the images it displays. The different types of monitor resolution are described with such acronyms as CGA (color graphics adapter), EGA (enhanced graphics adapter), VGA (video graphics adapter), and Super VGA. When you install 1-2-3, you have to select the type of display you want based on the monitor's resolution and manufacturer.

Printers

1-2-3 can use a variety of output devices for creating printed copies of your 1-2-3 data. These output devices include dot-matrix printers, laser printers, and plotters.

To connect any of these output devices to your system, you also need a cable and an available port. It is possible to connect printers to both parallel and serial ports so long as they are compatible, but you must use some special settings if you use a serial connection. First, you must set the printer's baud rate to control the speed of data transfer. At any baud rate except 110, you should also set one stop bit, eight data bits, and no parity. With a speed of 110, you should use two stop bits. Once 1-2-3 is loaded, use the /Worksheet Global Default Printer Interface command described in Chapter 6 to select the baud rate that matches your printer's rate.

Adding Disk Drives

1-2-3 offers several possibilities for storing the 1-2-3 programs and your data. You can store the 1-2-3 programs on your hard disk and use a hard disk or a floppy disk to store your data. Before you can store data on a floppy disk, the disk must be formatted with the FORMAT command described in your operating system manual or in the section "Using Operating System Commands" in Chapter 8.

Although releases before Release 2.3 can run solely on floppy disks, the best configuration for using 1-2-3 is a hard disk drive along with a floppy disk drive so you can load all of the 1-2-3 programs on the hard disk and have the flexibility of storing data files on either the hard disk or a floppy disk. You can then switch from 1-2-3 to Translate or PrintGraph without having to search for the proper disk, since all three programs are on your hard disk. Also, with a hard disk you can store files that exceed a floppy disk's capacity.

With Releases 2.3 and 2.4, you need hard drives. Using floppy disks to run Release 2.3 is feasible only through great effort and a very good understanding of how the programs are structured. Wysiwyg, the spreadsheet publishing add-in included with these releases of 1-2-3, cannot run without a hard drive. Release 2.4 requires you to have a hard disk to install 1-2-3.

The Operating System

The operating system is the control program that resides in the memory of your computer regardless of the software you are working with. It controls the interface between the various devices and establishes the format for data storage on disk. For 1-2-3 Releases 2 and higher, you need to use DOS Release 2.1 or higher. For 1-2-3 Release 1A, you can use an earlier version of DOS. Some computer systems may be unable to run on the earlier versions of DOS and so require a later version.

Noting Your Equipment

You are almost ready to install your 1-2-3 disks. First, however, make a note of your hardware configuration. You want this information available when you use 1-2-3's Install program.

Installing 1-2-3

Installing Release 2.4 of 1-2-3 registers your disks with your name and company name, copies files to the hard disk, and tailors your 1-2-3 disks to run with your specific hardware configuration. If 1-2-3 ran with only one type of hardware, this step would not be necessary. Since it is necessary, however, you should remember that it offers you an advantage: you can continue to use the package even if you change your hardware configuration to include a plotter, a new printer, or a different monitor.

When you purchase 1-2-3, the package you receive contains an envelope with several disks. These disks contain all of the files that 1-2-3 and its accessory programs need to run. Use these disks as you follow the steps to install 1-2-3 on your computer.

These instructions are based on the assumption that DOS is already installed on your system. If this is not the case, install DOS before you install 1-2-3.

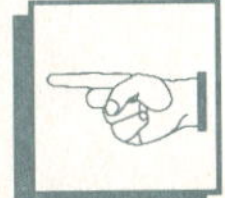

1. To start the Install program, insert the Install disk into drive A. Type A: and press ENTER to make the drive current. (You can also use drive B if you wish.) Then type **INSTALL** and press ENTER to start the installation program. Press ENTER after viewing the opening screen.

2. When prompted to register, enter your name on the first line and your company's on the second. Press INS. When prompted, press Y and ENTER to confirm.

3. Install prompts for the programs you want to transfer to your hard disk. You now select the parts of 1-2-3 and its accessory programs you want to install. As you highlight each option, you see the disk space required. The files on the disk are compressed, so you must use Install to transfer them to your hard disk. You can add programs later by running Install again from drive A or B. To include or remove a program to be transferred to your hard disk, use the arrow keys to highlight it and press the spacebar. Press ENTER when you have the programs you want selected.

4. Next, 1-2-3 prompts for the disk drive 1-2-3 will use and displays C. If you want to use 1-2-3 on another hard disk, enter the drive letter. Press ENTER to accept the default value or your new entry. If the disk you select does not have enough room, the Install program displays an error message. You can press ENTER to specify a new drive or press ESC to leave Install. From the screen where you select the drive, you can also press ESC to return to the screen from which you select the programs to transfer to your hard disk.

5. The program now prompts for the directory that 1-2-3 will use. Either use 1-2-3's suggested directory of \123R24 or supply a subdirectory name and press ENTER.

    a. If the directory you chose does not exist, the installation program displays a confirmation box, prompting you to type a Y to create the subdirectory and transfer files, or an N to return to the previous screen to select a new directory. Press ENTER.

    b. If you provide an existing empty directory, Install immediately starts copying files.

c. If the directory exists and contains files and you are installing the 1-2-3 program files, press ENTER after reading the error message and specify a new directory; 1-2-3 program files cannot be installed in a directory that contains other files. If you are not installing the 1-2-3 program files, Install starts transferring the files.

6. After you select a directory, 1-2-3 starts copying files from the Install disk. The Install program prompts you for the next disk it needs when it has finished copying files to your hard disk. Replace the disk with the one Install requests and press ENTER.

7. Once Install has finished copying files to your hard drive, it displays an introductory screen for the second part of the installation process: specifying your equipment. Press ENTER to continue.

8. At the main Install menu, highlight the Select Your Equipment menu option and press ENTER.

9. Install displays a screen describing what it has identified as the correct screen display. For most monitors, it is correct. Press ENTER to display the screen listing the available screen displays. Unless you know that the suggestion is incorrect, press ENTER to accept the suggestion. If the suggestion is wrong, highlight the correct display and press ENTER. Some monitor selections have a second menu that offers additional display options. Select the one you want and press ENTER.

10. Install next asks if you have a text printer so that it can find out which you want to use. Unless you do not have a printer, select Yes. Then select the printer manufacturer or one with which your printer is compatible. Select a model from the list Install displays. Highlight the option that is appropriate for your printer and press ENTER. Then select Yes and press ENTER to select another text printer and repeat the printer manufacturer and model selections, or select No and press ENTER to finish selecting text printers.

11. You can select the graphics printer for printing graphs and worksheets with Wysiwyg. Select No and press ENTER if your printer cannot print graphics or select Yes and press ENTER if it can. If you select Yes, you need to choose a printer manufacturer and model from the lists Install displays. After selecting a graphics printer, Install asks whether you want to select another one. You can highlight No and press ENTER to finish selecting graphics printers, or you can highlight Yes, press ENTER, and repeat the printer manufacturer and model selections.

12. After the printers are selected, Install asks you if you want to change the name of the driver set. If you select No, the installation program names the driver set 123.SET. If you select Yes, you must provide a filename.

13. If you are installing Wysiwyg, Install now displays an introductory screen for the third part of installation, generating fonts for you to use in your

spreadsheet. Press ENTER after reading the introductory screen. Highlight Basic, Medium, or Extended for the set of fonts that you want to install and then press ENTER. Install asks if you want to generate the fonts immediately or if you want to wait to generate them. If you select Yes, the fonts are generated immediately. Once the fonts are generated, press any key to leave Install. You are now ready to run 1-2-3. If you are not installing Wysiwyg or generating the fonts immediately, you see a screen that tells you the installation is complete. At this point, you can press ENTER to return to the DOS prompt. With 1-2-3 installed, you can start 1-2-3 by typing 123 and pressing ENTER.

Using Install After Installing 1-2-3

Once you have installed 1-2-3, you may continue to use the Install program. Use the Install program if you want to create more than one driver set with different hardware settings. You may need to change the hardware configuration to include another printer or screen display. You may also want to change the sort order that 1-2-3 uses for the /Data Sort command.

In Releases 2.3 and 2.4, using Install to change 1-2-3 settings requires that you start Install from the directory containing the 1-2-3 program files on your hard disk. You only start Install from a floppy disk when you want to add 1-2-3 or its accessory programs to your hard disk. In other releases, you start Install to change a driver set from the drive and directory where your 1-2-3 files are located.

Creating More Than One Driver Set

If you use your Lotus software on more than one computer or if you frequently alter the configuration of your system, you may want more than one driver set. This allows you to switch from one driver set to another without having to change the installation parameters each time.

If you use more than one driver set, pick a meaningful driver name for each, such as 2MONITOR, PLOTTER, or HOME. You can use up to eight characters for the file name. You must avoid the following symbols:

```
, . ; : / ? * = <> [ ] \ '
```

Install adds a .SET extension to the filename, as in COLOR.SET.

Use the Select Your Equipment menu option to create each driver set. Save each driver set under a different name. You may want to store each driver set on a separate disk or in a different directory, if you want to use different drivers with the files in different drives or directories. To use a driver set other than 123.SET, specify the pathname of the driver set when you start 1-2-3, as in 123 C:\BUDGET\HOME.SET.

Modifying the Current Driver

To modify the existing 1-2-3 driver sets, select Change Selected Equipment. To select a driver set to change, select Make Another Driver Set Current and supply a driver set filename. If you do not select a driver set file, Install uses 123.SET. Then select Modify the Current Driver Set. This displays a menu of settings you can change. 1-2-3 uses separate drivers for the text screen and the graph screen. Install selected the graphics screen driver and text screen driver based on the selection you made for the screen display. This screen also includes other options that you did not select when you created the driver set; you can change these now.

One of the options that is listed when you select Change Selected Equipment does not change driver sets. The Switch Mouse Buttons option switches how the right and left buttons on a mouse are used (a middle button is ignored). Select Left if you hold the mouse in your right hand; select Right if you hold the mouse in your left hand. Changing which mouse button you use to make selections is saved in 1-2-3's configuration file. A configuration file contains 1-2-3's default settings, such as the directory it searches for files and whether 1-2-3 beeps to alert you to errors.

Changing the Display

The display driver may need to be changed if you want to change the initial display driver or if you want to use different drivers for graphs and text. Several of the monitors can use more than one display driver. For example, if you are using a monitor with a VGA display, you may want to see how your graphs will look to someone with an EGA monitor. To change a display driver, select Text Display or Graphics Display. The Install program lists the possible selections with a triangle next to the display driver that is currently selected. When you select a different driver, Install replaces the current selection with the new selection.

Changing the Printer

The printer driver may need to be changed if you change the printer or if you want to add another one. 1-2-3 allows up to four text printer drivers and twelve graphics print drivers. To add or change a printer driver, select Text Printer or Graphics Printer. The Install program lists the possible printer manufacturers with a triangle next to the printer manufacturer that you have selected. To add another printer driver, select the printer driver you want to add. Then make the additional menu selections appropriate for the printer. This selects the printer driver that you added as the secondary printer driver. To remove a printer driver, select Text Printer or Graphics Printer and press DEL after highlighting the manufacturer and the model.

To select a printer driver from 1-2-3, use the /Worksheet Global Default Printer Name command. Then type the number that represents the selected driver. To select a printer driver for Wysiwyg, use the :Print Config Printer command. Then highlight the appropriate printer in the Printer List pop-up dialog box and press ENTER. To select a printer driver for PrintGraph, use the /Settings Hardware Printer command and select the printer driver from the list that PrintGraph displays. Notice that some printer selections made in Install have two or more selections in Wysiwyg and PrintGraph because some printers have multiple density or color selections for printing.

Changing the Sort Order

The Collating Sequence option allows you to change the collating sequence for the existing driver set. Install provides three options: ASCII, Numbers first, and Numbers last. The sort order for each option is as follows:

- *ASCII* Blank cells, followed by labels and values in ASCII order. Capitalization affects the sort order with this choice. This selection also makes functions case-sensitive and can have serious implications for formulas containing string functions that are used in computations or for the criteria area with /Data Query commands.

- *Numbers last* Blank cells, label entries with letters in alphabetical order, label entries beginning with numbers in numeric sequence, labels beginning with special characters, and then values.

- *Numbers first* Blank cells, labels beginning with numbers in numeric sequence, labels beginning with letters in alphabetical order, labels beginning with special characters, and then values.

To change the collating sequence, select Collating from the Modify Current Driver Set menu and then select the sort order you want from the submenu.

Saving the Driver Files

Once you have changed your driver file's display, printer, and sort configurations, you need to save them so that the driver file will contain your new selections. To save the driver file, select Return to Previous Menu and then select Save the Current Driver Set. When 1-2-3 displays the filename, edit it if you want the new settings saved with a different filename. When the filename is correct, press ENTER to save the updated changes. When the new driver set file is saved, you are instructed to press F9 to return to the last menu or to press ENTER to leave Install. After pressing ENTER, you must select Yes to confirm that you want to leave Install.

If Wysiwyg is installed and you change the printer or display in a driver set, you have to generate fonts again. The menu selections and process are identical to installing fonts when you install Wysiwyg.

Installing 1-2-3 in Earlier Releases

If you are installing a prior release of 1-2-3, the steps you perform are different. In Releases 2.2 and 2.01, you must run a program called INIT to register your System disk before you copy the 1-2-3 files onto floppy backup disks or to your hard disk. After the disks are registered, you can use the DOS COPY command to copy them to floppy or hard disks.

Before starting 1-2-3, you must run the Install program on the same disk as your 1-2-3 program files and tell 1-2-3 what equipment you have. Select First-Time Installation to tell 1-2-3 the type of equipment you are using. These selections are very similar to the ones described in this appendix in steps 8 through 11 under "Installing 1-2-3." If you are installing Allways, which is included with Release 2.2, you must install it separately using the menu-driven AWSETUP program. You will need to select First-Time Installation and the display and printer you are using so AWSETUP can copy the appropriate files to your hard disk.

Installing 1-2-3 in Windows

You can use Releases 2.3 and 2.4 in Windows. Windows allows you to switch between applications without having to exit one to get into another. To install 1-2-3 with Windows, you can either add the program to Windows yourself or have Windows do it for you. You will first need to install 1-2-3, as described earlier in this appendix.

To add the program to Windows yourself, activate the group window to which you want to add 1-2-3 and select New from the File menu. Select Program Item and click OK. In the next dialog box displayed, enter 1-2-3 Release 2.4 in the Description text box and C:\123R24\123 in the Command Line text box before you select OK to add the program item to the program group.

To have Windows add 1-2-3 for you, select Windows Setup from the Main group window. Select Set Up Applications from the Options menu. Select OK to search all directories or change the option selected to limit the search. After the search is completed, highlight Lotus 1-2-3, select it, and select the Add command button. Finally, select the OK command button and follow any further instructions Windows displays on the screen.

LICS Codes

You can use the Lotus International Character Set codes to create special characters within your worksheets. These special characters can create boxes or special letters that are used in various languages. Use LICS codes to create characters unavailable on your keyboard. Each possible character has an LICS code. LICS codes do not use numbers 0 to 31 because these numbers actually represent control codes used internally by 1-2-3. Their use in the worksheet is not supported. The codes 32 through 127 represent standard ASCII codes and are found in the table. The third set of codes is 128 through 255, which provides special characters and symbols.

Some monitors and printers cannot display all LICS character codes. When a worksheet contains an LICS character that the monitor cannot display or the printer cannot print, 1-2-3 substitutes a different character for displaying and printing.

Table B-1 lists the LICS codes and the key codes you use to create them. The Xsymbols column shows the characters as they will appear when printed with the Xsymbols font.

Creating LICS Characters

You can create LICS characters three different ways. The method you use depends on the task you are performing when you want the LICS character.

- **Enter the character directly from the keyboard** The LICS characters represented by codes 32 through 127 (such as letters, numbers, and common punctuation) can be entered by typing a key.

- **Use the COMPOSE** (ALT-F1) **key**   Press ALT-F1 and type the Compose sequence. For example, to create a trademark symbol (™), press ALT-F1 (COMPOSE) and type a **T** and an **M**. 1-2-3 converts these entries into a trademark symbol.

- **Use the @CHAR function**   Enter the appropriate LICS code for the function's argument. For example, to include the trademark symbol (™) in a note for a cell formula, enter **@CHAR(184)**. 1-2-3 converts the function into a trademark symbol. The @CHAR function is used within formulas, especially when you cannot enter the character using another method, such as double quotation marks.

Printing Characters that Are Not in the LICS Set

You can create characters that are not part of the LICS set by printing two characters in the same location on the printed page. You use ALT-F1 (COMPOSE) with the Merge Code (mg) option and then type the two characters you want in the current location. For example, to underline an X, you would press ALT-F1 (COMPOSE), type **mg**, then type _X. When the character prints, it looks like this: <u>X</u>.

LICS Code	Normal Character	Xsymbols Character	Compose Sequence	Description of Normal Character
32				Space
33	!	♩		Exclamation point
34	"	⁝		Double quotes
35	#	❧	+	Pound sign
36	$	♥		Dollar sign
37	%	♣		Percent
38	&	❦		Ampersand
39	'	❧		Close quote
40	(	♣		Open parenthesis
41	)	♦		Close parenthesis
42	*	♥		Asterisk
43	+	♠		Plus sign
44	,	①		Comma

* Indicates a character where the order of the compose characters is important

---

Table B-1.   *Lotus International Character Set (LICS) Codes*

LICS Code	Normal Character	Xsymbols Character	Compose Sequence	Description of Normal Character
45	–	②		Minus sign
46	.	③		Period
47	/	④		Slash
48	0	⑤		Zero
49	1	⑥		One
50	2	⑦		Two
51	3	⑧		Three
52	4	⑨		Four
53	5	⑩		Five
54	6	❶		Six
55	7	❷		Seven
56	8	❸		Eight
57	9	❹		Nine
58	:	❺		Colon
59	;	❻		Semicolon
60	<	❼		Less than
61	=	❽		Equal sign
62	>	❾		Greater than
63	?	❿		Question mark
64	@	①	aa or AA	At sign
65	A	②		A, uppercase
66	B	③		B, uppercase
67	C	④		C, uppercase
68	D	⑤		D, uppercase
69	E	⑥		E, uppercase
70	F	⑦		F, uppercase
71	G	⑧		G, uppercase
72	H	⑨		H, uppercase
73	I	⑩		I, uppercase
74	J	❶		J, uppercase
75	K	❷		K, uppercase
76	L	❸		L, uppercase
77	M	❹		M, uppercase
78	N	❺		N, uppercase

* Indicates a character where the order of the compose characters is important

Table B-1.   *Lotus International Character Set (LICS) Codes* (continued)

LICS Code	Normal Character	Xsymbols Character	Compose Sequence	Description of Normal Character
79	O	❻		O, uppercase
80	P	❼		P, uppercase
81	Q	❽		Q, uppercase
82	R	❾		R, uppercase
83	S	❿		S, uppercase
84	T	→		T, uppercase
85	U	→		U, uppercase
86	V	↔		V, uppercase
87	W	↕		W, uppercase
88	X	↘		X, uppercase
89	Y	→		Y, uppercase
90	Z	↗		Z, uppercase
91	[	→	((	Open bracket
92	\	→	//	Backslash
93	]	→	))	Close bracket
94	^	→	vv	Caret
95	_	→		Underscore
96	'	→		Open single quote
97	a	→		a, lowercase
98	b	➤		b, lowercase
99	c	➤		c, lowercase
100	d	➤		d, lowercase
101	e	➡		e, lowercase
102	f	➡		f, lowercase
103	g	▶		g, lowercase
104	h	➡		h, lowercase
105	i	⇨		i, lowercase
106	j	⇨		j, lowercase
107	k	⇦		k, lowercase
108	l	⇦		l, lowercase
109	m	⇨		m, lowercase
110	n	⇨		n, lowercase
111	o	⇨		o, lowercase
112	p			p, lowercase

* Indicates a character where the order of the compose characters is important

Table B-1.   *Lotus International Character Set (LICS) Codes* (continued)

LICS Code	Normal Character	Xsymbols Character	Compose Sequence	Description of Normal Character
113	q	⇨		q, lowercase
114	r	⊃		r, lowercase
115	s	➤→		s, lowercase
116	t	➘		t, lowercase
117	u	➢→		u, lowercase
118	v	➚		v, lowercase
119	w	➘		w, lowercase
120	x	➤→		x, lowercase
121	y	➚		y, lowercase
122	z	➡		z, lowercase
123	{	➡	(–	Open brace
124	|	➤➤	^/	Bar
125	}	➤➤	–)	Close brace
126	~	⇒	– –	Tilde
127	⬠			Delete
128	`	⊀	`(space)	Grave accent, uppercase*
129	´		´(space)	Acute accent, uppercase*
130	^		^(space)	Circumflex accent
131	"		"(space)	Umlaut accent, uppercase
132	~		~(space)	Tilde accent, uppercase*
133	▮			Not used
134	▮			Not used
135	▮			Not used
136	▮			Not used
137	▮			Not used
138	▮			Not used
139	▮			Not used
140	▮			Not used
141	▮			Not used
142	▮			Not used
143	▮			Not used

* Indicates a character where the order of the compose characters is important

Table B-1.   *Lotus International Character Set (LICS) Codes* (continued)

LICS Code	Normal Character	Xsymbols Character	Compose Sequence	Description of Normal Character
144	`		(space)`	Grave accent, lowercase*
145	´		(space)´	Acute accent, lowercase*
146	^		(space)^	Circumflex accent
147	"		(space)"	Umlaut accent, lowercase
148	~		(space)~	Tilde accent, lowercase*
149	ı		i(space)	i without dot (lowercase)
150	‾		_(space)	Ordinal indicator
151	▲		ba	Begin attribute
152	▼		ea	End attribute
153	■			Not used
154	•		(space)(space)	Hard space (display only)
155	←		mg	Merge character (display only)
156	■			Not used
157	■			Not used
158	■			Not used
159	■			Not used
160	ƒ		ff	Guilder
161	¡		!!	Exclamation point, inverted
162	¢		cl c/ Cl or C/	Cent sign
163	£		L= l= L– or l–	British pound sterling symbol
164	„		"^	Low double quotes, opening
165	¥		Y= y= Y– or y–	Yen sign
166	Pt		PT Pt or pt	Peseta sign
167	§		SO, so, So, or S0	Section symbol
168	¤		XO or xo	International currency sign
169	©		CO, C0, co, or c0	Copyright symbol
170	ª		a_ or A_	Feminine ordinal indicator
171	«		<<	Left angle quotes
172	Δ		dd or DD	Delta
173	π		PI, pi, or Pi	Pi*
174	≥		>=	Greater-than-or-equal-to sign*
175	÷		:-	Division sign
176	°		^0	Degree symbol

* Indicates a character where the order of the compose characters is important

Table B-1.   *Lotus International Character Set (LICS) Codes* (continued)

LICS Code	Normal Character	Xsymbols Character	Compose Sequence	Description of Normal Character
177	±		+−	Plus or minus sign
178	²		^2	Two superscript
179	³		^3	Three superscript
180	”		"v	Low double quotes, closing
181	μ		/u	Greek mu, lowercase*
182	¶		!P or !p	Paragraph symbol
183	•		^.	Center dot
184	™		TM, Tm, or tm	Trademark symbol*
185	¹		^1	One superscript
186	º		o_ or O_	Masculine ordinal indicator
187	»		>>	Right angle quotes
188	¼		14	One quarter*
189	½		12	One half*
190	≤		=<	Less-than-or-equal-to-sign
191	¿		??	Question mark inverted
192	À		A‘	A with grave accent, uppercase
193	Á		A’	A with acute accent, uppercase
194	Â		A^	A with circumflex, uppercase
195	Ã		A~	A with tilde, uppercase
196	Ä		A"	A with umlaut, uppercase
197	Å		A*	A with ring, uppercase
198	Æ		AE	AE with diphthong, uppercase
199	Ç		C,	C with cedilla, uppercase
200	È		E‘	E with grave accent, uppercase
201	É		E’	E with acute accent, uppercase
202	Ê		E^	E with circumflex, uppercase
203	Ë		E"	E with umlaut, uppercase
204	Ì		I‘	I with grave accent, uppercase
205	Í		I’	I with acute accent, uppercase
206	Î		I^	I with circumflex, uppercase
207	Ï		I"	I with umlaut, uppercase
208	Ð		D -	Icelandic eth, uppercase
209	Ñ		N~	N with tilde, uppercase
210	Ò		O‘	O with grave accent, uppercase

* Indicates a character where the order of the compose characters is important

Table B-1.   *Lotus International Character Set (LICS) Codes* (continued)

LICS Code	Normal Character	Xsymbols Character	Compose Sequence	Description of Normal Character
211	Ó		O'	O with acute accent, uppercase
212	Ô		O^	O with circumflex, uppercase
213	Õ		O~	O with tilde, uppercase
214	Ö		O"	O with umlaut, uppercase
215	Œ		OE	OE ligature, uppercase
216	Ø		O/	O with slash, uppercase
217	Ù		U`	U with grave accent, uppercase
218	Ú		U'	U with acute accent, uppercase
219	Û		U^	U with circumflex, uppercase
220	Ü		U"	U with umlaut, uppercase
221	Ÿ		Y"	Y with umlaut, uppercase
222	Þ		P_	Icelandic thorn, uppercase
223	β		ss	German sharp, lowercase or Beta
224	à		a`	a with grave accent, lowercase
225	á		a'	a with acute accent, lowercase
226	â		a^	a with circumflex, lowercase
227	ã		a~	a with tilde, lowercase
228	ä		a"	a with umlaut, lowercase
229	å		a*	a with ring, lowercase
230	æ		ae	ae diphthong, lowercase
231	ç		c, c with cedilla, lowercase	
232	è		e`	e with grave accent, lowercase
233	é		e'	e with acute accent, lowercase
234	ê		e^	e with circumflex, lowercase
235	ë		e"	e with umlaut, lowercase
236	ì		i`	i with grave accent, lowercase
237	í		i'	i with acute accent, lowercase
238	î		i^	i with circumflex, lowercase
239	ï		i"	i with umlaut, lowercase
240	ð		d-	Icelandic eth, lowercase
241	ñ		n~	n with tilde, lowercase
242	ò		o`	o with grave accent, lowercase
243	ó		o'	o with acute accent, lowercase

* Indicates a character where the order of the compose characters is important

Table B-1.   *Lotus International Character Set (LICS) Codes* (continued)

LICS Code	Normal Character	Xsymbols Character	Compose Sequence	Description of Normal Character
244	ô		o^	o with circumflex, lowercase
245	õ		o~	o with tilde, lowercase
246	ö		o"	o with umlaut, lowercase
247	œ		oe	oe diphthong, lowercase
248	ø		o/	o with slash, lowercase
249	ù		u`	u with grave accent, lowercase
250	ú		u'	u with acute accent, lowercase
251	û		u^	u with circumflex, lowercase
252	ü		u"	u with umlaut, lowercase
253	ÿ		y"	y with umlaut, lowercase
254	þ		p-	Icelandic thorn, lowercase
255	■			Not used

* Indicates a character where the order of the compose characters is important

Table B-1.   ***Lotus International Character Set (LICS) Codes*** (continued)

Menu Trees

1-2-3 provides a hierarchical menu system that allows you to access many features of the package. 1-2-3's main menu is displayed whenever you press the slash (/). In Releases 2.3 and 2.4, you can also activate the menu by moving the mouse into the control panel. The choices in this main menu are basic because they are designed to provide an overview of 1-2-3 features and allow you to access more complex submenus. As you choose additional selections from lower-level submenus, you will be making your instructions more specific since the lower level menu selections allow you to refine and limit your main menu choice. If you are ever uncertain what a menu selection does, you can highlight a choice in the menu and read the description of this item in the second line of the menu display.

The main menu branches into seven major menus, as shown here:

/WORKSHEET

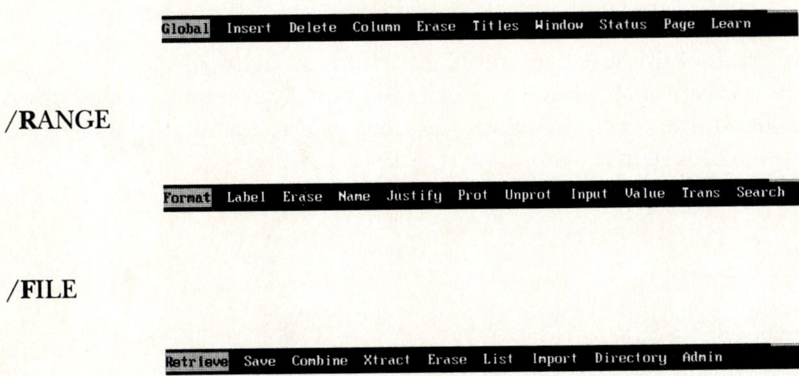

/RANGE

/FILE

/PRINT

/GRAPH

/DATA

/ADD-IN

Figures C-1 through Figure C-7 show the first level menu and the submenus presented after you make a selection from the main menu.

The Wysiwyg Add-In was a new feature with 1-2-3 Release 2.3. For you to access it, it must be attached. Once the Add-In is attached you can access Wysiwyg's menu at any time by typing a colon (:). The main menu selections for Wysiwyg look like this:

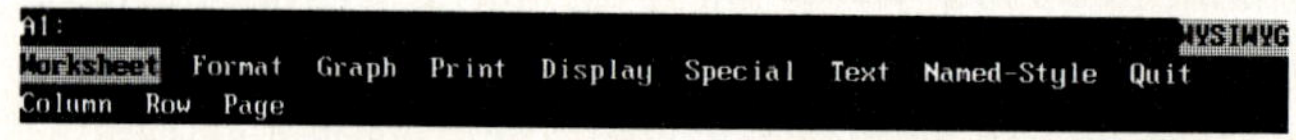

The first two levels of the Wysiwyg Add-In are shown in Figure C-8.

Once you select an option from this menu, a submenu of selections will pull down from the main menu. Repeated selections will cause additional menus and lists to overlay portions of the screen as you refine your selections.

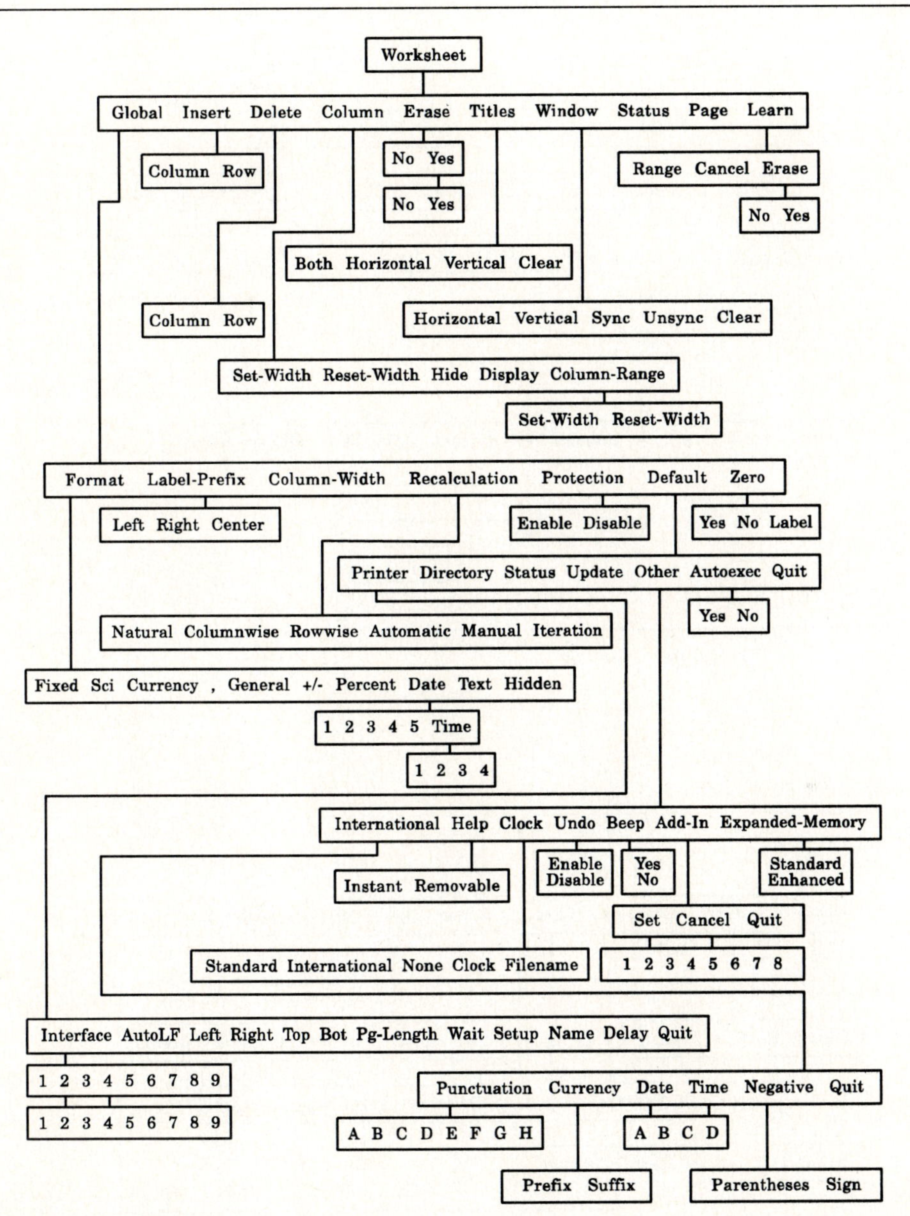

Figure C-1.   *The Worksheet menu tree*

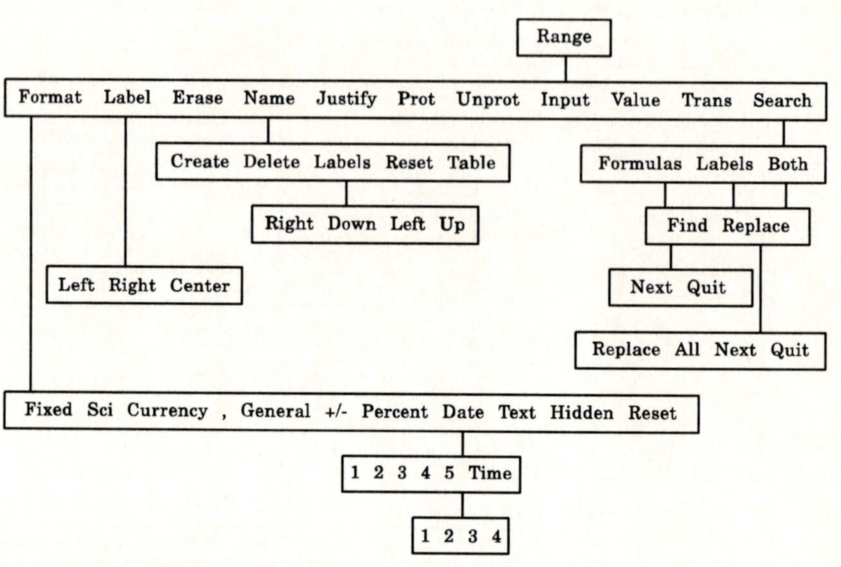

Figure C-2.   *The Range menu tree*

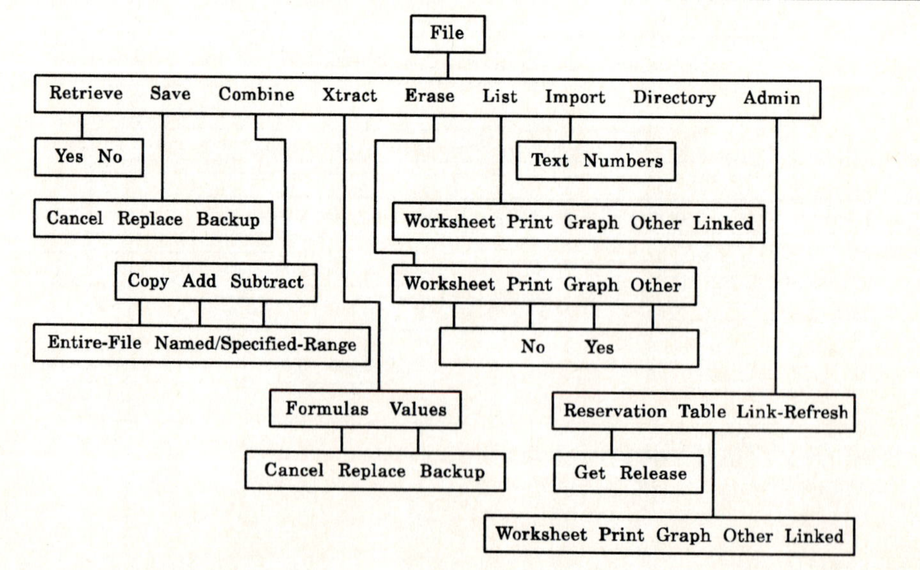

Figure C-3.   *The File menu tree*

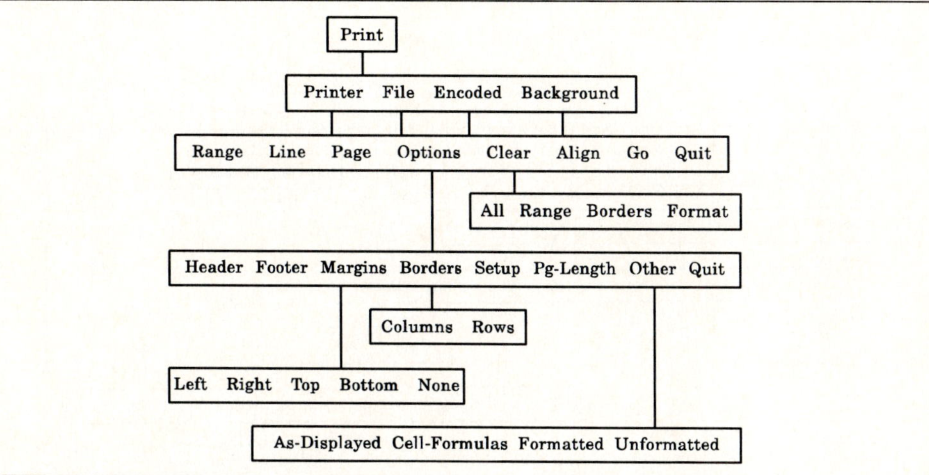

Figure C-4.   *The Print menu tree*

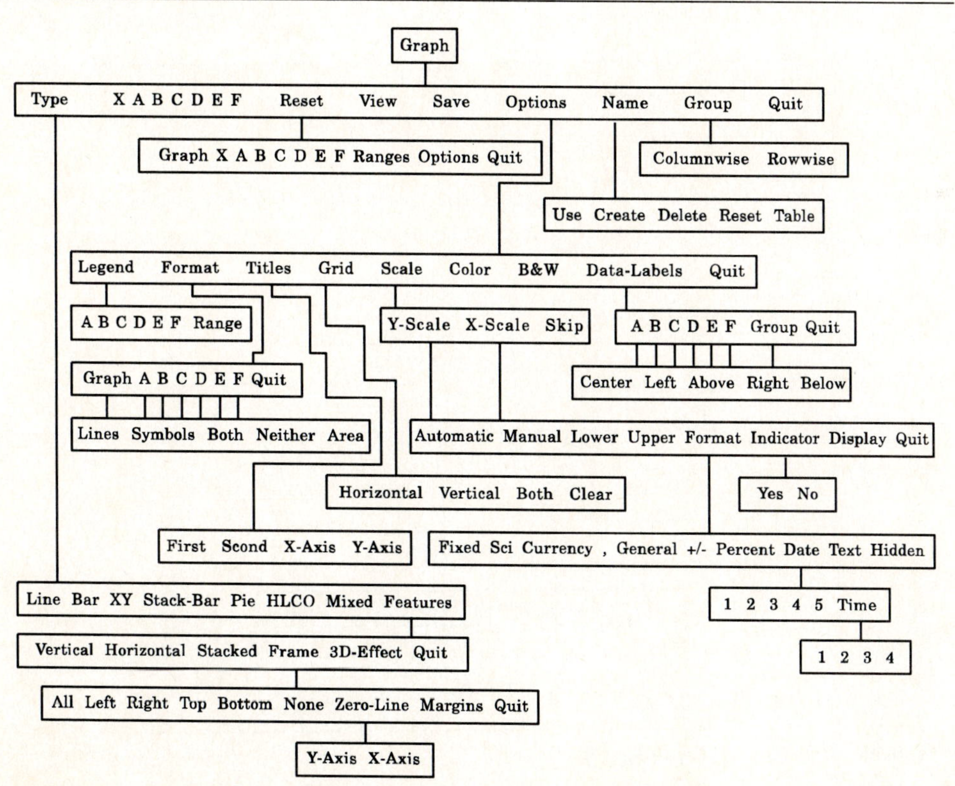

Figure C-5.   *The Graph menu tree*

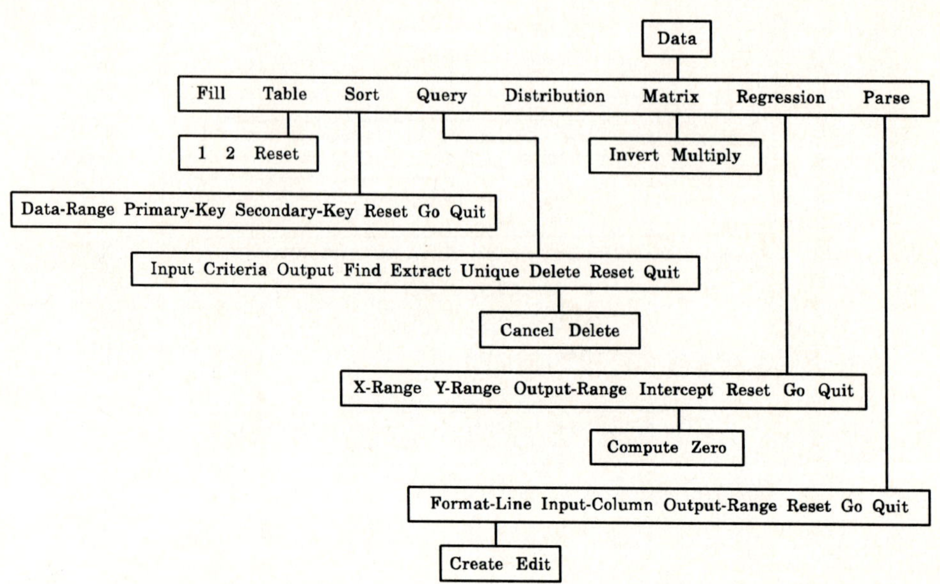

Figure C-6.   *The Data menu tree*

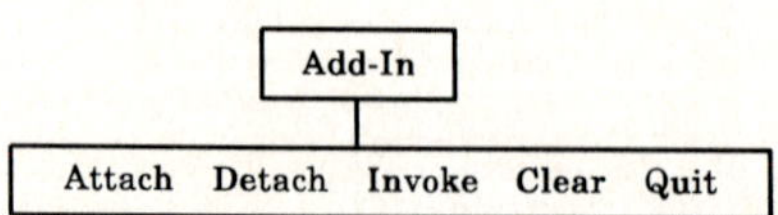

Figure C-7.   *The Add-In menu tree*

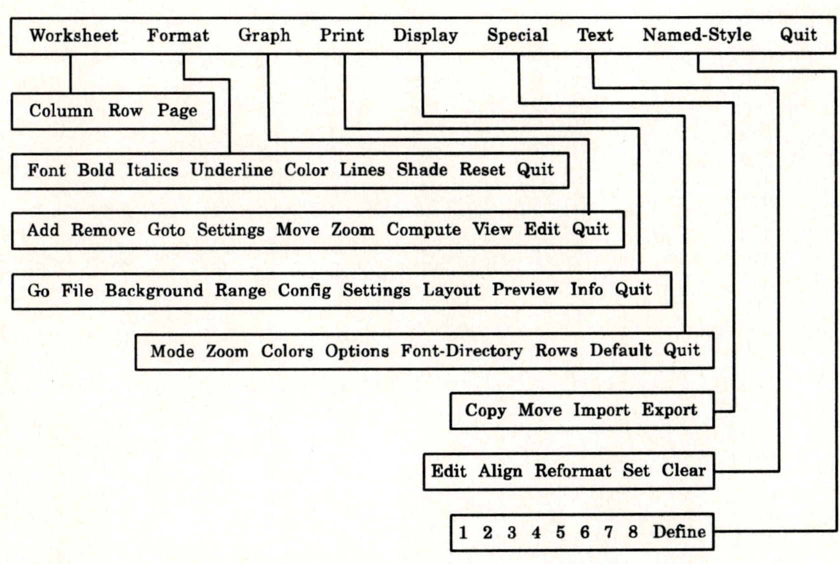

Figure C-8.   *The first two levels of the Wysiwyg menu tree*

The SmartIcons

The Icons add-in available with 1-2-3 Release 2.4 contains 77 icons you can use to simplify various operations performed with 1-2-3 and Wysiwyg. Selecting a SmartIcon is like selecting the same menu command. You can use this appendix as a quick reference for the identification of the various SmartIcons. Note that two icons appear beside each description. The first is the graphic form of the icon, the way the icon appears when Wysiwyg is attached to 1-2-3. The second icon is the text form, the way the icon appears when Wysiwyg is not attached. Note that the asterisked icons are Wysiwyg icons; that is, they activate Wysiwyg features. They cannot be used unless Wysiwyg is attached.

The number of icons appearing on each icon palette is controlled by the type of monitor you have and whether Wysiwyg is attached. With a VGA monitor and Wysiwyg attached, you will have seven palettes of icons, but with a VGA monitor without Wysiwyg attached, you will have ten palettes. In this table, the icons are divided by the palettes they would appear on if you had a VGA monitor with Wysiwyg attached. If you are using another monitor, you will find that these icons are still in the correct order, but the breaks between the palettes are in different places than indicated here. The File Save icon, which is only described on palette 1 in this table, appears at the top of every icon palette. All of the icons that appear on the first palette, which is the custom palette, also appear on one of the other palettes, but are only described on the first palette in this table.

The icons that appear when Wysiwyg is not attached or when you are using text mode appear in a different order than they do when you are in a graphical mode with Wysiwyg attached. Therefore, icon descriptions for text icons are not given in order of the palette on which they appear.

Palette 1

Graphic Icon	Text Icon	Description
		Saves the worksheet to a disk
		Retrieves a worksheet from a disk
		SmartSum
		Displays the current range as a graph
		Prints a range
		Previews print output
		Adds or removes bold*
		Adds or removes italic*
		Adds or removes single underlining*
		Displays the text in the next font*
		Formats as currency or returns to the default format
		Deletes the entries in the highlighted range

Palette 1 (*continued*)

Graphic Icon	**Text Icon**	**Description**
	COPY	Copies the highlighted range
	MOVE	Moves the highlighted range
	REP DATA	Duplicates the current cell
	A→Z	Sorts a database in ascending order

Palette 2

Graphic Icon	**Text Icon**	**Description**
U	U =	Adds or removes double underlining*
0,0	0,0	Formats with a comma or returns the format to the default
%	%	Formats as a percentage or restores the default format
A→A	FGRD	Displays in the next color*
A→A	BGRD	Displays the background in the next color*
		Adds or removes outlining with a drop shadow*

Palette 2 (*continued*)

Graphic Icon	Text Icon	Description
		Adds a single-, double-, or wide-line outline*
		Adds light, dark, or solid shading*
		Left-aligns all the labels in the selected range
		Centers all the labels in the selected range
		Right-aligns all the labels in the selected range
		Cycles through text range alignment options*

Palette 3

Graphic Icon	Text Icon	Description
		Inserts one row above the selected range
		Inserts one column left of the selected range
		Deletes all rows in the selected range
		Deletes all columns in the selected range
		Inserts a 1-2-3 or Wysiwyg page break in the row

Palette 3 (*continued*)

Graphic Icon	Text Icon	Description
		Inserts a Wysiwyg page break in the column*
		Sorts a database in descending order
		Fills the selected range with a series of values
		Recalculates all of the formulas
		Enters the current date and time*
		Adds a graph that is a circle around the selected range
		Zooms up to the worksheet
		Turns on the STEP mode used for macros
		Lets you choose a macro to run

Palette 4

Graphic Icon	Text Icon	Description
		Moves the cell pointer one cell to the left
		Moves the cell pointer one cell to the right

Palette 4 (*continued*)

Graphic Icon	Text Icon	Description
		Moves the cell pointer one cell up
		Moves the cell pointer one cell down
		Starts the Help system
		Moves the cell pointer to cell A1
		Moves the cell pointer to the lower- right corner of the active area
		Moves the cell pointer down to the intersection of a blank and a filled cell
		Moves the cell pointer up to the intersection of a blank and a filled cell
		Moves the cell pointer right to the intersection of a blank and a filled cell
		Moves the cell pointer left to the intersection of a blank and a filled cell

Palette 4 (*continued*)

Graphic Icon	Text Icon	Description
	GOTO	Prompts for the new location for the cell pointer
	FIND	Activates the Search feature
	UNDO	If Undo is enabled, cancels your last action

Palette 5

Graphic Icon	Text Icon	Description
		Places the current graph in the worksheet*
	VIEW GRPH	Displays the current graph
	EDIT TEXT	Defines a range as text*
	COPY FRMT	Applies the Wysiwyg formats of the selected range*
	N	Removes all Wysiwyg formatting*

Palette 6

Graphic Icon	Text Icon	Description
		Adds an icon to the custom palette
		Removes an icon from your custom palette
		Moves an icon on your custom palette
		Displays the descriptions of user icons

Palette 7

Graphic Icon	Text Icon	Description
U1	U1	Runs the macro attached to the user icon
U2	U2	Runs the macro attached to the user icon
U3	U3	Runs the macro attached to the user icon
U4	U4	Runs the macro attached to the user icon
U5	U5	Runs the macro attached to the user icon

Palette 7 (*continued*)

Graphic Icon	Text Icon	Description
U6	U6	Runs the macro attached to the user icon
U7	U7	Runs the macro attached to the user icon
U8	U8	Runs the macro attached to the user icon
U9	U9	Runs the macro attached to the user icon
UIO	U10	Runs the macro attached to the user icon
UII	U11	Runs the macro attached to the user icon
UI2	U12	Runs the macro attached to the user icon

H

I

LAN Times Buyers Directory

How many network products are there to choose from?

THOUSANDS!

How do you find and compare them?

There is only ONE SOURCE—The LAN Times Buyers Directory. IT'S NEW!

The LAN Times Buyers Directory contains descriptions of thousands network hardware and software products and network services. Each listing contains product specifications, pricing, and company contact information. If you only want to have one resource for network products and services, the LAN Times Buyers Directory is it!

And now its available in two formats: PRINTED and ELECTRONIC.

The printed version includes all descriptions of products and services plus indexes by product type, company, and region. It is printed annually.

The electronic version comes as a runtime hypertext diskette (DOS / Folio). You can instantly search on product names, specifications, or compatibility standards as well as company names or locations. It's simple and intuitive to use. The electronic version is available on a subscription basis with monthly updates.

ORDER TODAY! Call (801) 565-5812 or mail the attatched form.

LAN TIMES BUYERS DIRECTORY
7050 Union Park Center
Suite 240
Midvale, UT 84047